Good Reasons with Contemporary Arguments

Reading, Designing, and Writing Effective Arguments

Third Edition

Lester Faigley
University of Texas at Austin

Jack Selzer
The Pennsylvania State University

PEARSON
Longman

New York San Francisco Boston
London Toronto Sydney Tokyo Singapore Madrid
Mexico City Munich Paris Cape Town Hong Kong Montreal

Senior Acquisitions Editor: Lynn M. Huddon
Development Editor: Leslie Taggart
Senior Supplements Editor: Donna Campion
Media Supplements Editor: Jenna Egan
Senior Marketing Manager: Sandra McGuire
Production Manager: Eric Jorgensen
Project Coordination, Text Design, and Electronic Page Makeup: Pre-Press Company, Inc.
Cover Design Manager: John Callahan
Cover Image: ©Stone/Getty Images, Inc.
Photo Researcher: Chrissy McIntyre
Senior Manufacturing Buyer: Dennis J. Para
Printer and Binder: Courier Corporation
Cover Printer: Coral Graphics

For permission to use copyrighted textual material, grateful acknowledgment is made to the copyright holders on pages 700–703, which are hereby made part of this copyright page.

Library of Congress Cataloging-in-Publication Data
Faigley, Lester, 1947–
   Good reasons with contemporary arguments : reading, designing, and writing effective arguments / Lester Faigley, Jack Selzer.-- 3rd ed.
      p. cm.
   Includes bibliographical references and index.
   ISBN 0-321-36496-1 (pbk.) -- ISBN 1-4130-1981-1
   1. English language--Rhetoric. 2. Persuasion (Rhetoric) 3. Report writing. I. Selzer, Jack. II. Title.
   PE1431.F35 2006b
   808'.042--dc22   2005036681

Please visit us at www.ablongman.com

ISBN 0-321-36496-1
1 2 3 4 5 6 7 8 9 10—CRW—09 08 07 06

In memory of our teacher and friend,
James L. Kinneavy (1920–1999)

Contents

Chapter 5: Understanding Visual Arguments   85

PART 2   Putting Good Reasons into Action: Options for Arguments   105

Chapter 6: Definition Arguments   109

Chapter 24: Media   631

Alternate Table of Contents: Types of Arguments

Evaluation Arguments

Narrative Arguments

Rebuttal Arguments

Proposal Arguments

Visual Arguments

Irony and Satire in Arguments

Arguments That Cite Sources

Preface

L ike many other college writing teachers, we have come to believe that a course focusing on argument is an essential part of a college writing curriculum. Most students come to college with very little experience in reading and writing extended arguments. Because so much writing in college concerns arguments in the various disciplines, a basic course in writing arguments is part of the foundation of an undergraduate education. You will find that college courses frequently require you to analyze the structure of arguments, to identify competing claims, to weigh the evidence offered, to recognize assumptions, to locate contradictions, and to anticipate opposing views. The ability to write cogent arguments is also highly valued in most occupations that require college degrees. Just as important, you need to be able to read arguments critically and write arguments skillfully if you are to participate in public life after you leave college. The long-term issues that will affect your life after your college years—education, the environment, social justice, and the quality of life, to name a few—have many diverse stakeholders and long, complex histories. They cannot be reduced to slogans and sound bites. If you are to help make your views prevail in your communities, you must be able to participate in sustained give-and-take on a range of civic issues.

A Straightforward Approach to Argument

Good Reasons with Contemporary Arguments begins by considering why people take the time to write arguments in the first place. People write arguments because they want to change attitudes and beliefs about particular issues, and they want things done about problems they identify. We start out by asking you to examine exactly why you might want to write an argument and how what you write can lead to extended discussion and long-term results. We then provide you with practical means to find good reasons that support convincingly the positions you want to advocate.

A Rhetorical Approach to Finding Good Reasons

You won't find a lot of complicated terminology in *Good Reasons*. The only technical terms this book uses are the general classical concepts of *pathos, ethos,* and *logos*—sources of good reasons that emerge from the audience's most passionately held values, from the speaker's expertise and credibility, or from reasonable, common sense thinking. The crux of teaching argument, in our view, is to get you to appreciate its rhetorical nature. A reason becomes a *good reason* when the audience accepts the writer or speaker as credible and accepts the assumptions and evidence on which the argument is based.

The Oral and Visual Aspects of Argument

Good Reasons is also distinctive in its attention to the delivery and presentation of arguments—to oral and visual aspects of argument in addition to the written word. We encourage you to formulate arguments in different genres and different media. Commonly used word processing programs and Web page editors now allow you to include pictures, icons, charts, and graphs—making design an important part of an argument. While the heart of an argument course should be the critical reading and critical writing of prose, we also believe that you should understand and use visual persuasion when appropriate.

The Value of Argument

The popularity of argument courses is not an accident. Even though we hear frequently that people have become cynical about politics, they are producing self-sponsored writing in quantities never before seen. It's almost as if people have rediscovered writing. While writing personal letters is perhaps becoming a lost art, participating in online discussion groups, writing Web logs (blogs), putting up Web sites, and sending email have become commonplace. Citizen participation in local and national government forums, in a multitude of issue-related online discussions and blogs, and in other forms such as online magazines is increasing daily. You already have many opportunities to speak in the electronic polis. We want you to recognize and value the breadth of information available on the Internet and to evaluate, analyze, and synthesize that information. And we want to prepare you for the changing demands of the professions and public citizenship in your future.

Argument as a Social Act

So that you can see how argument is a social act—that is, how arguments develop out of and respond to other arguments—we have grouped Part 4 reading selections around interesting current issues: the environment, sexual difference, globalization, science and ethics, privacy, regulating substances, and media. In each chapter, we present a range of viewpoints so that you can see how arguers develop their points in response to the perspectives of others—and so that you might develop your own arguments around those various points of view. So that you can observe the range of argumentative styles and approaches that we discuss in the book, you will notice an unusual diversity of opinions and genres (including ads, cartoons, and photos as well as print arguments) but also a diversity of writers and writing styles. You will see arguments that originally appeared on the Internet and others from magazines and newspapers. You will encounter well-known citizens such as Edward O. Wilson, N. Scott Momaday, Alice Walker, Anna Quindlen, and Ted Koppel as well as ordinary citizens who make extraordinary cases. And you will find examples of the kinds of arguments that we discuss throughout Parts 1 through 3: definitions, evaluations, causal arguments, narratives, refutations, and proposals.

Features New to This Edition

- Visual argument is emphasized throughout in order to respond to the need for greater visual literacy in our media-saturated culture.

  Chapter 1 introduces the new emphasis by including a new visual argument to accompany the chapter from Rachel Carson's classic *Silent Spring.*

  A new chapter in Part 1, Chapter 5 on "Understanding Visual Arguments," discusses visual persuasion and how visuals are used as supports for textual arguments. Twenty-five photographs, icons, charts, graphs, and advertisements illustrate major points. A new student paper, "Got Roddick?" demonstrates rhetorical analysis of an advertisement.

  More visuals illustrate concepts throughout Parts 1 and 2. In Chapter 4, for example, two photos of a Roman statue exemplify textual and contextual analysis. All the photo openers in Part 2 serve a pedagogical function. In all, over 75 new visuals, including 35 by Lester Faigley, appear in this edition.

- Three new chapters in Part 1 aid students in the process of creating and analyzing arguments.

  A new chapter on invention, Chapter 2 on "Finding Arguments," helps students decide what to argue about, how to think about audience, and how to craft a thesis statement for the argument.

The chapter introduces invention strategies such as freewriting, brainstorming, using online subject directories, and making idea maps in addition to reading in the subject area. The thesis discussion includes both focusing the thesis and evaluating it.

A new chapter on rhetorical analysis, Chatper 4 on "Understanding Written Arguments: Rhetorical Analysis," gives an overview of two main forms of rhetorical analysis: textual analysis (via classical rhetorical theory) and contextual analysis (text as a part of a larger conversation). Each type of analysis is demonstrated by analyzing a narrative argument from Part 2, Leslie Marmom Silko's "The Border Patrol State." A student uses both kinds of analysis in her paper "The NRA Blacklist: A Project Gone Mad."

A new chapter on visual analysis, Chapter 5 on "Understanding Visual Arguments," discusses visuals that make explicit claims, photos and ads whose claims must be inferred or co-created by the viewer, and visual metaphor. The section on visual evidence discusses current and past evidence, how the significance of images can be debated, and how the contexts of images, producers, and viewers can create controversy around the use of visuals as evidence.

■ A greater emphasis on student work throughout encourages students to understand themselves as agents and to see the range of topics their colleagues are investigating.

Five new student essays appear in Parts 1 and 2, along with student-produced Web sites in Part 3.

■ Expanded discussions of the process of research and MLA and APA documentation guidelines.

Particular attention is given to using library databases and to documenting sources from library databases. A new sample student paper using MLA style, "Need a Cure for Tribe Fever? How About a Dip in the Lake" can be found in Chapter 11.

■ An expanded and revised selection of arguments in Part 4, "Contemporary Arguments," engages students in issues that are fresh and provocative. "Contemporary Arguments" includes a great many new visual arguments (ads, cartoons, Web sites, photos); new chapters on globalization, privacy issues, science and ethics, and media; and more than fifty new selections in all.

■ Five new "Issues in Focus" target specific issues within the chapter topics in Part 4. Issues in Focus are detailed argumentative exchanges on habitat loss, same sex marriage, stem cell research, surveillance and security, and the regulation of tobacco. All five Issues in Focus feature short essays, speeches, cartoons, photos, commentaries, and questions for reflection and discussion. The Issues in Focus will invite student responses, direct student analyses, and represent various positions that students might take on those issues.

■ A new glossary of terms helps students remember important concepts.

Companion Website and Instructor's Manual

The Companion Website to accompany *Good Reasons with Contemporary Arguments,* Third Edition (**http://www.ablongman.com/faigley**), revised by Matt Newcomb, offers a wealth of resources for both students and instructors. Students can access detailed chapter summaries and objectives, writing exercises, chapter review quizzes, and links to additional Web resources for further study. Instructors will find sample syllabi, additional activities for classroom use, Web resources, and more.

The *Instructor's Manual* that accompanies this text was revised by Iris Ralph and is designed to be useful for new and experienced instructors alike. Available to qualified adopters of this text, it briefly discusses the ins and outs of teaching the material in each chapter. Also provided are in-class exercises, homework assignments, discussion questions for each reading selection, and model paper assignments and syllabi. This revised *Instructor's Manual* will make your work as a teacher a bit easier. Teaching argumentation and composition becomes a process that has genuine—and often surprising—rewards.

Acknowledgments

We are much indebted to the work of many outstanding scholars of argument and to our colleagues who teach argument at Texas and at Penn State. In particular, we thank the following reviewers for sharing their expertise: Anita Daniels, University of Florida; Dan Ferguson, Amarillo College; Lynda Haas, University of California, Irvine; Jeffrey D. Harris, Somerset Community College; Tom Molanphy, Academy of Art University; Kerry Newman, Pennsylvania State University; Doreen Piano, Georgia Institute of Technology; Iris Ralph, University of Texas at Austin; Ingrid Schreck,

College of Marin; Rebecca G. Smith, Barton College; Michael Stancliff, Arizona State University West; and Jacqueline Thomas, University of Texas at Austin. We are especially grateful to our students, who have given us opportunities to test these materials in class and who have taught us a great deal about the nature of argument.

Our editor, Eben Ludlow, convinced us we should write this book and gave us wise guidance throughout two editions. Lynn Huddon's support and guidence on this edition have been invaluable. We are extremely fortunate to have Leslie Taggart as our development editor for this edition. Leslie not only brings great ideas but she also makes writing the book fun. Kelly Kessler worked with us in the revision and made many fine contributions, and Matt Newcomb made essential suggestions for Part 4, Contemporary Arguments. Melissa Mattson at Pre-Press and Eric Jorgensen at Pearson Longman did splendid work in preparing our book for publication. Finally we thank our families, who make it all possible.

LESTER FAIGLEY
JACK SELZER

PART 1

Persuading with Good Reasons

What Do We Mean by Argument?

For over thirty years, the debate over legalized abortion has raged in the United States. The following scene is a familiar one: Outside an abortion clinic, a crowd of pro-life activists has gathered to try to stop women from entering the clinic. They carry signs that read "ABORTION = MURDER" and "A BABY'S LIFE IS A HUMAN LIFE." Pro-choice supporters are also present in a counterdemonstration. Their signs read "KEEP YOUR LAWS OFF MY BODY" and "WOMEN HAVE THE RIGHT TO CONTROL THEIR BODIES." Police keep the two sides apart, but they do not stop the shouts of "Murderer!" from the pro-life side and "If you're anti-abortion, don't have one!" from the pro-choice side.

When you imagine an argument, you might think of two people engaged in a heated exchange, or two groups of people with different views, shouting back and forth at each other like the pro-choice and pro-life demonstrators. Or you might think of the arguing that occurs in the courthouse, where district attorneys and defense lawyers debate strenuously. Written arguments can resemble these oral arguments in being heated and one sided. For example, the signs that the pro-choice and pro-life demonstrators carry might be considered written arguments.

But in college courses, in public life, and in professional careers, written arguments are not thought of as slogans. Bumper stickers require no supporting evidence or reasons. Many other kinds of writing do not offer reasons either. An instruction manual, for example, does not try to persuade you. It assumes that you want to do whatever the manual tells you how to do; indeed, most people are willing to follow the advice, or else they would not be consulting the manual. Likewise, an article written by someone who is totally committed to a particular cause or belief often assumes that everyone should think the same way. These writers can count on certain phrases and words to produce predictable responses.

Effective arguments do not make the assumption that everyone should think the same way or hold the same beliefs. They attempt to change people's minds by convincing them of the validity of new ideas or that a particular course of action is the best one to take. Written arguments not only offer evidence and reasons but also often examine the assumptions on which they are based, think through opposing arguments, and anticipate objections. They explore positions thoroughly and take opposing views into account.

Extended written arguments make more demands on their readers than most other kinds of writing. Like bumper stickers, they often appeal to our emotions. But they typically do much more. They expand our knowledge with the depth of their analysis and lead us through a complex set of claims by providing networks of logical relations and appropriate evidence. They explicitly build on what has been written before by offering trails of sources, which also demonstrates that they can be trusted because the writers have done their homework. They cause us to reflect on what we read, in a process that we will shortly describe as *critical reading*.

Our culture is a competitive culture, and often the goal is to win. If you are a professional athlete, a top trial lawyer, or a candidate for president of the United States, it really is win big or lose. But most of us live in a world in which the opponents don't go away when the game is over. Even professional athletes have to play the team they beat in the championship game the next year.

In real life, most of us have to deal with people who disagree with us at times but with whom we have to continue to work and live in the same communities. The idea of winning in such situations can only be temporary. Soon enough other situations will come up in which we will need the support of those who were on the other side of the current issue. Probably you can think of times when friendly arguments ended up with everyone involved coming to a better understanding of the others' views. And probably you can think of other times when someone was so concerned with winning an argument that even though the person might have been technically right, hard feelings were created that lasted for years.

Usually, listeners and readers are more willing to consider your argument seriously if you cast yourself as a respectful partner rather than as a competitor and put forth your arguments in the spirit of mutual support and negotiation—in the interest of finding the *best* way, not "my way." How can you be the person that your reader will want to cooperate with rather than resist? Here are a few suggestions, both for your writing and for discussing controversial issues in class.

Strategies for Being a Respectful Partner in Argument

- **Try to think of yourself as engaged not so much in winning over your audience as in courting your audience's cooperation.** Argue vigorously, but not so vigorously that opposing views are vanquished or silenced. Remember that your goal is to invite a response that creates a dialog.

- **Show that you understand and genuinely respect your listener's or reader's position even if you think the position is ultimately wrong.** Often, that amounts to remembering to argue against opponents' positions, not against the opponents themselves. It often means representing an opponent's position in terms that he or she would accept. Look for ground that you already share with your reader, and search for even more. See yourself as a mediator. Consider that neither you nor the other person has arrived at a best solution, and carry on in the hope that dialog will lead to an even better course of action than the one you now recommend. Expect and assume the best of your listener or reader, and deliver your own best yourself.

- **Cultivate a sense of humor and a distinctive voice.** Many textbooks on argument emphasize using a reasonable voice. But a reasonable voice doesn't have to be a dull one. Humor is a legitimate tool of argument. Although playing an issue strictly for laughs risks not having the reader take it seriously, nothing creates a sense of goodwill quite so much as good humor. You will be seen as open to new possibilities and to cooperation if you occasionally show a sense of humor. And a sense of humor can sometimes be especially welcome when the stakes are high, the sides have been chosen, and tempers are flaring.

Consider that your argument might be just one move in a larger process that might end up helping *you*. Most times we argue because we think we have something to offer. But in the process of developing and presenting your views, realize also that you might learn something in the course of your research or from an argument that answers your own. Holding onto that attitude will keep you from becoming too overbearing and dogmatic.

What to Argue About

A Book That Changed the World

In 1958, Rachel Carson received a copy of a letter that her friend Olga Huckens had sent to the *Boston Herald*. The letter described what had happened during the previous summer when Duxbury, Massachusetts, a small town just north of

Rachel Carson

Cape Cod where Huckens lived, was sprayed several times from an airplane with the chemical pesticide DDT to kill mosquitoes. The mosquitoes came back as hungry as ever, but the songbirds, bees, and other insects vanished except for a few dead birds that Huckens had to pick up out of her yard. Huckens asked Carson if she knew anyone in Washington who could help to stop the spraying.

The letter from Olga Huckens struck a nerve with Rachel Carson. Carson was a marine biologist who had worked for many years for the U.S. Fish and Wildlife Service and who had written three highly acclaimed books about the sea and wetlands. In 1944 she published an article on how bats use radarlike echoes to find insects, which was reprinted in *Reader's Digest* in 1945. The editors at *Reader's Digest* asked whether she could write something else for them, and Carson replied in a letter that she wanted to write about experiments using DDT. DDT was being hyped as the solution for controlling insect pests, but Carson knew in 1945 that fish, waterfowl, and other animals would also be poisoned by widespread spraying and that eventually people could die too. *Reader's Digest* was not interested in Carson's proposed article, so she dropped the idea and went on to write about other things.

Huckens's letter brought Carson back to the subject of chemical spraying. In the late 1940s and 1950s, pesticides—especially the chlorinated hydrocarbons

DDT, aldrin, and dieldrin—were sprayed on a massive scale throughout the United States and were hailed as a panacea for world hunger and famine. In 1957 much of the greater New York City area, including Long Island, was sprayed with DDT to kill gypsy moths. But there were noticeable side effects. Many people complained about not only birds, fish, and useful insects being killed but also their plants, shrubs, and pets. Other scientists had written about the dangers of massive spraying of pesticides, but they had not convinced the public of the hazards of pesticides and of the urgency for change.

Rachel Carson decided that she needed to write a magazine article about the facts of DDT. When she contacted *Reader's Digest* and other magazines, she found that they still would not consider publishing on the subject. Carson then concluded that she should write a short book. She knew that her job was not going to be an easy one because people in the United States still trusted science to solve all problems. Science had brought the "green revolution" that greatly increased crop yields through the use of chemical fertilizers and chemical pesticides. Carson's subject matter was also technical and difficult to communicate to the general public. At that time the public did not think much about air and water pollution, and most people were unaware that pesticides could poison humans as well as insects. And she was sure to face opposition from the pesticide industry, which had become a multimillion-dollar business. Carson knew the pesticide industry would do everything it could to stop her from publishing and to discredit her if she did.

Rachel Carson nonetheless wrote her book, *Silent Spring*. It sounded the alarm about the dangers caused by the overuse of pesticides, and the controversy it raised has still not ended. No book has had a greater impact on our thinking about the environment. *Silent Spring* was first published in installments in *The New Yorker* in the summer of 1962, and it created an immediate furor. Chemical companies threatened to sue Carson, and the trade associations that they sponsored launched full-scale attacks against the book in pamphlets and magazine articles. The chemical companies treated *Silent Spring* as a public relations problem; they hired scientists whose only job was to ridicule the book and to dismiss Carson as a "hysterical woman." Some even accused *Silent Spring* of being part of a communist plot to ruin U.S. agriculture.

Brown pelicans are again common along the coasts of the South and in California after they were nearly made extinct by the effects of DDT.

But the public controversy over *Silent Spring* had another effect. It helped to make the book a success shortly after it was published in September 1962. A half-million hardcover copies of *Silent Spring* were sold, keeping it on the best-seller list for thirty-one weeks. President John F. Kennedy read *Silent Spring* and met with Carson and other scientists to discuss the pesticide problem. Kennedy requested that the President's

> That we still talk so much about the environment is testimony to the lasting power of *Silent Spring*.

Scientific Advisory Committee study the effects of pesticides and make a report. This report found evidence around the world of high levels of pesticides in the environment, including the tissues of humans. The report confirmed what Carson had described in *Silent Spring*.

In the words of a news commentator at the time, *Silent Spring* "lit a fire" under the government. Many congressional hearings were held on the effects of pesticides and other pollutants on the environment. In 1967 the Environmental Defense Fund was formed; it developed the guidelines under which DDT was eventually banned. Three years later, President Richard Nixon became convinced that only an independent agency within the executive branch could operate with enough independence to enforce environmental regulations. Nixon created the Environmental Protection Agency (EPA) in December 1970, and he named William Ruckelshaus as its first head. One of the missions of the EPA, according to Ruckelshaus, was to develop an environmental ethic.

The United States was not the only country to respond to *Silent Spring*. The book was widely translated and inspired legislation on the environment in nearly all industrialized nations. Moreover, it changed the way we think about the environment. Carson pointed out that the nerve gases that were developed for use on our enemies in World War II were being used as pesticides after the war. She criticized the view of the environment as a battlefield where people make war on those natural forces that they believe impede their progress. Instead, she advocated living in coexistence with the environment because we are part of it. She was not totally opposed to pesticides, but she wanted to make people more aware of the environment as a whole and how changing one part would affect other parts. Her message was to try to live in balance with nature. That we still talk so much about the environment is testimony to the lasting power of *Silent Spring*. In 1980, Rachel Carson was posthumously awarded the highest civilian decoration in the nation: the Presidential Medal of Freedom. The citation accompanying the award expresses the way she is remembered:

Never silent herself in the face of destructive trends, Rachel Carson fed a spring of awareness across America and beyond. A biologist with a gentle, clear voice, she welcomed her audiences to her love of the sea, while with an equally clear voice she warned Americans of the dangers human beings themselves pose for their own environment. Always concerned, always eloquent, she created a tide of environmental consciousness that has not ebbed.

Why *Silent Spring* Became a Classic

A book titled *Our Synthetic Environment*, which covered much of the same ground as *Silent Spring*, had been published six months earlier. The author, Murray Bookchin, writing under the pen name Lewis Herber, also wrote about the pollution of the natural world and the effects on people. Bookchin was as committed to warning people about the hazards of pesticides as Carson, but *Our Synthetic Environment* was read by only a small community of scientists. Why, then, did Carson succeed in reaching a larger audience?

Rachel Carson had far more impact than Murray Bookchin not simply because she was a more talented writer or because she was a scientist while Bookchin was not. She also thought a great deal about who she was writing for—her **audience**. If she was going to stop the widespread spraying of dangerous pesticides, she knew she would have to connect with the values of a wide audience, an audience that included a large segment of the public as well as other scientists.

The opening chapter in *Silent Spring* begins not by announcing Carson's thesis or giving a list of facts. Instead, the book starts out with a short fable about a small town located in the middle of prosperous farmland, where wildflowers bloomed much of the year, trout swam in the streams, and wildlife was abundant. Suddenly, a strange blight came on the town, as if an evil spell had been cast upon it. The chickens, sheep, and cattle on the farms grew sick and died. The families of the townspeople and farmers alike developed mysterious illnesses. Most of the birds disappeared, and the few that remained could neither sing nor fly. The apple trees bloomed, but there were no bees to pollinate the trees, and so they bore no fruit. The wildflowers withered as if they had been burned. Fishermen quit going to the streams because the fish had all died.

But it wasn't witchcraft that caused everything to grow sick and die. Carson writes that "the people had done it to themselves." She continues, "I know of no community that has experienced all the misfortunes I describe. Yet every one of these disasters has actually happened somewhere, and many real communities have already suffered a substantial number of them. A grim specter has crept upon us almost unnoticed, and this imagined tragedy may easily become a stark reality." Carson's fable did happen several times after the book was published. In July 1976, a chemical reaction went out of control at a plant near Seveso, Italy, and a cloud of powdery white crystals of almost pure dioxin fell on the town. The children ran out to play in the powder because it looked like snow. Within four days, plants, birds, and animals began dying, and the next week, people started getting sick. Most of the people had to go to the hospital, and everyone had to move out of the town. An even worse disaster happened in December 1984, when a storage tank in a pesticide plant exploded near Bhopal, India, showering the town. Two thousand people died quickly, and another fifty thousand became sick for the rest of their lives.

Perhaps if Rachel Carson were alive today and writing a book about the dangers of pesticides, she might begin differently. But remember that at the time she was writing, people trusted pesticides and believed that DDT was a miracle solution for all sorts of insect pests. She first had to make people aware that DDT could be harmful to them. In the second chapter of *Silent Spring* (reprinted at the end of this chapter), Carson continued appealing to the emotions of her audience. People in 1962 knew about the dangers of radiation even if they were ignorant about pesticides. They knew that the atomic bombs that had been dropped on Hiroshima and Nagasaki at the end of World War II were still killing Japanese people through the effects of radiation many years later, and they feared the fallout from nuclear bombs that were still being tested and stockpiled in the United States and Soviet Union.

Getting people's attention by exposing the threat of pesticides wasn't enough by itself. There are always people writing about various kinds of threats, and most aren't taken seriously except by those who already believe that the threats exist. Carson wanted to reach people who didn't think that pesticides were a threat but might be persuaded to take this view. To convince these people, she had to explain why pesticides are potentially dangerous, and she had to make readers believe that she could be trusted.

Rachel Carson was an expert marine biologist. To write *Silent Spring*, she had to read widely in sciences that she had not studied, including research about insects, toxic chemicals, cell physiology, biochemistry, plant and soil science, and public health. Then she had to explain complex scientific processes to people who had very little or no background in science. It was a very difficult and frustrating task. While writing *Silent Spring*, Carson confided in a letter to a friend the problems she was having: "How to reveal enough to give understanding of the most serious effects of the chemicals without being technical, how to simplify without error—these have been problems of rather monumental proportions."

TACTICS OF *SILENT SPRING*

Chapter 1 of *Silent Spring* tells a parable of a rural town where the birds, fish, flowers, and plants die and people become sick after a white powder is sprayed on the town. At the beginning of Chapter 2, Rachel Carson begins her argument against the mass aerial spraying of pesticides. Most of her readers were not aware of the dangers of pesticides, but they were well aware of the harmful effects of radiation. Let's look at her tactics:

The interrelationship of people and the environment provides the basis for Carson's argument.

The history of life on earth has been a history of interaction between living things and their surroundings. To a large extent, the physical form and the habits of earth's vegetation and its animal life have been molded by the environment. Considering the whole span of earthly time, the opposite effect, in which life actually modifies its surroundings, has been relatively slight. Only within the moment of time represented by the present century has one species—man—acquired significant power to alter the nature of his world.

During the past quarter century this power has not only increased to one of disturbing magnitude but it has changed in character. The most alarming of all man's assaults upon the environment is the contamination of air, earth, rivers, and sea with dangerous and even lethal materials. This pollution is for the most part irrecoverable; the chain of life it initiates not only in the world that must support life but in living tissues is for the most part irreversible. In this now universal contamination of the environment, chemicals are the sinister and little-recognized partners of radiation in changing the very nature of the world—the very nature of its life. Strontium 90, released through nuclear explosions into the air, comes to earth in rain or drifts down as fallout, lodges in the soil, enters into the grass or corn or wheat grown there, and in time takes its abode in the bones of a human being, there to remain until his death. Similarly, chemicals sprayed on croplands or forests or gardens lie long in soil, entering into living organisms, passing from one to another in a chain of poisoning and death. Or they pass mysteriously by underground streams until they emerge and, through the alchemy of air and sunlight, combine into new forms that kill vegetation, sicken cattle, and work unknown harm on those who drink from once-pure wells. As Albert Schweitzer has said, "Man can hardly even recognize the devils of his own creation."

Carson shifts her language to a metaphor of war against the environment rather than interaction with the natural world.

In 1963 the first treaty was signed by the United States and the Soviet Union that banned the testing of nuclear weapons above ground, under water, and in space.

The key move: Carson associates the dangers of chemical pesticides with those of radiation.

Albert Schweitzer (1875–1965) was a concert musician, philosopher, and doctor who spent most of his life as a medical missionary in Africa.

To make people understand the bad effects of pesticides required explaining what is not common sense: why very tiny amounts of pesticides can be so harmful. The reason lies in how pesticides are absorbed by the body. DDT is fat-soluble and gets stored in organs such as the adrenals, thyroid, liver, and kidneys. Carson explains how pesticides build up in the body:

> This storage of DDT begins with the smallest conceivable intake of the chemical (which is present as residues on most foodstuffs) and continues until quite high levels are reached. The fatty storage deposits act as biological magnifiers, so that an intake of as little as 1/10 of 1 part per million in the diet results in storage of about 10 to 15 parts per million, an increase of one hundredfold or more. These terms of reference, so commonplace to the chemist or the pharmacologist, are unfamiliar to most of us. One part in a million sounds like a very small amount—and so it is. But such substances are so potent that a minute quantity can bring about vast changes in the body. In animal experiments, 3 parts per million has been found to inhibit an essential enzyme in the heart muscle; only 5 parts per million has brought about necrosis or disintegration of liver cells.

Throughout the book, Carson succeeds in translating scientific facts into language that, to use her words, "most of us" can understand. Of course, Carson was a scientist and quite capable of reading scientific articles. She establishes her credibility as a scientist by using technical terms such as *necrosis*. But at the same time she identifies herself with people who are not scientists and gains our trust by taking our point of view.

To accompany these facts, Carson tells about places that have been affected by pesticides. One of the more memorable stories is about Clear Lake, California, in the mountainous country north of San Francisco. Clear Lake is popular for fishing, but it is also an ideal habitat for a species of gnat. In the late 1940s the state of California began spraying the lake with DDD, a close relative of DDT. Spraying had to be repeated because the gnats kept coming back. The western grebes that lived on the lake began to die, and when scientists examined their bodies, the grebes were loaded with extraordinary levels of DDD. Microscopic plants and animals filtered the lake water for nutrients and concentrated the pesticides at 20 times their level in the lake water. Small fish ate these tiny plants and animals and again concentrated the DDD at levels 10 to 100 times that of their microscopic food. The grebes that ate the fish suffered the effects of this huge magnification.

Although DDT is still used in parts of the developing world, the influence of *Silent Spring* led to the banning of it and most other similar pesticides in the United States and Canada. Rachel Carson's book eventually led people to stop relying only on pesticides and to look instead to other methods of controlling pests, such as planting crops that are resistant to insects and disease. When pesticides are used today, they typically are applied much more selectively and in lower amounts than was common when Carson was writing.

Rachel Carson's more lasting legacy is our awareness of our environment. She urges us to be aware that we share this planet with other creatures and that "we are dealing with life—with living populations and all their pressures and counterpressures, their surges and recessions." She warns against dismissing the balance of nature. She writes:

> The balance of nature is not the same today as in Pleistocene times, but it is still there: a complex, precise, and highly integrated system of relation-ships between living things which cannot safely be ignored any more than the law of gravity can be defied with impunity by a man perched on the edge of a cliff. The balance of nature is not a *status quo*; it is fluid, ever shifting, in a constant state of adjustment.

Since the publication of *Silent Spring*, we have grown much more con-scious of large-scale effects on ecosystems caused by global warming, acid rain, and the depleted ozone layer in addition to the local effects of pesticides described in Carson's book. The cooperation of nations today in attempting to control air and water pollution, in encouraging more efficient use of energy and natural resources, and in promoting sustainable patterns of con-sumption is due in no small part to the long-term influence of *Silent Spring*.

ANALYZING ARGUMENTS: PATHOS, ETHOS, AND LOGOS

When the modern concept of democracy was developed in Greece in the fifth century BCE, the study of rhetoric also began. It's not a coincidence that the teaching of rhetoric was closely tied to the rise of democracy. In the Greek city-states, all citizens had the right to speak and vote at the popular assembly and in the committees of the assembly that functioned as the criminal courts. Citizens took turns serving as the officials of government. Because the citizens of Athens and other city-states took their responsibilities quite seriously, they highly valued the ability to speak effectively in public. Teachers of rhetoric were held in great esteem.

In the next century, the most important teacher of rhetoric in ancient Greece, Aristotle (384–323 BCE), made the study of rhetoric systematic. He defined **rhetoric** as the art of finding the best available means of persuasion in any situation. Aristotle set out three primary tactics of argument: appeals to the emotions and deepest-held values of the audience (**pathos**), appeals based on the trustworthiness of the speaker (**ethos**), and appeals to good reasons (**logos**).

ANALYZING ARGUMENTS: PATHOS, ETHOS, AND LOGOS *(continued)*

Carson makes these appeals with great skill in *Silent Spring*. Very simply, her purpose is to stop pesticide pollution. She first appeals to *pathos*, engaging her readers in her subject. She gives many specific examples of how pesticides have accumulated in the bodies of animals and people. But she also engages her readers through her skill as a writer, making us care about nature as well as concerned about our own safety. She uses the fate of robins to symbolize her crusade. Robins were the victims of spraying for Dutch elm disease. Robins feed on earthworms, which in turn process fallen elm leaves. The earthworms act as magnifiers of the pesticide, which either kills the robins outright or renders them sterile. Thus when no robins sang, it was indeed a silent spring.

Carson is also successful in creating a credible *ethos*. We believe her not just because she establishes her expertise. She convinces us also because she establishes her ethos as a person with her audience's best interests at heart. She anticipates possible objections, demonstrating that she has thought about opposing positions. She takes time to explain concepts that most people do not understand fully, and she discusses how everyone can benefit if we take a different attitude toward nature. She shows that she has done her homework on the topic. By creating a credible ethos, Carson makes an effective moral argument that humans as a species have a responsibility not to destroy the world they live in.

Finally, Carson supports her argument with good reasons, what Aristotle called *logos*. She offers "because clauses" to support her main claims. She describes webs of relationships among the earth, plants, animals, and humans, and she explains how changing one part will affect the others. Her point is not that we should never disturb these relationships but that we should be as aware as possible of the consequences.

Reading Arguments

If you have ever been coached in a sport or have been taught an art such as dancing or playing a musical instrument, you likely have viewed a game or a performance in two ways. You might enjoy the game or performance like everyone else, but at the same time, you might be especially aware of something that you know from your experience is difficult to do and therefore appreciated the skill and the practice necessary to develop it. A similar distinction can be made about two kinds of reading. For the sake of convenience, the first can be called **ordinary reading**, although we don't really think there is a single kind of ordinary reading. In ordinary reading, on the first time through, the reader forms a sense of content and gets an initial impression: whether it's interesting, whether the author has something important to say, whether you agree or disagree.

For most of what you read, one time through is enough. When you read for the second or third time, you start to use different strategies because you have some reason to do so. You are no longer reading to form a sense of the overall content. Often, you are looking for something in particular. If you reread a textbook chapter, you might want to make sure you understand how a key concept is being used. When you reread your apartment contract, you might want to know what is required to get your deposit back. This second kind of reading can be called **critical reading**. Critical reading does not mean criticizing what the writer has to say (although that's certainly possible). Critical reading begins with questions and specific goals.

T I P S

Become a Critical Reader

Before you start reading, find out when the argument was written, where it first appeared, and who wrote it.

Arguments don't appear in vacuums. They most often occur in response to something else that has been written or some event that has happened. You also have a title, which suggests what the argument might be about. This information will help you to form an initial impression about why the writer wrote this particular argument, who the writer imagined as the readers, and what purposes the writer might have had in mind. Then pick up your pencil and start reading.

Become a Critical Reader *(continued)*

Ask Questions

On the first time through, you need to understand what's in the argument. So circle the words and references that you don't know and look them up. If a statement part of the argument isn't clear, note that section in the margin. You might figure out what the writer is arguing later, or you might have to work through it slowly a second time through.

Analyze

On your second reading, you should start analyzing the structure of the argument. Here's how to do it:

- Identify the writer's main claim or claims. You should be able to paraphrase it if it doesn't appear explicitly.
- What are the reasons that support the claim? List them by number in the margins. There might be only one reason, or there could be several (and some reasons could be supported by others).
- Where is the evidence? Does it really support the reasons? Can you think of contradictory evidence?
- Does the writer refer to expert opinion or research about this subject? Do other experts see this issue differently?
- Does the writer acknowledge opposing views? Does the writer deal fairly with opposing views?

Respond

Write down your thoughts as you read. Often you will find that something you read reminds you of something else. Jot that down. It might be something to think about later, and it might give you ideas for writing. Think also about what else you should read if you want to write about this topic. Or you might want to write down whether you are persuaded by the argument and why.

Writers of arguments engage in critical reading even on the first time through. They know that they will have to acknowledge what else has been written about a particular issue. If the issue is new (and few are), then the writer will need to establish its significance by comparing it to other issues on which much has been written. Writers of arguments, therefore, begin reading with *questions*. They want to know *why* a particular argument was written. They want to know *what* the writer's basic assumptions are. They want to know *who* the writer had in mind when the argument was written. Critical readers most often read with pen or pencil in hand or with a window open on their computer. They write their questions in the margins or in the file.

Critical readers do more than just question what they read. They analyze how the argument works. Critical readers look at how an argument is laid out. They identify key terms and examine how the writer is using them. They consider how the writer appeals to our emotions, represents himself or herself, and uses good reasons. They analyze the structure of an argument—the organization—and the way in which it is written—the style.

Finally, critical readers often *respond* as they read. They don't just take in what they read in a passive way. They jot down notes to themselves in the margins or on the blank pages at the front and back of a book. They use these notes later when they start writing. Reading is often the best way to get started writing.

POSITION AND PROPOSAL ARGUMENTS

In *Silent Spring*, Rachel Carson made an effective argument against the massive use of synthetic pesticides. Arguing against the indiscriminate use of pesticides, however, did not solve the problem of what to do about harmful insects that destroy crops and spread disease. Carson also did the harder job of offering solutions. In her final chapter, "The Other Road," Carson gives alternatives to the massive use of pesticides. She describes how a pest organism's natural enemies can be used against it instead.

These two kinds of arguments can be characterized as *position* and *proposal* arguments.

Position Arguments

In a **position argument**, the writer makes a claim about a controversial issue.

- **The writer first has to define the issue**. Carson had to explain what synthetic pesticides are in chemical terms and how they work, and she had to give a history of their increasing use after World War II before she could begin arguing against pesticides.
- **The writer should take a clear position**. Carson wasted no time setting out her position by describing the threat that high levels of pesticides pose to people worldwide.

POSITION AND PROPOSAL ARGUMENTS *(continued)*

■ **The writer should make a convincing argument and acknowledge opposing views**. Carson used a variety of strategies in support of her position, including research studies, quotes from authorities, and her own analyses and observations. She took into account opposing views by acknowledging that harmful insects needed to be controlled and conceded that selective spraying is necessary and desirable.

Proposal Arguments

In a **proposal argument**, the writer proposes a course of action in response to a recognizable problem situation. The proposal says what can be done to improve the situation or change it altogether.

■ **The writer first has to define the problem**. The problem Carson had to define was complex. Not only was the overuse of pesticides killing helpful insects, plants, and animals and threatening people, but the harmful insects the pesticides were intended to eliminate were becoming increasingly resistant. More spraying and more frequent spraying produced pesticide-resistant "superbugs." Mass spraying resulted in actually helping bad bugs such as fire ants by killing off their competition.

■ **The writer has to propose a solution or solutions**. Carson did not hold out for one particular approach to controlling insects, but she did advocate biological solutions. She proposed biological alternatives to pesticides, such as sterilizing and releasing large numbers of male insects and introducing predators of pest insects. Above all, she urged that we work with nature rather than being at war with it.

■ **The solution or solutions must work, and they must be feasible**. The projected consequences should be set out, arguing that good things will happen, bad things will be avoided, or both. Carson discussed research studies that indicated her solutions would work, and she argued that they would be less expensive than massive spraying. Today, we can look at Carson's book with the benefit of hindsight. Not everything Carson proposed ended up working, but her primary solution—learn to live with nature—has been a powerful one. Mass spraying of pesticides has stopped in the United States, and species that were threatened by the excessive use of pesticides, including falcons, eagles, and brown pelicans, have made remarkable comebacks.

RACHEL CARSON

The Obligation to Endure

Rachel Carson (1907–1964) was born and grew up in Springdale, Pennsylvania, 18 miles up the Allegheny River from Pittsburgh. When Carson was in elementary school, her mother was fearful of infectious diseases that were sweeping through the nation and often kept young Rachel out of school. In her wandering on the family farm, Rachel developed the love of nature that she maintained throughout her life. At 22 she began her career as a marine biologist at Woods Hole, Massachusetts, and she later went to graduate school at Johns Hopkins University in Baltimore. She began working for the U.S. government in 1936 in the agency that later became the Fish and Wildlife Service, and she was soon recognized as a talented writer as well as a meticulous scientist. She wrote three highly praised books about the sea and wetlands: Under the Sea Wind *(1941),* The Sea Around Us *(1951), and* The Edge of the Sea *(1954).*

Carson's decision to write Silent Spring *marked a great change in her life. For the first time, she became an environmental activist rather than an inspired and enthusiastic writer about nature. She had written about the interconnectedness of life in her previous three books, but with* Silent Spring *she had to convince people that hazards lie in what had seemed familiar and harmless. Although many people think of birds when they hear Rachel Carson's name, she was the first scientist to make a comprehensive argument that links cancer to environmental causes. Earlier in this chapter, you saw how Carson associated pesticides with the dangers of radiation from nuclear weapons. Notice how else she gets her readers to think differently about pesticides in this selection, which begins Chapter 2 of* Silent Spring.

1   The history of life on earth has been a history of interaction between living things and their surroundings. To a large extent, the physical form and the habits of the earth's vegetation and its animal life have been molded by the environment. Considering the whole span of earthly time, the opposite effect, in which life actually modifies its surroundings, has been relatively slight. Only within the moment of time represented by the present century has one species—man—acquired significant power to alter the nature of his world.

2   During the past quarter century this power has not only increased to one of disturbing magnitude but it has changed in character. The most alarming of all man's assaults upon the environment is the contamination of air, earth, rivers, and sea with dangerous and even lethal materials. This pollution is for the most part irrecoverable; the chain of evil it initiates not only in the world that must support life but in living tissues

is for the most part irreversible. In this now universal contamination of the environment, chemicals are the sinister and little recognized partners of radiation in changing the very nature of the world—the very nature of its life. Strontium 90, released through nuclear explosions into the air, comes to earth in rain or drifts down as fallout, lodges in soil, enters into the grass or corn or wheat grown there, and in time takes up its abode in the bones of a human being, there to remain until his death. Similarly, chemicals sprayed on croplands or forests or gardens lie long in soil, entering into living organisms, passing from one to another in a chain of poisoning and death. Or they pass mysteriously by underground streams until they emerge and, through the alchemy of air and sunlight, combine into new forms that kill vegetation, sicken cattle, and work unknown harm on those who drink from once-pure wells. As Albert Schweitzer has said, "Man can hardly even recognize the devils of his own creation."

3   It took hundreds of millions of years to produce the life that now inhabits the earth—eons of time in which that developing and evolving and diversifying life reached a state of adjustment and balance with its surroundings. The environment, rigorously shaping and directing the life it supported, contained elements that were hostile as well as supporting. Certain rocks gave out dangerous radiation; even within the light of the sun, from which all life draws its energy, there were short-wave radiations with power to injure. Given time—time not in years but in millennia—life adjusts, and a balance has been reached. For time is the essential ingredient; but in the modern world there is no time.

4   The rapidity of change and the speed with which new situations are created follow the impetuous and heedless pace of man rather than the deliberate pace of nature. Radiation is no longer merely the background radiation of rocks, the bombardment of cosmic rays, the ultraviolet of the sun that have existed before there was any life on earth; radiation is now the unnatural creation of man's tampering with the atom. The chemicals to which life is asked to make its adjustment are no longer merely the calcium and silica and copper and all the rest of the minerals washed out of the rocks and carried in rivers to the sea; they are the synthetic creations of man's inventive mind, brewed in his laboratories, and having no counterparts in nature.

5   To adjust to these chemicals would require time on the scale that is nature's; it would require not merely the years of a man's life but the life of generations. And even this, were it by some miracle possible, would be futile, for the new chemicals come from our laboratories in an endless stream; almost five hundred annually find their way into actual use in the United States alone. The figure is staggering and its implications are not easily grasped—500 new chemicals to which the bodies of men and animals are required somehow to adapt each year, chemicals totally outside the limits of biologic experience.

6   Among them are many that are used in man's war against nature. Since the mid-1940s over 200 basic chemicals have been created for use in killing insects, weeds, rodents, and other organisms described in the modern vernacular as "pests"; and they are sold under several thousand different brand names.

7   These sprays, dusts, and aerosols are now applied almost universally to farms, gardens, forests, and homes—nonselective chemicals that have the power to kill every insect, the "good" and the "bad," to still the song of birds and the leaping of fish in the streams, to coat the leaves with a deadly film, and to linger on in soil—all this though the intended target may be only a few weeds or insects. Can anyone believe it is possible to lay down such a barrage of poisons on the surface of the earth without making it unfit for all life? They should not be called "insecticides," but "biocides."

8   The whole process of spraying seems caught up in an endless spiral. Since DDT was released for civilian use, a process of escalation has been going on in which ever more toxic materials must be found. This has happened because insects, in a triumphant vindication of Darwin's principle of the survival of the fittest, have evolved super races immune to the particular insecticide used, hence a deadlier one has always to be developed—and then a deadlier one than that. It has happened also because, for reasons to be described later, destructive insects often undergo a "flareback," or resurgence, after spraying, in numbers greater than before. Thus the chemical war is never won, and all life is caught in its violent crossfire.

9   Along with the possibility of the extinction of mankind by nuclear war, the central problem of our age has therefore become the contamination of man's total environment with such substances of incredible potential for harm—substances that accumulate in the tissues of plants and animals and even penetrate the germ cells to shatter or alter the very material of heredity upon which the shape of the future depends.

10   Some would-be architects of our future look toward a time when it will be possible to alter the human germ plasm by design. But we may easily be doing so now by inadvertence, for many chemicals, like radiation, bring about gene mutations. It is ironic to think that man might determine his own future by something so seemingly trivial as the choice of an insect spray.

11   All this has been risked—for what? Future historians may well be amazed by our distorted sense of proportion. How could intelligent beings seek to control a few unwanted species by a method that contaminated the entire environment and brought the threat of disease and death even to their own kind? Yet this is precisely what we have done. We have done it, moreover, for reasons that collapse the moment we examine them. We are told that the enormous and expanding use of

pesticides is necessary to maintain farm production. Yet is our real problem not one of *overproduction?* Our farms, despite measures to remove acreages from production and to pay farmers *not* to produce, have yielded such a staggering excess of crops that the American taxpayer in 1962 is paying out more than one billion dollars a year as the total carrying cost of the surplus-food storage program. And is the situation helped when one branch of the Agriculture Department tries to reduce production while another states, as it did in 1958, "It is believed generally that reduction of crop acreages under provisions of the Soil Bank will stimulate interest in use of chemicals to obtain maximum production on the land retained in crops."

12 All this is not to say there is no insect problem and no need of control. I am saying, rather, that control must be geared to realities, not to mythical situations, and that the methods employed must be such that they do not destroy us along with the insects. ■

UNION OF CONCERNED SCIENTISTS

The Impact of Global Warming in North America

In 1969 faculty members and students at the Massachusetts Institute of Technology founded the Union of Concerned Scientists dedicated to building a cleaner, healthier environment and a safer world. The UCS offers the insights of scientific analysis to both government policy makers and the general public.

One topic the UCS has addressed is global warming. Ten of the warmest years on record have occurred since 1987, and the mean surface temperature of the earth has increased 0.5 °F over the past forty years. In January 2003, Dr. Sharon Locke of the University of Southern Maine and Dr. Susanne Moser of the Union of Concerned Scientists updated a world map to show the effects of global warming based on the latest scientific findings < www.climatehotmap.org/namerica.html >.

The map of North America reproduced here is one part of the world map. The map indicates "fingerprints," the documented effects of a widespread and long-term trend toward higher temperatures, with the darker shade. "Harbingers," events that foreshadow impacts that are likely to become more frequent and widespread, are indicated with the lighter shade. Direct links for the harbingers to global warming cannot be confirmed or eliminated at this time.

The world map on global warming makes an argument by accumulation of details. It attempts to convince you by supplying a mass of evidence. If you don't believe one particular piece of evidence is connected to global warming, there are still many others. This method of argument is particularly well suited to the Web because a visitor to the Web site can click on the many links the site provides.

Global warming fingerprint

Ocean warming, sea-level rise and coastal flooding

Chesapeake Bay

Marsh and island loss. The current rate of a sea level rise is three times the historical rate and appears to be accelerating. Since 1938, about one-third of the marsh at Blackwater National Wildlife Refuge has been submerged.

Global warming harbinger

Earlier spring arrival

Southeast Arizona

Mexican jays are laying eggs 10 days earlier than in 1971. The earlier breeding coincides with a nearly 5°F (2.8°C) increase in average nighttime temperatures from 1971 to 1998.

CHAPTER 2

Finding Arguments

What Exactly Is an Argument?

Many people think of the term *argument* as a synonym for *debate*. College courses and professional careers, however, require a different kind of argument—one that, most of the time, is cooler in emotion and more elaborate in detail than oral debate. At first glance an **argument** in writing doesn't seem have much in common with debate. But the basic elements and ways of reasoning used in written arguments are similar to those we use in everyday conversations. Let's look at an example of an informal debate.

When the pain in his abdomen didn't go away, Jeff knew he had torn something while lifting his friend's heavy speakers up a flight of stairs. He went to the student health center, and called his friend Maria when he returned home.

> An argument must have a claim and one or more reasons to support that claim.

JEFF: I have good news and bad news. The pain is a minor hernia that can be repaired with day surgery. The bad news is that the fee we pay for the health center doesn't cover hospital visits. We should have health coverage.

MARIA: Jeff, you didn't buy the extra insurance. Why should you get it for nothing?

JEFF: Because health coverage is a right.

MARIA: No it's not. Everyone doesn't have health insurance.

JEFF: Well, because in some other countries like Canada, Germany, and Britain, they do.

MARIA: Yes, and people who live in those countries pay a bundle in taxes for the government-provided insurance.

JEFF: It's not fair in this country because some people have health insurance and others don't.

MARIA: Jeff, face the facts. You could have bought the extra insurance. Instead you chose to buy a new car.

> JEFF: It would be better if the university provided health insurance because students could graduate in four years. I'm going to have to get a second job and drop out for a semester to pay for the surgery.
>
> MARIA: Neat idea, but who's going to pay for it?
>
> JEFF: OK, all students should be required to pay for health insurance as part of their general fee. Most students are healthy, and it wouldn't cost that much more.

In this discussion, Jeff starts out by making a **claim** that students should have health coverage. Maria immediately asks him why students should not have to pay for health insurance. She wants a reason to accept his claim. Scholars who study argument maintain that *an argument must have a claim and one or more reasons to support that claim.* Something less might be persuasive, but it isn't an argument.

A bumper sticker that says "NO TOLL ROADS" is a claim, but it is not an argument because the statement lacks a reason. Many reasons are possible for arguing against building toll roads:

- We don't need new roads but should build light-rail instead.
- We should raise the gas tax to pay for new roads.
- We should use gas tax revenue only for roads—rather than using it for other purposes.

When a claim has a reason attached, then it becomes an argument.

The Basics of Arguments

A reason is typically offered in a **because clause**, a statement that begins with the word *because* and that provides a supporting reason for the claim. Jeff's first attempt is to argue that students should have health insurance *because* health insurance is a right.

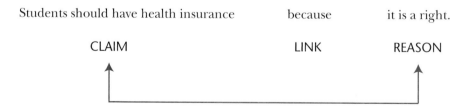

Students should have health insurance   because   it is a right.

CLAIM   LINK   REASON

The word *because* signals a **link** between the reason and the claim. Every argument that is more than a shouting match or a simple assertion has to have one or more reasons. Just having a reason for a claim, however, doesn't mean that the audience will be convinced. When Jeff tells Maria that students have a right to health insurance, Maria replies that students don't have that right. Maria will accept Jeff's claim only if she accepts that his reason supports his claim. Maria challenges Jeff's links and keeps asking "So what?" For her, Jeff's reasons are not good reasons.

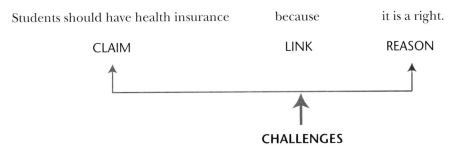

(Other people in the United States do not have free health insurance. Why should students get free insurance?)

By the end of this short discussion, Jeff has begun to build an argument. He has had to come up with another claim to support his main claim: All students should be required to pay for health insurance as part of their general fee. If he is to convince Maria, he will probably have to provide a *series of claims* that she will accept as linked to his primary claim. He will also need to find evidence to support these claims.

Benjamin Franklin observed, "So convenient a thing it is to be a rational creature, since it enables us to find or make a reason for every thing one has a mind to do." It is not hard to think of reasons. What *is* difficult is to convince your audience that your reasons are **good reasons**. In a conversation, you get immediate feedback that tells you whether your listener agrees or disagrees. When you are writing, you usually don't have someone reading who can question you immediately. Consequently, you have to (1) be more specific about what you are claiming, (2) connect with the values you hold in common with your readers, and (3) anticipate what questions and objections your readers might have, if you are going to convince someone who doesn't agree with you or know what you know already.

When you write an argument, imagine a reader like Maria who is going to listen carefully to what you have to say but who is not going to agree with you automatically. Readers like Maria will expect to see:

1. A *claim* that is interesting and makes them want to find out more about what you have to say
2. At least one *good reason* that makes your claim worth taking seriously
3. Some *evidence* that the good reason or reasons are valid
4. Some acknowledgment of the *opposing views and limitations* of the claim

The remainder of this chapter will guide you through the process of finding a topic and making a claim. Chapter 3 will help you find good reasons and evidence and anticipate objections to your claim.

WHAT IS NOT ARGUABLE

Statements of *facts* are usually not considered arguable. Most facts can be verified by doing research. But even simple facts can sometimes be argued. For example, Mount Everest is usually acknowledged to be the highest mountain in the world at 29,028 feet above sea level. But if the total height of a mountain from base to summit is the measure, then the volcano Mauna Loa in Hawaii is the highest mountain in the world. Although the top of Mauna Loa is 13,667 feet above sea level, the summit is 31,784 above the ocean floor. Thus the "fact" that Mount Everest is the highest mountain on the earth depends on a definition of *highest* being the point farthest above sea level. You could argue for this definition.

Another category of claims that are not arguable are those of *personal taste*. Your favorite food and your favorite color are examples of personal taste. If you hate fresh tomatoes, no one can convince you that you actually like them. But many claims of personal taste turn out to be value judgments using arguable criteria. For example, if you think that *Alien* is the best science fiction movie ever made, you can argue that claim using evaluative criteria that other people can consider as good reasons (see Chapter 8). Indeed, you might not even like science fiction and still argue that *Alien* is the best science fiction movie ever.

Finally, many claims rest on *beliefs* or *faith*. If someone accepts a claim as a matter of religious belief, then for that person, the claim is true and cannot be refuted. Of course, people still make arguments about the existence of God and which religion reflects the will of God. Whenever an audience will not consider an idea, it's possible but very difficult to construct an argument. Many people claim to have evidence that UFOs exist, but most people refuse to acknowledge that evidence as even being possibly factual.

▣ Find a Topic

When your instructor gives you a writing assignment, look closely at what you are asked to do. Assignments typically contain a great deal of information, and you have to *sort* that information. First, circle all the instructions about the length, the due date, the format, the grading criteria, and anything else about the production and conventions of the assignment. This information is important to you, but it doesn't tell you what the paper is supposed to be about.

Read Your Assignment Carefully

Often your assignment will contain key words such as *analyze, define, evaluate*, or *propose* that will assist you in determining what direction to take. *Analyze* can mean several things. Your instructor might want you to analyze a piece of writing (see Chapter 4), an image (see Chapter 5), or the causes of something (see Chapter 7). *Define* usually means a **definition argument**, where you argue for a definition based on the criteria you set out (see Chapter 6). *Evaluate* indicates an **evaluation argument**, where you argue that something is good, bad, best, or worst in its class according to criteria that you set out (see Chapter 8). *Write about an issue using your personal experience* indicates a **narrative argument** (see Chapter 9). *Take a position in regard to a reading* might lead you to write a **rebuttal argument** (see Chapter 10). *Propose* means that you should identify a particular problem and explain why your solution is the best one (see Chapter 11).

If you remain unclear about the purpose of the assignment after reading it carefully, talk with your instructor.

Think about What Interests You

Your assignment may specify the topic you are to write about. If your assignment gives you a wide range of options and you don't know what to write about, look first at the materials for your course: the readings, your lecture notes, and discussion boards. Think about what subjects came up in class discussion.

If you need to look outside class for a topic, think about what interests you. Subjects we argue about often find us. There are enough of them in daily life. We're late for work or class because the traffic is bad or the bus doesn't run on time. We can't find a place to park when we get to school or work. We have to negotiate through various bureaucracies for almost anything we do—making an appointment to see a doctor, getting a course added or dropped, or correcting a mistake on a bill. Most of the time we grumble and let it go at that. But sometimes we stick with a subject. Neighborhood groups in cities and towns have been especially effective in getting something done by writing about it—for example, stopping a new road from being built, getting better police and fire protection, and having a vacant lot turned into a park.

List and Analyze Issues

A good way to get started is to list possible issues to write about. Make a list of questions that can be answered "YES, because . . ." or "NO, because. . . ." (Following are some lists to get you started.) You'll find out that often before you can make a claim, you first have to analyze exactly what is meant by a phrase like *censorship of the Internet*. Does it mean censorship of the World Wide Web or of everything that goes over the Internet, including private email? To be convincing, you'll have to argue that one thing causes another, for good or bad.

Think about issues that affect your campus, your community, the nation, and the world. Which ones interest you? In which could you make a contribution to the larger discussion?

Campus

- Should students be required to pay fees for access to computers on campus?
- Should smoking be banned on campus?
- Should varsity athletes get paid for playing sports that bring in revenue?
- Should admissions decisions be based exclusively on academic achievement?
- Should knowledge of a foreign language be required for all degree plans?
- Should your college or university have a computer literacy requirement?
- Should fraternities be banned from campuses if they are caught encouraging alcohol abuse?

Community

- Should people who ride bicycles and motorcycles be required to wear helmets?
- Should high schools be allowed to search students for drugs at any time?
- Should high schools distribute condoms?
- Should bilingual education programs be eliminated?
- Should the public schools be privatized?
- Should bike lanes be built throughout your community to encourage more people to ride bicycles?
- Should more tax dollars be shifted from building highways to funding public transportation?

Nation/World

- Should advertising be banned on television shows aimed at preschool children?
- Should capital punishment be abolished?
- Should the Internet be censored?
- Should the government be allowed to monitor all phone calls and all email to combat terrorism?
- Should handguns be outlawed?
- Should beef and poultry be free of growth hormones?
- Should a law be passed requiring that the parents of teenagers who have abortions be informed?
- Should people who are terminally ill be allowed to end their lives?
- Should the United States punish nations with poor human rights records?

After You Make a List

1. Put a check beside the issues that look most interesting to write about or the ones that mean the most to you.
2. Put a question mark beside the issues that you don't know very much about. If you choose one of these issues, you will probably have to do in-depth research—by talking to people, by using the Internet, or by going to the library.

3. Select the two or three issues that look most promising. For each issue, make another list:

- Who is most interested in this issue?
- Whom or what does this issue affect?
- What are the pros and cons of this issue? Make two columns. At the top of the left one, write "YES, because." At the top of the right one, write "NO, because."
- What has been written about this issue? How can you find out what has been written?

You can get help with finding a topic, drafting a thesis, and organizing and revising your paper at your writing center.

Explore Your Topic

Once you have identified a general topic, the next step is to explore that topic. You don't have to decide exactly what to write about at this stage. Your goal is to find out how much you already know and what you need to learn more about. Experienced writers use several strategies for exploring a topic.

Freewrite

The goal of **freewriting** is to write as quickly as you can without stopping for a set time—usually five or ten minutes. Set a timer and then write as fast as you can, even if you wander off the topic. Don't stop to correct mistakes. Write the same sentence again if you get stuck momentarily. The constant flow of words will generate ideas—some useful and some not. After you've finished, read what you have written and single out any key ideas.

Freewrite on privacy

I get so much junk email and junk mail. How did so many people get my email and mail addresses? How is it collected? How does it get passed around? How do I find this out? Friend told me about a question in an interview—they had done a Google search on him. A lot of people have the same names. Easy to mix up people. Scary. How could you fix it? Amazon account tracks what I buy. Do they sell that information? What are the laws? Read that Florida made it illegal to keep track of who owns guns but they have a government list of prescription drug users. Why are prescription drug users more dangerous than gun owners?

Ideas to Use

1. *The sharing of personal information.*
2. *The misuse of personal information by corporations.*
3. *Government collected personal information.*

You may want to take one of the ideas you have identified to start another freewrite. After two or three rounds of freewriting, you should begin to identify how you might develop your topic.

Brainstorm

Another method of discovery is to brainstorm. The end result of **brainstorming** is usually a list—sometimes of questions, sometimes of statements. These questions and statements give you ways to develop your topic. Below is a list of questions on the issue of secondhand smoke.

- How much of a risk is secondhand smoke?
- What are the effects of secondhand smoke on children?

- How do the risks of secondhand smoke compare to other kinds of pollution?
- Which states ban all exposure to secondhand smoke? exposure in restaurants? exposure in the workplace?
- Who opposes banning exposure to secondhand smoke?

Use an Online Subject Directory

Online subject directories can help you identify the subtopics of a large, general topic. Try the subject index of your library's online catalog. You'll likely find subtopics listed under large topics.

Yahoo! Issues and Causes directory
(dir.yahoo.com/Society_and_Culture/Issues_and_Causes/)

One of the best Web subject directories for finding arguments is Yahoo's Issues and Causes directory. This directory provides subtopics for major issues and provides links to the Web sites of organizations interested in particular issues.

Read about Your Topic

Read about your topic extensively before writing about it. Most of the writing you will do in college will be in response to what others have written about that topic. Reading will often give you ideas about where to begin in writing about your topic and will help you think of ways of developing it. Chapter 15 gives you ways of finding material to read about your topic.

Write notes as you read—in the margins, in a notebook, or on a computer. Identify the main ideas and write questions and comments. Good reading notes are like a gift when you start to write. "Talking" to a text by writing questions and comments will help you to become familiar with it. Imagine the author sitting across the table from you. What would you say to her or him? Writing responses can bring that text to life, and it can also help you realize that the author is, like you, a person with a point of view.

Make an Idea Map

When you have a number of facts and ideas about a topic, you need to begin making connections. One method of assembling ideas is an **idea map**, which describes visually how the many aspects of a particular issue relate to each other. Idea maps are useful because you can see everything at once and make connections among the different aspects of an issue—definitions, causes, proposed solutions, and opposing points of view.

A good way to get started is to write down ideas on sticky notes. Then you can move the sticky notes around until you figure out which ideas fit together. The accompanying illustration shows what an idea map on childhood obesity might look.

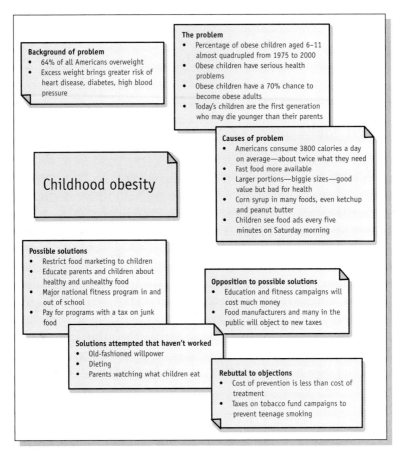

Idea map on childhood obesity

Think about Your Audience

Thinking about your audience doesn't mean telling them what they might want to hear. Instead, imagine yourself in a dialog with your audience. What questions will they likely have? How might you address any potential objections?

What Does Your Audience Know—and Not Know?

Critical to your argument is your audience's knowledge of your subject. If they are not familiar with the background information, they probably won't understand your argument fully. If you know that your readers will be unfamiliar with your subject, you will have to supply background information before attempting to convince them of your position. A good tactic is to tie your new information to what your readers already know. Comparisons and analogies can be very helpful in linking old and new information.

Another critical factor is your audience's level of expertise. How much technical language can you use? For example, if you are writing a proposal to put high-speed Internet connections into all dormitory rooms, will your readers know the difference between a T1 line and a T3 line? The director of the computation center should know the difference, but the vice president for student affairs might not. If you are unsure of your readers' knowledge level, it's better to include background information and explain technical terms. Few readers will be insulted, and they can skip over this information quickly if they are familiar with your subject.

What Is Your Audience's Attitude Toward You?

Does your audience know you at all, either by reputation or from previous work? Are you considered your reader's equal, superior, or subordinate? How your audience regards you will affect the tone and presentation of your message. Does your audience respect you and trust you? What can you include in your presentation to build trust? In many cases, your audience will know little about you. Especially in those circumstances, you can build trust in your reader by following the advice on building credibility, discussed in Chapter 3.

What Is Your Audience's Attitude Toward Your Subject?

People have prior attitudes about controversial issues that you must take into consideration as you write or speak. Imagine, for instance, that you are preparing an argument for a guest editorial in your college newspaper advocating that your state government provide parents with choices between public and private schools. You plan to argue that the tax dollars that now automatically go to public schools should go to private schools if the parents so choose. You have evidence that the sophomore-to-senior dropout rate in private schools is less than half the rate of public schools. Furthermore, students from private schools attend college at nearly twice the rate of public school graduates. You intend to argue that one of the reasons private schools are more successful is that they spend more money on instruction and less on administration. And you believe that school choice speaks to the American desire for personal freedom.

Not everyone on your campus will agree with your stand. How might the faculty at your college or university feel about this issue? the administrators? the staff? other students? interested people in the community who read the student newspaper? What attitudes toward public funding of private schools will they have before they start reading what you have to say? How are you going to deal with the objection that because many students in private schools come from more affluent families, it is not surprising that they do better?

Even when you write about a much less controversial subject, you must think carefully about your audience's attitudes toward what you have to say or write. Sometimes, your audience may share your attitudes; other times, your audience may be neutral; at still other times, your audience will have attitudes that differ sharply from your own. Anticipate these various attitudes and act accordingly. Show awareness of the attitudes of your audience, and if those attitudes are very different from yours, you will have to work hard to counter them without insulting your audience.

Write a Thesis

Once you have identified a topic and have a good sense of how to develop it, the next critical step is to write a **working thesis**. Your **thesis** states your main idea. Much writing that you will do in college and later in your career will have an explicit thesis, usually stated near the beginning. The thesis announces your topic and indicates what points you want to make about that topic.

Focus Your Thesis

The thesis can make or break your paper. If the thesis is too broad, you cannot do justice to the argument. Who wouldn't wish for fewer traffic accidents, better medical care, more effective schools, or a cleaner environment? Simple solutions for these complex problems are unlikely.

Stating something that is obvious to everyone isn't an arguable thesis. Don't settle for easy answers. It's easy to make broad generalization or make predictable statements when your topic is too broad. Narrow your focus and concentrate on the areas where you have the most questions. Those places are likely the ones where your readers will have the most questions too.

The opposite problem is less common: a too-narrow thesis. If your thesis is only a statement of a commonly known fact, then it is too narrow. For example, the growth rate of the population in the United States has doubled since 1970 because of immigration. The Census Bureau provides reasonably accurate statistical information, so this claim is not arguable. But the policies that allow increased immigration and the effects of a larger population on more crowding, congestion, and the costs of housing, education, and transportation are arguable.

NOT ARGUABLE: The population of the United States grew faster in the 1990s than in any previous decade because Congress increased the level of legal immigration and the government stopped enforcing most laws against illegal immigration in the interior of the country.

ARGUABLE: Allowing a high rate of immigration helps the United States deal with the problems of an increasingly aging society and helps provide funding for millions of Social Security recipients.

ARGUABLE: The increase in the number of visas to foreign workers in technology industries is the major cause of unemployment in those industries.

Evaluate Your Thesis

Once you have a working thesis, ask these questions:

1. Is it arguable?
2. Is it specific?
3. Is it manageable in the length and time you have?
4. Is it interesting to your intended readers?

Example 1

Sample thesis:
We should take action to resolve the serious traffic problem in our city.

Arguable? The thesis is arguable, but it lacks a focus.

Specific? The thesis is too broad.

Manageable? Transportation is a complex issue. New highways and rail systems are expensive and take many years to build. Furthermore, citizens don't want new roads running through their neighborhoods.

Interesting? The topic has the potential to be interesting if the writer can propose a specific solution to a problem everyone in the city recognizes.

When a thesis is too broad, it needs to be revised to address a specific aspect of an issue. Make the big topic smaller.

Revised thesis:
The existing freight railway that runs through the center of the city should be converted to a passenger railway because it is the cheapest and quickest way to decrease traffic congestion downtown.

Example 2

Sample thesis:
Over 60% of Americans play video games on a regular basis.

Arguable? The thesis states a commonly acknowledged fact.

Specific? The thesis is too narrow.

Manageable? A known fact is stated in the thesis, so there is little to research. Several surveys report this finding.

Interesting? Video games are interesting as a cultural trend, but nearly everyone is aware of the trend. The popularity of video games is well established.

There's nothing original or interesting about stating that Americans love video games. Think about what is controversial. One debatable topic is the effects of video games on children.

Revised thesis:
Video games are valuable because they improve children's visual attention skills, their literacy skills, and their computer literacy skills.

CHAPTER 3

Finding and Supporting Good Reasons

The Basics of Reasoning

You decide to pick up a new pair of prescription sunglasses at the mall on your way to class. The company promises that it can make your glasses in an hour, but what you hadn't counted on was how long it would take you to park and how long you would have to wait in line at the counter. You jog into the mall, drop off your prescription, and go out of the store to wait. There's a booth nearby where volunteers are checking blood pressure. You don't have anything better to do, so you have your blood pressure checked.

After the volunteer takes the blood pressure cuff off your arm, he asks how old you are. He asks you whether you smoke, and you say no. He tells you that your reading is 150 over 100. He says that's high for a person your age and that you ought to have it checked again. "This is all I need," you think. "I have a test coming up tomorrow, a term paper due Friday, and if I don't make it to class, I won't get my homework turned in on time. And now something bad is wrong with me."

When you get your blood pressure checked again at the student health center after your test the next day, it turns out to be 120/80, which the nurse says is normal. When you think about it, you realize that you probably had a high reading because of stress and jogging into the mall.

Your blood pressure is one of the most important indicators of your health. When the volunteer checking your blood pressure tells you that you might have a serious health problem because your blood pressure is too high, he is relying on his knowledge of how the human body works. If your blood pressure is too high, it

> A good reason works because it includes a link to your claim that your readers will find valid.

eventually damages your arteries and puts a strain on your entire body. But he used the word *might* because your blood pressure is not the same all the time. It can go up when you are under stress or even when you eat too much salt. And blood pressure varies from person to person and even in different parts of your body. For example, your blood pressure is higher in your legs than in your arms.

Doctors use blood pressure and other information to make diagnoses. Diagnoses are claims based on evidence. But as the blood pressure example shows, often the link is not clear, at least from a single reading. A doctor will collect several blood pressure readings over many weeks or even years before concluding that a patient has a condition of high blood pressure called *hypertension*. These readings will be compared to readings from thousands of other patients in making a diagnosis. Doctors are trained to rely on **generalizations** from thousands of past observations in medical science and to make diagnoses based on probability. In everyday life, you learn to make similar generalizations from which you make decisions based on probability. If you are in a hurry in the grocery store, you likely will go to the line that looks the shortest. You pick the shortest line because you think it will probably be the fastest.

Sometimes we don't have past experience to rely on, and we have to reason in other ways. When we claim that one thing is like something else, we make a link by **analogy**. When a United States court ruled against Microsoft in an antitrust case, Microsoft's lawyers argued by analogy against the decision. They maintained that requiring Microsoft to bundle the rival browser Netscape Navigator with their own browser, Internet Explorer, was as irrational as expecting Coca-Cola to put three cans of Pepsi in every six-pack of Coke. The analogy drew on the fierce rivalry between Coca-Cola and Pepsi, where no one would expect either to help the other to sell its product.

Another way we reason is by using **cultural assumptions**, which we often think of as common sense. For example, you walk down the street and see a 280Z speed around a car that is double-parked, cross the double line, and sideswipe a truck coming the other way. A police officer arrives shortly, and you tell her that the 280Z is at fault. Maybe you've seen many accidents before, but the reason you think the 280Z is at fault is because in the United States, drivers are supposed to stay on the right side of two-way roads. It is a part of our culture that you take for granted—that is, until you try to drive in Japan, Great Britain, or India, where people drive on the left. Driving on the left will seem unnatural to you, but it's natural for the people in those countries.

Particular cultural assumptions can be hard to challenge because you often have to take on an entire system of belief. It is much easier to use the metric system to calculate distances than it is to employ the English system of miles, feet, and inches. Nonetheless, people in the United States have strongly resisted efforts to convert to metric measures. When cultural assumptions become common sense, people accept them as true even though they often can be questioned. It seems like common sense to say that salad is good for you, but in reality it depends on what's in the salad. A salad consisting of lettuce and a mayonnaise-based dressing has little nutritional value and too much fat.

Find Good Reasons

A **good reason** works because it includes a link to your claim that your readers will find valid. Your readers are almost like a jury that passes judgment on your good reasons. If they accept them and cannot think of other, more compelling good reasons that oppose your position, you will convince them.

Most good reasons derive from mulling things over "reasonably," or, to use the technical term, from logos. *Logos* refers to the logic of what you communicate; in fact, logos is the root of our modern word *logic*. Good reasons are thus commonly associated with logical appeals. Over the years, rhetoricians have devised questions to help speakers and writers find good reasons to support their arguments. These questions will equip you to communicate more effectively when you are speaking before a group as well as writing an argument. But do not expect every question to be productive in every case. Sometimes, a certain question won't get you very far; and often, the questions will develop so many good reasons and strategies that you will not be able to use them all. You will ultimately have to select from among the best of your good reasons to find the ones that are most likely to work in a given case.

If a certain question does not seem to work for you at first, do not give up on it the next time. Get in the habit of asking these questions in the course of developing your arguments. If you ask them systematically, you will probably have more good reasons than you need for your arguments.

Can You Argue by Definition?

Probably the most powerful kind of good reason is an **argument from definition**. You can think of a definition as a simple statement: _____ *is a* _____.

You use these statements all the time. When you need a course to fulfill your social science requirement, you look at the list of courses that are defined as social science courses. You find out that the anthropology class you want to take is one of them. It's just as important when _____ *is not a* _____. Suppose you are taking College Algebra this semester, which is a math course taught by the math department, yet it doesn't count for the math requirement. The reason it doesn't count is because College Algebra is not defined as a college-level math class. So you have to enroll next semester in Calculus I.

Many definitions are not nearly as clear cut as the math requirement. If you want to argue that figure skaters are athletes, you will need to define what an athlete is. You start thinking. An athlete competes in an activity, but that definition alone is too broad, since many competitions do not require physical activity. Thus, an athlete must participate in a competitive physical activity and must train for it. But that definition is still not quite narrow enough, since soldiers train for competitive physical activity. You decide to add that the activity must be a sport and that it must require special competence and precision. Your *because clause* turns out as follows: *Figure skaters are athletes because true athletes train for and compete in physical sporting competitions that require special competence and precision.*

If you can get your audience to accept your definitions of things, you've gone a long way toward convincing them of the validity of your claim. That is why the most controversial issues in our culture—abortion, affirmative action, gay rights, pornography, women's rights, gun control, the death penalty—are argued from definition. Is abortion a crime or a medical procedure? Is pornography protected by the First Amendment, or is it a violation of women's rights? Is the death penalty just or cruel and inhuman? You can see from these examples that definitions often rely on cultural assumptions for their links.

Because cultural assumptions about controversial issues are strongly held, people usually don't care about the practical consequences. Arguing that it is much cheaper to execute prisoners who have been convicted of first-degree murder than to keep them in prison for life does not convince those who believe that it is morally wrong to kill. (See Chapter 6.)

Can You Argue from Value?

A special kind of argument from definition, one that often implies consequences, is the **argument from value**. You can support your claim with a because clause (or several of them) that includes a sense of evaluation. Arguments from value follow from claims like _____ *is a good* _____, or _____ *is not a good* _____.

You make arguments from value every day. Your old TV set breaks, so you go to your local discount store to buy a new one. When you get there, you find too many choices. You have to decide which one to buy. You have only $200 to spend, but there are still a lot of choices. Which is the best TV for $200 or less? The more you look, the more confusing it gets. There are several 20-inch TVs in your price range. All have remote control. Some have features such as front surround sound, multilingual on-screen display, and A/V inputs. But you realize that there is one test that will determine the best TV for you: the picture quality. You buy the one with the best picture.

Evaluative arguments usually proceed from the presentation of certain criteria. These criteria come from the definitions of good and bad, of poor and not so poor, that prevail in a given case. A really good 20-inch TV fulfills certain criteria; so does an outstanding movie, an excellent class, or, if you work in an office, an effective telephone system. Sometimes the criteria are straightforward, as in the TV example. The TV that you select has to be under a certain cost, equipped with a remote, and ready to hook up to your cable. After those criteria are met, the big ones are picture and sound quality. But if your boss asks you to recommend a new telephone system, then it's not quite so straightforward. You are presented with many options, and you have to decide which of them are worth paying for. You have to decide how the phone system is going to be used, examine which features will be important for your office, and then rate the systems according to the criteria you have set out. The key to evaluation arguments is identifying and arguing for the right criteria. If you can convince your readers that you have the right criteria and that your assessments are correct, then you will be convincing. (See Chapter 8).

Can You Compare or Contrast?

Evaluative arguments can generate comparisons often enough. But even if they don't generate comparisons, your argument might profit if you get in the habit of thinking in comparative terms—in terms of what things are like or unlike the topic you are discussing. **Claims of comparisons** take the form _____ *is like* _____ or _____ *is not like* _____. If you are having trouble coming up with good reasons, think of comparisons that help your readers agree with you. If you want to argue that figure skaters are athletes, you might think about how their training and competitions resemble those of other athletes. Making comparisons is an effective way of building common ground.

A particular kind of comparison is an analogy. An analogy is an extended comparison—one that is developed over several sentences or paragraphs for explanatory or persuasive purposes. Analogies take different forms. A historical analogy compares something that is going on now with a similar case in the past. One of the most frequently used historical analogies is a comparison of a current situation in which one country attacks or threatens another with Germany's seizing of Czechoslovakia in 1938 and then invading Poland in 1939, which started World War II. The difficulty with this analogy is that circumstances today are not the same as those in 1939, and it is easy to point out how the analogy fails.

Other analogies make literal comparisons. A literal analogy is a comparison between current situations, in which you argue that what is true or works in one situation should be true or should work in another. Most advanced nations provide basic health care to all their citizens either free or at minimal charge. All citizens of Canada are covered by the same comprehensive health care system, which is free for both rich and poor. Canadians go to the doctor more frequently than citizens of the United States do, and they receive what is generally regarded as better care than their southern neighbors, who pay the most expensive health care bills on the planet.

The Canadian analogy has failed to convince members of the U.S. Congress to vote for a similar system in the United States. Opponents of adopting the Canadian system argue that health care costs are also high in Canada, but Canadians pay the costs in different ways. They pay high taxes, and the Canadian national debt has increased since the universal health system was approved. These opponents of adopting the Canadian system for the United States believe that the best care can be obtained for the lowest cost if health care is treated like any other service and consumers decide what they are willing to pay. Comparisons can always work both ways.

Analogies are especially valuable when you are trying to explain a concept to a willing listener or reader, but analogies are far from foolproof if the reader does not agree with you from the outset. Using an analogy can be risky if the entire argument depends on the reader's accepting it.

Can You Argue from Consequence?

Another powerful source of good reasons comes from considering the possible consequences of your position: Can you sketch out the good things that will follow from your position? Can you establish that certain bad things will be avoided if your position is adopted? If so, you will have other good reasons to use.

Arguments from consequence take the basic form of _____ *causes* _____ (or _____ *does not cause* _____). Very often, arguments from consequence are more complicated, taking the form _____ *causes* _____ *which, in turn, causes* _____ and so on. In Chapter 1 we describe how *Silent Spring* makes powerful arguments from consequence. Rachel Carson's primary claim is that *DDT should not be sprayed on a massive scale because it will poison animals and people.* The key to her argument is the causal chain that explains how animals and people are poisoned. Carson describes how nothing exists alone in nature. When a potato field is sprayed with chemical poison such as DDT, some of that poison is absorbed by the skin of the potatoes and some washes into the groundwater, where it contaminates drinking water. Other poisonous residue is absorbed into streams, where it is ingested by insect larvae, which in turn are eaten by fish. Fish are eaten by other fish, which are then eaten by waterfowl and people. At each stage, the poisons become more concentrated. Carson shows why people are in danger from drinking contaminated water and eating contaminated vegetables and fish. Even today, over thirty years after DDT stopped being used in the United States, dangerous levels exist in the sediment at the bottom of many lakes and bays. (See Chapter 7.)

Proposal arguments are future-oriented arguments from consequence. In a proposal argument, you cannot stop with naming good reasons; you also have to show that these consequences would follow from the idea or course of action that you are arguing. As an example, let's say you want to argue that all high school graduates in your state should be computer literate. You want a computer requirement more substantial than the one computer literacy course you had in the eighth grade. You want all high school graduates to be familiar with basic computer concepts and terminology, to be able to use a word processing application and at least two other applications, and to understand issues of ethics and privacy raised by new electronic technologies.

Your strongest good reason is that high school graduates should be competent in the use of computers, the tool that they will most certainly use for most writing tasks and many other activities during their lifetime. Even if your readers accept that good reason, you still have to prove that the requirement will actually give students the competency they require. Many students pass language requirements without being able to speak, read, or write the language they have studied.

Furthermore, you have to consider the feasibility of any proposal that you make. A good idea has to be a practical one. If you want to impose a computer literacy requirement, you have to argue for increased funding for expensive technology. High school students in poor communities cannot become computer literate unless they have access to computers. More teachers might also need to be hired. And you will need to figure out how to fit the computer requirement into an already crowded curriculum. Sometimes, feasibility is not a major issue (for example, if you're proposing that the starting time for basketball games be changed by thirty minutes), but if it is, you must address it. (See Chapter 11.)

Can You Counter Objections to Your Position?

Another good way to find convincing good reasons is to think about possible objections to your position. If you can imagine how your audience might counter or respond to your argument, you will probably include in your argument precisely the points that will address your readers' particular needs and objections. If you are successful, your readers will be convinced that you are right. You've no doubt had the experience yourself of mentally saying to a writer in the course of your reading, "Yeah, but what about this other idea?"—only to have the writer address precisely this objection.

You can impress your readers that you've thought about why anyone would oppose your position and exactly how that opposition would be expressed. If you are writing a proposal argument for a computer literacy requirement for all high school graduates, you might think about why anyone would object, since computers are becoming increasingly important to our jobs and lives. What will the practical objections be? What philosophical ones? Why hasn't such a requirement been put in place already? By asking such questions in your own arguments, you are likely to develop robust because clauses that may be the ones that most affect your readers.

Sometimes, writers pose rhetorical questions such as "You might say, 'But won't paying for computers for all students make my taxes go up?'" Stating objections explicitly can be effective if you make the objections as those of a reasonable person with an alternative point of view. But if the objections you state are ridiculous ones, then you risk being accused of setting up a *straw man*—that is, making the position opposing your own so simplistic that no one would likely identify with it. (See Chapter 10.)

QUESTIONS FOR FINDING GOOD REASONS

1. Can you argue by definition—from "the nature of the thing"?

- Can you argue that while many (most) people think X is a Y, X is better thought of as a Z?
  Example: Most people do not think of humans as an endangered species, but small farmers have been successful in comparing their way of life to an endangered species and thus have extended the definition of an endangered species to include themselves.

- Can you argue that while X is a Y, X differs from other Ys and might be thought of as a Z?
  Example: Colleges and universities are similar to public schools in having education as their primary mission, but unlike public schools, colleges and universities receive only part of their operating costs from tax revenues and therefore, like a business, must generate much of their own revenue.

2. Can you argue from value?

- Can you grade a few examples of the kind of thing you are evaluating as good, better, and best (or bad and worse)?
  Example: There have been lots of great actors in detective films, but none compare to Humphrey Bogart.

- Can you list the features you use to determine whether something is good or bad and then show why one is most important?
  Example: Coach Powers taught me a great deal about the skills and strategy of playing tennis, but most of all, she taught me that the game is fun.

3. Can you compare or contrast?

- Can you think of items, events, or situations that are similar or dissimilar to the one you are writing about?
  Example: We should require a foreign language for all students at our college because our main competitor does not have such a requirement.

(continued)

QUESTIONS FOR FINDING GOOD REASONS *(continued)*

- Can you distinguish why your subject is different from one usually thought of as similar?
  Example: While poor people are often lumped in with the unemployed and those on welfare, the majority of poor people do work in low-paying jobs.

4. Can you argue from consequence?

- Can you argue that good things will happen if a certain course of action is followed or that bad things will be avoided?
  Example: Eliminating all income tax deductions would save every taxpayer many hours and would create a system of taxation that does not reward people for cheating.

- Can you argue that while there were obvious causes of Y, Y would not have occurred had it not been for X?
  Example: A 17-year-old driver is killed when her car skids across the grass median of an interstate highway and collides with a pickup truck going the other direction. Even though a slick road and excessive speed were the immediate causes, the driver would be alive today if the median had had a concrete barrier.

- Can you argue for an alternative cause rather than the one many people assume?
  Example: Politicians take credit for reducing the violent crime rate because of "get-tough" police policies, but in fact, the rate of violent crime is decreasing because more people are working.

5. Can you counter objections to your position?

- Can you think of the most likely objections to your claim and turn them into your own good reasons?
  Example: High school administrators might object to requiring computer literacy because of cost, but schools can now lease computers and put them on a statewide system at a cost less than they now pay for textbooks.

- Can the *reverse* or opposite of an opposing claim be argued?
  Example: A proposed expressway through a city is claimed to help traffic, but it also could make traffic worse by encouraging more people to drive to the city.

Find Evidence to Support Good Reasons

Good reasons are essential ingredients of good arguments, but they don't do the job alone. You must support or verify good reasons with evidence. **Evidence** consists of hard data or examples or narratives or episodes or tabulations of episodes (known as *statistics*) that are seen as relevant to the good reasons that you are putting forward. To put it another way, a writer of arguments puts forward not only claims and good reasons but also evidence that those good reasons are true. And that evidence consists of examples, personal experiences, comparisons, statistics, calculations, quotations, and other kinds of data that a reader will find relevant and compelling.

How much supporting evidence should you supply? How much evidence is enough? That is difficult to generalize about; as is usual in the case of rhetoric, the best answer is to say, "It depends." If a reader is likely to find one of your good reasons hard to believe, then you should be aggressive in offering support. You should present detailed evidence in a patient and painstaking way. As one presenting an argument, you have a responsibility not just to *state* a case but to *make* a case with evidence. Arguments that are unsuccessful tend to fail not because of a shortage of good reasons; more often, they fail because the reader doesn't agree that there is enough evidence to support the good reason that is being presented.

If your good reason isn't especially controversial, you probably should not belabor it. Think of your own experiences as a reader. How often do you recall saying to yourself, as you read a passage or listened to a speaker, "OK! OK! I get the point! Don't keep piling up all of this evidence for me because I don't want it or need it." However, such a reaction is rare, isn't it? By contrast, how often do you recall muttering under your breath, "How can you say that? What evidence do you have to back it up?" When in doubt, err on the side of offering too much evidence. It's an error that is seldom made and not often criticized.

When a writer doesn't provide satisfactory evidence for a because clause, readers might feel that there has been a failure in the reasoning process. In fact, in your previous courses in writing and speaking, you may have learned about various **fallacies** associated with faulty arguments (which are listed on page 51–52).

Strictly speaking, there is nothing false about these so-called logical fallacies. The fallacies most often refer to failures in providing evidence; when you don't provide enough good evidence to convince your audience, you might be accused of committing a fallacy in reasoning. You will usually avoid such accusations if the evidence that you cite is both *relevant* and *sufficient*.

Relevance refers to the appropriateness of the evidence to the case at hand. Some kinds of evidence are seen as more relevant than others for particular audiences. For example, in science and industry, personal testimony is seen as having limited relevance, while experimental procedures and controlled observations have far more credibility. Compare someone who defends the use of a particular piece of computer software because "it worked for me" with someone who defends it because "according to a journal article published last month, 84 percent of the users of the software were satisfied or very satisfied with it." On the other hand, in writing to the general public on controversial issues such as gun control, personal experience is often considered more relevant than other kinds of data. The so-called Brady Bill, which requires a mandatory waiting period for the purchase of handguns, was named for President Ronald Reagan's press secretary, James Brady, who was permanently disabled when John W. Hinckley, Jr., made an assassination attempt on the president in 1981. James Brady's wife, Sarah, effectively told the story of her husband's suffering in lobbying for the bill.

Sufficiency refers to the amount of evidence cited. Sometimes a single piece of evidence or a single instance will carry the day if it is especially compelling in some way—if it represents the situation well or makes a point that isn't particularly controversial. More often, people expect more than one piece of evidence if they are to be convinced of something. Convincing readers that they should approve a statewide computer literacy requirement for all high school graduates will require much more evidence than the story of a single graduate who succeeded with her computer skills. You will likely need statistical evidence for such a broad proposal.

If you anticipate that your audience might not accept your evidence, face the situation squarely. First, think carefully about the argument you are presenting. If you cannot cite adequate evidence for your assertions, perhaps those assertions must be modified or qualified in some way. If you remain convinced of your assertions, then think about doing more research to come up with additional evidence. If you anticipate that your audience might suspect you have overlooked or minimized important information, reassure them that you have not and deal explicitly with conflicting arguments. Another strategy is to acknowledge explicitly the limitations of your evidence. Acknowledging limitations doesn't shrink the limitations, but it does build your credibility and convinces your audience that alternatives have indeed been explored fully and responsibly. If you are thinking of your reader as a partner rather than as an adversary, it is usually easy to acknowledge limitations because you are looking not for victory and the end of debate but for a mutually satisfactory situation that might emerge as a result of the communication process that you are part of.

FALLACIES IN ARGUMENTS

Reasoning in arguments depends less on *proving* a claim than it does on finding evidence for the claim that readers will accept as valid. Logical fallacies in argument reflect a failure to provide adequate evidence for the claim that is being made. Among the most common fallacies are the following.

- **Bandwagon appeals.** *It doesn't matter if I cheat on a test because everyone else does.* This argument suggests that everyone is doing it, so why shouldn't you? Close examination may reveal that in fact everyone really isn't doing it—and in any case, it may not be the right thing to do.

- **Begging the question.** *People should be able to use land any way they want to because using land is an individual right.* The fallacy of begging the question occurs when the claim is restated and passed off as evidence.

- **Either-or.** *Either we build a new freeway crossing downtown or else there will be perpetual gridlock.* The either-or fallacy suggests that there are only two choices in a complex situation. This is rarely, if ever, the case. (In this example, the writer ignores other transportation options besides freeways.)

- **False analogies.** *The Serbian seizure of Bosnian territory was like Hitler's takeover of Czechoslovakia in 1938, and having learned the hard way what happens when they give in to dictators, Western nations stood up to Serbian aggression.* Analogies always depend on the degree of resemblance of one situation to another. In this case, the analogy fails to recognize that Serbia in 1993 was hardly like Nazi Germany in 1938.

- **Hasty generalization.** *We had three days this summer when the temperature reached an all-time high; that's a sure sign of global warming.* A hasty generalization is a broad claim made on the basis of a few occurrences. The debate over global warming takes into account climate data for centuries. Individual climate events such as record hot days do not confirm trends.

- **Name calling.** Name calling is as frequent in political argument as on the playground. Candidates are "accused" of being tax-and-spend liberals, ultraconservatives, radical feminists, and so on. Rarely are these terms defined; hence they are meaningless.

- **Non sequitur.** *A university that can afford to build a new football stadium should not have to raise tuition.* A non sequitur (a Latin term meaning "it does not follow") ties together two unrelated ideas. In this case, the argument fails to recognize that the money for new stadiums is often donated for that purpose and is not part of a university's general revenue.

(continued)

FALLACIES IN ARGUMENTS *(continued)*

- **Oversimplification.** *No one would run stop signs if we had a mandatory death penalty for doing it.* This claim may be true, but the argument would be unacceptable to most citizens. More complex, if less definitive, solutions are called for.

- **Polarization.** *Feminists are all man haters.* Polarization, like name calling, exaggerates positions and groups by representing them as extreme and divisive.

- **Post hoc fallacy.** *I ate a hamburger last night and got deathly sick—must have been food poisoning.* The post hoc fallacy (from the Latin *post hoc ergo hoc,* "after this, therefore this") assumes that things that follow in time have a causal relationship. In this example, you may have simply started coming down with the flu—as would be obvious two days later.

- **Rationalization.** *I could have done better on the test if I thought the course mattered to my major.* People frequently come up with excuses and weak explanations for their own and others' behavior that avoid actual causes.

- **Slippery slope.** *We shouldn't grant amnesty to illegal immigrants now living in the United States because it will mean opening our borders to a flood of people from around the world who want to move here.* The slippery slope fallacy assumes that if the first step is taken, other steps necessarily follow.

- **Straw man.** *Environmentalists won't be satisfied until not a single human being is allowed to enter a national park.* A straw man argument is a diversionary tactic that sets up another's position in a way that can be easily rejected. In fact, only a small percentage of environmentalists would make an argument even close to this one.

Organize Good Reasons

Asking a series of questions can generate a list of because clauses, but even if you have plenty, you still have to decide which ones to use and in what order to present them. How can you decide which points are likely to be most persuasive? In choosing which good reasons to use in your arguments, consider your readers' attitudes and values and the values that are especially sanctioned by your community.

When people communicate, they tend to present their own thinking—to rely on the lines of thought that have led them to believe as they do. That's natural enough, since it is reasonable to present to others the reasons that make us believe what we are advocating in writing or speech. People have much in common, and it is natural to think that the evidence and patterns of thought that have guided your thinking to a certain point will also guide others to the same conclusions.

But people are also different, and what convinces you might not always convince others. When you are deciding what because clauses to present to others, try not so much to recapitulate your own thinking process as to influence the thinking of others. Ask yourself not just why you think as you do but also what you need to convince others to see things your way. Don't pick the because clauses that seem compelling to you; pick those that will seem compelling to your audience.

Create Credibility

You have probably noticed that many times in the course of reading, you get a very real sense of the kind of person who is doing the writing. Even if you have never read this person's writing before, even if you really know nothing about the actual person behind the message, you still often get a sense of the character and personality of the writer just by reading. How you respond to the message to some extent depends on how you respond to the person who delivers it.

In March 1997, scientists at the Oregon Regional Primate Research Center held a press conference to announce that they had successfully cloned two rhesus monkeys from early-stage embryos. They had taken a set of chromosomes from cells in a primitive monkey embryo and inserted them into egg cells from which the original DNA had been removed. These embryos were then implanted in the wombs of host mothers using in vitro fertilization techniques. The monkeys were born normally and were expected to live as long as twenty years. Donald Wolf, a senior scientist at the center, called the cloning a major breakthrough, since it would remove some of the uncertainties in animal research that might have been attributed to genetic differences among animals.

Other people were greatly alarmed by the cloning of the monkeys that followed closely the announcement of the successful cloning of sheep. The U.S. Congress organized hearings that began in March 1997 to examine the implications of cloning research. Following are two examples of letters sent to the House Science Subcommittee on Technology following the hearings. What persona did the writer of each of the following letters create? Both letters contain the same major points, and both are passionate in demanding legislation to end cloning of animals. Both assert that cloning monkeys for research purposes is wrong because it lacks scientific and ethical justification. But they stand apart in the ethos of the writer.

The writer of the first letter, Helen Barnes, attempts to establish common ground by noting that nearly everybody is opposed to the cloning of humans. Barnes makes a bridge to her issue by noting that the terms used for human cloning—*repulsive, repugnant, offensive*—should also be used for the cloning of animals. She urges Representative Morella to look at monkeys as beings rather than genetic material for the use of researchers. She points out the absence of any voices opposed to the use of monkeys for experiments at the hearings on cloning. She takes a strong stand at the end, but she uses "we," inviting Representative Morella to join her.

Rep. Connie Morella, Chairperson
House Science Subcommittee on Technology
2319 Rayburn House Office Building
Washington, DC 20515

Dear Representative Morella:

I am pleased to see among members of Congress great concern that humans should not be cloned. What perplexes me is the lack of protest against cloning animals. "Repulsive," "repugnant," "offensive"—scientists and politicians alike have used these words to describe human cloning experiments, but these adjectives should also be invoked to describe cloning experiments on animals.

There are both ethical and scientific reasons to oppose the cloning of animals. Animals are simply not commodities with whose genetic material we can tamper in pursuit of human ends. M. Susan Smith, director of the Oregon Primate Research Center, where Rhesus monkeys were cloned from embryo cells, says that we should be glad that scientists will now need to use "only" 3 or 4 animals instead of 20 or 30. But Smith and other proponents of animal experimentation really just don't get it. What about the 3 or 4 beings who will suffer and die in experiments? We don't bargain with lives—3 or 40—it's their use in experiments that's wrong.

Smith and other scientists justify their work by stating that genetically identical monkeys will help research into AIDS, alcoholism, depression and other illnesses. Scientists can clone a million monkeys, but they still won't be good models for human disease. It is not genetic variability that limits the effectiveness of animal experimentation—it's that the physiology of animal species differs. Animals are not "little humans," and there's no way that researchers can clone themselves around that reality.

At the recent Congressional hearings on the ethics of cloning, testimony was heard from the following: the director of National Institutes of Health, the largest funding agency of animal experimentation in the country; the head of Genzyme Transgenics Corporation, a company that seeks to profit from genetically manipulated animals; a representative from the U.S. Department of Agriculture, which is interested in the potential of cloning animals for food; Smith of Oregon Primate Research Center; and an ethicist who declared (and numerous exposés of animal experiments refute) that we do not permit research that is cruel to animals in our society.

There was a voice missing from this panel biased in favor of animal cloning: someone to represent the animals, whose lives and interests are so readily dismissed. We all need to speak up for them now and demand legislation to ban all cloning experiments.

Sincerely,
Helen Barnes

The writer of the second letter, by contrast, is confrontational from the outset. Ed Younger accuses Representative Morella of stacking the deck by inviting only proponents of cloning to the hearing. He insinuates that she is stupid if she doesn't realize the cloned monkeys will be killed and that the use of animals for testing has not produced cures for diseases such as cancer and AIDS. He suggests that she is a dupe of high-tech companies by taking their side. He ends with a threat to vote her out of office. His persona is clearly that of angry citizen.

Rep. Connie Morella, Chairperson
House Science Subcommittee on Technology
2319 Rayburn House Office Building
Washington, DC 20515

Dear Representative Morella:

I cannot believe you actually pretended to have a hearing on animal cloning and only invited people in favor of cloning. Why didn't you invite someone to speak for the animals? What a waste of our tax dollars! You should be passing laws against cloning instead of trying to justify it.

Don't you understand that the monkeys are being cloned to be killed? Thousands of monkeys have died in research on cancer and AIDS, and we're still no closer to finding cures. Don't you see that such research is useless? It's not that difficult to figure out. Monkeys are not people. It doesn't matter if they have identical genes or not.

We see what's happening. This is another example of government protecting big business over the interests of the people. The only people who will benefit from cloning animals are the big executives of the high-tech companies and a few scientists who will make big profits.

Haven't you read the polls and noticed that the great majority of Americans are opposed to cloning? You'll find out how we feel when you have to run for reelection!

Sincerely,
Ed Younger

Representatives often receive more than a thousand letters, faxes, and emails each day, and they have to deal with letters from angry people all the time. Usually, staff members answer the mail and simply tally up who is for and against a particular issue. Often, the reply is a form letter thanking the writer for his or her concern and stating the representative's position. But sometimes, representatives personally write detailed answers to letters from their constituents. Imagine that you are Representative Morella and you have to answer these two letters. Ed Younger's persona makes it difficult to say more than "I appreciate hearing your opinion on this issue." Helen Barnes's persona leaves open the possibility of an exchange of ideas.

People make judgments about you that are based on how you represent yourself when you write. Sometimes the angry voice is the one to present if you believe that your readers need a wake-up call. However, most people don't like to be yelled at. Just as you can change your voice orally when the situation calls for it—just as you can speak in a friendly way, in an excited way, or in a stern way in different circumstances—so too you should be able to modulate your voice in writing, depending on what is called for. Some important factors are the following:

- **Your relationship with your audience** (Your voice can be less formal when you know someone well or when you are communicating with people in the same circumstances than when you are communicating with a relative stranger or with someone above or below you in an organization.)
- **Your audience's personality** (Different people respond sympathetically to different voices.)
- **Your argument** (Some arguments are more difficult to make than others.)

ARGUE RESPONSIBLY

In Washington, D.C., cars with diplomatic license plates often park illegally. Their drivers know they will not be towed or have to pay a ticket. For people who abuse the diplomatic privilege, the license plate says in effect, "I'm not playing by the rules."

In a similar way, you announce you are not playing by the rules when you begin an argument by saying "in my opinion." First, a reader assumes that if you make a claim in writing, you believe that claim. More important, it is rarely *only* your opinion. Most beliefs and assumptions are shared by many people. If it is only your opinion, it can be easily dismissed. But if your position is likely to be held by at least a few other members of your community, then a responsible reader must consider your position seriously.

- **Your purpose** (You may take a more urgent tone if you want your readers to act immediately.)
- **Your genre** (Arguments in formal proposals usually have a different voice from arguments in newspaper sports and opinion columns.)

Choose an Appropriate Voice

Arguments that are totally predictable quickly lose their effectiveness. Being aware of your options in creating a **voice** when you write is one of the secrets of arguing successfully. Before those options are described for a specific argument, a little background for the case in point will be useful. In June 1989, the Supreme Court ruled in *Texas v. Johnson* to uphold the First Amendment right to burn the U.S. flag as symbolic political speech. An outraged Congress approved the Flag Protection Act of 1989, but the Senate voted down an amendment to the Constitution. After the Flag Protection Act became law, there were many protests against it. Some protesters were arrested, but the courts ruled that the Flag Protection Act was unconstitutional. Pressure built to get a flag protection amendment into the Constitution, and legislation has been introduced for such an amendment in every session of Congress since 1995. Imagine that you have decided to argue that flag burning should be protected as free speech. You think that people could find better ways to protest than by burning the flag, but nonetheless, they still should have that right. When you start researching the issue and look at the text of laws that have been passed against flag burning, you discover that the laws are vague about defining what a flag is. You realize that people could be arrested and put in prison for cutting a cake with an image of the flag in the icing at a Fourth of July picnic. You decide that examining definitions of the U.S. flag is a great way to begin your paper because if the flag cannot be defined, then you have a good argument that attempts to ban burning of the flag are doomed to failure. Congress cannot pass an amendment against something that it cannot accurately define. You look up the U.S. Code about the flag that was federal law from 1968 to 1989, when it was overturned in the Supreme Court case of *Texas v. Johnson*. It reads:

> Whoever knowingly casts contempt upon any flag of the United States by publicly mutilating, defacing, defiling, burning, or trampling upon it shall be fined not more than $1,000 or imprisoned for not more than one year, or both.
>
> The term "flag of the United States" as used in this section, shall include any flag, standard colors, ensign, or any picture or representation of either, or of any part or parts of either, made of any substance or represented on any substance, of any size evidently purporting to be either of said flag, standard, color, or ensign of the United States of America, or a picture or a representation of either, upon which shall be shown the colors, the stars and the stripes, in any number of either thereof, or of any part or parts of either, by which the average person seeing the same without deliberation may believe the same to represent the flag, standards, colors, or ensign of the United States of America.

You think the definition in the second paragraph is ridiculous. It could apply to red-and-white striped pants or almost anything that has stars and is red, white, and blue. But the question is how to make the point effectively in your analysis. Here are three versions of an analysis paragraph that would come after you quote the above law:

Version 1 (Distant, balanced)
The language of the 1968 law, passed in the midst of the protest over the Vietnam War, demonstrates the futility of passing laws against flag burning. Congress realized that protesters could burn objects that resembled the American flag and evade prosecution, so they extended the law to apply to anything "the average person" believed to represent the flag. The great irony was that the major violators of this law were the most patriotic people in America, who put flags on their cars and bought things with images of flags. When they threw away their flag napkins, they desecrated the flag and violated the law.

Version 2 (Involved, angry)
The 1968 law against flag burning is yet another example of why the Washington bureaucrats who love big government always get it wrong.

They see on TV something they don't like—protesters burning a flag. So they say, "Let's pass a law against it." But for the law to have teeth, they realize that it has to be far reaching, including every imagined possibility. So they make the law as broad as possible so the police can bust the heads of anyone they want to. The attempt to ban flag burning shows how people with good intentions take away your liberties.

Version 3 (Comedic)

"Wait a second!" you're probably saying to yourself. "Any number of stars? Any part or parts of either? On any substance? Or a picture or representation?" You bet. Burning a photo of a drawing of a three-starred red, white, and blue four-striped flag would land you in jail for a year. I'm not making this up. Do you still trust them to define what a flag is? I don't.

You can hear the differences in voices of these paragraphs. The first is the modulated voice of a radio or television commentator, appearing to give a distanced and balanced perspective. The second is the voice of an angry libertarian, asserting that the government that governs best is the one that governs least. The third is the voice of Comedy Central or the alternative press, laughing at what government tries to do. Once again, the point is not which one is most effective, because each could be effective for different audiences. The point is to be aware that you can take on different voices when you write and to learn how to control these voices.

CHAPTER 4

Understanding Written Arguments: Rhetorical Analysis

What Is Rhetorical Analysis?

To many people, the term *rhetoric* means speech or writing that is highly ornamental or deceptive or manipulative. You might hear someone say, "That politician is just using a bunch of rhetoric" or "the rhetoric of that advertisement is very deceptive." But as you have already learned, the term **rhetoric** is also used in a positive sense. It is commonly used as a neutral synonym for all kinds of writing or speech, for instance ("*Silent Spring* is one of the most influential pieces of environmental rhetoric ever written"), and it is sometimes used as the name of a college course ("English 101: Rhetoric and Composition") or even a college major. As a subject of study, rhetoric is usually associated with how to produce effective pieces of communication, following Aristotle's classic definition of rhetoric as "the art of finding in any given case the available means of persuasion." But in recent years rhetoric has also taken on an interpretive or analytical function. It has come to be used not just as a means of *producing* effective communications but also as a way of *understanding* communication. The two aspects mutually support one another: Becoming a better writer makes you a better interpreter, and becoming a better interpreter makes you a better writer. This chapter is designed to give you a good understanding of the key concepts involved in rhetorical analysis and to make you comfortable conducting rhetorical analyses on your own.

The Goals of Rhetorical Analysis

Aristotle's emphasis on persuasion has been influential in the history of rhetoric. It is now common to understand rhetoric as fundamentally involved in the study of persuasion. **Rhetorical analysis**, therefore, can be defined as an effort to understand how people in specific social situations attempt to influence others through language. But not *just* through language: Rhetoricians today attempt to understand better every kind of important symbolic action—speeches and articles, yes, but also architecture (isn't it clear that the U.S. Capitol in Washington makes an argument as a building?), movies and television shows (doesn't *The Bachelor* have designs on viewers' values and attitudes?), memorials (don't the AIDS quilt and the Vietnam Veterans Memorial make arguments about AIDS and about our national understanding of the Vietnam war?), as well as visual art, Web sites, advertisements, photos and other images, dance, and popular songs.

Through rhetorical analysis, people strive to understand better how particular rhetorical acts are persuasive. They get a better sense of the values and beliefs and attitudes that are conveyed in specific rhetorical moments. It might be helpful to think of rhetorical analysis as a kind of critical reading: Whereas "ordinary" reading involves experiencing firsthand a speech or text or TV show or advertisement and then reacting (or not reacting) to it, **critical reading**—rhetorical analysis, that is—involves studying carefully some kind of symbolic action in order to understand it better and appreciate its tactics. The result is a heightened awareness of the message and an appreciation for the ways people manipulate language and other symbols for persuasive purposes.

Rhetorical analysis examines how an idea is shaped and presented to an audience in a particular form for a specific purpose. There are many approaches to rhetorical analysis and no one "correct" way to

The statue of Castor stands at the entrance of the Piazza del Campidoglio in Rome. A textual analysis focuses on the statue itself. The size and realism of the statue makes it a masterpiece of classical Roman sculpture.

do it. But generally approaches to rhetorical analysis can be placed between two broad extremes—not mutually exclusive categories but extremes along a continuum. At the one end of the continuum are analyses that concentrate more on texts than contexts. They typically use rhetorical concepts to analyze the features of texts. Let's call this approach **textual analysis**. At the other extreme are approaches that emphasize **context** over text. These emphasize reconstructing the cultural environment or context that existed when a particular rhetorical event took place, and then to depend on that re-creation to produce clues about the persuasive tactics and appeals. Those who undertake **contextual analysis**—as we'll call this second approach—regard particular rhetorical acts as parts of larger communicative chains, or "conversations."

> Rhetorical analysis examines how an idea is shaped and presented to an audience in a particular form for a specific purpose.

Now let's discuss those two approaches in detail.

A contextual analysis focuses on the surroundings and the history of the statue. Legend has Castor and his twin brother Pollux, the mythical sons of Leda, assisting Romans in an early battle. Romans built a large temple in the Forum to honor them. The statues of Castor and Pollux were uncovered in sixteenth-century excavations and brought in 1583 to stand at the top of the Cordonata, a staircase designed by Michelangelo as part of a renovation of the Piazza del Campidoglio commissioned by Pope Paul III Farnese in 1536.

Textual Analysis: Using Rhetorical Concepts as an Analytical Screen

Just as expert teachers in every field of endeavor—from baseball to biology— devise vocabularies to facilitate specialized study, rhetoricians too have developed a set of key concepts to permit them to describe rhetorical activities. A fundamental concept in rhetoric, of course, is *audience*. But there are many others. Classical rhetoricians in the tradition of Aristotle, Quintilian, and Cicero developed a range of terms around what they called the "canons" of rhetoric in order to describe some of the actions of communicators: *inventio* (invention—the finding or creation of information for persuasive acts, and the planning of strategies), *dispostio* (or arrangement), *elocutio* (or style), *memoria* (the recollection of rhetorical resources that one might call upon, as well as the memorization of what has been invented and arranged), and *pronuntiatio* (or delivery). These five canons generally describe the actions of any persuader, from preliminary planning to final delivery.

Over the years, and as written discourse gained in prestige against oral discourse, four canons (excepting *memoria*) especially encouraged the development of concepts and terms useful for rhetorical analysis. Terms like *ethos, pathos,* and *logos,* all associated with invention, account for features of texts related to the trustworthiness and credibility of the writer or speaker (ethos), for the persuasive good reasons in an argument that derive from a community's mostly deeply and emotionally held values (pathos), and for the good reasons that emerge from intellectual reasoning (logos). Arrangement has required terms like *exordium* (introduction), *narratio* (generally equivalent to what we refer to today as "forecasting"), *confirmatio* (proof), *refutatio* (answering the objections of others), and *peroration* (conclusion) to describe the organization of speeches and essays. Delivery has given rise to a discussion of things like voice, gesture, and expression (in oral discourse) and to voice and visual impact (in written). And a whole series of technical terms developed over the years to describe effective maneuvers of style (*elocutio*)—many of them still in common use, such as antithesis, irony, hyperbole, and metaphor. Fundamental to the classical approach to rhetoric is the concept of *decorum*, or "appropriateness": Everything within a persuasive act can be understood as in keeping with a central rhetorical goal that any communicator consistently keeps in mind and that governs consistent choices according to occasion and audience. The concept of decorum lies behind rhetorical analysis in that decisions by a communicator are understood as rational and consistent and thus, available for systematic analysis.

Perhaps an example will make textual rhetorical analysis clearer. If you have not done so already, take a few minutes to read "The Border Patrol State" by Leslie Marmon Silko (pp. 164–169). We use the concepts of classical rhetoric to understand it better.

Silko's Purpose and Argument

What is the purpose of Silko's essay? Silko wrote the essay well over a decade ago, but you probably find it to be interesting and readable still, in part at least because it concerns the perennial American issue of civil rights. In this case, Silko is taking issue with practices associated with the Border Patrol of the Immigration and Naturalization Service (INS): They are reenacting, she feels, the long subjugation of native peoples by the Anglo majority. Silko proposes that the power of the Border Patrol be sharply reduced so that the exploitation of her people might be curtailed, and she supports that thesis with an essay that describes and condemns the Border Patrol tactics. Essentially the argument comes down to this: The Border Patrol must be reformed for two good reasons: because "the Immigration and Naturalization Service and Border Patrol have implemented policies that interfere with the rights of U.S. citizens to travel freely within our borders" (para. 8), and because efforts to restrict immigration are ineffective, doomed to fail ("It is no use; borders haven't worked, and they won't work" in para. 16). Her essay amounts to an evaluation of the Border Patrol's activities, an evaluation that finds those activities wanting on ethical and practical grounds.

Silko's Use of Logos, Pathos, and Ethos

All that is easy enough to see. But note that the because-clauses used by Silko that we have just named derive from logos and pathos. When she condemns the unethical actions of the border police early in the essay, she does so in a way that is full of evidence and other appeals to readers' minds—including appeals to our sense of what is legal, constitutional, fair, and honorable. When she explains the futility of trying to stop immigration, she appeals again to her readers' reasonableness: Constructing walls across the border with Mexico is foolish because "border entrepreneurs have already used blowtorches to cut passageways through the fence" (para. 15), because "a mass migration is already under way" (para. 16), and because "The Americas are Indian country, and the 'Indian problem' is not about to go away" (para. 17). The bulk of "The Border Patrol State" amounts to an argument by example wherein the single case—Silko's personal experience, as a native American, with the border police—stands for many such cases. This case study persuades as other case studies and narratives do—by being presented as representative. Silko creates through her narrative a representative example that stands for the treatment of many native Americans. The particular details provided in the essay are not mere "concrete description" but hard, logical evidence summoned to support Silko's thesis.

Those logical appeals are reinforced by Silko's more emotional good reasons:

- The border patrol is constructing an "Iron Curtain" that is as destructive of human rights as the Iron Curtain that the Soviet Union constructed around Eastern Europe after World War II (para. 15).
- "Proud" and "patriotic" Native American citizens are being harassed, such as "old Bill Pratt [who] used to ride his horse 300 miles overland ... every summer to work as a fire lookout" (para. 1).
- American citizens can be terrified by border police in a way that is chillingly reminiscent of "the report of Argentine police and military officers who became addicted to interrogation, torture, and murder" (paras. 3–5).

The most emotional moment of all in the essay may be when Silko describes how the border patrol dog, trained to find illegal drugs and other contraband, including human contraband, seems to sympathize with her and those she is championing: "I saw immediately from the expression in her eyes that the dog hated them" (para. 6); "the dog refused to accuse us: She had an innate dignity that did not permit her to serve the murderous impulses of those men" (para. 7). Clearly the good reasons in "The Border Patrol State" appeal in a mutually supportive way to the reason and emotions of Silko's audience. She appeals to the whole person.

Why do we take Silko's word about the stories she tells? It is because she establishes her ethos, her trustworthiness, early in the article. Of course any item in print gains a certain credibility from being printed, and Silko can also count on being widely recognized for her accomplishments as a writer. But just to be sure that she comes off as credible, Silko reminds her readers that she is a respected, published author who has been on a book tour to publicize her novel *Almanac of the Dead* (para. 3). She quotes widely, if unobtrusively, from books and reports to establish that she has studied the issues thoroughly; note how much she displays her knowledge of INS policies in paragraph 9, for instance. She cites the stories not only of her own encounters with the border police (experiences that are a source of great credibility), but also of others whom she lists, name after careful name, in order that we might trust her account. She knows history and geography. She also ties herself to traditional American values such as freedom (para. 1), ethnic pride, tolerance, and even the love of dogs. While her political biases and values might be known from other sources and while even this essay, because of its anti-authoritarian strain, might seem to display politically progressive attitudes at times, in general Silko comes off as hard-working, honest, educated, even patriotic. And definitely credible.

Silko's Arrangement

Silko arranges her essay appropriately as well. In general the essay follows a traditional pattern. She begins with a long concrete introductory story that "hooks" the reader and leads to her thesis in paragraph 8. Next, in the body of her essay, she supports her thesis by evaluating the unethical nature of INS policies: She cites their violation of constitutional protections, their similarity to tactics used in nations that are notorious for violating the rights of citizens, and their fundamental immorality; and she emphasizes how those policies are racist in nature (e.g., paras. 11–13). After completing her moral evaluation of INS policy, she turns beginning with paragraph 14 to the practical difficulties of halting immigration: NAFTA permits the free flow of goods, and even drugs are impossible to stop, so how can people be stopped from crossing borders; efforts to seal borders are "pathetic" in their ineffectuality (para. 15). This all lays the groundwork for the surprising and stirring conclusion: "The great human migration within the Americas cannot be stopped; human beings are natural forces of the earth, just as rivers and winds are natural forces" (para. 16); "the Americas are Indian country, and the 'Indian problem' is not about to go away" (para. 17); the mythic "return of the Aztlan" is on display in the box cars that go by as the essay closes. In short, this essay unfolds in a conventional way: It has a standard beginning, middle, and end.

Silko's Style

What about Silko's style? How is it appropriate to her purposes? Take a look at paragraphs 3 and 4: you will notice that nearly all of the fourteen sentences in those paragraphs are simple in structure. There are only five sentences that use any form of *subordination* (clauses that begin with *when*, *that*, or *if*). Many of the sentences either consist of one clause or of two clauses joined by simple *coordination* (such as *and* or *but* or a semicolon).

Several of the sentences and clauses are unusually short. Furthermore, Silko never in these paragraphs uses metaphors or other sorts of poetic language, and her **diction**—the words she uses—is as simple as her sentences. It all reminds you of the daily newspaper, doesn't it? Silko chooses a style similar to one used in newspaper reporting—simple, straightforward, unadorned— because she wants her readers to accept her narrative as credible and trust-worthy. Her tone and voice reinforce her ethos.

There is more to say about the rhetorical choices that Silko made in crafting "The Border Patrol State." But this analysis is enough to illustrate our main point. Textual rhetorical analysis employs rhetorical terminology— in this case, terms borrowed from classical rhetoric such as ethos, pathos, logos, arrangement, style, and tone—as a way of helping us to understand a piece of writing better, as a way of understanding how a writer makes choices to achieve certain effects. And it cooperates with contextual analysis.

METAPHORS IN ADS

Advertisers have long understood the critical role that words play in persuading people. The writers of advertising copy are well aware that the average American is exposed to over three thousand ads a day and that such oversaturation has made people cynical about ads. Advertisers have to be clever to get our attention, so ads often use the tactics of poets and comedians. Words in ads often use puns and metaphors to draw our attention to the products they promote. A watch ad runs with the banner "Every second counts." An ad for a coffeemaker asks, "Who better to handle his ugly mug in the morning?" A plastic wrap ad shows two chicken legs under the headline "Stop our legs from drying out." A used-car ad appears under the words "Born again."

But it is not just clever plays on words that do the work in the language of advertising. We often find words in ads that do not make much sense at first reading. For example, a Nikon camera ad displays in big bold letters, "It's a stealth bomber with fuzzy dice." Calling a camera a "stealth bomber with fuzzy dice" is an example of metaphor. **Metaphor** is a Greek term that means "carry over," which describes what happens when you encounter a metaphor. You carry over the meaning from one word to another. Metaphor is but one kind of **figurative language**. Also common in advertising are **synecdoche**, in which the part is used to represent the whole (a hood ornament represents a car), and **metonymy**, in which something stands for something else with which it is closely associated (using flowers to represent a product's fresh scent).

METAPHORS IN ADS *(continued)*

There are other kinds of figurative language, but all involve the transfer of meaning from one word or phrase to another. How this transfer works is complicated. If we encounter an unfamiliar metaphor such as the stealth bomber example, we do our best to make sense of what the writer means. What meanings, then, is the reader supposed to carry over from "stealth bomber with fuzzy dice" to a Nikon camera? Cameras don't have wings, wheels, jet engines, or bomb bays, nor are they covered with fake fur. The advertisers didn't want the reader to work too hard, so they put in fine print at the bottom their interpretation of the metaphor: "The technology of a serious camera. The spontaneity of a point-and-shoot. Now you don't have to choose between the two."

Contextual Analysis: Communication as Conversation

Notice that in the previous discussion the fact that Leslie Marmon Silko's "The Border Patrol State" was originally published in the magazine *The Nation* did not matter too much. Nor did it matter when the essay was published (October 17, 1994) or who exactly read it or what their reaction was or what other people at the time were saying. Textual analysis, strictly speaking, need not attend to such matters; it can proceed as if the item under consideration "speaks for all time" somehow, as if it is a sort of museum piece unaffected by time and space just as surely as, say, an ancient altarpiece once housed in a church might be placed on a pedestal in a museum. There's nothing wrong with museums, of course; they certainly permit people to observe and appreciate objects in an important way. But just as certainly museums often fail to retain a vital sense of an artwork's original context and cultural meaning; in that sense museums can diminish understanding as much as they contribute to it. Contextual rhetorical analysis, however, as an attempt to understand communications through the lens of their environments, does examine the setting or scene out of which any communication emerges.

And, as in the case of textual analysis, contextual analysis may be conducted in any number of ways. But *contextual rhetorical analysis always proceeds from a description of the **rhetorical situation*** that motivated the item in question. It demands an appreciation of the social circumstances that call rhetorical events into being and that orchestrate the course of those events. It regards communications as anything but self-contained:

■ Each communication is considered as a response to other communications (and to other social practices).

■ Communications (and social practices more generally) are considered to reflect the attitudes and values of the communities that sustain them.

■ Evidence is sought about how those other communications (and social practices) are reflected in texts.

Rhetorical analysis from a contextualist perspective understands individual pieces as parts of ongoing conversations.

The challenge is to reconstruct the conversation surrounding a specific piece of writing or speaking. Sometimes it is fairly easy to do so. You may have good background information on the topic and a feel for what is behind what people are writing or saying about it. People who have strong feelings about the environment or stem cell research (or about same-sex marriage, the lack of competitive balance in major league baseball, or any number of other current issues) are well informed about the arguments that are converging around those topics.

But other times it takes some research to reconstruct the conversations and social practices related to a particular issue. You need to see how the debate is conducted in current magazines, newspapers, talk shows, movies and TV shows, Web sites, and so forth (if the issue concerns current events), or do archival research into historical collections of newspapers, magazines, books, letters, and other documentary sources (if the item being analyzed was from an earlier time period). That research usually involves libraries, special research collections, or film and television archives where it is possible to learn quite a bit about context.

Again, an example will clarify how contextual analysis works to "open up" an argument to analysis: let's return again to a discussion of Silko's "The Border Patrol State." It will take a bit of research to reconstruct some of the "conversations" that Silko is participating in, but the result will be an enhanced understanding of the essay as well as an appreciation for how you might do a contextual rhetorical analysis.

Silko's Life and Works

You can begin by learning more about Silko herself. The essay itself gives some facts about her (e.g., that she is a native American writer of note who has lived in the Southwest); the headnote on page 164 gives additional information (that her writing usually develops out of native American traditions and tales); and you can learn still more about her from the Internet. Thus Silko's credibility, her ethos, is established not just by her textual moves but by her prior reputation, especially for readers of *The Nation* who would recognize and appreciate her accomplishments. Perhaps the most relevant information on the Web is about *Almanac of the Dead*, the novel Silko refers to in paragraph 3. That novel, set mainly in Tucson, revolves around a native American woman psychic who is in the process of transcribing the lost histories of her dead ancestors into "an almanac of the dead"—into a history of her people. That history is from the point of view of the conquered, not the conqueror; "The Border Patrol State," it seems, is an essayistic version of *Almanac of the Dead* in that like the novel it protests what has been lost—and what is still being lost—in the clash between Anglo and native cultures. It is a protest against the tactics of the border police. Or is it?

The Context of Publication

Through a consideration of the conversations swirling around it, contextual analysis actually suggests that "The Border Patrol State" is just as much about immigration policy as it is about the civil rights of native Americans. The article first appeared in *The Nation*, a respected, politically progressive magazine that has been appearing weekly for decades. Published in New York City, it is a magazine of public opinion that covers the theater, film, music, fiction, and other arts; politics and public affairs; and contemporary culture. If you want to know what left-leaning people are thinking about an issue, *The Nation* is a good magazine to consult. You can imagine that Silko's essay therefore reached an audience of sympathetic readers—people who would be receptive to her message. They would be inclined to sympathize with Silko's complaints and to heed her call for a less repressive border patrol.

But what is interesting is that Silko's essay appeared on October 17, 1994 in a special issue of *The Nation* given over to "The Immigration Wars," a phrase very visible on the cover of that issue. Hers was one of several articles that appeared under that banner, an indication that Silko's argument is not just about the violation of the civil rights of native Americans but also about the larger issue of immigration policy. "The Border Patrol State" appeared after David Cole's "Five Myths about Immigration"; Elizabeth Kadetsky's "Bashing Illegals in California"; Peter Kwong's "China's Human Traffickers"; two editorials about immigration policy; and short columns on immigration by *Nation* regulars Katha Pollitt, Aryeh Neier, and Christopher Hitchens. Together the articles in this issue of *The Nation* mounted a sustained argument in favor of a liberal immigration policy.

The Larger Conversation

Why did *The Nation* entitle its issue "The Immigration Wars"? Immigration was a huge controversy in October 1994, just before the 1994 elections. When the 1965 Immigration Act was amended in 1990, the already strong flow of immigrants to the United States became a flood. While many immigrants previously came to the United States from Europe, most recent immigrants have come from Asia, Latin America, and the Caribbean islands, and Africa. While those earlier immigrants typically passed through Ellis Island and past the Statue of Liberty that welcomed them, most recent immigrants in 1994 were coming to Florida, Texas, and California. The arrival of all those new immigrants revived old fears about immigrants that have been in the air for decades (that they take away jobs from native-born Americans, that they undermine national values by resisting assimilation and clinging to their own cultures, that they reduce standards of living by stressing educational and social welfare budgets). Many people countered those claims by indicating that immigrants create jobs and wealth, enhance the vitality of American culture, become among the proudest of Americans, and contribute to the tax base of their communities. But those counterarguments were undermined when a tide of illegal immigrants—up to 300,000 per year—was arriving at the time Silko was writing.

The Immigration Wars were verbal wars. In the 1994 election, Republicans had united under the banner of a "Contract with America." Some three hundred Republican congressional candidates, drawn together by conservative leader Newt Gingrich, agreed to run on a common platform in an ultimately successful effort to gain control of the House of Representatives. The Contract offered a number of conservative initiatives, among them a reduction in the size of government, a balanced budget amendment, crime legislation, a reduction in welfare benefits and capital gains taxes, and benefits increases for seniors on social security. More to the point here, it also proposed changes in laws in order to curtail immigration, reduce illegal immigration, and deny benefits to illegal residents, including health care and education. Title IV of the proposed Personal Responsibility Act would have declared resident aliens ineligible for welfare assistance and restricted their eligibility for health, social service, and education benefits (see www.house.gov/house/Contract/CONTRACT.html). In this way, the

Contract with America offered support for California's Proposition 187, another important 1994 proposal. This so-called "Save Our State" initiative was designed to "prevent California's estimated 1.7 million undocumented immigrants from partaking of every form of public welfare including non-emergency medical care, pre-natal clinics and public schools," as Kadetsky explained her essay in *The Nation*. In the words of the proposition itself, "The People of California find and declare as follows: That they have suffered and are suffering economic hardship caused by the presence of illegal aliens in this state. That they have suffered and are suffering personal injury and damage caused by the criminal conduct of illegal aliens. That they have a right to the protection of their government from any person or persons entering this country illegally." The Republican Contract for America and California's proposed Proposition 187 together constituted the nation's leading domestic issue in October 1994. A war of words about them was evident in the magazines, books, newspapers, talk shows, barber shops, and hair salons of America.

Silko's Political Goals

In this context, it is easy to see that Silko's essay is against more than the border patrol. It is an argument in favor of relatively unrestricted immigration, especially from Mexico and especially for native Americans. Moreover, it is a direct refutation of the Contract for America in general and Proposition 187 in particular. Where the proposition stated "that [the People of California] have suffered and are suffering economic hardship caused by the presence of illegal aliens in this state, that they have suffered and are suffering personal injury and damage caused by the criminal conduct of illegal aliens, [and] that they have a right to the protection of their government from any person or persons entering this country illegally," Silko turns the claim around. It is the border patrol that is behaving illegally. It is the border patrol that is creating economic hardship. It is the border police that is creating personal injury and damage through criminal conduct. Finally, it is the U.S. government that is acting illegally by ignoring the treaty of Guadalupe Hidalgo, which "recognizes the right of the Tohano O'Odom (Papago) people to move freely across the U.S.-Mexico border without documents," as Silko puts it in her footnote. Writing just before the election of 1994, then, and in the midst of a spirited national debate (and in the pages of an immigration issue of *The Nation*), Silko had specific political goals in mind. A contextual analysis of "The Border Patrol State" reveals that the essay is, at least in part, an eloquent refutation of the Contract for America and Proposition 187—two items that are not even named explicitly in the essay!

We could do more in the way of contextual analysis here. We could cite many more articles and books and reports and TV broadcasts that can be compared with "The Border Patrol State," including speeches and television interviews by Pat Buchanan, who ran for the Republican presidential nomination in 1992 and 1996 on an anti-immigration stance and who was in the process of writing an incendiary book entitled *The Death of the West: How Mass Immigration, Depopulation, and a Dying Faith Are Killing Our Culture and the Country*. A discussion of the conversation about immigration in 1994 and about Leslie Marmon Silko's specific contribution to that conversation could be extended for a long time—indefinitely, in fact. There is no need to belabor the point, however: our purpose has been simply to illustrate that contextual analysis of a piece of rhetoric can enrich our understanding.

 # Write a Rhetorical Analysis

Effective rhetorical analysis, as we have seen, can be generally textual or contextual in nature. But we should emphasize again that these two approaches to rhetorical analysis are not mutually exclusive. Indeed, many if not most analysts operate some place between these two extremes; they consider the details of the text, but they also attend to the particulars of context as well. Textual analysis and contextual analysis inevitably complement each other. Getting at what is at stake in "The Border Patrol State" or any other sophisticated argument takes patience and intelligence. Like Silko's essay, many arguments have designs on the attitudes and beliefs of audiences. Rhetorical analysis, as a way of understanding how people argue, is both enlightening and challenging.

Try to use elements of both kinds of analysis whenever you want to understand a rhetorical event more completely. Rhetoric is "inside" texts, but it is also "outside": specific rhetorical performances are an irreducible mixture of text and context, and so interpretation and analysis of those performances must account for both as well. Remember, however, the limitations of your analysis; realize that your analysis will always be somewhat partial and incomplete, ready to be deepened, corrected, modified, and extended by the insights of others. Rhetorical analysis can itself be part of an unending conversation—a way of learning and teaching within a community.

Sample Student Rhetorical Analysis

Erica Strausner is a sophomore at Pennsylvania State University, where she majors in psychology and minors in Spanish. She is a member of the Phi Eta Sigma honor society and the National Society of Collegiate Scholars. Strausner's professional goal is to earn a PhD in order to pursue a career as a clinical psychologist. She wrote this essay in a first-year composition course.

Strausner 1

Erica Strausner

Ms. Kale

English 15

November 11, 2003

The NRA Blacklist: A Project Gone Mad

The National Rifle Association is naming names? Recently the NRA decided to assign its staff researchers to dig up every anti-gun remark ever made, no matter how slight, and to put those who made the remark on a nineteen-page list accessible through the NRA Web site. It's called the NRA blacklist. How are people reacting to that list? Bob Herbert, an editorial columnist for The New York Times and one of those named on the list, isn't too happy at all. An examination of how Herbert writes his response to the NRA blacklist, "The NRA Is Naming Names," combined with another essay by Herbert in the same New York Times, "More Guns for Everyone!," will indicate how Herbert persuades his readers to reject the NRA.

"More Guns for Everyone!" indicates without a doubt Herbert's views on gun control. In commenting on a ruling by Attorney General John Ashcroft, he states,

---

The NRA has seldom had a better friend in the
government than Mr. Ashcroft. That was proved
again on Monday, when the Justice Department,
in a pair of briefs, rejected the long-held
view of the court, the Justice Department
itself, and most legal scholars that the
Second Amendment protects only the right of
state-owned militias to own firearms.

This passage indicates that Herbert is anti-NRA, but
not that he is necessarily anti-gun. In fact, he even
refers to his days in the army, when he "had a .45
caliber pistol hanging low on my hip," to show that he
is not completely against guns. Rather, Herbert
believes only that not everyone has a legitimate reason
to own a gun and that there should be some restrictions
on them. It would be safer to say that Herbert is
cautious about gun distribution because he has seen
that guns in the wrong hands can be detrimental to
society. "No gun is more suited to criminal misuse than
a handgun, and that's exactly the type of weapon that
Mr. Ashcroft and his NRA pals are trying to make
available," Herbert notes in "More Guns for Everyone";
but "I'm not anti-gun."

With this background in mind, one can see that
Herbert wrote "The NRA Is Naming Names" at a crucial
time. Gun laws have always been an issue, and there will
always be proposals to restrict gun distribution as long
as people use firearms to kill other people. Particularly
in recent days, however, there have been crucial

Strausner 3

high-spirited arguments between NRA supporters and
detractors. The NRA posted its list in a secluded space
on its Web site on July 17, 2003, but quite possibly
Herbert saw the list only much later because it was
buried deep within the organization's Library of the
Institute for Legislative Action. According to Andrew
Arulanandum, Director of Public Affairs for the NRA, the
posting of the list was a "response to many requests by
our members wanting to know which organizations support
the rights of law-abiding Americans to keep and bear
arms" (NRA). Herbert found himself on the NRA hate list
even though he supports only some restrictions on
handguns—along with responsible people like football
player Doug Flutie and admired organizations like Ben and
Jerry's.

To defend himself, Herbert wrote his response to the
NRA in the New York Times. His voice and tone express
exactly how he feels and how vehemently he stands up for
himself and others on the blacklist. Because readers of
the New York Times can be considered informed on current
affairs and generally educated, Herbert uses language
that is appropriate to them. His vocabulary is not
difficult or pedantic; his language is suited to the
average person. Editorial opinion columns are much more
opinionated in tone than objective news stories, but
Herbert strengthens his argument in the fashion of a news
report by using sources and interviewing critical people.

Actually, Herbert addresses several kinds of
readers in his essay, all of them within the readership

of the Times. Most importantly, he addresses NRA
members. He addresses the irrational assumptions made by
the NRA about others and about himself. Gun lobbyists
will also read Herbert's essay, so Herbert makes
comments about legislation currently under consideration
in Congress. Lastly and mainly, Herbert addresses those
who are sympathetic to his own views on gun legislation.
For all these readers Herbert establishes his
credibility very carefully. He has experience,
obviously, or else he would not be on the NRA list. He
responds to the list as any wronged person would, with
well-placed outrage. Since he is a regular New York
Times writer, he obviously has already established some
credibility with his readers as well, and they have come
to trust him because he produces hard facts, not just
opinions, and is knowledgeable about current events.

    Herbert also appeals to his readers logically. He
burrows down into the root of the problem, the NRA, by
interviewing the Director of Public Affairs about why
the list was compiled and what significance it holds. The
interview also affects his argument positively because
he sheds light on both sides of the story. Herbert also
depends on statistics: e.g., "more than one million
Americans were killed by firearms" (NRA). He also cites
as evidence important pieces of current legislation,
such as President Clinton's 1994 bill banning the
distribution of assault weapons: he explains how gun
lobbyists will do anything to kill any piece of gun
control legislation. Herbert also supplies several

Strausner 5

logical reasons why his being listed is unfair, most
notably the fact that "I am not anti-gun." By saying
that he believes people should have a legitimate reason
to own a gun, and that city slickers or suburbanites
seldom have any reason to have a gun, he establishes
that he is not really an enemy of guns, just an enemy of
their abuse. What he says makes sense because
suburbanites and city dwellers do not hunt for food.
Yes, they do have a right to protect their homes, and in
some areas that might be necessary; but the majority of
people have no use for guns.

　　Finally, Herbert appeals to his readers' emotions.
Since the essay is an op-ed piece, a slightly sarcastic
or pejorative air hangs on some of Herbert's phrases:
e.g., "I'm sure there's a method to the NRA's madness,
but to tell you the truth, all I can see is the madness."
After that comment he drops the cynicism and turns to a
description of The Year the Dream Died: Revisiting 1968
in America by Jules Witcover. The book movingly describes
the assassinations of Robert Kennedy and Martin Luther
King, Jr. Just as he has his readers hooked on the
tragedy of these deaths, he returns to a cynical tone by
remarking, "Both were killed by freaks with guns." He
then returns to a somber tone by offering cold statistics
on deaths by firearms and details on gun legislation.
Then, just as quickly, he gives his final, clinching quip:
"Ah, free expression." It is this alternation of two
opposite emotions that strengthens his argument because
it forces readers to think about his and their feelings.

Strausner 6

By examining how Herbert writes his response to the
NRA blacklist and comparing it to another essay by him
that states his views on gun control, one can see that
Herbert has intrigued not only his usual readers but the
members of the NRA. Herbert effectively argues his
point, and he provides every reason for the NRA to
remove him from its blacklist. In fact, he makes it seem
that the NRA cannot be considered responsible since it
keeps a blacklist in the first place, and then includes
people on it inaccurately. Such an organization cannot
be trusted or taken seriously.

Strausner 7

Works Cited

Herbert, Bob. "More Guns for Everyone!" Editorial. New
    York Times 9 May 2002, late ed.: A39.

———. "The NRA Is Naming Names" Editorial. New York
    Times 13 Oct. 2003, late ed.: A17.

National Rifle Association. "National Organizations with
    Anti-Gun Policies." NRA-ILA Fact Sheets. 2003.
    National Rifle Association Institute for Legislative
    Action. 14 Oct. 2003 <http://www.nraila.org//issues/
    factsheets/read.aspx?id=15>.

Steps to a Rhetorical Analysis

Step 1 Select an argument to analyze

Find an argument to analyze: a speech or sermon designed to persuade, an op-ed item in a newspaper, an ad in a magazine designed for a particular audience, a commentary on a talk show.

Examples

- You can find arguments on the editorial pages of newspapers; in opinion features in magazines such as *Time, Newsweek,* and *U.S. News & World Report;* in magazines that take political positions such as *National Review, Mother Jones, New Republic, Nation,* and the online journal *Slate;* and the Web sites of activist organizations.
- Letters to the editor and online newsgroup postings probably won't work for this assignment unless they are long and detailed.

Step 2 Analyze the context

Who is the author?

Through research in the library or on the Web, learn all you can about the author of the argument.

- How does the argument you are analyzing repeat arguments previously made by the author?
- Does the author borrow arguments and concepts from previous things he or she has written?
- What motivated the author to write?

Who is the audience?

Through research, learn all you can about the place where the argument appeared and the audience.

- Who is the anticipated audience?
- How do the occasion and forum for writing affect the argument?
- How would the argument have been written differently if it had appeared elsewhere?
- What motivated the newspaper or magazine (or other venue) to publish it?

What is the larger conversation?

Through research, find out what else was being said about the subject your selection discusses. Track down any references made in the text you are examining.

- When did the argument appear?
- Why did it get published at that particular moment?
- What other concurrent pieces of "cultural conversation" (e.g., TV shows, other articles, speeches, Web sites) does the item you are analyzing respond to or "answer"?

Step **3** Analyze the text

Summarize the argument

- What is the main claim?
- What reasons are given in support of the claim?
- How is the argument organized? What are the component parts, and why are the parts presented in that order?

What is the medium and genre?

- What is the medium? A newspaper? a scholarly journal? a Web site?
- What is the genre? An editorial? an essay? a speech? an advertisment? What expectations does the audience have about this genre?

What appeals are used?

- **Analyze the ethos**. How does the writer represent himself or herself? Does the writer have any credentials to be an authority on the topic? Do you trust the writer? Why or why not?
- **Analyze the logos**. Where do you find facts and evidence in the argument? What kinds of facts and evidence does the writer present? Direct observation? statistics? interviews? surveys? secondhand sources such as published research? quotations from authorities?
- **Analyze the pathos**. Are there any places where the writer attempts to invoke an emotional response? Where do you find appeals to shared values with the audience? You are a member of that audience, so what values do you hold in common with the writer? What values do you not hold in common?

How would you characterize the style?

- Is the style formal, informal, satirical, or something else?
- Are any metaphors used?

Step 4 Write a draft

Introduction

- Describe briefly the argument you are analyzing, including where it was published, how long it is, and who wrote it.
- If the argument is on an issue unfamiliar to your readers, you may have to supply some background.

Body

- Analyze the context, following Step 2.
- Analyze the text, following Step 3.

Conclusion

- Do more than simply summarize what you have said. You might, for example, end with an example that typifies the argument.
- You don't have to end by either agreeing or disagreeing with the writer. Your task in this assignment is to analyze the strategies the writer uses.

Step 5 Revise, edit, proofread

- For detailed instructions, see Chapter 12.
- For a checklist to use to evaluate your draft, see pages 217–222.

CHAPTER 5

Understanding Visual Arguments

What Is a Visual Argument?

We live in a world where we are surrounded by images. They pull on us, compete for our attention, push us to do things. But unlike verbal arguments, we rarely think about how they do their work.

Arguments in written language are in one sense visual: We use our eyes to read the words on the page. But without words, can there be a visual argument? Certainly some visual symbols take on conventional meanings. Think about the signs in airports or other public places, designed to communicate with speakers of many languages.

Some visual symbols even make explicit claims. A one-way street sign says that drivers should travel in the same direction. But are such signs arguments? In Chapter 2 we point out that scholars of argument do not believe that everything's an argument. Most scholars define an argument as a claim supported by one or more reasons. A one-way sign has a claim: All drivers should go in the same direction. But is there a reason? Of course we all know an

> Visual arguments are often powerful because they invite viewers to co-create the claims and links.

unstated reason the sign carries: Drivers who go the wrong way violate the law and risk a substantial fine (plus they risk a head-on collision with other drivers).

Visual arguments often are powerful because they invite viewers to co-create claims and links. For example, the artists who decorated medieval cathedrals taught religious lessons. The facade of the Last Judgment on the front pillar of the Duomo in Orvieto, Italy, depicts Christ as judge damning sinners to hell. The facade makes a powerful visual argument about the consequences that await the unfaithful.

Facade of Last Judgment, Orvieto, Italy. ca. 1310–1330.

Other visual arguments cannot be explained this easily, even ones that purport to make claims. Beginning in 1935, the Farm Security Administration, a U.S. government agency, hired photographers to document the effects of the Great Depression and the drought years on Americans. One of the photographers, Dorothea Lange, shot a series of photographs of homeless and destitute migrant workers in California that have become some of the most familiar images of America in the 1930s. Lange had an immediate goal—getting the government to build a resettlement camp for the homeless workers. She wrote to her boss in Washington that her images were "loaded with ammunition."

Lange titled one of her images *Eighteen-year-old mother from Oklahoma, now a California migrant.* The young woman and child in the photograph are obviously quite poor if we assume the tent is where they live. Yet the image doesn't seem one of suffering. Dorothea Lange was a portrait

Eighteen-year-old mother from Oklahoma, now a California migrant. Photo by Dorothea Lange. March 1937.

photographer before becoming a documentary photographer, and her experience shows. She takes advantage of the highlighting of the woman's hair from the sun behind her contrasted with the dark interior of the tent to draw our eyes to the woman's face. She doesn't appear to be distressed—just bored. Only later do we notice the dirty face of the child and other details. With another caption—perhaps "Young mother on a camping trip left behind while the father went for a hike"— we might read the photograph to say something else. And even if we take the image as evidence of poverty, the claim is not evident, just as images of homeless people today do not necessarily make arguments.

Visual Persuasion

The Italian clothing retailer Benetton for many years has run ad campaigns intended to raise social awareness on issues including AIDS, hunger, pollution, and racism. The campaign against racism featured images of black and white children playing together, black and white hands overlapping, black and white arms handcuffed together, and similar contrasting themes. One ad shows three human hearts with the labels "BLACK," "WHITE," and "YELLOW," with a small label "United Colors of Benetton" on one side. The image of the three hearts makes a straightforward visual argument. The claim and reason might be phrased in words: "Prejudice based on skin color is wrong because we're all alike inside."

Hearts. Benetton Ad Campaign. 1996.

The particular genre—an advertisement—suggests there may be more arguments in the ad than the one that is most apparent. Benetton advertises for the same reason other companies advertise—to get consumers to buy their products. They do place their name on all their ads. The question then becomes how the controversial ads influence consumers to purchase Benetton clothing. Perhaps consumers identify with the messages in Benetton's ads and consequently identify with their clothing. Benetton says on its Web site that its ad campaigns "have succeeded in attracting the attention of the public and in standing out amid the current clutter of images." At the very least the ads give Benetton name-recognition. You may have other ideas about why the Benetton ads have been successful, but here's the point we're making: Explicit claims and reasons are often hard to extract from images.

Indeed, most ads lack explicit reasons and claims beyond "Buy this product." Throughout most of the 1900s, print ads and broadcast ads associated something desirable with purchase of a product. Romantic fulfillment was one common theme, financial success another. Unglamorous products were often placed in glamorous settings. Arthur Rothstein, a colleague of Dorothea Lange in documenting the Great Depression, photographed steelworkers' children in a homemade swimming pool in front of a billboard depicting beer as a family beverage for the wealthy.

By the 1980s advertisers realized that the old tactics would not work for an audience saturated with advertising. Advertisers began to create ads

Homemade swimming pool for steelworkers' children, Pittsburgh, Pennsylvania. Photo by Arthur Rothstein. July 1938.

that were entertaining, often recirculating images from the media and the larger culture. Many ads today base their images on something else—familiar images (for example, the *Mona Lisa* has been used many times in ads), old television shows, movies, even other ads.

One attention-getting tactic is **visual metaphor**—the use of an image that represents an abstract concept to make a visual analogy. The viewer is invited to make the connection between the image and the concept. Antidrug ads have used visual metaphors extensively, especially to portray the effects of drugs on the brain. The image of the brain as a scrambled egg is one example. Other metaphors represent drugs as self-destructive weapons.

Marijuana can slow a child's emotional development. Marijuana can interfere with academic performance, cause short-term memory loss and hurt your child's ability to cope with the problems of life. Call 1-800-729-6686 for a free copy of "Marijuana: Facts Parents Need to Know."

Antidrug ads often use visual metaphors.

Public Service Announcements
provided courtesy of the
Partnership for a Drug Free America ®

 # Visual Evidence

Photographs

Images and graphics seldom make arguments on their own, but they are frequently used to support arguments. Photographs are commonly used as

Saddam Hussein shortly after he was captured on December 13, 2003. Photo by Staff Sgt. David Bennett.

factual evidence. When United States soldiers captured Saddam Hussein on December 13, 2003, the military immediately released photographs of the former leader of Iraq, whom they declared a prisoner of war, even though releasing images of a POW is technically a violation of Geneva Convention rules. But even nations critical of the United States didn't raise this issue. The demand for proof of Saddam's capture was overwhelming.

Photographs also provide evidence of the past. They provide a cultural memory of earlier times. The segregation of white and African Americans in the South before the 1960s would now be hard to imagine without images from the time that depict separate water fountains and separate entrances to public buildings.

Just as for other kinds of evidence, the significance of images can be contested. In 1936, 21-year-old Arthur Rothstein worked as a photographer for the Resettlement Administration, a federal agency created to help people living in rural poverty. Rothstein sent a photograph of a bleached cow's

"Colored" entrance to a movie theater, Belzoni, Mississippi, October 1939. Photo by Marion Post Wolcott.

skull lying on cracked dirt to Roy Stryker, his boss in Washington. Stryker saw the image as representing the plight of Midwestern plains states in the midst of a severe drought.

But not all people living in plains states found the image and others like it representative. A newspaper in Fargo, North Dakota, published one of Rothstein's photographs on the front page under the headline, "It's a fake." The newspaper accused journalists in general of making the situation on the plains appear worse than it was and accused Rothstein in particular of using a movable prop to make a cheap point. Furthermore, the newspaper contended that the cracked earth was typical of the badlands at all times but didn't represent the soil condition in most of the state. Close examination of the set of photographs of the skull revealed the skull had been moved about 10 feet, which Rothstein admitted. But he protested that the drought was real enough and there were plenty of cow bones on the ground. Rothstein followed a long practice among photographers in altering a scene for the purpose of getting a better photograph.

Photographs were often manipulated in the darkroom, but realistic results required a high skill level. Digital photography and the image editing software have made it relatively easy to alter photographs. Thousands of altered images are circulated daily that put heads on different bodies and put people in different places, often within historical images. The ease of cropping digital photographs reveals an important truth about photography. A high-resolution picture of a crowd can be divided into many smaller images that each say something different about the event. The act of pointing the camera in one direction and not in another shapes how photographic evidence will be interpreted.

The bleached skull of a steer on the dry, sun-baked earth of the South Dakota Badlands, 1939. Photo by Arthur Rothstein.

Tables

Statistical information is frequently used as evidence in arguments. For example, gun control advocates point to comparisons between the United States and other advanced nations of the world, all of which have much stricter gun laws than the United States and much lower rates of deaths by firearms. The rate of firearm deaths in the United States is three times higher than Canada's, four times higher than Australia's, nine times higher than Germany's, twenty-four times higher than the United Kingdom's (even including Northern Ireland), and almost two hundred times higher than Japan's.

The problem with giving many statistics in words is that readers shortly lose track of the numbers. Readers require formats where they can take in a mass of numerical data at once. Tables are useful for presenting an array of numerical data. Below is a comparison of the death rates due to firearms in the United States and other advanced nations.

Deaths Due to Firearms
(rates are per 100,000 people)

	Total Firearm Deaths		Firearm Homicides		Firearm Suicides		Fatal Firearm Accidents	
	Rate	Number	Rate	Number	Rate	Number	Rate	Number
United States (1995)	13.7	35,957	6	15,835	7	18,503	0.5	1,225
Australia (1994)	3.05	536	0.56	96	2.38	420	0.11	20
Canada (1994)	4.08	1,189	0.6	176	3.35	975	0.13	38
Germany (1995)	1.47	1,197	0.21	168	1.23	1,004	0.03	25
Japan (1995)	0.07	93	0.03	34	0.04	49	0.01	10
Sweden (1992)	2.31	200	0.31	27	1.95	169	0.05	4
Spain (1994)	1.01	396	0.19	76	0.55	219	0.26	101
United Kingdom (1994)	0.57	277	0.13	72	0.33	193	0.02	12

Source: United Nations. *United Nations International Study on Firearms Regulation.* Vienna, Austria: United Nations Crime Prevention and Criminal Justice Division, 1997. 109.

Charts and Graphs

While tables can present an array of numbers at once, they too lack the dramatic impact of charts. Charts visually represent the magnitude and proportion of data. The differences in death rates due to firearms is striking when presented as a chart.

Column and Bar Charts

One of the easiest charts to make is a simple column or bar chart (column charts are vertical; bar charts are horizontal).

The options in creating charts involve rhetorical decisions. The lengths of the axes on a column or bar chart either exaggerate or minimize differences. The unit of measurement also determines the appearance of a chart.

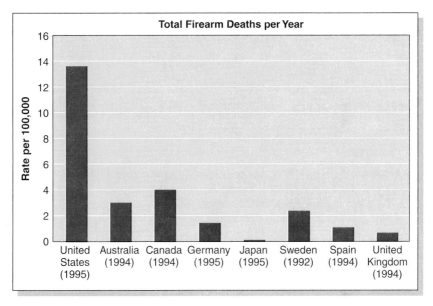

Figure 5.1 Column chart of firearm deaths by country.

Line Graphs

People have difficulty visualizing trends if they are given a long list of numbers, but they can recognize a visual pattern at a glance, which is why line graphs are commonly used to represent statistical trends across time. In Figure 5.2, it's easy to see that the number of handgun homicides rose in the early 1990s but then declined in the late 1990s.

Pie Charts

Pie charts are especially useful for representing percentages, but they work only if the percentages of the parts add up to one hundred percent. Gun control advocates frequently cite a study done in Seattle that identified all gunshot

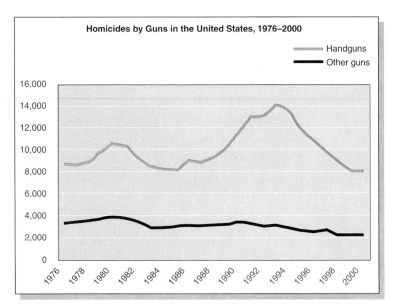

Figure 5.2 Line graph of homicides by guns in the United States, 1976–2000 Source: United States. Department of Justice. *Homicide Trends in the U.S.* 21 Nov. 2002. 2 Dec. 2003 <http://www.ojp.usdoj.gov/bjs/homicide/weapons.htm>.

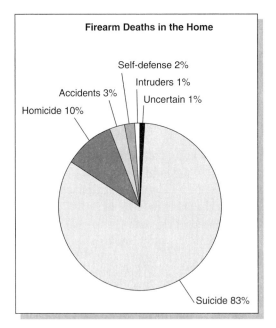

Figure 5.3 Pie chart of causes of firearm deaths in the home.

deaths over a six-year period (A. L. Kellermann and D. L. Reay. "Protection or Peril: An Analysis of Firearm-Related Deaths in the Home." *New England Journal of Medicine* 314 (1986): 1557–60). Of the 733 deaths by firearms, a majority of 398 occurred in the home in which the firearm involved was kept. Of that 398,333 (83.6%) were suicides, 41 (10.3%) were criminal homicides, 12 (3.0%) were accidental, 7 (1.7%) were justifiable self-defense, and only 2 (0.5%) involved an intruder shot during an attempted entry.

Gun control advocates use this study to question the advisability of keeping firearms in the home for protection. Gun rights advocates, however, fault the study because there is no evidence for how many attempts to enter the home might be prevented because intruders fear that the owner is armed.

EVALUATING CHARTS AND GRAPHS

Computer software makes it simple to create charts and graphs. This ease, however, does not tell you which kind of chart or graph is best to use and the purpose of including a chart or graph. Ask these questions when you are analyzing charts and graphs.

1. Is the type of chart appropriate for the information presented? For example, a pie chart is inappropriate if the parts do not add up to 100 percent of the whole.

Bar and column charts — make comparisons in particular categories

Line graphs — show proportional trends over time

Pie charts — show the proportion of parts in terms of the whole

(Continued)

> **EVALUATING CHARTS AND GRAPHS** *(continued)*
>
> 2. Does the chart have a clear purpose?
> 3. Does the title indicate the purpose?
> 4. What do the units represent (dollars, people, voters, percentages, and so on)?
> 5. What is the source of the data?
> 6. Is there any distortion of information? A bar chart can exaggerate small differences if intervals are manipulated (for example, 42 can look twice as large as 41 on a bar chart if the numbering begins at 40).

 # Write a Visual Analysis

Few images and graphics by themselves convey definite meanings. But words often don't have definite meanings either. Consider this sentence: "Sheila will give you a ring tomorrow." Is Sheila going to call you or give you a piece of jewelry to wear on your finger? Usually we never think of the alternative meaning because the context makes clear which meaning of *ring* is intended.

Many signs are highly abstract, but we seldom confuse their meaning. Look again at a common sign in an airport. The symbols for man and woman are part of an international system of hieroglyphics and are endorsed by the U.S. Department of Transportation. People around the world interpret these symbols to indicate toilets for men and women, even though gender is marked by a garment worn only sometimes by women in Western nations.

Sign in an airport.

But if we place this symbol in a different context—for example, placing it over a graffiti drawing of closed fists—the meaning changes. Perhaps the composite image could be interpreted as suggesting an ongoing war between the sexes. If so, the line between the two symbols changes to a wall. The immediate context often gives a way of interpreting an image, and if the image is placed in a strange context, the meaning often isn't as clear.

A conventional symbol placed in a new context.

We use more than the immediate context to interpret images. We use our knowledge of images to classify them into types or genres. We recognize the image of the three individuals shown here as a snapshot, a kind of image that has been enormously popular since the appearance of the inexpensive Brownie camera in 1888. We know from how cameras are typically used in our culture that the woman in the center is probably a tourist who asked the two police officers to pose with her.

A tourist in New York City.

Another detail gives an important clue to how to read the photograph. The woman is wearing an NYPD cap, which were seldom worn by people other than police officers before September 11, 2001. The cap tells us that the location is probably New York City and the date of the photo was sometime after September 11. In addition to the immediate context, we use our knowledge of the broader historical and cultural contexts to interpret an image.

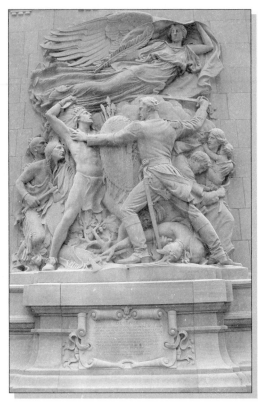

Relief sculpture of the Fort Dearborn Massacre on the Michigan Avenue Bridge, Chicago.

The great majority of visual arguments we see each day are advertisements, but there are other important kinds of visual arguments. One is public art and sculpture, which often celebrates the importance of people and events. On one of the bridge houses of the Michigan Avenue Bridge crossing the Chicago River in downtown Chicago is a large relief sculpture depicting the massacre of settlers fleeing Fort Dearborn in 1812. The size of the sculpture and its placement on the busiest and most famous street in Chicago attests to its significance at the time it was commissioned.

Two central figures— an American soldier and a Potawatomi Indian— battle as an angel hovers above. On the left another Indian is stealthily approaching, crouched with a tomahawk in hand. On the right a man shields a woman and a child from the threat. The sculpture uses a familiar stereotype of American Indians to make a visual argument: the Indians are attacking because they are bloodthirsty and sneaky; the innocent white people bravely resist. The sculpture does not speak to the circumstances of the massacre. The Potawatomis allied with the British during the War of 1812 to resist settlers who were taking their land. The settlers waited too long to evacuate Fort Dearborn in the face of growing numbers of Indians surrounding the fort.

It's not surprising that the sculpture represents the settlers as heroic. The bridge and monument were part of a grand plan to enhance Chicago's waterfront, begun in 1909. Thus the monument plays its part in obscuring the actual history of the area. Viewers who are unaware of the facts may feel a sense of patriotic pride in the actions of the soldier and the woman. Viewers who are familiar with the whole story may take a more cynical view of the intended message.

Sample Student Visual Analysis

Angela Yamashita wrote the following essay while a first-year student at Pennsylvania State University. Yamashita is majoring in bioengineering and is an avid lacrosse player.

Angela Yamashita

Dr. Sanchez

English 15

12 December 2003

Got Roddick?

Andy Roddick is one of the hottest up-and-coming athletes of today. In 2003 he became the youngest American to finish ranked number one in the ATP rankings, and he's known not only for his excellent playing skills but also for his good looks and easygoing attitude. Boyfriend to popular singer Mandy Moore, Roddick has been thrown into the spotlight and is now a teenage crush. It was his picture that stopped me while leafing through Seventeen and made me take a longer look. Roddick stands staring at the viewer, racquet over his shoulder, leaning against the net on the court. More prominent than his

Yamashita 2

white pants, white tennis shirt, and white towel draped
around his neck is the white milk mustache above his
upper lip. The ad reads: "Now serving. I'm into power. So
I drink milk. It packs 9 essential nutrients into every
glass. Which comes in handy whether you're an athlete or
an energetic fan." At the bottom of the page is the ad
slogan (also in white) "Got Milk?"

The "Got Milk?" campaign has been going on since
1993 and has published numerous ads that try to convince
adults to drink more milk. Everyone from rock groups to
actors to athletes have participated in this campaign.
In today's caffeine-obsessed society of coffee and soda
drinkers, America's Dairy Farmers and Milk Processors
(the association that sponsors the "Got Milk?" campaign)
felt the need to reverse the decline in milk consumption
by advertising milk in a new way. The catchy "Got Milk?"
proved to be highly successful, and the campaign has
been mimicked by many others including "Got cookies?"

"Got fish?" "Got sports?" and even "Got Jesus?"
(Philpot). The Andy Roddick ad is typical of the "Got
Milk?" series, urging people young and old to drink milk
to remain healthy and strong. The Roddick ad primarily
uses the appeals ethos and pathos to persuade its
audience. (The one gesture toward logos in the ad is the
mention that milk has nine nutrients.)

America's Dairy Farmers and Milk Processors use
celebrity endorsements to establish the ethos of their
ads. The "Got Milk?" campaign has enlisted a range of
celebrities popular with young audiences from Amy Grant
to Austin Powers, Britney Spears to Brett Farve, T-Mac
(Tracy McGrady) to Bernie Mac. Choosing Andy Roddick,
the dominant young male player in American tennis, fits
squarely in this lineup. Admired by a strong following
of young adults (girls for his looks, boys for his
athletic ability), Roddick is an ideal spokesman for
establishing that milk is a healthy drink. Implicit in
the ad is that milk will help you become a better
athlete and better looking too.

Pathos in the ad is conveyed not simply through
Roddick's good looks. His pose is casual, almost
slouching, yet his face is serious, one that suggests
that he not only means business about playing tennis but
also about his drink of choice. The words "I'm into
power" don't mess around. They imply that you too can be
more powerful by drinking milk. "Now serving" is also in
your face, making a play on the word "serving" both as a
tennis and a drink term.

Yamashita 4

The effectiveness of the "Got Milk?" campaign is demonstrated in gallons of milk sold. The campaign began in California in 1993 at a time when milk sales were rapidly eroding. A San Francisco ad agency developed the milk mustache idea, which is credited for stopping the downward trend in milk consumption in California. In 1995 the campaign went national. By 2000 national sales of milk remained consistent in contrast to annual declines in the early 1990s (Stamler). "Got Milk?" gave milk a brand identity that it had previously lacked, allowing it to compete with the well-established identities of Pepsi and Coca-Cola. Milk now has new challengers with more and more people going out to Starbuck's and other breakfast bars. Nonetheless, the original formula of using celebrities like Andy Roddick who appeal to younger audiences continues to work. Milk isn't likely to go away soon as a popular beverage.

Yamashita 5

Works Cited

"Andy Roddick." Got Milk? 2003. Milk Processor
    Education Program. 18 Nov. 2003
    <http://www.whymilk.com/celebrity_archive.htm>.

Philpot, Robert. "Copycats Mimic 'Got Milk' Ads."
    Milwaukee Journal Sentinel 12 May 2002, final ed.: D3.

Stamler, Bernard. "Got Sticking Power?" New York Times
    30 July 2001, late ed.: C11.

Steps to a Visual Analysis

Step 1 Select an example of visual persuasion to analyze

Many visual objects and images intend to persuade. Of course, all forms of advertising fall into the category of persuasion.

Examples

- Analyze a map. What is represented on a map? What is most prominent? What is left out? Maps most often do not make explicit claims, but they are persuasive nonetheless.
- Analyze a popular consumer product. Why did iPods became the hottest-selling MP3 player? What made the iPod stand out?
- Analyze a public building in your city or town. What messages does it convey?
- Analyze images on an online real estate site. Why are particular pictures of a house displayed? What arguments do those images make?

Step 2 Analyze the context

What is the context?

- Why was this image made or object created?
- What was the purpose?
- Where did it come from?

Who is the audience?

- What can you infer about the intended audience?
- What did the designer(s) assume the audience knew or believed?

Who is the designer?

- Do you know the identity of the author?
- What else has the designer done?

Step 3 Analyze the text

What is the subject?

- Can you describe the content?
- How is the image or object arranged?

What is the medium and genre?

- What is the medium? A printed photograph? an oil painting? an outdoor sign? a building?
- What is the genre? An advertisement? a monument? a portrait? a cartoon? What expectations does the audience have about this genre?

Are words connected to the image or object?

- Is there a caption attached to the image or words in the image?
- Are there words on the building or object?

What appeals are used?

- Are there appeals to ethos—the character of what is represented?
- Are there appeals to logos—the documentation of facts?
- Are there appeals to pathos—the values of the audience? Are there elements that can be considered as symbolic?

How would you characterize the style?

- Is the style formal, informal, comic, or something else?
- Are any visual metaphors used?

Step 4 Write a draft

- Introduce the image or object and give the background.
- Make a claim about the image or object you are analyzing. For example, *the "Got Milk?" ad featuring Andy Roddick relies on the appeals of ethos and pathos.*
- Support your claim with close analysis of the image or object. Describe key features.

Step 5 Revise, edit, proofread

- For detailed instructions, see Chapter 12.
- For a checklist to use to evaluate your draft, see pages 217–222.

PART 2

Putting Good Reasons into Action

Options for Arguments

Imagine that you bought a new car in June and you are taking some of your friends to your favorite lake over the Fourth of July weekend. You have a great time until, as you are heading home, a drunk driver—a repeat offender—swerves into your lane and totals your new car. You and your friends are lucky not to be hurt, but you're outraged because you believe that repeat offenders should be prevented from driving, even if that means putting them in jail. You also remember going to another state that had sobriety checkpoints on holiday weekends. If such a checkpoint had been at the lake, you might still be driving your new car. You live in a town that encourages citizens to contribute to the local newspaper, and you think you could get a guest editorial published. The question is: How do you want to write the editorial?

- You could tell your story about how a repeat drunk driver endangered the lives of you and your friends.
- You could define driving while intoxicated (DWI) as a more legally culpable crime.
- You could compare the treatment of drunk drivers in your state with the treatment of drunk drivers in another state.

- You could cite statistics that drunk drivers killed 17,013 people in 2003, a figure that was down from previous years but still represented too many needless deaths.

- You could evaluate the present drunk driving laws as insufficiently just or less than totally successful.

- You could propose taking vehicles away from repeat drunk drivers and forcing them to serve mandatory sentences.

- You could argue that your community should have sobriety checkpoints at times when drunk drivers are likely to be on the road.

- You could do several of the above.

You're not going to have much space in the newspaper, so you decide to argue for sobriety checkpoints. You know that they are controversial. One of your friends in the car with you said that they are unconstitutional because they involve search without cause. However, after doing some research to find out whether checkpoints are defined as legal or illegal, you learn that on June 14, 1990, the U.S. Supreme Court upheld the constitutionality of using checkpoints as a deterrent and enforcement tool against drunk drivers. But you still want to know whether most people would agree with your friend that sobriety checkpoints are an invasion of privacy. You find opinion polls and surveys going back to the 1980s that show that 70 to 80 percent of those polled support sobriety checkpoints. You also realize that you can argue by analogy that security checkpoints for alcohol are similar in many ways to airport security checkpoints that protect the passengers. You decide you will finish by making an argument from consequence. If people who go to the lake with plans to drink a lot know in advance that there will be checkpoints, they will find a designated driver or some other means of safe transportation, and everyone else will also be a little safer.

The point of this example is that people very rarely set out to define something in an argument for the sake of definition, compare for the sake of comparison, or adopt any of the other ways of structuring an argument. Instead, they have a purpose in mind, and they use the kinds of arguments that are discussed in Part 2—most often in combination—as means to an end. Most arguments use multiple approaches and multiple sources of good reasons. Proposal arguments in particular often analyze a present situation with definition, causal, and evaluative arguments before advancing a course of future action to address that situation. The advantage of thinking explicitly about the structure of arguments is that you often find other ways to argue. Sometimes you just need a way to get started writing about complex issues.

Using Different Approaches to Construct an Argument

An even greater advantage of thinking explicitly about specific kinds of arguments is that they can often give you a *sequence* for constructing arguments. Take affirmative action policies for granting admission to college as an example. No issue has been more controversial on college campuses during the last ten years.

Definition

What exactly does *affirmative action* mean? You know that it is a policy that attempts to address the reality of contemporary inequality based on past injustice. But injustice to whom and by whom? Do all members of minorities, all women, and all people with disabilities have equal claims for redress of past injustices? If not, how do you distinguish among them? And what exactly does affirmative action entail? Do all students who are admitted by affirmative action criteria automatically receive scholarships? Clearly, you need to define affirmative action first before proposing any changes in the policy.

Cause and Effect

Since affirmative action policies have been around for a few years, you might next investigate how well they have worked. If you view affirmative action as a cause, then what have been its effects? You might find, for example, that the percentage of African Americans graduating from college dropped from 1991 through 2001 in many states. Furthermore, affirmative action policies have created a backlash attitude among many whites who believe, rightly or wrongly, that they are victims of reverse racism. But you might find that enrollment of minorities at your university has increased substantially since affirmative action policies were instituted. And you might come across a book by the then-presidents of Princeton and Harvard, William G. Bowen and Derek Bok, entitled *The Shape of the River: Long-Term Consequences of Considering Race in College and University Admissions*, which examines the effects of affirmative action policies at twenty-eight of the nation's most select universities. They found that African American graduates of elite schools were more likely than their white counterparts to earn graduate degrees and to take on civic responsibilities after graduation.

Evaluation

With a definition established and evidence collected, you can move to evaluation. Is affirmative action fair? Is affirmative action just? Is the goal of achieving diversity through affirmative action admissions policies a worthy one because white people enjoyed preferential treatment until the last few decades? Or are affirmative action admissions policies bad because they continue the historically bad practice of giving preference to people of certain races and because they cast into the role of victims the people they are trying to help?

Proposal

When you have a definition with evidence and have made an evaluation, you have the groundwork for making a recommendation in the form of a proposal. A proposal argues what should be done in the future or what should not be done and what good or bad consequences will follow.

Your Goals for Argument

Even though types of argument are distinguished in Part 2, they are closely linked parts of a whole. Each type of argument can stand alone but always involves multiple aspects. If you are clear in your purpose for your argument and have a good sense of the knowledge and attitudes of the people your argument is aimed toward, then the most effective types of arguments will be evident to you. You might find yourself using several different approaches at once.

CHAPTER 6

Definition Arguments

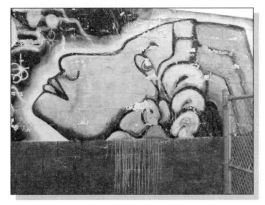

> What a quintessential marriage of cool and style to write your name in giant separate living letters, large as animals, lithe as snakes, mysterious as Arabic and Chinese curls of alphabet.
>
> NORMAN MAILER,
> THE FAITH OF GRAFFITI, 1973

> "It's expression, you know," one 15-year-old tagger, who would give his name only as Chris, said. "Most taggers aren't in gangs," he added. "They're not shooting people. It's not that big a problem, if you stop and think. It's really art."
>
> No, Chris, it's not art—it's vandalism when you deface the property of another without permission.
>
> EDITORIAL, DENVER POST,
> JUNE 10, 2003

From cave paintings made over thirty thousand years ago to artwork spanning from Egyptian and Roman times to the present, people have been writing and painting on walls. The present trend in graffiti grew up along with
hip-hop in New York City in the 1970s and has evolved from simple "tagging" of names to large, sophisticated murals.

But what is graffiti—art or vandalism? Some graffiti artists have been
hired to paint murals in public spaces and some even have been honored
with exhibits in major art museums. Yet graffiti is also defined as a crime,
either a misdemeanor or a felony. For some, graffiti is a means of self-
expression and a vibrant form of urban diversity. For others, graffiti is
visual pollution, even a kind of domestic terrorism that says no one is safe
and that blights neighborhoods and destroys small businesses.

The continuing controversy about
graffiti illustrates why definitions often
matter more that we might think at first.
People argue about definitions because

> Definition arguments are the
> most powerful arguments.

of the consequences of something being defined in a certain way. The controversy over graffiti also illustrates three very important principles that operate
when definitions are used in arguments.

First, people make definitions that benefit their interests. You learned
very early in life the importance of defining actions as "accidents." Windows
can be broken through carelessness, especially when you are tossing a ball
against the side of the house, but if it's an accident, well, accidents just happen (and don't require punishment).

Second, most of the time when you are arguing a definition, your audience will either have a different definition in mind or be unsure of the definition. Your mother or father probably didn't think breaking the window
was an accident, so you had to convince Mom or Dad that you were really
being careful, but the ball just slipped out of your hand. It's your job to get
them to accept your definition.

Third, if you can get your audience to accept your definition, then usually you succeed. For this reason, definition arguments are the most powerful arguments.

Kinds of Definitions

Rarely do you get far into an argument without having to define something. Imagine that you are writing an argument about the United States'
decades-old and largely ineffective "war on drugs." We all know that the

war on drugs is being waged against drugs that are illegal, like cocaine and marijuana, and not against the legal drugs produced by the multibillion-dollar drug industry. Our society classifies drugs into two categories: "good" drugs, which are legal, and "bad" drugs, which are illegal.

How exactly does our society arrive at these definitions? Drugs would be relatively easy to define as good or bad if the difference could be defined at the molecular level. Bad drugs would contain certain molecules that define them as bad. The history of drug use in the United States, however, tells us that it is not so simple. In the last century alcohol was on the list of illegal drugs for over a decade, while opium was considered a good drug and distributed in many patent medicines by pharmaceutical companies. Similarly, LSD and MDMA (ecstasy) were developed by the pharmaceutical industry but later placed in the illegal category. In a few states marijuana is now crossing over to the legal category for medicinal use.

If drugs cannot be classified as good or bad by their molecular structure, then perhaps society classifies them by effects. It might be reasonable to assume that drugs that are addictive are illegal, but that's not the case. Nicotine is highly addictive and is a legal drug; so too are many prescription medicines. Neither are drugs taken for the purpose of offering pleasure necessarily illegal (think of alcohol and Viagra), nor are drugs that alter consciousness or change personality (Prozac).

How a drug is defined as legal or illegal apparently is determined by *example*. The nationwide effort in the United States to stop people from drinking alcohol during the first decades of the twentieth century led to the passage of the Eighteenth Amendment and the ban on sales of alcohol from 1920 to 1933, known as Prohibition. Those who argued for Prohibition used examples of drunkenness, especially among the poor, to show how alcohol broke up families and left mothers and children penniless in the street. Those who opposed Prohibition initially pointed to the consumption of beer and wine in many ethnic traditions. Later they raised examples of the bad effects of Prohibition—the rise of organized crime, the increase in alcohol abuse, and the general disregard for laws.

When you make a definitional argument, it's important to think about what kind of definition you will use. Descriptions of three types follow.

Formal Definitions

Formal definitions typically categorize an item into the next higher classification and give distinguishing criteria from other items within that classification. Most dictionary definitions are formal definitions. For example, fish are cold-blooded aquatic vertebrates that have jaws, fins, and scales and are distinguished from other cold-blooded aquatic vertebrates (such as sea snakes) by the presence of gills. If you can construct a formal definition with specific criteria that your audience will accept, then likely you will have a strong argument. The key is to get your audience to agree to your criteria.

Operational Definitions

Many concepts cannot be easily defined by formal definitions. Researchers in the natural and social sciences must construct operational definitions that they use for their research. For example, researchers who study binge drinking among college students define a binge as five or more drinks in one sitting for a man, and four or more drinks for a woman. Some people think this standard is too low and should be raised to six to eight drinks to distinguish true problem drinkers from the general college population. No matter what the number, researchers must argue that the particular definition is one that suits the concept.

Definitions from Example

Many human qualities such as honesty, courage, creativity, deceit, and love must be defined by examples that the audience accepts as representative of the concept. Few would not call the firemen who entered the World Trade Center on September 11, 2001, courageous. Most people would describe someone with a diagnosis of terminal cancer who refuses to feel self-pity as courageous. But what about a student who declines to go to a concert with her friends so she can study for an exam? Her behavior might be admirable, but most people would hesitate to call it courageous. The key to arguing a definition from examples is that the examples must strike the audience as in some way typical of the concept, even if the situation is unusual.

Building a Definitional Argument

Because definition arguments are the most powerful arguments, they are often at the center of the most important debates in American history. The major arguments of the civil rights movement were definition arguments, none more

Martin Luther King, Jr.

eloquent than Martin Luther King, Jr.'s "Letter from Birmingham Jail." From 1957 until his assassination in April 1968, King served as president of the Southern Christian Leadership Conference, an organization of primarily African American clergymen dedicated to bringing about social change. King, who was a Baptist minister, tried to put into practice Mahatma Gandhi's principles of nonviolence in demonstrations, sit-ins, and marches throughout the South. During Holy Week in 1963, King led demonstrations and a boycott of downtown merchants in Birmingham, Alabama, to end racial segregation at lunch counters and discriminatory hiring practices.

On Wednesday, April 10, the city obtained an injunction directing the demonstrations to cease until their legality could be argued in court. But after meditation, King decided, against the advice of his associates, to defy the court order and proceed with the march planned for Good Friday morning. On Friday morning, April 12, King and fifty followers were arrested. King was held in solitary confinement until the end of the weekend, allowed neither to see his attorneys nor to call his wife. On the day of his arrest, King read in the newspaper a statement objecting to the demonstrations signed by eight white Birmingham clergymen of Protestant, Catholic, and Jewish faiths, urging that the protests stop and that grievances be settled in the courts.

On Saturday morning, King started writing an eloquent response that addresses the criticisms of the white clergymen, who are one primary audience of his response. But King intended his response to the ministers for widespread publication, and he clearly had in mind a larger readership. The clergymen gave him the occasion to address moderate white leaders in the South as well as religious and educated people across the nation and supporters of the civil rights movement. King begins "Letter from Birmingham Jail" by addressing the ministers as "My Dear Fellow Clergymen," adopting a conciliatory and tactful tone from the outset but at the same time offering strong arguments for the necessity of acting now rather than waiting for change. A critical part of King's argument is justifying disobedience of certain laws. The eight white clergymen asked that laws be obeyed until they are changed. Here's how King responds:

> You express a great deal of anxiety over our willingness to break laws. This is certainly a legitimate concern. Since we so diligently urge people to obey the Supreme Court's decision of 1954 outlawing segregation in the public schools, at first glance it may seem rather paradoxical for us consciously to break laws. One may well ask: "How can you advocate breaking some laws and obeying others?" The answer lies in the fact that there are two types of laws: just and unjust. I would be the first to advocate obeying just laws. One has not only a legal but a moral responsibility to obey just laws. Conversely, one has a moral responsibility to disobey unjust laws. I would agree with St. Augustine that "an unjust law is no law at all."
>
> Now, what is the difference between the two? How does one determine whether a law is just or unjust? A just law is a man-made code that squares with the moral law or the law of God. An unjust law is a code that is out of harmony with the moral law. To put it in the terms of St. Thomas Aquinas: An unjust law is a human law that is not rooted in eternal law and natural law. Any law that uplifts human personality is just. Any law that degrades human personality is unjust. All segregation statutes are unjust because segregation distorts the soul and damages the personality. It gives the segregator a false sense of superiority and the segregated a false sense of inferiority. Segregation, to use the terminology of the Jewish philosopher Martin Buber, substitutes an "I-it" relationship and ends up relegating persons to the status of things. Hence segregation is not only politically, economically and sociologically unsound, it is morally wrong and sinful. Paul Tillich has said that sin is separation. Is not segregation an existential expression of man's tragic separation, his awful estrangement, his terrible sinfulness? Thus it is that I can urge men to obey the 1954 decision of the Supreme Court, for it is morally right; and I can urge them to disobey segregation ordinances, for they are morally wrong.

Martin Luther King's analysis of just and unjust laws is a classic definitional argument. Definitional arguments take this form:

> SOMETHING is a _____ if it possesses certain criteria that differentiate it from other similar things in its general class.

According to King, a *just law* possesses the criteria of being consistent with moral law and uplifting human personality. Just as important, King sets out the criteria of an *unjust law*, when something is not a _____. Unjust laws have the criteria of being out of harmony with moral law and damaging human personality. The criteria are set out in because-clauses: *SOMETHING is a _____ because it has these criteria.* The criteria provide the link shown in Figure 6.1. The negative can be argued in the same way, as shown in Figure 6.2.

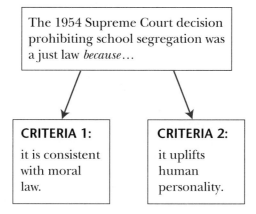

Figure 6.1

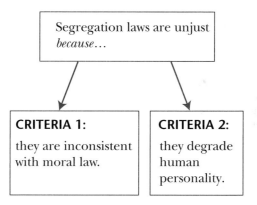

Figure 6.2

An extended definition like King's is a two-step process. First you have to determine the criteria. Then you have to argue that what you are defining possesses these criteria. If you want to argue that housing prisoners in unheated and non-air-conditioned tents is cruel and unusual punishment, then you have to make exposing prisoners to hot and cold extremes one of the criteria of cruel and unusual punishment. The keys to a definitional argument are getting your audience to accept your criteria and getting your audience to accept that the case in point meets those criteria. King's primary audience was the eight white clergymen; therefore, he used religious criteria and cited Protestant, Catholic, and Jewish theologians as his authority. His second criterion about just laws uplifting the human personality was a less familiar concept than the idea of moral law. King therefore offered a more detailed explanation drawing on the work of Martin Buber.

But King was smart enough to know that not all of his potential readers would put quite so much stock in religious authorities. Therefore, he follows the religious criteria with two other criteria that appeal to definitions of democracy:

> Let us consider a more concrete example of just and unjust laws. An unjust law is a code that a numerical or power majority group compels a minority group to obey but does not make binding on itself. This is *difference* made legal. By the same token, a just law is a code that a majority compels a minority to follow and that it is willing to follow itself. This is *sameness* made legal.
>
> Let me give another explanation. A law is unjust if it is inflicted on the minority that, as a result of being denied the right to vote, has no part in enacting or devising the law. Who can say that the legislature of Alabama which set up that state's segregation laws was democratically elected? Throughout Alabama all sorts of devious methods are used to prevent Negroes from becoming registered voters, and there are some counties in which, even though Negroes constitute a majority of the population, not a single Negro is registered. Can any law enacted under such circumstances be considered democratically structured?

King expands his criteria for just and unjust laws to include four major criteria, and he defines both by classifying and by giving examples. (See Figure 6.3.)

King's "Letter from Birmingham Jail" draws much of its rhetorical power from its reliance on a variety of arguments that are suited for different readers. An atheist could reject the notion of laws made by God but could still be convinced by the criteria that segregation laws are undemocratic and therefore unjust.

To make definitional arguments work, often you must put much effort into identifying and explaining your criteria. You must convince your readers that your criteria are the best ones for what you are defining and that they apply to the case you are arguing. King backs up his assertion—that Alabama's segregation laws in 1963 were unjust because the Alabama legislature was not democratically elected—by pointing to counties that had African American majorities but no African American voters.

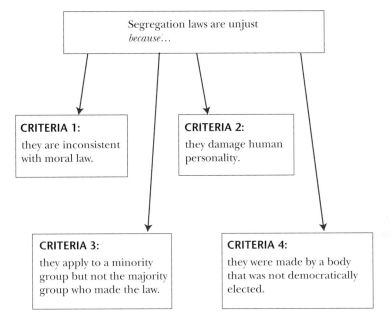

Figure 6.3

SCOTT MCCLOUD

Setting the Record Straight

*Scott McCloud is the pseudonym of Scott Willard McLeod, who was born
in Boston in 1960 and graduated from Syracuse University in 1982. After
a short stint in the production department at DC Comics, he quickly
became a highly regarded writer and illustrator of comics. His works
include the ten-issue series* Zot! *(1984–1985)* Destroy!! *(1986), and the
nonfiction* Understanding Comics: The Invisible Art *(Northampton, MA:
Tundra, 1993), from which this selection is taken.*

    Understanding Comics *is a brilliant explanation of how comics
combine words and pictures to achieve effects that neither words nor
pictures can do alone. At the beginning of the book, McCloud finds it
necessary to define what comics are and are not before he can begin to
analyze the magic of comics. Notice how he has to refine his criteria
several times before he has an adequate definition.*

Understanding Comics *Copyright © 1993, 1994 by Scott McCloud. Published by Kitchen Sink Press. Reprinted by permission of HarperCollins Publishers Inc.*

IN LESS THAN A *YEAR*, I BECAME *TOTALLY* **OBSESSED** WITH COMICS! I DECIDED TO BECOME A *COMICS ARTIST* IN *10th GRADE* AND BEGAN TO *PRACTICE, PRACTICE,* **PRACTICE!**

I FELT THAT THERE WAS SOMETHING *LURKING* IN COMICS... SOMETHING THAT HAD *NEVER BEEN DONE.*

SOME KIND OF *HIDDEN* **POWER!**

BUT WHENEVER I TRIED TO *EXPLAIN* MY FEELING, I FAILED *MISERABLY.*

COMIC BOOKS?! HA! HA! HA!

BUT IT-- BUT IT'S-- BUH...

SURE, I REALIZED THAT COMIC BOOKS WERE USUALLY *CRUDE, POORLY-DRAWN, SEMILITERATE, CHEAP, DISPOSABLE KIDDIE FARE--*

--BUT--

THEY DON'T **HAVE** TO BE!

THE *PROBLEM* WAS THAT FOR *MOST PEOPLE,* THAT WAS WHAT "COMIC BOOK" *MEANT!*

DON'T GIMME THAT *COMIC BOOK* TALK, BARNEY!

IF PEOPLE FAILED TO *UNDERSTAND* COMICS, IT WAS BECAUSE THEY DEFINED WHAT COMICS COULD BE *TOO NARROWLY!*

A *PROPER DEFINITION,* IF WE COULD *FIND* ONE, MIGHT GIVE *LIE* TO THE STEREOTYPES--

--AND SHOW THAT THE *POTENTIAL* OF COMICS IS *LIMITLESS* AND *EXCITING!*

THIS IS WHERE OUR JOURNEY *BEGINS.*

* EISNER'S OWN *COMICS AND SEQUENTIAL ART* BEING A HAPPY EXCEPTION.

*JUXTAPOSED= ADJACENT, SIDE-BY-SIDE.
GREAT ART SCHOOL WORD.

CHAPTER 7

Causal Arguments

In a 5–4 decision, the U.S. Supreme Court has ruled that the U.S. Corps of Army Engineers cannot regulate isolated wetlands merely because passing birds might land on such property. . . . The decision, says the National Association of Home Builders (NAHB), is "a major legal victory for home builders and other private property owners."

REALTY TIMES, JANUARY 10, 2001

According to the U.S. Fish and Wildlife Service, more than 120,000 acres of wetlands are destroyed annually. And with the leveling of these wetlands go entire delicate ecosystems—and the plants, insects, and animals they support.

NATIONAL PARKS CONSERVATION ASSOCIATION, 2004
http://www.npca.org/marine%5Fand %5Fcoastal/wetlands/

Many biologists now believe that within one hundred years as many as half the species on earth will become extinct or else be relegated to ghost status, surviving in zoos or as DNA samples. It's not that plants and animals are going to vanish; they will still be abundant but the number of different species will be radically fewer. Why is this mass extinction occurring? And why are many animal and plant species now thriving when so many others are disappearing?

Biologists have found a complex set of factors that are changing the composition of living things on earth: rising human population, habitat destruction, habitat fragmentation, overkill, pollution, the disruption of ecosystems, and invasive species. The species that survive will be ones that can thrive in human-dominated environments. Wildlife will consist of rats, roaches, squirrels, house sparrows, crows, starlings, pigeons, and white-tailed deer. For example, the population of raccoons is five times greater in suburban areas than in wild areas. David Quammen compares these species to weeds, ones that reproduce quickly, spread widely, tolerate a broad range of conditions, and resist efforts at eradication. Even when land is set aside in preserves, often it is surrounded by human development and weedy species to eventually overrun the species the preserve was created to protect.

To slow the loss of biological diversity we will require far more knowledge than we possess today about the intricate connections of the causes of species decline. But even in our daily lives, we are confronted with numerous questions of causation. Why did the driver who passed you on a blind curve risk his life to get one car ahead at the next traffic light? Why is it hard to recognize people you know when you run into them unexpectedly in an unfamiliar setting? Why do nearly all kids want the same toy each Christmas, forcing their parents to stand in line for hours at—sometimes outside—the toy store? Why does your mother or father spend an extra hour plus the extra gas driving to a supermarket across town just to save a few pennies on one or two items on sale? Why do some of your friends keep going to horror films when they can hardly sit through them and have nightmares afterward?

> Effective causal arguments move beyond the obvious to get at underlying causes.

Life is full of big and little mysteries, and people spend a lot of time speculating about the causes. Most of the time, however, they don't take the time to analyze in depth what causes a controversial trend, event, or phenomenon. But before and after you graduate, you likely will have to write causal arguments that require in-depth analysis. In a professional career you will have to make many detailed causal analyses: Why did a retail business fail when it seemed to have an ideal location? What causes cost overruns in the development of a new product? What causes people in some circumstances to prefer public transportation over driving? What causes unnecessary slowdowns in a local computer network? Answering any of these questions requires making a causal argument, which takes a classic form:

SOMETHING causes (or does not cause) SOMETHING ELSE.

The causal claim is at the center of a causal argument. Therefore, to get started on a causal argument, you need to propose one or more causes.

Methods of Finding Causes

The big problem with causal arguments is that any topic worth writing about is likely to be complex. Identifying causes usually isn't easy. The philosopher John Stuart Mill recognized this problem long ago and devised four methods for finding causes:

1. *The Common Factor Method.* When the cause-and-effect relationship occurs more than once, look for something in common in the events and circumstances of each effect; any common factor could be the cause. Scientists have used this method to explain how seemingly different phenomena are associated. There were a variety of explanations of fire until, in the 1700s, Joseph Priestley in England and Antoine Lavoisier in France discovered that oxygen was a separate element and that burning was caused by oxidation.

2. *The Single Difference Method.* This method works only when there are at least two similar situations, one that leads to an effect and one that does not. Look for something that was missing in one case and present in another—the single difference. The writer assumes that if everything is substantially alike in both cases, then the single difference is the (or a) cause. At the Battle of Midway in 1942, the major naval battle of World War II in the Pacific, the Japanese Navy had a 4-to-1 advantage over the U.S. Navy. Both fleets were commanded by competent, experienced leaders. But the U.S. commander, Admiral Nimitz, had a superior advantage in intelligence, which proved to be decisive.

3. *Concomitant Variation.* This tongue twister is another favorite method of scientists. If an investigator finds that a possible cause

and a possible effect have a similar pattern of variation, then one can suspect that a relationship exists. For example, scientists noticed that peaks in the eleven-year sunspot cycle have predictable effects on high-frequency radio transmission on the earth.

4. *Process of Elimination.* Many possible causes can be proposed for most trends and events. If you are a careful investigator, you have to consider all that you can think of and eliminate the ones that cannot be causes.

For an example of how these methods might work for you, suppose you want to research the causes of the increase in legalized lotteries in the United States. You might discover that lotteries go back to colonial times. Harvard and Yale have been longtime rivals in football, but the schools' rivalry goes back much further. Both ran lotteries before the Revolutionary War! In 1747 the Connecticut legislature voted to allow Yale to conduct a lottery to raise money to build dormitories, and in 1765 the Massachusetts legislature gave Harvard permission for a lottery. Lotteries were common before and after the American Revolution, but they eventually ran into trouble because they were run by private companies that failed to pay the winners. After 1840, laws against lotteries were passed, but they came back after the Civil War in the South. The defeated states of the Confederacy needed money to rebuild the bridges, buildings, and schools that had been destroyed in the Civil War, and they turned to selling lottery tickets throughout the nation, tickets that ironically were very popular in the North. Once again, the lotteries were run by private companies, and scandals eventually led to their banning.

In 1964 the voters in New Hampshire approved a lottery as a means of funding education—in preference to an income tax or sales tax. Soon other northeastern states followed this lead, establishing lotteries with the reasoning that if people are going to gamble, the money should remain at home. During the 1980s, other states approved not only lotteries but also other forms of state-run gambling such as keno and video poker. By 1993 only Hawaii and Utah had no legalized gambling of any kind.

If you are analyzing the causes of the spread of legalized gambling, you might use the **common factor method** to investigate what current lotteries have in common with earlier lotteries. That factor is easy to identify: It's economic. The early colonies and later the states have turned again and again to lotteries as a way of raising money that avoids unpopular tax increases. But why have lotteries spread so quickly and seemingly become so permanent since 1964, when before that, they were used only sporadically and were eventually banned? The **single difference method** points us to the major difference between the lotteries of today and those of previous eras:

Lotteries in the past were run by private companies, and inevitably someone took off with the money instead of paying it out. Today's lotteries are owned and operated by state agencies or else contracted under state control, and while they are not immune to scandals, they are much more closely monitored than lotteries were in the past.

The controversies over legal gambling now focus on casinos. In 1988 Congress passed the Indian Gaming Regulatory Act, which started a new era of casino gambling in the United States. The world's largest casino, Foxwoods Casino in Connecticut, owned by the Mashantucket Pequot Tribe, became a huge moneymaker—paying along with nearby Mohegan Sun Casino over $400 million into the Connecticut state treasury. Other tribes and other states were quick to cash in on casino gambling. Iowa legalized riverboat gambling in 1989, followed shortly by Louisiana, Illinois, Indiana, Mississippi, and Missouri. As with lotteries, the primary justification for approving casino gambling has been economic. States have been forced to fund various programs that the federal government used to pay for.

The 350 tribal casinos in the United States produce over $16 billion in revenues each year.

Especially in states where lottery revenues had begun to sag, legislatures and voters turned to casinos to make up the difference.

Casinos, however, have been harder to sell to voters than lotteries. For many voters, casinos are a NIMBY ("not in my back yard") issue. They may believe that people should have the right to gamble, but they don't want a casino in their town. Casino proponents have tried to overcome these objections by arguing that casinos bring added tourist dollars, benefiting the community as a whole. Opponents argue the opposite: that people who go to casinos spend their money on gambling and not on tourist attractions. The cause-and-effect benefit of casinos to community businesses can be examined by **concomitant variation**. Casino supporters argue that people who come to gamble spend a lot of money elsewhere. Opponents of casinos claim that people who come for gambling don't want to spend money elsewhere. Furthermore, they point out that gambling represents another entertainment option for people within easy driving distance and can hurt area businesses such as restaurants, amusement parks, and bowling alleys. So far, the record has been mixed, some businesses being helped and others being hurt when casinos are built nearby.

Many trends don't have causes as obvious as the spread of legalized gambling. One such trend is the redistribution of wealth in the United States since 1970. During the 1950s and 1960s, businesses in the United States grew by 90 percent, and the resulting wealth benefited all income classes. Since 1970, however, almost all the growth in wealth has gone to people at the top of the economic ladder. Analysis of census data by the Congressional Budget Office found that the richest 1 percent of American households received $515,600 in after-tax income adjusted for inflation in 1999 compared with $234,700 in 1977. The incomes of the bottom 20 percent of households fell from $10,000 in 1977 to $8,800 in 1999. The higher on the economic ladder, the more extreme the gains. Those on the very highest rung in the 99.9 percentile—13,400 households out of 134 million taxpaying households—received 5% of the total income of the country, almost $24 million per household. In 1970, this top group received 1% of the total national income with $3.6 million per household.

The increasing divide between the rich and the rest of the people in the United States is well documented, but economists don't agree about the reasons why the richest Americans have become astonishingly more wealthy and why those who are in the bottom 90 percent have lost ground since 1970. The explanations that have been given include the tax cuts of 1986, the decline of labor unions, the downsizing of corporations, the increase in corporate mergers, automation, competition from low-wage nations, and simple greed. Although each of these may be a contributing cause, there must be other causes too.

The **process of elimination method** can be a useful tool when several possible causes are involved. The shift in income to the wealthy started before the tax cuts of 1986, so the tax cuts cannot be the only cause. Low-wage nations now produce cheap exports, but the sectors of the U.S. economy that compete directly with low-wage nations make up a small slice of the total pie (about 2 percent). And it's hard to explain why people might be greedier now than in earlier decades; greed has always been a human trait.

In a book published in 1995 entitled *The Winner-Take-All Society*, Robert H. Frank and Phillip J. Cook argue that changes in attitudes help to account for the shifts in wealth since 1973. In an article summarizing their book, published in *Across the Board* (33:5 [May 1996]: 4), they describe what they mean by the winner-take-all society:

Our claim is that growing income inequality stems from the growing importance of what we call "winner-take-all markets"—markets in which small differences in performance give rise to enormous differences in economic reward. Long familiar in entertainment, sports, and the arts, these markets have increasingly permeated law, journalism, consulting, medicine, investment banking, corporate management, publishing, design, fashion, even the hallowed halls of academe.

An economist under the influence of the human-capital metaphor might ask: Why not save money by hiring two mediocre people to fill an important position instead of paying the exorbitant salary required to attract the best? Although that sort of substitution might work with physical capital, it does not necessarily work with human capital. Two average surgeons or CEOs or novelists or quarterbacks are often a poor substitute for a single gifted one.

The result is that for positions for which additional talent has great value to the employer or the marketplace, there is no reason to expect that the market will compensate individuals in proportion to their human capital. For these positions—ones that confer the greatest leverage or "amplification" of human talent—small increments of talent have great value and may be greatly rewarded as a result of the normal competitive market process. This insight lies at the core of our alternative explanation of growing inequality.

A winner-take-all market is one in which reward depends on relative, not absolute, performance. Whereas a farmer's pay depends on the absolute amount of wheat he produces and not on how that compares with the amounts produced by other farmers, a software developer's pay depends largely on her performance ranking. In the market for personal income-tax software, for instance, the market reaches quick consensus on which among the scores or even hundreds of competing programs is the most comprehensive and user-friendly. And although the best program may be only slightly better than its nearest rival, their developers' incomes may differ a thousandfold.

Frank and Cook find that technology has accelerated the trend toward heaping rewards on those who are judged best in a particular arena. In the 1800s, for example, a top tenor in a major city such as London might have commanded a salary many times above that of other singers, but the impact of the tenor was limited by the fact that only those who could hear him live could appreciate his talent. Today, every tenor in the world competes with Luciano Pavarotti because opera fans everywhere can buy Pavarotti's CDs. This worldwide fan base translates into big money. It's no surprise that Michael Jordan received more money for promoting Nike shoes than the combined annual payrolls for all six factories in Indonesia that made the shoes bearing his name. What is new is how other professions have become more like sports and entertainment.

The Winner-Take-All Society is a model of causal analysis that uses the process of elimination method. The authors

- Describe and document a trend
- Set out the causes that have been previously offered and show why together they are inadequate to explain the trend, and then
- Present a new cause, explaining how the new cause works in concert with those that have been identified

But it's not enough just to identify causes. They must be connected to effects. For trends in progress, such as the growing divide between the rich and the rest in the United States, the effects must be carefully explored to learn about what might lie ahead. Frank and Cook believe that the winner-take-all attitude is detrimental for the nation's future because, like high school basketball players who expect to become the next Kobe Bryant, many people entering college or graduate school grossly overestimate their prospects for huge success and select their future careers accordingly:

> The lure of the top prizes in winner-take-all markets has also steered many of our most able graduates toward career choices that make little sense for them as individuals and still less sense for the nation as a whole. In increasing numbers, our best and brightest graduates pursue top positions in law, finance, consulting, and other overcrowded arenas, in the process forsaking careers in engineering, manufacturing, civil service, teaching, and other occupations in which an infusion of additional talent would yield greater benefit to society.
>
> One study estimated, for example, that whereas a doubling of enrollments in engineering would cause the growth rate of the GDP to rise by half a percentage point, a doubling of enrollments in law would actually cause a decline of three-tenths of a point. Yet the number of new lawyers admitted to the bar each year more than doubled between 1970 and 1990, a period during which the average standardized test scores of new public-school teachers fell dramatically.
>
> One might hope that such imbalances would fade as wages are bid up in underserved markets and driven down in overcrowded ones, and indeed there have been recent indications of a decline in the number of law-school applicants. For two reasons, however, such adjustments are destined to fall short.
>
> The first is an informational problem. An intelligent decision about whether to pit one's own skills against a largely unknown field of adversaries obviously requires a well-informed estimate of the odds of winning. Yet people's assessments about these odds are notoriously inaccurate. Survey evidence shows, for example, that some 80 percent of us think we are better-than-average drivers and that more than 90 percent of workers

consider themselves more productive than their average colleague. Psychologists call this the "Lake Wobegon Effect," and its importance for present purposes is that it leads people to overestimate their odds of landing a superstar position. Indeed, overconfidence is likely to be especially strong in the realm of career choice, because the biggest winners are so conspicuous. The seven-figure NBA stars appear on television several times each week, whereas the many thousands who fail to make the league attract little notice.

The second reason for persistent overcrowding in winner-take-all markets is a structural problem that economists call "the tragedy of the commons." This same problem helps explain why we see too many prospectors for gold. In the initial stages of exploiting a newly discovered field of gold, the presence of additional prospectors may significantly increase the total amount of gold that is found. Beyond some point, however, additional prospectors contribute very little. Thus, the gold found by a newcomer to a crowded gold field is largely gold that would have been found by others.

This short example illustrates why causal arguments for any significant trend that involves people almost necessarily have to be complex. Most people don't quit their day job expecting to hit it big in the movies, the record business, or professional athletics, yet people do select fields such as law that have become in many ways like entertainment, with a few big winners and the rest just getting by. Frank and Cook point to the "Lake Wobegon Effect" (named for Garrison Keillor's fictional town where "all children are above average") to give an explanation of why people are realistic about their chances in some situations and not in others.

Building a Causal Argument

Effective causal arguments move beyond the obvious to get at underlying causes. The immediate cause of the growing income inequality in the United States is that people at the top make a lot more now than they did thirty years ago, while people in the middle make the same and people at the bottom make less. Those changes are obvious to anyone who has looked at the numbers. What isn't obvious is why those changes occurred.

Insightful causal analyses of major trends and events avoid oversimplification by not relying on only one direct cause but instead showing how that cause arises from another cause or works in combination with other causes. Indeed, Frank and Cook have been criticized for placing too much emphasis on the winner-take-all hypothesis.

The great causal mystery today is global warming. Scientists generally agree that the average surface temperature on earth has gone up by one degree Fahrenheit or 0.6 degrees Celsius over the last hundred years and that the amount of carbon dioxide has increased by 25 percent. But the causes of those facts are much disputed. Some people believe that the rise in temperature is a naturally occurring climate variation and that the increase in carbon dioxide is only minimally the cause or not related at all. Others argue that the burning of fossil fuels and the cutting of tropical forests have led to the increase in carbon dioxide, which in turn traps heat, thus increasing the temperature of the earth. The major problem for all participants in the global warming debate is that the causation is not a simple, direct one.

Scientists use powerful computer models to understand the causes and effects of climate change. These models predict that global warming will affect arctic and subarctic regions more dramatically than elsewhere. In Iceland, average summer temperatures have risen by 0.5 to 1.0 degrees Celsius since the early 1980s. All of Iceland's glaciers except a few that surge and ebb independent of weather are now in rapid retreat, a pattern observed throughout regions in the far north. Arctic sea ice shrank by 6 percent from 1978 to 1998, and Greenland's massive ice sheet has been thinning by more than three feet a year. Environmentalists today point to the melting of the glaciers and sea ice as proof that human-caused global warming is taking place.

Scientists, however, are not so certain. Their difficulty is to sort human causes from naturally recurring climate cycles. Much of the detailed data about the Great Melt in the north goes back only to the early 1990s—not long enough to rule out short-term climate cycles. If we are in a regular, short-term warming cycle, then the question becomes how does greenhouse warming interact with that cycle? Computer models suggest there is a very low probability that such rapid change could occur naturally. But the definitive answers to the causes of the Great Melt are probably still a long way off.

Another pitfall common in causal arguments using statistics is mistaking correlation for causation. For example, the FBI reported that criminal victimization rates in the United States in 1995 dropped 13 percent for personal crimes and 12.4 percent for property crimes, the

Glaciers in retreat

largest decreases ever. During that same year, the nation's prison and jail populations reached a record high of 1,085,000 and 507,000 inmates, respectively. The easy inference is that putting more people behind bars lowers the crime rate, but there are plenty of examples to the contrary. The drop in crime rates in the 1990s remains quite difficult to explain. Others have argued that the decline in SAT verbal scores during the late 1960s and 1970s reflected a decline in literacy caused by an increase in television viewing. But the fact that the number of people who took the SAT during the 1970s greatly increased suggests that there was not an actual decline in literacy, only a great expansion in the population who wanted to go to college.

Sample Student Causal Argument

Jennifer May majors in communication disorders and intends to go to graduate school to study speech pathology. She wrote this essay for a composition course at Pennsylvania State University. After the semester in which she wrote it, May studied in Sydney, Australia, where she paraglided, snorkelled, and parasailed her way through the semester.

May 1

Jennifer May

Professor Reynolds

English 102

20 April 2002

Why Are Teenage Girls Dying to Be Thin?

Imagine waking up every morning, looking into the mirror, and thinking no one loves you because you are overweight. Imagine stepping onto a scale, weighing in at 80 pounds, and thinking that is too high. Imagine staring at the food on your plate, trying to eat and thinking about the number of calories in each bite. Imagine that this is your life. It is hard to picture a life without food, self-confidence, and love. Anorexia, which commonly affects girls, is a mental disease that becomes physical and a physical disease that becomes emotional. What causes a person to slowly kill herself in an effort to be thin? Are the principal causes nature (biological) or nurture (environmental)? While there are many reasons that may lead a girl to become anorexic, the causes depend on the individual and usually include a combination of both nature and nurture.

Eating disorders, especially anorexia nervosa, consume health and body one bite at a time. The American Academy of Arts and Sciences stated in 1992 that "the disorder affects 10 out of every 100 American females at some time in their life" (qtd. in Verdon 158). Anorexia is characterized by excessive activity or exercise along with self-starvation, fear of gaining weight, and a distorted body image (Verdon 160). This disorder usually affects white adolescent females of normal weight. They become "15% or more underweight," yet still feel fat and thus continue to starve (Myers 371). Anorexia is the relentless pursuit of a perfect body, a constant struggle to stay thin, and if left untreated, a life-threatening obsession.

Nurture, the surrounding environment, is a major influence on anorexia. Nurture involves parents and family upbringing, social pressures, and cultural influences. A family can give a child support, love, and trust; or a family can pressure, reject, and become detached. Parents or caregivers may exhibit one or all of these characteristics during the child's upbringing.

May 3

An anorexic person cannot accept the love that a caregiver may offer and feels only neglect. Parents must show support, hoping that the feeling of abandonment and loneliness will vanish.

The pressures surrounding an adolescent each day are immense and sometimes too difficult for someone with an eating disorder to handle. In a culture that admires Barbie doll figures and is infatuated with dieting, it is difficult not to become self-conscious about your body. Beautiful women in magazines and on television, singers with perfect voices, dancers and athletes with gorgeous bodies, parents who expect straight As, coaches who believe winning is everything, and peers who say "you're fat" are all contributors to adolescent stress.

Nature refers to the innate biological aspects of a person. Along with genetic make-up, nature includes the personality of an individual. Low self-confidence and perfectionism are prominent personality traits among anorexics, who fear failing, getting fat, and letting people down. Roger Verdon says that many anorexics "are perfectionists in an imperfect world" (161). Perfectionists often are high achievers, but they are never satisfied by their performance.

Feeling that one's life is ruled by others (parents, media, school) leads to a need for control of something else. Anorexics become obsessed with numbers on the scale or if their pants are fitting a little too tight. It is an ongoing struggle in the mind, a seclusion from the rest of the world, a battle that is fought alone. Here is a journal entry from a friend (I'll refer to her

May 4

as "Jessica") who is contemplating whether to tell people about her illness.

> Everyone will be watching me, noticing,
> thinking, wondering . . . questioning why this
> is happening to me, why I let it happen to me,
> why I don't stop it. People don't realize the
> difficulty involved, the emotional pain, the
> physical risks and consequences, the deep,
> dark truth behind it. Why can't I just be
> normal? Everybody else thinks I am. I am
> living a lie, and I know it. Should I keep it
> this way? How can I impose on other people by
> telling them my problems, making them witness
> it, make them feel obligated to help.

Female athletes, especially gymnasts, are at risk for anorexia. Training for nine hours a day, eating only one apple, and getting little sleep leads to anorexia because the body adapts to deprivation. Christy Hendrich, champion of the 1989 Gymnastic World Games, was both anorexic and bulimic. Although the causes are different for each individual, similar feelings and emotions are common. Before dying at the weight of sixty pounds, Hendrich said: "My life is a horrifying nightmare; there feels like a beast is inside of me" (qtd. in Myers 372).

The effects of anorexia range from short-term hospitalization to death from malnutrition. Because anorexia nervosa usually occurs during puberty, a time when bone growth is crucial, those who suffer from this disease may have bone fractures and osteoporosis at a young age from lack of calcium. Reproductive organs

May 5

may not fully develop, so menstrual abnormalities may occur and lead to pregnancy problems later in life. Malnutrition can also lead to brain damage and can affect mood and behavior (Seidenfeld and Rickert 444).

Recovery from anorexia is a long process. Relapses are common, and complete recovery can take years. Jessica says: "Mentally, I'm doing worse; my physical signs are better, but underneath the outer parts, it's doing worse. My body has adjusted to a lower caloric intake, and my metabolism has dropped again regardless of running every day." As much as Jessica wants to be cured, she keeps getting pulled back into this destructive pattern. I've learned from Jessica that anorexia can happen to any young woman, and for even those as aware as she is of what is happening, the pattern is not easy to break.

May 6

Works Cited

"Jessica." Email to the author. 2 Oct. 2001.

Myers, David G. Psychology. New York: Worth, 1998.

Seidenfeld, Margorie, and Vaugh Rickert. "Impact of Anorexia, Bulimia, and Obesity on the Gynecologic Health of Adolescents." American Family Physician 64 (2000): 444-45.

Verdon, Roger. "Mirror, Mirror on the Wall, Who Is the Thinnest of Them All?" Reclaiming Children and Youth 9.3 (2000): 157-61.

Steps in a Causal Argument

Step **1** Make a claim

Make a causal claim on a controversial trend, event, or phenomenon.

Formula

- SOMETHING does (or does not) cause SOMETHING ELSE.
  –or–
- SOMETHING causes SOMETHING ELSE, which, in turn, causes SOMETHING ELSE.

Examples

- One-parent families (or television violence, bad diet, and so on) is (or is not) the cause of emotional and behavioral problems in children.
- Firearms control laws (or right-to-carry-handgun laws) reduce (or increase) violent crimes.
- The trend toward home schooling (or private schools) is (or is not) improving the quality of education.
- The length of U.S. presidential campaigns forces candidates to become too much influenced by big-dollar contributors (or prepares them for the constant media scrutiny that they will endure as president).
- Putting grade school children into competitive sports teaches them how to succeed in later life (or puts undue emphasis on winning and teaches many who are slower to mature to have a negative self-image).

Step **2** What's at stake in your claim?

- If the cause is obvious to everyone, then it probably isn't worth writing about.

Step **3** Think of possible causes

- Which are the immediate causes?
- Which are the background causes?
- Which are the hidden causes?
- Which are the causes that most people have not recognized?

Step 4 Analyze your potential readers

- Who are your readers?
- How familiar will they be with the trend, event, or phenomenon that you're writing about?
- What are they likely to know and not know?
- How likely are they to accept your causal explanation?
- What alternative explanation might they argue for?

Step 5 Write a draft

Introduction

- Describe the controversial trend, event, or phenomenon.
- Give the background that your intended readers will need.

Body

- For a trend, event, or phenomenon that is unfamiliar to your readers, you can explain the cause or chain of causation. Remember that providing facts is not the same thing as establishing causes, although facts can help to support your causal analysis.
- Another way of organizing the body is to set out the causes that have been offered and reject them one by one. Then you can present the cause that you think is most important.
- A third way is to treat a series of causes one by one, analyzing the importance of each.

Conclusion

- Do more than simply summarize. You might consider additional effects beyond those that have been previously noted.

Step 6 Revise, edit, proofread

- For detailed instructions, see Chapter 12.
- For a checklist to use to evaluate your draft, see pages 217–222.

CHAPTER 8

Evaluation Arguments

The solar-powered Field Integrated Design and Operations (FIDO) rover is tested in the Nevada desert to simulate driving conditions on Mars.

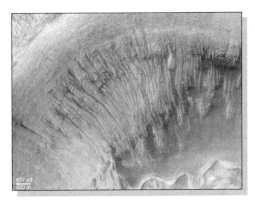

The Mars Orbiter Camera found evidence of water recently on the surface of Mars. Scientists believe that the gullies and finger-like deposits at the base of the wall were formed by flowing water and debris flows.

Robots have dug in the dirt on Mars, flown in the atmosphere of Jupiter, driven by the moons of Neptune and plopped down on an asteroid. A few are even flirting with the boundary of the solar system. Humans, on the other hand, have been relegated mostly to going in circles, barely above the surface of the planet. . . . Given the danger, the costs and the setbacks, why send humans into space at all?

RICHARD STENGER, CNN.COM, FEBRUARY 18, 2003

Returning to the moon is an important step for our space program. . . . With the experience and knowledge gained on the moon, we will then be ready to take the next steps of space exploration: human missions to Mars and to worlds beyond. . . . Probes, landers and other vehicles of this kind continue to prove their worth, sending spectacular images and vast amounts of data back to Earth. Yet the human thirst for knowledge ultimately cannot be satisfied by even the most vivid pictures or the most detailed measurements. We need to see and examine and touch for ourselves.

PRESIDENT GEORGE W. BUSH, SPEECH, JANUARY 14, 2004

The tragic loss of seven space shuttle astronauts in February 2003 revived a long-running debate over the value of sending humans into space. Humans must carry their environment with them when they venture into space. Robotic probes do not require water, air, and food and can travel for a fraction of the cost. Space shuttle missions typically cost around $500 million, while a satellite can be launched for $20 million. Even unmanned flights to Mars have cost as little as $250 million.

Many people argue that the extra money needed to put people into space would be better spent at home. Furthermore, flights to Mars and beyond would require years, subjecting humans to the risks of solar radiation exposure and prolonged weightlessness, which over months leads to breakdowns of the immune system and bone structure.

Others, however, believe there are reasons besides scientific research for sending people into space. John Logsdon, director of the Space Policy Institute at George Washington University, says, "We do not give parades for robots. There are intangible benefits from human presence in space—national pride, role models for youth—that are real if not measurable."

The debate about sending people into space is an evaluation argument. People make evaluations all the time. Newspapers and magazines have picked up on this love of evaluation by running "best of" polls. They ask their readers what's the best Mexican, Italian, or Chinese restaurant; the best pizza; the best local band; the best coffeehouse; the best dance club; the best neighborhood park; the best swimming hole; the best bike ride (scenic and challenging); the best volleyball court; the best place to get married; and so on. If you ask one of your friends who voted in a "best" poll why she picked a particular restaurant as the best of its kind, she might respond by saying simply, "I like it." But if you ask her why she likes it, she might start offering good reasons such as these: The food is good, the service prompt, the prices fair, and the atmosphere comfortable. It's really not a mystery why these polls are often quite predictable and why the same restaurants tend to win year after year. Many people think that evaluations are matters of personal taste, but when we begin probing the reasons, we often discover that the criteria that different people use to make evaluations have a lot in common.

People opposed to sending humans into space use the criteria of cost and safety. Those who argue for sending people into space use the criteria of expanding human presence and human experience. The key to convincing other people that your judgment is sound is establishing the criteria you will use to make your evaluation. Sometimes it will be necessary to argue for the validity of those criteria that

> Evaluation arguments depend on the criteria you select.

you think your readers should consider. If your readers accept your criteria, it's likely they will agree with your conclusions.

Kinds of Evaluations

Arguments of evaluation are structured much like arguments of definition. Recall that the criteria in arguments of definition are set out in because clauses: *SOMETHING is a_____ because it has these criteria*. In arguments of evaluation the claim takes the form

> SOMETHING is a good (bad, the best, the worst) _____ if measured by these criteria

The key move in writing most evaluative arguments is first deciding what kind of criteria to use.

Imagine that the oldest commercial building in your city is about to be torn down. Your goal is to get the old store converted to a museum, which is a proposal argument. First you will need to make an evaluative argument that will form the basis of your proposal. You might argue that a downtown museum would be much better than more office space because it would draw more visitors. You might argue that the stonework in the building is of excellent quality and deserves preservation. Or you might argue that it is only fair that the oldest commercial building be preserved because the oldest house and other historic buildings have been saved.

Each of these arguments uses different criteria. An argument that a museum is better than an office building because it would bring more visitors to the downtown area is based on **practical criteria**. An argument that the old building is beautiful and that beautiful things should be preserved uses **aesthetic criteria**. An argument that the oldest store building deserves the same treatment as the oldest house is based on fairness, a concept that relies on **ethical criteria**. The debate over the value of sending people versus sending robots into space employs all these criteria but with different emphases. Both those who favor and those who oppose human space travel make practical arguments that much scientific knowledge and many benefits result from space travel. Those who favor sending humans use aesthetic arguments: Space travel is essential to the way we understand ourselves as humans and Americans. Those who oppose sending humans question the ethics of spending so much money for manned space vehicles when there are pressing needs at home and point out that robots can be used for a fraction of the cost. (See Figure 8.1.)

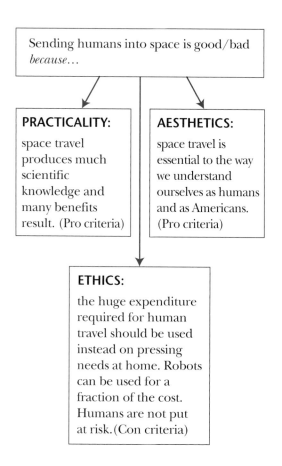

Figure 8.1

WHERE DO CRITERIA COME FROM?

The basic advice of this chapter probably makes sense to you: Making an evaluation argument is essentially a matter of finding appropriate criteria for evaluation and then measuring the topic or issue against those criteria. The criteria are, in effect, the basis for one or more because-clauses that support the overall judgment of the argument. Such-and-such is good *because of* x and *because of* y; or such-and-such is better than something else *because of* x and *because of* y. "Cleveland is a surprisingly good vacation spot *because* there's a lot to do, *because* there's a lot of beauty around Lake Erie, *because* the crowds and prices are reasonable, *and because* there are no friendlier people anywhere." "Despite his failure with the Vietnam War, President Johnson was actually a good president *because* the Civil

WHERE DO CRITERIA COME FROM? *(continued)*

Rights Act of 1964 and Voting Rights Act of 1965 made lasting improvements in American life, *because* Johnson presided with honor during calamitous times, *and because* his War on Poverty was actually a huge success."

But where do you find those criteria?

Traditionally evaluative criteria emerge from three sources: practicality, aesthetics, and ethics. Things are usually judged as good (or not so good) either because they work well (practicality), because they are beautiful (aesthetics), or because they are fair or morally just (ethics). All three of these sources of criteria may not appear in every evaluative argument, but one of them certainly will—and often all three will show up.

Practicality means that the thing being evaluated works efficiently or leads to good outcomes: Things are seen as good if they improve conditions, work well, are cost effective, and so forth. *Aesthetics* refers to beauty, but it also has to do with matters often associated with beauty, such as image and tradition. *Ethics* has to do with moral rightness, with legality or constitutionality, with fair play and human decency: Things are rarely evaluated positively if there are ethical improprieties to worry about.

Try out those sources of criteria on a few simple examples. Are you evaluating a consumer product, like a pair of skis, before you buy them? Of course you'll consider how well they work and fit and how much they cost; but you will also consider whether they are good looking and perhaps what image they project. And before you buy you will probably think about ethical issues as well. Were the skis manufactured in a sweatshop of some kind, for example? Does the store selling them have a good reputation? Or maybe you are evaluating various study-abroad programs to support your major in Spanish. Of course you will consider the quality of the educational experience (where will you learn the most?), cost, safety, and other practical matters; but you will also think about how beautiful or interesting the possible locations are as well as ethical issues such as the kind of government that is in place in the country or how the institution treats students.

Or maybe you are evaluating a public policy of some kind. A new gun control measure proposed for a certain community, for example, will have to be measured against its cost, enforceability, and effectiveness, of course. But you will also have to consider legal and constitutional issues—and even aesthetic considerations (such as what kind of community you wish to project your community to be, or what kind of traditions your community stands for). Or recall how you chose the college or university you attended: You evaluated it according to the quality of education it offered, according to cost, and according to other practical considerations (e.g., dorm quality, the availability of work opportunities), but you

(continued)

WHERE DO CRITERIA COME FROM? *(continued)*

also thought about other, less practical matters: Does it offer an aesthetically pleasing environment? Does it project a respected image? Does it have a tradition of encouraging certain values? Is it respected as an institution that is fair and honorable? Colleges and universities generally enjoy good reputations, so fairness and morality do not often show up in discussions of the relative merits of colleges; but if a college or university does something to compromise its reputation— because its sports teams are caught up in sports recruiting scandals, for example, or because it misuses research funds or is involved in a discrimination suit—its quality is perceived to be profoundly affected.

Or even take the example of a movie or book or musician. Typically those things are evaluated according to aesthetic merit, and evaluations of those things will therefore depend on aesthetic criteria like the ones celebrated in the Academy Awards or Grammy Awards shows: cinematography, acting, writing, direction, musical quality. And yet it is also true that movies, music, and other forms of entertainment are also evaluated on moral grounds. Look at the arguments that erupt daily over the work of Britney Spears or Eminem, for example. When a movie or song is truly controversial, as in the case of the recent movie by Mel Gibson, *The Passion of the Christ*, you can be sure that discussions about it will be based on aesthetics (e.g., was the torture of Christ in the movie too prolonged for it to be considered beautiful? was the acting inspirational or overly melodramatic?), on morality (e.g., is the movie anti-Semitic? does it promote values that run contrary to post–Vatican II Catholic values? is it sadistic?), and on pragmatics (e.g., will the movie inspire imitations? will it encourage church attendance, increase devotionalism, and renew Christian faith? is it really true to the Gospel accounts?).

Later in this chapter you will find a sample evaluative essay that considers an institutional policy: the quality of a university's health care plan. Examine it carefully to see whether it bases its evaluation on all three sources of criteria— practicality, aesthetics, and ethics—or whether it depends on one or two of them. Does it look at the health plan only as a question of practicality (e.g., affordability and effectiveness), or does it bring ethics and even aesthetics into the argument? Are certain criteria missing—and if they are, does that matter?

Building an Evaluation Argument

Most people have a lot of practice making consumer evaluations, and when they have enough time to do their homework, they usually make an informed decision. But sometimes, criteria for evaluations are not so obvious, and evaluations are much more difficult to make. Sometimes, one set of criteria favors one choice, while another set of criteria favors another. You might have encountered this problem when you chose a college. If you were able to leave home to go to school, you had a potential choice of over 1,400 accredited colleges and universities. Until twenty years ago, there wasn't much information about choosing a college other than what colleges said about themselves. You could find out the price of tuition and what courses were offered, but it was hard to compare one college with another.

In 1983 the magazine *U.S. News & World Report* began ranking U.S. colleges and universities from a consumer's perspective. Those rankings have remained highly controversial ever since. Many college officials have attacked the criteria that *U.S. News* uses to make its evaluations. In an August 1998 *U.S. News* article, Gerhard Casper, the president of Stanford University (which is consistently near the top of the rankings), says, "Much about these rankings—particularly their specious formulas and spurious precision—is utterly misleading." Casper argues that using graduation rates as a criterion of quality rewards easy schools. Other college presidents have called for a national boycott of the *U.S. News* rankings (without much success).

U.S. News replies in its defense that colleges and universities themselves do a lot of ranking, beginning with ranking students for admissions, using their SAT or ACT scores, high school GPA, ranking in high school class, quality of high school, and other factors, and then grading the students and ranking them against each other when they are enrolled in college. Furthermore, schools also evaluate faculty members and take great interest in the national ranking of their departments. They care very much about where they stand in relation to each other. Why, then, *U.S. News* argues, shouldn't people be able to evaluate colleges and universities, since colleges and universities are so much in the business of evaluating people?

Arguing for the right to evaluate colleges and universities is one thing; actually doing comprehensive and reliable evaluations is quite another. *U.S. News* uses a formula in which 25 percent of a school's ranking is based on a survey of reputation in which the president, provost, and dean of admissions at each college rate the quality of schools in the same category, and the remaining 75 percent is based on statistical criteria of quality. These statistical criteria fall into six major categories: retention of students, faculty resources, student selectivity, financial resources, alumni giving, and (for national universities and liberal arts colleges only) "graduation rate performance," the difference between the proportion of students who are expected to graduate and the proportion that actually do. These major categories are made up of factors that are weighted for their importance. For example, the faculty resources category is determined by the size of classes (the proportion of classes with fewer than twenty students and the proportion of classes with fifty or more students), the average faculty pay weighted by the cost of living in different regions of the country, the percentage of professors with the highest degree in their field, the overall student-faculty ratio, and the percentage of faculty who are full time.

Those who have challenged the *U.S. News* rankings argue that the magazine should use different criteria or weight the criteria differently. *U.S. News* answers those charges on its Web site (http://www.usnews.com/usnews/edu/college/corank.htm) by claiming that it has followed a trend toward emphasizing outcomes such as graduation rates. If you are curious about where your school ranks, take a look at the *U.S. News* Web site.

Sample Student Evaluation Argument

Houston native DeMarcus Taylor wrote "An Unhealthy Practice" in his first-year composition course at the University of Texas at Austin. DeMarcus is a government major who intends to go to law school. He is a member of the Beta Alpha Rho Pre-Law fraternity and loves to play volleyball.

```
                                                       Taylor 1

    DeMarcus Taylor

    Professor Kim

    RHE 306

    9 March 2004

                        An Unhealthy Practice

         Let me tell you a story. During my second semester

    at the University of Texas, I began having headaches.

    Taking Tylenol helped, but the headaches returned. So I

    made an appointment with one of the doctors at

    University Health Services. This facility provides fully

    certified doctors and nurses for students as part of

    mandatory fees that are tacked on to each semester's
```

tuition bill. (As it stands, the university charges
students approximately sixty dollars each semester for
what it dubs a "medical services fee.") The doctor told
me that the headaches could be caused by many different
things and recommended that I get an MRI to rule out any
serious physical problems. I soon found out that that it
stands for Magnetic Resonance Imaging and that I would
have to go off campus to a radiology facility to have
the procedure done. I had the MRI and the results
brought a sigh of relief—no brain tumor. To my surprise,
however, I then received a bill for $1,642 that my
student medical plan did not cover. I called the
accounting office and was told that I had to have
purchased additional coverage to pay for the MRI. I had
improperly assumed that my medical fees would cover any
procedures directly ordered by the health center. In
fact, these fees only cover minor treatment and office
visits, though the specifics are quite vague and answers
are hard to find.

Inconsistent with other university policies,
detrimental to students' academic growth, and a threat
to parents' and students' well-being, the current
university policy for medical services falls short of
being efficient, effective, or educational. Overall, UT
has established an admirable tradition of providing—free
of charge—various programs and services to aid students
in expanding their minds within and beyond the classroom
and coping with the challenges of college life. As the
university fosters an image of paternal compassion and

Taylor 3

concern, programs such as Freshman Interest Groups (FIGs) and Achieving College Excellence (ACE) strive to provide new and at-risk students with tools helpful in reaching their academic and social goals. Similarly, academic services such as the Undergraduate Writing Center help students augment their in-class learning and bolster their writing skills, while the Counseling and Mental Health Center provides students with onsite psychiatrists and psychologists. A student will never receive a surprise bill for two hours of help on a writing assignment for Introduction to Biology or two sessions of counseling for depression. Sessions are either totally free or limits are clearly articulated through staff interaction or program literature. These types of offerings stand as a symbol of a university that cares about its enrollees as people, not just tuition payers.

In contrast, the current medical services plan keeps students in the dark. Aside from my personal experience with the unexpected MRI charge, I have heard other students discussing issues such as nurses, doctors, and administrators ordering laboratory tests and directly stating that they did not know if the student would owe any additional fees. Even if students do carefully read the university Web site and talk to representatives, he or she has no guarantee that either source will provide an accurate answer to questions. All in all, the school's health services protocol fails to encourage its students to excel in the university's main goal: learning.

Taylor 4

In addition to being at odds with the university's other policies and programs, the current medical services plan places students, parents, and the university at risk of suffering various levels of economic and educational hardships. Though my family was able to pull together funds to pay the MRI charge, incurring exorbitant and unexpected health costs could force and has forced students to drop out of school altogether. Many students (and often those who are targeted for special programs) come from lower socio-economic backgrounds and would be hard-pressed to cover surprise medical bills. Very possibly, many of these same students come from one of the millions of American families who are lacking employer- or personally funded family health insurance. For these two reasons, a non-communicative staff and unclear billing policies could result in students dropping out of the university because money saved for tuition and fees must be used to pay medical bills. One unexpected MRI bill could devastate a family. Is it fair for these students to have to risk their educations and futures because of an inefficient and ineffectively articulated policy? Moreover, this policy can result not only in students suffering as they are forced to give up their educational dreams, but can also cause the university to forfeit the tuition and other revenue it would be earning from continuing students. While this may seem like small change to such a big school, when coupled with the poor public image this policy produces, the stakes are high.

Finally and on the most human and practical of levels, the current policy puts each individual student's health at risk. Bitten once by expensive fees or afraid of the unknowns attached to a vague system and an evasive staff, students may simply forego treatment. On their own for the first time, uninformed about medical costs, anxious about the university policy, and lacking personal insurance, some students may simply ignore health problems, resulting in poor attendance records, undiagnosed severe medical problems, or even the spread of contagions throughout the university community.

As young adults leave their homes to begin forging their own futures at UT, the university must be accountable for the physical—not just mental and educational—well being of the fifty-thousand plus students in its charge. The current health care policy of the University of Texas at Austin highlights its size and lack of intimacy and diminishes its ongoing attempts to welcome and cultivate the young minds and bodies of a culturally, ethnically, and economically diverse student body. By tweaking its procedures and training its staff, the university could convert its lackluster health services program into one which protects students and families, encourages the learning of life skills, and presents UT as an organization that seeks to go beyond the role of educator to one of overall mentor. As it currently stands, the program falls short on all counts.

Steps to Evaluation Argument

Step **1** Make a claim

Make an evaluative claim based on criteria.

Formula

- SOMETHING is good (bad, the best, the worst) ___ if measured by certain criteria (practicality, aesthetics, ethics).

Examples

- Write a book review or a movie review.
- Write a defense of a particular kind of music or art.
- Evaluate a controversial aspect of sports (e.g., the current system of determining who is champion in Division I college football by a system of bowls and polls) or evaluate a sports event (e.g., this year's WNBA playoffs) or a team.
- Evaluate the effectiveness of an educational program (such as your high school honors program or your college's core curriculum requirement) or some other aspect of your campus.
- Evaluate the effectiveness of a social policy or law such as legislating 21 as the legal drinking age, current gun control laws, or environmental regulation.

Step **2** Think about what's at stake

- Would nearly everyone agree with you? Then your claim probably isn't interesting or important. If you can think of people who would disagree, then something is at stake.
- Who argues the opposite of your claim?
- Why do they make a different evaluation?

Step **3** List the criteria

- Which criteria make something either good or bad?
- Which criteria are the most important?
- Which are fairly obvious and which will you have to argue for?

Step **4** Analyze your potential readers

- Who are your readers?
- How familiar will they be with what you are evaluating?
- What are they likely to know and not know?
- Which criteria are they most likely to accept with little explanation, and which will they disagree with?

Step **5** Write a draft

Introduction

- Introduce the person, group, institution, event, or object that you are going to evaluate. You might want to announce your stance at this point or wait until the concluding section.
- Give the background that your intended readers will need.

Body

- Describe each criterion and then analyze how well what you are evaluating meets that criterion.
- If you are making an evaluation according to the effects someone or something produces, describe each effect in detail.
- Anticipate where readers might question either your criteria or how they apply to your subject.
- Address opposing viewpoints by acknowledging how their evaluations might differ and by showing why your definition is better.

Conclusion

- If you have not yet announced your stance, then you can conclude that, on the basis of the criteria you set out or the effects you have analyzed, something is good (bad, best, worst).
- If you have made your stance clear from the beginning, then you can end with a compelling example or analogy.

Step **6** Revise, edit, proofread

- For detailed instructions, see Chapter 12.
- For a checklist to use to evaluate your draft, see pages 217–222.

CHAPTER 9

Narrative Arguments

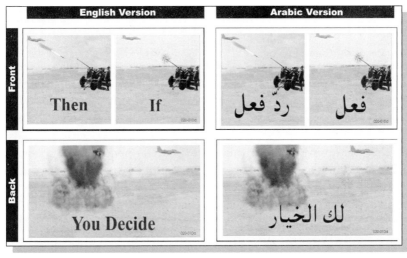

In the months leading up to the second war against Iraq, which began on March 20, 2003, the United States and its allies enforced "no-fly" zones in northern and southern Iraq by increasing the number of surveillance flights. Occasionally, Iraqis shot at Coalition planes, which led to bombings of anti-aircraft sites. In October 2002, Coalition planes began dropping hundreds of thousands of propaganda leaflets on Iraqi military bases depicting what would happen if Iraqi soldiers shot at Coalition planes. (Notice that the "If" panel is on the right because Arabic is read from right to left.)

In 1980, 53,172 people were killed in traffic accidents in the United States, and over half the deaths involved alcohol. Americans had become accustomed to losing around 25,000 to 30,000 people every year to drunk drivers. But it was the tragic death in 1980 of Cari Lightner, a 13-year-old California girl who was killed by a hit-and-run drunk driver while walking along a city street, that made people start asking whether this carnage could be prevented. The driver had been out on bail only two days for another hit-and-run drunk driving crash, and he had three previous drunk driving arrests. He was allowed to plea-bargain for killing Cari and avoided going to prison. Cari's mother, Candy Lightner, was outraged that so little was being done to prevent needless deaths and injuries. She and a small group of other women founded Mothers Against Drunk Driving (MADD) with the goals of getting tougher laws against drunk driving, stiffer penalties for those who kill and injure while driving drunk, and greater public awareness of the seriousness of driving drunk.

Cari Lightner's story aroused to action other people who had been injured themselves or lost loved ones to drunk drivers. Chapters of MADD spread quickly across the country, and it has become one of the most effective citizen groups ever formed, succeeding in getting much new legislation against drunk driving on the books. These laws and changing attitudes about drunk driving have had a significant impact. The National Highway Traffic Safety Administration reported that in 2002, 17,419 people were killed in alcohol-related traffic accidents in the United States compared to 24,045 in 1986, a 30 percent reduction.

The success of MADD points to why arguing by narrating succeeds sometimes when other kinds of arguments have little effect. The story of Cari Lightner appealed to shared community values in ways that statistics did not. The story vividly illustrated that something was very wrong with the criminal justice system if a repeat drunk driver was allowed to run down and kill a child on a sidewalk only days after committing a similar crime.

> Like visual arguments, narrative arguments invite the audience to co-create the claims and links.

Martin Luther King, Jr., was another master of using narratives to make his points. In "Letter from Birmingham Jail," he relates in one sentence the disappointment of his 6-year-old daughter when he had to explain to her why, because of the color of her skin, she could not go to an amusement park in Atlanta advertised on television. This tiny story vividly illustrates the pettiness of segregation laws and their effect on children.

Kinds of Narrative Arguments

Using narratives for advocating change is nothing new. As far back as we have records, we find people telling stories and singing songs about their own lives that argue for change. Folk songs have always given voice to political protest and have celebrated marginalized people. When workers in the United States began to organize in the 1880s, they adapted melodies that soldiers had sung in the Civil War. In the 1930s, performers and songwriters such as Paul Robeson, Woody Guthrie, Huddie Ledbetter (Leadbelly), and Aunt Molly Jackson relied on traditions of hymns, folk songs, and African American blues to

Folk singer/songwriter Shawn Colvin is one of many contemporary folk and blues singers who continue the tradition of making narrative arguments in their songs.

protest social conditions. In the midst of the politically quiet 1950s, folk songs told stories that critiqued social conformity and the dangers of nuclear war. In the 1960s, the civil rights movement and the movement against the Vietnam War brought a strong resurgence of folk music. The history of folk music is a continuous recycling of old tunes, verses, and narratives to engage new political situations. What can be said for folk songs is also true for any popular narrative genre, be it the short story, novel, drama, movies, or even rap music.

Narrative arguments work in a way different from those that spell out their criteria and argue for explicit links. A narrative argument succeeds if the experience being described invokes the life experiences of the readers. Anyone who has ever been around children knows that most kids love amusement parks. Martin Luther King, Jr., did not have to explain to his readers why going to an amusement park advertised on television was so important for his daughter. Likewise, the story of Cari Lightner was effective because even if you have not known someone who was killed by a drunk driver, most people have known someone who died tragically and perhaps needlessly. Furthermore, you often read about and see on television many people who die in traffic accidents. Narrative arguments allow readers to fill in the conclusion. In the cases of King's arguments against segregation laws and MADD's campaign against drunk drivers, that's exactly what happened. Public outcry led to changes in laws and public opinion.

Narrative arguments can be representative anecdotes, as we have seen with the examples from MADD and Martin Luther King, Jr., or they can be longer accounts of particular events that express larger ideas. One such story is George Orwell's account of a hanging in Burma (the country that is now known as Myanmar) while he was a colonial administrator in the late 1920s. In "A Hanging," first published in 1931, Orwell narrates an execution of a nameless prisoner who was convicted of a nameless crime. Everyone quietly and dispassionately performs their jobs—the prison guards, the hangman, the superintendent, and even the prisoner, who offers no resistance when he is bound and led to the gallows. All is totally routine until a very small incident makes Orwell aware of what is happening:

> It was about forty yards to the gallows. I watched the bare brown back of the prisoner marching in front of me. He walked clumsily with his bound arms, but quite steadily, with that bobbing gait of the Indian who never straightens his knees. At each step his muscles slid neatly into place, the lock of hair on his scalp danced up and down, his feet printed themselves on the wet gravel. And once, in spite of the men who gripped him by each shoulder, he stepped lightly aside to avoid a puddle on the path.
>
> It is curious; but till that moment I had never realized what it means to destroy a healthy, conscious man. When I saw the prisoner step aside to avoid the puddle, I saw the mystery, the unspeakable wrongness, of cutting a life short when it is in full tide. This man was not dying, he was alive just as we are alive. All the organs of his body were working—bowels digesting food, skin renewing itself, nails growing, tissues forming—all toiling away in solemn foolery. His nails would still be growing when he stood on the drop, when he was falling through the air with a tenth-of-a-second to live. His eyes saw the yellow gravel and gray walls, and his brain still remembered, foresaw, reasoned—even about puddles. He and we were a party of men walking together, seeing, hearing, feeling, understanding the same world; and in two minutes, with a sudden snap, one of us would be gone—one mind less, one world less.

Orwell's narrative leads to a dramatic moment of recognition, which gives this story its lasting power.

Building a Narrative Argument

The biggest problem with narrative arguments is that anyone can tell a story. On the one hand, there are compelling stories that argue against capital punishment. For example, a mentally retarded man who was executed in Arkansas had refused a piece of pie at his last meal, telling the guards that he wanted to save the pie for later. On the other hand, there are also many stories about the victims of murder and other crimes. Many families have Web sites on which they call for killing those responsible for murdering their loved ones. They too have compelling stories to tell.

Violent deaths of all kinds make for especially vivid narrative arguments. In the late 1990s, there were several incidents in which school-children used guns taken from the family home to kill other students. Stories of these tragedies provided strong arguments for gun control. Gun rights organizations, including the National Rifle Association (NRA), attempted to counter these stories by claiming that they are not truly representative. The NRA claims that between sixty million and sixty-five million Americans own guns and thirty million to thirty-five million own handguns. They argue that more than 99.8 percent of all guns and 99.6 percent of handguns will not be used to commit crimes in any given year. Thus, the NRA argues that narratives of tragic gun deaths are either not representative or the result of allowing too many criminals to avoid prison or execution.

There are two keys to making effective narrative arguments: establishing credibility and establishing representativeness. It's easy enough to make up stories that suit the point you want to make. Writing from personal experience can give you a great deal of impact, but that impact vanishes if your readers doubt that you are telling the truth. Second, the story you tell may be true enough, but the question remains how representative the incident is. We don't ban bananas because someone once slipped on a banana peel. Narratives are often useful for illustrating how people are affected by particular issues or events, but narrative arguments are more effective if you have more evidence than just one incident. The death of Cari Lightner was a tragedy, but the deaths of over 25,000 people a year caused by drunk drivers made Cari Lightner's death representative of a national tragedy, a slaughter that could be prevented. Cari Lightner's tragic story had power because people understood it to be representative of a much larger problem.

LESLIE MARMON SILKO

The Border Patrol State

*Leslie Marmon Silko (1948–) was born in Albuquerque and graduated
from the University of New Mexico. She now teaches at the University of
Arizona. She has received much critical acclaim for her writings about
Native Americans. Her first novel,* Ceremony *(1977), describes the
struggles of a veteran returning home after World War II to civilian life on
a New Mexico reservation. Her incorporation of Indian storytelling
techniques in* Ceremony *drew strong praise. One critic called her "the most
accomplished Indian writer of her generation." She has since published
two more novels,* Almanac of the Dead *(1991) and* Gardens in the Dunes
(1999); a collection of essays, Yellow Woman and a Beauty of the Spirit:
Essays on Native American Life Today *(1996); two volumes of poems and
stories; and many shorter works. Silko's talents as a storyteller are evident
in this essay, which first appeared in the magazine* Nation *in 1994.*

1   I used to travel the highways of New Mexico and Arizona with a wonderful sensation of absolute freedom as I cruised down the open road
and across the vast desert plateaus. On the Laguna Pueblo reservation,
where I was raised, the people were patriotic despite the way the U.S.
government had treated Native Americans. As proud citizens, we grew
up believing the freedom to travel was our inalienable right, a right that
some Native Americans had been denied in the early twentieth century.
Our cousin, old Bill Pratt, used to ride his horse 300 miles overland
from Laguna, New Mexico, to Prescott, Arizona, every summer to work
as a fire lookout.

2   In school in the 1950s, we were taught that our right to travel from
state to state without special papers or threat of detainment was a right that
citizens under communist and totalitarian governments did not possess.
That wide open highway told us we were U.S. citizens; we were free. . . .

3   Not so long ago, my companion Gus and I were driving south from
Albuquerque, returning to Tucson after a book promotion for the paper-
back edition of my novel *Almanac of the Dead*. I had settled back and
gone to sleep while Gus drove, but I was awakened when I felt the car
slowing to a stop. It was nearly midnight on New Mexico State Road 26,
a dark, lonely stretch of two-lane highway between Hatch and Deming.
When I sat up, I saw the headlights and emergency flashers of six vehicles—Border Patrol cars and a van were blocking both lanes of the highway. Gus stopped the car and rolled down the window to ask what was
wrong. But the closest Border Patrolman and his companion did not
reply; instead, the first agent ordered us to "step out of the car." Gus

asked why, but his question seemed to set them off. Two more Border Patrol agents immediately approached our car, and one of them snapped, "Are you looking for trouble?" as if he would relish it.

4   I will never forget that night beside the highway. There was an awful feeling of menace and violence straining to break loose. It was clear that the uniformed men would be only too happy to drag us out of the car if we did not speedily comply with their request (asking a question is tantamount to resistance, it seems). So we stepped out of the car and they motioned for us to stand on the shoulder of the road. The night was very dark, and no other traffic had come down the road since we had been stopped. All I could think about was a book I had read—*Nunca Mas*—the official report of a human rights commission that investigated and certified more than 12,000 "disappearances" during Argentina's "dirty war" in the late 1970s.

5   The weird anger of these Border Patrolmen made me think about descriptions in the report of Argentine police and military officers who became addicted to interrogation, torture and the murder that followed. When the military and police ran out of political suspects to torture and kill, they resorted to the random abduction of citizens off the streets. I thought how easy it would be for the Border Patrol to shoot us and leave our bodies and car beside the highway, like so many bodies found in these parts and ascribed to "drug runners."

6   Two other Border Patrolmen stood by the white van. The one who had asked if we were looking for trouble ordered his partner to "get the dog," and from the back of the van another patrolman brought a small female German shepherd on a leash. The dog apparently did not heel well enough to suit him, and the handler jerked the leash. They opened the doors of our car and pulled the dog's head into it, but I saw immediately from the expression in her eyes that the dog hated them, and that she would not serve them. When she showed no interest in the inside of the car, they brought her around back to the trunk, near where we were standing. They half-dragged her up into the trunk, but still she did not indicate any stowed-away human beings or illegal drugs.

7   The mood got uglier; the officers seemed outraged that the dog could not find any contraband, and they dragged her over to us and commanded her to sniff our legs and feet. To my relief, the strange violence the Border Patrol agents had focused on us now seemed shifted to the dog. I no longer felt so strongly that we would be murdered. We exchanged looks—the dog and I. She was afraid of what they might do, just as I was. The dog's handler jerked the leash sharply as she sniffed us, as if to make her perform better, but the dog refused to accuse us: She had an innate dignity that did not permit her to serve the murderous impulses of those men. I can't forget the expression in the dog's eyes; it was as if she were embarrassed to be associated with them. I had a small amount of medicinal marijuana in

my purse that night, but she refused to expose me. I am not partial to dogs, but I will always remember the small German shepherd that night.

8   Unfortunately, what happened to me is an everyday occurrence here now. Since the 1980s, on top of greatly expanding border checkpoints, the Immigration and Naturalization Service and the Border Patrol have implemented policies that interfere with the rights of U.S. citizens to travel freely within our borders. I.N.S. agents now patrol all interstate highways and roads that lead to or from the U.S.-Mexico border in Texas, New Mexico, Arizona and California. Now, when you drive east from Tucson on Interstate 10 toward El Paso, you encounter an I.N.S. check station outside Las Cruces, New Mexico. When you drive north from Las Cruces up Interstate 25, two miles north of the town of Truth or Consequences, the highway is blocked with orange emergency barriers, and all traffic is diverted into a two-lane Border Patrol checkpoint—ninety-five miles north of the U.S.-Mexico border.

9   I was detained once at Truth or Consequences, despite my and my companion's Arizona driver's licenses. Two men, both Chicanos, were detained at the same time, despite the fact that they too presented ID and spoke English without the thick Texas accents of the Border Patrol agents. While we were stopped, we watched as other vehicles—whose occupants were white—were waved through the checkpoint. White people traveling with brown people, however, can expect to be stopped on suspicion they work with the sanctuary movement, which shelters refugees. White people who appear to be clergy, those who wear ethnic clothing or jewelry and women with very long hair or very short hair (they could be nuns) are also frequently detained; white men with beards or men with long hair are likely to be detained, too, because Border Patrol agents have "profiles" of "those sorts" of white people who may help political refugees. (Most of the political refugees from Guatemala and El Salvador are Native American or mestizo because the indigenous people of the Americas have continued to resist efforts by invaders to displace them from their ancestral lands.) Alleged increases in illegal immigration by people of Asian ancestry mean that the Border Patrol now routinely detains anyone who appears to be Asian or part Asian, as well.

10   Once your car is diverted from the Interstate Highway into the checkpoint area, you are under the control of the Border Patrol, which in practical terms exercises a power that no highway patrol or city patrolman possesses: They are willing to detain anyone, for no apparent reason. Other law-enforcement officers need a shred of probable cause in order to detain someone. On the books, so does the Border Patrol; but on the road, it's another matter. They'll order you to stop your car and step out; then they'll ask you to open the trunk. If you ask why or request a search warrant, you'll be told that they'll have to have a dog sniff the car before they can request a search warrant, and the dog might not get there

for two or three hours. The search warrant might require an hour or two past that. They make it clear that if you force them to obtain a search warrant for the car, they will make you submit to a strip search as well.

11   Traveling in the open, though, the sense of violation can be even worse. Never mind high-profile cases like that of former Border Patrol agent Michael Elmer, acquitted of murder by claiming self-defense, despite admitting that as an officer he shot an "illegal" immigrant in the back and then hid the body, which remained undiscovered until another Border Patrolman reported the event. (Last month, Elmer was convicted of reckless endangerment in a separate incident, for shooting at least ten rounds from his M-16 too close to a group of immigrants as they were crossing illegally into Nogales in March 1992.) Or that in El Paso a high school football coach driving a vanload of players in full uniform was pulled over on the freeway and a Border Patrol agent put a cocked revolver to his head. (The football coach was Mexican-American, as were most of the players in his van; the incident eventually caused a federal judge to issue a restraining order against the Border Patrol.) We've a mountain of personal experiences like that which never make the newspapers. A history professor at U.C.L.A. told me she had been traveling by train from Los Angeles to Albuquerque twice a month doing research. On each of her trips, she had noticed that the Border Patrol agents were at the station in Albuquerque scrutinizing the passengers. Since she is six feet tall and of Irish and German ancestry, she was not particularly concerned. Then one day when she stepped off the train in Albuquerque, two Border Patrolmen accosted her, wanting to know what she was doing, and why she was traveling between Los Angeles and Albuquerque twice a month. She presented identification and an explanation deemed "suitable" by the agents, and was allowed to go about her business.

12   Just the other day, I mentioned to a friend that I was writing this article and he told me about his 73-year-old father, who is half Chinese and who had set out alone by car from Tucson to Albuquerque the week before. His father had become confused by road construction and missed a turnoff from Interstate 10 to Interstate 25; when he turned around and circled back, he missed the turnoff a second time. But when he looped back for yet another try, Border Patrol agents stopped him and forced him to open his trunk. After they satisfied themselves that he was not smuggling Chinese immigrants, they sent him on his way. He was so rattled by the event that he had to be driven home by his daughter.

13   This is the police state that has developed in the southwestern United States since the 1980s. No person, no citizen, is free to travel without the scrutiny of the Border Patrol. In the city of South Tucson, where 80 percent of the respondents were Chicano or Mexicano, a joint research project by the University of Wisconsin and the University of Arizona recently concluded that one out of every five people there had

been detained, mistreated verbally or nonverbally, or questioned by I.N.S. agents in the past two years.

14   Manifest Destiny may lack its old grandeur of theft and blood— "lock the door" is what it means now, with racism a trump card to be played again and again, shamelessly, by both major political parties. "Immigration," like "street crime" and "welfare fraud," is a political euphemism that refers to people of color. Politicians and media people talk about "illegal aliens" to dehumanize and demonize undocumented immigrants, who are for the most part people of color. Even in the days of Spanish and Mexican rule, no attempts were made to interfere with the flow of people and goods from south to north and north to south. It is the U.S. government that has continually attempted to sever contact between the tribal people north of the border and those to the south.[1]

15   Now that the "Iron Curtain" is gone, it is ironic that the U.S. government and its Border Patrol are constructing a steel wall ten feet high to span sections of the border with Mexico. While politicians and multinational corporations extol the virtues of NAFTA and "free trade" (in goods, not flesh), the ominous curtain is already up in a six-mile section at the border crossing at Mexicali; two miles are being erected but are not yet finished at Naco; and at Nogales, sixty miles south of Tucson, the steel wall has been all rubber-stamped and awaits construction likely to begin in March. Like the pathetic multimillion-dollar "antidrug" border surveillance balloons that were continually deflated by high winds and made only a couple of meager interceptions before they blew away, the fence along the border is a theatrical prop, a bit of pork for contractors. Border entrepreneurs have already used blowtorches to cut passageways through the fence to collect "tolls," and are doing a brisk business. Back in Washington, the I.N.S. announces a $300 million computer contract to modernize its record-keeping and Congress passes a crime bill that shunts $255 million to the I.N.S. for 1995, $181 million earmarked for border control, which is to include 700 new partners for the men who stopped Gus and me in our travels, and the history professor, and my friend's father, and as many as they could from South Tucson.

16   It is no use; borders haven't worked, and they won't work, not now, as the indigenous people of the Americas reassert their kinship and solidarity with one another. A mass migration is already under way; its roots are not simply economic. The Uto-Aztecan languages are spoken as far north as Taos Pueblo near the Colorado border, all the way south to Mexico City. Before the arrival of the Europeans, the indigenous communities throughout this region not only conducted commerce, the people shared

---

[1]The Treaty of Guadalupe Hidalgo, signed in 1848, recognizes the right of Tohano O'Odom (Papago) people to move freely across the U.S.-Mexico border without documents. A treaty with Canada guarantees similar rights to those of the Iroquois nation in traversing the U.S.-Canada border. [Author's note]

cosmologies, and oral narratives about the Maize Mothers, the Twin Brothers and their Grandmother, Spider Woman, as well as Quetzalcoatl the benevolent snake. The great human migration within the Americas cannot be stopped; human beings are natural forces of the Earth, just as rivers and winds are natural forces.

17   Deep down the issue is simple: The so-called "Indian Wars" from the days of Sitting Bull and Red Cloud have never really ended in the Americas. The Indian people of southern Mexico, of Guatemala and those left in El Salvador, too, are still fighting for their lives and for their land against the "cavalry" patrols sent out by the governments of those lands. The Americas are Indian country, and the "Indian problem" is not about to go away.

18   One evening at sundown, we were stopped in traffic at a railroad crossing in downtown Tucson while a freight train passed us, slowly gaining speed as it headed north to Phoenix. In the twilight I saw the most amazing sight: Dozens of human beings, mostly young men, were riding the train; everywhere, on flat cars, inside open boxcars, perched on top of boxcars, hanging off ladders on tank cars and between boxcars. I couldn't count fast enough, but I saw fifty or sixty people headed north. They were dark young men, Indian and mestizo; they were smiling and a few of them waved at us in our cars. I was reminded of the ancient story of Aztlán, told by the Aztecs but known in other Uto-Aztecan communities as well. Aztlán is the beautiful land to the north, the origin place of the Aztec people. I don't remember how or why the people left Aztlán to journey farther south, but the old story says that one day, they will return. ∎

Steps to a Narrative Argument

Step **1** Identify an experience that makes an implicit argument

Think about experiences that made you realize that something is wrong or that things need to be changed. The experience does not have to be one that leads to a moral lesson at the end, but it should be one that makes your readers think.

Examples

- Being arrested and hauled to jail for carrying a glass soft drink bottle in a glass-free zone made you realize how inefficiently your police force is being used.
- After going through a complicated system of getting referrals for a serious medical condition and then having the treatment your physician recommends denied by your HMO, you want to tell your story to show just how flawed the HMO system really is.
- When you moved from a well-financed suburban school to a much poorer rural school, you came to realize what huge differences exist among school systems in your state.
- If you have ever experienced being stereotyped in any way, narrate that experience and describe how it affected you.

Step **2** List all the details you can remember

- When did it happen?
- How old were you?
- Why were you there?
- Who else was there?
- Where did it happen? If the place is important, describe what it looked like.

Step **3** Examine the significance of the event

- How did you feel about the experience when it happened?
- How did it affect you then?
- How do you feel about the experience now?
- What long-term effects has it had on your life?

Step **4** Analyze your potential readers

- Who are your readers?
- How much will your readers know about the background of the experience you are describing?
- Are they familiar with the place where it happened?
- Would anything similar ever likely have happened to them?
- How likely are they to agree with your feelings about the experience?

Step **5** Write a draft

- You might need to give some background first, but if you have a compelling story, often it's best to launch right in.
- You might want to tell the story as it happened (chronological order), or you might want to begin with a striking incident and then go back to tell how it happened (flashback).
- You might want to reflect on your experience at the end, but you want your story to do most of the work. Avoid drawing a simple moral lesson. Your readers should share your feelings if you tell your story well.

Step **6** Revise, edit, proofread

- For detailed instructions, see Chapter 12.
- For a checklist to use to evaluate your draft, see pages 217–222.

CHAPTER 10

Rebuttal Arguments

The Media Foundation, a Canadian media activist organization, challenges advertising it sees as harmful by subverting it. The Media Foundation publishes an ad-free magazine, *Adbusters*, and it supports the Adbusters Web site, both of which take on specific advertising campaigns with clever spoofs.

When you hear the word *rebuttal*, you might think of a debate team or the part of a trial when the attorney for the defense answers the plaintiff's accusations. Although rebuttal has those definitions, a **rebuttal argument** can be thought of in much larger terms. Indeed, much of what people know about the world today is the result of centuries of arguments of rebuttal.

In high school and college, you no doubt have taken many courses that required the memorization of knowledge and evidence, which you demonstrated by repeating these facts on tests. You probably didn't think much about how the knowledge came about. Once in a while, though, something happens that makes people think consciously about a piece of knowledge that they have learned. For example, in elementary school, you learned that the earth rotates on its axis once a day. Maybe you didn't think about it much at the time, but once, years later, you were out on a clear night and noticed the Big Dipper in one part of the sky, and then you looked for it later and found it in an-

> Effective rebuttal arguments depend on critical thinking.

other part of the sky. Perhaps you became interested enough that you watched the stars for a few hours. If you've ever spent a clear night out stargazing, you have observed that the North Star, called Polaris, stays in the same place. The stars near Polaris appear to move in a circle around Polaris, and the stars farther away move from east to west until they disappear below the horizon.

If you are lucky enough to live in a place where the night sky is often clear, you can see the same pattern repeated night after night. And if you stop to think about why you see the stars circling around Polaris, you remember what you were taught long ago—that you live on a rotating ball, so the stars appear to move across the sky, but in fact, stars are so distant from the earth that their actual movement is not visible to humans over a short term.

An alternative explanation for these facts not only is possible but is the one that people believed from ancient times until about five hundred years ago. People assumed that their position on the earth was fixed and that the entire sky rotated on an axis connecting Polaris and the earth. The flaw in this theory for people in ancient times is the movement of the planets. If you watch the path of Mars over several nights, you will observe that it also moves across the sky from east to west, but it makes an anomalous backward movement during its journey and then goes forward again. The other planets also seem to wander back and forth as they cross the night sky. The ancient Greeks developed an explanation of the strange wanderings of the planets by theorizing that the planets move in small circles imposed on larger orbits. By graphing little circles on top of circles, the course of planets could be plotted and predicted. This theory culminated in the work of Ptolemy, who lived in Alexandria in the second century AD. Ptolemy proposed displaced centers for the small circles called *epicycles,* which gave a better fit for predicting the path of planets.

Because Ptolemy's model of the universe was numerically accurate in its predictions, educated people for centuries assumed its validity, even though there was evidence to the contrary. For example, Aristarchus of Samos, who lived in the fourth century BCE, used the size of the earth's shadow cast on the moon during a lunar eclipse to compute the sizes of the moon and sun and their distances from the earth. Even though his calculations were inaccurate, Aristarchus recognized that the sun is much bigger than the earth, and he advanced the heliocentric hypothesis: that the earth orbits the sun.

Many centuries passed, however, before educated people believed that the sun, not the earth, was the center of the solar system. In the early sixteenth century, the Polish astronomer Nicolas Copernicus recognized that Ptolemy's model could be greatly simplified if the sun was at the center of the solar system. He kept his theory a secret for much of his life and saw the published account of his work only a few hours before his death in 1543. Even though Copernicus made a major breakthrough, he was not able to take full advantage of the heliocentric hypothesis because he followed the tradition that orbits are perfect circles; thus, he still needed circles on top of circles to explain the motion of the planets but far fewer than did Ptolemy.

The definitive rebuttal of Ptolemy came a century later with the work of the German astronomer Johannes Kepler. Kepler performed many tedious calculations, which were complicated by the fact that he had to first assume an orbit for the earth before he could compute orbits for the planets. Finally he made a stunning discovery: All the orbits of the planets could be described as an ellipse with the sun at the center. The dominance of the Ptolemaic model of the universe was finally over.

Critical Thinking

The relationship of facts and theories lies at the heart of the scientific method. Both Ptolemy's theory and Kepler's theory explain why the stars appear to move around Polaris at night. Kepler made a convincing argument by rebuttal to the Ptolemaic model because he could give a much simpler analysis. The history of astronomy is a history of arguments of rebuttal. Modern astronomy was made possible because Copernicus challenged the established relationship of theory and evidence in astronomy. This awareness of the relationship of factual and theoretical claims in science is one definition of *critical thinking* in the sciences. What is true for the history of astronomy is true for the sciences; critical thinking in the sciences relies on arguments of rebuttal.

Similar kinds of arguments of rebuttal are presented today in the debate over global warming. One of the main sources of data for arguments of rebuttal against global warming is the twenty-year record of temperature readings from NASA weather satellites orbiting the earth at the North and South Poles. These satellites use microwave sensors to measure temperature variation in the atmosphere from the surface to about six miles above the earth. Computer models predict a gradual warming in the earth's lower atmosphere along with the surface because of the buildup of carbon dioxide and other greenhouse gases, the gases produced from burning fossil fuels. But while temperatures measured on the earth's surface have gradually increased, the corresponding rises in the atmosphere as recorded by satellites didn't appear to happen. In August 1998, however, two scientists discovered a flaw in the satellites that was making them lose altitude and therefore misreport temperature data. When adjusted, the satellite data confirm what thermometers on the ground tell us: The earth is getting warmer.

In some cases, particular disciplines have specialized training to assess the relationship of theory and evidence. But more often, people must engage in *general critical thinking* to assess the validity of claims based on evidence. Often, one has to weigh competing claims of people who have excellent qualifications. One group of nutritional experts says that people should take calcium supplements to strengthen their bones. Another group warns that people are in danger of suffering from kidney stones if they take too much calcium. Critical thinking is involved in all the kinds of arguments that are discussed in this book, but it is especially important in arguments of rebuttal.

Two Ways of Rebutting

When you rebut the argument of someone else, you can do one of two things. You can *refute* the argument, or you can *counterargue*. In the first case, **refutation**, you emphasize the shortcomings of the argument that you wish to undermine without really making a positive case of your own. In the second case, **counterargument**, you emphasize not so much the shortcomings of the argument that you are rebutting but the positive strengths of the position you wish to support. Often there is considerable overlap between refutation and counterargument, and often both are present in a rebuttal.

Refutation

If you think back to the basic model of how arguments work, you can quickly see that there are two primary strategies for refutation arguments. First, *you can challenge the assumptions* on which a claim is based. Copernicus did not question Ptolemy's data concerning how the stars and planets appear in the sky to an observer on the earth. Instead, he questioned Ptolemy's central assumption that the earth is the center of the solar system.

Second, *you can question the evidence* supporting the claim. Sometimes, the evidence presented is simply wrong, as was the case for the satellites that lost altitude and reported faulty temperature data. Sometimes, the evidence is incomplete or unrepresentative, and sometimes, counterevidence can be found. Often when you refute an argument, you make the case that your opponent has been guilty of one or more **fallacies of arguments** (see pages 51–52). Your opponent has engaged in the either-or fallacy, or jumped to a hasty generalization, or created a straw man. So you indicate how the conclusions do not follow from the reasons offered, or you show that the evidence in support of the reasons is faulty or incomplete.

Take, for example, the case of arguments about drug policy in the United States. Today, almost everyone who writes about illegal drugs in the United States says that the current drug policy is flawed in some way. Even though U.S. jails and prisons are bursting with people who have been convicted and sentenced for drug offenses, millions of people still use illegal drugs. The social, political, and economic costs of illegal drugs are staggering, and the debate continues over what to do about these substances. On one side are those who want more police, more drug users in jail, and military forces sent to other countries to stop the drug traffic. On the other are those who compare current efforts to stop the flow of drugs to those of failed efforts under Prohibition (1919–1933) to halt the sale of alcohol. They want most illegal drugs to be legalized or decriminalized.

On September 7, 1989, Nobel prize–winning economist Milton Friedman published in the *Wall Street Journal* an open letter to William Bennett, then the drug czar (director of the Office of National Drug Policy) under President George H. W. Bush. Friedman wrote this as his refutation:

Dear Bill:

In Oliver Cromwell's eloquent words, "I beseech you, in the bowels of Christ, think it possible you may be mistaken" about the course you and President Bush urge us to adopt to fight drugs. The path you propose of more police, more jails, use of the military in foreign countries, harsh penalties for drug users, and a whole panoply of repressive measures can only make a bad situation worse. The drug war cannot be won by those tactics without undermining the human liberty and individual freedom that you and I cherish.

You are not mistaken in believing that drugs are a scourge that is devastating our society. You are not mistaken in believing that drugs are tearing asunder our social fabric, ruining the lives of many young people, and imposing heavy costs on some of the most disadvantaged among us. You are not mistaken in believing that the majority of the public share your concerns. In short, you are not mistaken in the end you seek to achieve.

Your mistake is failing to recognize that the very measures you favor are a major source of the evils you deplore. Of course the problem is demand, but it is not only demand, it is demand that must operate through repressed and illegal channels. Illegality creates obscene profits that finance the murderous tactics of the drug lords; illegality leads to the corruption of law enforcement officials; illegality monopolizes the efforts of honest law forces so they are starved for resources to fight the simpler crimes of robbery, theft and assault.

Drugs are a tragedy for addicts. But criminalizing their use converts that tragedy into a disaster for society, for users and non-users alike. Our experience with the prohibition of drugs is a replay of our experience with the prohibition of alcoholic beverages. . . .

Had drugs been decriminalized 17 years ago [when Friedman first made an appeal that drugs be decriminalized], "crack" would never have been invented (it was invented because the high cost of illegal drugs made it profitable to provide a cheaper version) and there would today be far fewer addicts. The lives of thousands, perhaps hundreds of thousands of innocent victims would have been saved, and not only in the U.S. The ghettos of our major cities would not be drug-and-crime-infested no-man's-lands. Fewer people would be in jails, and fewer jails would have been built.

Colombia, Bolivia, and Peru would not be suffering from narco-terror, and we would not be distorting our foreign policy because of narco-terror. Hell would not, in the words with which Billy Sunday welcomed Prohibition, "be forever for rent," but it would be a lot emptier.

In the first two paragraphs, Friedman carefully identifies the common ground he shares with Bennett. Both are political conservatives, as Friedman reminds Bennett when he mentions the "human liberty and individual freedom that you and I cherish." Friedman also agrees with Bennett about the severity of the drug problem, noting that it is "tearing asunder our social fabric, ruining the lives of many young people, and imposing heavy costs on some of the most disadvantaged among us."

Where Friedman differs from Bennett is in Bennett's central assumption: Friedman feels that Bennett's conclusion—"more police, more jails, use of the military in foreign countries, harsh penalties for drug users, and a whole panoply of repressive measures"—does not follow from the evidence about drugs. Bennett has cause and effect reversed, says Friedman: "Your mistake is failing to recognize that the very measures you favor are a major source of the evils you deplore." If drugs are now illegal and still being used, then how can the solution be to make them even more illegal by increasing penalties and extending law enforcement beyond U.S. borders? Friedman calls attention to the centrality of Bennett's assumptions when he quotes Oliver Cromwell's famous words: "I beseech you, in the bowels of Christ, think it possible you may be mistaken." If, in fact, Bennett's central assumption is flawed, then the reason to spend millions of dollars, to violate civil liberties, and to antagonize other nations is suddenly taken away.

William Bennett responded to Friedman quickly. On September 19, 1989, the *Wall Street Journal* published another refutation, an open letter of reply from Bennett to Friedman. Here is part of Bennett's response, which has a much more strident tone than Friedman's letter:

Dear Milton:

There was little, if anything, new in your open letter to me calling for the legalization of drugs. As your 1972 article made clear, the legalization argument is an old and familiar one, which has recently been revived by a small number of journalists and academics who insist that the only solution to the drug problem is no solution at all. What surprises me is that you would continue to advocate so unrealistic a proposal without pausing to consider seriously its consequences.

If the argument for drug legalization has one virtue it is its sheer simplicity. Eliminate laws against drugs, and street crime will disappear. Take the profit out of the black market through decriminalization and regulation, and poor neighborhoods will no longer be victimized by drug dealers. Cut back on drug enforcement, and use the money to wage a public health campaign against drugs, as we do with tobacco and alcohol.

The basic premise of all these propositions is that using our nation's laws to fight drugs is too costly. To be sure, our attempts to reduce drug use do carry with them enormous costs. But the question that must be asked—and which is totally ignored by the legalization advocates—is, what are the costs of *not* enforcing laws against drugs?

In my judgment, and in the judgment of virtually every serious scholar in this field, the potential costs of legalizing drugs would be so large as to make it a public policy disaster.

Of course, no one, including you, can say with certainty what would happen in the U.S. if drugs were suddenly to become a readily purchased product. We do know, however, that wherever drugs have become cheaper and more easily obtained, drug use—and addiction—has skyrocketed. In opium and cocaine producing countries, addiction is rampant among the peasants involved in drug production.

Professor James Q. Wilson tells us that during the years in which heroin could be legally prescribed by doctors in Britain, the number of addicts increased forty-fold. And after the repeal of Prohibition—an analogy favored but misunderstood by legalization advocates—consumption of alcohol soared by 350%.

Could we afford such dramatic increases in drug use? I doubt it. Already the toll of drug use on American society—measured in lost productivity, in rising health insurance costs, in hospitals flooded with drug overdose emergencies, in drug caused accidents, and in premature death—is surely more than we would like to bear.

You seem to believe that by spending just a little more money on treatment and rehabilitation, the costs of increased addiction can be avoided. That hope betrays a basic misunderstanding of the problems facing drug treatment. Most addicts don't suddenly decide to get help. They remain addicts either because treatment isn't available or because they don't seek it out. . . .

As for the connection between drugs and crime, your unswerving commitment to a legalization solution prevents you from appreciating the complexity of the drug market. Contrary to your claim, most addicts do not turn to crime to support their habit. Research shows that many of them were involved in criminal activity before they turned to drugs. Many former addicts who have received treatment continue to commit crimes during their recovery. And even if drugs were legal, what evidence do you have that the habitual drug user wouldn't continue to rob and steal to get money for clothes, food or shelter? Drug addicts always want more drugs than they can afford, and no legalization scheme has yet come up with a way of satisfying that appetite.

In refuting Friedman, Bennett contends that Friedman has not told the whole story. He has omitted important information, namely the likelihood that drug use would increase (and with tragic consequences) if drugs are legalized: "the potential costs of legalizing drugs would be so large as to make it a public policy disaster."

Bennett goes on to maintain that "a true friend of freedom under-stands that government has a responsibility to craft and uphold laws that help educate citizens about right and wrong. That, at any rate, was the Founders' view of our system of government." He ends by describing Friedman's proposal as "irresponsible and reckless public policy."

Friedman was not content to let Bennett have the last word, so he in turn wrote another reply—yet another refutation—that appeared on September 29, 1989, in the *Wall Street Journal*. At this point, Friedman drops the open-letter strategy and writes instead a more conventional response, referring to Bennett as *he* instead of *you*:

> William Bennett is entirely right (editorial page, Sept. 19) that "there was little, if anything, new in" my open letter to him—just as there is little, if anything, new in his proposed program to rid this nation of the scourge of drugs. That is why I am so disturbed by that program. It flies in the face of decades of experience. More police, more jails, more-stringent penal-ties, increased efforts at interception, increased publicity about the evils of drugs—all this has been accompanied by more, not fewer, drug addicts; more, not fewer, crimes and murders; more, not less, corruption; more, not fewer, innocent victims.
>
> Like Mr. Bennett, his predecessors were "committed to fighting the problem on several fronts through imaginative policies and hard work over a long period of time." What evidence convinces him that the same policies on a larger scale will end the drug scourge? He offers none in his response to me, only assertion and the conjecture that legalizing drugs would produce "a public policy disaster"—as if that is not exactly what we already have.

Friedman, that is, challenges Bennett's lack of evidence: "What evi-dence convinces him that the same policies on a larger scale will end the drug scourge? He offers none in his response to me." Friedman then adds that "legalizing drugs is not equivalent to surrender" but rather the precon-dition for an effective fight against drug use. He concedes that the number of addicts might increase, but he argues that it is certain that the total num-ber of innocent victims would drop drastically, including innocent victims in foreign nations when we base our foreign policy on drug control.

Friedman's sharpest refutation of Bennett comes over Bennett's claim to represent the tradition of the Founders of the United States. Friedman completely rejects Bennett's assertion that the Founders wanted govern-ment to educate citizens about what is right and what is wrong. Friedman says "that is a totalitarian view utterly unacceptable to the Founders. I do not believe, and neither did they, that it is the responsibility of government to tell free citizens what is right and wrong."

Counterargument

Rebuttals, therefore, frequently involve refutation: a demonstration of where an argument has gone wrong. Refuters say, in effect, "I hear your argument, and here is where you are in error." What follows that thesis in a refutation is a challenge to the reasoning process (to show that a conclusion does not necessarily follow from the premises offered) or a challenge to the evidence that supports the premises (to show that the premise itself is not necessarily true). A person who engages in refutation does not necessarily say what is right—though certainly Bennett and Friedman leave no doubt about what they think is right—only that the other party is wrong.

Another way to rebut, however, is to counterargue. In a counterargument, you do not really show the shortcomings of your opponent's point of view; you may not refer to the details of the other argument at all. Rather, you offer an argument of the other point of view, in the hope that it will outweigh the argument that is being rebutted. A counterarguer, in effect, says "I hear your argument. But there is more to it than that. Now listen while I explain why another position is stronger." A counterargument offered to Friedman might go this way, in effect: "I hear your argument about the benefits of decriminalizing illegal drugs. You contend that the war on drugs threatens civil liberties and creates crime problems when drug abusers need money to support their bad habits. I accept your argument, as far as it goes. But what you have not called sufficient attention to is the negative consequences of legalizing drugs. Now listen as I explain how a policy of decriminalization will be a disaster, especially because it will encourage many, many more people to abuse harmful substances."

The counterarguer depends on the wisdom of audience members to hear all sides of an issue and to make up their minds about the merits of the case. In the following short poem, Wilfred Owen, a veteran of the horrors of World War I trench warfare, offers a counterargument to those who argue that war is noble, to those who believe along with the Latin poet Horace that "dulce et decorum est pro patria mori"—that it is sweet and fitting to die for one's country. This poem gains in popularity whenever there is an unpopular war, for it rebuts the belief that it is noble to die for one's country in modern warfare.

Dulce Et Decorum Est
Bent double, like old beggars under sacks,
Knock-kneed, coughing like hags, we cursed through sludge,
Till on the haunting flares we turned our backs

And towards our distant rest began to trudge.
Men marched asleep. Many had lost their boots
But limped on, blood-shod. All went lame; all blind;
Drunk with fatigue; deaf even to the hoots
Of disappointed shells that dropped behind.

Gas! Gas! Quick, boys!—An ecstacy of fumbling,
Fitting the clumsy helmets just in time;
But someone still was yelling out and stumbling
And floundering like a man in fire or lime.—
Dim, through the misty panes and thick green light
As under a green sea, I saw him drowning.
In all my dreams, before my helpless sight,
He plunges at me, guttering, choking, drowning.

If in some smothering dreams you too could pace
Behind the wagon that we flung him in,
And watch the white eyes writhing in his face,
His hanging face, like a devil's sick of sin;
If you could hear, at every jolt, the blood
Come gargling from the froth-corrupted lungs,
Obscene as cancer, bitter as the cud
Of vile, incurable sores on innocent tongues,—
My friend, you would not tell with such high zest
To children ardent for some desperate glory,
The old Lie: Dulce et decorum est
Pro patria mori.

Wilfred Owen does not summarize the argument in favor of being willing to die for one's country and then refute that argument, premise by premise. Rather, his poem presents an opposing argument, supported by a narrative of the speaker's experience in a poison gas attack, that he hopes will more than counterbalance what he calls "the old lie." Owen simply ignores the good reasons that people give for being willing to die for one's country and essentially argues instead that there are also good reasons not to do so. And he hopes that the evidence that he summons for his countering position will outweigh for his audience ("My friend") the evidence in support of the other side.

Of course, this example, like the Friedman-Bennett exchange, shows that it can be artificial to oppose refutation and counterargument, particularly because all arguments, in a broad sense, are counterarguments. Rebuttal arguments commonly frequently offer both refutation and counterargument. In short, people who write rebuttals work like attorneys do in a trial: They make their own cases with good reasons and hard evidence, but they also do what they can to undermine their opponent's argument. In the end the jury, the audience, decides.

LINDA CHAVEZ

The "Separation of Church and State" Myth

Linda Chavez (1947–), the author of An Unlikely Conservative: The
Transformation of an Ex-Liberal *(2002) and* Out of the Barrio: Toward a
New Politics of Hispanic Assimilation *(1991), has been outspoken in the
service of contemporary conservatism for many years. Director of the U.S.
Commission on Civil Rights from 1983 to 1985, she frequently appears on
television talk shows and news programs, and she writes for a variety of
publications about affirmative action, immigration, bilingual education,
voting rights, and other issues. The following rebuttal essay appeared in the*
Jewish World Review *in July 2002 after a federal appeals court ruled that
the words "under God" in the Pledge of Allegiance ought to be stricken
because they are forbidden by the First Amendment clause that requires a
separation of church and state. (In 2004, the Supreme Court reversed that
court of appeals judgment, as Chavez had hoped.)*

1   As soon as the Ninth Circuit Court of Appeals handed down its decision
on the Pledge of Allegiance last week, the e-mails started pouring into
my mailbox. Most railed against the idea that a couple of judges on "the
Left Coast," as one person put it, could strike down the words "under
God," which Congress added to the pledge in 1954. But a few, mostly from
readers of my column, suggested that if I didn't like the decision, maybe I
should try thinking about how I'd feel if Congress had inserted the words
"under no God" instead—a sentiment echoed by the Ninth Circuit. In
order to protect religious liberty, they implied, we have to make sure government divorces itself from any expression of religious belief.

2   "Why did the Founding Fathers, a group of basically conservative,
property-owning religious men find it necessary at all to put the separation of Church and State into the Constitution, if not because of the persecution suffered in the lands they left from those who felt that only
they knew the truth?" wrote one of my interlocutors.

3   Good question, because it exposes one of the most widely held
myths in modern America.

4   Ask most Americans what the First Amendment says about religion, and you'll get the standard reply (if you're lucky enough to get
any answer at all) that it guarantees the separation of church and
state.

5   It says no such thing, of course. What it says is careful and precise:
"Congress shall make no law respecting an establishment of religion, or
prohibiting the free exercise thereof."

6   The First Amendment guarantees the freedom of religion, not from
religion.

7   The Founders understood that religious belief was not incidental to the American experiment in liberty but was the foundation on which it was built. The whole idea that individuals were entitled to liberty rests on the Judeo-Christian conception of man. When the colonists rebelled against their king—an action that risked their very lives—they did so with the belief that they were answering to a higher law than the king's. They were emboldened by "the laws of nature and nature's God," in Thomas Jefferson's memorable phrase to declare their independence.

8   "We hold these truths to be self-evident that all men are created equal and that they are endowed by their Creator with certain unalienable rights," he wrote.

9   It is impossible to overstate how important the Judeo-Christian tradition was guiding the Founder's deliberations. Yet, in recent years, we've virtually ignored this aspect of our history.

10   As scholar Michael Novak points out in his excellent little book *On Two Wings: Humble Faith and Common Source at the American Founding*, "Professor Donald Lutz counted 3,154 citations in the writings of the founders; of these nearly 1,100 references (34 percent) are to the Bible, and about 300 each to Montesquieu and Blackstone, followed at considerable distance by Locke and Hume and Plutarch."

11   Perhaps the most eloquent argument on behalf of the role of religion in preserving our democracy was George Washington's, who cautioned in his Farewell Address on Sept. 19, 1794, that virtue and morality were necessary to popular government.

12   "And let us with caution indulge the supposition, that morality can be maintained without religion" he said. "Whatever may be conceded to the influence of refined education on minds of peculiar structure, reason and experience both forbid us to expect that national morality can prevail in exclusion of religious principle."

13   The Constitutional Convention of 1787 opened with a prayer, as does each session of Congress today. The motto "In God We Trust" is on our currency, and similar expressions adorn public buildings across the Nation. Even the U.S. Supreme Court, which has been the locus of so much recent confusion on the First Amendment, begins its proceedings with the phrase "God save the United States and this honorable court."

14   Perhaps our plea should be "God save us from the courts."

15   As Jefferson, perhaps the least devout of our Founders, once said to the Rev. Ethan Allen, as recorded in Allen's diary now in the Library of Congress, and quoted by Michael Novak: "No nation has ever yet existed or been governed without religion. Nor can be."

16   Let us hope the Supreme Court in reviewing the Ninth Circuit's opinion does not insist on testing whether Jefferson was right. ■

Linda Chavez, "The 'Separation of Church and State' Myth" as appeared in *Jewish World Review*, July 3, 2002. By permission of Linda Chavez and Creators Syndicate, Inc.

Steps to a Rebuttal Argument

Step 1 Identify an argument to argue against as well as its main claim(s)

- What exactly are you arguing against?
- Are there secondary claims attached to the main claim?
- A fair summary of your opponent's position should be included in your finished rebuttal.

Example

- If you are taking on affirmative action admissions policies for colleges and universities, then what do those policies involve and whom do they affect?

Step 2 Examine the facts on which the claim is based

- Are the facts accurate?
- Are the facts a truly representative sample?
- Are the facts current?
- Is there another body of facts that you can present as counterevidence?
- If the author uses statistics, is evidence for the validity of those statistics presented?
- Can the statistics be interpreted differently?
- If the author quotes from sources, how reliable are those sources?
- Are the sources treated fairly, or are quotations taken out of context?
- If the author cites outside authority, how much trust can you place in that authority?

Step 3 Examine the assumptions on which the claim is based

- What is the primary assumption of the claim you are rejecting?
- What other assumptions support that claim?
- How are those assumptions flawed?
- If you are arguing against a specific piece of writing, then how does the author fall short?
- Does the author resort to name calling? use faulty reasoning? ignore key facts?
- What fallacies is the author guilty of committing?

Step 4 Analyze your potential readers

- To what extent do your potential readers support the claim that you are rejecting?
- If they strongly support that claim, then how might you appeal to them to change their minds?
- What common assumptions and beliefs do you share with them?

Step 5 Decide whether to write a refutation, a counterargument—or both

- Make your aim clear in your thesis statement.
- For example, a thesis statement like this one promises a refutation and a counterargument: "Friedman's argument is flawed in several ways. Not only that, he ignores the fact that laws in the United States are frequently developed in order to protect individuals against themselves."

Step 6 Write a draft

Identify the issue and the argument you are rejecting

- If the issue is not familiar to most of your readers, you might need to provide some background.
- Even if it is familiar, it might be helpful to give a quick summary of the competing positions.
- Remember that offering a fair and accurate summary is a good way to build credibility with your audience.

Take on the argument that you are rejecting

- You might want to question the evidence that is used to support the argument.
- You can challenge the facts, present counterevidence and countertestimony, cast doubt on the representativeness of the sample, cast doubt on the currency and relevance of the examples, challenge the credibility of any authorities cited, question the way in which statistical evidence is presented and interpreted, and argue that quotations are taken out of context.

Conclude on a firm note

- In your conclusion you should have a strong argument that underscores your objections.
- You might wish to close with a counterargument or counterproposal.

Step 7 Revise, edit, proofread

- For detailed instructions, see Chapter 12.
- For a checklist to use to evaluate your draft, see pages 217–222.

CHAPTER 11

Proposal Arguments

The major football programs in NCAA Division I generate millions of dollars in ticket and television revenue.

Not all NCAA Division I football programs are financially successful. Some lose millions every year.

The amateur tradition in college athletics continues at colleges in NCAA Division III, which do not offer athletic scholarships. The Williams College Ephs compete against the Tufts University Jumbos in a Division III game on a crisp fall Saturday in Williamston, Massachusetts.

Student athletes in big-time college football programs earn millions of dollars for their schools in ticket and television revenues, yet besides their scholarships, they receive barely enough money to live on. Should college athletes be paid? The Nebraska legislature thought so in April 2003 when it passed a bill allowing universities to pay student athletes. But the National Collegiate Athletic Association (NCAA) argues strongly to the contrary. The NCAA claims that paying players would destroy amateurism in college sports and make players third-rate professionals. Furthermore, only a handful of schools in NCAA Division I make a profit from athletics. At many schools athletics lose money, forcing administrators to cover these expenses from other revenues. Some people have proposed that schools should reduce expenses by offering fewer scholarships and by capping the salaries of coaches. These kinds of arguments are called proposal arguments, and they take the classic form:

We should (or should not) do SOMETHING.

At this moment, you might not think that there is anything you feel strongly enough about to write a proposal argument. But if you make a list of things that make you mad or at least a little annoyed, then you have a start toward writing a proposal argument. Some things on your list are not going to produce proposal arguments that many people would want to read. If your roommate is a slob, you might be able to write a proposal for that person to start cleaning up more, but who else would be interested? Similarly, it might be annoying to you that where you live it stays too hot for too long in the summer or too cold for too long in the winter, but unless you have a direct line to God, it is hard to imagine a serious proposal to change the climate. (Cutting down on air pollution, of course, is something that people *can* change.) Short of those extremes, however, are a lot of things that you might think, "Why hasn't someone done something about this?" If you believe that others have something to gain if a problem is solved or at least the situation made a little better, then you might be able to develop a good proposal argument.

For instance, suppose you are living off campus, and you buy a student parking sticker when you register for courses so that you can park in the student lot. However, you quickly find out that there are too many cars and trucks for the number of available spaces, and unless you get to campus by 8:00 AM, you aren't going to find a place to park in your assigned lot. The situation makes you angry because you believe that if you pay for a sticker, you should have a reasonable chance of finding a space to park. You see that there are unfilled lots reserved for faculty and staff next to the student parking lot, and you wonder why more spaces aren't allotted to students. You decide to write to the president of your college. You want her to direct parking and traffic services to give more spaces to students or else build a parking garage that will accommodate more vehicles.

But when you start talking to other students on campus, you begin to realize that the problem may be more complex than your first view of it. Your college has taken the position that the fewer students who drive to campus, the less traffic there will be on and around your campus. The administration wants more students to ride shuttle buses, form car pools, or bicycle to campus instead of driving alone. You also find out that faculty and staff members pay ten times as much as students for their parking permits, so they pay a very high premium for a guaranteed space—much too high for most students. If the president of your college is your primary audience, you first have to argue that a problem really exists. You have to convince the president that many students have no choice but to drive if they are to attend classes. You, for example, are willing to ride the shuttle buses, but they don't run often enough for you to make your classes, get back to your car that you left at home, and then drive to your job.

> Proposal arguments often include definition, causal, evaluation, narrative, and rebuttal arguments.

Next, you have to argue that your solution will solve the problem. An eight-story parking garage might be adequate to park all the cars of students who want to drive, but parking garages are very expensive to build. Even if a parking garage is the best solution, the question remains: Who is going to pay for it? Many problems in life could be solved if you had access to unlimited resources, but very few people have such resources at their command. It's not enough to have a solution that can resolve the problem. You have to be able to argue for the feasibility of your solution. If you want to argue that a parking garage is the solution to the parking problem on your campus, then you must also propose how the garage will be financed.

Components of Proposals

Proposal arguments are often complex and involve the kinds of arguments that are discussed in Chapters 5 through 9. Successful proposals have four major components:

1. *Identifying the problem.* Sometimes, problems are evident to your intended readers. If your city is constantly tearing up the streets and then leaving them for months without doing anything to

repair them, then you shouldn't have much trouble convincing the citizens of your city that streets should be repaired more quickly. But if you raise a problem that will be unfamiliar to most of your readers, you will first have to argue that the problem exists. Recall that in Chapter 1, Rachel Carson had to use several kinds of arguments in *Silent Spring* to make people aware of the dangers of pesticides, including narrative arguments, definition arguments, evaluation arguments, and arguments of comparison. Often, you will have to do similar work to establish exactly what problem you are attempting to solve. You will have to define the scope of the problem. Some of the bad roads in your city might be the responsibility of the state, not city government.

2. *Stating your proposed solution.* You need to have a clear, definite statement of exactly what you are proposing. You might want to place this statement near the beginning of your argument, or later, after you have considered and rejected other possible solutions.

3. *Convincing your readers with good reasons that your proposed solution is fair and will work.* When your readers agree that a problem exists and a solution should be found, your next task is to convince them that your solution is the best one to resolve the problem. If you're writing about the problem your city has in getting streets repaired promptly, then you need to analyze carefully the process that is involved in repairing streets. Sometimes there are mandatory delays so that competing bids can be solicited, and unexpected delays when tax revenue falls short of expectations. You should be able to put your finger on the problem in a detailed causal analysis. You should be able to make an evaluation argument that your solution is fair to all concerned. You should also be prepared to make arguments of rebuttal against other possible solutions.

4. *Demonstrating that your solution is feasible.* Your solution not only has to work; it must be feasible to implement. Malaysia effectively ended its drug problem by imposing mandatory death sentences for anyone caught selling even small amounts of drugs. Foreign nationals, teenagers, and grandmothers have all been hanged under this law. Malaysia came up with a solution for its purposes, but this solution probably would not work in most countries because the punishment seems too

extreme. If you want a parking garage built on your campus and you learn that no other funds can be used to construct it, then you have to be able to argue that the potential users of the garage will be willing to pay greatly increased fees for the convenience of parking on campus.

Building a Proposal Argument

Proposal arguments don't just fall out of the sky. For any problem of major significance—gun control, poverty, teenage pregnancy, abortion, capital punishment, drug legalization—you will find long histories of debate. An issue with a much shorter history can also quickly pile up mountains of arguments if it gains wide public attention. In 1972, for example, President Richard Nixon signed into law the Education Amendments Act, including Title IX, which prohibits sex discrimination at

Girls' sports leagues were a rarity in many communities just thirty years ago.

colleges that receive federal aid. Few people at the time guessed that Title IX would have the far-reaching consequences it did. When Title IX was first passed, 31,000 women participated in intercollegiate athletics. In the academic year 2002–2003, over 160,000 women athletes participated in varsity college sports. Even more striking is the increase in girls' participation in high school sports. The number of boy athletes has risen gradually from about 3.6 million in 1971 to approximately 4 million 2003–2004, while the number of girl athletes increased tenfold—from 294,000 in 1971 to 2.9 million in 2003–2004.

Proponents of Title IX are justifiably proud of the increased level of participation of women in varsity athletics. But for all the good that Title IX has done to increase athletic opportunities for women, critics blame Title IX for decreasing athletic opportunities for college men. According to the U.S. General Accounting Office (GAO), more than three hundred men's teams have been eliminated in college athletics since 1993. In 2000 the University of Miami dropped its men's swimming team, which had produced many Olympians, including Greg Louganis, who won gold medals in both platform and springboard diving in two consecutive Olympics. In 2001 the University of Nebraska also discontinued its men's swimming team, which had been in place since 1922, and the University of Kansas dropped men's swimming and tennis. Wrestling teams have been especially hard hit, dropping from 363 in 1981 to 192 in 1999. The effects were noticeable at the 2000 Olympics in Australia, where U.S. freestyle wrestlers failed to win any gold medals for the first time since 1968.

College and university administrators claim that they have no choice but to drop men's teams if more women's teams are added. Their belief comes not from the original Title IX legislation, which does not mention athletics, but from a 1979 clarification by the Office of Civil Rights (OCR), the agency that enforces Title IX. OCR set out three options for schools to comply with Title IX:

1. Bring the proportion of women in varsity athletics roughly equal to the percentage of women students.
2. Prove a "history and continuing practice" of creating new opportunities for women.
3. Prove that the school has done everything to "effectively accommodate" the athletic interests of women students.

University administrators have argued that the first option, known as *proportionality*, is the only one that can be argued successfully in a courtroom if the school is sued.

Proportionality is difficult to achieve at schools with football programs. Universities that play NCAA Division I-A football offer eighty-five football scholarships to men. Since there is no equivalent sport for women, football throws the gender statistics way out of balance. Defenders of football ask that it be exempted from Title IX because it is the cash cow that pays most of the bills for both men's and women's sports. Only a handful of women's basketball programs make money. All other women's sports are money losers and, like men's "minor" sports, depend on men's football and basketball revenues and student fees to pay their bills. College officials maintain that if they cut the spending for football, football will bring in less revenue, and thus all sports will be harmed.

Those who criticize Title IX argue that it assumes that women's interest in athletics is identical to men's. They point out that male students participate at much higher rates in intramural sports, which have no limitations on who can play. In contrast, women participate at much higher rates in music, dance, theater, and other extracurricular activities, yet Title IX is not being applied to those activities.

Defenders of Title IX argue that women's interest in athletics cannot be determined until they have had equal opportunities to participate. They claim Title IX is being used as a scapegoat for college administrators who do not want to make tough decisions. They point out that in 2001, women made up 53 percent of all college students but only 42 percent of all college athletes. At major colleges and universities, men still received 73 percent of the funds devoted to athletics. Without Title IX, in their view, schools would have no incentive to increase opportunities for women. The battle over Title IX is not likely to go away soon.

Sample Student Proposal Argument

Lifetime Cleveland Indians fan Brian Witkowski wrote this proposal argument in spring 2004 for a research paper assignment in the Rhetoric of Sports. Brian is a computer sciences major who enjoys playing video games and riding mountain bikes.

Brain Witkowski

Professor Mendelsohn

RHE 309K

2 May 2004

Need a Cure for Tribe Fever?

How About a Dip in the Lake?

Everyone is familiar with the Cleveland Indians'
Chief Wahoo logo and I do mean everyone, not just
Clevelanders. Across America one can see individuals
sporting the smiling mascot on traditional Indians caps
and jerseys, and recent trends in sports merchandise have
popularized new groovy multicolored Indians sportswear.
In fact, Indians merchandise recently was ranked just
behind the New York Yankees' merchandise in terms of
sales (Adams). Because of lucrative merchandising
contracts between major league baseball and Little
League, youth teams all over the country don Cleveland's
famous (or infamous) smiling Indian each season as fresh-
faced kids scamper onto the diamonds looking like mini
major leaguers ("MLBP"). Various incarnations of the
famous Chief Wahoo—described by sportswriter Rick
Telander as "the red-faced, big-nosed, grinning, drywall-
toothed moron who graces the peak of every Cleveland
Indians cap"—have been around since the 1940s (qtd. in
Eitzen). Now redder and even more cartoonish than the
original hooknosed, beige Indian with a devilish grin,
Wahoo often passes as a cheerful baseball buddy like the
San Diego Chicken or the St. Louis Cardinals' Fredbird.
(See Fig. 1.)

Witkowski 2

Fig. 1. Many youth baseball and softball teams use the Chief Wahoo logo, including teams with American Indian players.

Though defined by its distinctive logo, Cleveland baseball far preceded its famous mascot, changing from the Forest Citys to the Spiders to the Bluebirds/Blues to the Broncos to the Naps and finally to the Indians. Dubbed the Naps in 1903 in honor of their star player and manager Napoleon Lajoie, the team finally arrived at their current appellation in 1915. After Lajoie was traded, the team's president challenged sportswriters to devise a suitable "temporary" label for the floundering club. Publicity material has it that the writers decided on the Indians to celebrate Louis Sockalexis, a Penobscot Indian who played for the team from 1897 to 1899. With a heck of a batting average and the notability of being the first Native American in professional baseball, Sockalexis was immortalized by the new Cleveland label (Schneider 10-23). (Contrary to popular lore, some cite alternate—and less reverent—motivations behind the team's naming and point to a lack of Sockalexis publicity in period newspaper articles discussing the team's naming process [Staurowsky 95-97].) Almost ninety years later, the "temporary" name continues to raise eyebrows, both in its marketability and ideological questionability.

Witkowski 3

Today the logo is more than a little embarrassing. Since the high-profile actions of the American Indian Movement (AIM) in the 1970s, sports teams around the country—including the Indians—have been criticized and cajoled over their less than racially sensitive mascots. Native American groups question the sensitivity of such caricatured displays—not just because of grossly stereotyped mascots, but also because of what visual displays of team support say about Native American culture. Across the country, professional sporting teams, as well as high schools and colleges, perform faux rituals in the name of team spirit. As Tim Giago, publisher of The Lakota Times, a weekly South Dakotan Native American newspaper, has noted, "The sham rituals, such as the wearing of feathers, smoking of so-called peace pipes, beating of tomtoms, fake dances, horrendous attempts at singing Indian songs, the so-called war whoops, and the painted faces, address more than the issues of racism. They are direct attacks upon the spirituality of the Indian people" (qtd. in Wulf). Controversy over such performances still fuels the fire between activists and alumni at schools such as the University of Illinois at Champaign-Urbana where the "Fighting Illini" observe football halftimes with a performance by an (often white) student dressed as Chief Illiniwek. For fifteen years, the symbol has been dividing alumni, students, faculty, and administration; one alumnus has spent upward of ten thousand dollars to preserve the Chief (Selingo A20). Since 1969, when

Oklahoma disavowed its "Little Red" mascot, more than 600 school and minor league teams have followed a more ethnically sensitive trend and ditched their "tribal" mascots for ones less publicly explosive (Price). High-profile teams such as Berkeley, St. Johns University, and Miami (Ohio) University have buckled to public pressure, changing their team names from the Indians to the Cardinals (1972), the Redmen to the Red Storm (1993), and the Redskins to the Redhawks (1996), respectively. While many see such controversies as mere bowing to the PC pressures of the late twentieth and early twenty-first centuries, others see the mascot issue as a topic well worthy of debate.

Cleveland's own Chief Wahoo has far from avoided controversy. Protests regarding the controversial figure have plagued the city. Multiple conflicts between Wahoo devotees and dissenters have arisen around the baseball season. At the opening game of 1995, fifty Native Americans and supporters took stations around Jacobs Field to demonstrate against the use of the cartoonish smiling crimson mascot. While protestors saw the event as a triumph for first amendment rights and a strike against negative stereotyping, one befuddled fan stated, "I never thought of [Chief Wahoo] that way. It's all how you think of it" (Kropk). Arrests were made in 1998 when demonstrators from the United Church of Christ burned a three-foot Chief Wahoo doll in effigy ("Judge"). Wedded to their memorabilia, fans proudly stand behind their Indian as others lobby vociferously for its removal. Splitting government officials, fans, social and religious groups, this issue draws hostility from both sides of the argument. In 2000 Cleveland Mayor Michael White came out publicly against the team mascot, joining an already established group of religious leaders, laypersons, and civil rights activists who had demanded Wahoo's retirement. African American religious and civic leaders such as the Rev. Gregory A. Jacobs had been speaking out throughout the 1990s and highlighting the absurdity of minority groups who embrace the Wahoo symbol. "Each of us has had to fight its [sic] own battle, quite frankly," Jacobs stated. "We cannot continue to live in this kind of hypocrisy that says, Yes, we are in solidarity with my [sic] brothers and sisters, yet we continue to exploit them" (qtd. in Briggs). These words clash with those of individuals such as former Indians owner Dick Jacobs, who said amidst protest that the Wahoo logo would remain as long as he was principal owner of the club (Bauman 1) and a delegate of the East Ohio Conference of the United Methodist Church, who quipped, "I would cease being a United Methodist before I would cease wearing my Chief Wahoo clothing" (Briggs).

This controversy also swirls outside of the greater Cleveland area. Individual newspapers in Nebraska, Kansas, Minnesota, and Oregon have banned the printing of Native American sports symbols and team names such as the Braves, Indians, or Redmen (Wulf), while the Seattle Times went so far as to digitally remove the Wahoo symbol from images of the Cleveland baseball cap

("Newspaper"). As other teams make ethnically sensitive and image conscious choices to change their mascots, Cleveland stands firm on its resolve to retain the Chief. Despite internal division and public ridicule fueled by the team icon, the city refuses to budge. Clevelanders consequently appear as insensitive and backward as those who continue to support the Redmen, Redskins, or Illini.

As the city of Cleveland continues to enjoy its recent improved image and downtown revitalization, must the plague of the Wahoo controversy continue? As a native of Cleveland, I understand the power of "Tribe Fever" and the unabashed pride one feels when wearing Wahoo garb during a winning (or losing) season. Often it is not until we leave northeastern Ohio that we realize the negative image that Wahoo projects. What then can Cleveland do to simultaneously save face and bolster its burgeoning positive city image? I propose that the team finally change the "temporary" Indians label. In a city so proud of its diverse ethnic heritage—African American, Italian American, and Eastern European American to name a few—why stand as a bearer of retrograde ethnic politics? Cleveland should take this opportunity to link its positive midwestern image to the team of which it is so proud. Why not take the advice of the 1915 Cleveland management and change the team's "temporary" name? I propose a shift to the Cleveland Lakers.

The city's revival in the last twenty years has embraced the geographic and aesthetic grandeur of Lake

Erie. Disavowing its "mistake on the lake" moniker of
the late 1970s, Cleveland has traded aquatic pollution
fires for a booming lakeside business district.
Attractions such as the Great Lakes Science Center, the
Rock and Roll Hall of Fame, and the new Cleveland Browns
Stadium take advantage of the beauty of the landscape
and take back the lake. Why not continue this trend
through one of the city's biggest and highest-profile
moneymakers: professional baseball? By changing the
team's name to the Lakers, the city would gain national
advertisement for one of its major selling points, while
simultaneously announcing a new ethnically inclusive
image that is appropriate to our wonderfully diverse
city. It would be a public relations triumph for the
city.

Of course this call will be met with many
objections. Why do we have to buckle to pressure? Do we
not live in a free country? What the fans and citizens
alike need to keep in mind is that ideological pressures
would not be the sole motivation for this move. Yes,
retiring Chief Wahoo would take Cleveland off of AIM's
hit list. Yes, such a move would promote a kinder and
gentler Cleveland. At the same time, however, such a
gesture would work toward uniting the community. So much
civic division exists over this issue that a renaming
could help start to heal these old wounds.

Additionally, this type of change could bring added
economic prosperity to the city. First, a change in name
will bring a new wave of team merchandise. Licensed

Witkowski 8

sports apparel enjoys more than a 10 billion dollar
annual retail business in the U.S., and teams have
repeatedly proven that new uniforms and logos can provide
new capital. After all, a new logo for the Seattle
Mariners bolstered severely slumping merchandise sales
(Lefton). Wahoo devotees need not panic; the booming
vintage uniform business will keep him alive, as is
demonstrated by the current ability to purchase replica
1940s jerseys with the old Indians logo. Also, good press
created by this change will hopefully help increase
Cleveland tourism. If the good will created by the
Cleveland Lakers can prove half as profitable as The Drew
Carey Show or the Rock and Roll Hall of Fame, then local
businesses will be humming a happy tune. Finally, if
history repeats itself, a change to a more culturally
inclusive logo could, in and of itself, prove to be a
cash cow. When Miami University changed from the Redskins
to the Redhawks, it saw alumni donations skyrocket to an
unprecedented 25 million dollars (Price). Perhaps a less
divisive mascot would prove lucrative to the ball club,
city, and players themselves. (Sluggers with inoffensive
logos make excellent spokesmen.)

Perhaps this proposal sounds far fetched: Los
Angeles may seem to have cornered the market on Lakers.
But where is their lake? (The Lakers were formerly the
Minneapolis Lakers, where the name makes sense in the
"Land of 10,000 Lakes.") Various professional and
collegiate sports teams—such as baseball's San Francisco
Giants and football's New York Giants—share the same team

name, so licensing should not be an issue. If Los Angeles has qualms about sharing the name, perhaps Cleveland could persuade them to become the Surfers or the Stars—after all, Los Angeles players seem to spend as much time on the big and small screen as on the court.

Now is the perfect time for Cleveland to make this jump. Sportscasters continue to tout the revitalized young Cleveland team as an up-and-coming contender. Perhaps a new look will help usher in a new era of Cleveland baseball. The team has already begun to minimize the presence of Wahoo on new Wahoo-less caps and jerseys, and the owners should introduce a new look and ethnically sensitive image to its upstart team. Like expansion teams such as the Florida Marlins and the Arizona Diamondbacks, Cleveland's new look could bring with it a vital sense of civic pride and a World Series ring to boot. Through various dry spells, the Cleveland Indians institution has symbolically turned to the descendants of Sockalexis, asking for good will or a latter-generation Penobscot slugger (Fleitz 3). Perhaps the best way to win good will, fortunes, and their first World Series title since 1948 would be to eschew a grinning life-size Chief Wahoo for the new and improved Cleveland Laker, an oversized furry monster sporting water wings, cleats, and a catcher's mask. His seventh-inning-stretch show could include an air guitar solo with a baseball bat as he quietly reminds everyone that the Rock Hall is just down the street. Go Lakers and go Cleveland!

Witkowski 10

Works Cited

Adams, David. "Cleveland Indians Investors Watch Case on

Native American Names." Akron Beacon Journal

6 Apr. 1999. LexisNexis Academic. LexisNexis.

Perry-Casteñeda Lib., U of Texas at Austin. 20 Apr.

2004 <http://www.lexisnexis.com/>.

Bauman, Michael. "Indians Logo, Mascot Are the Real

Mistakes." Milwaukee Journal Sentinel 23 Oct. 1997:

Sports 1.

Briggs, David. "Churches Go to Bat Against Chief Wahoo."

Cleveland Plain Dealer 25 Aug. 2000: 1A.

Eitzen, D. Stanley and Maxine Baca Zinn. "The Dark Side

of Sports Symbols." USA Today Magazine Jan. 2001:

48.

Fleitz, David L. Louis Sockalexis: The First Cleveland

Indian. Jefferson: McFarland, 2002.

"Judge Dismisses Charges Against City in Wahoo Protest."

Associated Press 6 Aug. 2001. LexisNexis Academic.

LexisNexis. Perry-Casteñeda Lib., U of Texas at

Austin. 19 Apr. 2004 <http://www.lexisnexis.com/>.

Kropk, M. R. "Chief Wahoo Protestors Largely Ignored by

Fans." Austin American Statesman 6 May 1995: D4.

Lefton, Terry. "Looks Are Everything: For New

Franchises, Licensing Battles Must Be Won Long

Before the Team Even Takes the Field." Sport

89 (May 1998): 32.

"MLBP Reaches Youth League Apparel Agreements with

Majestic Athletic, Outdoor Cap." 25 June 2004.

Major League Baseball. 28 June 2004.

Witkowski 11

<http://mlb.mlb.com/NASApp/mlb/mlb/news/mlb_press_
release.jsp?ymd=20040625&content_id=780105&vkey=pr_
mlb&fext=.jsp>.

"Newspaper Edits Cleveland Indian Logo from Cap Photo."
Associated Press 31 Mar. 1997. LexisNexis Academic.
LexisNexis. Perry-Casteñeda Lib., U of Texas at
Austin. 17 Apr. 2004 <http://www.lexisnexis.com/>.

Price, S. L. "The Indian Wars." Sports Illustrated
4 Mar. 2002: 66+. Expanded Academic ASAP. Thomson
Gale. Perry-Casteñeda Lib., U of Texas at Austin.
20 Apr. 2004 <http://www.gale.com/>.

Schneider, Russell. The Cleveland Indians Encyclopedia.
Philadelphia: Temple UP, 1996.

Selingo, Jeffrey. "An Honored Symbol to Some, a Racist
Mascot to Others." Chronicle of Higher Education
18 June 2004: A20-23.

Staurowsky, Ellen J. "Sockalexis and the Making of the
Myth at the Core of the Cleveland's 'Indian'
Image." Team Spirits: The Native American Mascots
Controversy. Eds. C. Richard King and Charles
Fruehling Springwood. Lincoln: U of Nebraska P,
2001. 82-106.

Wulf, Steve. "A Brave Move." Sports Illustrated
24 Feb. 1992: 7.

Steps to a Proposal Argument

Step **1** Make a claim

Make a proposal claim advocating a specific change or course of action.

Formula

- *We should (or should not) do* SOMETHING. In an essay of five or fewer pages, it's difficult to propose solutions to big problems such as continuing poverty. Proposals that address local problems are not only more manageable; sometimes, they get actual results.

Examples

- The process of registering for courses (getting appointments at the health center, getting email accounts) should be made more efficient.
- Your community should create bicycle lanes to make bicycling safer and to reduce traffic (build a pedestrian overpass over a dangerous street; make it easier to recycle newspapers, bottles, and cans).

Step **2** Identify the problem

- What exactly is the problem?
- Who is most affected by the problem?
- What causes the problem?
- Has anyone tried to do anything about it? If so, why haven't they succeeded?
- What is likely to happen in the future if the problem isn't solved?

Step **3** Propose your solution

State your solution as specifically as you can.

- What exactly do you want to achieve?
- How exactly will your solution work?
- Can it be accomplished quickly, or will it have to be phased in over a few years?
- Has anything like it been tried elsewhere?
- Who will be involved?
- Can you think of any reasons why your solution might not work?
- How will you address those arguments?
- Can you think of any ways of strengthening your proposed solution in light of those possible criticisms?

Step **4** Consider other solutions

- What other solutions have been or might be proposed for this problem, including doing nothing?
- What are the advantages and disadvantages of those solutions?
- Why is your solution better?

Step **5** Examine the feasibility of your solution

- How easy is your solution to implement?
- Will the people most affected by your solution be willing to go along with it? (For example, lots of things can be accomplished if enough people volunteer, but groups often have difficulty getting enough volunteers to work without pay.)
- If it costs money, how do you propose to pay for it?
- Who is most likely to reject your proposal because it is not practical enough?
- How can you convince your readers that your proposal can be achieved?

Step **6** Analyze your potential readers

- Whom are you writing for?
- How interested will your readers be in this problem?
- How much does this problem affect them?
- How would your solution benefit them directly and indirectly?

Step **7** Write a draft

Define the problem
- Set out the issue or problem. You might begin by telling about your experience or the experience of someone you know. You might need to argue for the seriousness of the problem, and you might have to give some background on how it came about.

Present your solution
- You might want to set out your solution first and explain how it will work, then consider other possible solutions and argue that yours is better; or you might want to set out other possible solutions first, argue that they don't solve the problem or are not feasible, and then present your solution.

- Make clear the goals of your solution. Many solutions cannot solve problems completely. If you are proposing a solution for juvenile crime in your neighborhood, for example, you cannot expect to eliminate all juvenile crime.
- Describe in detail the steps in implementing your solution and how they will solve the problem you have identified. You can impress your readers by the care with which you have thought through this problem.
- Explain the positive consequences that will follow from your proposal. What good things will happen and what bad things will be avoided if your advice is taken?

Argue that your proposal is feasible

- Your proposal for solving the problem is a truly good idea only if it can be put into practice. If people have to change the ways they are doing things now, explain why they would want to change. If your proposal costs money, you need to identify exactly where the money would come from.

Conclude with a call for action

- Your conclusion should be a call for action. You should put your readers in a position such that if they agree with you, they will take action. You might restate and emphasize what exactly they need to do.

Step 8 Revise, edit, proofread

- For detailed instructions, see Chapter 12.
- For a checklist to use to evaluate your draft, see pages 217–222.

CHAPTER 12

Revision: Putting It All Together

S killed writers know that one secret to writing well is rethinking and rewriting. Even the best writers often have to reconsider their aims and methods in the course of writing and to revise several times to get the result they want. If you want to become a better writer, therefore, take three words of advice: revise, revise, revise.

The biggest trap you can fall into is seeking a fast resolution and skipping revision. The quality of an argument varies in direct proportion to the amount of time devoted to it. You cannot revise a paper effectively if you finish it at the last minute. You have to allow your ideas to develop, and you have to allow what you write to sit for a while before you go back through it. So try your best to write your arguments over a period of several days. Be patient. Test your ideas against your reading and the informal advice of trusted friends and advisors. And once you are satisfied with what you have written, allow at least a day to let what you write cool off. With a little time you gain enough distance to "resee" it, which, after all, is what revision means. To be able to revise effectively, you have to plan your time.

> Revise, revise, revise.

Most of all, keep your eyes focused on the big picture, especially early in the process of making your argument. Don't sweat the small stuff at the beginning. If you see a word that's wrong or if you are unsure about a punctuation mark, you may be tempted to drop everything and fix the errors first. Don't do that: If you start searching for the errors early in the process, then it's hard to get back to the larger concerns that ultimately make your argument successful or unsuccessful.

Over time you have to develop effective strategies for revising if you're going to be successful. These strategies include the following:

1. Keep your goals in mind—but stay flexible about them.
2. Read as you write.
3. Take the perspective of your reader.

211

4. Focus on your argument.

5. Attend to your style and proofread carefully.

In addition, plan to get responses to what you write in time for you to revise your work based on those responses.

Keep Your Goals in Mind—But Stay Flexible

People who argue effectively know what they want to achieve. They understand their readers' needs, know what they want to accomplish, and keep their goals in mind as they write and revise. But they also know that writing about a subject likely will change how they think about it, often in productive ways. Thus they remain flexible enough to modify their goals as they write. You may begin writing an argument because you have strong feelings about an issue; in fact, a rush of strong feelings can often motivate you to compose a strong statement at one sitting. That's good. But at some point before you commit what you write to a final version, give yourself a chance to rethink your goals. It may be that you can make a better argument in the end if you leave yourself open to adjustments in what you are arguing and to whom you are arguing it.

Consider, for example, the case of a student at a northeastern university, Nate Bouton (not his real name), who arrived on his campus in the midst of a controversy in 2000 over the raising of the Confederate Battle Flag over the South Carolina state capitol building. You may recall the controversy: In 1999 the NAACP, in the conviction that the Confederate flag was a symbol of racism, called on citizens to boycott South Carolina tourist venues until the flag no longer was displayed over the state capitol building. After contentious debate and considerable thought, legislators decided to remove the flag. On July 1, 2000, it was taken down and displayed instead in a nearby memorial to Confederate soldiers. But public opinion within and outside South Carolina remained divided: Some citizens continued to ask that the flag be restored to the capitol, while others demanded that it be removed from the Confederate memorial as well.

As a native of South Carolina, Nate felt that students at his university were coming to uninformed, premature conclusions, which stemmed from faulty assumptions about the flag issue in particular and South Carolinians in general. When the players on the baseball team at Nate's university decided not to play previously scheduled games in South Carolina, he was ready to join the argument. He decided to write about the flag issue, in his words, "in order to straighten people out. People in the northeast just didn't know the facts and that ticked me off. I wanted to write an argument supporting what was being done in South Carolina."

Nate's interest and enthusiasm for his topic generated a series of notes and several draft paragraphs, and he was able to explain his goals forcefully in class. Here is what he wrote when his teacher asked for an account of what he planned to do in his essay: "I would like to evaluate the decision to remove the Confederate Battle Flag from the statehouse dome in Columbia, South Carolina. I do not believe it was handled properly and I do not think the valiant soldiers that fought in the war between the states and defended their way of life should be dishonored by a bunch of politicians who use people's feelings to their disadvantage. Now that politicians have won a battle, many more are springing up all over the South wanting to destroy a way of life and turn it into a politically correct zombie. I want to show that the flag is about pride, not prejudice."

But as Nate wrote a first draft, his goals gradually changed. In the course of discussing his ideas with his classmates and with his friends, he discovered that they had a number of what he considered to be misperceptions. They did not know much about the South and its traditions, and their conclusions on the flag issue, he was convinced, followed from their lack of knowledge. Nate also learned that several of his friends and classmates had different notions of what the Confederate flag stood for. African Americans in his dorm explained that when they stopped at a restaurant and saw the Confederate flag in the window, they understood from experience that it meant, "We don't want black people eating here."

Nate decided that one of his goals would be to educate people about the thinking of many South Carolinians and that the Confederate flag was not necessarily a symbol of racism. He would defend the decision of the South Carolina legislature, which had attempted to find some middle ground on the issue. Rather than calling for the return of the flag to the capitol, he would support the legislature's decision to raise the flag only at the monument to Confederate soldiers.

Read as You Write

Nate's conversations with his friends indicated to him that he had to become more knowledgeable before he could complete his argument. He continued reading in the library as he developed his points, using many of the search strategies we discuss in Chapter 15. Nate's decision reflects an important fact about effective arguments: They usually emerge from substantial knowledge. If you have not explored your topic fully, then you must read widely about the subject before going further. Not only will your reading alert you to arguments that you can cite in support of your own points, but it will also clarify for you the thinking of those who disagree with you so that you can take into account their points of view. Finally, reading will allow you to take seriously what we advise early in this book: that arguing is often more a contribution to a continuing conversation than a final resolution of all doubts, and that you can sometimes do far more good by persuading people to cooperate with you than by fervently opposing them.

Nate's reading gave him a number of insights into the flag issue. He learned about the original design of the flag, which was related to the crosses of St. Andrew and St. George. He also learned about the history of the flag's display at the capitol—including the fact that the flag was first raised there in 1962, in the midst of the civil rights movement. He also found that George Wallace began displaying the Battle Flag in Alabama shortly after his confrontations with Robert Kennedy over the issue of segregation. Nate read about the NAACP and the reasons for its opposition to the flag. He sampled Web sites that supported the flag's display over the capitol (including one that quoted the famous historian Shelby Foote), and he considered others that opposed that position. After several hours of note taking, Nate was ready to assemble a serious draft.

Take the Perspective of Your Reader

In most first drafts, it makes sense to get your ideas on paper without thinking about readers. Such a practice makes positive use of strong feelings and reveals the skeleton of an argument. (Nate's first draft expressed ideas that he had been formulating for some time.) The first draft, however, is only the beginning. You need to take time to think about how your argument will come across to your readers.

First, pretend you are someone who is either uninformed about your subject or informed but holding an opposing viewpoint. If possible think of an actual person and pretend to be that person. (Nate could easily imagine a person holding an opposing view because he knew people in his dorm who disagreed with him on this issue.) Then read your argument aloud all the way through. When you read aloud, you often hear clunky phrases and catch errors, but do no more in this stage than put checks in the margins that you can return to later. Once again, you don't want to get bogged down with the little stuff. Rather, what you are after in this stage is getting an overall sense of how well you accomplished what you set out to do. Think in particular about these things:

1. *Your claim.* When you finish reading, can you summarize in one sentence what you are arguing? If you cannot, then you need to focus your claim. Then ask yourself what's at stake in your claim. Who benefits by what you are arguing? Who doesn't? How will readers react to what you are arguing? If what you are arguing is obvious to everyone and if all or nearly all would agree with you, then you need to identify an aspect on which people would disagree and restate your claim.

2. *Your good reasons.* What are the good reasons for your claim? Would a reader have any trouble identifying them? Will those readers be likely to accept your reasons? What evidence is offered to support these good reasons and how is the evidence relevant to the claim (the "so what?" question in Chapter 2)? Note any places where you might add evidence and any places where you need to explain why the evidence is relevant.

3. *Your representation of yourself.* To the extent you can, forget for a moment that you wrote what you are reading. What impression do you have of you, the writer? Is the writer believable? Trustworthy? Has the writer done his or her homework on the issue? Does the writer take an appropriate tone? Note any places where you can strengthen your credibility as a writer.

4. *Your consideration of your readers.* Do you give enough background if your readers are unfamiliar with the issue? Do you acknowledge opposing views that they might have? Do you appeal to common values that you share with them? Note any places where you might do more to address the concerns of your readers.

Here is a sample paragraph from a first draft of Nate's essay on the Confederate flag:

The Confederate Battle Flag is not a racist sign; it is the most powerful and widely recognized symbol of Southern valor and independence. The flag honors the Confederate dead, who fought for their way of life and defended their homes from Northern aggression in the War Between the States. People today owe it to the men and women who fought for their belief in liberty and states' rights, a sacrifice rarely seen today. People ought to honor the memories of the Confederate fallen just as they remember people involved in every other war. While people are making monuments to war dead in Washington, including monuments to those who died in Vietnam and Korea, there are those who are trying to dishonor Confederate dead by taking the Battle Flag from the Confederate monument in Columbia.

When Nate put himself in the shoes of his readers, he quickly saw the need for substantial changes in that paragraph. He still felt strongly about his belief in the symbolism of the flag, but he also realized that people who disagreed with him—the people he was trying to persuade—would not appreciate his use of the term "War Between the States" because they would suspect him of thinking that the war was not fought over the issue of slavery and accuse him of resisting any racist notions associated with the flag. "States' rights" is a phrase that is honorable, but not when one of the rights is the right to own slaves. Here is how he revised his paragraph:

The Confederate Battle Flag is not a racist sign; it is the most powerful and widely recognized symbol of Southern valor and independence. It is true, unfortunately, that many racists today display the Confederate flag. But that unfortunate truth should not permit us to discontinue to honor the flag, any more than the use of the cross by the Ku Klux Klan should permit us to discontinue honoring the cross in our churches. It is also true that the Civil War was conducted in large part because of the issue of slavery, that many people therefore associate the Confederate flag with white supremacy, and that many whites during the Civil Rights era flew the flag as a sign of resistance to the end of segregation. But the Civil War was also fought for other reasons in the South by many people who neither owned slaves nor who had any use for slavery. The flag honors the Confederate dead who fought for their way of life and who believed they were defending their homes from Northern aggression. People today owe it to those who fought for their belief in liberty (our nation's most basic belief) to permit their monuments to include the flag they fought under. The Confederate flag needs to be restored to its original symbolism, and that can only take place if it continues to be displayed in honorable places. To change the Confederate monument in Columbia by taking away the Confederate flag would be to dishonor those who died under it. People ought to honor the memories of the Confederate fallen just as they remember people involved in every other war. Shelby Foote, the well known Southern historian and author of a three-volume history of the Civil War, said it best: "Many among the finest people this country ever produced died [under the Confederate flag]. To take it as a symbol of evil is a misrepresentation" (www.southerninitiative.com, April 30, 2001).

Do you think Nate's revisions were successful in answering his reader's objections and in creating a more effective ethos? How will his quotation from the Southern historian go over with his Northern readers?

REVISION CHECKLIST

 # Focus on Your Argument

1. Find your main claim.

What kind of claim is it? Are you writing a proposal, an evaluation, a rebuttal, a narrative, or what? What things follow from that? (All arguments, as we have emphasized in Chapters 6 through 11, tend to develop in certain ways, depending on their kind.) Nate's argument that the Confederate flag ought to be permitted to remain on the Confederate monument (but not over the state capitol building) is a proposal argument. Identifying the type of claim helps you to think about how it might be developed further (see Chapter 11).

2. How will you support your claim?

What good reasons will you use? Will you use definitions, an evaluation, a causal argument, a list of consequences, a comparison or contrast, or a combination of these? Nate's paragraph, one segment of his overall proposal, offers a definition: "The Confederate Battle Flag is not a racist sign; it is the most powerful and widely recognized symbol of Southern valor and independence." If Nate can get his readers to accept that definition—that "good reason" for agreeing to his overall thesis—he will have gone a long way toward achieving his goals. It may take him several paragraphs to argue for the definition, but eventually it will be worth the effort. Nate might also use other good reasons to support his overall position on the flag issue: the good consequences that will follow if his advice is heeded (e.g., goodwill; an end to polarization in the community), the bad consequences that might be avoided (e.g., continued controversy and divisiveness in South Carolina), the useful comparisons or contrasts that can be cited as support (e.g., the comparison between the Klan's use of the cross and racists' use of the Confederate flag), and so forth. Altogether, those good reasons will make up a complete and satisfactory argument.

3. Analyze your organization.

Turn to one of the writing guides at the end of Chapters 6 though 11 that best fits your argument (or Chapter 4 if you are doing an rhetorical analysis or Chapter 5 if you are doing a visual analysis). The guides will help you determine what kind of overall organization you need. For example, if you have a definition argument, go to the Steps at the end of Chapter 6. You should be able to identify the criteria for your definition. How many criteria do you offer? Where are they located? Are they clearly connected to your claim? In what order should they be offered?

In addition, think about other effective ordering principles. Since readers often remember things that come first or last, do you want to put your strongest good reasons early and repeat them toward the end? Or do you want to build toward a climactic effect by ordering your reasons from least important to most important? Can you group similar ideas? Should you move from least controversial to most controversial? Or from most familiar to least familiar?

4. Examine your evidence.

If you noted places where you could use more evidence when you first read through your draft, now is the time to determine what kinds of additional evidence you need. Evidence can come in the shape of examples, personal experiences, comparisons, statistics, calculations, quotations, and other kinds of data that a reader will find relevant and compelling. Decide what you need and put it in.

5. Consider your title and introduction.

Many students don't think much about titles, but titles are important: A good title makes the reader want to discover what you have to say. Be as specific as you can in your title and, if possible, suggest your stance. In the introduction get off to a fast start and convince your reader to keep reading. You may need to establish right away that a problem exists. You may have to give some background. You may need to discuss an argument presented by someone else. But above all, you want to convince your reader to keep reading.

6. Consider your conclusion.

Restating your claim usually isn't the best way to finish. The worst endings say something like "in my paper I've said this." Think about whether there is a summarizing point you can make, an implication you can draw, or another example you can include that sums up your position. If you are writing a proposal, your ending might be a call for action or a challenge. If you have a telling quotation from an authority, sometimes that can make an effective clincher.

7. Analyze the visual aspects of your text.

Do the font and layout you selected look attractive? Do you use the same font throughout? If you use more than one font, have you done so consistently? Would headings and subheadings help to identify key sections of your argument? If you include statistical data, would charts be effective? Would illustrations help to establish key points? For example, a map could be very useful if you are arguing about the location of a proposed new highway.

REVISION CHECKLIST

 # Focus on Your Style and Proofread Carefully

In our advice about revision, we have ignored so far issues of style and correctness. We did that not because we think style and correctness are unimportant but because some people forget that revision can involve much more than those things. In your final pass through your text, you should definitely concentrate on the style of your argument and eliminate as many errors as you can. Here are some suggestions that may help.

1. Check the connections between sentences.

Notice how your sentences are connected. If you need to signal the relationship from one sentence to the next, use a transitional word or phrase. For example, compare the following:

> *Silent Spring* was widely translated and inspired legislation on the environment in nearly all industrialized nations. *Silent Spring* changed the way we think about the environment. ⟶

> *Silent Spring* was widely translated and inspired legislation on the environment in nearly all industrialized nations. **Moreover**, the book changed the way we think about the environment.

2. Check your sentences for emphasis.

When most people talk, they emphasize points by speaking louder, using gestures, and repeating themselves. You should know that it is possible to emphasize ideas in writing too.

■ **Things in main clauses tend to stand out more than things in subordinate clauses.** Compare these two sentences: "Kroger, who studied printing in Germany, later organized a counterfeiting ring"; and "Before he organized a counterfeiting ring, Kroger studied printing in Germany." These two sentences contain exactly the same information, but they emphasize different things. The second sentence suggests Kroger studied printing in order to organize a counterfeiting ring. Signal what you want to emphasize by putting it into main clauses, and put less important information in subordinate clauses or in modifying phrases. (If two things are equally important, signal that by using coordination: "Kroger studied printing in Germany; he later organized a counterfeiting ring.")

■ **Things at the beginning and at the end of sentences tend to stand out more than things in the middle.** Compare these three sentences: "After he studied printing in Germany, Kroger organized a counterfeiting ring"; "Kroger, after he studied printing in Germany, organized a counterfeiting ring"; and "Kroger organized a counterfeiting ring after he studied printing in Germany." All three sentences contain the exact same words and use the same main clause and subordinate clause, but they emphasize different things, depending on which items are placed in the beginning, middle, and end.

■ **Use punctuation for emphasis.** Dashes add emphasis; parentheses de-emphasize. Compare these two sentences: "Kroger (who studied printing in Germany) organized a counterfeiting ring"; and "Kroger—who studied printing in Germany—organized a counterfeiting ring."

3. Eliminate wordiness.

Drafts often contain unnecessary words. When you revise, often you can find long expressions that can easily be shortened ("at this point in time" ⟶ "now"). Sometimes you become repetitive, saying about the same thing you said a sentence or two before. See how many words you can take out without losing the meaning.

4. Use active verbs.

Anytime you can use a verb besides a form of *be* (*is, are, was, were*), take advantage of the opportunity to make your style more lively. Sentences that begin with "There is (are)" and "It is" often have better alternatives:

> "It is true that exercising a high degree of quality control in the manufacture of our products will be an incentive for increasing our market share."
> ⟶ "If we pay attention to quality when we make our products, more people will buy them."

Notice too that active verbs often cut down on wordiness.

5. Know what your spelling checker can and can't do.

Spelling checkers are the greatest invention since peanut butter. They turn up many typos and misspellings that are hard to catch. But spelling checkers do not catch wrong words (e.g., "to much" should be "too much"), incorrect word endings ("three dog" should be "three dogs"), and other, similar errors. You still have to proofread carefully to eliminate misspellings and word choice errors.

6. Use your handbook to check items of mechanics and usage.

Nothing hurts your credibility more than leaving mechanics and usage errors in what you write. A handbook will help you identify the most common errors and answer questions of usage. Readers probably shouldn't make such harsh judgments when they find errors, but in real life they do. We've seen job application letters tossed in the rejected pile because an applicant made a single, glaring error. The conventions of punctuation, mechanics, and usage aren't that difficult to master, and you'll become a lot more confident when you know the rules or at least know how to look up the rules. You should also trust your ear: If you noticed that a sentence was hard to read aloud or that it doesn't sound right, think about how you might rephrase it. If a sentence seems too long, then you might break it into two or more sentences. If you notice a string of short sentences that sound choppy, then you might combine them. If you notice any run-on sentences or sentence fragments, fix them.

Get Help on Your Draft

Don't trust your own ears (and eyes) exclusively. Most good writers let someone else—a trusted advisor or several of them—read what they write before they share it with their audience. You too need to develop a way of getting advice that you can use to shape your revisions. Be sure to leave enough time for someone else to review your work and for you to make revisions.

A good reviewer is one who is willing to give you her time and honest opinion, and who knows enough about the subject of your paper to make useful suggestions. A roommate or close friend can serve, but often such a friend will be reluctant to give negative evaluations. Perhaps you can develop a relationship with people with whom you can share drafts—you read theirs; they read yours. Whomever you choose, give that person time to read your work carefully and sympathetically. You need not take every piece of advice you get, but you do need to consider suggestions with an open mind.

PART 3

Making Effective Arguments

Designing, Presenting, and Documenting

Advances in digital technology have made it possible for almost anyone to publish color images along with text, both on paper and on the World Wide Web. Programs such as PowerPoint make it easy to prepare visuals for oral presentations. Furthermore, many students now routinely publish animations, audio, and video clips along with images on Web sites. What is now possible using relatively common and inexpensive computers and software is staggering in comparison to what could be done just a decade ago.

But if new technologies for writing have given us a great deal of potential power, they have also presented us with a variety of challenges. Designing a piece of writing wasn't much of an issue with a typewriter. You could either single or double space, and increase or decrease the margins. But today with a word processing program you can change the typeface, insert illustrations, create charts and other graphics, and print in color. If you are publishing on the Web, you can introduce sound, animation, and video. Sometimes it seems like there are too many choices.

Likewise when you do research on the Web, you often find too much rather than too little. Much of what you find is of little value for a serious argument. And if the physical act of making changes to what you write is easier with a computer, the mental part is still hard work. Even experienced writers struggle with getting what they write into the shape they want it. In the chapters in Part 3, we offer you strategies for creating effective arguments using both new and old technologies.

CHAPTER 13

Effective Visual Design

Arguments do not communicate with words alone. Even written arguments that do not contain graphics or images have a look and feel that also communicates meaning. In daily life we infer a great deal from what we see. Designers are well aware that, like people, all writing has a body language that often communicates a strong message. Designers organize words, graphics, and images to achieve a desired effect for a particular audience and purpose. The principles of graphic design are not so very different from the rhetorical principles that were discussed in the previous chapters. It all has to do with understanding how particular effects can be achieved for particular readers in particular situations. Becoming more attentive to design will make your arguments more effective.

Perhaps the most important thing to know about design is that there are very few hard-and-fast rules. As for all arguments, everything depends on the rhetorical situation. All your decisions hinge on your purpose, your subject, the type of document you are writing, your intended audience(s), and how you want your reader(s) to perceive you. Sometimes, you succeed by breaking the rules.

Design Basics

Before discussing principles of graphic design, it is important to think about how language and visual design work. Language is extremely well adapted for describing things that fall into a linear order. Because humans perceive time as linear, language allows us from a very young age to tell stories. But when you describe a place, you have to decide what to tell about first. Suppose someone asks you how your house is laid out. You might begin by saying that inside the front door, there is an entryway that goes to the living room. The dining room is on the right, and the kitchen is adjacent. On the left is a hallway, which connects to two bedrooms on the right, one on the left, and a bathroom at the end. But if you draw a floor plan, you can show at once how the house is arranged. That's the basic difference between describing with spoken language and describing with visual images. Spoken language forces you to put things in a *sequence*; visual design forces you to arrange things in *space*. Written language—especially writing on a computer—permits you to do both: to use sequence and space simultaneously. Some of the same principles apply for both language and design when you write. Three of the most important groups of design principles are arrangement, consistency, and contrast.

Arrangement

Many people get through high school by mastering the five-paragraph theme. When they get the assignment, they first have to figure out exactly three points about the topic. Then they write an introduction announcing that they have three points, write a paragraph on each of the three points, and conclude with a paragraph that repeats the three points. It

> Place every item on a page in a visual relationship with the other items.

is amazing how useful that formula is. The basic structure of announcing the subject, developing it sequentially, and concluding with a summary works well enough in a great many circumstances—from business letters to short reports. Even many PhD dissertations are five-paragraph themes on a larger scale.

But if you translate the five-paragraph formula to space, it's not so simple. Think about putting it on a business card. How would you do it?

Introduction		Point 1
	My Topic	
Conclusion	Point 3	Point 2

Your eyes naturally go to the center, where the topic is boldfaced. But where do they go after that? It's not a given that a reader will start in the upper left-hand corner and go clockwise around the card.

Let's switch to an example of a business card.

(919) 684-2741	23 Maple Street Durham, NC 27703

Todd Smith

Westin Associates	Management Consulting

Again, the name in the middle is where you go first, but where do your eyes go after that? The problem is that nothing on the card has any obvious visual relationship with anything else.

The way beginning designers often solve this problem is to put everything in the center. This strategy forces you to think about what is most important, and you usually put that at the top. On the next card, the information is grouped so that the relationship of the elements is clear. One of the most important design tools—white space—separates the main elements.

Todd Smith

Westin Associates

Management Consulting

23 Maple Street
Durham, NC 27703
(919) 684-2741

But centering everything isn't the only solution for showing the relationship of elements. Another way is by *alignment*. In the next example, the elements are aligned on the right margin and connected by an invisible line. This alignment is often called *flush right*.

If you are in the habit of centering title pages and other elements, try using the flush left and flush right commands in your word processing program along with grouping similar elements. You'll be surprised what a difference it makes and how much more professional and persuasive your work will appear.

Consistency

You learned the principle of consistency in elementary school when your teacher told you to write on the lines, make the margins even, and indent your paragraphs. When you write using a computer, your word processing program takes care of these small concerns. However, too many people stop there when they use a computer to write. You can do a whole lot more.

> Make what is similar look similar.

Sometime during your college years, you likely will write a report or paper that uses headings. Readers increasingly expect you to divide what you write into chunks and label those chunks with headings.

It's easy enough to simply center every heading so that your report looks like this:

Title

Saepe et multum hoc mecum cogitavi, bonine an mali plus attulerit hominibus et civitatibus copia dicendi ac summum eloquentiae studium.

Heading 1

Ac me quidem diu cogitantem ratio ipsa in hanc potissimum sententiam ducit, ut existimem sapientiam sine eloquentia parum prodesse civitatibus, eloquentiam vero sine sapientia nimium obesse plerumque, prodesse numquam.

Heading 2

Ac si volumus huius rei, quae vocatur eloquentia, sive artis sive studii sive exercitationis cuiusdam sive facultatis ab natura profectae considerare principium, reperiemus id ex honestissimis causis natum atque optimis rationibus profectum.

If you write a report that looks like this one, you can make it much more visually appealing by devising a system of consistent headings that indicates the overall organization. You first have to determine the level of importance of each heading by making an outline to see what fits under what. Then you make the headings conform to the different levels so that what is equal in importance will have the same level of heading.

Title

Saepe et multum hoc mecum cogitavi, bonine an mali plus attulerit hominibus et civitatibus copia dicendi ac summum eloquentiae studium.

Major Heading

Ac me quidem diu cogitantem ratio ipsa in hanc potissimum sententiam ducit, ut existimem sapientiam sine eloquentia parum prodesse civitatibus, eloquentiam vero sine sapientia nimium obesse plerumque, prodesse numquam.

Level 2 Heading   Ac si volumus huius rei, quae vocatur eloquentia, sive artis sive studii sive exercitationis cuiusdam sive facultatis ab natura profectae considerare principium, reperiemus id ex honestissimis causis natum atque optimis rationibus profectum.

Other useful tools that word processing programs offer are ways of making lists. Bulleted lists are used frequently to present good reasons for claims and proposals. For example:

The proposed new major in Technology, Literacy, and Culture will:

- Prepare our students for the changing demands of the professions and public citizenship
- Help students to move beyond technical skills and strategies to understand the historical, economic, political, and scientific impacts of new technologies
- Allow students to practice new literacies that mix text, graphics, sound, video, animation, hypermedia, and real-time communication
- Help to ensure that wise decisions are made about the collection, organization, storage, and distribution of and access to information via new technologies
- Provide students with a deeper, richer, and more profound understanding of the dynamic relationships among technology, culture, and the individual

---

A bulleted list is an effective way of presenting a series of items or giving an overview of what is to come. However, bulleted lists can be ineffective if the items in the list are not similar.

Contrast

We tend to follow the principle of consistency because that's what we've been taught and that's what writing technologies—from typewriters to computers—do for us. But the principle of contrast takes some conscious effort on our part to implement. Take a simple résumé as an example.

> Make what is different look different.

Roberto Salazar

Address: 3819 East Jefferson Avenue, Escondido, CA 92027

Send email to: salazar@capaccess.org

Job Title: Financial Consultant, Credit Reviewer, Financial Analyst

Relocation: Yes—particular interest in Central and South America.

Experience

2004–present. Credit Services Group, Carpenter & Tokaz LLP, 3000 Wilshire Boulevard, Los Angeles, California 90017

CONSULTING: Presented Directorate with report findings, conclusions, and recommendations for operation improvements. Coordinated a process improvement engagement for a large finance company, which resulted in the consolidation of credit operations.

SUPERVISION: Supervised, trained, and assessed the work of staff (1–4) involved in audit assists. Reviewed real estate investments, other real estate owned, and loan portfolios for documentation, structure, credit analysis, risk identification, and credit scoring.

Education

2004 San Diego State University, San Diego, California, Bachelor of Business Administration

Languages

Fluent in English and Spanish. Experience in tutoring students with Spanish lessons at San Diego State University, San Diego, California

Computers

Proficient with Microsoft Word and Excel, Lotus Notes, AmiPro, Lotus 1-2-3, WordPerfect, and Sendero SV simulation modeling software. Familiarity with several online information retrieval methods.

References available on request.

The résumé has consistency, but there is no contrast between what is more important and what is less important. The overall impression is that the person is dull, dull, dull.

Your résumé, along with your letter of application, might be the most important piece of persuasive writing you'll do in your life. It's worth taking some extra time to distinguish yourself. Your ability to write a convincing letter and produce a handsome résumé is a good reason for an employer to hire you. Remember why you are paying attention to graphic design. You want your readers to focus on certain elements, and you want to create the right image. Use of contrast can emphasize the key features of the résumé and contribute to a much more forceful and dynamic image.

Roberto Salazar

3819 East Jefferson Avenue
Escondido, CA 92027
salazar@capaccess.org

Position Titles Sought

Financial Consulting
Credit Reviewer
Financial Analyst
(Willing to relocate, especially to Central or South America)

Education

2004	**Bachelor of Business Administration.** San Diego State University.

Experience

2004–present	**Credit Services Group, Carpenter & Tokaz, LLP.** 3000 Wilshire Boulevard Los Angeles, California 90017
	Consulting: Presented Directorate with report findings, conclusions, and recommendations for operation improvements. Coordinated a process improvement engagement for a large finance company, which resulted in the consolidation of credit operations.
	Supervision: Supervised, trained, and assessed the work of four staff involved in audit assists. Reviewed real estate investments, other real estate owned, and loan portfolios for documentation, structure, credit analysis, risk identification, and credit scoring.

Languages

Fluent in English and Spanish. Experience as a Spanish Tutor at SDSU.

Computer Skills

Proficient with Microsoft Word & Excel, Lotus Notes, AmiPro, Lotus 1-2-3, WordPerfect, and Sendero SV simulation modeling software. Familiarity with several online information retrieval methods.

References

Available on request.

Notice that arrangement and consistency are also important to the revised résumé. Good design requires that all elements be brought into play to produce the desired results.

Understanding Typefaces and Fonts

Until computers and word processing software came along, most writers had little or no control over the type style they used. If they typed, they likely used Courier, a fact that many typists didn't even know. Furthermore, the typewriter gave no choice about type size. Writers worked with either 10-point type or 12-point type. (A point is a printer's measure. One inch equals 72 points.) You had no way to include italics. The convention was to underline the word so that the printer would later set the word in italics. Boldfacing could be accomplished only by typing the word over again, making it darker.

Even if the general public knew little about type styles and other aspects of printing before computers came along, printers had five hundred years' experience learning about which type styles were easiest to read and what effects different styles produced. Type styles are grouped into families of **typefaces**. When you open the pull-down font menu of your word processing program, you see a small part of that five-hundred-year tradition of developing typefaces. At first, many of the typefaces will look about the same to you, but after you get some practice with using various typefaces, you will begin to notice how they differ.

The two most important categories of typefaces are **serif** and **sans serif**. Serif (rhymes with "sheriff") type was developed first, imitating the strokes of an ink pen. Serifs are the little wedge-shaped ends on letter forms, which scribes produced with wedge-tipped pens. Serif type also has thick and thin transitions on the curved strokes. Five of the most common serif typefaces are the following:

Times

Palatino

Bookman

Garamond

New Century Schoolbook

If these typefaces look almost alike to you, it's not an accident. Serif typefaces were designed to be easy to read. They don't call attention to themselves. Therefore, they are well suited for long stretches of text and are used frequently.

Sans serif type (*sans* is French for "without") doesn't have the little wedge-shaped ends on letters, and the thickness of the letters is the same. Popular sans serif typefaces include the following:

Helvetica

Verdana

Arial

Sans serif typefaces work well for headings and short stretches of text. They give the text a crisp, modern look. And some sans serif typefaces are easy to read on a computer screen.

Finally, there are many script and decorative typefaces. These typefaces tend to draw attention to themselves. They are harder to read, but sometimes they can be used for good effects. Some script and decorative typefaces include the following:

Zapf Chancery

STENCIL

Mistral

Tekton

Changing typefaces will draw attention. It is usually better to be consistent in using typefaces within a text unless you want to signal something.

It's easy to change the size of type when you compose on a computer. A specific size of a typeface is called a **font**. The font size displays on the menu bar. For long stretches of text, you probably should use at least 10-point or 12-point type. For headings, you can use larger type.

type	8 point
type	10 point
type	12 point
type	14 point
type	18 point
type	24 point
type	36 point

type
48 point

type
72 point

Fonts also have different weights. *Weight* refers to the thickness of the strokes. Take a look at the fonts on your font menu. You probably have some fonts that offer options ranging from light to bold, such as Arial Condensed Light, Arial, Arial Rounded MT Bold, and Arial Black. Here's what each of these looks like as a heading:

1. Arial Condensed Light

Position Titles Sought

Financial Consultant

Credit Reviewer

Financial Analyst

(Willing to relocate, especially to Central or South America)

2. Arial

Position Titles Sought

Financial Consultant

Credit Reviewer

Financial Analyst

(Willing to relocate, especially to Central or South America)

3. Arial Rounded MT Bold

Position Titles Sought

Financial Consultant

Credit Reviewer

Financial Analyst

(Willing to relocate, especially to Latin America)

4. Arial Black

Position Titles Sought

Financial Consultant

Credit Reviewer

Financial Analyst

(Willing to relocate, especially to Latin America)

You can get strong contrasts by using heavier weights of black type for headings and using white space to accent what is different.

Finally, most word processing programs have some special effects that you can employ. The three most common are **boldface**, *italics*, and underlining. All three are used for emphasis, but underlining should be avoided because it makes text harder to read.

Creating Images and Other Graphics

Pictures, drawings, and other graphics can have powerful impacts on readers. They can support or emphasize your claims and make concrete the ideas you express in words. They can introduce additional details and even show other points of view.

The main thing you want to avoid is using images strictly for decoration. Readers quickly get tired of pictures and other graphics that don't contribute to the content. Think of pictures, charts, and graphics as alternative means of presenting information. Good use of images contributes to your overall argument.

Pictures

Digital cameras and scanners enable you to create digital images, which you can then easily insert into a word processing file or a Web site. Having the capability to create and publish images, however, doesn't tell you when to use images or for what purposes.

The first step is to determine what images you might need. The majority of images should be used to illustrate content. After you decide that you need a particular image, the next step is to find or create it. If you use someone else's images, including those you find on the Web, you need to obtain permission from the owner, and you need to credit the image just as you would a quotation (see Chapter 15).

When you have images in a digital format, you may need to edit or resize them. Many computers now come equipped with image editors, and you can also download shareware from the Web. If you own a digital camera, it likely includes some type of image editor. Before you begin working, make a copy from the original image. Once you alter and save the original, you cannot get its original image again.

One feature on all image editors is a **cropping** command, which allows you to select part of an image to keep while discarding the rest. You can crop out distracting or unneeded detail and thus create a stronger focus on what you want to emphasize. Cropping also reduces file size, allowing images to load faster on a Web site. To crop an image, select the rectangle or cropping tool, and when you have identified the area you want to keep, select the crop or trim command to discard the rest.

Other Graphics

Charts and graphs create visual summaries of data and are especially useful for illustrating comparisons, patterns, and trends. Popular software, including Microsoft Excel and PowerPoint, allows you to make charts and graphs by typing the data into a datasheet and then selecting the type of graph or chart. The program then creates the chart or graph. You must provide labels for the data, and you should include a caption that describes the content. See pages 92–96 for a discussion of charts and graphs.

Cropping enables you to select the part of the image that is important and to discard the rest.

Writing Arguments for the Web

The Web is a grassroots medium with millions of people putting up Web sites, so it's no surprise that the Web has turned out to be a vast forum for arguments. It seems that if anyone has an opinion about anything, there's a Web site representing that position. If you have strong feelings about any broad issue, you can find on the Web people who think like you do.

The problem with many argument sites on the Web is that they don't provide much depth. Their links, if any, take you to similar sites, with no context for making the link. It's up to you to figure out the relevance of the link. This strategy works for people who are already convinced of the position being advocated, but it's not a strategy that works well with people who haven't made up their mind. When you create a Web site that advocates a position, the ease of linking on the Web doesn't make your work any easier. Good arguments still require much thought and careful planning. You cannot expect your readers to do your work for you. You still have to supply good reasons.

Web authoring software makes it easy to compose Web pages, but the software doesn't tell you how reading on the Web is different from reading print materials. In most printed books, magazines, and newspapers, the text is continuous. Even though printed text isn't necessarily linear—witness the boxes and sidebars in this book—the basic movement in print is linear and the basic unit is the paragraph. By contrast, the basic movement on the Web is nonlinear and the basic unit is the screen. Perhaps the most important fact to remember when composing for the Web is that fewer than 10 percent of people who click on a Web site ever scroll down the page. Their eyes stop at the bottom of the screen. And those who do scroll down usually don't scroll down very far.

The First Page Is the Most Important

People who browse Web sites don't stay long if they aren't interested or if it takes too long to find out what's on the Web site. That's why the first page is critical. If you have something to tell your visitors, tell them right away. They probably aren't going to click or scroll through a bunch of pages to find out where you stand on an issue. You have to let your readers know on the first page what your site is about.

The first page is also the front door to your site, and when visitors enter your front door, they need to know where to go next. Supplying navigation tools on the first page is critical. These can take the form of menu bars, buttons, or clickable images. Whatever form you choose, the labels should indicate what the visitor will find on the next screen.

The Web page in Figure 13.1 was created by Grace Bernhardt for a class project on the conflict surrounding the Balcones Canyonlands Preserve (BCP), a nature reserve located within the city limits of Austin, Texas, and the habitat for six endangered species. The text on the first page describes the place and the various stakeholders in the Balcones Canyonlands Preserve. It also provides a menu to the main areas of the site.

Divide Your Text into Chunks

Long stretches of text on the Web tend not to get read. Effective Web designers try to divide text into chunks whenever possible. For example, when they present a list of facts, they often put space between items or use a bulleted list rather than a long paragraph. The page in Figure 13.2 is from a student Web site designed by Chungpei Hu on safety issues for Sixth Street, the entertainment district in Austin, Texas. It uses a bulleted list to enumerate frequent fire code violations in bars and clubs along Sixth Street.

You can put a great deal of background information about a topic on a Web site, connected by links to the main argument. You can thus offer a short summary on the main page, with links to other pages that give background and evidence. One advantage of this strategy is that you

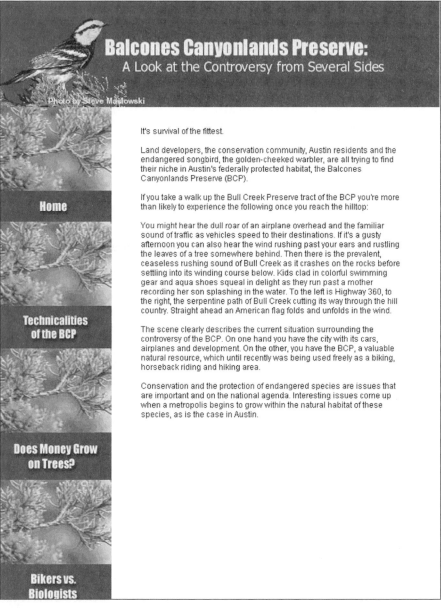

Figure 13.1 Balcones Canyonlands Preserve: A Look at the Controversy from Several Sides

Figure 13.2 Sixth Street Safety & Awareness

design a single site both for those who know a great deal about the subject and want to skip the background information, and for those who know little and need to know the background. You can include additional evidence that would be hard to work into a paper otherwise. Furthermore, the act of clicking on particular words can make readers aware of the links in an argument.

Make the Text Readable

Above all, make your text readable. Remember that other people's monitors may be smaller than yours; thus what appears as small type on your monitor may require a magnifying glass for others. Also, dark backgrounds make for tough reading. If you use a dark background and want people to read what you write, be sure to increase the font size, make sure the contrast between text and background is adequate, and avoid using all caps and italics.

TEXT IN ALL CAPS IS HARD TO READ ON A BLACK BACKGROUND, *ESPECIALLY IF THE TEXT IS IN ITALICS.*

Determine the Visual Theme of Your Site

Most Web sites contain more than one page, and because it is so easy to move from one site to another on the Web, it's important to make your site as unified as possible. Using common design elements, such as color, icons, typeface, and layout, contributes to the unity of the site. The Balcones Canyonlands Preserves site shown in Figure 13.1 repeats the image of its most famous resident—the endangered golden-cheeked warbler—on each page, along with images of foliage. Even without the text, the images on the site make it evident that the site deals with environmental issues.

Keep the Visuals Simple

The students who produced the Web sites in this chapter could have included many large pictures if they had chosen to. But they deliberately kept the visual design simple. A less complicated site is not only more friendly because it loads faster, but if it is well designed, it can be elegant. Simple elements are also easier to repeat. Too many icons, bullets, horizontal rules, and other embellishments give a page a cluttered appearance. A simple, consistent design is always effective for pages that contain text.

Finally, keep in mind that although good graphic design provides visual impact and can help the visitor navigate a Web site, it has little value if it is not supported by substance. People still expect to come away from a Web site with substantial information. Good visual design makes your Web site more appealing, but it does not do the work of argument for you.

Make Your Site Easy to Navigate

People don't read Web sites the same way they read a book. They scan quickly and move around a lot. They don't necessarily read from top to bottom. If you are trying to make an argument on the Web, you have to think differently about how the reader is going to encounter your argument. If you put the argument on more than one page, you have to plan the site so that readers can navigate easily.

First, you should determine the overall structure of your Web site, assuming you plan to include more than one page. Web sites that have a main page should have clear navigation tools. For example, the transportation section of Sixth Street Safety & Awareness (Figure 13.3) offers sections for both the general public and University of Texas students. The navigation icons make the possibilities obvious.

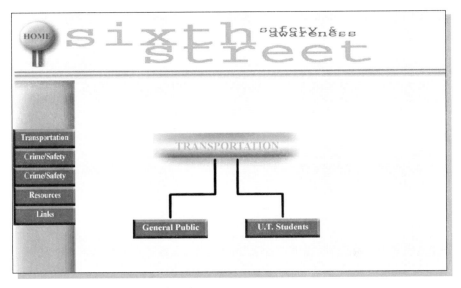

Figure 13.3 Sixth Street Safety & Awareness

EVALUATING A WEB SITE

You can use the following criteria to evaluate Web sites you have designed or those designed by others.

1. **Audience:** How does the site identify its intended audience? How does it indicate what else is on the site?

2. **Content:** How informative is the content? Where might more content be added? What do you want to know more about? Are there any mechanical, grammar, or style problems?

3. **Readability:** Is there sufficient contrast between the text and the background to make the text legible? Are the margins wide enough? Are there any paragraphs that go on too long and need to be divided? Are headings inserted in the right places, and if headings are used for more than one level, are these levels indicated consistently? Is text in boldface and all caps kept short?

4. **Visual Design:** Does the site have a consistent visual theme? Where is the focal point on each page? Do the images contribute to the visual appeal or do they detract from it?

5. **Navigation:** How easy or difficult is it to move from one page to another on the site? Are there any broken links?

CHAPTER 14

Effective Oral Presentations

B ecoming effective in oral communication is just as important as in written communication. You may be asked to give oral presentations in your later life and perhaps in your college career. Oral presentations can be developed from written assignments and supported by visual elements such as slides, overheads, video clips, and other media.

Planning an Oral Presentation

Getting Started

Successful oral arguments, like written arguments, require careful planning. You first step is to find out what kind of oral presentation you are being asked to give. Look closely at your assignment for key words such as *analyze, evaluate,* and *propose,* which often indicate what is expected.

Another important consideration is length. How much time you have to give a speech determines the depth you can go into. Speakers who ignore this simple principle often announce near the end of their time that they will have to omit major points and rush to finish. Their presentations end abruptly and leave the audience confused about what the speaker had to say.

You also should consider early on where you will be giving the speech. If you want to use visual elements to support your presentation, you need to make sure the room has the equipment you need. If you know the room is large or has poor acoustics, you may need to bring audio equipment.

Selecting Your Topic

Choosing and researching a topic for an oral presentation is similar to choosing and researching a topic for a written assignment. If you have a broad choice of topics, make a list of subjects that interest you. Then go through your list and ask yourself these questions:

- Will you enjoy speaking on this topic?
- Will your audience be interested in this topic?
- Does the topic fit the situation for your presentation?
- Do you know enough to speak on this topic?
- If you do not know enough, are you willing to do research to learn more about the topic?

Remember that enthusiasm is contagious, so if you are excited about a topic, chances are your audience will become interested too.

Research for an oral presentation is similar to the research you must do for a written argument. You will find guidelines in Chapter 15 for planning your research. Remember that you will need to develop a bibliography for an oral presentation that requires research, just as you would for a written argument. You will need to document the sources of your information and provide those sources in your talk.

Thinking About Your Audience

Unlike writing, when you give a speech, you have your audience directly before you. They will give you concrete feedback during your presentation by smiling or frowning, by paying attention or losing interest, by asking questions or sitting passively.

When planning your presentation, you should think about your audience in relation to your topic.

- What is your audience likely to know or believe about your topic?
- What does your audience probably not know about your topic?
- What key terms will you have to define or explain?
- What assumptions do you hold in common with your audience?
- Where is your audience most likely to disagree with you?
- What questions are they likely to ask?

Supporting Your Presentation

The steps for writing various kinds of arguments, listed at the ends of Chapters 4–11, can be used to organize an oral presentation. When you have organized your main points, you need to decide how to support those points. Look at your research notes and think about how best to incorporate the information you found. Consider using one or more of these strategies:

- **Facts.** Speakers who know their facts build credibility.
- **Statistics.** Good use of statistics gives the impression that the speaker has done his or her homework. Statistics also can indicate that a particular example is representative. One tragic car accident doesn't mean a road is dangerous, but an especially high accident rate relative to other nearby roads does make the case.
- **Statements by authorities.** Quotations from credible experts are another common way of supporting key points.
- **Narratives.** Narratives are small stories that can illustrate key points. Narratives are a good way of keeping the attention of the audience. Keep them short so they don't distract from your major points.
- **Humor.** In most situations audiences appreciate humor. Humor is a good way to convince an audience that you have common beliefs and experiences, and that your argument may be one they can agree with.

Planning Your Introduction

No part of your speech is more critical than the introduction. You have to get the audience's attention, introduce your topic, convince the audience that it is important to them, present your thesis, and give your audience either an overview of your presentation or a sense of your direction. Accomplishing all this in a short time is a tall order, but if you lose your audience in the first two minutes, you won't recover their attention. You might begin with a compelling example or anecdote that both introduces your topic and indicates your stance.

Planning Your Conclusion

The next most important part of your speech is your conclusion. You want to end on a strong note. First, you need to signal that you are entering the conclusion. You can announce that you are concluding, but you also can give signals in other ways. Touching on your main points again will help your audience to remember them. But simply summarizing is a dull way to close. Think of an example or an idea that captures the gist of your speech, something that your audience can take away with them.

Delivering an Oral Presentation

The Importance of Practice

There is no substitute for rehearsing your speech several times in advance. You will become more confident and have more control over the content. The best way to overcome nervousness about speaking in front of others is to be well prepared. When you know what you are going to say, you can pay more attention to your audience, making eye contact and watching body language for signals about how well you are making your points. When you rehearse you can also become comfortable with any visual elements you will be using. Finally, rehearsing your speech is the only reliable way to find out how long it will take to deliver.

Practice your speech in front of others. If possible, go to the room where you will be speaking and ask a friend to sit in the back so you can learn how well you can be heard. You can also learn a great deal by videotaping your rehearsal and watching yourself as an audience member.

Speaking Effectively

Talking is so much a part of our daily lives that we rarely think about our voices as instruments of communication unless we have some training in acting or public speaking. You can become better at speaking by becoming more aware of your delivery. Pay attention to your breathing as you practice your speech. When you breathe at your normal rate, you will not rush your speech. Plan where you will pause during your speech. Pauses allow you to take a sip of water and give your audience a chance to sum up mentally what you have said. And don't be afraid to repeat key points. Repetition is one of the easiest strategies for achieving emphasis.

Most of the time nervousness is invisible. You can feel nervous and still impress your audience as being calm and confident. If you make mistakes while speaking, know that the audience understands and will be forgiving. Stage fright is normal; sometimes it can be helpful in raising the energy level of a presentation.

Nonverbal Communication

While you are speaking, you are also communicating with your presence. Stand up unless you are required to sit. Move around instead of standing behind the podium. Use gestures to emphasize main points, and only main points; if you gesture continually, you may appear nervous.

Maintaining eye contact is crucial. Begin your speech by looking at the people directly in front of you and then move your eyes around the room, looking to both sides. Attempting to look at each person during a speech may seem unnatural, but it is the best way to convince all the members of your audience that you are speaking directly to them.

T I P S

For Effective Speeches

Usually more effective	Usually less effective
Practice in advance	Don't practice
Talk	Read
Stand	Sit
Make eye contact	Look down
Move around	Stand still
Speak loudly	Mumble
Use visual elements	Lack visual elements
Focus on main points	Get lost in details
Give an overview of what you are going to say in the introduction	Start your talk without indicating where you are headed
Give a conclusion that summarizes your main points and ends with a key idea or example	Stop abruptly
Finish on time	Run overtime

Handling Questions

Your presentation doesn't end when you finish. Speakers are usually expected to answer questions afterward. How you handle questions is also critical to your success. Speakers who are evasive or fail to acknowledge questions sometimes lose all the credibility they have built in their speech. But speakers who listen carefully to questions and answer them honestly build their credibility further.

Keep in mind a few principles about handling questions:

■ Repeat the question so that the entire audience can hear it and to confirm you understood it.

■ Take a minute to reflect on the question. If you do not understand the question, ask the questioner to restate it.

■ Some people will make a small speech instead of asking a question. Acknowledge their point of view but avoid getting into a debate.

■ If you cannot answer a question, don't bluff and don't apologize. You can offer to research the question or you can ask the audience if they know the answer.

■ If you are asked a question during your speech, answer it if it is a short, factual question or one of clarification. Postpone questions that require long answers until the end to avoid losing the momentum of your speech.

Multimedia Presentations

Visual Elements

Visual elements can both support and reinforce your major points. They give you another means of reaching your audience and keeping them stimulated. Visual elements range from simple transparencies and handouts to elaborate multimedia presentations. Some of the more easily created visual elements are

■ Outlines
■ Statistical charts
■ Flow charts
■ Photographs
■ Maps

At the very minimum, you should consider putting an outline of your talk on an overhead transparency. Some speakers think that they will kill interest in their talk if they show the audience what they are going to say in advance. Just the opposite is the case. An outline allows an audience to keep track of where you are in your talk. Outlines also help you to make transitions to your next point. Most printers can make transparencies from blank transparency sheets fed through the paper feeder. Charts, maps, photographs, and other graphics in digital format can thus be printed onto transparencies. Many photocopiers can also make transparencies.

Keep the amount of text short. You don't want your audience straining to read long passages on the screen and neglecting what you have to say. Except for quotations, use single words and short phrases—not sentences—on transparencies and slides.

One major difficulty with visual elements is that they tempt you to look at the screen instead of at your audience. You have to face your audience while your audience is looking at the screen. Needless to say, you have to practice to feel comfortable.

T I P S

Readable Transparencies and Slides

If you put text on transparencies or slides, make sure that the audience can read the text from more than 10 feet away. You may depend on your transparencies and slides to convey important information, but if your audience cannot read the slides, not only will the information be lost but the audience will become frustrated.

Use these type sizes for transparencies and slides.

	Transparencies	Slides
Title:	36 pt	24 pt
Subtitles:	24 pt	18 pt
Other text:	18 pt	14 pt

Preview your transparencies and slides from a distance equal to the rear of the room where you will be speaking. If you cannot read them, increase the type size.

Presentation Software

You likely have seen many presentations that use Microsoft PowerPoint because it has become a favorite of faculty who lecture. If you have Microsoft Word on your computer, you likely have PowerPoint since they are often sold together. PowerPoint is straightforward to use, which is one of the reasons it has become so popular. You can quickly get an outline of your presentation onto slides, and if projection equipment is available in the room where you are speaking, the slides are easily displayed.

PowerPoint offers a choice of many backgrounds, which is a potential pitfall. Light text on a dark background is hard to read. It forces you to close every window and turn off all the lights in order for your audience to see the text. Darkened rooms create problems. You may have difficulty reading your notes in a dark room, and your audience may fall asleep. Instead, always use dark text on a white or light-colored background. Usually your audience can read your slides with a light background in a room with the shades up or lights on.

You can leave a slide on the screen for about one to two minutes, which allows your audience time to read and connect the slide to what you are saying. You will need to practice to know when to display a new slide. Without adequate practice, you can easily get too far ahead or behind in your slide show and then be forced to interrupt yourself to get your slides back in sync with your speech. You also need to know how to darken the screen if you want the audience to focus on you during parts of your presentation.

Another pitfall of PowerPoint is getting carried away with all the special effects possible such as fade-ins, fade-outs, and sound effects. Presentations heavy on the special effects often come off as heavy on style and light on substance. They also can be time-consuming to produce.

CHAPTER 15

Effective Research

💻 Research: Knowing What Information You Need

The writing that you do in school sometimes seems isolated from the real world. After all, when you write for a class, your real audience is usually the teacher. For the same reason, the research associated with writing for school tends to get isolated from real-world problems. Instead of asking questions such as "How may compounds that mimic estrogen be causing reproductive abnormalities in certain animal species?" students ask questions such as "What do I need to know to write this paper?" This approach tends to separate research from writing. If you've ever said to yourself, "I'll get on the Web or go to the library to do the research tonight, and then tomorrow afternoon I'll start writing the paper," you might be making some assumptions about the nature of research and writing that will actually make your task harder instead of easier. For now, set aside what you already know about how to do research and think instead in terms of gathering information to solve problems and answer questions.

Effective research depends on two things: knowing what kind of information you are looking for and knowing where to get it. What you already know about writing arguments will help you to make some decisions about what kind of information you should be looking for. For instance, if you have decided to write a proposal for solving the problem of HMOs limiting subscribers' health care options, you already know that you will need to find statistics (to help your readers understand the urgency and scope of the problem) and several different analyses of the situation by writers from different camps (to help you make sure your own understanding of the situation is accurate, complete, and fair to all participants). But if you keep thinking about the demands of the proposal as a type of argument, you might also decide that you need to look at how this problem has been solved in the British or Canadian health system or how programs like Medicare and Medicaid are dealing with it.

Even if you don't yet know enough about your subject to know what type of argument you will want to write, there are still some basic questions you can use to plan your research. To make a thoughtful and mature contribution to any debate in the realm of public discourse, you will need to know the background of the issue. As you begin your research, then, you can use the following questions as a guide.

1. Who are the speakers on this issue and what are they saying?

Subdividing the group of everyone who has something to say on this issue and everything that is being said into narrower categories will help you to gain a better understanding of what the debate looks like. For example, you might make the following divisions:

- Who are the experts on this issue? What do the experts say?
- Who else is talking about it? What do they say?
- Are the people whose interests are most at stake participating in the debate? What are they saying?

In addition to the categories of experts, nonexpert speakers, and those whose interests are at stake, there are other general categories you can begin from, such as supporters and opponents of a position, liberals and conservatives, and so on.

Also remember that any given debate will have its own specific set of opponents. In a debate about constructing a storage facility for nuclear waste in Nevada, for instance, conservationists and proponents of growth in the state of Nevada are lining up against the federal government. On another significant issue—water usage—proponents of growth stand in opposition to conservationists, who object to the demands Las Vegas makes on the waters of the Colorado River. On yet other issues, conservationists depend on the federal government to use its power to protect land, water, and other resources that are vulnerable to the activities of businesses and individuals.

2. What is at stake?

Political debates often boil down to arguments about control of, or access to, resources or power. Therefore, resources and power are good places to start looking for what is at stake in any given debate. Depending on the nature of the debate, you might also look at what is at stake in terms of ethical and moral issues. For example, as a country and as a human community, what does this nation stand to lose if many young Americans can no longer afford to go to college? To help narrow down your search, you might rephrase this question in several different ways:

- How or why does this issue matter: to the world, to the citizens of this country, to the people whose interests are at stake, to me?

- What stands to be gained or lost for any of these stakeholders?
- Who is likely to be helped and hurt the most?

3. What kinds of arguments are being made about this issue?

Just as it is helpful to subdivide the whole field of speakers on your issue into narrower groups that line up according to sides, it is also helpful to subdivide the whole field of what is being said according to types or categories of arguments. It might help to set up a chart of speakers and their primary arguments to see how they line up.

- What are the main claims being offered?
- What reasons are offered in support of these claims?
- What are the primary sources of evidence?
- Is some significant aspect of this issue being ignored or displaced in favor of others?
- If so, why?

4. Who are the audiences for this debate?

Sometimes, the audience for a debate is every responsible member of society, everyone living in a certain region, or everyone who cares about the fate of the human species on this planet. More often, however, arguments are made to specific types of audiences, and knowing something about those audiences can help you to understand the choices that the writers make. Even more important, knowing who is already part of the audience for a debate can help you to plan your own strategies.

- Do you want to write to one of the existing audiences to try to change its mind or make it take action?
- Or do you want to try to persuade a new, as-yet-uninvolved audience to get involved in the debate?
- How much do they know about the issues involved?
- Where do they likely stand on these issues?
- Will they define the issues the same way you do?

5. What is your role?

At some point, as you continue to research the issue and plan your writing strategies, you will need to decide what your role should be in this debate. Ask yourself:

- What do I think about it?
- What do I think should be done about it?
- What kind of argument should I write, and to whom?

Use these questions to take inventory of how much you already know about the issue and what you need to find out more about. When you have worked through these questions, you are ready to make a claim that will guide your research efforts. See steps in writing arguments at the ends of Chapters 6 through 11 to get started.

WHAT MAKES A GOOD SUBJECT FOR RESEARCH

- **Find a subject that you are interested in.** Research can be enjoyable if you are finding out new things rather than just confirming what you already know. The most exciting part of doing research is making small discoveries.
- **Make sure that you can do a thorough job of research.** If you select a topic that is too broad, such as proposing how to end poverty, you will not be able to do an adequate job.
- **Develop a strategy for your research early on.** If you are researching a campus issue such as a parking problem, then you probably will rely most on interviews, observations, and possibly a survey. But if you find out that one of the earliest baseball stadiums, Lakefront Park in Chicago (built in 1883), had the equivalent of today's luxury boxes and you want to make an argument that the trend toward building stadiums with luxury boxes is not a new development, then you will have to do library research.
- **Give yourself enough time to do a thorough job.** You should expect to find a few dead ends, and you should expect to better focus your subject as you proceed. If you are going to do research in the field, by survey, or in the library, remember the first principle of doing research: *Things take longer than you think they will.*

🖥 Planning Your Research

Once you have a general idea about the kind of information you need to make your argument, the next step is to decide where to look for it. People who write on the job—lawyers preparing briefs, journalists covering news stories, policy analysts preparing reports, engineers describing a manufacturing process, members of Congress reporting to committees, and a host of others—have general research strategies available to them. The first is to gather the information themselves, which is called **primary** or **firsthand evidence**. We can distinguish two basic kinds of primary research.

Experiential research involves all the information you gather just through observing and taking note of events as they occur in the real world. You meet with clients, interview a candidate, go to a committee meeting, talk to coworkers, read a report from a colleague, observe a manufacturing process, witness an event, or examine a patient. In all these ways, you are adding to your store of knowledge about a problem or issue. In many cases, however, the knowledge that is gained through experience is not enough to answer all the questions or solve all the problems. In those cases, writers supplement experiential research with empirical research and research in the library.

Empirical research is a way of gathering specific and narrowly defined data by developing a test situation and then observing and recording events as they occur in the test situation. Analysis of tissue samples and cell cultures in a laboratory, for instance, can add important information to what a doctor can learn by examining a patient. Crash tests of cars help automakers and materials engineers understand why crumpling is an important part of a car's ability to protect its passengers in a crash. Surveys of adult children of divorced parents make it possible for psychologists to identify the long-term effects of divorce on family members. Many people believe that this kind of research is what adds new information to the store of human knowledge; so for many audiences, reporting the results of empirical research is an important part of making a strong argument. (Therefore, writers often use statistics and reports of research done by experts in the field to support their claims.)

For the most part, however, debates about public issues occur outside the fairly narrow intellectual spaces occupied by the true experts in any given field. Experts do, of course, participate in public debates, but so do all other interested citizens and policymakers. The majority of speakers on an issue rely on the work of others as sources of information—what is known as **secondary** or **secondhand evidence**. Many people think of library research as secondary research—the process of gathering information by reading what other people have written on a subject. In the past, library research was based almost exclusively on collections of printed materials housed in libraries; in addition to public and university libraries, organizations of all kinds had their own collections of reference materials specific to their work. Today, the Web has brought significant changes in the way people record, store, view, distribute, and gain access to documents. For most issues, searching the Web will be an important part of your research.

INTERVIEWS, OBSERVATIONS, AND SURVEYS

Interviews

- Decide first why one or more interviews could be important for your argument. Knowing the goals of your interview will help you to determine whom you need to interview and to structure the questions in the interview. You might, for example, learn more about the history of a campus issue than you were able to find out in the campus newspaper archives.

- Schedule each interview in advance, preferably by email or letter. Let the person know why you are conducting the interview. Then follow up with a phone call to find out whether the person is willing and what he or she might be able to tell you.

- Plan your questions. You should have a few questions in mind as well as written down. Listen carefully so that you can follow up on key points.

- Come prepared with at least a notebook and pencil. If you use a tape recorder, be sure to get the person's permission in advance and be sure that the equipment is working.

Observations

- Make detailed observations that you can link to your claim. For example, if you believe that the long lines in your student services building are caused by inefficient use of staff, you could observe how many staff members are on duty at peak and slack times.

- Choose a place where you can observe without intrusion. Public places work best because you can sit for a long time without people wondering what you are doing.

- Carry a notebook and write extensive notes whenever you can. Write down as much as you can. Be sure to record where you were, the date, exactly when you arrived and left, and important details such as the number of people present.

INTERVIEWS, OBSERVATIONS, AND SURVEYS *(continued)*

Surveys

- Like interview questions, questions on surveys should relate directly to the issue of your argument. Take some time to decide what exactly you want to know first.

- Write a few specific, unambiguous questions. The people you contact should be able to fill out your survey quickly, and they should not have to guess what a question means. It's always a good idea to test the wording of the questions on a few people to find out whether your questions are clear before you conduct the survey.

- You might include one or two open-ended questions, such as "What do you like about X?" or "What don't you like about X?" Answers to these questions can be difficult to interpret, but sometimes they provide insights.

- Decide whom you want to participate in your survey and how you will contact them. If you are going to use your survey results to claim that the people surveyed represent the views of undergraduates at your school, then you should match the gender, ethnic, and racial balance to the proportions at your school.

- If you are going to mail or email your survey, include a statement about what the survey is for and how the results will be used.

- Interpreting your results should be straightforward if your questions require definite responses. Multiple-choice formats make data easy to tabulate, but they often miss key information. If you included one or more open-ended questions, you need to figure out a way to analyze responses.

Finding Library Sources

Large libraries can be intimidating, even to experienced researchers when they begin working on a new subject. You can save time and frustration if you have some idea of how you want to proceed when you enter the library. Libraries have two major kinds of sources: books and periodicals. Periodicals include a range of items from daily newspapers to scholarly journals that are bound and put on the shelves like books.

Most books are shelved according to the Library of Congress Classification System, which uses a combination of letters and numbers to direct you to a book's location in the library. The Library of Congress call number begins with a letter or letters that represent the broad subject area into which the book is classified. The Library of Congress system has the advantage of shelving books on the same subject together, so you can sometimes find additional books by browsing in the stacks. You can use the *Library of Congress Subject Headings,* available in print in your library's reference area or on the Web (http://lcweb.loc.gov), to help you find out how your subject might be indexed.

If you want to do research on cloning, you might type "cloning" in the subject index of your online card catalog, which would yield something like the following results:

1 Cloning—23 item(s)

2 Cloning—Bibliography.—1 item(s)

3 Cloning—Congresses.—2 item(s)

4 Cloning—Fiction.—6 item(s)

5 Cloning—Government policy—United States.—2 item(s)

6 Cloning—History.—1 item(s)

7 Cloning, Molecular—36 item(s) Indexed as: MOLECULAR CLONING

8 Cloning—Moral and ethical aspects.—13 item(s)

9 Cloning—Moral and ethical aspects—Government policy—United States.—1 item(s)

10 Cloning—Moral and ethical aspects—United States.—2 item(s)

11 Cloning—Religious aspects—Christianity.—2 item(s)

12 Cloning—Research—History.—1 item(s)

13 Cloning—Research—Law and legislation—United States.—1 item(s)

14 Cloning—Research—United States—Finance.—1 item(s)

15 Cloning—Social aspects.—1 item(s)

16 Cloning—United States—Religious aspects.—1 item(s)

This initial search helps you to identify more precisely what you are looking for. If you are most interested in the ethical aspects of cloning, then the books listed under number 8 would be most useful to you.

Finding articles in periodicals is accomplished in much the same way. To find relevant newspaper and magazine articles, use a periodical index. Print indexes are located in the reference area of your library, but many are now available on your library's Web site. These general indexes are now commonly known as databases because they often have full-text versions of the articles they index. Databases are sometimes listed on your library's Web site under the name of the vendor—the company that sells the database to your library (e.g., EBSCO, FirstSearch). Some of the more useful general databases include

Academic Search Premier (EBSCO). Provides full text for over 3,000 scholarly publications, including social sciences, humanities, education, computer sciences, engineering, language and linguistics, literature, medical sciences, and ethnic studies journals.

ArticleFirst (FirstSearch). Indexes over 15,000 journals in business, the humanities, medicine, science, and social sciences.

Expanded Academic ASAP (Thomson Gale). Indexes 2,300 periodicals from the arts, humanities, sciences, social sciences, and general news, some with full-text articles available.

Factiva (Dow Jones). Gives full-text access to major newspapers, market research reports, and business journals, including *The Wall Street Journal*.

Ingenta.com (Ingenta). Gives citations to over 20,000 multidisciplinary journals.

LexisNexis Academic (LexisNexis). Provides full text of a wide range of newspapers, magazines, government and legal documents, and company profiles from around the world.

WorldCat (FirstSearch). Contains over 52 million records of books and other materials in libraries throughout the world but very few articles in journals.

In addition to these general periodical indexes, there are many specialized indexes that list citations to journal articles in various fields.

Follow these steps to find articles:

1. Select an index that is appropriate to your subject.
2. Search the index using the relevant subject heading(s).
3. Print or copy the complete citation to the article(s).
4. Check the periodicals holdings to see whether your library has the journal.

SCHOLARLY, TRADE, AND POPULAR JOURNALS

Some indexes give citations for only one kind of journal. Others include more than one type. Although the difference between types of journals is not always obvious, you should be able to judge whether a journal is scholarly, trade, or popular by its characteristics.

Characteristics of Scholarly Journals

- Articles are long with few illustrations.
- Articles are written by scholars in the field, usually affiliated with a university or research center.
- Articles have footnotes or a works-cited list at the end.
- Articles usually report original research.
- Authors write in the language of their discipline, and readers are assumed to know a great deal about the field.
- Scholarly journals contain relatively few advertisements.

Examples: *American Journal of Mathematics, College English, JAMA: Journal of the American Medical Association, Plasma Physics*

Characteristics of Trade Journals

- Articles are frequently related to practical job concerns.
- Articles usually do not report original research.
- Articles usually do not have footnotes or have relatively few footnotes.

SCHOLARLY, TRADE, AND POPULAR JOURNALS *(continued)*

■ Items of interest to people in particular professions and job listings are typical features.

■ Advertisements are aimed at people in the specific field.

Examples: *Advertising Age, Industry Week, Macworld, Teacher Magazine*

Characteristics of Popular Journals

■ Articles are short and often illustrated with color photographs.

■ Articles seldom have footnotes or acknowledge where their information came from.

■ Authors are usually staff writers for the magazine or freelance writers.

■ Advertisements are aimed at the general public.

■ Copies can be bought at newsstands.

Examples: *Cosmopolitan, Newsweek, Sports Illustrated, GQ, People*

Finding Web Sources

Searches for sources on databases on your library's Web site and searches on Google may look similar on your computer, but there is a world of difference. Sources on library databases have the advantage of being screened by librarians along with the convenience of Web delivery. Your library pays for access to most databases, which is why they aren't available to the public. The results of a Google search, by contrast, often give you a series of commercial sites selling books and products related to the words you typed in.

Nonetheless, some important databases, including ERIC, Ingenta.com, and MEDLINE, have many resources available free of charge both through library Web sites and through the Web. Furthermore, a huge selection of government documents is available on the Web. Often it takes skill and patience to find what is valuable on the Web. The key to success is knowing where you are most likely to find current and accurate information about the particular question you are researching.

Traditional Criteria for Evaluating Print Sources

Over the years librarians have developed criteria for evaluating print sources.

1. **Source.** Who printed the book or article? Scholarly books that are published by university presses and articles in scholarly journals are assessed by experts in the field before they are published. Because of this strict review process, they contain generally reliable information. But since the review process takes time, scholarly books and articles are not the most current sources. For people outside the field, they also have the disadvantage of being written for other experts. Serious trade books and journals are also generally reliable, though magazines devoted to politics often have an obvious bias. Popular magazines and books vary in quality. Often, they are purchased for their entertainment value, and they tend to emphasize what is sensational or entertaining at the expense of accuracy and comprehensiveness. Many magazines and books are published to represent the viewpoint of a particular group or company, so that bias should be taken into account. Newspapers also vary in quality. National newspapers, such as the *New York Times, Washington Post*, and *Los Angeles Times*, employ fact checkers and do a thorough editorial review and thus tend to be more reliable than newspapers that lack such resources.

2. **Author.** Who wrote the book or article? Is the author's name mentioned? Are the author's qualifications listed?

3. **Timeliness.** How current is the source? Obviously, if you are researching a fast-developing subject such as cloning, then currency is very important. But if you are interested in an issue that happened years ago, then currency might not be as important.

4. **Evidence.** How adequate is the evidence to support the author's claims? Where does the evidence come from—interviews, observations, surveys, experiments, expert testimony, or counterarguments? Does the author acknowledge any other ways in which the evidence might be interpreted?

5. **Biases.** Can you detect particular biases of the author? Is the author forthright about his or her biases? How do the author's biases affect the interpretation that is offered?

6. **Advertising.** Is the advertising prominent in the journal or newspaper? Is there any way that ads might affect what gets printed? For example, some magazines that ran many tobacco ads refused to run stories about the dangers of smoking.

Traditional print criteria can be helpful in evaluating some Internet sources. For example, most messages sent to a list or newsgroup do not mention the qualifications of the author or offer any support for the validity of evidence. For this reason any information you gather via such a newsgroup should be verified with a more reliable source.

Sources on the Web present other difficulties. Some of these are inherent in the structure of the Web, with its capability for linking to other pages. When you are at a site that contains many links, you will often find that some links go to pages on the same site but others take you off the site. You have to pay attention to the URLs to know where you are in relation to where you started. Furthermore, when you find a Web page using a search engine, often you go deep into a complex site without having any sense of the context of that page. You might have to spend thirty minutes or more just to get some idea of what is on the overall site.

Additional Criteria for Evaluating Web Sources

Traditional criteria for evaluating print sources remain useful for evaluating sources on the Web, but you should keep in mind how the Web can be different.

1. **Source.** If a Web site indicates what organization or individual is responsible for the information found on it, then you can apply the traditional criteria for evaluating print sources. For example, most major newspapers maintain Web sites where you can read some of the articles that appear in print. If a Web site doesn't indicate ownership, then you have to make judgments about who put it up and why. Documents are easy to copy and put up on the Web, but they are also very easily quoted out of context or altered. For example, you might find something represented as an "official" government document that is in fact a fabrication.

2. **Author.** Often, it is difficult to know who put up a particular Web site. Even when an author's name is present, in most cases the author's qualifications are not listed.

3. **Timeliness.** Many Web pages do not list when they were last updated; therefore, you do not know how current they are. Furthermore, there are thousands of ghost sites on the Web—sites that the owners have abandoned but have not bothered to remove. You can stumble onto these old sites and not realize that the organization might have a more current site elsewhere.

4. **Evidence.** The accuracy of any evidence found on the Web is often hard to verify. There are no editors or fact checkers guarding against mistakes or misinformation. The most reliable information on the Web stands up to the tests of print evaluation, with clear indication of an edited source, credentials of the author, references for works cited, and dates of publication.

5. **Biases.** Many Web sites are little more than virtual soapboxes. Someone who has an ax to grind can potentially tell millions of people why he or she is angry. Other sites are equally biased but conceal their attitude with a reasonable tone and seemingly factual evidence such as statistics.

6. **Advertising.** Many Web sites are "infomercials" of one sort or another. While they can provide useful information about specific products or services, the reason the information was placed on the Web is to get you to buy the product or service. Advertising on the Web costs a fraction of broadcast ads, so it's no wonder that advertisers have flocked to the Web.

Taking Notes

Before personal computers became widely available, most library research projects involved taking notes on notecards. This method was cumbersome, but it had some big advantages. You could spread out the notecards on a table or pin them to a bulletin board and get an overview of how the information that you gathered might be connected. Today, many people make notes in computer files. If you make notes in a computer file, then you don't have to retype when you write your paper. For example, if you copy a direct quote and decide to use it, you can cut and paste it. It is, of course, possible to print all your notes from your computer and then spread them out, or you can even paste your notes on cards, which will let you enjoy the best of both systems. Whatever way works best for you, there are a few things to keep in mind.

Make sure you get the full bibliographic information when you make notes. For books, you should get the author's name, title of the book, place of publication, publisher, and date of publication. This information is on the front and back of the title page. For journals, you need the author's name, title of the article, title of the journal, issue of the journal, date of the issue, and page numbers. For Web sites, you need the name of the page, the author if listed, the sponsoring organization if listed, the date the site was posted, the date you visited, and the complete URL.

Make photocopies or print copies of sources you plan to use in your paper. Having a copy of the source lessens the chances you'll make mistakes. If you do take notes, be sure to indicate which words are the author's and which words are yours. It's easy to forget later. Attach the bibliographic information to photocopies and printouts so that you won't get mixed up about which source the material came from.

Finally, know when to say you have enough information. Many topics can be researched for a lifetime. It's not just the quantity of sources that counts. You should have enough diversity that you are confident you know the major points of view on a particular issue. When you reach a possible stopping point, group your notes and see whether a tentative organization for your paper becomes evident. People who like to work with notecards sometimes write comment cards to attach to each card, indicating how that piece of information fits. People who work with computer files sometimes type in caps how they see their notes fitting together. The method doesn't matter as much as the result. You should have a sketch outline by the time you finish the information-gathering stage.

CHAPTER 16

MLA Documentation

Intellectual Property and Scholastic Honesty

In the 1970s cassette tapes met with the ire of the recording industry, while the video recorder soon thereafter drove the motion picture studios to distraction. Why? These new technologies were enabling individuals to create unauthorized copies of music and movies. In 1999 the entertainment industry found a new foe in Shawn Fanning, the 19-year-old programmer and founder of Napster. Fanning's service allowed Internet users to "swap" MP3 formatted music files, circumventing royalty fees for each new copy of a song or album. While users reveled in the freedom of the new cyber-trend, musicians such as Metallica and Dr. Dre and trade organizations such as the Record Industry Association of America and the National Music Publishers Association hurled accusations of piracy. Ultimately, the courts upheld the rights of the artists and those who licensed their music, ruling that copyrighted music is property and that file "sharing" is "stealing." The Napster altercation—as well as the ongoing controversy over illegal file sharing—indicates the complexity of the concept of intellectual property and its applications. Copyright laws were established in the 1700s to protect the financial interests of publishers and authors, but over the last century, the domain of intellectual property has spread to company trademarks, photographs, films, radio and television broadcasts, computer software, and—as the courts forced Fanning and users to acknowledge—music scores, lyrics, and recordings. With the rising ubiquity of the Internet, conflict over the unauthorized distribution of intellectual property continues to increase as art, scholarship, and countless other cerebral creations find their way onto the crowded information superhighway.

Intellectual property rights, however, are not the main reason that college writing requires strict standards of documentation. Writing at the college level follows a long tradition of scholarly writing that insists on accuracy in referencing other work so that a reader can consult a writer's sources. Often, scholarly arguments build on the work of others, and experiments almost always identify an area that other researchers have addressed. Sometimes, other pieces of writing are the primary data, as when a historian uses letters and public documents to construct what happened in the past. It is important for other historians to be able to review the same documents to confirm or reject a particular interpretation.

There is also a basic issue of fairness in recognizing the work of others. If you find an idea in someone else's work that you want to use, it seems only fair to give that person proper credit. In Chapter 7, we discuss Robert H. Frank and Phillip J. Cook's controversial argument that changes in attitudes help to account for the increasing divide between rich and poor people since 1973, a shift that they summarize as the winner-take-all society. The phrase "winner-take-all society" has become common enough that you might hear it in news features describing the contemporary United States, but certainly any extended treatment of the concept should acknowledge Frank and Cook for coming up with the idea. Many students now acknowledge the work of other students if they feel that their classmates have made an important contribution to their work. And why not? It's only fair.

In our culture in general and in the professions in particular, work that people claim is their own is expected to be their own. Imagine that you are the director of marketing at a company that paid a consulting firm to conduct a survey, only to find out that the work the firm presented to you had been copied from another survey. Wouldn't you be on the phone right away to your company's attorneys? Even though the unethical copying of the survey might have been the failure of only one employee, surely the reputation of the consulting firm would be damaged, if not ruined. Many noteworthy people in political and public life have been greatly embarrassed by instances of plagiarism; in some cases, people have lost their positions as a result. Short of committing a felony, plagiarism is one of the few things that can get you expelled from your college or university if the case is serious enough. So it's worth it to you to know what plagiarism is and isn't.

Avoiding Plagiarism

Stated most simply, you would be guilty of plagiarizing if you used the words or ideas of someone else without acknowledging the source. That definition seems easy enough, but when you think about it, how many new ideas are there? And how could you possibly acknowledge where all your ideas came from? In practical terms, you are not expected to acknowledge everything. You do not have to acknowledge what is considered general knowledge, such as facts that you could find in a variety of reference books. For example, if you wanted to assert that Lyndon Johnson's victory over

Barry Goldwater in the 1964 presidential election remains the largest popular vote percentage (61 percent) in presidential election history, you would not have to acknowledge the source. This information should be available in encyclopedias, almanacs, and other general sources.

But if you cite a more obscure fact that wouldn't be as readily verifiable, you should let your readers know where you found it. Likewise, you should acknowledge the sources of any arguable statements, claims, or judgments. The sources of statistics, research findings, examples, graphs, charts, and illustrations also should be acknowledged. People are especially skeptical about statistics and research findings if the source is not mentioned.

Where most people get into plagiarism trouble is when they take words directly from a source and use them without quotation marks, or else change a few words and pass them off as their own words. It is easiest to illustrate where the line is drawn with an example. Suppose you are writing an argument about attempts to censor the Internet, and you want to examine how successful other nations have been. You find the following paragraph about China:

> China is encouraging Net use for business, but not what it considers seditious or pornographic traffic and "spiritual pollution." So the state is building its communications infrastructure like a mammoth corporate system—robust within the country, but with three gateways to the world, in Beijing, Shanghai, and Shenzhen. International exchanges can then be monitored and foreign content "filtered" at each information chokepoint, courtesy of the Public Security Bureau.
>
> —Jim Erickson. "WWW.POLITICS.COM." *Asiaweek* 2 Oct. 1998: 42.

You want to mention the point about the gateways in your paper. You have two basic options: to paraphrase the source or to quote it directly.

If you quote directly, you must include all words you take from the original inside quotation marks:

```
According to one observer, "China is encouraging Net use for

business, but not what it considers seditious or pornographic

traffic and 'spiritual pollution'" (Erickson 42).
```

This example is typical of MLA style. The citation goes outside the quotation marks but before the period. The reference is to the author's last name, which refers you to the full citation in the works-cited list at the end. Following the author's name is the page number where the quotation can be located. Notice also that if you quote material that contains quotation marks, then the double quotation marks around the original quotation change to the single quotation mark. If you include the author's name, then you need to include only the page number in the parentheses:

> According to Jim Erickson, "China is encouraging Net use for business, but not what it considers seditious or pornographic traffic and 'spiritual pollution'" (42).

If an article appears on one page only, you do not need to include the page number:

> According to Jim Erickson, "China is encouraging Net use for business, but not what it considers seditious or pornographic traffic and 'spiritual pollution.'"

If the newspaper article did not include the author's name, you would include the first word or two of the title. The logic of this system is to enable you to find the reference in the works-cited list.

The alternative to quoting directly is to paraphrase. When you paraphrase, you change the words without changing the meaning. Here are two examples:

Plagiarized

> China wants its citizens to use the Internet for business, but not for circulating views it doesn't like, pornography, and "spiritual pollution." So China is building its communications infrastructure like a mammoth corporate system—well linked internally but with only three ports to the outside world. The Public Security Bureau will monitor the foreign traffic at each information choke-point (Erickson).

This version is unacceptable. Too many of the words in the original are used directly here, including much of one sentence: "is building its communications infrastructure like a mammoth corporate system." If an entire string of words is lifted from a source and inserted without using quotation marks, then the passage is plagiarized. The first sentence is also too close in structure and wording to the original. Changing a few words in a sentence is not a paraphrase. Compare the following example:

Acceptable paraphrase

```
The Chinese government wants its citizens to take advantage
of the Internet for commerce while not allowing foreign
political ideas and foreign values to challenge its
authority. Consequently, the Chinese Internet will have
only three ports to the outside world. Traffic through
these ports will be monitored and censored by the Public
Security Bureau (Erickson).
```

There are a few words from the original in this paraphrase, such as *foreign* and *monitored,* but these sentences are original in structure and wording while accurately conveying the meaning of the original.

Using Sources Effectively

The purpose of using sources is to *support* your argument, not to make your argument for you. Next to plagiarism, the worst mistake you can make with sources is stringing them together without building an argument of your own. Your sources help to show that you've done your homework and that you've thought in depth about the issue.

One choice you have to make when using sources is when to quote and when to paraphrase. Consider the following example about expressways:

```
Urban planners of the 1960s saw superhighways as the means to
prevent inner cities from continuing to decay. Inner-city
blight was recognized as early as the 1930s, and the problem
was understood for four decades as one of circulation (hence
expressways were called "arterials"). The planners argued
that those who had moved to the suburbs would return to the
city on expressways. By the end of the 1960s, the engineers
were tearing down thousands of units of urban housing and
small businesses to build expressways with a logic that was
similar to the logic of mass bombing in Vietnam—to destroy
the city was to save it (Patton 102). Shortly the effects
were all too evident. Old neighborhoods were ripped apart,
```

```
the flight to the suburbs continued, and the decline of inner

cities accelerated rather than abated.

    Not everyone in the 1950s and 1960s saw expressways as

the answer to urban dilapidation. Lewis Mumford in 1958

challenged the circulation metaphor. He wrote: "Highway

planners have yet to realize that these arteries must not be

thrust into the delicate tissue of our cities; the blood they

circulate must rather enter through an elaborate network of

minor blood vessels and capillaries" (236). Mumford saw that

new expressways produced more congestion and aggravated the

problem they were designed to overcome, thus creating demand

for still more expressways. If road building through cities

were allowed to continue, he predicted the result would be "a

tomb of concrete roads and ramps covering the dead corpse of

a city" (238).
```

Notice that two sources are cited: Phil Patton, *Open Road: A Celebration of the American Highway.* New York: Simon, 1986; and Lewis Mumford, "The Highway and the City," *The Highway and the City.* New York: Harcourt, 1963. 234–46.

The writer decided that the point from Patton about tearing down thousands of units of urban housing and small businesses to build expressways in the 1960s should be paraphrased, but Mumford's remarks should be quoted directly. In both direct quotations from Mumford, the original wording is important. Mumford rejects the metaphor of arteries for expressways and foresees in vivid language the future of cities as paved-over tombs. As a general rule, you should use direct quotations only when the original language is important. Otherwise, you should paraphrase.

If a direct quotation runs more than four lines, then it should be indented one inch and double-spaced. But you still should *integrate* long quotations into the text of your paper. Long quotations should be attributed; that is, you should say where the quotation comes from in your text as well as in the reference. And it is a good idea to include at least a sentence or two after the quotation to describe its significance for your argument. The original wording in the long quotation in the following paragraph is important because it gives a sense of the language of the Port Huron Statement. The sentences following the quotation explain why many faculty members in the 1960s looked on the

Port Huron Statement as a positive sign (of course, college administrators were horrified). You might think of this strategy as putting an extended quotation in an envelope with your words before and after:

> Critiques of the staleness and conformity of American education made the first expressions of student radicalism in the 1960s such as the "Port Huron Statement" from the Students for a Democratic Society (SDS) in 1962 appear as a breath of fresh air. The SDS wrote:
>
> > Almost no students value activity as a citizen. Passive in public, they are hardly more idealistic in arranging their private lives; Gallup concludes they will settle for "low success, and won't risk high failure." There is not much willingness to take risks (not even in business), no setting of dangerous goals, no real conception of personal identity except one manufactured in the image of others, no real urge for personal fulfillment except to be almost as successful as the very successful people. Attention is being paid to social status (the quality of shirt collars, meeting people, getting wives or husbands, making solid contacts for later on); much, too, is paid to academic status (grades, honors, the med-school rat race). But neglected generally is real intellectual status, the personal cultivation of mind. (238)
>
> Many professors shared the SDS disdain for the political quietism on college campuses. When large-scale ferment erupted among students during the years of the Vietnam War, some faculty welcomed it as a sign of finally emerging from the intellectual stagnation of the Eisenhower years. For some it was a sign that the promise of John F. Kennedy's administration could be fulfilled, that young people could create a new national identity.

Note three points about form in the long quotation. First, there are no quotation marks around the extended quotation. Readers know that the material is quoted because it is blocked off. Second, words quoted in the original retain the double quotation marks. Third, the page number appears *after* the period at the end of the quotation.

Whether long or short, make all quotations part of the fabric of your paper while being careful to indicate which words belong to the original. A reader should be able to move through the body of your paper without having to stop and ask: Why did the writer include this quotation? or Which words are the writer's and which are being quoted?

MLA Works-Cited List

Different disciplines use different styles for documentation. The two styles that are used most frequently are the APA style and the MLA style. APA stands for American Psychological Association, which publishes a style manual used widely in the social sciences (see Chapter 17). MLA stands for the Modern Language Association, and its style is the norm for humanities disciplines, including English and rhetoric and composition.

Both MLA and APA styles use a works-cited list placed at the end of a paper. Here is an example of an MLA works-cited list.

Smith 10

Center "Works Cited."

Double-space all entries. Indent all but the first line five spaces.

Alphabetize entries by last name of authors or by title if no author is listed.

Works Cited

Bingham, Janet. "Kids Become Masters of Electronic Universe: School Internet Activity Abounds." Denver Post 3 Sept. 1996: A13.

Dyrli, Odvard Egil, and Daniel E. Kinnaman. "Telecommunications: Gaining Access to the World." Technology and Learning 16.3 (1995): 79–84.

Smith 11

Ellsworth, Jill H. <u>Education on the</u>

<u>Internet: A Hands-On Book of Ideas,</u>

<u>Resources, Projects, and Advice.</u>

Indianapolis: Sams, 1994.

National Center for Education Statistics.

"Internet Access in Public Education."

Feb. 1998. NCES. 4 Jan. 1999 <http://

nces.ed.gov/pubs98/98021.html>.

Romano, Allison. "Oxygen: It Lives! Now Can

It Breathe? After Some Stumbles, the

Women's Network Is Working to Refine

and Redefine Its Image." <u>Broadcasting</u>

<u>and Cable</u> 5 May 2003: 10.

"UK: A Battle for Young Hearts and Minds."

<u>Computer Weekly</u> 4 Apr. 1996: 20.

> Underline the titles of books and periodicals.

The works-cited list eliminates the need for footnotes. If you have your sources listed on notecards, then all you have to do when you finish your paper is to find the cards for all the sources that you cite, alphabetize the cards by author, and type your works-cited list. For works with no author listed, alphabetize by the first content word in the title (ignore *a*, *an*, and *the*).

Some of the more common citation formats in MLA style are listed in the following section. If you have questions that these examples do not address, you should consult the *MLA Handbook for Writers of Research Papers* (6th edition, 2003) and the *MLA Style Manual and Guide to Scholarly Publishing* (2nd edition, 1998).

For a sample MLA-style research paper, see pages 196–206.

Citing Books

The basic format for listing books in the works-cited list is

1. Author's name (last name first)
2. Title (underlined)
3. Place of publication
4. Short name of publisher
5. Date of publication

On the book's title page (not on the cover) you will find the exact title, the publisher, and the city (use the first city if several are listed). The date of publication is included in the copyright notice on the back of the title page.

Book by One Author

Lewis, Michael. Moneyball: The Art of Winning an Unfair Game.
   New York: Norton, 2003.

Book by Two or Three Authors

Sturken, Marita, and Lisa Cartwright. Practices of Looking: An
   Introduction to Visual Culture. New York: Oxford UP, 2001.

Book by Four or More Authors

Redkar, Arohi, et al. Pro MSMQ: Microsoft Message Queue
   Programming. Berkeley: Apress, 2004.

Two or More Books by the Same Author

Berger, John. About Looking. New York: Pantheon, 1980.

---. Ways of Seeing. New York: Viking, 1973.

Translation

Martin, Henri-Jean. The History and Power of Writing. Trans.
   Lydia G. Cochrane. Chicago: U of Chicago P, 1994.

Edited Book

Bizzell, Patricia, and Bruce Herzberg, eds. The Rhetorical
   Tradition: Readings from Classical Times to the Present.
   Boston: Bedford, 1990.

One Volume of a Multivolume Work

Arnold, Matthew. <u>Complete Prose Works</u>. Ed. R. H. Super.

    Vol. 2. Ann Arbor: U of Michigan P, 1960.

Selection in an Anthology or Chapter in an Edited Collection

Merritt, Russell. "Nickelodeon Theaters, 1905-1914: Building

    an Audience for the Movies." <u>The American Film Industry</u>.

    Rev. ed. Ed. Tino Balio. Madison: U of Wisconsin P,

    1985. 83-102.

Government Document

Malveaux, Julianne. "Changes in the Labor Market Status of

    Black Women." <u>A Report of the Study Group on Affirmative</u>

    <u>Action to the Committee on Education and Labor</u>. 100th

    Cong., 1st sess. H. Rept. 100-L. Washington: GPO, 1987.

    213-55.

Bible

Holy Bible. Revised Standard Version Containing the Old and

    New Testaments. New York: Collins, 1973. [Note that

    "Bible" is not underlined.]

Citing Articles in Periodicals

When citing periodicals, the necessary items to include are

1. Author's name (last name first)
2. Title of article inside quotation marks
3. Title of journal or magazine (underlined)
4. Volume number (for scholarly journals)
5. Date
6. Page numbers

Many scholarly journals are printed to be bound as one volume, usually by year, and the pagination is continuous for that year. If, say, a scholarly journal is printed in four issues and the first issue ends on page 278, then the second issue will begin with page 279. For journals that are continuously paginated, you do not need to include the issue number. Some scholarly journals, however, are paginated like magazines with each issue beginning on page 1. For journals paginated by issue, you should list the issue number along with the volume (e.g., for the first issue of volume 11, you would put "11.1" in the entry after the title of the journal).

Article in a Scholarly Journal—Continuous Pagination

Berlin, James A. "Rhetoric and Ideology in the Writing
    Class." College English 50 (1988): 477-94.

Article in a Scholarly Journal—Continuous Pagination, Two or Three Authors

Roach, Bill, and Mary Roach. "Horatio Alger, Jr.: Precursor
    of the Stratemeyer Syndicate." Journal of Popular
    Culture 37 (2004): 450-62.

Article in a Scholarly Journal—Continuous Pagination, Four or More Authors

Domke, David, et al. "Insights Into U.S. Racial
    Hierarchy: Racial Profiling, News Sources, and
    September 11." Journal of Communication 53 (2003): 606-23.

Article in a Scholarly Journal—Pagination by Issue

Kolby, Jerry. "The Top-Heavy Economy: Managerial Greed and
    Unproductive Labor." Critical Sociology 15.3 (1988): 53-69.

Review

Chomsky, Noam. Rev. of Verbal Behavior, by B. F. Skinner.
    Language 35 (1959): 26-58.

Magazine Article

Engardio, Pete. "Microsoft's Long March." Business Week 24
    June 1996: 52-54.

Newspaper Article

Bingham, Janet. "Kids Become Masters of Electronic Universe:

School Internet Activity Abounds." Denver Post 3 Sept.

1996: A13

Letter to the Editor

Luker, Ralph E. Letter. Chronicle of Higher Education 18 Dec.

1998: B9

Editorial

"An Open Process." Editorial. Wall Street Journal 30 Dec.

1998: A10

Citing Online Sources

Online sources pose special difficulties for systems of citing sources. Many online sources change frequently. Sometimes you discover to your frustration that what you had found on a Web site the previous day has been altered or in some cases no longer exists. Furthermore, basic information such as who put up a Web site and when it was last changed are often absent. Many print sources have also been put on the Web, which raises another set of difficulties. The basic format for citing a generic Web site is

1. Author's name (last name first)
2. Title of the document (in quotation marks)
3. Title of complete work or name of the journal (underlined)
4. Date of Web publication or last update
5. Sponsoring organization
6. Date you visited
7. URL (enclosed in angle brackets)

Book on the Web

Rheingold, Howard. Tools for Thought: The People and Ideas of

the Next Computer Revolution. New York: Simon, 1985. 14

Sept. 2004 <http://www.well.com/user/hlr/

texts/tftindex.html>.

Article in a Scholarly Journal on the Web

Browning, Tonya. "Embedded Visuals: Student Design in Web

Spaces." <u>Kairos</u> 2.1 (1997). 4 May 2004 <http://

www.as.ttu.edu/kairos/2.1/features/browning/index.html>.

Article in a Library Database

Pope, Nigel K. "The Impact of Stress in Self- and Peer

Assessment." <u>Assessment and Evaluation in Higher</u>

<u>Education</u> 30 (2005): 51-63. <u>Academic Search Premier.</u>

EBSCO. Zimmerman Lib., U of New Mexico. 14 Feb. 2005

<http://www.epnet.com/>.

Article in a Magazine on the Web

Layden, Tim. "Taking Action: Give Track and Field

Credit for Trying to Clean Up Its Doping

Problem." <u>SI.com</u> 3 July 2004. 28 July 2004

<http://sportsillustrated.cnn.com/2004/writers/

tim_layden/07/23/track.doping/index.html>.

Web Publication by an Organization

"ACLU Warns House Approval of Increased Indecency Fines Will

Have a Chilling Effect on Speech." 11 Mar. 2004.

American Civil Liberties Union. 28 July 2004 <http://

www.aclu.org/FreeSpeech/FreeSpeech.cfm?ID=15248&c=42>.

Personal Subscription Service (AOL)

Parascenzo, Marino A. "Zaharias, Babe Didrikson."

<u>World Book Online Reference Center</u>. 2004. America

Online. 29 July 2004. Keyword: Zaharias.

Newsgroup or Listserv Posting

Card, Lorin. "Re: <u>Fahrenheit 9/11—Fahrenheit 451</u>."

Online posting. 28 July 2004. H-NET List for

Scholarly Studies and Uses of Media. 28 July 2004

<http://h-net.msu.edu/>.

Entry in a Weblog (Blog)

Stereogum. "Dustin Hoffman Saves Bee Sting Victim." Weblog
    posting. 28 July 2004. The Best Week Ever. 30 July 2004
    <http://bestweekever.vh1.com/2004/07/
    dustin_hoffman_.html>.

Personal Email

Fung, Richard. "Re: Invitation to University of Texas Speaking
    Engagement." Email to the author. 13 Oct. 2003.

Course Web Site

Caristi, Dom. Programs and Audiences. Course home page
    Sept. 2004-Apr. 2005. Dept. of Telecommunications,
    Ball State U. 28 July 2004 <http://www.bsu.edu/classes/
    caristi/tcom306/>.

Personal Web Site

Vitanza, Victor. Home page. 24 Apr. 2002. 7 Sept. 2004
    <http://www.uta.edu/english/V/Victor_.html>.

CD-ROM

Boyer, Paul, et al. The Enduring Vision, Interactive Edition.
    1993 ed. CD-ROM. Lexington: Heath, 1993.

Citing Visual Sources

Film

Harry Potter and the Prisoner of Azkaban. Dir.
    Alfonso Cuarón. Perf. Daniel Radcliffe, Rupert
    Grint, Emma Watson, David Thewlis, Michael
    Gambon, Maggie Smith, Alan Rickman, Emma
    Thompson, Robbie Coltrane, and Gary Oldman.
    Warner Bros., 2004.

Television Program

"The Attitude." Perf. Calista Flockhart, Courtney
Thorne-Smith. Dir. Allan Arkush, Daniel Attias,
et al. Writ. David E. Kelley. Ally McBeal. Fox.
WFXT, Boston. 3 Nov. 1997.

Cartoon

Hamilton, Jane. "Little Rascals." Cartoon. Entertainment
Weekly. 14 Mar. 2003: 8.

Advertisement

"The Laughing Cow." Advertisement. People. 2 Aug. 2004: 20.

Painting, Sculpture, or Photograph

Hernandez, Anthony. Rome #17. Solomon R. Guggenheim Museum,
New York.

Citing Other Sources

Personal Interview

Williams, Errick Lynn. Telephone interview. 4 Jan. 1999.

Broadcast Interview

Reagan, Ron, Jr. Interview with Terry Gross. Fresh Air. Natl.
Public Radio. KUT-FM, Austin. 22 July 2004.

Unpublished Dissertation

Rouzie, Albert. "At Play in the Fields of Writing: Play and
Digital Literacy in a College-Level Computers and
Writing Course." Diss. U of Texas at Austin, 1997.

Recording

Glass, Phillip. "Low" Symphony. Point Music, 1973.

Speech

Khrushchev, Sergei. "Russia, Putin, and the War on Terrorism."
National Press Club, Washington. 6 Dec. 2001.

CHAPTER 17

APA Documentation

D isciplines in the social sciences (anthropology, government, linguistics, psychology, sociology) and in education most frequently use the APA (American Psychological Association) documentation style. This chapter offers a brief overview of the APA style. For a detailed treatment you should consult the *Publication Manual of the American Psychological Association*, fifth edition (2001).

The APA style has many similarities to the MLA style described in Chapter 16. Both styles use parenthetical references in the body of the text with complete bibliographical citations in the reference list at the end. The most important difference is the emphasis on the date of publication in the APA style. When you cite an author's name in the body of your paper with APA style, you always include the date of publication and the page number:

> By the end of the 1960s, the engineers were tearing down thousands of units of urban housing and small businesses to build expressways with a logic that was similar to the logic of mass bombing in Vietnam—to destroy the city was to save it (Patton, 1986, p. 102). Shortly the effects were all too evident. Old neighborhoods were ripped apart, the flight to the suburbs continued, and the decline of inner cities accelerated rather than abated.
>
> Not everyone in the 1950s and 1960s saw expressways as the answer to urban dilapidation. Mumford (1963) challenged the circulation metaphor: "Highway planners have yet to realize that these arteries must not be thrust into the delicate tissue of our cites; the blood they circulate must rather enter through an elaborate network of minor blood vessels and capillaries" (p. 236).

Notice that unlike MLA, a comma is placed after the author's name and the abbreviation for page is included (Patton, 1986, p. 102).

APA Reference List

The APA list of works cited is titled *References*:

Center "References"

Double-space all entries. Indent all but first line five spaces.

Alphabetize entries by last name of authors or by title if no author is listed.

Notice that author's initials are listed rather than first names.

Notice that only the first words and proper nouns are capitalized in titles and subtitles of articles and books.

Notice that article titles are not placed inside quotation marks.

If an author has more than one entry, put the earliest publication first.

New Technologies 5

References

Bingham, J. (1996, September 3). Kids
    become masters of electronic
    universe: School Internet activity
    abounds. *Denver Post,* p. A13.

Dyrli, O. E., & Kinnaman, D. E. (1995).
    Telecommunications: Gaining access to
    the world. *Technology and Learning,*
    16(3), 79–84.

Engardio, P. (1996, June 24). Microsoft's
    long march. *Business Week,* 52–54.

The future just happened. (2001, July 29).
    BBC Online. Retrieved August 29,
    2001, from http://news.bbc.co.uk/hi/
    english/static/in_depth/programmes/
    2001/future/tv_series_1.stm

Lewis, M. (1989). *Liar's poker: Rising
    through the wreckage on Wall Street.*
    New York: Norton.

Lewis, M. (2000). *The next new thing: A
    Silicon Valley story.* New York: Norton.

Lewis, M. (2001). *Next: The future just
    happened.* New York: Norton.

```
                    New Technologies 6

National Center for Education Statistics.

     (1998, February). Internet access in

     public education. Retrieved May 21,

     1998, from http://nces.ed.gov/pubs98/

     98021.html

UK: A battle for young hearts and minds.

     (1996, April 4). Computer Weekly, 20.
```

Italicize the titles of books and periodicals.

The reference list eliminates the need for footnotes. If you have your sources listed on notecards, all you have to do when you finish your paper is find the cards for all the sources that you cite, alphabetize the cards by author (or title), and type your reference list. For works with no author listed, alphabetize by the first significant word in the title (ignore *a*, *an*, and *the*).

Citing Books

The basic format for listing books in the reference list is

1. Author's name (last name first, initials)
2. Year of publication (in parentheses)
3. Title (in italics)
4. Place of publication
5. Name of publisher

Use the abbreviation for pages (pp.) for chapters in a book. Note that unlike MLA, APA includes the full range of pages (pp. 151–158).

Book by One Author

```
Wolf, S. (2002). A problem like Maria: Gender and sexuality

     in the American musical. Ann Arbor, MI: University of

     Michigan Press.
```

Book by Two or More Authors

Scribner, S., & Cole, M. (1981). *The psychology of literacy.* Cambridge, MA: Harvard University Press.

Two or More Books by the Same Author

Stagier, J. (2000). *Perverse spectators: The practices of film reception.* New York: New York University Press.

Stagier, J. (2001). *Blockbuster TV: Must-see-sitcoms in the network era.* New York: New York University Press.

Edited Book

Inness, S. (Ed.). (2004). *Action chicks: New images of tough women in popular culture.* New York: Palgrave Macmillan.

Translated Book

Homer. (2004). *The odyssey: Homer.* (E. McCrorie, Trans.). Baltimore, MD: Johns Hopkins University Press.

One Volume of a Multivolume Work

de Selincourt, E., & Darbishire, H. (Eds.). (1958). *The poetical works of William Wordsworth* (Vol. 5). Oxford, England: Oxford University Press.

Selection in an Anthology or Chapter in an Edited Collection

Merritt, R. (1985). Nickelodeon theaters, 1905–1914: Building an audience for the movies. In T. Balio (Ed.), *The American film industry* (Rev. ed., pp. 83–102). Madison: University of Wisconsin Press.

Unpublished Dissertation

Rouzie, A. (1997). *At play in the fields of writing: Play and digital literacy in a college-level computers and writing course.* Unpublished doctoral dissertation, University of Texas at Austin.

Citing Articles in Periodicals

When citing periodicals, the necessary items to include are

1. Author's name (last name first, initials)
2. Date of publication (in parentheses). For scholarly journals, give the year. For newspapers and weekly magazines, give the year followed by the month and day (2001, December 13)
3. Title of the article
4. Title of the journal or magazine (in italics)
5. Volume number (in italics)
6. Page numbers

For articles in newspapers, use the abbreviation for page or pages (p. or pp.).

Many scholarly journals are printed to be bound as one volume, usually by year, and the pagination is continuous for that year. If, say, a scholarly journal is printed in four issues and the first issue ends on page 278, then the second issue will begin with page 279. For journals that are continuously paginated, you do not need to include the issue number. Some scholarly journals, however, are paginated like magazines with each issue beginning on page 1. For journals paginated by issue, you should list the issue number along with the volume (e.g., for the first issue of volume 11, you would put *11*(1) in the entry after the title of the journal).

Article in a Scholarly Journal—Continuous Pagination

Berlin, J. A. (1988). Rhetoric and ideology in the writing
class. *College English, 50*, 477–494.

Article in a Scholarly Journal—Pagination by Issue

Kolby, J. (1988). The top-heavy economy: Managerial greed
and unproductive labor. *Critical Sociology,*
15(3), 53–69.

Article by Two Authors

Roach, B., & Roach, M. (2004). Horatio Alger, Jr.: Precursor
of the Stratemeyer syndicate. *Journal of Popular*
Culture, 37(3), 450–462.

Article by Three or More Authors (if more than six, the seventh and subsequent authors can be abbreviated to *et al.*)

Domke, D., Garland, P., Billeaudeaux, A., & Hutcheson, J.

(2003). Insights into U.S. racial hierarchy: Racial

profiling, news sources, and September 11. *Journal of*

Communication, *53*, 606–623.

Review

Chomsky, N. (1959). [Review of the book *Verbal behavior*].

Language, 35, 26–58.

Magazine Article

Engardio, P. (1996, June 24). Microsoft's long march.

Business Week, 52–54.

Magazine Article—No Author Listed

UK: A battle for young hearts and minds. (1996, April 4).

Computer Weekly, 20.

Newspaper Article

Bingham, J. (1996, September 3). Kids become masters of

electronic universe: School Internet activity abounds.

Denver Post, p. A13.

Citing Online Sources

The *Publication Manual of the American Psychological Association* specifies that those citing Web sources should direct readers to the exact source page if possible, not to menu or home pages. URLs have to be typed with complete accuracy to identify a Web site. If you type an uppercase letter for a lowercase letter, a browser will not find the site. To avoid typos in URLs, load the page in your browser, highlight the URL, and copy it (Control C on Windows or Command C on a Mac), and then paste it into the reference. You may have to change the font to match your text, but you will have the accurate URL.

The basic format for citing online sources is as follows:

1. Author's last name, initials
2. Date of document or last revision in parentheses
3. Title of document. Capitalize only the first word and any proper nouns.
4. Title of periodical (if applicable). Use italics and capitalize only the first word and any proper nouns.
5. Date of retrieval
6. URL or access path from a database. Notice that there is no period after a URL.

Article in a Scholarly Journal on the Web

Agre, P. (1998). The Internet and public discourse.

First Monday, 3(3). Retrieved July 10, 2001, from

http://www.firstmonday.dk/issues/issue3_3/agre/

Article Retrieved from a Database

Schott, G., & Selwyn, N. (2001). Examining the "male,

antisocial" stereotype of high computer users. Journal

of Educational Computing Research, 23, 291—303.

Retrieved November 2, 2004, from PsychINFO database.

Abstract Retrieved from a Database

Putsis, W. P., & Bayus, B. L. (2001). An empirical analysis

of firms' product line decisions. Journal of Marketing

Research, 37(8), 110—118. Abstract retrieved December

31, 2004, from PsychINFO database.

Article in a Newspaper on the Web

Mendels, P. (1999, May 26). Nontraditional teachers

more likely to use the Net. New York Times on

the Web. Retrieved September 19, 2001, from

http://www.nytimes.com/library/tech/99/05/cyber/

education/26education.html

Article from an Online News Service

Rao, M. (1999, February 10). WorldTel in $100 M community
    initiative for Indian state. *Asia InternetNews*.
    Retrieved April 15, 2001, from http://asia.internet.com/
    1999/2/1003-india.html

Article in a Magazine on the Web

Happy new Euro. (1998, December 30). *Time Daily*. Retrieved
    May 10, 2000, from http://www.time.com/
    time/nation/article/0,8599,17455,00.html

Online Encyclopedia

Semiconductor. (1999). In *Encyclopaedia Britannica Online*.
    Retrieved November 30, 2000, from http://search.eb.com/
    bol/topic?eu=68433&sctn=1#s_top

Document on a Web Site

Kaplan, N. (1997, December 17). E-literacies:
    Politexts, hypertexts and other cultural
    formations in the late age of print. Retrieved
    July 2, 2001, from http://raven.ubalt.edu/
    staff/kaplan/lit/

Document on the Web Site of an Organization

National Audubon Society. (2001). Cowbirds and
    conservation. Retrieved August 15, 2001,
    from http://www.audubon.org/bird/research/

Electronic Version of a U.S. Government Report

U.S. Public Health Service. Office of the Surgeon
    General.(2001, January 11). *Clean indoor air regulations
    fact sheet*. Retrieved February 12, 2001,
    from http://www.cdc.gov/tobacco/sgr/sgr_2000/factsheets/
    factsheet_clean.htm

Graphic, Audio, or Video Files

East Timor awaits referendum. (1999, August 31). *NPR Online*.

Retrieved August 31, 1999, from http://www.npr.org/

ramfiles/atc/19990830.atc.10.ram

Electronic Mailing List Posting

Selzer, J. (1998, July 4). Ed Corbett. Message posted to

WPA-L@lists.asu.edu

Entry in a Weblog

Stereogum. (2004, July 28). Dustin Hoffman saves bee sting

victim. Message posted to http://bestweekever.vh1.com/

2004/07/dustin_hoffman_.html

Newsgroup Posting

Brody, P. (1999, May 9). Chamax. Message posted to news:

sci.archaeology.mesoamerican

Personal Email

APA omits personal email from the list of references. Personal communication can be cited in parenthetical references in the text. Provide a date if possible.

S. Wilson (personal communication, April 6, 2004)

Citing Other Sources

Government Report

U.S. Environmental Protection Agency. (1992). *Respiratory*

health effects of passive smoking: Lung cancer and other

disorders. (EPA Publication No. 600/6-90/006 F).

Washington, DC: Author.

Film

Spielberg, S. (Director). (1998). *Saving Private Ryan* [Motion

picture]. United States: Paramount Pictures.

Television Broadcast

Burns, K. (Writer). (1992, January 29). *Empire of the air:*
The men who made radio [Television broadcast]. Walpole,
NH: Florentine Films.

Television Series

Connelly, J. (Producer). (1957). *Leave it to Beaver*
[Television series]. New York: CBS Television.

Music Recording

Glass, P. (1973). *"Low" symphony* [CD]. New York: Point Music.

Contemporary Arguments

CHAPTER 18

Negotiating the Environment

American Environmentalism

As noted in the first chapter, Rachel Carson's *Silent Spring* in 1962 stimulated the environmental movement in the United States. Carson's book explicitly indicted pesticides commonly used in the agriculture industry, particularly DDT, but implicitly she was arguing for something broader—for a new sense of our relation to our environment, for the conviction that we should be living in balance with nature, not in domination over it. Thus, Carson's book ultimately influenced not just agricultural practice but also efforts to protect endangered species, to regulate population growth, and to clean up our air and water resources. When President Richard Nixon created the Environmental Protection Agency in 1973, environmental concern became institutionalized in the United States; most states created their own departments of natural resources or environmental protection soon after.

In part, Rachel Carson was successful because her appeals struck a chord deep within many Americans. For in a very real sense environmental-

> We are the most dangerous species of life on the planet, and every other species, even the earth itself, has cause to fear our power to exterminate. But we are also the only species which, when it chooses to do so, will go to great effort to save what it might destroy.
>
> —WALLACE STEGNER

ism is ingrained within the American character. It derives from a respect for the land—the American Eden—that is evident in the legend of Rip Van Winkle, in the work of Hudson River painters such as Thomas Cole, in the landscape architecture of Frederick Law Olmsted, in Henry David Thoreau's *Walden* and in Ralph Waldo Emerson's Transcendentalist writings in the 1850s, in John Muir's testimonials about Yosemite, and in Theodore Roosevelt's withdrawals into the Badlands and his campaign to begin a system

Thomas Cole's American Lake Scene (1844)
Source: *American Lake Scene,* 1844 by Thomas Cole, gift of Douglas R. Roby, photograph © 1986 The Detroit Institute of the Arts.

of national parks. Of course, the exploitation of the American green world for profit is also ingrained in our national character. Even as some Americans were reverencing the land as a special landscape that sustained them physically and spiritually, pioneers moving westward were subduing it for their own purposes, in the process spoiling rivers and air and virgin forests—and native peoples—in the name of development.

Contemporary Arguments

The tension between the uses of nature and its protection is persistent. This tension helps to explain why arguments about environmental issues are so prevalent in public discourse today.

- Are science and technology friends or foes of the environment?
- What is the proper relationship between people and the natural environment?

- What is a suitable balance between resource development and resource protection—resources including everything from timber and coal to streams and animals?

- How serious a problem is global warming, and what should be done about it?

- To what extent should we invest scarce resources in the protection of little-known species or lands whose benefit to people has not been demonstrated?

- How can poorer nations develop economically without global environmental repercussions?

- Is it already too late to avoid such repercussions?

Such questions are debated each day in every kind of media, especially as organized environmental groups are legion, ranging from the activist Earth First! (whose ten thousand members sometimes advocate direct action in support of environmental aims) to more mainstream groups such as the Sierra Club or the Nature Conservancy, which has created a membership of nearly one million in an explicit effort to create partnerships between scientists and businesspersons in the interests of environmental reform. On the other hand, conservatives such as Rush Limbaugh have often ridiculed the efforts of environmentalists in the interest of a relatively unbridled developmentalism that is in the optimistic tradition of nineteenth-century free enterprise.

Debates about environmental issues, in other words, are part and parcel of American culture. What follows is a sampling of several arguments on which our future depends. The first ones (by Edward O. Wilson, N. Scott Momaday, Alice Walker, and

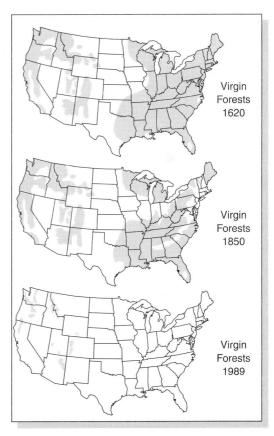

How Virgin Forests Have Diminished in the Continental United States

Wendell Berry) present for approval one or another aspect of what might be called "the environmental ethic." In a very real sense, these essays provide a context for a great many of the environmental arguments that are offered in the United States.

Next, in the tradition of Rachel Carson's warnings about environmental catastrophe comes James Howard Kunstler's "The Long Emergency"—a dire causal argument that worries about our national dependence on fossil fuels. Kunstler's essay provides an apt introduction to the arguments that follow it, on global warming. Scientific evidence continues to contribute to the conclusion that the burning of fossil fuel is causing the earth's atmosphere to warm, and so in December 1997 representatives from about 150 nations, meeting in Kyoto, Japan, signed a protocol to combat global warming by limiting fossil fuel emissions. But many nations, including the United States, have not ratified that agreement (negotiations are continuing)

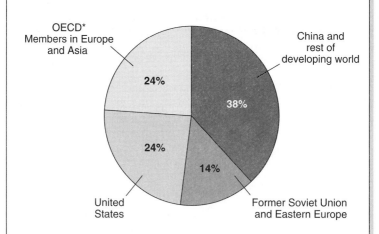

The United States Produces Most Greenhouse Gases

The United States produces about a quarter of the world's carbon dioxide emissions—the major cause of global warming. While U.S. emissions are expected to drop to 21 percent of the total by 2020, those from China and the rest of the developing world will rise from the current 38 percent to 50 percent.

Worldwide Carbon Emissions by Region, 1996

OECD* Members in Europe and Asia — 24%

China and rest of developing world — 38%

United States — 24%

Former Soviet Union and Eastern Europe — 14%

* Organization for Economic Cooperation and Development

Source: Environmental Protection Agency Web site on global warming: www.epa.gov/global_missions/international/projections.html.
Reproduced in *CQ Researcher* issue on global warming, January 26, 2001.

because many people still contend that the rise in temperatures may be due to natural causes or that the consequences need not be dire. Here we present arguments on both sides of the issue. (See also pages 21–22.)

The section concludes with a focus on a particular issue that is a prototype for many others in the same vein—habitat loss and restoration in the Yellowstone National Park area. Should wolves, victimized by habitat loss in the nineteenth and twentieth centuries, be reintroduced into the West in the twenty-first? More broadly, what are our responsibilities to animals and plants in particular—and to environmental protection in general? Is it possible to have both economic development and a healthy environment, or must hard choices be made? And if it comes to choices, which ones must be made?

EDWARD O. WILSON

The Conservation Ethic

Edward O. Wilson, a long-time Harvard professor and an entomologist with a special interest in ants, is one of the world's leading naturalists. He has won the Pulitzer Prize (twice) and the National Medal of Science, among other awards. Many of his books, including The Diversity of Life, Naturalist, *and* Biophilia, *emphasize the vitality of species diversity and decry activities that cause the extinction of particular species. Wilson points out the value of even the smallest bugs and plants as integral parts of life-systems. The following text, from* Biophilia *(1984), outlines important connections between ecology and ethics.*

1   When very little is known about an important subject, the questions people raise are almost invariably ethical. Then as knowledge grows, they become more concerned with information and amoral, in other words more narrowly intellectual. Finally, as understanding becomes sufficiently complete, the questions turn ethical again. Environmentalism is now passing from the first to the second phase, and there is reason to hope that it will proceed directly on to the third.

2   The future of the conservation movement depends on such an advance in moral reasoning. Its maturation is linked to that of biology and a new hybrid field, bioethics, that deals with the many technological advances recently made possible by biology. Philosophers and scientists are applying a more formal analysis to such complex problems as the allocations of scarce organ transplants, heroic but extremely expensive efforts to prolong life, and the possible use of genetic engineering to alter human heredity. They have only begun to consider the relationships

between human beings and organisms with the same rigor. It is clear that the key to precision lies in the understanding of motivation, the ultimate reasons why people care about one thing but not another—why, say, they prefer a city with a park to a city alone. The goal is to join emotion with the rational analysis of emotion in order to create a deeper and more enduring conservation ethic.

3   Aldo Leopold, the pioneer ecologist and author of *A Sand County Almanac,* defined an ethic as a set of rules invented to meet circumstances so new or intricate, or else encompassing responses so far in the future, that the average person cannot foresee the final outcome. What

ALDO LEOPOLD

Excerpts from The Land Ethic

Aldo Leopold (1887–1948) was one of the most influential nature writers of the twentieth century and one of the founders of modern ecology. He was completing his essay "The Land Ethic" when he died while fighting a brushfire in a neighbor's field. It appeared in Leopold's posthumously published A Sand County Almanac *(1949). As the following excerpts illustrate, the essay offers a new way of understanding our relationship with the environment—an understanding which has powerfully influenced environmental policy debates in the United States.*

The Ethical Sequence

The first ethics dealt with the relation between individuals; the Mosaic Decalogue is an example. Later accretions dealt with the relation between the individual and society. The Golden Rule tries to integrate the individual to society; democracy to integrate social organization to the individual.

There is as yet no ethic dealing with man's relation to land and to the animals and plants which grow upon it.

The Community Concept

All ethics so far evolved rest upon a single premise: that the individual is a member of a community of interdependent parts. His instincts prompt him to compete for his place in that community, but his ethics prompt him also to co-operate (perhaps in order that there may be a place to compete for).

The land ethic simply enlarges the boundaries of the community to include soils, waters, plants, and animals, or collectively: the land.

is good for you and me at this moment might easily sour within ten years, and what seems ideal for the next few decades could ruin future generations. That is why any ethic worthy of the name has to encompass the distant future. The relationships of ecology and the human mind are too intricate to be understood entirely by unaided intuition, by common sense—that overrated capacity composed of the set of prejudices we acquire by the age of eighteen.

4   Values are time-dependent, making them all the more difficult to carve in stone. We want health, security, freedom, and pleasure for ourselves and our families. For distant generations we wish the same but

The Ecological Conscience

Obligations have no meaning without conscience, and the problem we face is the extension of the social conscience from people to land.

Substitutes for a Land Ethic

A system of conservation based solely on economic self-interest is hopelessly lopsided. It tends to ignore, and thus eventually to eliminate, many elements in the land community that lack commercial value, but that are (as far as we know) essential to its healthy functioning.

The Land Pyramid

Land, then, is not merely soil; it is a fountain of energy flowing through a circuit of soils, plants, and animals. Food chains are the living channels which conduct energy upward; death and decay return it to the soil.

Land Health and the A–B Cleavage

We see repeated the same basic paradoxes: man the conqueror *versus* man the biotic citizen; science the sharpener of his sword *versus* science the searchlight on his universe; land the slave and servant *versus* land the collective organism.

The Outlook

Examine each question in terms of what is ethically and esthetically right, as well as what is economically expedient. A thing is right when it tends to preserve the integrity, stability, and beauty of the biotic community. It is wrong when it tends otherwise. ■

not at any great personal cost. The difficulty created for the conservation ethic is that natural selection has programmed people to think mostly in physiological time. Their minds travel back and forth across hours, days, or at most a hundred years. The forests may all be cut, radiation slowly rise, and the winters grow steadily colder, but if the effects are unlikely to become decisive for a few generations, very few people will be stirred to revolt. Ecological and evolutionary time, spanning centuries and millennia, can be conceived in an intellectual mode but has no immediate emotional impact. Only through an unusual amount of education and reflective thought do people come to respond emotionally to far-off events and hence place a high premium on posterity.

5   The deepening of the conservation ethic requires a greater measure of evolutionary realism, including a valuation of ourselves as opposed to other people. What do we really owe our remote descendants? At the risk of offending some readers I will suggest: Nothing. Obligations simply lose their meaning across centuries. But what do we owe ourselves in planning for them? Everything. If human existence has any verifiable meaning, it is that our passions and toil are enabling mechanisms to continue that existence unbroken, unsullied, and progressively secure. It is for ourselves, and not for them or any abstract morality, that we think into the distant future. The precise manner in which we take this measure, how we put it into words, is crucially important. For if the whole process of our life is directed toward preserving our species and personal genes, preparing for future generations is an expression of the highest morality of which human beings are capable. It follows that the destruction of the natural world in which the brain was assembled over millions of years is a risky step. And the worst gamble of all is to let species slip into extinction wholesale, for even if the natural environment is conceded more ground later, it can never be reconstituted in its original diversity. The first rule of the tinkerer, Aldo Leopold reminds us, is to keep all the pieces.

6   This proposition can be expressed another way. What event likely to happen during the next few years will our descendants most regret? Everyone agrees, defense ministers and environmentalists alike, that the worst thing possible is global nuclear war. If it occurs the entire human species is endangered; life as normal human beings wish to live it would come to an end. With that terrible truism acknowledged, it must be added that if no country pulls the trigger the worst thing that will *probably* happen—in fact is already well underway—is not energy depletion, economic collapse, conventional war, or even the expansion of totalitarian governments. As tragic as these catastrophes would be for us, they can be repaired within a few generations. The one process now going on that will take millions of years to correct is the loss of genetic and species diversity by the destruction of natural habitats. This is the folly our descendants are least likely to forgive us.

7   Extinction is accelerating and could reach ruinous proportions during the next twenty years. Not only are birds and mammals vanishing but such smaller forms as mosses, insects, and minnows. A conservative estimate of the current extinction rate is one thousand species a year, mostly from the destruction of forests and other key habitats in the tropics. By the 1990s the figure is expected to rise past ten thousand species a year (one species per hour). During the next thirty years fully one million species could be erased.

8   Whatever the exact figure—and the primitive state of evolutionary biology permits us only to set broad limits—the current rate is still the greatest in recent geological history. It is also much higher than the rate of production of new species by ongoing evolution, so that the net result is a steep decline in the world's standing diversity. Whole categories of organisms that emerged over the past ten million years, among them the familiar condors, rhinoceros, manatees, and gorillas, are close to the end. For most of their species, the last individuals to exist in the wild state could well be those living there today. It is a grave error to dismiss the hemorrhaging as a "Darwinian" process, in which species autonomously come and go and man is just the latest burden on the environment. Human destructiveness is something new under the sun. Perhaps it is matched by the giant meteorites thought to smash into the Earth and darken the atmosphere every hundred million years or so (the last one apparently arrived 65 million years ago and contributed to the extinction of the dinosaurs). But even that interval is ten thousand times longer than the entire history of civilization. In our own brief lifetime humanity will suffer an incomparable loss in aesthetic value, practical benefits from biological research, and worldwide biological stability. Deep mines of biological diversity will have been dug out and carelessly discarded in the course of environmental exploitation, without our even knowing fully what they contained.

Bonobo chimps like this one, close relative to humans, are threatened with extinction due to destruction of their habitat.

9   The time is late for simple answers and divine guidance, and ideological confrontation has just about run its course. Little can be gained by throwing sand in the gears of industrialized society, even less by perpetuating the belief that we can solve any problem created by earlier spasms of human ingenuity. The need now is for a great deal more knowledge of the true biological dimensions of our problem, civility in

the face of common need, and the style of leadership once characterized by Walter Bagehot as agitated moderation.

10   Ethical philosophy is a much more important subject than ordinarily conceded in societies dominated by religious and ideological orthodoxy. It faces an especially severe test in the complexities of the conservation problem. When the time scale is expanded to encompass ecological events, it becomes far more difficult to be certain about the wisdom of any particular decision. Everything is riddled with ambiguity; the middle way turns hard and general formulas fail with dispiriting consistency. Consider that a man who is a villain to his contemporaries can become a hero to his descendants. If a tyrant were to carefully preserve his nation's land and natural resources for his personal needs while keeping his people in poverty, he might unintentionally bequeath a rich, healthful environment to a reduced population for enjoyment in later, democratic generations. This caudillo will have improved the long-term welfare of his people by giving them greater resources and more freedom of action. The exact reverse can occur as well: today's hero can be tomorrow's destroyer. A popular political leader who unleashes the energies of his people and raises their standard of living might simultaneously promote a population explosion, overuse of resources, flight to the cities, and poverty for later generations. Of course these two extreme examples are caricatures and unlikely to occur just so, but they suffice to illustrate that, in ecological and evolutionary time, good does not automatically flow from good or evil from evil. To choose what is best for the near future is easy. To choose what is best for the distant future is also easy. But to choose what is best for both the near and distant futures is a hard task, often internally contradictory, and requiring ethical codes yet to be formulated. ■

N. SCOTT MOMADAY

The Way to Rainy Mountain

N. Scott Momaday (1934–) tells us something about himself in the following introductory chapter from his 1969 book The Way to Rainy Mountain, *an account of his homeland in the Wichita Mountains of Oklahoma. Momaday's father was a Kiowa and his mother was a descendant of white pioneers, and hence a concern with the uneasy relations between American subcultures has always permeated his work. In addition to essays and fiction, Momaday has created paintings, memoirs, and plays. He is now Regents Professor of English at the University of Arizona.*

1 A single knoll rises out of the plain in Oklahoma, north and west of the Wichita Range. For many people, the Kiowas, it is an old landmark, and they gave it the name Rainy Mountain. The hardest weather in the world is there. Winter brings blizzards, hot tornadic winds arise in the spring, and in summer the prairie is an anvil's edge. The grass turns brittle and brown, and it cracks beneath your feet. There are green belts along the rivers and creeks, linear groves of hickory and pecan, willow and witch hazel. At a distance in July or August the steaming foliage seems almost to writhe in fire. Great green and yellow grasshoppers are everywhere in the tall grass, popping up like corn to sting the flesh, and tortoises crawl about on the red earth, going nowhere in the plenty of time. Loneliness is an aspect of the land. All things in the plain are isolate; there is no confusion of objects in the eye, but *one* hill or *one* tree or *one* man. To look upon that landscape in the early morning, with the sun at your back, is to lose the sense of proportion. Your imagination comes to life, and this, you think, is where Creation was begun.

2 I returned to Rainy Mountain in July. My grandmother had died in the spring, and I wanted to be at her grave. She had lived to be very old and at last infirm. Her only living daughter was with her when she died, and I was told that in death her face was that of a child.

3 I like to think of her as a child. When she was born, the Kiowas were living that last great moment of their history. For more than a hundred years they had controlled the open range from the Smoky Hill River to the Red, from the headwaters of the Canadian to the fork of the Arkansas and Cimarron. In alliance with the Comanches, they had ruled the whole of the southern plains. War was their sacred business, and they were among the finest horsemen the world has ever known. But warfare for the Kiowas was preeminently a matter of disposition rather than of survival, and they never understood the grim, unrelenting advance of the U.S. Cavalry. When at last, divided and ill-provisioned, they were driven onto the Staked Plains in the cold rains of autumn, they fell into panic. In Palo Duro Canyon they abandoned their crucial stores to pillage and had nothing then but their lives. In order to save themselves, they surrendered to the soldiers at Fort Sill and were imprisoned in the old stone corral that now stands as a military museum. My grandmother was spared the humiliation of those high gray walls by eight or ten years, but she must have known from birth the affliction of defeat, the dark brooding of old warriors.

4 Her name was Aho, and she belonged to the last culture to evolve in North America. Her forebears came down from the high country in western Montana nearly three centuries ago. They were a mountain people, a mysterious tribe of hunters whose language has never been

positively classified in any major group. In the late seventeenth century they began a long migration to the south and east. It was a journey toward the dawn, and it led to a golden age. Along the way the Kiowas were befriended by the Crows, who gave them the culture and religion of the Plains. They acquired horses, and their ancient nomadic spirit was suddenly free of the ground. They acquired Tai-me, the sacred Sun Dance doll, from that moment the object and symbol of their worship, and so shared in the divinity of the sun. Not least, they acquired the sense of destiny, therefore courage and pride. When they entered upon the southern Plains they had been transformed. No longer were they slaves to the simple necessity of survival; they were a lordly and dangerous society of fighters and thieves, hunters and priests of the sun. According to their origin myth, they entered the world through a hollow log. From one point of view, their migration was the fruit of an old prophecy, for indeed they emerged from a sunless world.

5   Although my grandmother lived out her long life in the shadow of Rainy Mountain, the immense landscape of the continental interior lay like memory in her blood. She could tell of the Crows, whom she had never seen, and of the Black Hills, where she had never been. I wanted to see in reality what she had seen more perfectly in the mind's eye, and traveled fifteen hundred miles to begin my pilgrimage.

6   Yellowstone, it seemed to me, was the top of the world, a region of deep lakes and dark timber, canyons and waterfalls. But, beautiful as it is, one might have the sense of confinement there. The skyline in all directions is close at hand, the high wall of the woods and deep cleavages of shade. There is a perfect freedom in the mountains, but it belongs to the eagle and the elk, the badger and the bear. The Kiowas reckoned their stature by the distance they could see, and they were bent and blind in the wilderness.

7   Descending eastward, the highland meadows are a stairway to the plain. In July the inland slope of the Rockies is luxuriant with flax and buckwheat, stonecrop and larkspur. The earth unfolds and the limit of the land recedes. Clusters of trees, and animals grazing far in the distance, cause the vision to reach away and wonder to build upon the mind. The sun follows a longer course in the day, and the sky is immense beyond all comparison. The great billowing clouds that sail upon it are shadows that move upon the grain like water, dividing light. Farther down, in the land of the Crows and Blackfeet, the plain is yellow. Sweet clover takes hold of the hills and bends upon itself to cover and seat the soil. There the Kiowas paused on their way; they had come to the place where they must change their lives. The sun is at home on the plains. Precisely there does it have the certain character of a god. When

the Kiowas came to the land of the Crows, they could see the dark lees of the hills at dawn across the Bighorn River, the profusion of light on the grain shelves, the oldest deity ranging after the solstices. Not yet would they veer southward to the caldron of the land that lay below; they must wean their blood from the northern winter and hold the mountains a while longer in their view. They bore Tai-me in procession to the east.

8   A dark mist lay over the Black Hills, and the land was like iron. At the top of a ridge I caught sight of Devil's Tower upthrust against the gray sky as if in the birth of time the core of the earth had broken through its crust and the motion of the world was begun. There are things in nature that engender an awful quiet in the heart of man; Devil's Tower is one of them. Two centuries ago, because they could not do otherwise, the Kiowas made a legend at the base of the rock. My grandmother said:

> Eight children were there at play, seven sisters and their brother. Suddenly the boy was struck dumb; he trembled and began to run upon his hands and feet. His fingers became claws, and his body was covered with fur. Directly there was a bear where the boy had been. The sisters were terrified; they ran, and the bear after them. They came to the stump of a great tree, and the tree spoke to them. It bade them climb upon it, and as they did so it began to rise into the air. The bear came to kill them, but they were just beyond its reach. It reared against the tree and scored the bark all around with its claws. The seven sisters were borne into the sky, and they became the stars of the Big Dipper.

From that moment, and so long as the legend lives, the Kiowas have kinsmen in the night sky. Whatever they were in the mountains, they could be no more. However tenuous their well-being, however much they had suffered and would suffer again, they had found a way out of the wilderness.

9   My grandmother had a reverence for the sun, a holy regard that now is all but gone out of mankind. There was a wariness in her, and an ancient awe. She was a Christian in her later years, but she had come a long way about, and she never forgot her birthright. As a child she had been to the Sun Dances; she had taken part in those annual rites, and by them she had learned the restoration of her people in the presence of Tai-me. She was about seven when the last Kiowa Sun Dance was held in 1887 on the Washita River above Rainy Mountain Creek. The buffalo were gone. In order to consummate the ancient sacrifice— to impale the head of a buffalo bull upon the medicine tree—a delegation of old men journeyed into Texas, there to beg and barter for an animal from the Goodnight herd. She was ten when the Kiowas came

together for the last time as a living Sun Dance culture. They could find no buffalo; they had to hang an old hide from the sacred tree. Before the dance could begin, a company of soldiers rode out from Fort Sill under orders to disperse the tribe. Forbidden without cause the essential act of their faith, having seen the wild herds slaughtered and left to rot upon the ground, the Kiowas backed away forever from the medicine tree. That was July 20, 1890, at the great bend of the Washita. My grandmother was there. Without bitterness, and for as long as she lived, she bore a vision of deicide.

10   Now that I can have her only in memory, I see my grandmother in the several postures that were peculiar to her: standing at the wood stove on a winter morning and turning meat in a great iron skillet; sitting at the south window, bent above her beadwork, and afterwards, when her vision failed, looking down for a long time into the fold of her hands; going out upon a cane, very slowly as she did when the weight of age came upon her; praying. I remember her most often at prayer. She made long, rambling prayers out of suffering and hope, having seen many things. I was never sure that I had the right to hear, so exclusive were they of all mere custom and company. The last time I saw her she prayed standing by the side of her bed at night, naked to the waist, the light of a kerosene lamp moving upon her dark skin. Her long, black hair, always drawn and braided in the day, lay upon her shoulders and against her breasts like a shawl. I do not speak Kiowa, and I never understood her prayers, but there was something inherently sad in the sound, some merest hesitation upon the syllables of sorrow. She began in a high and descending pitch, exhausting her breath to silence then again and again—and always the same intensity of effort, of something that is, and is not, like urgency in the human voice. Transported so in the dancing light among the shadows of her room, she seemed beyond the reach of time. But that was illusion; I think I knew then that I should not see her again.

11   Houses are like sentinels in the plain, old keepers of the weather watch. There, in a very little while, wood takes on the appearance of great age. All colors wear soon away in the wind and rain, and then the wood is burned gray and the grain appears and the nails turn red with rust. The windowpanes are black and opaque; you imagine there is nothing within, and indeed there are many ghosts, bones given up to the land. They stand here and there against the sky, and you approach them for a longer time than you expect. They belong in the distance; it is their domain.

12   Once there was a lot of sound in my grandmother's house, a lot of coming and going, feasting and talk. The summers there were full of excitement and reunion. The Kiowas are a summer people; they abide the cold and keep to themselves, but when the season turns and the

land becomes warm and vital they cannot hold still; an old love of go-ing returns upon them. The aged visitors who came to my grand-mother's house when I was a child were made of lean and leather, and they bore themselves upright. They wore great black hats and bright ample shirts that shook in the wind. They rubbed fat upon their hair and wound their braids with strips of colored cloth. Some of them painted their faces and carried the scars of old and cherished enmities. They were an old council of warlords, come to remind and be re-minded of who they were. Their wives and daughters served them well. The women might indulge themselves; gossip was at once the mark and compensation of their servitude. They made loud and elabo-rate talk among themselves, full of jest and gesture, fright and false alarm. They went abroad in fringed and flowered shawls, bright bead-work and German silver. They were at home in the kitchen, and they prepared meals that were banquets.

13   There were frequent prayer meetings, and great nocturnal feasts. When I was a child I played with my cousins outside, where the lamp-light fell upon the ground and the singing of the old people rose up around us and carried away into the darkness. There were a lot of good things to eat, a lot of laughter and surprise. And afterwards, when the quiet returned, I lay down with my grandmother and could hear the frogs away by the river and feel the motion of the air.

14   Now there is a funeral silence in the rooms, the endless wake of some final word. The walls have closed in upon my grandmother's house. When I returned to it in mourning, I saw for the first time in my life how small it was. It was late at night, and there was a white moon, nearly full. I sat for a long time on the stone steps by the kitchen door. From there I could see out across the land; I could see the long row of trees by the creek, the low light upon the rolling plains, and the stars of the Big Dipper. Once I looked at the moon and caught sight of a strange thing. A cricket had perched upon the handrail, only a few inches away from me. My line of vision was such that the creature filled the moon like a fossil. It had gone there, I thought, to live and die, for there, of all places, was its small definition made whole and eternal. A warm wind rose up and purled like the longing within me.

15   The next morning I awoke at dawn and went out on the dirt road to Rainy Mountain. It was already hot, and the grasshoppers began to fill the air. Still, it was early in the morning, and the birds sang out of the shadows. The long yellow grass on the mountain shone in the bright light, and a scissortail hied above the land. There, where it ought to be, at the end of a long and legendary way, was my grandmother's grave. Here and there on the dark stones were ancestral names. Look-ing back once, I saw the mountain and came away. ◼

Am I Blue?

Alice Walker (1944–) is best known for her award-winning 1982 novel
The Color Purple, *which was made into a movie by Steven Spielberg. But
Walker has also written a great deal of other material—poems, essays,
short stories, other novels—in the past three decades, material that is a
reflection of her upbringing in rural Georgia and a product of her
commitments to social justice and women's issues. Walker included "Am I
Blue?" in her 1988 collection of essays called* Living by the Word, *which
meditates on the insidious effects of power in our relationships with
animals.*

1   For about three years my companion and I rented a small house in
the country that stood on the edge of a large meadow that appeared
to run from the end of our deck straight into the mountains. The mountains, however, were quite far away, and between us and them there
was, in fact, a town. It was one of the many pleasant aspects of the
house that you never really were aware of this.

2   It was a house of many windows, low, wide, nearly floor to ceiling
in the living room, which faced the meadow, and it was from one of
these that I first saw our closest neighbor, a large white horse, cropping
grass, flipping its mane, and ambling about—not over the entire
meadow, which stretched well out of sight of the house, but over the
five or so fenced-in acres that were next to the twenty-odd that we had
rented. I soon learned that the horse, whose name was Blue, belonged
to a man who lived in another town, but was boarded by our neighbors
next door. Occasionally, one of the children, usually a stocky teenager,
but sometimes a much younger girl or boy, could be seen riding Blue.
They would appear in the meadow, climb up on his back, ride furiously
for ten or fifteen minutes, then get off, slap Blue on the flanks, and not
be seen again for a month or more.

3   There were many apple trees in our yard, and one by the fence
that Blue could almost reach. We were soon in the habit of feeding him
apples, which he relished, especially because by the middle of summer
the meadow grasses—so green and succulent since January—had dried
out from lack of rain, and Blue stumbled about munching the dried
stalks half-heartedly. Sometimes he would stand very still just by the
apple tree, and when one of us came out he would whinny, snort
loudly, or stamp the ground. This meant, of course: I want an apple.

4   It was quite wonderful to pick a few apples, or collect those that
had fallen to the ground overnight, and patiently hold them, one by

one, up to his large, toothy mouth. I remained as thrilled as a child by his flexible dark lips, huge, cubelike teeth that crunched the apples, core and all, with such finality, and his high, broad-breasted *enormity;* beside which, I felt small indeed. When I was a child, I used to ride horses, and was especially friendly with one named Nan until the day I was riding and my brother deliberately spooked her and I was thrown, head first, against the trunk of a tree. When I came to, I was in bed and my mother was bending worriedly over me; we silently agreed that perhaps horseback riding was not the safest sport for me. Since then I have walked, and prefer walking, to horseback riding—but I had forgotten the depth of feeling one could see in horses' eyes.

5   I was therefore unprepared for the expression in Blue's. Blue was lonely. Blue was horribly lonely and bored. I was not shocked that this should be the case; five acres to tramp by yourself, endlessly, even in the most beautiful of meadows—and his was—cannot provide many interesting events, and once rainy season turned to dry that was about it. No, I was shocked that I had forgotten that human animals and nonhuman animals can communicate quite well; if we are brought up around animals as children we take this for granted. By the time we are adults we no longer remember. However, the animals have not changed. They are in fact *completed* creations (at least they seem to be, so much more than we) who are not likely *to* change; it is their nature to express themselves. What else are they going to express? And they do. And, generally speaking, they are ignored.

6   After giving Blue the apples, I would wander back to the house, aware that he was observing me. Were more apples not forthcoming then? Was that to be his sole entertainment for the day? My partner's small son had decided he wanted to learn how to piece a quilt; we worked in silence on our respective squares as I thought. . . .

7   Well, about slavery: about white children, who were raised by black people, who knew their first all-accepting love from black women, and then when they were twelve or so, were told they must "forget" the deep levels of communication between themselves and "mammy" that they knew. Later they would be able to relate quite calmly, "My old mammy was sold to another good family." "My old mammy was _____ _____." Fill in the blank. Many more years later a white woman would say: "I can't understand these Negroes, these blacks. What do they want? They're so different from us."

8   And about the Indians, considered to be "like animals" by the "settlers" (a very benign euphemism for what they actually were), who did not understand their description as a compliment.

9   And about the thousands of American men who marry Japanese, Korean, Filipina, and other non-English-speaking women and of how happy they report they are, *"blissfully,"* until their brides learn to speak

English, at which point the marriages tend to fall apart. What then did the men see, when they looked into the eyes of the women they married, before they could speak English? Apparently only their own reflections.

10   I thought of society's impatience with the young. "Why are they playing the music so loud?" Perhaps the children have listened to much of the music of oppressed people their parents danced to before they were born, with its passionate but soft cries for acceptance and love, and they have wondered why their parents failed to hear.

11   I do not know how long Blue had inhabited his five beautiful, boring acres before we moved into our house; a year after we had arrived— and had also traveled to other valleys, other cities, other worlds—he was still there.

12   But then, in our second year at the house, something happened in Blue's life. One morning, looking out the window at the fog that lay like a ribbon over the meadow, I saw another horse, a brown one, at the other end of Blue's field. Blue appeared to be afraid of it, and for several days made no attempt to go near. We went away for a week. When we returned, Blue had decided to make friends and the two horses ambled or galloped along together, and Blue did not come nearly as often to the fence underneath the apple tree.

13   When he did, bringing his new friend with him, there was a different look in his eyes. A look of independence, of self-possession, of inalienable *horse*ness. His friend eventually became pregnant. For months and months there was, it seemed to me, a mutual feeling between me and the horses of justice, of peace. I fed apples to them both. The look in Blue's eyes was one of unabashed "this is *it*ness."

14   It did not, however, last forever. One day, after a visit to the city, I went out to give Blue some apples. He stood waiting, or so I thought, though not beneath the tree. When I shook the tree and jumped back from the shower of apples, he made no move. I carried some over to him. He managed to half-crunch one. The rest he let fall to the ground. I dreaded looking into his eyes—because I had of course noticed that Brown, his partner, had gone—but I did look. If I had been born into slavery, and my partner had been sold or killed, my eyes would have looked like that. The children next door explained that Blue's partner had been "put with him" (the same expression that old people used, I had noticed, when speaking of an ancestor during slavery who had been impregnated by her owner) so that they could mate and she conceive. Since that was accomplished, she had been taken back by her owner, who lived somewhere else.

15   Will she be back? I asked.

16   They didn't know.

17   Blue was like a crazed person. Blue *was*, to me, a crazed person. He galloped furiously, as if he were being ridden, around and around his five beautiful acres. He whinnied until he couldn't. He tore at the ground with

his hooves. He butted himself against his single shade tree. He looked always and always toward the road down which his partner had gone. And then, occasionally, when he came up for apples, or I took apples to him, he looked at me. It was a look so piercing, so full of grief, a look so *human,* I almost laughed (I felt too sad to cry) to think there are people who do not know that animals suffer. People like me who have forgotten, and daily forget, all that animals try to tell us. "Everything you do to us will happen to you; we are your teachers, as you are ours. We are one lesson" is essentially it, I think. There are those who never once have even considered animals' rights: those who have been taught that animals actually want to be used and abused by us, as small children "love" to be frightened, or women "love" to be mutilated and raped. . . . They are the great-grandchildren of those who honestly thought, because someone taught them this: "Women can't think," and "niggers can't faint." But most disturbing of all, in Blue's large brown eyes was a new look, more painful than the look of despair: the look of disgust with human beings, with life; the look of hatred. And it was odd what the look of hatred did. It gave him, for the first time, the look of a beast. And what that meant was that he had put up a barrier within to protect himself from further violence; all the apples in the world wouldn't change that fact.

18 And so Blue remained, a beautiful part of our landscape, very peaceful to look at from the window, white against the grass. Once a friend came to visit and said, looking out on the soothing view: "And it *would* have to be a *white* horse; the very image of freedom." And I thought, yes, the animals are forced to become for us merely "images" of what they once so beautifully expressed. And we are used to drinking milk from containers showing "contented" cows, whose real lives we want to hear nothing about, eating eggs and drumsticks from "happy" hens, and munching hamburgers advertised by bulls of integrity who seem to command their fate.

19 As we talked of freedom and justice one day for all, we sat down to steaks. I am eating misery, I thought, as I took the first bite. And spit it out. ■

WENDELL BERRY

Manifesto: The Mad Farmer Liberation Front

The writer, teacher, and land-lover Wendell Berry (born 1934) grew up (and still lives) on a farm in Kentucky. His poetry and essays explore the connections between people and nature and typically endorse a simple lifestyle, at odds with new technologies that threaten agrarian ways. His

many published works include the essays "What Are People For?" and
"Why I Am Not Going to Buy a Computer." His books of poetry include
Sabbaths *and* The Country of Marriage *(1973), from which the following*
poetic argument is taken.

Love the quick profit, the annual raise,
vacation with pay. Want more
of everything ready-made. Be afraid
to know your neighbors and to die.

5   And you will have a window in your head.
Not even your future will be a mystery
any more. Your mind will be punched in a card
and shut away in a little drawer.

When they want you to buy something
10   they will call you. When they want you
to die for profit they will let you know.
So, friends, every day do something
that won't compute. Love the Lord.
Love the world. Work for nothing.
15   Take all that you have and be poor.
Love someone who does not deserve it.

Denounce the government and embrace
the flag. Hope to live in that free
republic for which it stands.
20   Give your approval to all you cannot
understand. Praise ignorance, for what man
has not encountered he has not destroyed.

Ask the questions that have no answers.
Invest in the millenium. Plant sequoias.
25   Say that your main crop is the forest
that you did not plant,
that you will not live to harvest.

Say that the leaves are harvested
when they have rotted into the mold.
30   Call that profit. Prophesy such returns.
Put your faith in the two inches of humus
that will build under the trees
every thousand years.

Listen to carrion—put your ear
35   close, and hear the faint chattering
of the songs that are to come.
Expect the end of the world. Laugh.

Laughter is immeasurable. Be joyful
   though you have considered all the facts.
40   So long as women do not go cheap
for power, please women more than men.

Ask yourself: Will this satisfy
a woman satisfied to bear a child?
Will this disturb the sleep
45   of a woman near to giving birth?

Go with your love to the fields.
Lie down in the shade. Rest your head
in her lap. Swear allegiance
to what is nighest your thoughts.

50   As soon as the generals and the politicos
can predict the motions of your mind,
lose it. Leave it as a sign
to mark the false trail, the way
you didn't go.

55   Be like the fox
who makes more tracks than necessary,
some in the wrong direction.
Practice resurrection.

JAMES HOWARD KUNSTLER

The Long Emergency

James Howard Kunstler, the author of The Geography of Nowhere, Home
from Nowhere, *and* The City in Mind: Notes on the Urban Condition,
*writes about places and spaces in America. His work often addresses the
aesthetics of the suburban environment. Born in New York City and a
resident of New York's suburbs for a number of years, Kunstler has written
novels such as* Maggie Darling *and* An Embarrassment of Riches, *but he
has mainly worked as a reporter and feature writer for magazines. Often
his essays meditate on the links between economics and the environment.
The following selection is from his 2005 book* The Long Emergency:
Surviving the Converging Catastrophes of the Twenty-First Century.

1   A few weeks ago, the price of oil ratcheted above fifty-five dollars a
barrel, which is about twenty dollars a barrel more than a year ago.
The next day, the oil story was buried on page six of the *New York
Times* business section. Apparently, the price of oil is not considered

significant news, even when it goes up five bucks a barrel in the span of ten days. That same day, the stock market shot up more than a hundred points because, CNN said, government data showed no signs of inflation. Note to clueless nation: Call planet Earth.

2   Carl Jung, one of the fathers of psychology, famously remarked that "people cannot stand too much reality." What you're about to read may challenge your assumptions about the kind of world we live in, and especially the kind of world into which events are propelling us. We are in for a rough ride through uncharted territory.

3   It has been very hard for Americans—lost in dark raptures of non-stop infotainment, recreational shopping and compulsive motoring—to make sense of the gathering forces that will fundamentally alter the terms of everyday life in our technological society. Even after the terrorist attacks of 9/11, America is still sleepwalking into the future. I call this coming time the Long Emergency.

4   Most immediately we face the end of the cheap-fossil-fuel era. It is no exaggeration to state that reliable supplies of cheap oil and natural gas underlie everything we identify as the necessities of modern life—not to mention all of its comforts and luxuries: central heating, air conditioning, cars, airplanes, electric lights, inexpensive clothing, recorded music, movies, hip-replacement surgery, national defense—you name it.

5   The few Americans who are even aware that there is a gathering global-energy predicament usually misunderstand the core of the argument. That argument states that we don't have to run out of oil to start having severe problems with industrial civilization and its dependent systems. We only have to slip over the all-time production peak and begin a slide down the arc of steady depletion.

6   The term "global oil-production peak" means that a turning point will come when the world produces the most oil it will ever produce in a given year and, after that, yearly production will inexorably decline. It is usually represented graphically in a bell curve. The peak is the top of the curve, the halfway point of the world's all-time total endowment, meaning half the world's oil will be left. That seems like a lot of oil, and it is, but there's a big catch: It's the half that is much more difficult to extract, far more costly to get, of much poorer quality and located mostly in places where the people hate us. A substantial amount of it will never be extracted.

7   The United States passed its own oil peak—about 11 million barrels a day—in 1970, and since then production has dropped steadily. In 2004 it ran just above 5 million barrels a day (we get a tad more from natural-gas condensates). Yet we consume roughly 20 million barrels a day now. That means we have to import about two-thirds of our oil, and the ratio will continue to worsen.

8   The U.S. peak in 1970 brought on a portentous change in geoeconomic power. Within a few years, foreign producers, chiefly OPEC, were setting the price of oil, and this in turn led to the oil crises of the 1970s. In response, frantic development of non-OPEC oil, especially the North Sea fields of England and Norway, essentially saved the West's ass for about two decades. Since 1999, these fields have entered depletion. Meanwhile, worldwide discovery of new oil has steadily declined to insignificant levels in 2003 and 2004.

9   Some "cornucopians" claim that the Earth has something like a creamy nougat center of "abiotic" oil that will naturally replenish the great oil fields of the world. The facts speak differently. There has been no replacement whatsoever of oil already extracted from the fields of America or any other place.

10   Now we are faced with the global oil-production peak. The best estimates of when this will actually happen have been somewhere between now and 2010. In 2004, however, after demand from burgeoning China and India shot up, and revelations that Shell Oil wildly misstated its reserves, and Saudi Arabia proved incapable of goosing up its production despite promises to do so, the most knowledgeable experts revised their predictions and now concur that 2005 is apt to be the year of all-time global peak production.

11   It will change everything about how we live.

12   To aggravate matters, American natural-gas production is also declining, at five percent a year, despite frenetic new drilling, and with the potential of much steeper declines ahead. Because of the oil crises of the 1970s, the nuclear-plant disasters at Three Mile Island and Chernobyl and the acid-rain problem, the U.S. chose to make gas its first choice for electric-power generation. The result was that just about every power plant built after 1980 has to run on gas. Half the homes in America are heated with gas. To further complicate matters, gas isn't easy to import. Here in North America, it is distributed through a vast pipeline network. Gas imported from overseas would have to be compressed at minus-260 degrees Fahrenheit in pressurized tanker ships and unloaded (re-gasified) at special terminals, of which few exist in America. Moreover, the first attempts to site new terminals have met furious opposition because they are such ripe targets for terrorism.

13   Some other things about the global energy predicament are poorly understood by the public and even our leaders. This is going to be a permanent energy crisis, and these energy problems will synergize with the disruptions of climate change, epidemic disease and population overshoot to produce higher orders of trouble.

14   We will have to accommodate ourselves to fundamentally changed conditions.

15   No combination of alternative fuels will allow us to run American life the way we have been used to running it, or even a substantial fraction of it. The wonders of steady technological progress achieved through the reign of cheap oil have lulled us into a kind of Jiminy Cricket syndrome, leading many Americans to believe that anything we wish for hard enough will come true. These days, even people who ought to know better are wishing ardently for a seamless transition from fossil fuels to their putative replacements.

16   The widely touted "hydrogen economy" is a particularly cruel hoax. We are not going to replace the U.S. automobile and truck fleet with vehicles run on fuel cells. For one thing, the current generation of fuel cells is largely designed to run on hydrogen obtained from natural gas. The other way to get hydrogen in the quantities wished for would be electrolysis of water using power from hundreds of nuclear plants. Apart from the dim prospect of our building that many nuclear plants soon enough, there are also numerous severe problems with hydrogen's nature as an element that present forbidding obstacles to its use as a replacement for oil and gas, especially in storage and transport.

17   Wishful notions about rescuing our way of life with "renewables" are also unrealistic. Solar-electric systems and wind turbines face not only the enormous problem of scale but the fact that the components require substantial amounts of energy to manufacture and the probability that they can't be manufactured at all without the underlying support platform of a fossil-fuel economy. We will surely use solar and wind technology to generate some electricity for a period ahead but probably at a very local and small scale.

18   Virtually all "biomass" schemes for using plants to create liquid fuels cannot be scaled up to even a fraction of the level at which things are currently run. What's more, these schemes are predicated on using oil and gas "inputs" (fertilizers, weed-killers) to grow the biomass crops that would be converted into ethanol or bio-diesel fuels. This is a net energy loser—you might as well just burn the inputs and not bother with the biomass products. Proposals to distill trash and waste into oil by means of thermal depolymerization depend on the huge waste stream produced by a cheap oil and gas economy in the first place.

19   Coal is far less versatile than oil and gas, extant in less abundant supplies than many people assume and fraught with huge ecological drawbacks—as a contributor to greenhouse "global warming" gases and many health and toxicity issues ranging from widespread mercury poisoning to acid rain. You can make synthetic oil from coal, but the only time this was tried on a large scale was by the Nazis under wartime conditions, using impressive amounts of slave labor.

20   If we wish to keep the lights on in America after 2020, we may indeed have to resort to nuclear power, with all its practical problems and

eco-conundrums. Under optimal conditions, it could take ten years to get a new generation of nuclear power plants into operation, and the price may be beyond our means. Uranium is also a resource in finite supply. We are no closer to the more difficult project of atomic fusion, by the way, than we were in the 1970s.

21   The upshot of all this is that we are entering a historical period of potentially great instability, turbulence and hardship. Obviously, geopolitical maneuvering around the world's richest energy regions has already led to war and promises more international military conflict. Since the Middle East contains two-thirds of the world's remaining oil supplies, the U.S. has attempted desperately to stabilize the region by, in effect, opening a big police station in Iraq. The intent was not just to secure Iraq's oil but to modify and influence the behavior of neighboring states around the Persian Gulf, especially Iran and Saudi Arabia. The results have been far from entirely positive, and our future prospects in that part of the world are not something we can feel altogether confident about.

22   And then there is the issue of China, which, in 2004, became the world's second-greatest consumer of oil, surpassing Japan. China's surging industrial growth has made it increasingly dependent on the imports we are counting on. If China wanted to, it could easily walk into some of these places—the Middle East, former Soviet republics in central Asia—and extend its hegemony by force. Is America prepared to contest for this oil in an Asian land war with the Chinese army? I doubt it. Nor can the U.S. military occupy regions of the Eastern Hemisphere indefinitely, or hope to secure either the terrain or the oil infrastructure of one distant, unfriendly country after another. A likely scenario is that the U.S. could exhaust and bankrupt itself trying to do this, and be forced to withdraw back into our own hemisphere, having lost access to most of the world's remaining oil in the process.

23   We know that our national leaders are hardly uninformed about this predicament. President George W. Bush has been briefed on the dangers of the oil-peak situation as long ago as before the 2000 election and repeatedly since then. In March, the Department of Energy released a report that officially acknowledges for the first time that peak oil is for real and states plainly that "the world has never faced a problem like this. Without massive mitigation more than a decade before the fact, the problem will be pervasive and will not be temporary."

24   Most of all, the Long Emergency will require us to make other arrangements for the way we live in the United States. America is in a special predicament due to a set of unfortunate choices we made as a society in the twentieth century. Perhaps the worst was to let our towns and cities rot away and to replace them with suburbia, which had the additional side effect of trashing a lot of the best farmland in America.

Suburbia will come to be regarded as the greatest misallocation of resources in the history of the world. It has a tragic destiny. The psychology of previous investment suggests that we will defend our drive-in utopia long after it has become a terrible liability.

25   Before long, the suburbs will fail us in practical terms. We made the ongoing development of housing subdivisions, highway strips, fried-food shacks and shopping malls the basis of our economy, and when we have to stop making more of those things, the bottom will fall out.

26   The circumstances of the Long Emergency will require us to downscale and re-scale virtually everything we do and how we do it, from the kind of communities we physically inhabit to the way we grow our food to the way we work and trade the products of our work. Our lives will become profoundly and intensely local. Daily life will be far less about mobility and much more about staying where you are. Anything organized on the large scale, whether it is government or a corporate business enterprise such as Wal-Mart, will wither as the cheap energy props that support bigness fall away. The turbulence of the Long Emergency will produce a lot of economic losers, and many of these will be members of an angry and aggrieved former middle class.

27   Food production is going to be an enormous problem in the Long Emergency. As industrial agriculture fails due to a scarcity of oil- and gas-based inputs, we will certainly have to grow more of our food closer to where we live, and do it on a smaller scale. The American economy of the mid-twenty-first century may actually center on agriculture, not information, not high tech, not "services" like real estate sales or hawking cheeseburgers to tourists. Farming. This is no doubt a startling, radical idea, and it raises extremely difficult questions about the reallocation of land and the nature of work. The relentless subdividing of land in the late twentieth century has destroyed the contiguity and integrity of the rural landscape in most places. The process of readjustment is apt to be disorderly and improvisational. Food production will necessarily be much more labor-intensive than it has been for decades. We can anticipate the re-formation of a native-born American farm-laboring class. It will be composed largely of the aforementioned economic losers who had to relinquish their grip on the American dream. These masses of disentitled people may enter into quasi-feudal social relations with those who own land in exchange for food and physical security. But their sense of grievance will remain fresh, and if mistreated they may simply seize that land.

28   The way that commerce is currently organized in America will not survive far into the Long Emergency. Wal-Mart's "warehouse on wheels" won't be such a bargain in a non-cheap-oil economy. The national chain stores' 12,000-mile manufacturing supply lines could eas-

ily be interrupted by military contests over oil and by internal conflict in the nations that have been supplying us with ultra-cheap manufactured goods, because they, too, will be struggling with similar issues of energy famine and all the disorders that go with it.

29   As these things occur, America will have to make other arrangements for the manufacture, distribution and sale of ordinary goods. They will probably be made on a "cottage industry" basis rather than the factory system we once had, since the scale of available energy will be much lower—and we are not going to replay the twentieth century. Tens of thousands of the common products we enjoy today, from paints to pharmaceuticals, are made out of oil. They will become increasingly scarce or unavailable. The selling of things will have to be reorganized at the local scale. It will have to be based on moving merchandise shorter distances. It is almost certain to result in higher costs for the things we buy and far fewer choices.

30   The automobile will be a diminished presence in our lives, to say the least. With gasoline in short supply, not to mention tax revenue, our roads will surely suffer. The interstate highway system is more delicate than the public realizes. If the "level of service" (as traffic engineers call it) is not maintained to the highest degree, problems multiply and escalate quickly. The system does not tolerate partial failure. The interstates are either in excellent condition, or they quickly fall apart.

31   America today has a railroad system that the Bulgarians would be ashamed of. Neither of the two major presidential candidates in 2004 mentioned railroads, but if we don't refurbish our rail system, then there may be no long-range travel or transport of goods at all a few decades from now. The commercial aviation industry, already on its knees financially, is likely to vanish. The sheer cost of maintaining gigantic airports may not justify the operation of a much-reduced air-travel fleet. Railroads are far more energy efficient than cars, trucks or airplanes, and they can be run on anything from wood to electricity. The rail-bed infrastructure is also far more economical to maintain than our highway network.

32   The successful regions in the twenty-first century will be the ones surrounded by viable farming hinterlands that can reconstitute locally sustainable economies on an armature of civic cohesion. Small towns and smaller cities have better prospects than the big cities, which will probably have to contract substantially. The process will be painful and tumultuous. In many American cities, such as Cleveland, Detroit and St. Louis, that process is already well advanced. Others have further to fall. New York and Chicago face extraordinary difficulties, being oversupplied with gigantic buildings out of scale with the reality of declining energy supplies. Their former agricultural hinterlands have long been paved over. They will be encysted in a surrounding fabric of necrotic

suburbia that will only amplify and reinforce the cities' problems. Still, our cities occupy important sites. Some kind of urban entities will exist where they are in the future, but probably not the colossi of twentieth-century industrialism.

33   Some regions of the country will do better than others in the Long Emergency. The Southwest will suffer in proportion to the degree that it prospered during the cheap-oil blowout of the late twentieth century. I predict that Sunbelt states like Arizona and Nevada will become significantly depopulated, since the region will be short of water as well as gasoline and natural gas. Imagine Phoenix without cheap air conditioning.

34   I'm not optimistic about the Southeast, either, for different reasons. I think it will be subject to substantial levels of violence as the grievances of the formerly middle class boil over and collide with the delusions of Pentecostal Christian extremism. The latent encoded behavior of Southern culture includes an outsized notion of individualism and the belief that firearms ought to be used in the defense of it. This is a poor recipe for civic cohesion.

35   The Mountain States and Great Plains will face an array of problems, from poor farming potential to water shortages to population loss. The Pacific Northwest, New England and the Upper Midwest have somewhat better prospects. I regard them as less likely to fall into lawlessness, anarchy or despotism and more likely to salvage the bits and pieces of our best social traditions and keep them in operation at some level.

36   These are daunting and even dreadful prospects. The Long Emergency is going to be a tremendous trauma for the human race. We will not believe that this is happening to us, that 200 years of modernity can be brought to its knees by a world-wide power shortage. The survivors will have to cultivate a religion of hope—that is, a deep and comprehensive belief that humanity is worth carrying on. If there is any positive side to stark changes coming our way, it may be in the benefits of close communal relations, of having to really work intimately (and physically) with our neighbors, to be part of an enterprise that really matters and to be fully engaged in meaningful social enactments instead of being merely entertained to avoid boredom. Years from now, when we hear singing at all, we will hear ourselves, and we will sing with our whole hearts. ■

DANIEL GLICK

The Big Thaw

The September 2004 issue of National Geographic *magazine featured articles about the science and varied effects of global warming. In the wake of the Kyoto treaty on global warming, the articles treated global warming as a reality that required continuing study of its biological and atmospheric effects. One of those articles was the following by Daniel Glick. A reporter for* Newsweek *for much of his career, Glick has also written for many other magazines; has published* Powder Burn: Arson, Money, and Mystery on Vail Mountain *(2001); and has traveled extensively to research articles about glaciers, Alaskan ecology, and the geology of global warming.*

1   "If we don't have it, we don't need it," pronounces Daniel Fagre as we throw on our backpacks. We're armed with crampons, ice axes, rope, GPS receivers, and bear spray to ward off grizzlies, and we're trudging toward Sperry Glacier in Glacier National Park, Montana. I fall in step with Fagre and two other research scientists from the U.S. Geological Survey Global Change Research Program. They're doing what they've been doing for more than a decade: measuring how the park's storied glaciers are melting.

2   So far, the results have been positively chilling. When President Taft created Glacier National Park in 1910, it was home to an estimated 150 glaciers. Since then the number has decreased to fewer than 30, and most of those remaining have shrunk in area by two-thirds. Fagre predicts that within 30 years most if not all of the park's namesake glaciers will disappear.

3   "Things that normally happen in geologic time are happening during the span of a human lifetime," says Fagre. "It's like watching the Statue of Liberty melt."

4   Scientists who assess the planet's health see indisputable evidence that Earth has been getting warmer, in some cases rapidly. Most believe that human activity, in particular the burning of fossil fuels and the resulting buildup of greenhouse gases in the atmosphere, have influenced this warming trend. In the past decade scientists have documented record-high average annual surface temperatures and have been observing other signs of change all over the planet: in the distribution of ice, and in the salinity, levels, and temperatures of the oceans.

5   "This glacier used to be closer," Fagre declares as we crest a steep section, his glasses fogged from exertion. He's only half joking. A trailside sign notes that since 1901, Sperry Glacier has shrunk from more than 800 acres to 300 acres. "That's out of date," Fagre says, stopping to catch his breath. "It's now less than 250 acres."

6   Everywhere on Earth ice is changing. The famed snows of Kilimanjaro have melted more than 80 percent since 1912. Glaciers in the Garhwal Himalaya in India are retreating so fast that researchers believe that most central and eastern Himalayan glaciers could virtually disappear by 2035. Arctic sea ice has thinned significantly over the past half century, and its extent has declined by about 10 percent in the past 30 years. NASA's repeated laser altimeter readings show the edges of Greenland's ice sheet shrinking. Spring freshwater ice breakup in the Northern Hemisphere now occurs nine days earlier than it did 150 years ago, and autumn freezeup ten days later. Thawing permafrost has caused the ground to subside more than 15 feet in parts of Alaska. From the Arctic to Peru, from Switzerland to the equatorial glaciers of Man Jaya in Indonesia, massive ice fields, monstrous glaciers, and sea ice are disappearing, fast.

7   When temperatures rise and ice melts, more water flows to the seas from glaciers and ice caps, and ocean water warms and expands in volume. This combination of effects has played the major role in raising average global sea level between four and eight inches in the past hundred years, according to the Intergovernmental Panel on Climate Change (IPCC).

8   Scientists point out that sea levels have risen and fallen substantially over Earth's 4.6-billion-year history. But the recent rate of global sea level rise has departed from the average rate of the past two to three thousand years and is rising more rapidly—about one-tenth of an inch a year. A continuation or acceleration of that trend has the potential to cause striking changes in the world's coastlines.

9   Driving around Louisiana's Gulf Coast, Windell Curole can see the future, and it looks pretty wet. In southern Louisiana coasts are literally sinking by about three feet a century, a process called subsidence. A sinking coastline and a rising ocean combine to yield powerful effects. It's like taking the global sea-level-rise problem and moving it along at fast-forward.

10   The seventh-generation Cajun and manager of the South Lafourche Levee District navigates his truck down an unpaved mound of dirt that separates civilization from inundation, dry land from a swampy horizon. With his French-tinged lilt, Curole points to places where these bayous, swamps, and fishing villages portend a warmer world: his high school girlfriend's house partly submerged, a cemetery with water lapping against the white tombs, his grandfather's former hunting camp now afloat in a stand of skeleton oak snags. "We live in a place of almost land, almost water," says the 52-year-old Curole.

11   Rising sea level, sinking land, eroding coasts, and temperamental storms are a fact of life for Curole. Even relatively small storm surges in the past two decades have overwhelmed the system of dikes, levees, and

pump stations that he manages, upgraded in the 1990s to forestall the Gulf of Mexico's relentless creep. "I've probably ordered more evacuations than any other person in the country," Curole says.

12   The current trend is consequential not only in coastal Louisiana but around the world. Never before have so many humans lived so close to the coasts: More than a hundred million people worldwide live within three feet of mean sea level. Vulnerable to sea-level rise, Tuvalu, a small country in the South Pacific, has already begun formulating evacuation plans. Megacities where human populations have concentrated near coastal plains or river deltas—Shanghai, Bangkok, Jakarta, Tokyo, and New York—are at risk. The projected economic and humanitarian impacts on low-lying, densely populated, and desperately poor countries like Bangladesh are potentially catastrophic. The scenarios are disturbing even in wealthy countries like the Netherlands, with nearly half its landmass already at or below sea level.

13   Rising sea level produces a cascade of effects. Bruce Douglas, a coastal researcher at Florida International University, calculates that every inch of sea-level rise could result in eight feet of horizontal retreat of sandy beach shorelines due to erosion. Furthermore, when salt water intrudes into freshwater aquifers, it threatens sources of drinking water and makes raising crops problematic. In the Nile Delta, where many of Egypt's crops are cultivated, widespread erosion and saltwater intrusion would be disastrous—since the country contains little other arable land.

14   In some places marvels of human engineering worsen effects from rising seas in a warming world. The system of channels and levees along the Mississippi effectively stopped the millennia-old natural process of rebuilding the river delta with rich sediment deposits. In the 1930s, oil and gas companies began to dredge shipping and exploratory canals, tearing up the marshland buffers that helped dissipate tidal surges. Energy drilling removed vast quantities of subsurface liquid, which studies suggest increased the rate at which the land is sinking. Now Louisiana is losing approximately 25 square miles of wetlands every year, and the state is lobbying for federal money to help replace the upstream sediments that are the delta's lifeblood.

15   Local projects like that might not do much good in the very long run, though, depending on the course of change elsewhere on the planet. Part of Antarctica's Larsen Ice Shell broke apart in early 2002. Although floating ice does not change sea level when it melts (any more than a glass of water will overflow when the ice cubes in it melt), scientists became concerned that the collapse could foreshadow the breakup of other ice shelves in Antarctica and allow increased glacial discharge into the sea from ice sheets on the continent. If the West Antarctic ice sheet were to break up, which scientists consider very unlikely this century, it alone contains enough ice to raise sea level by nearly 20 feet.

16   Even without such a major event, the IPCC projected in its 2001 report that sea level will rise anywhere between 4 and 35 inches by the end of the century. The high end of that projection—nearly three feet—would be "an unmitigated disaster," according to Douglas.

17   Down on the bayou, all of those predictions make Windell Curole shudder. "We're the guinea pigs," he says, surveying his aqueous world from the relatively lofty vantage point of a 12-foot-high earthen berm. "I don't think anybody down here looks at the sea-level-rise problem and puts their heads in the sand." That's because soon there may not be much sand left.

18   Rising sea level is not the only change Earth's oceans are undergoing. The ten-year-long World Ocean Circulation Experiment, launched in 1990, has helped researchers to better understand what is now called the ocean conveyor belt.

19   Oceans, in effect, mimic some functions of the human circulatory system. Just as arteries carry oxygenated blood from the heart to the extremities, and veins return blood to be replenished with oxygen, oceans provide life-sustaining circulation to the planet. Propelled mainly by prevailing winds and differences in water density, which changes with the temperature and salinity of the seawater, ocean currents are critical in cooling, warming, and watering the planet's terrestrial surfaces—and in transferring heat from the Equator to the Poles.

20   The engine running the conveyor belt is the density-driven thermohaline circulation ("thermo" for heat and "haline" for salt). Warm, salty water flows from the tropical Atlantic north toward the Pole in surface currents like the Gulf Stream. This saline water loses heat to the air as it is carried to the far reaches of the North Atlantic. The coldness and high salinity together make the water more dense, and it sinks deep into the ocean. Surface water moves in to replace it. The deep, cold water flows into the South Atlantic, Indian, and Pacific Oceans, eventually mixing again with warm water and rising back to the surface.

21   Changes in water temperature and salinity, depending on how drastic they are, might have considerable effects on the ocean conveyor belt. Ocean temperatures are rising in all ocean basins and at much deeper depths than previously thought, say scientists at the National Oceanic and Atmospheric Administration (NOAA). Arguably, the largest oceanic change ever measured in the era of modern instruments is in the declining salinity of the subpolar seas bordering the North Atlantic.

22   Robert Gagosian, president and director of the Woods Hole Oceanographic Institution, believes that oceans hold the key to potential dramatic shifts in the Earth's climate. He warns that too much change in ocean temperature and salinity could disrupt the North Atlantic thermohaline circulation enough to slow down or possibly halt

the conveyor belt—causing drastic climate changes in time spans as short as a decade.

23   The future breakdown of the thermohaline circulation remains a disturbing, if remote, possibility. But the link between changing atmospheric chemistry and the changing oceans is indisputable, says Nicholas Bates, a principal investigator for the Bermuda Atlantic Time-series Study station, which monitors the temperature, chemical composition, and salinity of deep-ocean water in the Sargasso Sea southeast of the Bermuda Triangle.

24   Oceans are important sinks, or absorption centers, for carbon dioxide, and take up about a third of human-generated CO_2. Data from the Bermuda monitoring programs show that CO_2 levels at the ocean surface are rising at about the same rate as atmospheric CO_2. But it is in the deeper levels where Bates has observed even greater change. In the waters between 250 and 450 meters (820 and 1,476 feet) deep, CO_2 levels are rising at nearly twice the rate as in the surface waters. "It's not a belief system; it's an observable scientific fact," Bates says. "And it shouldn't be doing that unless something fundamental has changed in this part of the ocean."

25   While scientists like Bates monitor changes in the oceans, others evaluate CO_2 levels in the atmosphere. In Vestmannaeyjar, Iceland, a lighthouse attendant opens a large silver suitcase that looks like something out of a James Bond movie, telescopes out an attached 15-foot rod, and flips a switch, activating a computer that controls several motors, valves, and stopcocks. Two two-and-a-half-liter flasks in the suitcase fill with ambient air. In North Africa, an Algerian monk at Assekrem does the same. Around the world, collectors like these are monitoring the cocoon of gases that compose our atmosphere and permit life as we know it to persist.

26   When the weekly collection is done, all the flasks are sent to Boulder, Colorado. There, Pieter Tans, a Dutch-born atmospheric scientist with NOAA's Climate Monitoring and Diagnostics Laboratory, oversees a slew of sensitive instruments that test the air in the flasks for its chemical composition. In this way Tans helps assess the state of the world's atmosphere.

27   By all accounts it has changed significantly in the past 150 years.

28   Walking through the various labs filled with cylinders of standardized gas mixtures, absolute manometers, and gas chromatographs, Tans offers up a short history of atmospheric monitoring. In the late 1950s a researcher named Charles Keeling began measuring CO_2 in the atmosphere above Hawall's 13,679-foot Mauna Loa. The first thing that caught Keeling's eye was how CO_2 level rose and fell seasonally. That made sense since, during spring and summer, plants take in CO_2 during photosynthesis and produce oxygen in the atmosphere. In the fall

and winter, when plants decay, they release greater quantities of CO_2 through respiration and decay. Keeling's vacillating seasonal curve became famous as a visual representation of the Earth "breathing."

29 Something else about the way the Earth was breathing attracted Keeling's attention. He watched as CO_2 level not only fluctuated seasonally, but also rose year after year. Carbon dioxide level has climbed from about 315 parts per million (ppm) from Keeling's first readings in 1958 to more than 375 ppm today. A primary source for this rise is indisputable: humans' prodigious burning of carbon-laden fossil fuels for their factories, homes, and cars.

30 Tans shows me a graph depicting levels of three key greenhouse gases—CO_2, methane, and nitrous oxide—from the year 1000 to the present. The three gases together help keep Earth, which would otherwise be an inhospitably cold orbiting rock, temperate by orchestrating an intricate dance between the radiation of heat from Earth back to space (cooling the planet) and the absorption of radiation in the atmosphere (trapping it near the surface and thus warming the planet).

31 Tans and most other scientists believe that greenhouse gases are at the root of our changing climate. "These gases are a climate-change driver," says Tans, poking his graph definitively with his index finger. The three lines on the graph follow almost identical patterns: basically flat until the mid-1800s, then all three move upward in a trend that turns even more sharply upward after 1950. "This is what we did," says Tans, pointing to the parallel spikes. "We have very significantly changed the atmospheric concentration of these gases. We know their radiative properties," he says. "It is inconceivable to me that the increase would not have a significant effect on climate."

32 Exactly how large that effect might be on the planet's health and respiratory system will continue to be a subject of great scientific and political debate—especially if the lines on the graph continue their upward trajectory.

33 Eugene Brower, an Inupiat Eskimo and president of the Barrow Whaling Captains' Association, doesn't need fancy parts-per-million measurements of CO_2 concentrations or long-term sea-level gauges to tell him that his world is changing.

34 "It's happening as we speak," the 56-year-old Brower says as we drive around his home in Barrow, Alaska—the United States' northernmost city—on a late August day. In his fire chief's truck, Brower takes me to his family's traditional ice cellars, painstakingly dug into the permafrost, and points out how his stores of muktuk—whale skin and blubber—recently began spoiling in the fall because melting water drips down to his food stores. Our next stop is the old Bureau of Indian Affairs school building. The once impenetrable permafrost that kept the

foundation solid has bucked and heaved so much that walking through the school is almost like walking down the halls of an amusement park fun house. We head to the eroding beach and gaze out over open water. "Normally by now the ice would be coming in," Brower says, scrunching up his eyes and scanning the blue horizon.

35   We continue our tour. Barrow looks like a coastal community under siege. The ramshackle conglomeration of weather-beaten houses along the seaside gravel road stands protected from fall storm surges by miles-long berms of gravel and mud that block views of migrating gray whales. Yellow bulldozers and graders patrol the coast like sentries.

36   The Inupiat language has words that describe many kinds of ice. Piqaluyak is salt-free multiyear sea ice. Ivuniq is a pressure ridge. Sarri is the word for pack ice, tuvaqtaq is bottom-fast ice, and shore-fast ice is tuvaq. For Brower, these words are the currency of hunters who must know and follow ice patterns to track bearded seals, walruses, and bowhead whales.

37   There are no words, though, to describe how much, and how fast, the ice is changing. Researchers long ago predicted that the most visible impacts from a globally warmer world would occur first at high latitudes: rising air and sea temperatures, earlier snowmelt, later ice freeze-up, reductions in sea ice, thawing permafrost, more erosion, increases in storm intensity. Now all those impacts have been documented in Alaska. "The changes observed here provide an early warning system for the rest of the planet," says Amanda Lynch, an Australian researcher who is the principal investigator on a project that works with Barrow's residents to help them incorporate scientific data into management decisions for the city's threatened infrastructure.

38   Before leaving the Arctic, I drive to Point Barrow alone. There, at the tip of Alaska, roughshod hunting shacks dot the spit of land that marks the dividing line between the Chukchi and Beaufort Seas. Next to one shack someone has planted three eight-foot sticks of white driftwood in the sand, then crisscrossed their tops with whale baleen, a horny substance that whales of the same name use to filter life-sustaining plankton out of seawater. The baleen, curiously, looks like palm fronds.

39   So there, on the North Slope of Alaska, stand three makeshift palm trees. Perhaps they are no more than an elaborate Inupiat joke, but these Arctic palms seem an enigmatic metaphor for the Earth's future. ■

Тномаѕ Derr

Strange Science

Author of Environmental Ethics and Christian Humanism *(1996),*
Thomas Derr was a professor of religion at Smith College for many years.
He was twice awarded Danforth Foundation grants for religious study. His
essays frequently contribute to public discussions about global warming by
contending that popular media have not represented fully the scientific
data about the existence and significance of global warming. The
following article appeared in the November 2004 issue of First Things, *a*
journal about religion and public life.

1   Global warming has achieved the status of a major threat. It inspires nightmares of a troubled future and propels apocalyptic dramas such as the summer 2004 movie *The Day After Tomorrow.* Even were the Kyoto treaty to be fully implemented, it wouldn't make a dent in the warming trend, which seems to be inexorable. Doom is upon us.

2   Except that maybe it isn't. You might not know it from ordinary media accounts, which report the judgments of alarmists as "settled science," but there is a skeptical side to the argument. Scientists familiar with the issues involved have written critically about the theory of global warming. The puzzle is why these commentators, well-credentialed and experienced, have been swept aside to produce a false "consensus." What is it that produces widespread agreement among both "experts" and the general public on a hypothesis which is quite likely wrong?

3   The consensus holds that we are experiencing unprecedented global warming and that human activity is the main culprit. The past century, we are told, has been the hottest on record, with temperatures steadily rising during the last decades. Since human population and industrial activity have risen at the same time, it stands to reason that human activity is, one way or another, the cause of this observed warming. Anything wrong with this reasoning?

4   Quite a lot, as it turns out. The phrase "on record" doesn't mean very much, since most records date from the latter part of the nineteenth century. Without accurate records there are still ways of discovering the temperatures of past centuries, and these methods do not confirm the theory of a steady rise. Reading tree rings helps (the rings are further apart when the temperature is warmer and the trees grow faster). Core samples from drilling in ice fields can yield even older data. Some historical reconstruction can help, too—for example, we know that the Norsemen settled Greenland (and named it "green") a

millennium ago and grew crops there, in land which is today quite inhospitable to settlement, let alone to agriculture. Other evidence comes from coral growth, isotope data from sea floor sediment, and insects, all of which point to a very warm climate in medieval times. Abundant testimony tells us that the European climate then cooled dramatically from the thirteenth century until the eighteenth, when it began its slow re-warming.

5   In sum, what we learn from multiple sources is that the earth (and not just Europe) was warmer in the tenth century than it is now, that it cooled dramatically in the middle of our second millennium (this has been called the "little ice age"), and then began warming again. Temperatures were higher in medieval times (from about 800 to 1300) than they are now, and the twentieth century represented a recovery from the little ice age to something like normal. The false perception that the recent warming trend is out of the ordinary is heightened by its being measured from an extraordinarily cold starting point, without taking into account the earlier balmy medieval period, sometimes called the Medieval Climate Optimum. Data such as fossilized sea shells indicate that similar natural climate swings occurred in prehistoric times, well before the appearance of the human race.

6   Even the period for which we have records can be misread. While the average global surface temperature increased by about 0.5 degrees Celsius during the twentieth century, the major part of that warming occurred in the early part of the century, before the rapid rise in human population and before the consequent rise in emissions of polluting substances into the atmosphere. There was actually a noticeable cooling period after World War II, and this climate trend produced a rather different sort of alarmism—some predicted the return of an ice age. In 1974 the National Science Board, observing a thirty-year-long decline in world temperature, predicted the end of temperate times and the dawning of the next glacial age. Meteorologists, *Newsweek* reported, were "almost unanimous in the view that the trend will reduce agricultural productivity for the rest of the century." But they were wrong, as we now know (another caution about supposedly "unanimous" scientific opinion), and after 1975 we began to experience our current warming trend. Notice that these fluctuations, over the centuries and within them, do not correlate with human numbers or activity. They are evidently caused by something else.

7   What, then, is the cause of the current warming trend? As everyone has heard, the emission of so-called "greenhouse gasses," mostly carbon dioxide from burning fossil fuels, is supposed to be the major culprit in global warming. This is the anthropogenic hypothesis, according to which humans have caused the trouble. But such emissions correlate with human numbers and industrial development, so they could

not have been the cause of warming centuries ago, nor of the nineteenth-century rewarming trend which began with a much smaller human population and before the industrial revolution. Nor is there a very good correlation between atmospheric carbon dioxide levels and past climate changes. Thus, to many scientists, the evidence that greenhouse gasses produced by humans are causing any significant warming is sketchy.

8   The likeliest cause of current climate trends seems to be solar activity, perhaps in combination with galactic cosmic rays caused by supernovas, especially because there is some good observable correlation between solar magnetism output and terrestrial climate change. But that kind of change is not predictable within any usable time frame, not yet anyway, and, of course, it is entirely beyond any human influence. The conclusion, then, is that the climate will change naturally; aside from altering obviously foolish behavior, such as releasing dangerous pollutants into our air and water, we can and should do little more than adapt to these natural changes, as all life has always done.

9   That is not a counsel of despair, however, for global warming is not necessarily a bad thing. Increasing warmth and higher levels of carbon dioxide help plants to grow (carbon dioxide is not a pollutant), and, indeed, mapping by satellite shows that the earth has become about six percent greener overall in the past two decades, with forests expanding into arid regions (though the effect is uneven). The Amazon rain forest was the biggest gainer, despite the much-advertised deforestation caused by human cutting along its edges. Certainly climate change does not help every region equally and will probably harm some. That has always been true. But there are careful studies that predict overall benefit to the earth with increasing warmth: fewer storms (not more), more rain, better crop yields over larger areas, and longer growing seasons, milder winters, and decreasing heating costs in colder latitudes. The predictable change, though measurable, will not be catastrophic at all—maybe one degree Celsius during the twenty-first century. The news is certainly not all bad, and may on balance be rather good.

10   There is much more, in more detail, to the argument of those scientists who are skeptical about the threat of global warming. On the whole, their case is, I think, quite persuasive. The question, then, is why so few people believe it.

11   Part of the answer is that bad news is good news—for the news media. The media report arresting and frightening items, for that is what draws listeners, viewers, and readers. The purveyors of climate disaster theories have exploited this journalistic habit quite brilliantly, releasing steadily more frightening scenarios without much significant data to back them up. Consider the unguarded admission of Steven Schneider of

Stanford, a leading proponent of the global warming theory. In a now notorious comment, printed in *Discover* in 1989 and, surely to his discomfort, often cited by his opponents, Schneider admitted:

> To capture the public imagination, we have to offer up scary scenarios, make simplified dramatic statements, and make little mention of any doubts we may have. Each of us has to decide what the right balance is between being effective and being honest.

This sort of willingness to place the cause above the truth has exasperated Richard Lindzen, Sloan Professor of Meteorology at MIT, who is one of the authors of the science sections of the report of the International Panel on Climate Change (IPCC), the body responsible for an increasing crescendo of dire warnings. In testimony before the U.S. Senate's Environment and Public Works Committee, he called the IPCC's Summary for Policymakers, which loudly sounds the warming alarm, "very much a child's exercise of what might possibly happen . . . [which] conjures up some scary scenarios for which there is no evidence."

12   This brings us to the second part of the answer, which concerns the political and economic consequences of the policy argument. The IPCC is a UN body and reflects UN politics, which are consistently favorable to developing countries, the majority of its members. Those politics are very supportive of the Kyoto treaty, which not only exempts the developing countries from emissions standards but also requires compensatory treatment from the wealthier nations for any economic restraints that new climate management policies may impose on these developing countries. Were Kyoto to be implemented as written, the developing countries would gain lots of money and free technology. One need not be a cynic to grasp that a UN body will do obeisance to these political realities wherever possible.

13   The Kyoto treaty would not make a measurable difference in the climate—by 2050, a temperature reduction of maybe two-hundredths of a degree Celsius, or at most six-hundredths of a degree—but the sacrifices it would impose on the United States would be quite large. It would require us to reduce our projected 2012 energy use by 25 percent, a catastrophic economic hit. Small wonder that the Senate in 1997 passed a bipartisan resolution, the Byrd-Hagel anti-Kyoto resolution, by 95–0 (a fact rarely recalled by those who claim that America's refusal to sign on to the treaty was the result of the Bush administration's thralldom to corporate interests).

14   Most of the European countries that have ratified Kyoto are falling behind already on targets, despite having stagnant economies and falling populations. It is highly unlikely they will meet the goals they have signed on for, and they know it. Neither will Japan, for that matter. The European Union has committed itself to an eight percent reduction

in energy use (from 1990 levels) by 2012, but the European Environment Agency admits that current trends project only a 4.7 percent reduction. When Kyoto signers lecture non-signers for not doing enough for the environment, they invite the charge of hypocrisy. There is also the obvious fact that adherence to the treaty will hurt the U.S. economy much more than the European, which suggests that old-fashioned economic competitiveness is in the mix of motives at play here. The absurdity of the treaty becomes obvious when we recognize that it does not impose emissions requirements on developing countries, including economic giants such as China, India, and Brazil. (China will become the world's biggest source of carbon dioxide emissions in just a few years.)

15   A third reason why global warming fears seem to be carrying the day goes beyond these political interests; it involves intellectual pride. Academics are a touchy tribe (I'm one of them); they do not take it kindly when their theories, often the result of hard work, are contradicted. And sure enough, the struggle for the truth in this matter is anything but polite. It is intellectual warfare, entangled with politics, reputations, and ideology; and most of the anger comes from the side of the alarmists. People lose their tempers and hurl insults—"junk science," "willful ignorance," "diatribe," "arrogant," "stupid," "incompetent," "bias," "bad faith," "deplorable misinformation," and more. Consider the fiercely hateful reaction to Bjorn Lomborg's 2001 book, *The Skeptical Environmentalist.* He challenged the entrenched and politically powerful orthodoxy and did so with maddeningly thorough data. His critics, unable to refute his statistics, seem to have been enraged by their own weakness—a familiar phenomenon, after all. Or perhaps, with their reputations and their fund-raising ability tied to the disaster scenarios, they felt their livelihoods threatened. In any case, the shrillness of their voices has helped to drown out the skeptics.

16   Finally, there is a fourth cause: a somewhat murky antipathy to modern technological civilization as the destroyer of a purer, cleaner, more "natural" life, a life where virtue dwelt before the great degeneration set in. The global warming campaign is the leading edge of an environmentalism which goes far beyond mere pollution control and indicts the global economy for its machines, its agribusiness, its massive movements of goods, and above all its growing population. Picking apart this argument to show the weakness of its pieces does not go to the heart of the fear and loathing that motivate it. The revulsion shows in the prescriptions advanced by the global warming alarmists: roll back emissions to earlier levels; reduce production and consumption of goods; lower birth rates. Our material ease and the freedoms it has spawned are dangerous illusions, bargains with the devil, and now comes the reckoning. A major apocalypse looms, either to destroy or, paradoxically, to save us—if we come to our senses in the nick of time.

17   It is clear, then, given the deep roots of the scare, that it is likely to be pretty durable. It has the added advantage of not being readily falsifiable in our lifetimes; only future humans, who will have the perspective of centuries, will know for certain whether the current warming trend is abnormal. In the meantime, the sanest course for us would be to gain what limited perspective we can (remembering the global cooling alarm of a generation ago) and to proceed cautiously. We are going through a scare with many causes, and we need to step back from it, take a long second look at the scientific evidence, and not do anything rash. Though the alarmists claim otherwise, the science concerning global warming is certainly not settled. It is probable that the case for anthropogenic warming will not hold up, and that the earth is behaving as it has for millennia, with natural climate swings that have little to do with human activity. ■

ISSUE IN FOCUS

Habitat Loss

The Reintroduction of Wolves into Yellowstone

Habitat protection—the preservation and sometimes restoration of natural landscapes that are essential to the sustenance of various animal and plant species—has become the focus of much environmental debate in recent years. In communities large and small, in your own city or town meetings and in the debates in Congress, citizens have been weighing and debating the relative merits of protecting local habitats so that particular species (particularly endangered ones) might survive and flourish. Often the discussions turn to the management of local resources to encourage one or another kind of desirable environmental impact—though of course one group's desires frequently conflict with another's.

A Swan Lake pack wolf.
Source: *Yellowstone Science,*
Winter 2005, p. 7

A particular example, one that serves as a prototype for many others, is the case of wolves in Yellowstone National Park. Gray wolves once were prevalent across large portions of North America, but their population was gradually decimated after 1800 because hunters sought them and because their habitats were compromised as increasing numbers of settlers farmed the land. In the West, wolves were especially attacked because they were the enemy of ranchers, who wished to protect their livestock. According to a report by Ken Kostel of the Natural Resources Defense Council (published through its online magazine *OnEarth:* see <www.nrdc.org/onearth/04sum/briefings.asp>), wolves had been virtually eradicated from Yellowstone by 1910, just 38 years after the national park had been created, because they were regarded as a menace to prized herds of elk, deer, mountain sheep, and antelope, and because it was thought that predators were dangerous to human visitors. That wolves had gathered a bad reputation in popular lore—a scene in Willa Cather's famous novel *My Antonia,* for example, depicts a horrifying attack on a wedding party by wolves—did not help their cause. Sometime in the 1930s or 1940s the last wolf disappeared from Yellowstone, and so many disappeared from adjoining states that the wolf literally became an endangered species. Indeed, the wolf was included on the "threatened" species list protected by the Endangered Species Act of 1973. Meanwhile, without wolves to prey upon them, the elk in Yellowstone prospered—and began trampling on young aspen trees, willows, and cottonwoods; disrupting beaver populations; influencing the migrations of birds; and even ruining streams.

> "Die wolf"
>
> —BUMPER STICKER SEEN NEAR
> YELLOWSTONE PARK

Consequently, in 1995, after several years of heated debate between environmentalists and farmers, 31 wolves were reintroduced into Yellowstone under Secretary of the Interior Bruce Babbitt. In the ensuing decade, only the elk have apparently been losers: the wolves have prospered and multiplied, small animals and grizzly bears that feed on dead elk have done well too, elk are avoiding the open areas near streams so that stream quality has improved, and aspen have begun to return. Biodiversity has been enhanced. Ecologists are watching closely to determine the full effects of the reintroduction of wolves on the Yellowstone environment. And people are coming to Yellowstone expressly to see wolves: 153,000 visitors had reported seeing at least one wolf by 2005. (For a good summary of the wolf restoration and its effects, see the Winter 2005 issue of *Yellowstone Science.* Also authoritative is L. David Mech and Luigi Boitani's *Wolves: Behavior, Ecology, and Conservation.*)

> The last known North American case of a wolf killing a human being was in 1944, when an Alaskan native broke up a fight between a wolf and his sled dogs, got bit on the arm, and died of rabies.
>
> —*DENVER POST* EDITORIAL, JUNE 9, 2004

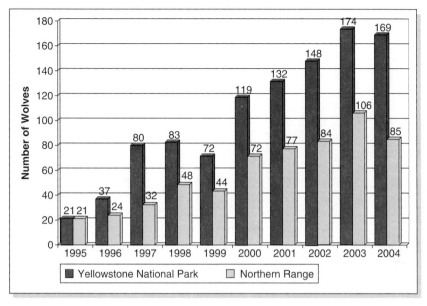

The increase in wolf population in and around Yellowstone National Park, 1995–2005. (The small drop in 1999 probably was due to disease.)
Source: *Yellowstone Science,* Winter 2005

But the debate has not grown less impassioned. While environmentalists have observed an increase in the number of animals that feed off wolf kills and while ecotourists enjoy viewing wolves in the wild, ranchers and farmers, under the auspices of the American Farm Bureau Federation, are worrying about the effect on cattle and sheep. While wolves, which live in packs, generally seem leery of mixing with humans, some people nevertheless fear that people and their pets will eventually be endangered by wolves. Livestock losses in the Yellowstone area have been modest so far and no humans have been attacked, but what will happen as the wolves increase in numbers and begin to roam beyond the borders of Yellowstone Park?

That question was raised dramatically when a wolf was killed on a Colorado highway in 2004, raising the fear that wolves were spreading far beyond the boundaries of Yellowstone and prompting the suggestion that wolves within the park should be protected as endangered while wolves that wander outside might be shot or chased off as predators. Currently ranchers are compensated for livestock losses, but can those compensations continue if losses grow? Should wolves remain officially "threatened," and therefore protected from harm? Or should they be carefully "managed" (i.e., selectively hunted) to prevent their becoming a menace? In short, what

A pack rally. Wolves howl for several reasons, one of which is social.
Source: *Jim & Jamie Dutcher/Getty Images*

should be done to keep the peace between humans and wolves? Is there room for both? More broadly, is this another case of the tension between personal rights and "big government intrusion"?

On the following pages you can sample some of the arguments that are revolving around habitat restoration in general and concerning wolves in particular. Dan Neal, writing in *National Geographic* (May 1998), presents the case in favor of the reintroduction of wolves, supported by a 1999 *Los Angeles Times* editorial, "Let the Gray Wolf Roam Free." William Norman Gregg articulates the opposing point of view, published in *The New American* on January 27, 2003, and supported by a photograph—a visual argument—of a frightening wolf. (Other photographs offer a more benign interpretation of the wolf.) As you read, think about habitat protection debates in your own communities. For wherever new highways, new developments, and new impacts on the land are proposed, proponents of habitat protection will be making their own arguments.

DAN NEAL

Who's Afraid of the Big Bad Wolf?

1   R estoring wolves to the northern Rocky Mountain region—an idea first floated in the 1970s—has always been more a political question than a biological decision.

2   In the American West, ranchers and farmers have held most of the trump cards since Europeans overran Native Americans. Backed by the Bureau of Reclamation and the Bureau of Land Management, they have won most of the battles over dams, development, and grazing rights on federal lands.

3   When conservationists began to win a few of the first battles over wolf reintroduction, the wolf became a symbol of the ranching industry's slipping influence and the rising power of environmentalists, both in the region and in Washington, D.C.

4   Once the federal government decided that it had the backing of enough people across the country to take on the region's agriculture interests, the decision was made to bring back the wolf to both Yellowstone and central Idaho under a plan that addressed the legitimate concerns of the livestock producers. The project was buttressed by a compensation fund administered by Defenders of Wildlife from which ranchers receive full payment for any verified wolf killing of livestock.

5   The U.S. Fish and Wildlife Service brought some 70 wolves from Canada to Yellowstone National Park and central Idaho in 1995 and 1996. The animals are thriving. Wolf experts had predicted success, but no one expected to see the wolves doing this well just three years into the program. Biologists in Yellowstone are only beginning to understand the cascading impacts of the large predators on the region's ecosystem.

6   One thing that is clear: Ranchers' worries that the wolves would drive them out of business were baseless. Since wolves were brought back to the Yellowstone region, they have killed only about 80 sheep and 5 cattle. Ranchers in Wyoming and Montana lose more sheep to "tipover"—when a sheep rolls on its back and can't get up again—than to wolves.

7   Those results show that wolves will not spell the end of western ranching as we know it. They make clear that the debate over wolf reintroduction is not really about wolves and their potential to kill livestock. The real issue is who controls the West, especially its public lands.

8   Indeed, some ranching interests still cannot stand the idea that the U.S. public forced them to accept a public policy decision they had fought so vigorously. The American Farm Bureau filed suit to block the plan.

This cartoon by Mike Keefe was published in *USA Today.*

9   In December 1997 a federal judge in Casper, Wyoming, declared that details of the reintroduction program violated the Endangered Species Act and ordered the removal of the wolves. Implementation of the order has been stayed pending appeal.

10   Should the courts back the Casper judge, the public should demand congressional action to ensure that these magnificent animals retain their rightful place in Yellowstone and the northern Rockies. ■

Los Angeles Times Editorial

Let the Gray Wolf Roam Free

1   The reintroduction of the gray wolf into Yellowstone National Park and nearby portions of Idaho and Montana has been a major success, and the worst fears of ranchers have come to nothing. The wolves are not killing off cattle and sheep as ranchers insisted would happen. Livestock losses since the program began in 1995 are but a fraction of the predictions in the environmental impact statement upon which the program was based. It's time for the ranchers to end their bitter political and legal opposition to the return of the gray wolf, which historically roamed Yellowstone until it was eradicated early in the century.

2   From the 31 wolves imported in 1995 and 1996 from Canada, the wolf population in the Greater Yellowstone ecosystem has risen to an estimated 160, say park biologists. At that rate, the Yellowstone wolf can be removed from the endangered species list not many years hence. That would mark an overwhelming success for the program.

3   The basic quarry for the wolves has been Yellowstone elk, primarily animals that are old or ill. Except for the depredation of two rogue wolves, livestock deaths have been minimal, park officials say. Conservation groups have compensated ranchers for any loss of stock.

4   But in spite of this success story, the American Farm Bureau Federation continues to pursue a lawsuit seeking to remove the Yellowstone wolves—they probably would have to be killed—based on a technically in the Endangered Species Act. The Farm Bureau won in the federal district court in Wyoming, and the case is now before the U.S. Circuit Court of Appeals in Denver.

5   At the outset of the program, the environmental impact statement forecast a loss of 40 to 50 sheep and 10 to 12 head of cattle to wolves each year. Biologist Doug Smith says only 83 sheep and eight head of cattle have been lost since the program started four years ago. Most involved wolves that were transplanted to Yellowstone and were not members of the original packs or their offspring. A single wolf was blamed for 63 of the sheep deaths.

6   "If you look at livestock mortality in Wyoming or Montana, it doesn't even register," Smith told the *Yellowstone Journal.* "Your average wolf doesn't kill livestock."

7   Smith's group now is measuring the impact of the wolves on other large predators in the park—grizzly bears, black bears and cougars. In the meantime, Yellowstone has become the premier place in the world to view wolves in the wild. ■

WILLIAM NORMAN GREGG

Thrown to the Wolves

1   Across the nation, particularly in western states, ranchers are feeling the bite of the so-called "wolf recovery" program, which began with reintroducing wolves to Yellowstone National Park in 1995. Stemming from the Endangered Species Act (ESA), this program was followed three years later with the return of Mexican gray wolves in the Southwest, and similar initiatives are underway in the Midwest and Northeast.

2   As the resurgent wolf packs thrive, they are inflicting serious economic damage on dairy and beef ranchers. Notes the November 9th *Milwaukee Journal-Sentinel*: "[B]eef cattle ranchers in northwestern Wisconsin say nighttime wolf raids cost them 92 calves [in 2001] alone. . . . They've found calves with their hindquarters shredded, still alive and trying to suckle. They have stumbled upon a pregnant cow ripped open and her fetus torn out. They have seen calves with crushed throats—dead without losing a drop of blood. Killed, they believe, simply for the thrill." "There is a reason the farmers made [wolves] extinct before, and this is probably the reason," comments Cortney Fornengo, whose family runs a beef cattle ranch in Wisconsin.

Protected killers: Federal "wolf recovery" efforts have resulted in devastating economic losses to ranchers in many states. Eco-radicals support reintroduction of wolves and other large predators as a way of advancing the UN-supported "Wildlands Project." [original caption and photo]

3   According to the December 30th *Salt Lake Tribune*, the impact of wolf recovery on the ranching industry in Idaho, Montana, and Wyoming is measured primarily by "an absence of calves coming home after hards graze [in] national forests." The family of Dick and Betty Baker, sixth-generation cattle ranchers in Salmon, Idaho, describe how wolves have literally intruded into their backyard to prey on cattle and sheep. Seeking to contain the predators, federal wildlife officials "got after them with rubber bullets and helicopters and spent a lot of money," Dick Baker recalled. Despite such cost-intensive efforts, "we [still] see wolves lay right up there on the bench watching the cattle and waiting for dark."

4   Jay Wiley owns a ranch located along Idaho's Salmon River. He points out that since 1995, "The [wolf] population just exploded, and [federal wildlife officials] have lost control." Wiley also points out that the owner of a neighboring ranch lost $12,000 worth of calves in wolf attacks during 2001. And with the feds looking to add local species such as the sage grouse and bull trout to the endangered species list, Wiley and other ranchers may be driven to sell off their land.

5   Heartbreaking though it is to lose a family ranch, losing a family member is incomparably worse. If not for their dog's protective instincts, the family of retired postal worker Richard Humphrey may have fallen prey to Mexican wolves during an April 1998 camping trip near Safford, Arizona. The family had set up camp in a well-known tourist location when their dog Buck discovered two Mexican wolves lurking nearby. The wolves backed off, and the family assumed that "the wolves were just passing through."

6   A little more than an hour later, Helen screamed for Richard to grab his rifle. A short distance from the camp Buck had become entangled in a life-and-death fight with several wolves. Armed with his rifle, Richard tried to chase the wolves away. One of them suddenly charged at the Humphreys, and Richard shot him down less than 50 feet from his family. The family gently gathered their seriously wounded dog and went to find a veterinarian. When they arrived at Safford, Richard—in compliance with federal law—reported the wolf shooting to an agent of the U.S. Fish & Wildlife Service (FWS).

7   The terrifying wolf attack was just the beginning of the Humphrey family's problems. Notes *Range* magazine, "Richard had accidentally become a political pawn and scapegoat." Eco-radical groups in Arizona demanded that the retired postal worker be slapped with a huge fine and sent to prison. After six weeks of relentless and invasive questioning by federal officials, no charges were filed against Humphrey, provoking eco-radical outrage.

8   "By refusing to prosecute Richard Humphrey . . . the U.S. Fish & Wildlife Service has sent a signal that killing wolves is not a serious crime," complained the Center for Biological Diversity. Bear in mind that the supposed crime committed by Humphrey was to defend himself, his wife, and two young daughters from a potentially lethal attack. It's also important to recognize that it was the FWS that had created the conditions for this near tragedy. As *Range* magazine points out, "wolves were being fed road-kill twice per week by [the] FWS" in release pens less than a mile away from the campsite where the attack occurred. "FWS had guaranteed in public meetings that 'Notice of general wolf locations will be publicized,'" reported the publication. "If they had followed through with their pledges to the public, the Humphreys' calamitous situation would not have occurred."

9   But such situations are the predictable—indeed, the intended—result of the federal government's wolf "re-colonization" effort. Renee Askins of the eco-radical Wolf Recovery Fund has admitted that "wolf recovery is not about wolves. [Instead] it is about control of the west."

10   Wildlife ecologist Dr. Charles F. Kay summarizes: "Simply put, environmentalists are using wolf recovery and the Endangered Species Act to run ranchers out of the country and to thwart multiple use of public

Lester Faigley took this photo of a Yellowstone wolf in August 2004. Note how it makes a decidedly different argument than the photo that accompanies the essay by William Norman Gregg, page 346.

lands. . . . Is this what Congress had in mind when it passed the Endangered Species Act?"

11   While Congress probably didn't intend for the Endangered Species Act to drive humans off their land, that is the act's inevitable effect. And this is entirely understandable considering that act's pedigree. Dr. Michael S. Coffman, a forest biologist and author of *Saviors of the Earth?*, points out that the Endangered Species Act is adapted from the UN's Convention on the International Trade in Endangered Species of Flora and Fauna.

12   The ESA's decades-long assault on property rights thus has its origins in UN mandates. And the "rural cleansing" campaign is part of an even more grandiose UN program called the "Wildlands Project," under which half of the U.S. land area would be converted into a vast biodiversity preserve. One supporter of re-wilding western lands explained that reintroducing wolves and other large predators was intended to "bring back another element that has been vanishing from the Western back country. That ingredient is fear. Wolves are killers. . . . People will think twice before traipsing into the back country."

13   Simply put, the "wolf recovery" program is a form of environmental terrorism. Thus while the U.S. government is working through the UN to fight a war against terrorism abroad. It is collaborating with UN-linked environmental radicals to wage an eco-terrorist campaign against rural property owners here at home. ∎

From Reading to Writing

1. Analyze the argument by either Dan Neal or William Norman Gregg: how is each argument the product of its audience and purpose, and what souces of argument (ethical appeal, emotional appeal, logical appeals, and good reasons) does each author choose and why? (See Chapter 4 for information on rhetorical analysis.)

2. Compare the various photos of wolves that appear on the preceding pages. What visual argument does each photo seem to make? (See Chapter 5 for information on analyzing visuals.)

3. Write an argument that makes its point by defining a key term related to environmental concerns. You might choose to change someone's attitude to a particular animal or plant or concept in order to defend or challenge it, for instance, by defining it in a certain way. Examples: "A field mouse isn't really much of a pest"; "the snail darter is just another nuisance fish"; "habitat loss is just another name for normal change." (See Chapter 6 for more on writing definition arguments.)

4. Propose a change in policy related to an environmental issue in your community. (See Chapter 11 for advice.)

5. Write a rebuttal of an article related to the environment in your local or school newspaper (see Chapter 10). Consider whether you wish to show the weakness in the article, whether you wish to counter-argue, or both.

6. Write an essay that recounts a personal experience of yours that makes an argumentative point related to the environment. It could be a story about a camping or hiking trip, for example, or a tale of your encounter with some environmental problem or challenge. See Chapter 9 for advice on narrative arguments.

CHAPTER 19

Confronting Sexual Difference

Sexual Difference in American Culture

It happened nearly a decade ago, but people still talk about it: In 1998 University of Wyoming political science major Matthew Shepard was beaten to a pulp and pistol-whipped to death in the town of Laramie, Wyoming. Russell Henderson, 21, and Aaron McKinney, 20, had lured Shepard from a bar (they knew he was gay), driven him to a deserted area, beaten him as he begged for mercy, and removed his shoes and tied him to a post, like a coyote, to warn off others. Henderson and McKinney took Shepard's wallet, left him to die, and then attacked two Latino men before they were arrested.

Matthew Shepard

Matthew Shepard, buried two days later before a crowd of 650 mourners (and a small group of protesters holding signs ridiculing "fags"), became a symbol of growing violence against gays in the United States. His murder and the subsequent trial of the perpetrators led many citizens and legislators to advocate a range of measures to protect gay, lesbian, and bisexual citizens, and to expand the rights and responsibilities that those citizens might enjoy.

A year before, in 1997, Ellen DeGeneres, star of the comedy series "Ellen," made public her character's (and her own) lesbianism and redirected her show toward an exploration of gay and lesbian identity. Before the series closed two years later, it consistently treated (typically as the material of comedy) the social and cultural tribulations faced by gays and lesbians, and challenged viewers to confront those tribulations in their own communities. Since then, a number of other television series have pursued the same end—most prominently, "Will and Grace," "Six Feet Under," and "Queer as Folk," but also soap operas, documentaries, variety shows (such as "Saturday Night Live"), and "reality" shows such as "Survivor" and "Boy Meets Boy." Television shows like these, as well as a range of movies, ads, and Web sites, have required American citizens to confront a range of cultural practices involving gay, lesbian, and bisexual people—practices including service in the military, same-sex marriage and other domestic issues, and even the ordination of priests.

Contemporary Arguments

This section of *Good Reasons* contains a range of arguments related to just those issues. Hate crimes in various communities in recent years have focused great attention on the violence that is often leveled at gays and on the issue of rights and protections for gay, lesbian, and bisexual citizens. The question of passing legislation to protect the rights and property and physical bodies of gays, lesbians, and bisexuals has animated citizens in many communities. Thus we present an argument by Carmen Vazquez about the predicament of gay and lesbian citizens in the United States that might have implications for legislation.

At the least, such legislation would prohibit hate speech and violent acts directed toward people on account of their sexual preference. Indeed, a number of states and cities have already moved to discourage hate crimes and to include sexual orientation along with provisions that protect people from discrimination based on race, religion, gender, and disability. In 2003 the Supreme Court struck down a Texas law criminalizing consensual sexual relations between people of the same gender. While proponents of such legal maneuvers feel that criminal conduct based on prejudice not only terrorizes victims and strips them of civil rights but also debilitates entire communities, critics note that law enforcement officials may remain indifferent to violence based on sexual orientation no matter what the law is. Critics also have other objections. Some feel that laws already prohibit violence and excessive harassment, that gay rights

The cast of "Queer as Folk."

legislation is really "special rights" legislation as opposed to "civil rights" legislation. Some regard sexual preferences as social behaviors, not inherent and immutable characteristics like gender or race that require protection (and some even believe that such behaviors can be modified through therapy). Some feel that legal protections somehow might grow into affirmative action for gays, lesbians, and bisexuals. And some even argue (based on passages in the Bible) that certain sexual activities not only do not deserve protection but are in fact immoral enough to deserve prosecution. There are even those who claim that gays, lesbians, and bisexuals prey on the young and constitute a threat to the stability of communities and families (especially in the light of the AIDS epidemic), a threat that hardly deserves protection and sanction. We therefore present here an argument (in two parts) by Jay Budziszewski resisting gay, lesbian, and bisexual rights that is based on many of these assumptions, as well as Peter J. Gomes's presentation countering them.

At most, so-called gay rights legislation might extend the rights of gays, lesbians, and bisexuals to permit a number of practices: the right to serve in the military, the right to marry, the right to be ordained into the clergy, the right to adopt and raise children (not to mention a host of related "marriage rights" relating to property and child rearing), the right to sexual freedom, and protections against discrimination based on AIDS.

The question of same-sex marriage is the most prominent of those issues right now, and so we devote an Issue in Focus segment to it here. The current controversy over gay marriage derives from years of efforts by gay, lesbian, and bisexual activists to achieve family rights on a piecemeal basis—through pressing for domestic partnership laws, for example, or through lawsuits to permit adoption by single persons. In 1993, the Hawaii Supreme Court suddenly ruled in support of the recognition of same-sex marriage. Since marriages in one state are usually recognized in all, the ruling in Hawaii made same-sex marriage into a national issue immediately. A federal law soon was passed—the Defense of Marriage Act—that said that states are not required to recognize Hawaiian marriages, but the issue has remained significant in many states because each must now decide whether to permit or at least recognize same-sex marriage. Subsequent court decisions, voter referendums, and new laws have only created additional controversies. Supporters of same-sex marriage, such as Andrew Sullivan and Anna Quindlen, point to practical consequences: the recognition of a personal, lasting, loving monogamous commitment (and the consequent freedom from prosecution for sexual behavior); the enjoyment of pension, insurance, and inheritance benefits; protection from child custody battles; and greater tolerance

SOME GAY RIGHTS WEB SITES

www.ngltf.org	The National Gay and Lesbian Task Force
www.glaad.org	Gay and Lesbian Alliance Against Defamation
www.actu.org/issues/gay/hmgl.html	American Civil Liberties Union
www.advocate.com	The *Advocate* magazine
www.lambdalegal.org	Lamba Legal Defense and Education Fund
www.theweddingparty.org	Seeks to secure equal marriage rights for same-sex couples
www.hrc.org	Human Rights Campaign
www.noah.cuny.edu/providers/gmhc.html	Gay Men's Health Crisis organization
www.glsen.org	Gay, Lesbian, Straight Education Network
www.buddybuddy.com	Partners Taskforce for Gay and Lesbian Couples
www.actwin.com/cahp	Citizens Against Homophobia
www.planetout.com	Collects news and commentary

for gay and lesbian citizens. In some ways, the movement to permit same-sex marriage is a conservative move in keeping with conservative times: one that would restrict gay lifestyles to monogamous relationships in the image of heterosexual marriage, and one that is consequently supported by many clergymen, including Peter J. Gomes in the selection we reprint. Thus, same-sex marriage statutes are often resisted by some gays and lesbians, who regard marriage as a straitjacket that enforces traditional sexual norms. Nevertheless, many staunch conservatives dismiss the idea of same-sex marriage outright, arguing that marriage as it is now constituted should remain a public sanctioning for the traditional family that has stood the test of time. Hadley Arkes's essay articulates that point of view.

We conclude our sampling of arguments by returning to where we began this introduction—with several pieces that discuss media representations and additional arguments about the prominence of sexual difference in American culture. James Poniewozik and William F. Jasper—with differing approval—comment on gay writers in the popular media; and Alexa Hackbarth wonders, with a sense of humor, what to make of the "metrosexual phenomenon."

CARMEN VAZQUEZ

Appearances

Carmen Vazquez (1949-) was born in Puerto Rico and raised in Harlem, a predominantly African American community in New York City. Active in the gay/lesbian movement for years, she has published many essays. The following piece was included in Warren J. Blumenfeld's 1992 book called Homophobia: How We All Pay the Price.

1 North of Market Street and east of Twin Peaks, where you can see the white fog mushroom above San Francisco's hills, is a place called the Castro. Gay men, lesbians, and bisexuals stroll leisurely up and down the bustling streets. They jaywalk with abandon. Night and day they fill the cafés and bars, and on weekends they line up for a double feature of vintage classics at their ornate and beloved Castro theater.

2 The 24 bus line brings people into and out of the Castro. People from all walks of life ride the electric-powered coaches. They come from the opulence of San Francisco's Marina and the squalor of Bayview projects. The very gay Castro is in the middle of its route. Every day, boys in pairs or gangs from either end of the city board the bus for a ride through the Castro and a bit of fun. Sometimes their fun is fulfilled with passionately obscene derision: "Fucking cocksucking faggots." "Dyke cunts." "Diseased butt fuckers." Sometimes, their fun is brutal.

3 Brian boarded the 24 Divisadero and handed his transfer to the driver one late June night. Epithets were fired at him the moment he turned for a seat. He slid his slight frame into an empty seat next to an old woman with silver blue hair who clutched her handbag and stared straight ahead. Brian stuffed his hands into the pockets of his worn brown bomber jacket and stared with her. He heard the flip of a skateboard in the back. The taunting shouts grew louder. "Faggot!" From the corner of his eye, he saw a beer bottle hurtling past the window and crash on the street. A man in his forties, wearing a Giants baseball cap and warmup jacket, yelled at the driver to stop the bus and get the hoodlums off. The bus driver ignored him and pulled out.

4 Brian dug his hands deeper into his pockets and clenched his jaw. It was just five stops to the top of the hill. When he got up to move toward the exit, the skateboard slammed into his gut and one kick followed another until every boy had got his kick in. Despite the plea of the passengers, the driver never called the police.

5 Brian spent a week in a hospital bed, afraid that he would never walk again. A lawsuit filed by Brian against the city states, "As claimant lay crumpled and bleeding on the floor of the bus, the bus driver tried

to force claimant off the bus so that the driver could get off work and go home. Claimant was severely beaten by a gang of young men on the #24 Divisadero Bus who perceived that he was gay."

6   On the south side of Market Street, night brings a chill wind and rough trade. On a brisk November night, men with sculptured torsos and thighs wrapped in leather walked with precision. The clamor of steel on the heels of their boots echoed in the darkness. Young men and women walked by the men in leather, who smiled in silence. They admired the studded bracelets on Mickey's wrists, the shine of his flowing hair, and the rise of his laughter. They were, each of them, eager to be among the safety of like company where they could dance with abandon to the pulse of hard rock, the hypnotism of disco, or the measured steps of country soul. They looked forward to a few drinks, flirting with strangers, finding Mr. or Ms. Right or, maybe someone to spend the night with.

7   At the end of the street, a lone black street lamp shone through the mist. The men in leather walked under the light and disappeared into the next street. As they reached the corner, Mickey and his friends could heal the raucous sounds of the Garden spill onto the street. They shimmied and rocked down the block and through the doors.

8   The Garden was packed with men and women in sweat-stained shirts. Blue smoke stung the eyes. The sour and sweet smell of beer hung in the air. Strobe lights pulsed over the dancers. Mickey pulled off his wash-faded black denim jacket and wrapped it around his waist. An iridescent blue tank top hung easy on his shoulders. Impatient with the wait for a drink, Mickey steered his girlfriend onto the crowded dance floor.

9   Reeling to the music and immersed in the pleasure of his rhythms Mickey never saw the ice pick plunge into his neck. It was just a bump with a drunk yelling, "Lame-assed faggot." "Faggot. Faggot. Faggot. Punk faggot." Mickey thought it was a punch to the neck. He ran after the roaring drunk man for seven steps, then lurched and fell on the dance floor, blood gushing everywhere. His girlfriend screamed. The dance floor spun black.

10   Mickey was rushed to San Francisco General Hospital, where thirty-six stitches were used by trauma staff to close the wound on his neck. Doctors said the pick used in the attack against him was millimeters away from his spinal cord. His assailant, charged with attempted murder, pleaded innocent.

11   Mickey and Brian were unfortunate stand-ins for any gay man. Mickey was thin and wiry, a great dancer clad in black denim, earrings dangling from his ear. Brian was slight of build, wore a leather jacket, and boarded a bus in the Castro. Dress like a homo, dance like a homo,

must be a homo. The homophobic fury directed at lesbians, gay men, and bisexuals in America most often finds its target. Ironclad evidence of sexual orientation, however, is not necessary for someone to qualify as a potential victim of deadly fury. Appearances will do.

12 The incidents described above are based on actual events reported to the San Francisco Police and Community United Against Violence (CUAV), an agency serving victims of antilesbian and antigay violence where I worked for four years. The names of the victims have been changed. Both men assaulted were straight.

13 Incidents of antilesbian and antigay violence are not uncommon or limited to San Francisco. A *San Francisco Examiner* survey estimates that over one million hate-motivated physical assaults take place each year against lesbians, gays, and bisexuals. The National Gay and Lesbian Task Force conducted a survey in 1984 that found that 94 percent of all lesbians and gay men surveyed reported being physically assaulted, threatened, or harassed in an antigay incident at one time or another. The great majority of these incidents go unreported.

14 To my knowledge, no agency other than CUAV keeps track of incidents of antigay violence involving heterosexuals as victims. An average of 3 percent of the over three hundred victims seen by CUAV each year identify as heterosexuals. This may or may not be an accurate gauge of the actual prevalence of antigay violence directed at heterosexuals. Most law enforcement agencies, including those in San Francisco, have no way of documenting this form of assault other than under a generic "harassment" code. The actual incidence of violence directed at heterosexuals that is motivated by homophobia is probably much higher than CUAV's six to nine victims a year. Despite the official paucity of data, however, it is a fact that incidents of antigay and antilesbian violence in which straight men and women are victimized do occur. Shelters for battered women are filled with stories of lesbian baiting of staff and of women whose husbands and boyfriends repeatedly called them "dykes" or "whores" as they beat them. I have personally experienced verbal abuse while in the company of a straight friend, who was assumed to be my lover.

15 Why does it happen? I have no definitive answers to that question. Understanding homophobic violence is no less complex than understanding racial violence. The institutional and ideological reinforcements of homophobia are myriad and deeply woven into our culture. I offer one perspective that I hope will contribute to a better understanding of how homophobia works and why it threatens all that we value as humane.

16 At the simplest level, looking or behaving like the stereotypical gay man or lesbian is reason enough to provoke a homophobic assault. Be-

neath the veneer of the effeminate gay male or the butch dyke, however, is a more basic trigger for homophobic violence. I call it *gender betrayal.*

17   The clearest expression I have heard of this sense of gender betrayal comes from Doug Barr, who was acquitted of murder in an incident of gay bashing in San Francisco that resulted in the death of John O'Connell, a gay man. Barr is currently serving a prison sentence for related assaults on the same night that O'Connell was killed. He was interviewed for a special report on homophobia produced by ABC's *20/20* (10 April 1986). When asked what he and his friends thought of gay men, he said, "We hate homosexuals. They degrade our manhood. We was brought up in a high school where guys are football players, mean and macho. Homosexuals are sissies who wear dresses. I'd rather be seen as a football player."

18   Doug Barr's perspective is one shared by many young men. I have made about three hundred presentations to high school students in San Francisco, to boards of directors and staff of nonprofit organizations, and at conferences and workshops on the topic of homophobia or "being lesbian or gay." Over and over again, I have asked, "Why do gay men and lesbians bother you?" The most popular response to the question is, "Because they act like girls," or, "Because they think they're men." I have even been told, quite explicitly. "I don't care what they do in bed, but they shouldn't act like that."

19   They shouldn't act like that. Women who are not identified by their relationship to a man, who value their female friendships, who like and are knowledgeable about sports, or work as blue-collar laborers and wear what they wish are very likely to be "lesbian baited" at some point in their lives Men who are not pursuing sexual conquests of women at every available opportunity, who disdain sports, who choose to stay at home and be a househusband, who are employed as hairdressers, designers, or housecleaners, or who dress in any way remotely resembling traditional female attire (an earring will do) are very likely to experience the taunts and sometimes the brutality of "fag bashing."

20   The straitjacket of gender roles suffocates many lesbians, gay men, and bisexuals, forcing them into closets without an exit and threatening our very existence when we tear the closet open. It also, however, threatens all heterosexuals unwilling to be bound by their assigned gender identity. Why, then, does it persist?

21   Suzanne Pharr's examination of homophobia as a phenomenon based in sexism and misogyny offers a succinct and logical explanation for the virulence of homophobia in Western civilization:

> It is not by chance that when children approach puberty and increased sexual awareness they begin to taunt each other by calling these names: "queer," "faggot," "pervert." It is at puberty that the full force of society's pressure to conform to heterosexuality and

prepare for marriage is brought to bear. Children know what we have taught them, and we have given clear messages that those who deviate from standard expectations are to be made to get back in line. . . .

To be named as lesbian threatens all women, not just lesbians, with great loss. And any woman who steps out of role risks being called a lesbian. To understand how this is a threat to all women, one must understand that any woman can be called a lesbian and there is no real way she can defend herself: there is no real way to credential one's sexuality. (*The Children's Hour,* a Lillian Hellman play, makes this point when a student asserts two teachers are lesbians and they have no way to disprove it.) She may be married or divorced, have children, dress in the most feminine manner, have sex with men, be celibate—but there are lesbians who do all these things. *Lesbians look like all women and all women look like lesbians.*[1]

I would add that gay men look like all men and all men look like gay men. There is no guaranteed method for identifying sexual orientation. Those small or outrageous deviations we sometimes take from the idealized mystique of "real men" and "real women" place all of us—lesbians, gay men, bisexuals, and heterosexuals alike—at risk of violence, derision, isolation, and hatred.

22   It is a frightening reality. Dorothy Ehrlich, executive director of the Northern California American Civil Liberties Union (ACLU), was the victim of a verbal assault in the Castro several years ago. Dorothy lives with her husband, Gary, and her two children, Jill and Paul, in one of those worn and comfortable Victorian homes that grace so many San Francisco neighborhoods. Their home is several blocks from the Castro, but Dorothy recalls the many times she and Gary could hear, from the safety of their bedroom, shouts of "faggot" and men running in the streets.

23   When Jill was an infant, Gary and Dorothy had occasion to experience for themselves how frightening even the threat of homophobic violence can be. One foggy, chilly night they decided to go for a walk in the Castro. Dorothy is a small woman whom some might call petite; she wore her hair short at the time and delights in the comfort of jeans and oversized wool jackets. Gary is very tall and lean, a bespectacled and bearded cross between a professor and a basketball player who wears jean jackets and tweed jackets with the exact same slouch. On this night they were crossing Castro Street, huddled close together with Jill in Dorothy's arms. As they reached the corner, their backs to the street, they heard a truck rev its engine and roar up Castro, the dreaded "faggot" spewing from young men they could not see in the fog. They

[1]Pharr, Suzanne. *Homophobia: A Weapon of Sexism* (Inverness, CA: Chardon, 1988), 17–19.

looked around them for the intended victims, but there was no one else on the corner with them. They were the target that night: Dorothy and Gary and Jill. They were walking on "gay turf," and it was reason enough to make them a target. "It was so frightening." Dorothy said. "So frightening and unreal."

24   But it is real. The *20/20* report on homophobia ends with the story of Tom and Jan Matarrase, who are married, have a child, and lived in Brooklyn, New York, at the time of their encounter with homophobic violence. On camera, Tom and Jan are walking down a street in Brooklyn lined with brown townhouses and black wrought-iron gates. It is snowing, and, with hands entwined, they walk slowly down the street where they were assaulted. Tom is wearing a khaki trenchcoat, slacks, and loafers. Snowflakes melt into the tight dark curls on his head. Jan is almost his height, her short bobbed hair moving softly as she walks. She is wearing a black leather jacket, a red scarf, and burnt orange cords. The broadness of her hips and softness of her face belie the tomboy flavor of her carriage and clothes, and it is hard to believe that she was mistaken for a gay man. But she was.

25   They were walking home, holding hands and engrossed with each other. On the other side of the street, Jan saw a group of boys moving toward them. As the gang approached, Jan heard a distinct taunt meant for her and Tom: "Aw, look at the cute gay couple." Tom and Jan quickened their step but it was too late. Before they could say anything, Tom was being punched in the face and slammed against a car. Jan ran toward Tom and the car, screaming desperately that Tom was her husband. Fists pummeled her face as well. Outnumbered and in fear for their lives, Tom yelled at Jan to please open her jacket and show their assailants that she was a woman. The beating subsided only when Jan was able to show her breasts.

26   For the *20/20* interview, Jan and Tom sat in the warmth of their living room, their infant son in Jan's lap. The interviewer asked them how they felt when people said they looked like a gay couple. "We used to laugh," they said. "But now we realize how heavy the implications are. Now we know what the gay community goes through. We had no idea how widespread it was. It's on every level."

27   Sadly, it *is* on every level. Enforced heterosexism and the pressure to conform to aggressive masculine and passive feminine roles place fag bashers and lesbian baiters in the same psychic prison with their victims, gay or straight. Until all children are free to realize their full potential, until all women and men are free from the stigma, threats, alienation, or violence that come from stepping outside their roles, we are all at risk.

28   The economic and ideological underpinnings of enforced heterosexism and sexism or any other form of systematic oppression are

formidable foes and far too complex for the scope of this essay. It is important to remember, however, that bigots are natural allies and that poverty or the fear of it has the power to seduce us all into conformity. In Castro graffiti, *faggot* appears right next to *nigger* and *kike.* Race betrayal or any threat to the sanctimony of light-skinned privilege engenders no less a rage than gender betrayal, most especially when we have a great stake in the elusive privilege of proper gender roles or the right skin color. *Queer lover* and *fag hag* are cut from the same mold that gave us *nigger lover,* a mold forged by fears of change and a loss of privilege.

29   Unfortunately, our sacrifices to conformity rarely guarantee the privilege or protection we were promised. Lesbians, gay men, and bisexuals who have tried to pass know that. Heterosexuals who have been perceived to be gay know that. Those of us with a vision of tomorrow that goes beyond tolerance to a genuine celebration of humanity's diversity have innumerable fronts to fight on. Homophobia is one of them.

30   But how will this front be won? With a lot of help, and not easily. Challenges to homophobia and the rigidity of gender roles must go beyond the visible lesbian and gay movement. Lesbians, gay men, and bisexuals alone cannot defuse the power of stigmatization and the license it gives to frighten, wound, or kill. Literally millions of us are needed on this front, straight and gay alike. We invite any heterosexual unwilling to live with the damage that "real men" or "real women" messages wreck on them, on their children, and on lesbians, gay men, and bisexuals to join us. We ask that you not let queer jokes go unchallenged at work, at home, in the media, or anywhere. We ask that you foster in your children a genuine respect for themselves and their right to be who and what they wish to be, regardless of their gender. We ask that you embrace your daughter's desire to swing a bat or be a carpenter, that you nurture your son's efforts to express affection and sentiment. We ask that you teach your children how painful and destructive words like *faggot* or *bulldyke* are. We ask that you invite your lesbian, gay, and bisexual friends and relatives into the routine of your lives without demanding silence or discretion from them. We invite you to study our history, read the literature written by our people, patronize our businesses, come into our homes and neighborhoods. We ask that you give us your vote when we need it to protect our privacy or to elect open lesbians, gay men, and bisexuals to office. We ask that you stand with us in public demonstrations to demand our right to live as free people, without fear. We ask that you respect our dignity by acting to end the poison of homophobia.

31   Until individuals are free to choose their roles and be bound only by the limits of their own imagination, *faggot, dyke,* and *pervert* will continue to be playground words and adult weapons that hurt and limit far many more people than their intended victims. Whether we like it

or not, the romance of virile men and dainty women, of Mother, Father, Dick, Jane, Sally, and Spot is doomed to extinction and dangerous in a world that can no longer meet the expectations conjured by history. There is much to be won and so little to lose in the realization of a world where the dignity of each person is worthy of celebration and protection. The struggle to end homophobia can and must be won, for all our sakes. Personhood is imminent. ◼

JAY BUDZISZEWSKI

Homophobia: An Unfinished Story

Jay Budziszewski (pronounced "Boojee-shefski"), who teaches government and philosophy at the University of Texas, Austin, is the author of several books, including True Tolerance. *Having experienced a conversion to Christianity, he now promotes "natural law" principles of ethics and government. In 1998 he offered two arguments—the ones that follow—to* Boundless, *in the format of the same "office hours" conversation that he frequently uses in his regular columns. (Boundless is a webzine designed for college students that offers a conservative Christian perspective on current issues.) The two essays, "Homophobia: An Unfinished Story" and "The Seeker," were written as companion pieces, so the second comments on the first. Both items indirectly rebut other essays in this segment, including the ones by Andrew Sullivan, Anna Quinden, and Peter J. Gomes.*

1   "Are you Professor Theophilus?"

2   I turned. "That's me. Come in."

3   "My name's Lawrence. I'm gay. I came to complain about your talk about constitutional liberties yesterday. It was bigoted and homophobic. I'm filing a formal protest to the people who run the Student Union speakers series."

4   *At least he's direct. I thought.* I waved him to a seat.

5   "Help me out, Mr. Lawrence. How could—"

6   "Just Lawrence."

7   "Thank you. Now how could my talk have been 'bigoted and homophobic' when it didn't mention homosexuality?"

8   "I didn't actually hear the talk itself. I came in during Q&A."

9   "I see. And what did I say during Q&A?"

10   "You said gays have sex with animals."

11   I'm used to this sort of thing, so I merely observed, "I'm afraid you weren't listening carefully."

12   "I remember distinctly," he declared. "A girl asked your opinion of laws against discrimination on the basis of sexual orientation, and you said gays have sex with animals."

13   "No, what I said was 'sexual orientation' can mean many things. Some people are 'sexually oriented' toward the opposite sex; others toward the same sex; others toward children; others toward animals; others toward cadavers. I said that I wondered where this trend will end."

14   "Then you admit that gays don't have sex with animals?"

15   "You brought that up," I reminded him. "I have no information on the point, I'm only suggesting that not all 'orientations' are morally equivalent."

16   He said nothing, but showed no inclination to leave. "Do *you* think all 'orientations' are morally equivalent?" I queried.

17   "I won't even dignify that question with an answer," he said. "But I know what you think of my orientation. I'm sick of you phony Christians with your filthy hypocrisy about the love of God."

18   "So you've heard that I'm a Christian."

19   "Who hasn't? The holy, the sanctimonious, the Most Excellent Professor Theophilus of Post-Everything State University—what else would he be? The whole school reeks of you, of you and the other so-called Christian so-called professors. That's why I walked in on your Q&A. I wanted to see you spit venom."

20   "My goodness. Have I said anything venomous?"

21   "It's what you're thinking that's venomous."

22   "I see." I smiled. "Why don't you stop being bashful, and tell me what's bothering you?"

23   "You must think you're funny."

24   "I'm serious. Tell your complaints one by one, and I'll answer them."

25   "You couldn't answer them. I have too many."

26   "Try me. I'll give short answers."

27   He cocked his head and peered at me. "You mean it, don't you?"

28   "I wouldn't say it if I didn't."

29   "One at a time?"

30   "One at a time."

31   "All right, here's the first. Christians are hypocrites. You're always running down gays, but what about the other things your Bible condemns, like divorce and remarriage? It's other people's sins that bother you, not your own."

32   I laughed. "If you'd spent any time around me, you'd know that I'm just as hard on the sins of heterosexuals as on those of homosexuals.

33   "Easy divorce is a prime example of how one bad thing leads to another—in our case the loss of the ability to make any distinctions about sexual acts at all."

34   Ignoring the reply, he went on to his next complaint. "You're intolerant. You reject people like me just because we're different than you."

35   "Me reject you?" I said. "Aren't you the one who rejects what is different than yourself? Don't you reject the challenge of the other sex?"

36   "I don't need the other sex. I have a committed relationship with my partner."

37   "Research shows that homosexuals with partners don't stop cruising, they just cruise less. When they don't think straights are listening, gay writers say the same."

38   "So what if it's true? There's nothing wrong with gay love anyway."

39   I spoke quietly. "Tell me what's loving about sex acts that cause bleeding, choking, disease and pain," I suggested. "You might start by explaining the meaning of the medical term 'Gay Bowel Syndrome,' or how people get herpes lesions on their tonsils."

40   "You're—how can you even say that?" he demanded. "How dare you tell me who to love?"

41   "I don't think I am telling you who to love."

42   "Oh, no? Then what are you telling me?"

43   "That there is nothing loving about mutual self-destruction."

44   "You must think my relationship with my partner is just dirt!"

45   "No, I respect friendship wherever I find it—your friendship with your partner included. It's just that sex doesn't make every kind of friendship better."

46   "Why not? Are you anti-sex or something?"

47   "Not at all," I said, "but would you say that sex improves the friendship of a father with his daughter?"

48   Seeing from his face that he didn't, I continued. "You get my point. Nor does sex improve the friendship of two men."

49   "That's where you're wrong. Gay sex is just as natural for some people as straight sex is for other people."

50   "What's 'natural'," I said, "is what unlocks our inbuilt potential instead of thwarting it. One of the purposes of marital sex is to get you outside your Self and its concerns, to achieve intimacy with someone who is Really Other."

51   *Was he listening to any of this*? "I'm sorry, Lawrence—I really am—but having sex with another man can't do that. It's too much like loving your reflection. That's what I meant before about refusing the challenge of the other sex."

52   I was about to go on, but abruptly he changed the subject: "It's attitudes like yours that killed Matthew Shepard."

53   "Surely you don't imagine that the thugs who killed Matthew Shepard were Christians, do you?" I smiled at the absurdity of the thought, but seeing that he misunderstood my smile I made my face serious and tried again.

54   "Lawrence, I deplore the violence that killed Matthew Shepard, and I'm glad those men were caught. But shouldn't we also grieve the urge which caused Matthew Shepard to be sexually attracted to violent strangers?"

55   He said only. "You hate me."

56   I paused to study him. Did he really believe that, or was it a smokescreen?

57   "I don't hate you," I said. "I love you." I paused. "I'd like to be with you forever, in heaven."

58   Lawrence's face displayed shock, as though he had been hit in the stomach. Then he looked confused. The expression of confusion was instantaneously replaced by an expression of anger.

59   For one split-second, it had looked as if the shutters were open. "*God in heaven,*" I thought, "*I need help.*" How could they be pried back up?

60   "My love isn't really the issue for you, is it?" I asked.

61   "What do you mean?"

62   "It's God's. God's love is the issue for you." For a few seconds there was no reaction.

63   Then it came. "You're bleeping right God's love is the issue for me," he said. "*Your* God's love. The lying God who says He loves man, but who hates me for loving men."

64   "Do you think God hates you?"

65   "Doesn't He?"

66   "What makes you say that?"

67   "Doesn't your Bible say that? It calls people like me an abomination."

68   "It calls what you *do* abomination. There's a difference."

69   "There's no difference. I do what I am."

70   I considered his point. "Could it be," I said, "that you want God to love you *less?*"

71   "Less!" he spat.

72   "Yes. Don't you know what love is?"

73   "Acceptance."

74   "Acceptance of what kills you? Consider another view. Love is a commitment of the will to the true good of the other person."

75   "What?"

76   "I said love is a commitment of the will to the true good of the other person."

77   "I don't get what you're saying."

78   "Sure you do. The lover wants what's good for the beloved."

79   He hesitated. "I suppose."

80   "Good. Now think. If that's what love is, then a *perfect* Lover would want the *perfect* good of the Beloved. Do you see what that

means? He would loathe and detest whatever destroyed the beloved's good—no matter how much the beloved desired it."

81   I couldn't read the look on his face, so I plowed on. "That's what sin does—it destroys us. Yours destroys you, mine destroys me. And so the Lover doesn't 'accept' it; He hates it with an inexorable hatred. To cut the cancer out of us, He will do whatever it takes—like a surgeon. No, more than like a surgeon. If you let Him, He will even take the cancer upon Himself and die in your place."

82   Still inscrutable, he kept his eyes in front of him, just avoiding my own.

83   I asked "What happens, then, if you refuse to let go of what destroys you? What happens if you say this to the divine and perfect Lover who wants your complete and perfect good—if you say, 'I bind myself to my destruction! Accept me, and my destruction with me! I refuse to enter heaven except in the company of Death!'"

84   Neither of us spoke.

85   Lawrence rose from his chair and walked out the door.

The Seeker

1   "**I**t wasn't easy finding your office," said my visitor as he took a seat. "This building is like a rabbit warren."

2   "Yes," I said, "for the first couple of years I worked here, I had to leave a trail of crumbs each day to find my way back out. We haven't met, have we?"

3   "No, I'm over in Antediluvian Studies—I'm a grad student. My name's Adam, Adam Apollolas."

4   "M.E. Theophilus." We shook hands.

5   "You are the same Theophilus who wrote the 'Homophobia' dialogue for Nounless Webzine, aren't you? I was hoping to talk with you about it."

6   "Busted," I smiled. "What would you like to know about it?"

7   "Was it based on a real conversation?"

8   "Yes and no; it was a composite. A homosexual student really did visit to accuse me of saying that 'gays have sex with animals,' and the rest is from real life too, but not necessarily from the same conversation."

9   "But it can't possibly be true that all of the homosexuals who speak with you are as angry and closed-minded as he was."

10   "No, of course not."

11   "Then why did you portray him that way in the dialogue?"

12   "Would you have me pretend that nobody in the homosexual life is angry and closed-minded? A good many are like that—you should see

my letters—and I try to show my readers the dynamics of more than one kind of conversation. You see, when people have honest questions you try to answer them, but when they only churn out smokescreens, then you blow the smoke away."

13 "So you'd be open to different kinds of conversation."

14 "Of course," I said. I smiled. "Are we, perhaps, having one right now?"

15 His eyebrows lifted. "Am I that obvious?"

16 "It was just a shot in the dark. So what did you really want to talk about?"

17 "I'm not very ideological, but I guess you could call me a Seeker. See, I've been in the gay life for five years, but lately I've been having second thoughts. I'm not asking you to convert me, understand? I thought I'd just hear what you have to say, then go away and think about it."

18 "What have you been having second thoughts about?"

19 He hesitated. "Are you going to use this conversation in one of your dialogues?"

20 "If I did, I'd make sure you couldn't be identified. You can speak freely."

21 "Well—" he hesitated. "One thing is intimacy. I've never had problems finding sex, but it's more or less anonymous. That didn't bother me at first, but now it's getting me down."

22 "Is the sex always anonymous?"

23 "No, the first time I had gay sex was in a steady relationship. I've been in two or three others, too—for a month, two months, a year. But they were never what you'd call faithful, know what I mean? It's as though there had to be other sexual outlets for the relationship to work at all. I'm starting to want—I don't know. Something else."

24 "I follow you."

25 He paused. "Another thing. I want to be a Dad. That doesn't fit the stereotype, does it? Are you surprised to hear me say it?"

26 "Not at all."

27 "In that case you're the only one. My friends don't get it. One said, 'Why don't you just get a turkey baster and make an arrangement with a lesbian?' But that's not what I want." Another pause. "I used to say to myself, 'Get used to it. You can't have everything you want.' But that doesn't work for me any more."

28 After a second he spoke again. "There's one more thing."

29 "What's that?"

30 "God."

31 "God? How so?"

32 "Oh, I go to church sometimes. Now that must surprise you."

33 "No. What kind of church?"

34   "Different kinds. I didn't go to any church at first. My family never went to church. Most of my gay friends don't have any use for God. Then I started going to a gay church, and that was okay for awhile. But I think I might want the real stuff, do you know what I mean? Or else nothing."

35   "I think so. You don't have any doubts about what the real stuff is?"

36   "No. I'm not saying I believe in Jesus, but—" He thought for a moment. "The gay church said you can be a Christian and still live a gay life. I don't think I ever really believed that. I read a book that the minister in the gay church recommended—"

37   "Yes?"

38   "The title was something like Sex and Dirt. I'm leaving something out. Hold on, it'll come to me."

39   "Never mind, I know the book."

40   "Oh, good. Then you probably remember how the author argues that when the Bible lays down rules about sex, they're just purity codes—not moral laws—so you don't have to keep them."

41   "Sure."

42   "He had me going for a while—right up to where he said 'that's why even having sex with animals is okay,' or words to that effect. Just what the guy in your dialogue accused you of saying gay people think. I could see that the author's conclusion followed from his premises—but after that, I didn't have any use for his premises, if you see what I mean."

43   "I see exactly what you mean. So where does all this leave you?"

44   "Like I said, I want to hear you out, and then I'll go away and think about it."

45   "That's fine, Adam, but just what is it that you want to hear me out about?"

46   "I think what I'm missing is the Big Picture about sex. If there is a Big Picture about sex."

47   "There is indeed a Big Picture about sex."

48   "Draw it, then. Paint it. Lecture me, even. That is," he added, "if you don't mind."

49   I had to laugh. "You asked me before if I was going to use this conversation in one of my dialogues. If I do, nobody will believe it. They'll call it contrived."

50   "Why?"

51   "Because you've set the stage too well. Your 'second thoughts' anticipate everything I'd like to say. And now you ask for a lecture!"

52   "After seven years of college, I'm used to lectures. You do your professor thing, and I'll listen. If I want to argue—believe me, I know how—I'll come back another day."

53   I collected my thoughts. "All right, Adam. The main point of Christian sexual morality is that human nature is designed. We need to live a certain way because we're designed to live that way."

54   He said, "I can see design in an organ like the heart. Human nature—that's a little too big for me."

55   "Then let's start with the heart. Do you see how every part works together toward its purpose, its function?"

56   "Sure. You've got nerves and valves and pumping chambers, all for moving blood."

57   "Right. If you think about the sexual powers instead of the heart, it's just the same. The key to understanding a design is to recognize its purposes. For the heart, the purpose is pumping blood; for the sexual powers—you tell me."

58   "Pleasure?"

59   "Think about it. Would you say pleasure is the purpose of eating?"

60   "No, I'd say nourishment is the purpose of eating, and pleasure is just the result."

61   "If you thought pleasure were the purpose of eating, what would you do if I offered you pleasant-tasting poison?"

62   "Eat it."

63   "And what would happen?"

64   "I'd get sick."

65   "But if you understood that nourishment were the purpose of eating and pleasure merely the result, then what would you do if I offered you pleasant-tasting poison?"

66   "Refuse it and ask for food instead."

67   "It's the same with the sexual powers. Pleasure is a result of their use, but not the purpose of their use. The purposes can tell you which kinds of sexual activity are good and which aren't; by itself, pleasure can't."

68   "So what are the purposes of the sexual powers?"

69   "You've told me already; you just didn't realize you were doing so."

70   "I have? When?"

71   "When you were telling me your second thoughts about the homosexual life. There were three of them. What was the first one about?"

72   "Intimacy. Bonding."

73   "And the second?"

74   "Having children."

75   "Then you won't be surprised to hear that one inbuilt purpose of the sexual powers is to bond a man with a woman, and another is to have and raise children."

76   "If bonding is good, why not use the sexual powers to bond a man with a man?"

77   "Has that worked in your case, Adam?"

78   "Well, no. That's what I was complaining about."

79   "You see, that's no accident. Bonding man with man is contrary to the design."

80   "You say that, but how do you know?"

81   "There are two reasons. First, man and woman are complementary. They're not just different, they match. There is something in male emotional design to which only the female can give completion, and something in female emotional design to which only the male can give completion. When same mates with same, that can't happen. Instead of balancing each other, they unbalance each other."

82   "What's the other reason?"

83   "The other reason is that the linkage of same with same is sterile. You've complained about that, too."

84   "But sometimes a man can't produce children with a woman, either."

85   "The mating of same with same isn't accidentally sterile, Adam, as the union of a particular man with a particular woman might be; it's inherently sterile. A husband and wife who are unable to have a baby haven't set themselves against their own inbuilt purposes. A man and man who have sex together have."

86   He grinned. "There's always the turkey baster."

87   "But when your friend made that suggestion, you refused, didn't you? What was your reason?"

88   "I'm not sure. I just think a kid needs a Mom and a Dad."

89   "That's exactly right. Male and female complement and complete each other not just in having children but in rearing them. Women are better designed for nurture, men are better designed for protection. Besides, two Dads can't model male-female relationships. Neither can two Moms. Neither can one."

90   Adam was silent as he digested this. "You know," he said finally, "this isn't at all what I expected you to talk about."

91   "What did you expect me to talk about?"

92   "Disease." He paused. "Now that I think about it, you didn't say much about disease in that dialogue I read either."

93   "I should think you already know the deadliness of your way of life."

94   "I suppose so. But it does seem unfair. Why should gay sex be less healthy than any other kind?"

95   "Don't we come right back to the design? Start with the fact that not all orifices are created equal."

96   "Hmmm."

97   "Hmmm?"

98   "I think I'll go do what I said I'd do: Go away and think about it all. In the meantime, Professor, I think you have a problem."

99   "Do I?"

100   "That is, if you do intend to use this chat of ours in one of your dialogues."

101   "And what might this problem be?"

102   "We've talked too long. Your dialogues are all 1500 words. This one is way over."

103   I smiled. "I'll talk to my editor about it." ∎

PETER J. GOMES

Homophobic? Read Your Bible

Peter J. Gomes (1942–) is an American Baptist minister. Widely regarded as one of the most distinguished preachers in the nation, he has served since 1970 in the Memorial Church at Harvard University. Since 1974 he has been Plummer Professor of Christian Morals at Harvard Divinity School as well. He wrote the following essay for the New York Times *in 1992.*

1   Opposition to gays' civil rights has become one of the most visible symbols of American civic conflict this year, and religion has become the weapon of choice. The army of the discontented, eager for clear villains and simple solutions and ready for a crusade in which political self-interest and social anxiety can be cloaked in morality, has found hatred of homosexuality to be the last respectable prejudice of the century.

2   Ballot initiatives in Oregon and Maine would deny homosexuals the protection of civil rights laws. The Pentagon has steadfastly refused to allow gays into the armed forces. Vice President Dan Quayle is crusading for "traditional family values." And Pat Buchanan, who is scheduled to speak at the Republican National Convention this evening, regards homosexuality as a litmus test of moral purity.

3   Nothing has illuminated this crusade more effectively than a work of fiction. *The Drowning of Stephan Jones,* by Bette Greene. Preparing for her novel, Ms. Greene interviewed more than 400 young men incarcerated for gay-bashing, and scrutinized their case studies. In an interview published in *The Boston Globe* this spring, she said she found that the gay-bashers generally saw nothing wrong in what they did, and, more often than not, said their religious leaders and traditions sanctioned their behavior. One convicted teen-age gay-basher told her that the pastor of his church had said. "Homosexuals represent the devil, Satan," and that the Rev. Jerry Falwell had echoed that charge.

4   Christians opposed to political and social equality for homosexuals nearly always appeal to the moral injunctions of the Bible, claiming that Scripture is very clear on the matter and citing verses that support their opinion. They accuse others of perverting and distorting texts contrary to their "clear" meaning. They do not, however, necessarily see quite as clear a meaning in biblical passages on economic conduct, the burdens of wealth, and the sin of greed.

5   Nine biblical citations are customarily invoked as relating to homosexuality. Four (Deuteronomy 23:17, I Kings 14:24, I Kings 22:46, and II Kings 23:7) simply forbid prostitution, by men and women.

6   Two others (Leviticus 18:19–23 and Leviticus 20:10–16) are part of what biblical scholars call the Holiness Code. The code explicitly bans homosexual acts. But it also prohibits eating raw meat, planting two different kinds of seed in the same field, and wearing garments with two different kinds of yarn. Tattoos, adultery, and sexual intercourse during a woman's menstrual period are similarly outlawed.

7   There is no mention of homosexuality in the four Gospels of the New Testament. The moral teachings of Jesus are not concerned with the subject.

8   Three references from St. Paul are frequently cited (Romans 1:26–2:1, I Corinthians 6:9–11, and I Timothy 1:10). But St. Paul was concerned with homosexuality only because in Greco-Roman culture it represented a secular sensuality that was contrary to his Jewish-Christian spiritual idealism. He was against lust and sensuality in anyone, including heterosexuals. To say that homosexuality is bad because homosexuals are tempted to do morally doubtful things is to say that heterosexuality is bad because heterosexuals are likewise tempted. For St. Paul, anyone who puts his or her interest ahead of God's is condemned, a verdict that falls equally upon everyone.

9   And lest we forget Sodom and Gomorrah, recall that the story is not about sexual perversion and homosexual practice. It is about inhospitality, according to Luke 10:10–13, and failure to care for the poor, according to Ezekiel 16:49–50: "Behold, this was the iniquity of thy sister Sodom, pride, fullness of bread, and abundance of idleness was in her and in her daughters, neither did she strengthen the hand of the poor and needy." To suggest that Sodom and Gomorrah is about homosexual sex is an analysis of about as much worth as suggesting that the story of Jonah and the whale is a treatise on fishing.

10   Part of the problem is a question of interpretation. Fundamentalists and literalists, the storm troopers of the religious right, are terrified that Scripture, "wrongly interpreted," may separate them from their values. That fear stems from their own recognition that their "values" are not derived from Scripture, as they publicly claim.

11   Indeed, it is through the lens of their own prejudices that they "read" Scripture and cloak their own views in its authority. We all

interpret Scripture: Make no mistake. And no one truly is a literalist, despite the pious temptation. The questions are, By what principle of interpretation do we proceed, and by what means do we reconcile "what it meant then" to "what it means now"?

12   These matters are far too important to be left to scholars and seminarians alone. Our ability to judge ourselves and others rests on our ability to interpret Scripture intelligently. The right use of the Bible, an exercise as old as the church itself, means that we confront our prejudices rather than merely confirm them.

13   For Christians, the principle by which Scripture is read is nothing less than an appreciation of the work and will of God as revealed in that of Jesus. To recover a liberating and inclusive Christ is to be freed from the semantic bondage that makes us curators of a dead culture rather than creatures of a new creation.

14   Religious fundamentalism is dangerous because it cannot accept ambiguity and diversity and is therefore inherently intolerant. Such intolerance, in the name of virtue, is ruthless and uses political power to destroy what it cannot convert.

15   It is dangerous, especially in America, because it is antidemocratic and is suspicious of "the other," in whatever form that "other" might appear. To maintain itself, fundamentalism must always define "the other" as deviant.

16   But the chief reason that fundamentalism is dangerous is that, at the hands of the Rev. Pat Robertson, the Rev. Jerry Falwell, and hundreds of lesser-known but equally worrisome clerics, preachers, and pundits, it uses Scripture and the Christian practice to encourage ordinarily good people to act upon their fears rather than their virtues.

17   Fortunately, those who speak for the religious right do not speak for all American Christians, and the Bible is not theirs alone to interpret. The same Bible that the advocates of slavery used to protect their wicked self-interests is the Bible that inspired slaves to revolt and their liberators to action.

18   The same Bible that the predecessors of Mr. Falwell and Mr. Robertson used to keep white churches white is the source of the inspiration of the Rev. Martin Luther King. Jr., and the social reformation of the 1960's.

19   The same Bible that antifeminists use to keep women silent in the churches is the Bible that preaches liberation to captives and says that in Christ there is neither male nor female, slave nor free.

20   And the same Bible that on the basis of an archaic social code of ancient Israel and a tortured reading of Paul is used to condemn all homosexuals and homosexual behavior includes metaphors of redemption, renewal, inclusion, and love—principles that invite homosexuals to accept their freedom and responsibility in Christ and demands that their fellow Christians accept them as well.

21 The political piety of the fundamentalist religious right must not be exercised at the expense of our precious freedoms. And in this summer of our discontent, one of the most precious freedoms for which we must all fight is freedom from this last prejudice. ■

ISSUE IN FOCUS

Same-Sex Marriage

Though the wisdom of allowing same-sex marriages in the United States has been debated for at least two decades now, the conversation surrounding the practice has become especially passionate in the past two years. In February 2004, the newly-elected mayor of San Francisco, Gavin Newsom, ordered the issuance of marriage licenses to same-sex couples. Newsome's order defied California's Proposition 22, accepted by 61 percent of California voters, which in the year 2000 had defined marriage as exclusively between one man and one woman. Gay couples rushed to obtain licenses, seizing what they knew might be a short-lived chance to marry—and short-lived it was: The California Supreme Court ordered a halt to such marriages.

Then, on May 17, 2004, Massachusetts became the first state to legally sanction gay marriage. Gay couples celebrated the moment on the steps of Boston's City Hall, counting down the minutes before their marriages could be sanctioned, while many other citizens decried the decision. Although these weddings were also stopped through court actions, all over the United States people saw images and read and heard words about this important current issue; some of those words and images, because they are burned into public memory, are reproduced here in these pages.

Across the country, actions in California and Massachusetts energized the long-standing debate about gay marriage. Proponents (such as Andrew

Phyllis Lyon, 79 (left), and Del Martin, 83, in San Francisco were the first same-sex couple to be officially married in the State of California. (Photo: Liz Margelsdorf in the *San Francisco Chronicle.*)

Davis Wilson (left) and Robert Compton were married at the Arlington Street Church in Boston. (Photo: Deanne Fitzmaurice in the *San Francisco Chronicle*.)

Sullivan and Anna Quindlen in essays reprinted here) point to practical consequences: the recognition and protection of a personal, lasting, and loving monogamous relationship; protection from prosecution for sexual behavior, the enjoyment of pension, insurance, tax, and inheritance benefits; protection from child custody battles. Other people, however, including President George W. Bush, called for a constitutional amendment defining marriage as strictly heterosexual in nature. They claim that marriage as it has been traditionally constituted protects children, they appeal to the Bible as authority (including to Biblical condemnations of homosexuality), and they feel that traditional marriage—already threatened by a high divorce rate—would somehow be undermined if same-sex marriages were permitted. Hadley Arkes's argument in this section articulates that point of view. That proposed constitutional amendment (the text of which

> "[This is a] huge relief. I can put my partner on my benefits. I don't have to check if a company offers domestic partner benefits. In the eyes of the law, I can stop carrying all those legal documents in my glove compartment, and if I get hit by a car, [my partner] Lane can come and see me in the emergency room."
>
> —STUART WELLS, AFTER THE PASSAGE OF LEGISLATION ALLOWING GAY MARRIAGE. *THE BOSTON GLOBE*, NOVEMBER 19, 2003.

PROPOSED AMENDMENT TO THE U.S. CONSTITUTION

108th CONGRESS, 1st Session

RESOLUTION 56 Proposing an amendment to the Constitution of the United States relating to marriage.

Resolved by the Senate and House of Representatives of the United States of America in Congress assembled (two-thirds of each House concurring therein). That the following article is proposed as an amendment to the Constitution of the United States, which shall be valid to all intents and purposes as part of the Constitution when ratified by the legislatures of three-fourths of the several States within seven years after the date of its submission for ratification:

"Article—

"SECTION 1. Marriage in the United States shall consist only of the union of a man and a woman. Neither this Constitution or the constitution of any State, nor state or federal law, shall be construed to require that marital status or the legal incidents thereof be conferred upon unmarried couples or groups."

is included below) failed to reach the Senate floor for debate, but opponents of gay marriage have fared better in some state legislatures. Massachusetts, for example, banned gay marriages while permitting domestic partnerships. At this point, at least 37 states and the federal government (under the Defense of Marriage Act. passed a decade ago and also reprinted below) have laws defining marriage as between a man and a woman. Missouri passed a constitutional amendment restricting marriage to one man and one woman, and similar legislation is pending in at least a dozen other states.

What follows, then, is just a sampling of the arguments associated with the same-sex marriage controversy. As you read, consider the arguments that you have heard and read in your own community, and consider entering into the debate yourself.

HOUSE OF REPRESENTATIVES

THE DEFENSE OF MARRIAGE ACT

Congress of the United States
House of Representatives
AS INTRODUCED ON MAY 7, 1996

Summary of the Act:

The Defense of Marriage Act (DOMA) does two things. First, it provides that no State shall be required to give effect to a law of any other State with respect to a same-sex "marriage." Second, it defines the words "marriage" and "spouse" for purposes of Federal law.

The first substantive section of the bill is an exercise of Congress' power under the "Effect" clause of Article IV, section I of the Constitution (the Full Faith and Credit Clause) to allow each State (or other political jurisdiction) to decide for itself whether it wants to grant legal status to same-sex "marriage." This provision is necessary in light of the possibility of Hawaii giving sanction to same-sex "marriage" under its state law, as interpreted by its state courts, and other states being placed in the position of having to give "full faith and credit" to Hawaii's interpretation of what constitutes "marriage." Although so-called "conflicts of law" principles do not necessarily compel such a result, approximately 30 states of the union are sufficiently alarmed by such a prospect to have initiated legislative efforts to defend themselves against any compulsion to acknowledge same-sex "marriage."

This is a problem most properly resolved by invoking Congress' authority under the Constitution to declare what "effect" one State's acts, records, and judicial proceedings shall have in another State. Congress has invoked this authority recently on two other occasions: in the Parental Kidnapping Prevention Act of 1980, which required each State to enforce child custody determinations made by the home State if made consistently with the provisions of the Act; and in the Full Faith and Credit for Child Support Order Act of 1994, which required each State to enforce child support orders made by the child's State if made consistently with the provisions of the Act.

The second substantive section of the bill amends the U.S. Code to make explicit what has been understood under federal law for over 200 years: that a marriage is the legal union of a man and a woman as husband and wife, and a spouse is a husband or wife of the opposite sex. The DOMA definition of marriage is derived most immediately from a Washington state case from 1974, Singer v. Hara, which is included in the 1990 edition of Black's Law Dictionary. More than a century ago, the U.S. Supreme Court spoke of the "union for life of one man and one woman in the holy estate of matrimony." Murphy v. Ramsey, 114 U.S. 15, 45 (1885).

DOMA is not meant to affect the definition of "spouse" (which under the Social Security law, for example, runs to dozens of lines). It ensures that whatever definition of "spouse" may be used in Federal law, the word refers only to a person of the opposite sex.

Provisions of the Act

4th CONGRESS 2D SESSION
H.R. 3396
IN THE HOUSE OF REPRESENTATIVES
Mr. BARR of Georgia (for himself, Mr. LARGENT, Mr. SENSEN-BRENNER, Ms. MYRICK, Mr. VOLKMER, Mr. SKELTON, Mr. BRYANT, and Mr. EMERSON) introduced the following bill, which was referred to the Committee

A BILL To define and protect the institution of marriage.

Be it enacted by the Senate and House of Representatives of the United States of America in Congress assembled,

SECTION 1. SHORT TITLE.

This Act may be cited as the "Defense of Marriage Act."

SECTION 2. POWERS RESERVED TO THE STATES.

(a) IN GENERAL.—Chapter 115 of title 28, United States Code, is amended by adding after section 1738B the following:

Section 1738C. Certain acts, records, and proceedings and the effect thereof "No State, territory, or possession of the United States, or Indian tribe, shall be required to give effect to any public act, record, or judicial proceeding of any other State, territory, possession, or tribe respecting a relationship between persons of the same sex that is treated as a marriage under the laws of such other State, territory, possession, or tribe, or a right or claim arising from such relationship."

(b) CLERICAL AMENDMENT.—The table of sections at the beginning of Chapter 115 of title 28, United States Code, is amended by inserting after the item relating to section 1738B the following new item: "1738C. Certain acts, records, and proceedings and the effect thereof."

SECTION 3. DEFINITION OF MARRIAGE.

(a) IN GENERAL.—Chapter 1 of title 1, United States Code, is amended by adding at the end the following:

"Section 7. Definition of 'marriage' and 'spouse'

"In determining the meaning of any Act of Congress, or of any ruling, regulation, or interpretation of the various administrative bureaus and agencies of the United States, the word 'marriage' means only a legal union between one man and one woman as husband and wife, and the word 'spouse' refers only to a person of the opposite sex who is a husband or a wife."

ANDREW SULLIVAN

Here Comes the Groom

Andrew Sullivan, the author of Virtually Normal: An Argument about Homosexuality *(1995),* Love Undetectable: Notes on Friendship, Sex, and Survival *(1998), and many essays, is one of the leading commentators on gay, lesbian, and bisexual issues in the nation. Openly gay himself, devotedly Catholic, critical of certain aspects of the gay community, and outspokenly conservative in many respects, he advocates full integration of gays and lesbians into American life. He regards prohibition of same-sex marriage as the most basic denial of civil rights in America. In 1996 he disclosed that he was receiving treatment for AIDS, entered graduate school to study government at Harvard, and reduced his editorial commitments to* The New Republic *(which had published the following argument in 1989). He subsequently completed his PhD in political science, and he lives and writes now (still for* The New Republic*) in Washington, D.C. To learn more about him and his work, see* < www.andrewsullivan.com > .

1   Last month in New York, a court ruled that a gay lover had the right to stay in his deceased partner's rent-control apartment because the lover qualified as a member of the deceased's family. The ruling deftly annoyed almost everybody. Conservatives saw judicial activism in favor of gay rent control: three reasons to be appalled. Chastened liberals (such as the *New York Times* editorial page), while endorsing the recognition of gay relationships also worried about the abuse of already stretched entitlements that the ruling threatened. What neither side quite contemplated is that they both might be right, and that the way to tackle the issue of unconventional relationships in conventional society is to try something both more radical and more conservative than putting courts in the business of deciding what is and is not a family. That alternative is the legalization of civil gay marriage.

2   The New York rent-control case did not go anywhere near that far, which is the problem. The rent-control regulations merely stipulated that a "family" member had the right to remain in the apartment. The judge ruled that to all intents and purposes a gay lover is part of his lover's family, inasmuch as a "family" merely means an interwoven social life, emotional commitment, and some level of financial interdependence.

3   It's a principle now well established around the country. Several cities have "domestic partnership" laws, which allow relationships that do not fit into the category of heterosexual marriage to be registered with the city and qualify for benefits that up till now have been reserved for straight married couples. San Francisco, Berkeley, Madison, and Los Angeles all have legislation, as does the politically correct Washington, D.C., suburb, Takoma Park. In these cities, a variety of interpersonal arrangements qualify for health insurance, bereavement leave, insurance, annuity and pension rights, housing rights (such as rent-control apartments), adoption and inheritance rights. Eventually, according to gay lobby groups, the aim is to include federal income tax and veterans' benefits as well. A recent case even involved the right to use a family member's accumulated frequent-flier points. Gays are not the only beneficiaries; heterosexual "live-togethers" also qualify.

4   There's an argument, of course, that the current legal advantages extended to married people unfairly discriminate against people who've shaped their lives in less conventional arrangements. But it doesn't take a genius to see that enshrining in the law a vague principle like "domestic partnership" [DP] is an invitation to qualify at little personal cost for a vast array of entitlements otherwise kept crudely under control.

5   To be sure, potential DPs have to prove financial interdependence, shared living arrangements, and a commitment to mutual caring. But they don't need to have a sexual relationship or even closely mirror old-style marriage. In principle, an elderly woman and her live-in nurse could qualify. A couple of uneuphemistically confirmed bachelors could

Two men exchanging rings during their same-sex wedding ceremony in Honolulu, Hawaii

be DPs. So could two close college students, a pair of seminarians, or a couple of frat buddies. Left as it is, the concept of domestic partnership could open a Pandora's box of litigation and subjective judicial decision-making about who qualifies. You either are or are not married; it's not a complex question. Whether you are in a "domestic partnership" is not so clear.

6   More important, the concept of domestic partnership chips away at the prestige of traditional relationships and undermines the priority we give them. This priority is not necessarily a product of heterosexism. Consider heterosexual couples. Society has good reason to extend legal advantages to heterosexuals who choose the formal sanction of marriage over simply living together. They make a deeper commitment to one another and to society; in exchange, society extends certain benefits to them. Marriage provides an anchor, if an arbitrary and weak one, in the chaos of sex and relationships to which we are all prone. It provides a mechanism for emotional stability, economic security, and the healthy rearing of the next generation. We rig the law in its favor not because we disparage all forms of relationship other than the nuclear family, but because we recognize that not to promote marriage would be to ask too much of human virtue. In the context of the weakened family's effect upon the poor, it might also invite social disintegration. One of the worst products of the New Right's "family values" campaign is that its extrem-

ism and hatred of diversity has disguised this more measured and more convincing case for the importance of the marital bond.

7   The concept of domestic partnership ignores these concerns, indeed directly attacks them. This is a pity, since one of its most important objectives—providing some civil recognition for gay relationship—is a noble cause and one completely compatible with the defense of the family. But the decision to go about it is not to undermine straight marriage; it is to legalize old-style marriage for gays.

8   The gay movement has ducked this issue primarily out of fear of division. Much of the gay leadership clings to notions of gay life as essentially outsider, anti-bourgeois, radical. Marriage, for them, is co-optation into straight society. For the Stonewall generation, it is hard to see how this vision of conflict will ever fundamentally change. But for many other gays—my guess, a majority—while they don't deny the importance of rebellion 20 years ago and are grateful for what was done, there's now the sense of a new opportunity. A need to rebel has quietly ceded to a desire to belong. To be gay and to be bourgeois no longer seems such an absurd proposition. Certainly, since AIDS, to be gay and to be responsible has become a necessity.

9   Gay marriage squares several circles at the heart of the domestic partnership debate. Unlike domestic partnership, it allows for recognition of gay relationships, while casting no aspersions on traditional marriage. It merely asks that gays be allowed to join in. Unlike domestic partnership, it doesn't open up avenues for heterosexuals to get benefits without the responsibilities of marriage, or a nightmare of definitional litigation. And unlike domestic partnership, it harnesses to an already established social convention the yearnings for stability and acceptance among a fast-maturing gay community.

10   Gay marriage also places more responsibilities upon gays; it says for the first time that gay relationships are not better or worse than straight relationships, and that the same is expected of them. And it's clear and dignified. There's a legal benefit to a clear, common symbol of commitment. There's also a personal benefit. One of the ironies of domestic partnership is that it's not only more complicated than marriage, it's more demanding, requiring an elaborate statement of intent to qualify. It amounts to a substantial invasion of privacy. Why, after all, should gays be required to prove commitment before they get married in a way we would never dream of asking of straights?

11   Legalizing gay marriage would offer homosexuals the same deal society now offers heterosexuals: general social approval and specific legal advantages in exchange for a deeper and harder-to-extract-yourself-from commitment to another human being. Like straight marriage, it would foster social cohesion, emotional security, and economic prudence. Since

there's no reason gays should not be allowed to adopt or be foster parents, it could also help nurture children. And its introduction would not be some sort of radical break with social custom. As it has become more acceptable for gay people to acknowledge their loves publicly, more and more have committed themselves to one another for life in full view of their families and their friends. A law institutionalizing gay marriage would merely reinforce a healthy social trend. It would also, in the wake of AIDS, qualify as a genuine public health measure. Those conservatives who deplore promiscuity among some homosexuals should be among the first to support it. Burke could have written a powerful case for it.

12   The argument that gay marriage would subtly undermine the unique legitimacy of straight marriage is based upon a fallacy. For heterosexuals, straight marriage would remain the most significant—and only legal—social bond. Gay marriage could only delegitimize straight marriage if it were a real alternative to it, and this is clearly not true. To put it bluntly, there's precious little evidence that straights could be persuaded by any law to have sex with—let alone marry—someone of their own sex. The only possible effect of this sort would be to persuade gay men and women who force themselves into heterosexual marriage (often at appalling cost to themselves and their families) to find a focus for their family instincts in a more personally positive environment. But this is clearly a plus, not a minus: gay marriage could both avoid a lot of tortured families and create the possibility for many happier ones. It is not, in short, a denial of family values. It's an extension of them.

13   Of course, some would claim that any legal recognition of homosexuality is a de facto attack upon heterosexuality. But even the most hardened conservatives recognize that gays are a permanent minority and aren't likely to go away. Since persecution is not an option in a civilized society, why not coax gays into traditional values rather than rail incoherently against them?

14   There's a less elaborate argument for gay marriage: it's good for gays. It provides role models for young gay people who, after the exhilaration of coming out, can easily lapse into short-term relationships and insecurity with no tangible goal in sight. My own guess is that most gays would embrace such a goal with as much (if not more) commitment as straights. Even in our society as it is, many lesbian relationships are virtual textbook cases of monogamous commitment. Legal gay marriage could also help bridge the gulf often found between gays and their parents. It could bring the essence of gay life—a gay couple—into the heart of the traditional straight family in a way the family can most understand and the gay offspring can most easily acknowledge. It could do as much to heal the gay-straight rift as any amount of gay rights legislation.

15   If these arguments sound socially conservative, that's no accident. It's one of the richest ironies of our society's blind spot toward gays that

essentially conservative social goals should have the appearance of being so radical. But gay marriage is not a radical step. It avoids the mess of domestic partnership; it is humane; it is conservative in the best sense of the word. It's also practical. Given the fact that we already allow legal gay relationships, what possible social goal is advanced by framing the law to encourage those relationships to be unfaithful, undeveloped, and insecure? ∎

HADLEY ARKES

The Closet Straight

Hadley Arkes (1944–) is a professor of law at Amherst College. His response to the arguments of Andrew Sullivan appeared in 1993 in the National Review *(which is resolute in publishing conservative viewpoints). Arkes's argument counters not the essay "Here Comes the Groom" but a similar essay that Sullivan published in 1993 titled "The Politics of Homosexuality."*

1   John Courtney Murray once observed that the atheist and the theist essentially agree in their understanding of the problem: The atheist does not mean to reject the existence of God only in Staten Island: he means to reject God universally, as a necessary truth. He accepts the same framework of reference, and he makes the same move to a transcendent standard of judgment. In a thoughtful, extended essay, Andrew Sullivan, the young, gay editor of *The New Republic,* has made a comparable concession for the advocate of "gay rights" ["The Politics of Homosexuality," *New Republic,* May 10]. For Sullivan has put into place, as the very ground and framework of his argument, a structure of understanding that must call into question any claims for the homosexual life as a rival good.

2   "The Politics of Homosexuality" confirms, at length, what anyone who has been with Andrew Sullivan can grasp within five minutes: he regards his erotic life as the center of his being, but he also conveys the most powerful need to seek that erotic fulfillment within a framework of domesticity, of the normal and the *natural.* The most persisting thread of anguish in the essay is the pain of awareness and reconciliation in his own family, with the recurring memory of his father weeping when Andrew declared, as he says, his sexuality. Sullivan reserves some of his most stinging words for the producers of a "queer" politics, aimed at "cultural subversion." That brand of politics would simply confirm the strangeness of homosexuals, and deepen the separation

from their families. Ironically, says Sullivan, "queer" politics "broke off dialogue with the heterosexual families whose cooperation is needed in every generation, if gay children are to be accorded a modicum of dignity and hope."

3   The delicacy barely conceals that "cooperation is needed in every generation" precisely because "homosexual families" cannot produce "gay children." Gay children must come into being through the only kind of family that nature knows. Those who wish to preserve, say, a Jewish people, know that Jews need to reproduce and raise their children as Jews. But what would be the comparable path of obligation for the person who is committed to the preservation of a "gay community"? Sullivan is convinced that there is something in our biology or chemistry that "determines" our sexuality, and in that case, the tendency to gay sex may be passed along to the next generation, as readily as temperament and allergies. The person who wishes to preserve, for the next generation, a gay community may be tempted then to render the ultimate service: For the good of the cause, he may cross the line and enter another domain of sex. But in crossing that line, he makes a decisive concession: implicitly, but unmistakably, he is compelled to acknowledge that homosexuality cannot even pretend to stand on the same plane as the way of life it would displace. We do not really find two kinds of "families" carrying out transactions with one another. But rather, we come to recognize again the primacy of "sexuality" in the strictest sense, the only sexuality that can produce "another generation."

4   It is evidently important to Sullivan to insist that homosexuality is rooted in "nature," that it is determined for many people by something in their makeup quite beyond their control. He would wish to draw to his side a certain strand of natural law to suggest that anything so rooted in nature cannot be wrong. And yet, he falls there into an ancient mistake. As the great expounders of natural law explained, we do not make our way to the "natural" simply by generalizing upon the mixed record of our species: by that reckoning, incest and genocide would be in accord with natural law, since they seem to form an intractable part of the human experience. And even if we could show, say, that some of us carried a gene for "arson," that would not settle the moral question on arson. We might not be as quick to blame the bearers of these genes, but we would expect them to exert more self-control, and we would hardly waive our moral reservations about arson.

5   In a passage of searing candor, Sullivan acknowledges that discrimination has not affected gays with the same kinds of deprivations that have been visited upon blacks. "[Gay] men and lesbians suffer no discernible communal economic deprivations and already operate at the highest levels of society." But when they call to their aid the levers of the law, they cultivate the sense of themselves as vulnerable and weak,

in need of protection, and they perpetuate, among gays, the tendencies to self-doubt. They suggest that the things most needful to gays are in the hands of other people to confer. In the sweep of his own conviction, Sullivan would soar past those demands altogether. He would stop demanding laws, which confer, upon straight people, the franchise of confirming, or discounting, the worth of gays.

Love and Marriage

6   Except for one, notable thing. What Andrew Sullivan wants, most of all, is marriage. And he wants it for reasons that could not have been stated more powerfully by any heterosexual who had been raised, as Sullivan was, in the Catholic tradition and schooled in political philosophy. "[T]he apex of emotional life," says Sullivan, "is found in the marital bond." The erotic interest may seek out copulation, but the fulfillment of eros depends on the integrity of a bond woven of sentiment and confirmed by law. Marriage is more than a private contract; it is "the highest public recognition of our personal integrity." Its equivalent will not be supplied by a string of sensual nights, accumulated over many years of "living together." The very existence of marriage "premises the core of our emotional development. It is the architectonic institution that frames our emotional life."

7   No one could doubt for a moment: as much as any of the "guys" in the Damon Runyon stories, the man who wrote those lines is headed, irresistibly, for marriage. What he craves—homosexual marriage—would indeed require the approval conferred by law. It would also require a benediction conferred by straight people, who would have to consent to that vast, new modeling of our laws. That project will not be undertaken readily, and it may not be undertaken at all. Still, there is something, rooted in the nature of Andrew Sullivan, that must need marriage.

8   But as Mona Charen pointed out, in an encounter with Sullivan at the National Review Institute conference this winter [*NR*, March 29], it is not marriage that domesticates men; it is women. Left to themselves, these forked creatures follow a way of life that George Gilder once recounted in its precise, chilling measures: bachelors were 22 times more likely than married men to be committed to hospitals for mental disease (and 10 times more likely to suffer chronic diseases of all kinds). Single men had nearly double the mortality rate of married men and 3 times the mortality rate of single women. Divorced men were 3 times more likely than divorced women to commit suicide or die by murder, and they were 6 times more likely to die of heart disease.

9   We have ample reason by now to doubt that the bipeds described in these figures are likely to be tamed to a sudden civility if they are

merely arranged, in sets of two or three, in the same house. I had the chance to see my own younger son, settled with three of his closest friends in a townhouse in Georgetown during his college years. The labors of the kitchen and the household were divided with a concern for domestic order, and the abrasions of living together were softened by the ties of friendship. And yet, no one, entering that house, could doubt for a moment that he was in a camp occupied for a while by young males, with their hormones flowing.

10   This is not to deny, of course, that men may truly love men, or commit themselves to a life of steady friendship. But many of us have continued to wonder just why any of these relations would be enhanced in any way by adding to them the ingredients of penetration—or marriage. The purpose of this alliance, after all, could not be the generation of children, and a marriage would not be needed then as the stable framework for welcoming and sheltering children. For gays, the ceremony of marriage could have the function of proclaiming to the world an exclusive love, a special dedication, which comes along with a solemn promise to forgo all other, competing loves. In short, it would draw its power from the romance of monogamy. But is that the vision that drives the movement for "gay rights"? An excruciating yearning for monogamy?

11   That may indeed be Andrew Sullivan's own yearning, but his position is already marking him as a curious figure in the camp of gay activists. When Sullivan commends the ideal of marriage for gays, he would seem to be pleading merely for the inclusion of gay "couples" in an institution that is indeed confined to pairs, of *adults,* in monogamous unions. But that is not exactly the vision of gay sex.

12   For many activists and connoisseurs, Sullivan would represent a rather wimpish, constricted view of the world they would open to themselves through sexual liberation. After all, the permissions for this new sexual freedom have been cast to that amorphous formula of "sexual orientation": the demand of gay rights is that we should recede from casting moral judgments on the way that people find their pleasure in engagements they regard as "sexual." In its strange abstraction, "sexual orientation" could take in sex with animals or the steamier versions of sado-masochism. The devotees of S&M were much in evidence during the recent march in Washington, but we may put aside for a moment these interests, to consider others which are even more exotic yet. There is, for example, the North American Man–Boy Love Association, a contingent of gay activists who identify themselves, unashamedly, as pedophiles. They insist that nothing in their "sexual orientation" should disqualify them to work as professional counselors, say, in the schools of New York, and to counsel young boys. And since they respect themselves, they will not hold back from commending their own way of life

to their young charges. If there is to be gay marriage, would it be confined then only to adults? And if men are inclined to a life of multiple partners, why should marriage be confined to two persons? Why indeed should the notion of gay marriage be sealed down to fit the notions held by Andrew Sullivan?

Sullivan's Dilemma

13 The sources of anguish run even deeper here than Sullivan may suspect, for his dilemma may be crystallized in this way: If he would preserve the traditional understanding of marriage and monogamy, he would not speak for much of a constituency among gays. But if the notion of "marriage" were enlarged and redefined—if it could take in a plurality of people and shifting combinations—it could hardly be the kind of marriage that Sullivan devoutly wishes as "the apex of emotional life" and "the highest public recognition of our personal integrity."

14   In traditional marriage, the understanding of monogamy was originally tied to the "natural teleology" of the body—to the recognition that only two people, no more and no fewer, can generate children. To that understanding of a union, or a "marriage," the alliance of two men would offer such an implausible want of resemblance that it would appear almost as a mocking burlesque. It would be rather like confounding, as Lincoln used to say, a "horse chestnut" and a "chestnut horse." The mockery would be avoided if the notion of marriage could be opened, or broadened, to accommodate the varieties of sexual experience. The most notable accommodation would be the acceptance of several partners, and the change could be readily reckoned precisely because it would hardly be novel: the proposal for gay marriage would compel us to look again—to look anew with eyes unclouded by prejudice—to the ancient appeal of polygamy. After all, there would be an Equal Protection problem now: we could scarcely confine this new "marital" arrangement only to members of one gender. But then, once the arrangement is opened simply to "consenting adults," on what ground would we object to the mature couplings of aunts and nephews, or even fathers and daughters—couplings that show a remarkable persistence in our own age, even against the barriers of law and sentiment that have been cast up over centuries? All kinds of questions, once placed in a merciful repose, may reasonably be opened again. They become live issues once we are willing to ponder that simple question, Why should marriage be confined, after all, to couples, and to pairs drawn from different sexes?

15   That question, if it comes to be treated as open and problematic, will not readily be closed, or not at least on the terms that Andrew Sullivan seeks. The melancholy news then is this: We cannot deliver to him

what he wants without introducing, into our laws, notions that must surely undercut the rationale and the justification for marriage. The marriage that he wants, he cannot practicably have: but in seeking it, he runs the risk of weakening even further the opinion that sustains marriage as "the architectonic institution that frames our emotional life."

16   But for marriage so understood, Sullivan does not seem to command a large following, or even a substantial interest, among gays. New York City must surely contain one of the largest concentrations of accomplished, successful gay men. Since March, New York has allowed the registering of "domestic partners," and by the first of June, 822 couples had come forth to register. By the unofficial estimate of people in the bureau, those couples have been just about evenly distributed between gays and lesbians. Four hundred gay couples would not be a trivial number, but in a city like New York, it does rather suggest that the craving for this public recognition may not be widely diffused. If all of the couples registered under the new law were collected in Yankee Stadium, they would hardly be noticeable in the crowd. Their numbers would not exactly suggest that there is a strong political constituency out there for gay marriage.

Unintended Consequence

17 In making then his own, heartfelt case for marriage, Andrew Sullivan is swept well past the interests and enthusiasms that mark most other people who now make up the "gay community." And he may earnestly put this question to himself: In the sweep of his own convictions, in the sentiment that draws him, powerfully, to marriage, has he not in fact swept past, and discarded, the rationales that sustain the homosexual life?

18   What comes through the writing, finally, is a man who finds his eros in domesticity, who will find pleasure in driving his own children to their soccer games on Saturday mornings. He will explain again to his friends that we must "cooperate" with heterosexual families; that if we would protect gay children we must raise them, and even produce them. There may be winks all around, and the sense that he is doing something for "the cause." But as Andrew Sullivan appreciates, "queer" politics always seeks to take "shame-abandonment to a thrilling conclusion." And what could be more exquisite and subtle than this reversal upon a reversal?: A man lives a highly visible public life as a homosexual, but he enters a marriage, which is taken as a kind of charade, and he is content to abet the jest with knowing glances. But the secret that dare not speak its name is that he really is, after all, a domesticated man, settled in his marriage. As a writer and a man, Andrew Sullivan is committed to an understanding of political life that finds its ground in nature. And he takes, as the core of our civic life, marriage and the laws that sustain marriage. For all of that, we here, composed, as we are, of eros and of dust, love him. ■

ANNA QUINDLEN

Evan's Two Moms

Anna Quindlen (1955–) won a Pulitzer prize in 1992 for the weekly
column she wrote for the New York Times *and other newspapers. Now she*
writes an essay for Newsweek *every other week and works on her fiction*
as well. Her essays, including the one that follows, have been collected
into several books, among them Thinking Out Loud: On the Personal, the
Political, the Public, and the Private *(1993).*

1   Evan has two moms. This is no big thing. Evan has always had two
moms in his school file, on his emergency forms, with his friends.
"Ooooh, Evan, you're lucky," they sometimes say. "You have two
moms." It sounds like a sitcom, but until last week it was emotional
truth without legal bulwark. That was when a judge in New York approved the adoption of a six-year-old boy by his biological mother's lesbian partner. Evan. Evan's mom. Evan's other mom. A kid, a psychologist, a pediatrician. A family.

2   The matter of Evan's two moms is one in a series of events over
the last year that led to certain conclusions. A Minnesota appeals court
granted guardianship of a woman left a quadriplegic in a car accident
to her lesbian lover, the culmination of a seven-year battle in which the
injured woman's parents did everything possible to negate the partnership between the two. A lawyer in Georgia had her job offer withdrawn
after the state attorney general found out that she and her lesbian lover
were planning a marriage ceremony: she's brought suit. The computer
company Lotus announced that the gay partners of employees would be
eligible for the same benefits as spouses.

3   Add to these public events the private struggles, the couples who
go from lawyer to lawyer to approximate legal protections their straight
counterparts take for granted, the AIDS survivors who find themselves
shut out of their partners' dying days by biological family members and
shut out of their apartments by leases with a single name on the dotted
line, and one solution is obvious.

4   Gay marriage is a radical notion for straight people and a conservative notion for gay ones. After years of being sledge-hammered by society, some gay men and lesbian women are deeply suspicious of participating in an institution that seems to have "straight world" written all
over it.

5   But the rads of twenty years ago, straight and gay alike, have other
things on their minds today. Family is one, and the linchpin of family
has commonly been a loving commitment between two adults. When
same-sex couples set out to make that commitment, they discover that

they are at a disadvantage: No joint tax returns. No health insurance coverage for an uninsured partner. No survivor's benefits from Social Security. None of the automatic rights, privileges, and responsibilities society attaches to a marriage contract. In Madison, Wisconsin, a couple who applied at the Y with their kids for a family membership were turned down because both were women. It's one of those small things that can make you feel small.

6   Some took marriage statutes that refer to "two persons" at their word and applied for a license. The results were court decisions that quoted the Bible and embraced circular argument: marriage is by definition the union of a man and a woman because that is how we've defined it.

7   No religion should be forced to marry anyone in violation of its tenets, although ironically it is now only in religious ceremonies that gay people can marry, performed by clergy who find the blessing of two who love each other no sin. But there is no secular reason that we should take a patchwork approach of corporate, governmental, and legal steps to guarantee what can be done simply, economically, conclusively, and inclusively with the words "I do."

8   "Fran and I chose to get married for the same reasons that any two people do," said the lawyer who was fired in Georgia. "We fell in love; we wanted to spend our lives together." Pretty simple.

9   Consider the case of *Loving* v. *Virginia,* aptly named. At the time, sixteen states had laws that barred interracial marriage, relying on natural law, that amorphous grab bag for justifying prejudice. Sounding a little like God throwing Adam and Eve out of paradise, the trial judge suspended the one-year sentence of Richard Loving, who was white, and his wife, Mildred, who was black, provided they got out of the State of Virginia.

10   In 1967 the Supreme Court found such laws to be unconstitutional. Only twenty-five years ago and it was a crime for a black woman to marry a white man. Perhaps twenty-five years from now we will find it just as incredible that two people of the same sex were not entitled to legally commit themselves to each other. Love and commitment are rare enough; it seems absurd to thwart them in any guise. ■

From Reading to Writing

Finding someone interested in reading or listening to arguments about same-sex marriage with you is not difficult; it is much on everyone's mind, it seems. No doubt particular proposals are being discussed in your own states and communities. The difficulty in making an argument on this issue, as with other topics that combine politics, morality, religion, and personal freedoms, is finding a way to focus those polarizing debates so that they are productive. Here are some suggested prompts for writing.

1. Write an essay defining "the ideal marriage" in a certain way in order to support or undermine the concept of same-sex marriage. Just what is marriage, anyway? (Chapter 6 has advice on definition arguments.)

2. If you are a member of a religious group, find out more about your church's stance on gay marriage and the reasoning behind it; then use what you have learned to support a specific position on same-sex marriage.

3. In the manner of Anna Quindlen, write an essay that describes a particular, monogamous, same-sex couple that you know—an essay that in the process supports or undermines the notion of legal same-sex unions.

4. Write an argument—a proposal argument like the ones discussed in Chapter 11—that is based on the positive or negative consequences that would follow from legalizing same-sex unions.

5. Do a rhetorical analysis of an essay or visual image associated with the same-sex marriage issue. It might be an argument reprinted here (such as those by Sullivan, Arkes, or Quindlen), or a photo or cartoon reprinted here; or it could be another argument that you are familiar with. How does the author of that argument use good reasons to support his or her point of view? How complete is the argument? How credible is the arguer? (Look again at Chapters 4 and 5, if you need to, to remind yourself how to do an effective rhetorical analysis.)

6. Though recent events in Massachusetts and San Francisco were important in the gay rights struggle, many other important incidents have occurred. Research one or more of those moments (gay marriage in Hawaii, the Stonewall revolt, the murder of Matthew Shepard, etc.) and compare those with the more recent events. How do the incidents that you study speak to the issue of same-sex marriage?

7. Find an argument on one side or the other of the same-sex marriage issue and write a rebuttal of that argument. You might use Peter J. Gomes's rebuttal argument as a model, and you can get other advice in Chapter 10.

8. Evaluate the Defense of Marriage Act or the proposed constitutional amendment banning same-sex marriage: based on aesthetic, ethical, and practical criteria (see pages 149–150), are these good laws or not?

JAMES PONIEWOZIK

Queer Eye for Straight TV

James Poniewozik writes as a media and television critic for Time *magazine and National Public Radio. Before joining the staff at* Time, *Poniewozik was the media section editor at Salon.com. A frequent contributor to numerous other publications, including* Rolling Stone *and* Fortune, *he writes about a variety of popular culture topics and continues to write short fiction as well. The following article appeared in the March 14, 2005, issue of* Time.

1   This is a tale of two elections. In November 2004, 11 states considered ballot measures banning gay marriage. All 11 passed. There was also an election, of sorts, in January 2005: the Golden Globe Awards. The TV awards for Best Comedy and Best Drama went, respectively, to ABC'S suburban mystery "Desperate Housewives" and FX's plastic-surgery saga "Nip/Tuck." The former is the highest-rated new series of the TV season; the latter, one of the highest-rated dramas on basic cable. Both are water-cooler shows about love, sex, fidelity and lies, mainly among heterosexual men and women.

2   And both were created by gay men.

3   A curious thing is going on in the U.S. Even as the nation is writing gays out of the definition of its most exalted relationship, gay writers—like "Housewives" creator Marc Cherry and "Nip/Tuck" creator Ryan Murphy—are behind the TV shows that are most provocatively defining straight relationships. HBO'S "Six Feet Under," the multilayered story of the lives and loves of a family that runs a funeral home, sprang from the mind of gay screenwriter Alan Ball ("American Beauty"). Before it, HBO'S "Sex and the City," which set the standard for frank talk about women and love, was created by Darren Star and later run by Michael Patrick King, both gay. (Later this year, King debuts "The Comeback," an HBO sitcom starring Lisa Kudrow as an actress trying to revive her career.)

4   Is all this coincidence? Gay TV writers will tell you that relationships are universal. (If they talk at all. King, Murphy and Star declined to be interviewed for this article.) They have good reasons for saying so. Gay writers run the risk of being labeled as, well, gay writers, and the idea of a gay sensibility conjures a monolithic image of campy queens quoting from *What Ever Happened to Baby Jane?*

5   In fact, these series represent a wide range of voices (as do more overtly gay-themed shows, from NBC's "Will & Grace" to Showtime's "The L Word" and "Queer as Folk"). "Housewives" is cartoony and parodic, "Nip/Tuck" slick and urbane, "Six Feet Under" moody and cerebral. "I don't think you could say they were all told from a specific perspective that comes from being gay," says ABC prime-time-entertainment president Stephen McPherson. "But if being gay makes you that talented, I'm going gay." In art, one could argue, sexual orientation shouldn't matter.

6   In life, though, it does. (See those November results, above.) If these gay writers are inclined to think creatively about love and identity, maybe it's because they didn't have the option of accepting the standard assumptions. Growing up gay, says "Six Feet Under" creator Alan Ball, "you have a pretty deeply ingrained sense of being an outsider. You don't swallow the mythology of pop culture hook, line and sinker because you know it's not true, for you, anyway."

7   Among the Fisher family members on "Six Feet Under," which returns for its fifth season this summer, only one, David (Michael C. Hall), is gay. (College-age Claire, played by Lauren Ambrose, has had flings with men and women.) But all, in a way, have been engaged in coming out. The funeral business they run is about the tidy management of emotions, and the repressed Fishers are continually struggling to open up to the people closest to them. Likewise, "Housewives" is rooted in mystery and enough lies to fill a three-car garage. "I certainly understand the nature of secrets," says Cherry. "If you grow up gay, you meet people and go on dates and find out the men are married. I'm conservative enough to be appalled. Secrets upon secrets upon secrets."

8   Truth and lies are unavoidable themes in the lives of gays, say "Will & Grace" co-creators Max Mutchnick and David Kohan. "The first 'real' moment for a gay man is when he comes out of the closet," says Mutchnick, who is gay. He says gays may have a special sensitivity to these issues "because in order to move forward, you have to live and tell the truth."

9   Bound up with lies and truth is a sensitivity to ambiguity in a world of black-and-white dualities: boy and girl, straight and gay. "Nip/Tuck" is literally about the idea that the flesh can tell lies, that identity is malleable, that a person is more than what is written on his or her anatomy. It also has an uncanny sensitivity for the stormy, complex relationship—like a platonic marriage—between the straight-male leads Christian (Julian McMahon) and Sean (Dylan Walsh). When Sean discovers, for instance, that Christian had an affair with Sean's wife and is the real father of his son, he tells his friend, heartbroken, "I loved you the most."

10   Ball's, Cherry's and Murphy's dramas are often compared to soap operas, which can often be code for "too girly." Says Cherry, whose

writing staff has five gays and six straights: "We push the boundaries in our lives by being gay. When we write, we are perfectly willing to write extreme behavior." Ilene Chaiken, the lesbian writer and creator of "The L Word," theorizes that gay men and women inevitably experience love as heightened drama. "One of the things that always make for a great love story is the obstacles," she says. "These writers are bringing to these stories not only their experiences of illicit love but enough illicit-ness to make the stories more exciting and infuse them with passion and intensity."

11   That passion, curiously, is expressed in each show through strong women. A gay man, says Ball, can see men through a straight woman's eyes—"We understand how weird men are"—but he believes he can also view women with greater detachment. "Once you remove the illu-sory screen of romantic projection, there is a person," he says, "and it's easier for a gay man to see the person in a female character." And, says Showtime entertainment president Robert Greenblatt, gay writers are more inclined to think about gender roles and stereotypes. "Straight men don't think about gender," he says. "Why should they? They're in the dominant position." (Of course, it's worth nothing that the male perspective, straight or gay, is much more common on TV than that of women, who still create far fewer prime-time shows.)

12   "Housewives" suburban hotties, like "Sex and the City's" urban ones, are unabashed straight stereotypes: the frazzled mom, the girl next door, the spicy Latina, the uptight homemaker. But, notes Paul Col-ichman, co-founder and CEO of Here! TV, a gay and lesbian premium channel, "Gay men have always loved sexy, ultrafeminine, exaggerated women like Marilyn Monroe. The women in 'Desperate Housewives' are caricatures and larger than life. That's why it works."

13   There's an old tradition of gay writers (not to mention actors) ex-pressing themselves through straight characters. Gay audiences saw themselves reflected in vivid women like Blanche DuBois in Tennessee Williams' *A Streetcar Named Desire*. TV and movie writers created themes and characters that were palatable to straight audiences but tripped the gaydar of knowing viewers—say, Paul Lynde's queeny Un-cle Arthur on "Bewitched." (In advertising, such dual signals are called gay vague.) Even "Sex and the City," with its witty, sexually assertive women, was reminiscent of the old maxim "Write gay, cast straight."

14   Shows like Cherry's, Murphy's and Ball's are not about sending coded messages from the closet to the living room. Yes, there are still barriers to gays on TV—"Survivor" last fall edited a kiss between two women. But Ball and Murphy work in cable, where they could create gay characters—and have. Even on network TV, "Housewives" recently had Susan (Teri Hatcher) stumbling across the teenage son of Bree (Marcia Cross) smooching another guy at a pool party. When he comes

out to Bree in a later episode, she says, "Well, I'd love you even if you were a murderer"—the precise response, Cherry says, that his mother gave when he came out at age 31.

15　　Mostly, though, these writers are asserting their right to be gay yet to write straight. Which raises the question, Couldn't straight men or women have created these shows? Probably. But they didn't. Instead, these writers have taken the idea of a gay sensibility beyond the old campy, gay stereotypes. Their shows have the subtler sensibility defined by gay film historian Vito Russo in *The Celluloid Closet*, his study of the influence of gays on the movies: "A natural conviction that difference exists but doesn't matter, that there's no such thing as normal even when a majority of people think so."

16　　This is a conviction you don't have to be gay to share. Whether set in an operating room or a funeral home, a leafy suburb or glittery Manhattan, these shows question our easy ideas of normality. They argue that knowing yourself can take a lifetime. And they tell us that truth is an essential part of life and art—but one that cannot always be told Straight. ■

WILLIAM F. JASPER

Subversion Through Perversion

William F. Jasper is a Senior Editor of The New American, *a biweekly magazine that is owned by the radically conservative John Birch Society, which claims to be "a valuable tool in confronting the liberal, mainstream media." It is a news and opinion publication focusing on national issues. Jasper is the author of* Global Tyranny . . . Step by Step: The United Nations and the Emerging New World Order *(1992) and* The United Nations Exposed *(2001). "Subversion Through Perversion" appeared in the March 21, 2005, edition of* The New American.

1　　**M**aybe you're like this writer and rarely sample the toxic television fare that parades under the false label of "entertainment." Even so, it's impossible to conduct even a brief, occasional audit of the tube without confronting the hard fact that the forces in control of this omnipresent and potent medium are hell-bent themselves, and are determined to take our whole society there with them.

2　　Nowhere is this more evident than in the incredible brazenness of the full-tilt campaign to homosexualize American culture. The organized sodomites, who constitute a tiny fraction of our society—1 to 2 percent, not the 10 percent they claim—have been given carte blanche to "overhaul straight America." You may not know it, but you are being psychologically overhauled to accept the homosexual revolution "whether you like it or not."

3   Welcome to the "queering of America." That's how the radical homosexual strategies themselves refer to their insidious crusade to remake our society and our entire culture in their image. They know they cannot succeed totally in the legislatures and the courts unless and until they have transformed our culture. This means saturating our popular cultural media with homosexual and lesbian characters, themes, styles, and symbols.

4   This also means placing homosexual and lesbian characters into virtually every sitcom, soap, and drama on television. And it has gone far beyond that, of course. Programs like *Queer Eye for the Straight Guy*, *Queer Eye for the Straight Girl*, and *The L Word* are total propaganda platforms for the superiority of homosexuals over straights.

"Velvet Mafia"

5   This subversive crafting of the program content of network and cable TV is dictated by a contingent of homo-lesbo executives, artists, and consultants known in the trade as the Velvet Mafia or the Lavender Mob.

6   When the Velvet Mafia determines that it's time to inoculate the American public with a few more doses of "gay" culture, we get another spate of "coming out" episodes or homo-lesbo kissing scenes. Thus, on February 10, *New York Times* writer Virginia Heffernan approvingly noted the recent wave of lesbian smooching during the network sweeps: "On *One Tree Hill*, *The O.C.* and even *Wife Swap*, Sapphic love is in the air. And why not? It's that extended prom night for television lesbians—sweeps."

7   According to Heffernan, "in the last decade television's masterminds have discovered the lesbian kiss" as a gimmick to gain viewership. Lesbian kisses, she claims, "offer something for everyone, from advocacy groups looking for role models to indignation-seeking conservatives, from goggle-eyed male viewers to progressive female ones, from tyrants who demand psychological complexity to plot buffs. Hooray for the all-purpose lesbian kiss, then, cynical though it may be."

8   Heffernan then runs through a historical list of television's lesbian kisses, from "L.A. Law" in 1991, up through "Picket Fences," "Roseanne," "Ellen," "Ally McBeal," and "Buffy the Vampire Slayer." Next up, then, are Marissa (Mischa Barton) and Alex (Olivia Wilde) on "The O.C." (Fox)," Heffernan reports, in apparent breathless anticipation. "The gorgeous California girls will finally kiss tonight."

9   Heffernan hit on the key element of the Velvet Mafia strategy when she said "gorgeous California girls." To sell their perversion to the targeted teen and young adult audiences, they have gone to great lengths to

Homersexualizing America: Homer performs "gay marriages" on "The Simpsons."

package lesbians as gorgeous, cool, hip, smart, chic. That is especially obvious in the new lesbian series, *The L Word,* now in its second season on the Showtime network. Giant billboards for *The L Word* show a bevy of beautiful actress/models posing naked in a group huddle.

10   Now comes Homer Simpson to further the revolution. In a special episode of "The Simpsons" on February 20, Homer, who has become a beloved cartoon icon, conducted "gay marriages" and one of the regular characters on the series, Patty, came out of the closet.

Televised Revolution

11   The revolutionary nature of these recent events was noted by the *Chicago Tribune*'s Web Behrens. "You probably didn't notice it at the time, but a revolution quietly took place a week and a half ago—and, yes, it was televised." After reciting a string of recent "gay" TV episodes, including "The Simpsons," Behrens wrote: "When you consider that, just a decade ago, any one of these recent episodes would have been cause for much hand-wringing, protests and even boycotts, the word 'revolution' is no exaggeration. So how did American culture arrive at this place?"

12   Behrens only partially answers that important question by reciting, like Heffernan, the chronology of landmark homo-lesbo TV
episodes over the past decade. But those episodes did not appear out of
thin air; they were part of a long-term, revolutionary program planned
by militant homosexuals and their insider sponsors in the industry.
Their entire strategy was laid out in minute detail in 1989, in a book entitled *After the Ball: How America Will Conquer Its Fear and Hatred of
Gays in the 90's.*

13   The authors, Marshall Kirk and Hunter Madsen, boasted that this
was an operational manual for the "overhauling of straight America,"
by which they meant "converting" America. Kirk and Madsen state: "By
conversion we actually mean something far more profoundly threatening to the American way of life. We mean conversion of the average
American's emotions, mind and will, through a planned psychological
attack. We mean 'subverting' the mechanism of prejudice to our own
ends—using the very process that made America hate us to turn their
hatred into warm regard—whether they like it or not."

14   And how would this be accomplished? Through a massive media,
public relations, and advertising "propaganda campaign." "Gays must
launch a large-scale campaign—we've called it the Waging Peace campaign—to reach straights through the mainstream media," the coau-
thors wrote. "We're talking about propaganda." They explained to their
deviate cohorts that "propaganda relies more upon emotional manipulation than upon logic, since its goal is, in fact, to bring about a change
in the public's feelings."

15   "The main thing," they asserted, "is to talk about gayness until
the issue becomes thoroughly tiresome." Accordingly, they said, the
"free and frequent discussion of gay rights by a variety of persons in a
variety of places gives the impression that homosexuality is commonplace. That impression is essential, because . . . the acceptability of any
new behavior ultimately hinges on the proportion of one's fellows accepting or doing it." And, the deviate duo opined, the "fastest way to
convince straights that homosexuality is commonplace is to get a lot of
people talking about the subject in a neutral or supportive way. Open,
frank talk makes gayness seem less furtive, alien, and sinful; more
aboveboard."

16   "At least at the outset," say Kirk and Madsen, "we seek desensitization and nothing more." The purpose of that phase is simply to get
straight folks to the "shoulder-shrug stage." The radical homo duo write
that "If you can get them to think that [homosexuality] is just another
thing—meriting no more than a shrug of the shoulders—then your battle for legal and social rights is virtually won."

17   However, the Kirk-Madsen program does not stop with mere societal acceptance of homosexuality. It goes on to "paint gay men and les-

bians as superior—veritable pillars of society." That is what we are see-ing now, with programming that portrays the homo-lesbo community as superior to the straight community.

18   Yes, Mr. Behrens was correct to use the word "revolution." That is precisely what Communist theoretician Antonio Gramsci intended in his strategy to achieve complete transformation of society through a complete transformation of the culture. For the past several decades, Gramsci's disciples have been applying his subversive strategy to under-mine the moral foundations that provide the bulwark of protection against that revolution. ■

ALEXA HACKBARTH

Vanity, Thy Name Is Metrosexual

In the last several years a new term, "metrosexual," has moved toward the center of discussions about sexuality and masculinity. Most likely coined by journalist Mark Simpson in 1994, the term "metrosexual" has been the subject of many definitional arguments on talk radio and TV and in the print media. Alexa Hackbarth, a research assistant and photo technician at the Washington Post *who has done freelance writing since 1999, invokes the term in her discussion of dating protocols that is reprinted below from the* November 17, 2003, *Post.*

1   At dinner the other night, my date listed the calorie count of the main entrees, raising an eyebrow at my chicken Alfredo selection after he had ordered a salad. I saw him check his reflection in the silver water pitcher three times. During dessert, he looked deeply into my eyes and told me he thought what we have together is very special. It was our third date.

2   It was then that I realized why my dating life has been as mysteri-ous as the Bermuda Triangle since I arrived in Washington. This city, unlike any other place I've lived, is a haven for the metrosexual. A met-rosexual, in case you didn't catch any of several newspaper articles about this developing phenomenon (or the recent "South Park" episode on Comedy Central), is a straight man who styles his hair using three different products (and actually calls them "products"), loves clothes and the very act of shopping for them, and describes himself as sensi-tive and romantic. In other words, he is a man who seems stereotypi-cally gay except when it comes to sexual orientation.

3   Gay men say they actually have a bit of trouble telling the straight from the gay anymore. But at least this new breed of man is more likely

to thank the gay man for the compliment than punch him in the face after being approached, which may indicate that metrosexuals are more accepting of other people's sexual preferences. Either that or they're afraid of breaking a nail when their fist makes contact.

4   My primary concern, however, is that women are also having a difficult time telling straight men from gay men. Maybe city girls really do want a boyfriend who can pick out a purse that goes with her outfit, who likes to talk about calorie intake and celebrity hook-ups. But there are just too many men in this city who know all the soap opera story lines and designer labels and too few who associate sweat with hard work instead of a stint in the sauna.

5   In the small western ranching town where I grew up, men wrangle cattle before sitting down to a breakfast of bacon and eggs. They're the strong and silent type, capable and calm in a crisis. They know how to fix a leaky faucet or rewire an electrical outlet. They drive pickup trucks. And when they cook, it's steak and potatoes, not wine-braised duck. They sure don't spend hours in front of the mirror only to emerge with prettier hair than mine.

6   Metrosexuals are overwhelmingly city-dwellers, which makes sense since Diesel, Banana Republic, Gap and Express Men are rarely found down dirt roads. The source of my confusion, however, is the overwhelming abundance of this type of man in Washington. This is a city of transplants, rural and urban alike. But for some reason, each of the nearly two dozen men I have dated over the past eight months has displayed metrosexual traits. I met quite a few of them in bars, some in coffeeshops and grocery stores, and one or two through mutual friends. I figure I've experienced a decent cross-section of the city's dating pool. So where, as Paula Cole sings, have all the cowboys gone?

7   I understand that men, like women, want to look their best in order to convey professionalism, attract lovers and improve their self-image. I just don't think they're going about it the right way. It's as if, in an effort to move far away from the image of a smelly, unshaven man smashing beer cans on his forehead and wiping his nacho cheese down the front of his stained T-shirt, these guys have swung too far in the opposite direction. It makes me uncomfortable when a man can discuss the new season's fashions in intimate detail. Perhaps I am unusually insensitive, but I don't want a man who pours out his heart on the fourth date. I lose interest in men who not only won't make the first move, but hesitate to make the second and third. I don't want my date to be tearing up at the end of a movie when I'm sitting there dry-eyed.

8   We're living in an exciting time. America's social fabric is being unraveled and rewoven as we become more accepting of the differences that make each individual unique and our country so great. I have no

arguments with expressions of individuality. But I will admit to worrying when I read the results of a survey of American men aged 21 to 48, conducted by Euro RSCG Worldwide, that says more than two-thirds of men value love over professional success. As it should be, you say. Perhaps. But only if the men surveyed were just those with families.

9   Who are the young, single men who say they value love over anything else? My guess is they're predominantly members of this new breed called metrosexuals: men in touch with their so-called feminine side who would rather "grow old with the woman they love," even if they haven't met her yet, than "head up a Fortune 500 company." This might be endearing and romantic, but it's not very productive. It doesn't make scientific and medical advances, it doesn't help develop solid foreign policy and it doesn't contribute to the gross national product.

10   So what is the motivation behind this metrosexual trend? A number of close male friends have told me that any secondary reasons for a straight man's behavior are completely overshadowed by their central motivation: to attract women. Men, they tell me, acquire money, status and distinguished job titles to impress and win the ladies, whether in droves or in terms of "till death do us part." They hear women describe the perfect man as being sensitive, sweet and romantic and aspire to that description.

11   But frank, open confessions of emotions on the first date? Poorly written poetry and a closet full of shoes? Plot-line knowledge of "The Bold and the Beautiful"? This just seems like way too much work to get a woman's attention, especially if the man is, indeed, looking to grow old with her. That's a long time to keep up the act. And while the theory that men are changing their images and priorities for love seems terribly flattering to us women, I find it hard to believe.

12   I'd hate to think that this is all the result of marketing and advertising pressure.

13   We all recognize the influence these methods have on people, both individually and en masse. That's why propaganda is an essential part of every war. That's why anorexia and bulimia were, and still are, such a problem in young girls. It is interesting to note that the term "metrosexual" was actually coined a few years ago by a writer in a satirical comment on "consumerism's toll on traditional masculinity." Marketers, like sharks in a feeding frenzy, grabbed on to the term and are currently masticating their way through the attached school of consumers who are willing to pay $150 for a pair of jeans. But even if this explains how a man can rationalize spending $75 on moisturizing cream, it still doesn't explain the mind-set that goes with it.

14   The metrosexual movement can't just be about love. Commercialism also can't be held solely responsible. And it's not just a heightened appreciation of the finer things in life.

15   These are all aspects of what drives this type of man, just as it motivates the women who consider shopping to be a form of therapy, who fall in love every other week, who live vicariously through the characters on TV. We all do this to some extent. But there's something more to it.

16   Perhaps this metrosexual trend indicates how far removed we've become from the real world.

17   Concrete cause-and-effect is becoming more and more disconnected from the lives of those of us fortunate enough to have the resources to be extravagant. Impracticality has become an indicator of progress. Money can provide every creature comfort, without requiring any skill or knowledge except that which earned the money in the first place. A man with money doesn't need to know how to install a water heater. He doesn't need to know his way around a sawhorse; he can pay someone else to build his cabinets.

18   Maybe the lack of a visible connection between hard work and the fruits of labor means that satisfaction in a job well done is much more elusive today than it used to be. And maybe, if fulfillment isn't being found in work, we end up looking to relationships to provide this sense of satisfaction and contentedness. But while I enjoy being in love as much as the next person, perhaps we shouldn't force its existence simply because we feel disconnected and adrift. It almost seems as if love and money and status are all just flimsy stand-ins for something more.

19   The emergence of metrosexuals, prevalent enough both to warrant a label and provoke discussion, indicates that something has been missing in the lives of these men. I just hope they find what they're looking for. ■

CHAPTER 20

Globalization: Importing and Exporting America

America's Place in the World

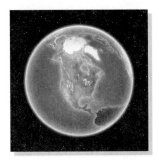

The place of America and Americans in relation to the rest of the world has always been an important topic in the national conversation, for the United States as a nation of immigrants has taken an increasing role in international affairs since its founding. But that topic has only grown more important, it seems, since the end of the Cold War (which seemed to leave the United States as the world's only superpower); since the development of economic reforms in China, in the European Union, and other parts of the world (which are challenging the primacy of American economic power); and especially since the events of September 11 and the subsequent war in Iraq (which have underscored the limits of the American military and compromised our will to work cooperatively with traditional allies). Indeed, according to a survey released on August 18, 2004, by the Pew Research Center for the People and the Press, the American public has a divided, even paradoxical opinion about the place of the United States in the world. On the one hand, Americans agree that the United States has assumed a more powerful role as a world leader, but, on the other, they concede that America also seems less respected around the world. Americans reject the role of the United States as a single world leader, but they also reject the pull toward isolation. More generally, then, Americans are confronting the issue of what has come to be known as globalization—that is, the general impact of various nations on each other—and more particularly the impact of American culture on other nations and cultures, and their impact on the United States.

403

"THE BAD NEWS IS OPERATION ANACONDA DEVASTATED OUR FORCES. THE GOOD NEWS IS THE AMERICAN INS APPROVED YOUR VISA."

Source: Henry Payne reprinted by permission of United Feature Syndicate, Inc.

Some of those impacts are economic, as the United States outsources manufacturing jobs to other nations and shifts in the direction of a "service" economy. Some of the impacts are military and political, as leaders and citizens debate the wisdom of various options. (For example, should our nation behave as a kind of "American empire," free to impose its wishes and will on others? Should our foreign policy be an effort to export democracy, even at the point of a gun? Or should we cooperate more broadly with allies, cultivate new friends, and respect the right of each nation to self-determination? Should the United States close off its borders, literally and figuratively, to follow a kind of neo-isolationism?) And some of those impacts are broadly cultural, as Americans import some of the cultural practices and values of others (as in popular songs, films, restaurants, fashions, and so forth) and export our own cultural values and traditions to others. This chapter of *Good Reasons with Contemporary Arguments* offers arguments on one or another aspect of these questions related to globalization.

Contemporary Arguments

The chapter begins with immigration. Just about everyone can quote the famous words that Emma Lazarus wrote for the pedestal of the Statue of Liberty ("Give me your tired, your poor, your huddled masses yearning to breathe free. The wretched refuse of your teeming shore. Send these, the homeless tempest-tost to me") because the United States prides itself on being a nation of immigrants. And recently we have made good on the promise: more than 10 percent of our people, over 30 million in all (and up from 10 million in 1970), were born in other countries. Indeed, according to the 2000 census, one in five U.S. citizens was either born abroad or to foreign-born parents. Steady increases in immigration after World War II developed into a boom during the 1980s and 1990s in part because the 1965 Immigration Act (amended in 1990) looked favorably on the immigration of relatives of U.S. citizens, repealed quotas on immigrants from certain nations,

Statue of Liberty

and therefore encouraged immigration from Asia, Latin America, and Africa. As a result, in 2000 and 2001 over a million people immigrated to the United States. While immigrants in the late nineteenth and early twentieth century mostly came from southern and central Europe, most of today's immigrants come from Mexico, the Caribbean islands, the former Soviet Union, and Asian nations such as China, Vietnam, the Philippines, and India. While those earlier immigrants typically passed by the Statue of Liberty and were processed at Ellis Island before going on to northern cities, more than half of recent immigrants have been attracted to Florida, Texas, and California.

Nevertheless, there has also been a long history of resistance to immigration in the United States, dating at least to those who proudly enrolled in the "Know Nothing" political party of the 1840s and 1850s. Members of that political faction resisted the immigrants from Ireland and Germany who were arriving in waves, and they tended to blame all the nation's ills on immigration—crime, economic problems, social stresses. The questions (and fears) raised by those early critics persist today, except that now they are raised in connection with Asians, Arabs, and Latin Americans. Just what are the social and economic effects of immigration? How quickly and how completely do immigrants become assimilated—learning the majority language, identifying themselves with American cultural values, participating in American political

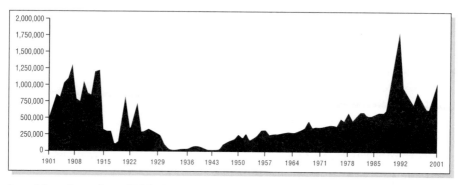

Legal Immigration, 1991–2001

Source: "Legal Immigration, Fiscal Year 2001." Immigration and Naturalization Service, U.S. Department of Justice.

life? What is our national responsibility to support, educate, and help assimilate immigrants? Do immigrants constitute a threat to the nation's economic well-being because they are commonly poor and less educated, because they take jobs away from native workers, and because they require expensive social services—welfare, education, health? Or do immigrants in fact increase the national wealth because they are highly motivated and because they supply labor to a perennially labor-hungry economy? Do immigrants endanger our national democracy because they cling to their original national identities, are slow to learn English, and participate only fitfully in political life—or do immigrants enrich the nation with their values and beliefs, ideas and ideals, hopes and hard work? Do immigrants pose a threat to national security?

Here we reprint two essays about immigration. Patrick J. Buchanan articulates the opposition to immigration in a speech that he delivered in 2000, during his third-party campaign for the presidency. Buchanan is countered by the item that follows his, Richard Rayner's "What Immigration Crisis?" Elsewhere in *Good Reasons*, on pages 164–169, Leslie Marmon Silko writes about im-

Cuban refugees stranded on a makeshift raft float between Key West, Florida, and Cuba, August 24, 1994

IMMIGRATION WEB SITES

You can learn more about immigration and read more arguments about it at a number of places on the World Wide Web. Here are a few:

U.S. Department of Homeland Security, U.S. Citizenship and Immigration Services, administers and enforces U.S. immigration policy. For information check the Office of Immigration Statistics at **<http://uscis.gov/graphics/shared/statistics/index.htm>**

For information about immigration from the U.S. Census Bureau, see **<www.census.gov/main/www/cen2000.html>**

The Cato Institute offers demographic and economic statistics about immigrants: **<www.cato/org/>**

The Alexis de Tocqueville Institution works to increase public understanding of the cultural and economic benefits of immigration: **<www.adti.net>**

The Center for Immigration Studies conducts research on the impact of immigration: **<www.cis.org>**

The Federation for American Immigration Reform (FAIR) lobbies in favor of placing restrictions on immigration: **<www.fairus.org>**

The National Council of La Raza lobbies on behalf of Latinos in the United States: **<www.nclr.org>**

The National Immigration Forum builds public support for immigration: **<www.immigrationforum.org>**

The Immigration History Research Center, based at the University of Minnesota, is a substantial resource on American immigration and ethnic history: **<www.ihrc.umn.edu/index.htm>**

migration from the point of view of immigrants themselves. These three arguments are framed by Emma Lazarus's famous poem that offers her 1883 invitation to immigrants and by a contrary poem, written by Thomas Bailey Aldrich in response to Lazarus, that proposes instead that the gates to immigration should be closed.

Next come arguments that reflect on the impact of globalization on national and ethic identity. James Baldwin's famous essay "Stranger in the Village" remains timely as Americans are pondering what it means to be uniquely American in the face of the emerging "global village." Gregory Rodriguez then argues that the American identity need not undergo fundamental changes even as large numbers of immigrants arrive.

A Time Line on Immigration

1607. First permanent English settlement at Jamestown, Virginia

1607–1776. "Open Door" era: individual colonies encourage immigration, restricting only criminals and "undesirables"

1776–1835. The "First Great Lull" in immigration: immigration numbers are low

1808. Importation of slaves is halted.

1840s. Irish immigration (as a result of famine) initiates an era of mass immigration that lasts until World War I.

1875. Supreme Court decides that immigration policy is the responsibility of the federal government, not the states.

1882–1917. Asian immigration is effectively interdicted. The 1882 Chinese Exclusion Act bars Chinese in particular.

1892. Ellis Island in New York harbor becomes the leading entry point for immigrants.

1890–1920. A wave of immigration from southern and eastern Europe peaks at 1.3 million in 1907.

1921. Quotas are initiated to reduce immigration sharply and to make immigration reflect the established face of the American community (i.e., white and European).

1920–1945. Second "Great Lull" in immigration. More restrictive immigration policies, the effects of the Great Depression, and the Second World War limit the number of immigrants who settle in the United States.

1940s. Restrictions dropped against Asian immigration.

1954. "Operation Wetback" effectively stops illegal immigration.

1965. Immigration and Nationality Act increases immigration quotas, abolishes the principle of taking into account immigrants' national origins, and emphasizes family unification.

1986. Immigration Reform and Control Act provides amnesty for many illegal immigrants.

1990s. Immigration numbers increase substantially—for both legal and illegal immigrants.

Basic sources: Peter Brimelow, *Alien Nation; CQ Researcher*

Finally, we offer a set of essays that make one or another argument about the immigration or emigration of ideas. What are the effects of American culture on global culture, and vice versa? Is American culture dominating world culture so pervasively that local cultures are being lost or irremediably altered? Todd Gitlin contends that the effect of Hollywood on global culture has indeed been profound, while Laura Carlsen, in an essay about Wal-Mart in Mexico, worries about the broader impact of American economic power on the cultures of other nations. On the other hand, what about American importation of cultural forms from other nations, and what about exportations of American culture that are welcomed, even sought out, in other nations? Are those importations and exportations dangerous or enriching? As if in response to Gitlin and Carlsen, Kishore Mahbubani offers a more benign interpretation of the effects of American culture on global culture. And Jeremy Rifkin, in an appropriate ending to the chapter, offers the possibility that American culture may in fact be in its descent in the face of developments in Europe.

To Reunite a Nation

Patrick J. Buchanan (1939–) grew up in Washington, D.C., attended Georgetown University, and received a master's degree in journalism from Columbia. During the 1970s he served as an advisor to Richard Nixon and Gerald Ford, and he was White House Communications Director under Ronald Reagan. He later served as a regular panelist on several national television shows. He made the sharp curtailing of immigration one of the key issues in his bids to secure the Republican Party and Reform Party nominations for the presidency in 1992, 1996, and 2000. Recently he published the incendiary book The Death of the West: How Mass Immigration, Depopulation, and a Dying Faith Are Killing Our Culture and Country. *"To Reunite a Nation" was given as a campaign speech on January 18, 2000, at the Richard Nixon Library in Yorba Linda, California.*

1   Let me begin with a story: In 1979, Deng Xiaoping arrived here on an official visit. China was emerging from the Cultural Revolution, and poised to embark on the capitalist road. When President Carter sat down with Mr. Deng, he told him he was concerned over the right of the Chinese people to emigrate. The Jackson-Vanik Amendment, Mr. Carter said, prohibited granting most favored nation trade status to regimes that did not allow their people to emigrate.

2   "Well, Mr. President," Deng cheerfully replied, "Just how many Chinese do you want? Ten million? Twenty million? Thirty million?" Deng's answer stopped Carter cold. In a few words, the Chinese leader had driven home a point Mr. Carter seemed not to have grasped: Hundreds of millions of people would emigrate to America in a eyelash, far more than we could take in, far more than our existing population of 270 million, if we threw open our borders. And though the U.S. takes in more people than any other nation, it still restricts immigration to about one million a year, with three or four hundred thousand managing to enter every year illegally.

3   There is more to be gleaned from this encounter. Mr. Carter's response was a patriotic, or, if you will, a nationalistic response. Many might even label it xenophobic. The President did not ask whether bringing in ten million Chinese would be good for them. He had suddenly grasped that the real issue was how many would be good for America? Mr. Carter could have asked another question: Which Chinese immigrants would be best for America? It would make a world of difference whether China sent over ten million college graduates or ten million illiterate peasants, would it not?

4   Since the Carter-Deng meeting, America has taken in twenty million immigrants, many from China and Asia, many more from Mexico, Central America and the Caribbean, and a few from Europe. Social scientists now know a great deal about the impact of this immigration.

5   Like all of you, I am awed by the achievements of many recent immigrants. Their contributions to Silicon Valley are extraordinary. The over-representation of Asian-born kids in advanced high school math and science classes is awesome, and, to the extent that it is achieved by a superior work ethic, these kids are setting an example for all of us. The contributions that immigrants make in small businesses and hard work in tough jobs that don't pay well merits our admiration and deepest respect. And many new immigrants show a visible love of this country and an appreciation of freedom that makes you proud to be an American.

6   Northern Virginia, where I live, has experienced a huge and sudden surge in immigration. It has become a better place, in some ways, but nearly unrecognizable in others, and no doubt worse in some realms, a complicated picture overall. But it is clear to anyone living in a state like California or Virginia that the great immigration wave, set in motion by the Immigration Act of 1965, has put an indelible mark upon America.

7   We are no longer a biracial society; we are now a multiracial society. We no longer struggle simply to end the divisions and close the gaps between black and white Americans; we now grapple, often awkwardly, with an unprecedented ethnic diversity. We also see the troubling signs of a national turning away from the idea that we are one people, and the emergence of a radically different idea, that we are separate ethnic nations within a nation.

8   Al Gore caught the change in a revealing malapropism. Mr. Gore translated the national slogan, "E Pluribus Unum," which means "Out of many, one," into "Out of one, many." Behind it, an inadvertent truth: America is Balkanizing as never before.

9   Five years ago, a bipartisan presidential commission, chaired by Barbara Jordan, presented its plans for immigration reform. The commission called for tighter border controls, tougher penalties on businesses that hire illegal aliens, a new system for selecting legal immigrants, and a lowering of the annual number to half a million. President Clinton endorsed the recommendations. But after ethnic groups and corporate lobbies for foreign labor turned up the heat, he backed away.

10   The data that support the Jordan recommendations are more refined today. We have a National Academy of Sciences report on the economic consequences of immigration, a Rand study, and work by Harvard's George Borjas and other scholars. All agree that new immigration to the United States is heavily skewed to admitting the less skilled. Un-

like other industrialized democracies, the U.S. allots the vast majority of its visas on the basis of whether new immigrants are related to recent immigrants, rather than whether they have the skills or education America needs. This is why it is so difficult for Western and Eastern Europeans to come here, while almost entire villages from El Salvador have come in.

11   Major consequences flow from having an immigration stream that ignores education or skills. Immigrants are now more likely than native-born Americans to lack a high school education. More than a quarter of our immigrant population receives some kind of welfare, compared to fifteen percent of native-born. Before the 1965 bill, immigrants were less likely to receive welfare. In states with many immigrants, the fiscal impact is dramatic. The National Academy of Sciences contends that immigration has raised the annual taxes of each native household in California by $1,200 a year. But the real burden is felt by native-born workers, for whom mass immigration means stagnant or falling wages, especially for America's least skilled.

12   There are countervailing advantages. Businesses can hire new immigrants at lower pay; and consumers gain because reduced labor costs produce cheaper goods and services. But, generally speaking, the gains from high immigration go to those who use the services provided by new immigrants.

13   If you are likely to employ a gardener or housekeeper, you may be financially better off. If you work as a gardener or housekeeper, or at a factory job in which unskilled immigrants are rapidly joining the labor force, you lose. The last twenty years of immigration have thus brought about a redistribution of wealth in America, from less-skilled workers and toward employers. Mr. Borjas estimates that one half of the relative fall in the wages of high school graduates since the 1980s can be traced directly to mass immigration.

14   At some point, this kind of wealth redistribution, from the less well off to the affluent, becomes malignant. In the 1950s and '60s, Americans with low reading and math scores could aspire to and achieve the American dream of a middle class lifestyle. That is less realistic today. Americans today who do poorly in high school are increasingly condemned to a low-wage existence; and mass immigration is a major reason why.

15   There is another drawback to mass immigration: a delay in the assimilation of immigrants that can deepen our racial and ethnic divisions. As in Al Gore's "Out of one, many."

16   Concerns of this sort are even older than the Republic itself. In 1751, Ben Franklin asked: "Why should Pennsylvania, founded by the English, become a Colony of Aliens, who will shortly be so numerous as to Germanize us instead of our Anglifying them?" Franklin would

never find out if his fears were justified. German immigration was halted by the Seven Years War; then slowed by the Great Lull in immigration that followed the American Revolution. A century and half later, during what is called the Great Wave, the same worries were in the air.

17   In 1915 Theodore Roosevelt told the Knights of Columbus: "There is no room in this country for hyphenated Americanism . . . . The one absolutely certain way of bringing this nation to ruin, of preventing all possibility of its continuing to be a nation at all, would be to permit it to become a tangle of squabbling nationalities." Congress soon responded by enacting an immigration law that brought about a virtual forty-year pause to digest, assimilate, and Americanize the diverse immigrant wave that had rolled in between 1890 and 1920.

18   Today, once again, it is impossible not to notice the conflicts generated by a new "hyphenated Americanism." In Los Angeles, two years ago there was an anguishing afternoon in the Coliseum where the U.S. soccer team was playing Mexico. The Mexican-American crowd showered the U.S. team with water bombs, beer bottles and trash. The "Star Spangled Banner" was hooted and jeered. A small contingent of fans of the American team had garbage hurled at them. The American players later said that they were better received in Mexico City than in their own country.

19   Last summer, El Cenizo, a small town in south Texas, adopted Spanish as its official language. All town documents are now to be written, and all town business conducted, in Spanish. Any official who cooperates with U.S. immigration authorities was warned he or she would be fired. To this day, Governor Bush is reluctant to speak out on this de facto secession of a tiny Texas town to Mexico.

20   Voting in referendums that play a growing part in the politics of California is now breaking down sharply on ethnic lines. Hispanic voters opposed Proposition 187 to cut off welfare to illegal aliens, and they rallied against it under Mexican flags. They voted heavily in favor of quotas and ethnic preferences in the 1996 California Civil Rights Initiative, and, again, to keep bilingual education in 1998. These votes suggest that in the California of the future, when Mexican-American voting power catches up with Mexican-American population, any bid to end racial quotas by referendum will fail. A majority of the state's most populous immigrant group now appears to favor set-asides and separate language programs, rather than to be assimilated into the American mainstream.

21   The list of troubling signs can be extended. One may see them in the Wen Ho Lee nuclear secrets case, as many Chinese-Americans immediately concluded the United States was prosecuting Mr. Lee for racist reasons.

22   Regrettably, a cultural Marxism called political correctness is taking root that makes it impossible to discuss immigration in any but the most

glowing terms. In New York City billboards that made the simple point that immigration increases crowding and that polls show most Americans want immigration rates reduced were forced down under circumstances that came very close to government-sponsored censorship. The land of the free is becoming intolerant of some kinds of political dissent.

23 Sociologist William Frey had documented an out-migration of black and white Americans from California, some of them seeking better labor market conditions, others in search of a society like the one they grew up in. In California and other high immigration states, one also sees the rise of gated communities where the rich close themselves off from the society their own policies produce.

24 I don't want to overstate the negatives. But in too many cases the American melting pot has been reduced to a simmer. At present rates, mass immigration reinforces ethnic subcultures, reduces the incentives of newcomers to learn English and extends the life of linguistic ghettos that might otherwise be melded into the great American mainstream. If we want to assimilate new immigrants—and we have no choice if we are to remain one nation—we must slow down the pace of immigration.

25 Whatever its shortcomings, the United States has done far better at alleviating poverty than most countries. But an America that begins to think of itself as made up of disparate peoples will find social progress far more difficult. It is far easier to look the other way when the person who needs help does not speak the same language, or share a common culture or common history.

26 Americans who feel it natural and right that their taxes support the generation that fought World War ll—will they feel the same way about those from Fukien Province or Zanzibar? If America continues on its present course, it could rapidly become a country with no common language, no common culture, no common memory and no common identity. And that country will find itself very short of the social cohesion that makes compassion possible.

27 None of us are true universalists: we feel responsibility for others because we share with them common bonds—common history and a common fate. When these are gone, this country will be a far harsher place.

28 That is why I am proposing immigration reform to make it possible to fully assimilate the thirty million immigrants who have arrived in the last thirty years. As president, I will ask Congress to reduce new entry visas to 300,000 a year, which is enough to admit immediate family members of new citizens, with plenty of room for many thousands with the special talents or skills our society needs. If after several years, it becomes plain that the United States needs more immigrants because of labor shortages, it should implement a point system similar to that of Canada and Australia, and allocate visas on a scale which takes into

account education, knowledge of English, job skills, age, and relatives in the United States.

29   I will also make the control of illegal immigration a national priority. Recent reports of thousands of illegals streaming across the border into Arizona, and the sinister and cruel methods used to smuggle people by ship into the United States, demand that we regain control of our borders. For a country that cannot control its borders isn't fully sovereign; indeed, it is not even a country anymore.

30   Without these reforms, America will begin a rapid drift into uncharted waters. We shall become a country with a dying culture and deepening divisions along the lines of race, class, income and language. We shall lose for our children and for the children of the thirty million who have come here since 1970 the last best hope of earth. We will betray them all—by denying them the great and good country we were privileged to grow in. We just can't do that.

31   With immigration at the reduced rate I recommend, America will still be a nation of immigrants. We will still have the benefit of a large, steady stream of people from all over the world whose life dream is to be like us—Americans. But, with this reform, America will become again a country engaged in the mighty work of assimilation, of shaping new Americans, a proud land where newcomers give up their hyphens, the great American melting pot does its work again, and scores of thousands of immigrant families annually ascend from poverty into the bosom of Middle America to live the American dream. ■

RICHARD RAYNER

What Immigration Crisis?

Richard Rayner, a writer born in England but now living in Los Angeles, contributed the following essay to the New York Times Magazine *on January 7, 1996.*

1   Maria T. bites her nails. At 31, with five children, she's one of the 1.7 million immigrants now estimated to be living in California illegally. She speaks almost no English, even though she has been in America for more than eight years. In her clean and sparsely furnished living room, her kids—Gustavo (11), Mario (7), Maribel (6), Cesar (5) and Joan (4)—are in front of the TV, laughing first at "Home Improvement," then at "The Simpsons."

2   The refrigerator is almost empty; it contains only a gallon of milk, some Kool-Aid, a few tortillas. Her life is frugal, a devotion to the future

of her children. Though there are three bedrooms in the apartment, all five sleep with her because she hates to let them out of her sight. Since she has no car and can rarely afford the bus, the family walks everywhere, Maria leading the way like Mother Goose with the kids behind toting Batman and Pocahontas backpacks. On a typical day she walks six miles, shuttling between her apartment and the local school in Van Nuys.

3   In Guadalajara her husband was a thief, a drug addict, a small-time street hustler who with friends jumped some guy and, during the robbery, knocked out his teeth. The man's friends came looking for him with a machete. They chopped off his hands. One was beyond repair, but doctors were able to sew back the other. He also sustained injuries to the head and neck. His brain was damaged, Maria says, and he began to abuse and beat her.

4   For her, as for so many, the decision to make the journey to El Norte was the beginning of an epic. Gustavo was 3 at the time, Mario was 8 months, and she was 5 months pregnant with Maribel. Maria crossed the border with the help of a "coyote," a guide, but when she arrived in San Diego the woman who'd paid for her brothers' crossings didn't have any money this time. Maria was kept a slave in the coyote's house. He beat and raped her until, after three months, her brother raised $300, half the sum agreed for the crossing, and the coyote let her go.

5   She stayed with her brother in Los Angeles, the Pico-Union district, and it was here that Maribel was born. "I'd come out of labor and I was staring at the wall and I said to my sister-in-law. 'Look, she's there.' She said, 'Who?' I said, 'The Virgin Mary.' She said: 'There's nothing there. You're crazy.' But it was true all the same. For eight months the Virgin would appear to me. She made me strong.

6   "At first I had to beg for food. Sometimes I did day work for Latinos, for $10 a day. I'd take off into the city on the bus, not really knowing where I was going, and get off to beg on the streets. I'm ashamed of that."

7   Slowly, she clawed her way up. It is in so many ways a classic immigrant's tale, although she has been the beneficiary not just of her own drive, but also of something equally important—welfare. She's here illegally, with fake ID, and she doesn't work. She receives $723 in cash and $226 in food stamps, and Section 8 takes care of more than two-thirds of her $1,000 rent (high, because landlords know illegals won't complain).

8   It's a myth, however, that anyone can come over the border and start milking the system. Only Medicaid and limited food benefits are available to illegal immigrants, and most don't apply for these because they fear detection by the Immigration and Naturalization Service. Maria T. gets what she does because of those of her children who were born here.

9   Local, state and federal governments spend about $11.8 billion a year educating legal and illegal immigrant children, according to the

Urban Institute, a nonpartisan research organization, compared with the $227 billion spent to educate all children. Generally, this is more than offset by the taxes that legal and illegal immigrant families pay— $70.3 billion a year, the Urban Institute says—while receiving $42.9 billion in total services. Illegal immigrants pay $7 billion in taxes.

10   Maria T., however, represents the nightmare scenario—an illegal immigrant who's sucking money from the system and putting nothing back. Even so, it's not clear that she's a villain. She hopes one day to go to work herself. She hopes and believes that her bright children will become outstanding. She believes in America, as the man said at the beginning of *The Godfather,* though it's the government that is helping her out, not Marlon Brando.

11   My wife, from Finland, has a green card; I'm English, in the process of applying for one myself; our son was born an American. When we moved into our house in Venice, California, one of our neighbors, an elderly white woman with whom we're now very friendly, said, "No Americans live on our block anymore."

12   Maybe she had the jitters about new neighbors, or maybe there was something else at play. I knew that her father had been born in Germany and had journeyed to Detroit, where she was born. I wanted to say that logically, therefore, our son is every bit as American as she is. But in any debate about nationality, I know, logic fades fast.

13   My own father once traced our family tree back to 1066, when one Baron de Rainier sailed from Normandy to help conquer England. Since then, give or take the occasional Irish excursion, my progenitors were all born within a hundred or so miles of one another in the north of England. So, when I came to America and found that nearly everyone was from somewhere else if they stepped back a generation or two, I found myself thrilled and oddly at ease. It explained America's drive, its generosity and up-for-anything energy. As Melville wrote, "We are not a nation, so much as a world."

14   Not everyone sees things this way. Many have drawn a line behind which they stand, *true* Americans, fearful and angry about the erosion of their identity. With unintended irony they talk of themselves as "natives." On immigration, they argue that enough is enough, that the borders must be secured and a drastic cutback enforced. Those who are allowed in, they say, must be professionals or skilled workers because the others—mobs of unskilled, third-world peasants—drain resources and take jobs. They cost billions and dilute the gene pool. They are mutating the face of America.

15   California itself, for instance, passed an anti-immigrant measure with scary ease. In last year's state election nearly 60 percent voted for Proposition 187, the so-called Save-Our-State initiative, which sought to deny public education, nonemergency health care and welfare to illegal

immigrants. By linking illegal immigration to joblessness and crime, Pete Wilson revived his flagging gubernatorial campaign and was swept back into office, even though, as an exit poll showed, few who voted for 187 actually thought it was going to work.

16 Wilson was avid for votes and a reaction and he got both. Many legal Latinos, fearful of deportation, refused to go near schools and emergency rooms. There was immigrant bashing and hate mail. Since the Republicans took control of the United States House and Senate, moreover, it seems as though all Washington has been grandstanding on the issue. Dozens of immigration-related bills were introduced last term, including two major vehicles, one from Senator Alan Simpson of Wyoming and the other from Representative Lamar Smith of Texas. At some point, the two bills could be rolled into one. Simpson aims to have the new law in force by October 1996. This is all happening at warp speed.

17 Many of the proposals are mean-spirited and, to a lot of observers, wrongheaded. One would impose a tax on employers who hire *legal* aliens. Others would deny citizenship to children born in this country to illegals, or eliminate some categories of family immigration. The anti-immigration forces have done an excellent job of creating an atmosphere of crisis in which the debate has focused on *how* to slow the "flood" of immigration, legal and illegal. But illegal immigration should not be folded over to scapegoat legals as well. The real point is that there isn't any immigration crisis.

18 Solving the problems we do have will require more than hastily drawn legislation. Demetrios Papademetriou, an immigration expert with the Carnegie Endowment for International Peace, says: "Polls tell us that Americans are worried about illegal immigration. Good. Let's take care of it. Polls say people think some employers are too unscrupulous with immigrants. Let's take care of that, too. But this requires patience and wisdom. Congress has neither at this time."

19 "The perception is that immigration is out of control," says Joel Kotkin, author of *Tribes* and a fellow at the Pepperdine University Institute of Public Policy. "It isn't. If you say to most Americans, 'We have 800,000 legal immigrants a year; they're going to reply. 'Hey, that's not so bad.' And this is the truth of the situation. But it's somehow been demonized so that people think there are millions coming across the border."

20 The Border Patrol logged 1,094,718 apprehensions in 1994. On page 26 of his *Alien Nation,* a leading restrictionist, Peter Brimelow, writes that legal immigration is "overwhelmed by an estimated 2 to 3 million illegal entries into the country in every recent year." He goes on to note, correctly, that many of these illegal entrants go back home, and that some trundle to and fro across the border every day. By page 33,

however, he's writing "a remarkable two to three million illegal immigrants may have succeeded in entering the country in 1993."

21   Within seven pages illegal entrants have mysteriously become illegal immigrants, attached to that hyperbolic 2 to 3 million, a figure vigorously disputed by I.N.S., which regards as preposterous the idea that for every border crosser caught another three get away. Indeed, throughout the 1970s there were some 8 million border apprehensions and during that time, according to the best estimates of I.N.S., about 1 million illegals came to reside—eight apprehensions per illegal immigrant.

22   So how many illegals are coming in and staying each year now? The Urban Institute says 250,000 to 300,000. The Center for Immigration Studies, a conservative research group, says 400,000, while I.N.S. says 300,000. The Census Bureau until recently guessed 200,000 to 400,000; now it agrees with the I.N.S.

23   The 300,000 figure is considered firm because it was based on the years following 1988, when the I.N.S. started to process the genuinely reliable data it amassed following the 1986 amnesty for illegals. Too much of this and the eyes glaze over, but the gist is, the further you get from 1988, the flakier the statistics become. And the argument over the number of illegal immigrants is nothing compared with the furor over how much they cost.

24   The fact is, no one knows for sure; there is simply no up-to-date research. "The issue has caught political fire," Papademetriou says. "But serious academics haven't got out into the field yet. They're reluctant to play into the hands of the politicians."

EMMA LAZARUS

The New Colossus

Emma Lazarus (1849–1887) wrote poetry and essays on a wide variety of topics that were published in the best known magazines of her time, and she became an influential figure in the rapidly changing New York art scene. She was born into a well-established Jewish family in New York City, was well educated, and worked to improve the conditions of Jews both at home and abroad by establishing programs to educate new immigrants and by founding the Society for the Improvement and Colonization of Eastern European Jews. Her most famous sonnet, reprinted here, was written in 1883 to help raise money for the Statue of Liberty Pedestal, and in 1901 was engraved on a tablet within the pedestal on which the Statue of Liberty now stands.

25   Immigration is in the spotlight not because of money but because it so impinges on issues like race, the role of government, national identity, and change. Name an issue and you can hook it to immigration. One side looks at crime, failing schools, and soaring welfare spending, and sees too many immigrants. The other sees America, the greatest nation on earth, built on the backs of immigrants and still benefiting enormously from the brains, energy, and determination (not to speak of low wages) of the next generation of newcomers. Right now the debate is more emotional than informed. It's all temper tantrums and red-hot sound bites.

26   When people complain about immigration, about the alien "flood," it's Latin Americans they mean, who from their entry points in California and Miami are fanning out through the country. There's concern about the small minority who are criminals, and the seeming reluctance of these people to learn English. Mixed in with this is the prejudice summarized by D. H. Lawrence in "Mornings in Mexico." They are other, he concluded, they are dirty, I don't trust them and they stink. There's also the suggestion that Latinos are lazy, though everywhere you look in Los Angeles you see evidence to the contrary.

27   Until recently the rough understanding was that, though you may have arrived illegally, if you manage to stay you get legal. There's desire to thwart that now, and an unanticipated effect of Proposition 187 was a record surge in citizenship applications. The Los Angeles district alone receives about 25,000 a month. This scramble for certainty of status prompted the I.N.S. to process 90,000 applications in 1994 and 125,000 in 1995, with 250,000 projected for 1996.

> Not like the brazen giant of Greek fame,
> With conquering limbs astride from land to land;
> Here at our sea-washed, sunset gates shall stand
> A mighty woman with a torch, whose flame
> 5 Is the imprisoned lightning, and her name
> Mother of Exiles. From her beacon-hand
> Glows world-wide welcome; her mild eyes command
> The air-bridged harbor that twin cities frame.
> "Keep ancient lands, your storied pomp!" cries she
> 10 With silent lips. "Give me your tired, your poor,
> Your huddled masses yearning to breathe free,
> The wretched refuse of your teeming shore.
> Send these, the homeless, tempest-tost to me,
> I lift my lamp beside the golden door!" ∎

28   On a hot September morning I visit the basement of the Federal Building on Los Angeles Street to sit in on preliminary interviews. Applicants must show that they have been law-abiding, tax-paying residents for at least seven years. They must be able to read, write, and speak English, and correctly answer a substantial proportion of a questionnaire about current affairs, history, and constitutional principles. In a little booth an I.N.S. interviewer asks Maria Elena Ortiz, a Mexican-born resident for 17 years, who the mayor of Los Angeles is.

29   She doesn't know.

"What is the highest law of the land?"

"The Ten Amendments." she says.

"What is the capital of the United States?"

"Sacramento."

"No," says the interviewer. "The capital of the *United* States."

She's unsure.

"Where does Bill Clinton live?"

"Washington, D.C.?" she answers. Still doubtful.

30   The next day, at the downtown convention center, 3,500 applicants who have successfully negotiated this interview and all the other I.N.S. hurdles attend a ceremony to become citizens. It's a feel-good affair, serious business mixed with Super Bowl hoopla and a celebration of the immigration myth. A guy from I.N.S. in a crisp and collarless white shirt stands up to sing "The Star Spangled Banner." An MTV-style video shows a farmer in the Kansas wheat fields, the Dallas Cowboys, a squadron of F-16's booming out above the Rockies. Federal Judge

THOMAS BAILEY ALDRICH

The Unguarded Gates

Thomas Bailey Aldrich (1836–1907) provides a poetic argument from the same time period as Emma Lazarus (his poem was published in 1895— two years after hers), but with a more guarded viewpoint. He was a prominent and prolific New England writer; originally from Portsmouth, New Hampshire, his 1883 book An Old Town by the Sea *was an important regional book. Aldrich's 1870 novel* Story of a Bad Boy *served as one inspiration for Mark Twain's* Tom Sawyer.

Wide open and unguarded stand our gates.
And through them press a wild, a motley throng—
Men from the Volga and the Tartar steppes,
Featureless figures of the Hoang Ho,
5 Malayan, Seythian, Teuton, Kelt, and Slav,

Dickran Tevrizian talks of the courage it takes to leave one's birthplace and fulfill one's dreams. "We Americans by birth can learn from you Americans by choice," he says. He then requests that these particular new citizens not go out and do graffiti. When the judge finishes, 3,500 fists, 40 percent of them Mexican until just a few moments before, raise high the Stars and Stripes and wave.

31   Maria T. takes me to meet some friends who live in the poor, densely populated, northeast section of the San Fernando Valley. I'm standing on the sidewalk when a skinny white guy comes up, offering a Makita power drill still in its box, for $20. The street is filled with drug dealers.

32   Behind a locked gate, the building's 32 apartments are cramped around a tiny concrete courtyard where all the young kids play. Two of the kids, maybe four or five years old, get excited when they hear the tinny music of an ice-cream truck and rush out toward the street. Beyond the gate it's gangsters and rap, urban America; inside you could be in Mexico.

33   Agustin C. and Maria V. have four children: Vanessa, Antonio, Alejandro and Catalina. Vanessa, the oldest, seven, is Maria's child by a previous relationship; all were born here. Agustin has a genuine green card valid until 2004, while Maria is here illegally. Her first fake green card, which cost $50, almost got her caught. The second was a much better buy at $150. She shows it to me proudly. "I've already got four jobs with this one."

> Flying the Old World's poverty and scorn;
> These bringing with them unknown gods and rites,
> Those tiger passions, here to stretch their claws.
> In street and alley what strange tongues are these.
> 10 Accents of menace alien to our air,
> Voices that once the tower of Babel knew!
> O, Liberty, white goddess, is it well
> To leave the gate unguarded? On thy breast
> Fold sorrow's children, soothe the hurts of fate,
> 15 Lift the downtrodden, but with the hand of steel
> Stay those who to thy sacred portals come
> To waste the fight of freedom. Have a care
> Lest from thy brow the clustered stars be torn
> And trampled in the dust. For so of old
> 20 The thronging Goth and Vandal trampled Rome,
> And where the temples of the Caesars stood
> The lean wolf unmolested made her lair. ■

34   They pay $600 a month for a ground-floor apartment with two bed-rooms, one bath and a small living room with kitchen attached. The TV is tuned, as always, to Channel 32, a Spanish-language station. The brown shag carpet is littered with crayons, empty soda cans and broken tortilla chips. Two fans—one on the floor, the other above the dining table—stir the stagnant air, while flies circle an open trash bin in the center of the room. A cockroach skitters down the wall.

35   "I came to America to work," says Agustin. "Before, I knew only what I was told, that it was easy to earn money. They said you could sweep dollars up from the streets like leaves."

36   With sly humor, Maria says: "And now it's true, he does—in a way. He's a gardener."

37   Agustin's smile shows a shattered top jaw, front teeth victims of a soccer game. He works for a landscape company that tends the lawns, sprinklers and hedges of corporate office buildings throughout the val-ley. He gets up at 6 in the morning and often doesn't return until 7 at night. For this he receives $300 a week, though his boss has just agreed to a raise to $350. His ultimate goal is citizenship for both him and Maria, though he says, "I'm proud to be Mexican."

38   He came to America in 1986, at age 20. By then he'd worked con-struction all over Mexico and had unloaded fish at Vera Cruz. He was already married, with two children, when—he's reluctant to admit—he discovered that his wife was cheating on him. His mother-in-law, who now looks after those two children, helped him with money for the journey.

39   Agustin is a hustler, an adventurous survivor. His grandfather died at 132, he says. When I express skepticism he springs out of his chair and hurries into the bedroom, returning with a cheap nylon gym bag, which, he says, contains his grandfather's birth certificate. Root-ing around inside, however, he can't find it. Instead, with pride he shows me the stub of the first paycheck he received in America; it's for $105.26, for a forty-hour week. He goes on pulling more and more stuff out of the bag. He has kept not just that first check stub, but every other one since. The bag holds nothing less than the history of his life here—letters and postcards from back home, copies of his tax returns and dealings with I.N.S. and the various fake ID's he used be-fore getting his legal green card. He did all the paperwork himself. He has friends who used lawyers, he says, but they ended up getting cheated.

40   I recall a visit to Room 1001 of the downtown Federal building to pick up my work permit and "advanced parole status" (preliminary green card approval). Room 1001 proved not to be a room at all but a huge induction and inquiry area in which 1,500 people stood in line or waited for their names to be called. More stood outside, around half the

block, trying to get in. The crowd was almost entirely Asian, Middle Eastern, and Hispanic. I spotted only two other whites, one an English hairdresser protesting so loudly at the indignity of being made to wait at all that I moved away and sat next to a middle-aged Mexican with a mustache and a cowboy hat who told me he'd been coming here five years now for his green card.

41 Five years! My heart plunged, but my expensive and very efficient Century City lawyer had provided an immigration specialist, a "facilitator" as he called himself, to walk me through. When, after an hour or so, a list of names mysteriously boomed out over a loudspeaker, mine was at the top. The fellow who had been in the mill all this time shrugged and smiled. It seemed like a miracle, although I knew this was exactly what it was not. Wheels had been oiled, though on this occasion, staring at all those faces dazed with boredom, I felt no guilt, merely gratitude. I waltzed out five minutes later bearing the employment card that made me legal.

42 Agustin doesn't resent his own difficulties. Whites have treated him pretty well, he says. He has no complaints. His mistrust and dislike are reserved for blacks, whom he believes are given all the breaks. "There's a system. You have to learn how to exist within the system."

43 He first heard about Proposition 187 when he came home one night, showered and turned on the TV. "I wasn't comfortable with it. Maria could be deported, with our kids, and it would totally destroy my family. Sure, there are cases of abuse. But nearly all of us want to work. Here in California they hire us happily for low wages. Then they throw immigration at us if we ask for more. I think they're scared that we might become them. We're the people that made California. We built it."

44 By the Treaty of Guadalupe Hidalgo in 1848, Mexico ceded California to the United States. It was just at this time that gold was discovered and lotus-land took on a new importance. Mexicans feel to this day that they were cheated; and that in coming to California they are asserting a historical right; with each payday and welfare check they claim revenge. "It's a scar, not a border," notes the Mexican writer Carlos Fuentes.

45 Sucking at his broken teeth, Agustin says, "Mexico is overshadowed by the U.S., which tends to use smaller countries for its own benefit. Americans buy our oil cheap, refine it and sell it for less. They exploit us and then they get upset when we come here." He goes quiet, and wipes his hands. He seems a little embarrassed. He says sadly. "I agree that the immigration problem is overwhelming."

46 It's true that illegal immigrants put a tremendous burden on the health and education systems. The Los Angeles Unified School District creaks under their influx. Vanessa, a fearless girl with an attention span as long as a rock video, attends a Van Nuys elementary school. She is

taken there each morning and collected each afternoon in a van by "the driver," as he's known in the neighborhood, to whom Maria and other mothers pay $12 a week. Ten years ago there were 750 pupils at the school. Now there are 1,550, and nearly 400 more are bused out. More than 85 percent are Hispanic, most from families like that of Agustin and Maria, for whom getting the kids dressed and out to school is sometimes too much. The school, accordingly, has a high rate of nonattendance and transiency. There's a constant influx of new students throughout the school year.

47   Vanessa's teacher is a chunky young guy with a mustache and a powerful, square jaw. He was born in Los Angeles to Mexican parents with little education. "A lot of people who come to El Norte, they think all their problems disappear," he says. "They know they'll get more money. But the hurricane of getting a job, paying the bills—that soon takes over, and they don't look after their kids' education. I know these people work so hard. But a child can fall behind and behind and behind and then that's it, they're lost."

48   Vanessa, in danger of this, might be sent to special ed. "Maybe she'll make it out," her teacher says. "But most likely she'll marry at a very young age, have kids and depend on the government, welfare."

49   One of the immigrant's implied bargains is this: I'll do your bad jobs for not much money, but you must educate my children. In return, the welcoming country expects that the immigrant and his or her family learn the national language. I remember that in Agustin and Maria's apartment the only reading material of any kind is *Bride's* magazine, from which Maria plots her wedding to Agustin next year. But then I also remember that Agustin and Maria work so hard they haven't time for much else. They're intimidated by the education system, perhaps even by books themselves.

50   Meanwhile, Vanessa, black-haired and beautiful, shoots up her hand to answer all the questions. She's eager, overeager, perhaps because I'm there with the photographer, and gets most of them wrong. Her T-shirt says, 'When I Grow Up I Want to Be a Movie Star."

51   By now I think I'm getting to know this family pretty well. I'm doing that writer's thing of congratulating myself on having got out there and actually *met* people. Then one morning out of the blue Maria says: "The other family who live here just had a baby the night before last. They came back from hospital today."

52   I say, "The *other* family?"

53   She gestures back toward the corridor that leads to the bedroom from which Agustin had produced his gym bag, to a shut door behind which I'd supposed the kids slept.

54   Another family lives in there? A whole family?

55   She nods.

56   I'm fascinated. It's not just that I've been naïve. Something has been revealed, one more barrier of mistrust cleared away. Of course, there must be others. And then there's something else: levels of hierarchy don't stop with immigrant and nonimmigrant, legal and illegal. Agustin and Maria have tenants who, it turns out, pay $250 a month for the smaller of the apartment's two bedrooms and use of the bathroom and kitchen. The arrangement doesn't seem to work. Maria is wishing they'd leave so she could bring in one of her sisters who has twin baby girls. Then her sister could baby-sit for her while she worked 13-hour night shifts at a local print shop, a job she had done before and to which she's been asked back.

57   In due course the young couple appear, Ruben and Lena, carrying their new baby in a car seat. Next day, at a wedding party for Maria's sister, Ruben explains that he, like Agustin, was born in a pueblo in the state of Hidalgo and came across when he was 15.

58   Now he's a dayworker, one of the many thousands in Los Angeles who stand on corners waiting to be hired. He takes a 90-minute bus ride each morning to the far southwest side of the valley, because that's where the white people are. "They pay better," he says. "And are less likely to cheat you."

59   At 7:30 in the morning, he stands on a street corner beneath a Bank of America sign that towers above the parking lot of the 7-Eleven. He spoons noodles into his mouth as a flatbed truck pulls in with two workers already in the back. The driver buys a Snapple and the truck heads out again and up into Topanga Canyon. "There's a lot of construction up there," says Ruben. "Many rich people. But they use legal workers. Those guys will get $20 an hour. I'm looking to get $7, $8 an hour." Sometimes, however, he has to take $4.

60   What *patrons* are doing is against the law as well. Negotiations happen in a blink, before the 7-Eleven security guard has a chance to jot down the license of the car, which he passes on to his boss, who'll give it to the police—at least that's the threat. It's a hustling scene. By 8 A.M. there are perhaps a hundred workers, grouped in various spots around the block. The security guard has been instructed to let them stay because, of course, they spend money at the 7-Eleven.

61   Historically, immigration has been tolerated, even encouraged during labor shortages. Labor migration has been going on for centuries and it's hard to see how 300,000 or so illegal immigrants per year will make or break the American economy. Indeed, in Los Angeles they're most likely an asset. The number of illegals in California is thought to be growing by 125,000 a year—hardly an economic catastrophe in a state of 31 million. In Los Angeles, where 80,000 jobs were created last year, it's a definite plus. The city has a thirst for people who will work for $5 or even $3 an hour.

62   The legal Chinese immigrants who have revitalized the San Gabriel Valley, the Latinos who are opening businesses in depressed areas of South Los Angeles, and the Russians and Iranians who are opening businesses all over are the principal reasons the city is so different from say, Detroit. Despite the fires, the earthquake, the riots, the decimation of the defense and aerospace industries, Los Angeles is very much alive. Says Joel Kotkin: "The only place where American society is evolving is where the immigrant influx is strong. Cities would have no future without them. But if you're sitting in Idaho, it looks different."

63   On Saturday Agustin and Maria and all four kids pile into the family car, a 20-year-old beige Datsun with more than 200,000 miles on it, a type of vehicle so common in Los Angeles that it has a name: Border Brothers' Cadillac. Agustin got it from a man he met through work, in exchange for doing the man's garden each Saturday for a month. Today is the fourth and final Saturday.

64   With Maria at the wheel the Datsun heads out onto Sepulveda Boulevard, and a cop car pulls up alongside. Inside the Datsun there's a sudden alarmed flurry because, it turns out, Maria has no California driver's license; if she's caught, therefore, her fake ID would most likely be discovered and she'd be in all sorts of trouble. But the black-and-white makes a left, and she smiles with nervous relief. I ask why she bothers, if every time she gets behind the wheel she risks deportation and the breakup of her family.

65   "I like to drive," she says.

66   I remember that Elton Gallegly, the Republican Representative for Ventura County, has added a provision to Lamar Smith's bill, to the effect that if you're here for 12 months, undocumented, you'll be prohibited from trying to become legal for 10 years. The motto is seek, bar, deport. He's hoping to make it impossible for illegals to stay.

67   "He's hallucinating," Maria says. "Does he think I'm just going to up and leave? Even if I am found and deported I'm going to crawl back here on my stomach if necessary to be with my children. He'll only push us deeper underground."

68   This is stupid, I say. You should get yourself legal: follow the procedures, marry Agustin, become a citizen—it's not that difficult.

69   "I know," she says, and explains how she dislikes governments telling her what to do. She hated it in Mexico as well. Governments are there to be mistrusted and got around, she says, sounding every bit a member of the Michigan militia. "I put more into this society than I get out," she says. "I work. I don't claim welfare, my children are Americans."

70   And so, meanwhile, she likes to drive.

71   We head west to a leafier, more prosperous section of the valley and stop outside a big house with a spanking new silver Lincoln in the

drive. The electronic garage doors open to reveal two more cars, a new BMW and a new Honda Civic, and Agustin steps inside to heft out the tools. He mows the lawns, front and back, adjusts the sprinklers, wields a buzzing trimmer at the edges.

72   The owner of the house, Antoine, a dapper middle-aged man dressed entirely in white, steps out with sodas for the kids and presents each of them with a crisp dollar bill. "Funny, isn't it?" says Antoine. "How something that means nothing to oneself can mean so much to someone else."

73   Los Angeles has more social gradations than a Henry James novel. People are kept separate by language, by geography, and mostly of course by money, a point Antoine has used $4 to make.

74   Antoine's kindly superiority is without thought or effort. He thinks of himself as a weary and saddened man of the world, not as an American, and certainly not as an immigrant. Yet he's of Armenian descent, born in Lebanon, where he worked in the hotel business. When the civil war really got going back in the 1970s, he was twice kidnapped by Muslim groups, and so he left to come here. His 24-year-old son was killed by shelling in Beirut a month ago, about the time the man decided to give Agustin the car. "I think there are too many immigrants," he says. "But Agustin is a nice guy and a hard worker. I like him."

75   Which pinpoints another problem: too many, but a nice guy and a hard worker. Immigration is typically an area where public pronouncement is at odds with private behavior. The whole debate is an onion. You can go on and on peeling back the layers and incongruities. Governor Wilson himself was embarrassed by the unsurprising revelation that he'd once hired an illegal. In California this is neither remarkable nor unusual, considering the available labor pool. Moreover, the distinction between legal and illegal starts getting fuzzy the moment they decide to stay and try to change their status, a process that—even as I.N.S. struggles manfully—often takes years.

76   South of San Diego I ride out with the Border Patrol, which prides itself on being bigger and much more visible these days. Federal money has boosted the number of agents in the San Diego sector to 1,500, compared with 798 in 1991. At a cost of $46 million, "Operation Gatekeeper" has been put into effect, a clampdown designed to squeeze border runners away from traditional crossing areas, like Imperial Beach, where they can easily hop onto a bus or train, and into others farther east where the journey is longer and more arduous.

77   The border was once chaotic and violent. Now it's surreal. The "coyotes" occupy the high ground, warning each other with bird calls when agents approach. A Vietnam-vintage Bell chopper, small enough to get into the canyons, whirls with its searchlight blazing. On a hill overlooking the ocean and a former K.G.B. listening station on the Mexican

side, a truck looms in the night with a huge, humming infrared periscope sticking out the top. Inside, in the eerie light, an agent stares into a screen on which humans are shown as white blobs, referred to as "glows."

78   Leaning against the hood of another truck, staring up at the ugly 10-foot-high steel wall that now snakes along 24 miles of the border, an agent speaks with regret of the wild days not so long ago when they'd come pouring over 1,000 at a time and he'd nab as many as 50 or even a 100 by himself. All the rest would get away. Now it's more of a cat-and-mouse game, he says, moving toward the fence as a figure clambers on top, spots him and then jumps back. "Do you think you could do this all night?"

79   A big friendship park dedicated by Pat Nixon in 1974 is deserted now, its picnic tables crumbling in the shadow of the wall. "It's a battle, it's a war," says Ed Head, night supervisor at the Imperial Beach station. "It's good to feel that we're winning for a change."

80   Coming up on midnight, an agent takes me on a long and bumpy ride, way out east into the San Ysidro Mountains, where we've heard that two or three groups of illegals, with perhaps as many as 15 or 20 in each group, are being chased by Border Patrol agents. In the end, this is what much of the new game comes down to—guys hoofing it after other guys across rough country in the pitch dark. By the time we arrive the bust has already gone down and 38 glows are sitting in the dirt in the glare of truck headlights.

81   Some have covered their eyes. Others have cuts on their hands and faces. Some have hiked for 12 hours up this 3,000-foot mountain wearing sneakers or toeless sandals. Some are from Central America, and have journeyed for months before that. Their dream to come to America must have been very strong. Within 40 minutes they'll be processed and dumped back over the border in Tijuana, where those who are O.T.M. (another Border Patrol usage: Other Than Mexican) will most likely be treated very unsympathetically indeed by a Mexican government that has its own savage ideas about what to do with aliens.

82   There's one young man with bulging brown eyes and mean, kinky hair. A Border Patrol guy says, "Yo, Prince!"

83   The young man's sad expression doesn't change. He says, "Que?"

84   The next day Arthur Ollman, director of San Diego's Museum of Photographic Arts, walks me through "A Nation of Strangers," an exhibit he has spent four years putting together. It documents the history of immigration in America; indeed, it is a moving and beautiful apologia for the same. "The bottom line is that the stuff we're going through today is not unique. We've been there before. We don't have to panic," he says.

85   One anti-immigration poster, circa 1850, says: "Native Americans! Arouse!" There have been immigrant floods before, at times of economic difficulty, and much the same fears concerning assimilation. Be-

neath a recent photograph by Don Bartletti of a beefy bleached blonde holding a placard that says, "Control Immigration or Lose America," I read the following quoted from a 1994 *Utne Reader*. "The rate of immigration relative to the nation's base population is far below historic levels. . . . Moreover the percentage of foreign-born people in the U.S. population has fallen from 8.89 in 1940 to 6.8 today."

86   America's not being overrun after all.

87   "It's true that we're changing to a more international place," says Ollman. "Americans will become more polyglot. The melting-pot metaphor doesn't work anymore. It's a mosaic. But we're not being overrun, and I find it almost offensive this idea that America is no longer strong enough to handle its immigrant influx."

88   I'm reassured.

89   My reactions, that is to say, are predictably liberal. Back home, in Los Angeles, I remind myself how much I like the diversity of the place. And yet we'd just hired a nanny. The only white applicant for the job was a disturbingly energetic 30-something woman with great rifts in her curriculum vitae, a self-confessed graduate of "12 Steps" whose hands were covered in paint and who exclaimed midway through the interview, "And in my spare time I'm a professional clown!"

90   We went the safe route. We hired a 22-year-old legal Mexican immigrant, Christine, who had already worked for three families, came with solid references and has a 2-year-old daughter who is a citizen. With Christine I find myself sympathetic and friendly one moment, a paranoid *patron* the next, questioning her stability, her hygiene, her habits. I can't imagine that Pete Wilson himself would be any crankier than I was when Christine came back with the stroller and told me that while she'd been walking our baby a man on the street had asked her for a date.

91   We've done more than invite Christine into our lives. We're trusting her with our child, our future. She meanwhile looks to me as a way in, a handhold on a society she doesn't understand and can't quite negotiate. She gets me to write to a lawyer with whom she's in dispute. She asks me to cash a check for her, because, she says, she's in between bank accounts. In a way, I suppose, she's after me to behave like a parent. I feel edgy, threatened. I hate it.

92   Pro-immigration forces have tended to keep their focus tight on the economic issues because they sense that Americans don't want to be told they're racist. Nobody does. Yet, one of the problems with the immigration issue is that it *does* impinge on the race issue, and thus appeals temptingly and dangerously to the worst side of all of us.

93   A central argument of Brimelow's *Alien Nation* is that America has always had an essential nature, an ethnic core, and that it's white. He writes that "the first naturalization law, in 1790, stipulated that an

applicant must be a 'free white person.' Blacks became full citizens only after the Civil War."

94   He goes on: "Maybe America should not have been like this. *But it was.*" And now: "Americans are being tricked out of their own identity."

95   Reading this, I'm overcome with a weird looking-glass giddiness. Someone's trying to change the rules here, to wipe a rag over history. America's identity is precisely that of mutation, its power drawn from an energetic and quite fearless ability to adapt and win. Its national book, after all, is *The Adventures of Huckleberry Finn,* about a beautiful and dangerous river that never stops changing.

96   Along with more than 7,000 others, Maria T. and her family stand in line outside the Fred Jordan Mission in downtown Los Angeles, where on a boiling August day they wait for a free handout of clothes and sneakers. They've been huddled in sleeping bags and under blankets all night, during the course of which a man was shot to death outside a Chinese food store on the opposite side of Fifth Street. This is Skid Row, a scary neighborhood.

97   The kids are tired, hot, and hungry, but still excited about getting new Nikes. Television crews from Japan, Spain, and Germany, as well as from local news programs, stand by to record the happy event. People hold umbrellas against the sun, and a man passes up and down the line with a garden hose, drenching upturned faces. Last year, about 8,000 children were helped. In 1995, however, corporate giving has slipped for the first time, and they have only 5,000 pairs of shoes.

98   Only 5,000 pairs of shoes, at least 7,000 children, and so outside, as the hours pass, the huge line gets anxious. Maria is scared because no one helped when a big group came surging up the street and muscled in ahead of them. Now her children are crying, and it looks as if they might not get sneakers after all. The smaller sizes have already run out. Maria talks to one of the mission workers, a man she has met before. Can he help? He's sorry, he says, but there's nothing he can do, and he turns away.

99   Other mission workers walk down the line, quietly inviting families to leave. Maria stands with her arms around her children gathered around her. By now she has waited for almost 24 hours. It's the end of a long and stressful day and her kids feel sick. "This isn't right," she says.

100   America is an immigrant nation; indeed, a nation of strangers. I like it that way, though the arguments in favor of the idea are not merely sentimental and historical. Corporate interests value immigration for something that troubles us—keeping wages lower, and these days not just at the level of busboys and dayworkers.

101   The American economy is in relatively good shape and has pretty much the legal immigration it needs. The system isn't broken, doesn't need fixing—and certainly not in the ways that are now being

proposed. Illegal immigration is touchier. Listening to academics makes it easy to forget the racially inflamed brush fire that is the debate in California.

102   Recent polls show a surprising sympathy even for illegal immigrants, provided they otherwise play by the rules; work, get documentation, learn English. Only 20 percent say immigrants take jobs away from citizens, and 69 percent say they do work that citizens don't necessarily want and that needs to be done. Few say that the American-born children of illegals should be deprived of education and welfare, let alone their citizenship. The message here is a sensible one: beef up the Border Patrol; deport criminals; don't break up families; target labor-enforcement at bad-guy sweatshop employers and make an effort to deal with temporary visa overstays, who surprisingly make up as much as 50 percent of all illegals; supply Federal assistance to heavily impacted areas such as Los Angeles, and forget the idea of a national verification system or an identification card.

103   Ultimately, this is a debate about values, not money. This is about how America feels about itself.

104   The last time I meet with Maria T. she has heard of the passing of the new Federal welfare bill, which will cut off welfare payments after five years, a measure that, in some respects, seems like a federalization of Proposition 187. Understanding the vulnerability of her position, she is panicked. I've had a hunch all along that she sends some little portion of the money she gets to her husband in Guadalajara, not so much to support him as to keep him away. "He doesn't understand how much our life has changed," she says. She asks if I know of anyone, an American, who'd be prepared to marry her.

105   I'm not sure this is the solution and, anyway, what about the guy in Guadalajara?

106   "He's not really my husband," she says. "I just call him that," and I reflect again how fluid human situations slop outside the bucket of any political oratory.

107   She bites her nails and gathers the kids around her for a walk to the store. Mario, already rebellious, is reluctant to come along. Soon he'll be at the age, Maria knows, where she'll have to start worrying about the danger and lure of the gangs: kids his age, or younger, get slammed in (eerily graphic usage for the youth trap of every poor neighborhood in Los Angeles). Maria believes in the American dream more than I do, at least to the extent that she trusts the uniquely American promise that her children will have a better life than she does. At the shrine outside a church on Cedros Avenue she lights a candle. She thanks the Virgin for a brand new day and asks for another one. Then she walks to JCPenney, where she buys socks for the kids and then, from another counter, an American flag, for hope. ■

JAMES BALDWIN

Stranger in the Village

Influential and admired essayist, novelist, poet, and playwright James Baldwin (1924–1987) grew up preaching in local churches in Harlem, New York City, before he turned to the pursuit of a writing career in Greenwich Village. His successful first novel, Go Tell It on the Mountain *(1953), allowed him to write full time, and he moved to France in 1948 to escape the oppression he felt in the United States. He continued to move between France, New York, and New England, and became active in the civil rights struggle in the late 1950s. His other important works include the essay collection* Notes of a Native Son *(1955), his 1956 novel dealing explicitly with homosexuality* Giovanni's Room, *and the strong civil rights statement* The Fire Next Time *(1963). Baldwin's lifelong interest in questions of racial identity and his concern with the experience of an immigrant are central to the following essay from his* Notes of a Native Son.

1   From all available evidence no black man had ever set foot in this tiny Swiss village before I came. I was told before arriving that I would probably be a "sight" for the village; I took this to mean that people of my complexion were rarely seen in Switzerland, and also that city people are always something of a "sight" outside of the city. It did not occur to me—possibly because I am an American—that there could be people anywhere who had never seen a Negro.

2   It is a fact that cannot be explained on the basis of the inaccessibility of the village. The village is very high, but it is only four hours from Milan and three hours from Lausanne. It is true that it is virtually unknown. Few people making plans for a holiday would elect to come here. On the other hand, the villagers are able, presumably, to come and go as they please—which they do: to another town at the foot of the mountain, with a population of approximately five thousand, the nearest place to see a movie or go to the bank. In the village there is no movie house, no bank, no library, no theater; very few radios, one jeep, one station wagon; and, at the moment, one typewriter, mine, an invention which the woman next door to me here had never seen. There are about six hundred people living here, all Catholic—I conclude this from the fact that the Catholic church is open all year round, whereas the Protestant chapel, set off on a hill a little removed from the village, is open only in the summertime when the tourists arrive. There are four or five hotels, all closed now, and four or five *bistros,* of which, however, only two do any business during the winter. These two do not do

a great deal, for life in the village seems to end around nine or ten o'clock. There are a few stores, butcher, baker, *épicerie,* a hardware store, and a money-changer—who cannot change travelers' checks, but must send them down to the bank, an operation which takes two or three days. There is something called the *Ballet Haus,* closed in the winter and used for God knows what, certainly not ballet, during the summer. There seems to be only one schoolhouse in the village, and this for the quite young children; I suppose this to mean that their older brothers and sisters at some point descend from these mountains in order to complete their education—possibly, again, to the town just below. The landscape is absolutely forbidding, mountains towering on all four sides, ice and snow as far as the eye can reach. In this white wilderness, men and women and children move all day, carrying washing, wood, buckets of milk or water, sometimes skiing on Sunday afternoons. All week long boys and young men are to be seen shoveling snow off the rooftops, or dragging wood down from the forest in sleds.

3   The village's only real attraction, which explains the tourist season, is the hot spring water. A disquietingly high proportion of these tourists are cripples, or semi-cripples, who come year after year—from other parts of Switzerland, usually—to take the waters. This lends the village, at the height of the season, a rather terrifying air of sanctity, as though it were a lesser Lourdes. There is often something beautiful, there is always something awful, in the spectacle of a person who has lost one of his faculties, a faculty he never questioned until it was gone, and who struggles to recover it. Yet people remain people, on crutches or indeed on deathbeds; and wherever I passed, the first summer I was here, among the native villagers or among the lame, a wind passed with me—of astonishment, curiosity, amusement, and outrage. The first summer I stayed two weeks and never intended to return. But I did return in the winter, to work; the village offers, obviously, no distractions whatever and has the further advantage of being extremely cheap. Now it is winter again, a year later, and I am here again. Everyone in the village knows my name, though they scarcely ever use it, knows that I come from America—though this, apparently, they will never really believe: black men come from Africa—and everyone knows that I am the friend of the son of a woman who was born here, and that I am staying in their chalet. But I remain as much a stranger today as I was the first day I arrived, and the children shout *Neger! Neger!* as I walk along the streets.

4   It must be admitted that in the beginning I was far too shocked to have any real reaction. In so far as I reacted at all, I reacted by trying to be pleasant—it being a great part of the American Negro's education (long before he goes to school) that he must make people "like" him. This smile-and-the-world-smiles-with-you routine worked about as well in this situation as it had in the situation for which it was designed,

which is to say that it did not work at all. No one, after all, can be liked whose human weight and complexity cannot be, or has not been, admitted. My smile was simply another unheard-of phenomenon which allowed them to see my teeth—they did not, really, see my smile and I began to think that, should I take to snarling, no one would notice any difference. All of the physical characteristics of the Negro which had caused me, in America, a very different and almost forgotten pain were nothing less than miraculous—or infernal—in the eyes of the village people. Some thought my hair was the color of tar, that it had the texture of wire, or the texture of cotton. It was jocularly suggested that I might let it all grow long and make myself a winter coat. If I sat in the sun for more than five minutes some daring creature was certain to come along and gingerly put his fingers on my hair, as though he were afraid of an electric shock, or put his hand on my hand, astonished that the color did not rub off. In all of this, in which it must be conceded there was the charm of genuine wonder and in which there was certainly no element of intentional unkindness, there was yet no suggestion that I was human: I was simply a living wonder.

5   I knew that they did not mean to be unkind, and I know it now; it is necessary, nevertheless, for me to repeat this to myself each time I walk out of the chalet. The children who shout *Neger!* have no way of knowing the echoes this sound raises in me. They are brimming with good humor and the more daring swell with pride when I stop to speak with them. Just the same, there are days when I cannot pause and smile, when I have no heart to play with them; when, indeed, I mutter sourly to myself, exactly as I muttered on the streets of a city these children have never seen, when I was no bigger than these children are now: *Your* mother *was a nigger.* Joyce is right about history being a nightmare—but it may be the nightmare from which no one *can* awaken. People are trapped in history and history is trapped in them.

6   There is a custom in the village—I am told it is repeated in many villages—of "buying" African natives for the purpose of converting them to Christianity. There stands in the church all year round a small box with a slot for money, decorated with a black figurine, and into this box the villagers drop their francs. During the *carnaval* which precedes Lent, two village children have their faces blackened—out of which bloodless darkness their blue eyes shine like ice—and fantastic horsehair wigs are placed on their blond heads; thus disguised, they solicit among the villagers for money for the missionaries in Africa. Between the box in the church and the blackened children, the village "bought" last year six or eight African natives. This was reported to me with pride by the wife of one of the *bistro* owners and I was careful to express astonishment and pleasure at the solicitude shown by the village for the souls of black folk. The *bistro* owner's wife beamed with a pleasure far

more genuine than my own and seemed to feel that I might now breathe more easily concerning the souls of at least six of my kinsmen.

7   I tried not to think of these so lately baptized kinsmen, of the price paid for them, or the peculiar price they themselves would pay, and said nothing about my father, who having taken his own conversion too literally never, at bottom, forgave the white world (which he described as heathen) for having saddled him with a Christ in whom, to judge at least from their treatment of him, they themselves no longer believed. I thought of white men arriving for the first time in an African village, strangers there, as I am a stranger here, and tried to imagine the astounded populace touching their hair and marveling at the color of their skin. But there is a great difference between being the first white man to be seen by Africans and being the first black man to be seen by whites. The white man takes the astonishment as tribute, for he arrives to conquer and to convert the natives, whose inferiority in relation to himself is not even to be questioned; whereas I, without a thought of conquest, find myself among a people whose culture controls me, has even, in a sense, created me, people who have cost me more in anguish and rage than they will ever know, who yet do not even know of my existence. The astonishment with which I might have greeted them, should they have stumbled into my African village a few hundred years ago, might have rejoiced their hearts. But the astonishment with which they greet me today can only poison mine.

8   And this is so despite everything I may do to feel differently, despite my friendly conversations with the *bistro* owner's wife, despite their three-year-old son who has at last become my friend, despite the *saluts* and *bonsoirs* which I exchange with people as I walk, despite the fact that I know that no individual can be taken to task for what history is doing, or has done. I say that the culture of these people controls me—but they can scarcely be held responsible for European culture. America comes out of Europe, but these people have never seen America nor have most of them seen more of Europe than the hamlet at the foot of their mountain. Yet they move with an authority which I shall never have; and they regard me, quite rightly, not only as a stranger in their village but as a suspect latecomer, bearing no credentials, to everything they have—however unconsciously—inherited.

9   For this village, even were it incomparably more remote and incredibly more primitive, is the West, the West onto which I have been so strangely grafted. These people cannot be, from the point of view of power, strangers anywhere in the world; they have made the modern world, in effect, even if they do not know it. The most illiterate among them is related, in a way that I am not, to Dante, Shakespeare, Michelangelo, Aeschylus, Da Vinci, Rembrandt, and Racine; the cathedral at Chartres says something to them which it cannot say to me, as

indeed would New York's Empire State Building, should anyone here ever see it. Out of their hymns and dances come Beethoven and Bach. Go back a few centuries and they are in their full glory—but I am in Africa, watching the conquerors arrive.

10   The rage of the disesteemed is personally fruitless, but it is also absolutely inevitable; this rage, so generally discounted, so little understood even among the people whose daily bread it is, is one of the things that makes history. Rage can only with difficulty, and never entirely, be brought under the domination of the intelligence and is therefore not susceptible to any arguments whatever. This is a fact which ordinary representatives of the *Herrenvolk,* having never felt this rage and being unable to imagine it, quite fail to understand. Also, rage cannot be hidden, it can only be dissembled. This dissembling deludes the thoughtless, and strengthens rage and adds, to rage, contempt. There are, no doubt, as many ways of coping with the resulting complex of tensions as there are black men in the world, but no black man can hope ever to be entirely liberated from this internal warfare—rage, dissembling, and contempt having inevitably accompanied his first realization of the power of white men. What is crucial here is that, since white men represent in the black man's world so heavy a weight, white men have for black men a reality which is far from being reciprocal; and hence all black men have toward all white men an attitude which is designed, really, either to rob the white man of the jewel of his näiveté, or else to make it cost him dear.

11   The black man insists, by whatever means he finds at his disposal, that the white man cease to regard him as an exotic rarity and recognize him as a human being. This is a very charged and difficult moment, for there is a great deal of will power involved in the white man's näiveté. Most people are not naturally reflective any more than they are naturally malicious, and the white man prefers to keep the black man at a certain human remove because it is easier for him thus to preserve his simplicity and avoid being called to account for crimes committed by his forefathers, or his neighbors. He is inescapably aware, nevertheless, that he is in a better position in the world than black men are, nor can he quite put to death the suspicion that he is hated by black men therefore. He does not wish to be hated, neither does he wish to change places, and at this point in his uneasiness he can scarcely avoid having recourse to those legends which white men have created about black men, the most usual effect of which is that the white man finds himself enmeshed, so to speak, in his own language which describes hell, as well as the attributes which lead one to hell, as being as black as night.

12   Every legend, moreover, contains its residuum of truth, and the root function of language is to control the universe by describing it. It is of quite considerable significance that black men remain, in the imagi-

nation, and in overwhelming numbers in fact, beyond the disciplines of salvation; and this despite the fact the West has been "buying" African natives for centuries. There is, I should hazard, an instantaneous necessity to be divorced from this so visibly unsaved stranger, in whose heart, moreover, one cannot guess what dreams of vengeance are being nourished; and, at the same time, there are few things on earth more attractive than the idea of the unspeakable liberty which is allowed the unredeemed. When, beneath the black mask, a human being begins to make himself felt one cannot escape a certain awful wonder as to what kind of human being it is. What one's imagination makes of other people is dictated of course, by the laws of one's own personality and it is one of the ironies of black-white relations that, by means of what the white man imagines the black man to be, the black man is enabled to know who the white man is.

13   I have said, for example, that I am as much a stranger in this village today as I was the first summer I arrived, but this is not quite true. The villagers wonder less about the texture of my hair than they did then, and wonder rather more about me. And the fact that their wonder now exists on another level is reflected in their attitudes and in their eyes. There are the children who make those delightful, hilarious, sometimes astonishingly grave overtures of friendship in the unpredictable fashion of children; other children, having been taught that the devil is a black man, scream in genuine anguish as I approach. Some of the older women never pass without a friendly greeting, never pass, indeed, if it seems that they will be able to engage me in conversation; other women look down or look away or rather contemptuously smirk. Some of the men drink with me and suggest that I learn how to ski— partly. I gather, because they cannot imagine what I would look like on skis—and want to know if I am married, and ask questions about my *métier.* But some of the men have accused *le sale négre*—behind my back—of stealing wood and there is already in the eyes of some of them that peculiar, intent, paranoiac malevolence which one sometimes surprises in the eyes of American white men when, out walking with their Sunday girl, they see a Negro male approach.

14   There is a dreadful abyss between the streets of this village and the streets of the city in which I was born, between the children who shout *Neger!* today and those who shouted *Nigger!* yesterday—the abyss is experience, the American experience. The syllable hurled behind me today expresses, above all, wonder: I am a stranger here. But I am not a stranger in America and the same syllable riding on the American air expresses the war my presence has occasioned in the American soul.

15   For this village brings home to me this fact: that there was a day, and not really a very distant day, when Americans were scarcely Americans at all but discontented Europeans, facing a great unconquered

continent and strolling, say, into a marketplace and seeing black men for the first time. The shock this spectacle afforded is suggested, surely, by the promptness with which they decided that these black men were not really men but cattle. It is true that the necessity on the part of the settlers of the New World of reconciling their moral assumptions with the fact—and the necessity—of slavery enhanced immensely the charm of this idea, and it is also true that this idea expresses, with a truly American bluntness, the attitude which to varying extents all masters have had toward all slaves.

16   But between all former slaves and slave owners and the drama which begins for Americans over three hundred years ago at Jamestown, there are at least two differences to be observed. The American Negro slave could not suppose, for one thing, as slaves in past epochs had supposed and often done, that he would ever be able to wrest the power from his master's hands. This was a supposition which the modern era, which was to bring about such vast changes in the aims and dimensions of power, put to death; it only begins, in unprecedented fashion, and with dreadful implications, to be resurrected today. But even had this supposition persisted with undiminished force, the American Negro slave could not have used it to lend his condition dignity, for the reason that this supposition rests on another: that the slave in exile yet remains related to his past, has some means—if only in memory—of revering and sustaining the forms of his former life, is able, in short, to maintain his identity.

17   This was not the case with the American Negro slave. He is unique among the black men of the world in that his past was taken from him, almost literally, at one blow. One wonders what on earth the first slave found to say to the first dark child he bore. I am told that there are Haitians able to trace their ancestry back to African kings, but any American Negro wishing to go back so far will find his journey through time abruptly arrested by the signature on the bill of sale which served as the entrance paper for his ancestor. At the time—to say nothing of the circumstances—of the enslavement of the captive black man who was to become the American Negro, there was not the remotest possibility that he would ever take power from his master's hands. There was no reason to suppose that his situation would ever change, nor was there, shortly, anything to indicate that his situation had ever been different. It was his necessity, in the words of E. Franklin Frazier, to find a "motive for living under American culture or die." The identity of the American Negro comes out of this extreme situation, and the evolution of this identify was a source of the most intolerable anxiety in the minds and the lives of his masters.

18   For the history of the American Negro is unique also in this: that the question of his humanity, and of his rights therefore as a human be-

ing, became a burning one for several generations of Americans, so burning a question that it ultimately became one of those used to divide the nation. It is out of this argument that the venom of the epithet *Nigger!* is derived. It is an argument which Europe has never had, and hence Europe quite sincerely fails to understand how or why the argument arose in the first place, why its effects are so frequently disastrous and always so unpredictable, why it refuses until today to be entirely settled. Europe's black possessions remained—and do remain—in Europe's colonies, at which remove they represented no threat whatever to European identity. If they posed any problem at all for the European conscience, it was a problem which remained comfortingly abstract: in effect, the black man, *as a man*, did not exist for Europe. But in America, even as a slave, he was an inescapable part of the general social fabric and no American could escape having an attitude toward him. Americans attempt until today to make an abstraction of the Negro, but the very nature of these abstractions reveals the tremendous effects the presence of the Negro has had on the American character.

19   When one considers the history of the Negro in America it is of the greatest importance to recognize that the moral beliefs of a person, or a people, are never really as tenuous as life—which is not moral—very often causes them to appear; these create for them a frame of reference and a necessary hope, the hope being that when life has done its worst they will be enabled to rise above themselves and to triumph over life. Life would scarcely be bearable if this hope did not exist. Again, even when the worst has been said, to betray a belief is not by any means to have put oneself beyond its power; the betrayal of a belief is not the same thing as ceasing to believe. If this were not so there would be no moral standards in the world at all. Yet one must also recognize that morality is based on ideas and that all ideas are dangerous—dangerous because ideas can only lead to action and where the action leads no man can say. And dangerous in this respect that confronted with the impossibility of becoming free of them, one can be driven to the most inhuman excesses. The ideas on which American beliefs are based are not, though Americans often seem to think so, ideas which originated in America. They came out of Europe. And the establishment of democracy on the American continent was scarcely as radical a break with the past as was the necessity, which Americans faced, of broadening this concept to include black men.

20   This was, literally, a hard necessity. It was impossible, for one thing, for Americans to abandon their beliefs, not only because these beliefs alone seemed able to justify the sacrifices they had endured and the blood that they had spilled, but also because these beliefs afforded them their only bulwark against a moral chaos as absolute as the physical chaos of the continent it was their destiny to conquer. But in the

situation in which Americans found themselves, these beliefs threatened an idea which, whether or not one likes to think so, is the very warp and woof of the heritage of the West, the idea of white supremacy.

21   Americans have made themselves notorious by the shrillness and the brutality with which they have insisted on this idea, but they did not invent it; and it has escaped the world's notice that those very excesses of which Americans have been guilty imply a certain, unprecedented uneasiness over the idea's life and power, if not, indeed, the idea's validity. The idea of white supremacy rests simply on the fact that white men are the creators of civilization (the present civilization, which is the only one that matters; all previous civilizations are simply "contributions" to our own) and are therefore civilization's guardians and defenders. Thus it was impossible for Americans to accept the black man as one of themselves, for to do so was to jeopardize their status as white men. But not so to accept him was to deny his human reality, his human weight and complexity, and the strain of denying the overwhelmingly undeniable forced Americans into rationalizations so fantastic that they approached the pathological.

22   At the root of the American Negro problem is the necessity of the American white man to find a way of living with the Negro in order to be able to live with himself. And the history of this problem can be reduced to the means used by Americans—lynch law and law, segregation and legal acceptance, terrorization and concession—either to come to terms with this necessity, or to find a way around it, or (most usually) to find a way of doing both these things at once. The resulting spectacle, at once foolish and dreadful, led someone to make the quite accurate observation that "the Negro-in-America is a form of insanity which overtakes white men."

23   In this long battle, a battle by no means finished, the unforeseeable effects of which will be felt by many future generations, the white man's motive was the protection of his identity, the black man was motivated by the need to establish an identity. And despite the terrorization which the Negro in America endured and endures sporadically until today, despite the cruel and totally inescapable ambivalence of his status in his country, the battle for his identity has long ago been won. He is not a visitor to the West, but a citizen there an American; as American as the Americans who despise him, the Americans who fear him, the Americans who love him—the Americans who became less than themselves, or rose to be greater than themselves by virtue of the fact that the challenge he represented was inescapable. He is perhaps the only black man in the world whose relationship to white men is more terrible, more subtle, and more meaningful than the relationship of bitter possessed to uncertain possessor. His survival depended, and his development depends, on his ability to turn his peculiar status in

the Western world to his own advantage and, it may be, to the very great advantage of that world. It remains for him to fashion out of his experience that which will give him sustenance, and a voice.

24   The cathedral at Chartres, I have said, says something to the people of this village which it cannot say to me; but it is important to understand that this cathedral says something to me which it cannot say to them. Perhaps they are struck by the power of the spires, the glory of the windows; but they have known God, after all, longer than I have known him, and in a different way, and I am terrified by the slippery bottomless well to be found in the crypt, down which heretics were hurled to death, and by the obscene, inescapable gargoyles jutting out of the stone and seeming to say that God and the devil can never be divorced. I doubt that the villagers think of the devil when they face a cathedral because they have never been identified with the devil. But I must accept the status which myth, if nothing else, gives me in the West before I can hope to change the myth.

25   Yet, if the American Negro has arrived at his identity by virtue of the absoluteness of his estrangement from his past, American white men still nourish the illusion that there is some means of recovering the European innocence, of returning to a state in which black men do not exist. This is one of the greatest errors Americans can make. The identity they fought so hard to protect has, by virtue of that battle, undergone a change; Americans are as unlike any other white people in the world as it is possible to be. I do not think, for example, that it is too much to suggest that the American vision of the world—which allows so little reality, generally speaking, for any of the darker forces in human life, which tends until today to paint moral issues in glaring black and white—owes a great deal to the battle waged by Americans to maintain between themselves and black men a human separation which could not be bridged. It is only now beginning to be borne in on us—very faintly, it must be admitted, very slowly, and very much against our will—that this vision of the world is dangerously inaccurate, and perfectly useless. For it protects our moral high-mindedness at the terrible expense of weakening our grasp of reality. People who shut their eyes to reality simply invite their own destruction, and anyone who insists on remaining in a state of innocence long after that innocence is dead turns himself into a monster.

26   The time has come to realize that the interracial drama acted out on the American continent has not only created a new black man, it has created a new white man, too. No road whatever will lead Americans back to the simplicity of this European village where white men still have the luxury of looking on me as a stranger. I am not, really, a stranger any longer for any American alive. One of the things that distinguishes Americans from other people is that no other people has ever

been so deeply involved in the lives of black men, and vice versa. This fact faced, with all its implications, it can be seen that the history of the American Negro problem is not merely shameful, it is also something of an achievement. For even when the worst has been said, it must also be added that the perpetual challenge posed by this problem was always, somehow, perpetually met. It is precisely this black-white experience which may prove of indispensable value to us in the world we face today. This world is white no longer, and it will never be white again. ■

GREGORY RODRIGUEZ

Why We're the New Irish

Gregory Rodriguez is a contributing editor of the Los Angeles Times *and serves as an Irvine Senior Fellow at the New America Foundation, a nonpartisan group that sponsors research, conferences, and writing on issues central to American life. Rodriguez writes for many other publications as well, on aspects of ethnicity, immigration, and shifts in American demographics. His* Atlantic Monthly *essay "Mongrel America" was noted as one of the best political writings of 2003. "Why We're the New Irish" appeared as the cover story for the May 30, 2005,* Newsweek.

1   Antonio Villaraigosa may not realize it, but his election as mayor of America's second largest city borrows a page from Al Smith. Like a lot of Irish-American politicians of his day, Smith knew how to play the ethnic card to great effect. After all, "shamrock politics" had helped the Irish establish a firm grasp on power throughout the Northeast in the late 19th and early 20th centuries. But as Smith rose through the ranks in New York politics, from speaker of the Assembly to the statehouse in the 1910s, both he and Irish-controlled Tammany Hall, the powerful Manhattan Democratic Party organization, agreed that he needed to build out his base. While never forgetting his ethnic roots, Smith broadened his outlook and became more politically independent, seeking allies in all corners of the state. Smith's political success helped normalize the image of the Irish as mainstream Americans throughout the Northeast.

2   As with the Irish, so too with Mexican-Americans, as Villaraigosa's comfortable margin of victory in the Los Angeles mayor's race attests. Villaraigosa, a onetime militant campus activist, fashioned his first race for the mayoralty in 2001 around a labor-left-Latino alliance. He lost. Four years later he broadened his message, built a more ideologically moderate multiethnic coalition and won by nearly 20 percentage points.

3   Villaraigosa's political ascent is a metaphor for the maturation of Mexican-American politics—a process that is more evolutionary than revolutionary, and, at bottom, a classic American story of ethnic integration into the mainstream.

4   Throughout American history, countless other ethnic groups have been stripped of their foreignness and have achieved mainstream acceptance. Political and cultural icons are often the vehicles for this cultural shift. In 1939, *Life* magazine complimented Italian-American ballplayer Joe DiMaggio for not reeking of garlic or using grease in his hair. By his retirement in 1951, however, it called him an all-American hero.

5   Of course, while European immigrant experiences generally had a beginning and an end, Mexican immigration has been virtually continuous for the past century. This has made the process of Mexican integration a perpetual one. But this dynamic hasn't so much retarded assimilation as it has sown confusion in the formulation of political and cultural identities. Though the self-definition of European-American groups gradually evolved from an immigrant to an ethnic American identity as time passed, Mexican-Americans have always had to contend with the presence of unassimilated newcomers as well as cyclical waves of anti-Mexican sentiment. Consequently, Mexican-Americans have had to battle against the presumption of foreignness longer than other ethnic groups.

6   What's happening with Mexican-Americans is happening to some extent among other Latino groups as well. In New York City, Puerto Rican mayoral hopeful Fernando Ferrer's only hope of catching the wealthy Republican incumbent Mayor Michael Bloomberg is to build bridges to blacks and other ethnic-minority groups in the metropolitan mosaic, while denting Bloomberg's base among middle- and upper-class whites. A growing number of immigrants from Latin America are flooding into south Florida, teaming with non-Latinos to chip away at the Cuban hold on political power there. Those groups pale in comparison to the political clout of Mexican-Americans, though. While Latinos now live in all parts of the country, two thirds of the nation's Hispanics are of Mexican origin—and their heavy concentration in Texas and California, the country's two most populous states, gives Mexican-Americans extraordinary clout.

7   Villaraigosa's overwhelming victory is a reminder that despite the uniqueness of Mexican immigration, the process of—and desire for—achieving "Americanness" is as strong as it ever was. Over the next generation, Mexican-Americans will only produce more of their own modern Smiths and DiMaggios. In so doing, they will be exchanging the now outdated language of multi-culturalism for an updated version of the melting pot. ■

TODD GITLIN

Under the Sign of Mickey Mouse & Co.

Todd Gitlin is a professor of journalism and sociology at Columbia University. A leading and longtime culture critic who writes for a variety of publications (including Mother Jones, *a popular magazine with a left-of-center appeal, especially to younger readers), he has received several prestigious grants and fellowships, including one from the MacArthur Foundation. His books include* Uptown: Poor Whites in Chicago *(1970),* The Whole World Is Watching: Mass Media in the Making and Unmaking of the New Left *(1981),* Inside Prime Time *(1983),* The Twilight of Common Dreams: Why America Is Wracked by Culture Wars *(1995),* Media Unlimited: How the Torrent of Images and Sounds Overwhelms Our Lives *(2002), and* Letters to a Young Activist *(2003). The selection below comes from the last chapter of* Media Unlimited.

1 Everywhere, the media flow defies national boundaries. This is one of its obvious, but at the same time amazing, features. A global torrent is not, of course, the master metaphor to which we have grown accustomed. We're more accustomed to Marshall McLuhan's *global village.* Those who resort to this metaphor casually often forget that if the world is a global village, some live in mansions on the hill, others in huts. Some dispatch images and sounds around town at the touch of a button; others collect them at the touch of *their* buttons. Yet McLuhan's image reveals an indispensable half-truth. If there is a village, it speaks American. It wears jeans, drinks Coke, eats at the golden arches, walks on swooshed shoes, plays electric guitars, recognizes Mickey Mouse, James Dean, E.T., Bart Simpson, R2-D2, and Pamela Anderson.

2 At the entrance to the champagne cellar of Piper-Heidsieck in Reims, in eastern France, a plaque declares that the cellar was dedicated by Marie Antoinette. The tour is narrated in six languages, and at the end you walk back upstairs into a museum featuring photographs of famous people drinking champagne. And who are they? Perhaps members of today's royal houses, presidents or prime ministers, economic titans or Nobel Prize winners? Of course not. They are movie stars, almost all of them American—Marilyn Monroe to Clint Eastwood. The symmetry of the exhibition is obvious, the premise unmistakable: Hollywood stars, champions of consumption, are the royalty of this century, more popular by far than poor doomed Marie.

3 Hollywood is the global cultural capital—capital in both senses. The United States presides over a sort of World Bank of styles and symbols, an International Cultural Fund of images, sounds, and

celebrities. The goods may be distributed by American-, Canadian-, European-, Japanese-, or Australian-owned multinational corporations, but their styles, themes, and images do not detectably change when a new board of directors takes over. Entertainment is one of America's top exports. In 1999, in fact, film, television, music, radio, advertising, print publishing, and computer software together *were* the top export, almost $80 billion worth, and while software alone accounted for $50 billion of the total, some of that category also qualifies as entertainment—video games and pornography, for example. Hardly anyone is exempt from the force of American images and sounds. French resentment of Mickey Mouse, Bruce Willis, and the rest of American civilization is well known. Less well known, and rarely acknowledged by the French, is the fact that *Terminator 2* sold 5 million tickets in France during the month it opened—with no submachine guns at the heads of the customers. The same culture minister, Jack Lang, who in 1982 achieved a moment of predictable notoriety in the United States for declaring that *Dallas* amounted to cultural imperialism, also conferred France's highest honor in the arts on Elizabeth Taylor and Sylvester Stallone. The point is not hypocrisy pure and simple but something deeper, something obscured by a single-minded emphasis on American power: dependency. American popular culture is the nemesis that hundreds of millions—perhaps billions—of people love, and love to hate. The antagonism and the dependency are inseparable, for the media flood—essentially American in its origin, but virtually unlimited in its reach—represents, like it or not, a common imagination.

4   How shall we understand the Hong Kong T-shirt that says "I Feel Coke"? Or the little Japanese girl who asks an American visitor in all innocence, "Is there really a Disneyland in America?" (She knows the one in Tokyo.) Or the experience of a German television reporter sent to Siberia to film indigenous life, who after flying out of Moscow and then traveling for days by boat, bus, and jeep, arrives near the Arctic Sea where live a tribe of Tungusians known to ethnologists for their bearskin rituals. In the community store sits a grandfather with his grandchild on his knee. Grandfather is dressed in traditional Tungusian clothing. Grandson has on his head a reversed baseball cap.

5   American popular culture is the closest approximation today to a global lingua franca, drawing the urban and young in particular into a common cultural zone where they share some dreams of freedom, wealth, comfort, innocence, and power—and perhaps most of all, youth as a state of mind. In general, despite the rhetoric of "identity," young people do not live in monocultures. They are not monocular. They are both local and cosmopolitan. Cultural bilingualism is routine. Just as their "cultures" are neither hard-wired nor uniform, so there is no

simple way in which they are "Americanized," though there are American tags on their experience—low-cost links to status and fun. Everywhere, fun lovers, efficiency seekers, Americaphiles, and Americaphobes alike pass through the portals of Disney and the arches of McDonald's wearing Levi's jeans and Gap jackets. Mickey Mouse and Donald Duck, John Wayne, Marilyn Monroe, James Dean, Bob Dylan, Michael Jackson, Madonna, Clint Eastwood, Bruce Willis, the multicolor chorus of Coca-Cola, and the next flavor of the month or the universe are the icons of a curious sort of one-world sensibility, a global semiculture. America's bid for global unification surpasses in reach that of the Romans, the British, the Catholic Church, or Islam; though without either an army or a God, it requires less. The Tungusian boy with the reversed cap on his head does not automatically think of it as "American," let alone side with the U.S. Army.

6　　The misleadingly easy answer to the question of how American images and sounds became omnipresent is: American imperialism. But the images are not even faintly force-fed by American corporate, political, or military power. The empire strikes from inside the spectator as well as from outside. This is a conundrum that deserves to be approached with respect if we are to grasp the fact that Mickey Mouse and Coke are everywhere recognized and often enough *enjoyed*. In the peculiar unification at work throughout the world, there is surely a supply side, but there is not only a supply side. Some things are true even if multinational corporations claim so: there is demand.

7　　What do American icons and styles mean to those who are not American? We can only imagine—but let us try. What young people graced with disposable income encounter in American television shows, movies, soft drinks, theme parks, and American-labeled (though not American-manufactured) running shoes, T-shirts, baggy pants, ragged jeans, and so on, is a way of being in the world, the experience of a flow of ready feelings and sensations bobbing up, disposable, dissolving, segueing to the next and the next after that. It is a quality of immediacy and casualness not so different from what Americans desire. But what the young experience in the video game arcade or the music megastore is more than the flux of sensation. They flirt with a loose sort of social membership that requires little but a momentary (and monetary) surrender. Sampling American goods, images, and sounds, they affiliate with an empire of informality. Consuming a commodity, wearing a slogan or a logo, you affiliate with disaffiliation. You make a limited-liability connection, a virtual one. You borrow some of the effervescence that is supposed to emanate from this American staple, and hope to be recognized as one of the elect. When you wear the Israeli version that spells *Coca-Cola* in Hebrew, you express some worldwide connection with unknown peers, or a sense of irony, or both—in any event, a marker of membership. In a world of ubiquitous images, of easy mobility and casual tourism, you get to feel not only local or national but global—without locking yourself in a box so confining as to deserve the name "identity."

8   We are seeing on a world scale the familiar infectious rhythm of modernity. The money economy extends its reach, bringing with it a calculating mentality. Even in the poor countries it stirs the same hunger for private feeling, the same taste for disposable labels and sensations on demand, the same attention to fashion, the new and the now, that cropped up earlier in the West. Income beckons; income rewards. The taste for the marketed spectacle and the media-soaked way of life spreads. The culture consumer may not like the American goods in particular but still acquires a taste for the media's speed, formulas, and frivolity. Indeed, the lightness of American-sponsored "identity" is central to its appeal. It imposes few burdens. Attachments and affiliations coexist, overlap, melt together, form, and re-form.

9   Marketers, like nationalists and fundamentalists, promote "identities," but for most people, the melange is the message. Traditional bonds bend under pressure from imports. Media from beyond help you have your "roots" and eat them, too. You can watch Mexican television in the morning and American in the afternoon, or graze between Kurdish and English. You can consolidate family ties with joint visits to Disney World—making Orlando, Florida, the major tourist destination in the United States, and the Tokyo and Marne-la-Vallée spin-offs massive attractions in Japan and France. You can attach to your parents, or children, by playing oldie music and exchanging sports statistics. You plunge back into the media flux, looking for—what? Excitement? Some low-cost variation on known themes? Some next new thing? You don't know just what, but you will when you see it—or if not, you'll change channels.

10   As devotees of Japanese video games, Hong Kong movies, and Mexican *telenovelas* would quickly remind us, the blends, juxtapositions, and recombinations of popular culture are not just American. American and American-based models, styles, and symbols are simply the most far-flung, successful, and consequential. In the course of a century, America's entertainment corporations succeeded brilliantly in cultivating popular expectations for entertainment—indeed, the sense of a *right* to be entertained, a right that belongs to the history of modernity, the rise of market economies and individualism. The United States, which began as Europe's collective fantasy, built a civilization to deliver the goods for playing, feeling, and meaning. Competitors ignore its success at their own peril, financial and otherwise. ■

LAURA CARLSEN

Wal-Mart vs. Pyramids

*Laura Carlsen is the director of the Americas Program for the
International Relations Center (formerly the Interhemispheric Resource
Center), which provides policy analysis and options for economic policy
involving North, Central, and South America. A graduate of Stanford
University, in 1986 she received a Fulbright Scholarship to study the
impact on women of the Mexican economic crisis. She continues to reside
in Mexico City. She has also written about trade agreements and other
economic issues impacting Mexico. The article reprinted below appeared in
several places in October and November of 2004, including New York
University's* Global Beat Syndicate, *the Common Dreams Web site
(< www.commondreams.org >), and* Human Quest, *an academic journal
of religion and philosophy.*

1   The showdown is rife with symbolism. Wal-Mart's expansion plans
in Mexico have brought about a modern-day clash of passions and
principles at the site of one of the earth's first great civilizations.

2   Several months ago Wal-Mart, the world's largest retail chain, quietly began constructing a new store in Mexico—the latest step in a phenomenal takeover of Mexico's supermarket sector. But the expansion
north of Mexico City is not just part of Wal-Mart's commercial conquest
of Mexico. It is infringing on the cultural foundations of the country.
The new store is just 3,000 meters from the Pyramid of the Sun, the
tallest structure in the ancient city of Teotihuacan.

3   The Teotihuacan Empire is believed to have begun as early as 200
B.C. Its dominion stretched deep into the heart of Mayan country in
Guatemala and throughout present-day Mexico. At its peak, Teotihuacan
was a thriving city of about 200,000 inhabitants, but the civilization declined in 700 A.D. under circumstances still shrouded in mystery.

4   Since then, other tribes and civilizations, including the Aztecs and
contemporary Mexican society, have claimed the "City of the Gods" as
their heritage. The grand human accomplishment it represents and the
power of its architectural, historical and, for many, spiritual legacy is
central to Mexico's history and culture.

5   While little is known for certain about the rise and fall of Teotihuacan, much is known about the rise of the Wal-Mart empire. From a
store in Rogers, Arkansas founded by the Walton brothers in 1962, the
enterprise grew in the breathtakingly short period of 42 years into the
world's largest company.

6   In Mexico, its conquest of the supermarket sector began by buying up the nation's extensive chain, Aurrerá, beginning in 1992. Today, with 657 stores, Mexico is home to more Wal-Marts and their affiliates than any other country outside the United States. Wal-Mart is now Mexico's largest private employer, with over 100,000 employees. But recent studies in the United States, where resistance to the megastores has been growing, show that job creation is often job displacement, because Wal-Marts put local stores out of business, leading to net job losses.

7   Wal-mart has revolutionized the labor and business world by working cheap and growing big. Labor costs are held down through anti-union policies, the hiring of undocumented workers in the United States, alleged discrimination against women and persons with disabilities, and cutbacks in benefits. Prices paid suppliers are driven down by outsourcing competition. Buoyed by $244.5 billion dollars in annual net sales, the chain can afford to make ever deeper incursions into Mexico's retail sector.

8   A diverse group of local merchants, artists, actors, academics and indigenous organizations are leading the opposition, protesting that the store damages Mexico's rich cultural heritage. Through ceremonies, hunger strikes, demonstrations and press coverage, the movement to defend the site has kept the conflict in the public eye and heightened the public-opinion costs to Wal-Mart. Now opponents have taken their concerns to the Mexican Congress and UNESCO.

9   Some ancient ruins have already been found on the store's new site, and Wal-Mart construction workers told the national daily, *La Jornada,* that they had orders to hide any archaeological relics they found. Normally, the presence of relics requires that further excavation be carried out painstakingly or halted altogether. But the booming Wal-Mart corporation clearly has no time for such delays.

10   The dispute in Teotihuacan today is not a battle between the past and the future. It is a struggle over a country's right to define itself. For defenders of the ancient site, the foremost symbol of the nation's cultural heritage also constitutes part of its contemporary integrity. Modern Mexico is still a country that defines itself by legends, and whose collective identity—unlike its neophyte northern neighbor—reaches back thousands of years.

11   In this context, Wal-Mart is a symbol of the cultural insensitivity of rampant economic integration. While its actions may be technically legal, in the end Wal-Mart could pay a high price for this insensitivity. . . and if there is anything Wal-Mart hates, it is high prices. ◼

KISHORE MAHBUBANI

American Culture: The People's Choice or a Form of Imperialism?

Kishore Mahbubani (born 1948) is Singapore's Permanent Representative to the United Nations. He also serves as the High Commissioner of Singapore to Canada. During his career he has been a diplomat in Cambodia, Malaysia, Washington, D.C., and New York. In January 2001 and May 2002 he was President of the UN Security Council. Mahbubani has published articles in numerous newspapers and journals, including the prestigious Foreign Affairs, *and some of his work has been collected in his 2002 book,* Can Asians Think? *On May 1, 2000, he gave the following speech to the International Press Institute's World Congress in Boston, Massachusetts. The IPI is a network of journalists concerned with freedom of the press, the global flow of information, and ethical journalistic practices.*

1   My answer to the question, "Is American culture the people's choice, or is it a form of imperialism?", is that it is neither and that I have a very different view of American culture as it is in the world today.

2   To explain my view on the role that American culture plays, I'm going to make a slight distinction between high culture and low culture, and I'll be speaking a bit more on high culture than low culture in my presentation today.

3   The view that I have, living outside the United States, is of the United States as a giant filtration machine that sucks in talent from all over the world, processes the talent, nurtures the talent, sometimes retains it in the United States, but often sends it back to the countries that it comes from. And of course there are two views outside on the results of this process. Is this good or bad?

4   I tend to view the role the United States plays as being a positive one, in a sense acting as a brain trust for the world, developing talent otherwise wasted in their own countries. Now does this mean that if the United States acts as the main source of trading of talent all over the world, does this mean that the whole world is going to become Americanized, that we're all going to wear jeans and drink Coca-Cola and go out and eat at McDonald's? My answer to that is "no." This will not happen and indeed the exact opposite will happen. If you trade and nurture talent from societies all over the world, and if, as I believe, this talent goes back to their respective societies, this talent will reinvigorate

these societies and indeed you'll see the revival of these societies, partly as a result of the process of American education. And I can assure you of one thing—one of the things that I say in my writings—namely that Asian societies will become as prosperous, as successful, over time, as European and North American societies, and I think this will be, in a sense, a more positive development because you'll have a diversity of civilizations, a diversity of successful societies, but all this is triggered maybe unconsciously by the United States, the educator of the world's talent.

5 But for the Asian societies to succeed and do well, what they have to do is make sure they pick the right viruses from American society and not the wrong viruses. And this is, in a sense, the challenge of those who come from outside to study in the U.S., to find out why is the U.S. the most successful economy in the world today? Why is it so dynamic? Why do you have nine years of growth? The emphasis that most American intellectuals put is on institutions like democracy, human rights, freedom of the press—these are the institutions that Americans emphasize as being important and critical success factors, and I don't deny that these are critical success factors. But let me suggest to you that for the countries that are at a lower stage of development there are other critical success factors in American society that they need to copy and emulate with equal vigor. And these are the institutions that you have built, institutions of government like the Treasury, the NASDAQ, the Securities Exchange Commission.

6 Without these institutions to regulate the market place, the market place wouldn't do so well. The weaknesses that other societies have is that they don't have the institutions in place that allow the foreign investors to come in, that allow them to invest in and develop these societies. So if they really want to copy what is good in American society, I suggest that they should also copy institutions that the United States has developed. And by the way, these institutions took years of development and they will be difficult to copy and transplant, but if they can do that then hopefully other societies will become as dynamic as American society.

7 One last point. There has been a lot of discussion here about the role of the Internet. I know that the conventional wisdom is that the Internet will be another source of transmission of American values—the world will become Americanized as a result of American domination of the Internet. I have, in a sense, the exact opposite vision on the role of the Internet today. The Internet, unlike previous media of mass communication, is not a one-way street. It's a two-way street. It means that if you can send a message to Tanzania, Tanzania can send a message back to you via the Internet. And that two-way street will play a very

important role in terms of empowering those who, in a sense, have been disempowered, disenfranchised, because of a lack of contact or access to the modern world. When I grew up as a child in Singapore, all I had access to was maybe 600 books in my local library and that was all. Today the same child in Singapore can get access to any book in the Library of Congress that he wants through the Internet. If you want to look for a quote from Plato, you can get a quote from Plato on the Internet, and if you want to get information on the seasons in Tanzania, you can get it anytime you want.

8   And incidentally, when you go to the Internet and you see what is available in the English language, you will see the connectivity is only in one language, but the Internet is also connecting other language communities. And the surprising thing I've discovered is that my sister in New Jersey gets more access to Indian culture than my family does in Singapore. She gets two 24-hour Hindi music stations, two 24-hour Hindi movie stations, all in New Jersey. And it's partly because there is a transmission of information and knowledge taking place. So with the Internet, I suggest to you that we will not have the Americanization of the world, we may have the world connecting in a way that hasn't happened in 500 years. ■

JEREMY RIFKIN

The European Dream

Jeremy Rifkin (born 1943), a long-time activist and President of the Foundation on Economic Trends, has authored numerous books on the impact of science and technology on economics, society, and the environment. His books include The End of Work *(1995),* The Biotech Century *(1998), and* The Age of Access *(2000). He has appeared on numerous news programs and has lectured at hundreds of colleges and universities. Rifkin is also the author of* The European Dream: How Europe's Vision of the Future is Quietly Eclipsing the American Dream *(2004).*
The following argument, a selection from that book, presents the possibility that the American dream is losing out to a new European dream that better fits a globalizing world.

1   What really separates America from all earlier political experiments is the unbounded hope and enthusiasm, the optimism that is so thick at times it can bowl you over. This is a land dedicated to possibilities, a place where constant improvement is the only meaningful compass and economic progress is regarded to be as certain as the rising

sun. We are a people who threw off the yoke of tyranny and vowed never to be ruled by arbitrary elites of any kind. We eschew class distinctions and the hereditary transmission of status, embrace the democratic spirit, and believe that everyone should be judged solely on merit.

2   Americans have long been aware of our special circumstance. We think of America as a refuge for every human being who has ever dreamed of a better life and been willing to risk his or her own to come here and start over.

3   That's why it saddens me to say that America is no longer a great country. Yes, it's still the most powerful economy in the world, with a military presence unmatched in all of history. But to be a great country, it is necessary to be a good country. It is true that people everywhere enjoy American cultural forms and consumer goods. America is even envied, but it is no longer admired as it once was. The American Dream, once so coveted, has increasingly become an object of derision. Our way of life no longer inspires; rather, it is now looked on as outmoded and, worse yet, as something to fear, or abhor.

4   Stripped to its bare essentials, the American Dream offers everyone a fair shot at prosperity if they're willing to work hard and cultivate self-reliance. But fulfillment of the dream is becoming more elusive. For Americans who have made every effort to succeed, only to be pulled down over and over again by a market economy and a society weighted against them, the dream can feel like a cruel hoax, a myth without substance. There may still be opportunity for both the native-born and newcomers, but the unfettered upward mobility that defined American life up until the early 1970s no longer exists. As the gap between rich and poor has widened, the sons and daughters of wealthier Americans have come to feel entitled to happiness and are less willing to work hard and make something of themselves. On all social levels, the dream is losing its cachet, casting many of its former believers adrift. One-third of all Americans say they no longer even believe in the American Dream.

5   While the American spirit languishes in the past, a compelling new dream is coming of age, driven by the rise of the world's other great superpower, the European Union (EU). Twenty-five nations, representing 455 million people, have joined together to create a "United States" of Europe. Like the United States of America, this vast cultural entity has its own founding documents and hopes for the future. It also has its own empowering myth. Although it is still in its adolescence, the European Dream is the first transnational vision, one far better suited to the next stage in the human journey. Europeans are beginning to adopt a new global consciousness that extends beyond, and below, the borders of their nation-states, deeply embedding them in an increasingly interconnected world.

Comparing Quality of Life

6   Americans are so used to thinking of our country as the most successful on earth, they might be surprised to learn that, by many measures, this is no longer the case. In just a few decades, the European Union has grown to become the third-largest governing institution in the world. Though its landmass is half the size of the continental United States, its $10.5 trillion gross domestic product now eclipses the U.S. GDP, making it the world's largest economy. The European Union is already the world's leading exporter and largest internal trading market. Sixty-one of the 140 biggest companies on the Global Fortune 500 rankings are European, while only 50 are U.S. companies.

7   The comparisons between the world's two great superpowers are even more revealing when it comes to the quality of life. For example, in the European Union, there are approximately 322 physicians per 100,000 people, whereas in the United States there are only 279. The United States ranks 26th among the industrial nations in infant mortality, well below the EU average. The average life span in the 15 most developed EU countries is now 78.01 years, compared to 76.9 years in the United States.

8   Children in 12 European nations now rank higher in mathematics literacy than their American peers, and in 8 European countries children outscore Americans in scientific literacy. When it comes to wealth distribution—a crucial measure of a country's ability to deliver on the promise of prosperity—the United States ranks 24th among the industrial nations. All 18 of the most developed European countries have less income inequality between rich and poor. There are now more poor people living in America than in the 16 European nations for which data are available. America is also a more dangerous place to live. The U.S. homicide rate is four times higher than the European Union's. Even more disturbing, the rates of childhood homicides, suicides, and firearm-related deaths in the United States exceed those of the other 25 wealthiest nations, including the 14 wealthiest European countries. Although the United States is only 4 percent of the world's population, it now contains one-quarter of the world's entire prison population. While the EU member states average 87 prisoners per 100,000 people, the U.S. averages an incredible 685 prisoners per 100,000 people.

9   Europeans often remark that Americans "live to work," while Europeans "work to live." The average paid vacation time in Europe is now six weeks a year. By contrast, Americans, on average, receive only two weeks. Most Americans would also be shocked to learn that the average commute to work in Europe is less than 19 minutes. When one considers what makes a people great and what constitutes a better way of life, Europe is beginning to surpass America.

Two Dreams, One Past

10   Though historians seldom allude to it, the American Dream is largely a European creation transported to American soil and frozen in time. The American Dream was born in the early modern era—a period that saw the flowering of the individual, the development of a sophisticated private property regime, the invention of market capitalism, and the creation of the nation-state. The Protestant Reformation and the Enlightenment idea of science as the relentless pursuit and exploitation of nature's secrets had begun to take hold in Europe. While much of Europe eventually tempered its religious fervor, its scientific zeal, and its enthusiasm for unbridled market capitalism, preferring a compromise in the form of democratic socialism, America did not. Instead, successive generations chose to live out those older traditions in their purest forms, making us the most devoutly Protestant people on Earth and the most committed to scientific pursuits, private property, capitalism, and the nation-state.

11   That difference is reflected in the American and European Dreams, which at their core are about two diametrically opposed ideas about freedom and security. For Americans, freedom has long been associated with autonomy. An autonomous person is not dependent on others or vulnerable to circumstances beyond his or her control. To be autonomous one needs to be propertied. The more wealth one amasses, the more independent one is in the world. One is free by becoming self-reliant and an island unto oneself. With wealth comes exclusivity, and with exclusivity comes security.

12   The new European Dream is based on different assumptions about what constitutes freedom and security. For Europeans, freedom is found not in autonomy but in embeddedness. To be free is to have access to many interdependent relationships. The more communities one has access to, the more options one has for living a full and meaningful life. It is *inclusivity* that brings security—belonging, not belongings.

13   The American Dream emphasizes economic growth, personal wealth, and independence. The new European Dream focuses more on sustainable development, quality of life, and interdependence. The American Dream pays homage to the work ethic. The European Dream is more attuned to leisure and "deep play." The American Dream is inseparable from the country's religious heritage and deep spiritual faith. The European Dream is secular to the core. The American Dream depends on assimilation: We associate success with shedding our former ethnic ties and becoming free agents in the great American melting pot. The European Dream, by contrast, is based on preserving one's cultural identity and living in a multicultural world. The American Dream is wedded to love of country and patriotism. The European Dream is more cosmopolitan and less territorial.

14   Americans are more willing to employ military force to protect what we perceive to be our vital self-interests. Europeans are more reluctant to use military force and instead favor diplomacy, economic assistance, and aid to avert conflict and favor peacekeeping operations to maintain order. Americans tend to think locally while Europeans' loyalties are more divided and stretch from the local to the global. The American Dream is deeply personal and little concerned with the rest of humanity. The European Dream is more expansive and systemic, and therefore more bound to the welfare of the planet.

15   That isn't to say that Europe has suddenly become a utopia. For all of its talk about preserving cultural identity, Europeans have become increasingly hostile toward newly arrived immigrants and asylum seekers. Ethnic strife and religious intolerance continue to flare up in pockets across Europe. Anti-Semitism is on the rise again, as is discrimination against Muslims and other religious minorities. While Europe's people and countries berate American military hegemony and what they regard as a trigger-happy foreign policy, they are more than willing, on occasion, to let the U.S. armed forces safeguard European security interests. Meanwhile, both supporters and critics say that the European Union's governing machinery, based in Brussels, is a maze of bureaucratic red tape. Its officials are often accused of being aloof and unresponsive to the needs of the European citizens they supposedly serve.

16   The point, however, is not whether the Europeans are living up to their dream. We Americans have never fully lived up to ours. Rather, what's important is that Europe has articulated a new vision for the future that differs from our own in fundamental ways. These basic differences are crucial to understanding the dynamic that has begun to unfold between the early 21st century's two great superpowers.

Forging a Union

17 Unlike past states and empires whose origins are embedded in the myth of heroic victories on the battlefield, the European Union is novel in being the first mega governing institution in history to be born out of the ashes of defeat. Rather than commemorate a noble past, it sought to ensure that the past would never again be repeated. After a thousand years of unremitting conflict, war, and bloodshed, the nations of Europe emerged from two world wars with their population maimed and killed, their ancient monuments and cities lying in ruins, their worldly treasures depleted, and their way of life destroyed. Determined that they would never again take up arms against each other, the nations searched for a political mechanism that could move them beyond their ancient rivalries.

18   In a series of treaties following World War II, Europe's political elites began the painstaking process of creating a united Europe, all the

while attempting to define the limits of power of the emerging European Community. The federalists argued for ceding more power to the European central authority. The confederalists, by contrast, tried to keep power in the hands of the member states, viewing the new governing structure as a means to strengthen and coordinate their national objectives. Every compromise along the way reflected the tensions and strains between these two divergent visions.

19   While the powers that be continue to jostle back and forth between federalism and confederalism, the very technological, economic, and social realities that gave rise to the European Community, and that continue to push it along its journey to union, have created a political dynamic of a different sort. Rather than becoming a super-state or a mechanism to represent the enlightened national self-interests, the European Union has metamorphosed into a third form. It has become a discursive forum whose function is to referee relationships and help coordinate activity among a range of players, of which the nation-state is only one. The European Union's primary role has become orchestral. It facilitates the coming together of networks of engagement that include nation-states, but also extend outward to transnational organizations and inward to municipal and regional governments, as well as civil society organizations.

20   The European Union, then, is less a place than a process. Its genius is its indeterminacy. Unlike the traditional nation-state, whose purpose is to integrate, assimilate, and unify the diverse interests inside its borders, the European Union has no such mission. To the contrary, its role is just the opposite of what nation-states do. Its political cachet is bound up in facilitating and regulating a competing flow of divergent activities and interests.

21   There has never been a governing institution like the European Union. True, the European Union maintains many of the trappings of a state. Its laws supersede those of its 25 nations. It has a currency (the euro), a flag, and a headquarters. It regulates commerce and trade and coordinates energy, transportation, communications, and, increasingly, education across its many national borders. Its citizens enjoy a common EU passport. It has a European Parliament, which makes laws, and a European Court, whose judicial decisions are binding on member countries and their citizens. It also has a president and a military force.

22   But though the European Union qualifies as a state in many important particulars, it isn't one. It cannot tax its citizens, and its member countries still enjoy a veto on any decision that would deploy their troops. Most important, the European Union is an extraterritorial governing institution. Although it regulates activity within its member states, it has no claim to territory. Its legitimacy is based exclusively on the continued trust and goodwill of its members and the treaties and directives—and soon a new constitution—they have pledged to uphold.

23   Today, two-thirds of the people living across the European Union say they feel "European." Six out of ten EU citizens say they feel "very attached" or "fairly attached" to Europe, while one-third of Europeans between the ages of 21 and 35 say they "now regard themselves as more European than as nationals of their home country." Although it is difficult to fathom, this extraordinary change in how Europe's people perceive themselves has occurred in less than 50 years.

A New Constitution

24   Europeans are in the midst of a historic debate over whether to ratify a proposed constitution. Much of that 265-page document probably would not be acceptable to most Americans. Although many passages are cribbed largely from our own Declaration of Independence and the U.S. Constitution's Bill of Rights, there are other ideas and notions that are so alien to the contemporary American psyche that they might be considered with suspicion or even thought of as somewhat bizarre.

25   To begin with, there is not a single reference to God and only a veiled reference to Europe's "religious inheritance." Strange, on a continent where great cathedrals grace the central plazas of most cities and small churches and chapels appear around every corner. Many Europeans no longer believe in God. While 82 percent of Americans say that God is very important to them, less than 20 percent of Europeans express similar religious convictions. God is not the only consideration to be given short shift. There is only one reference to private property tucked deep inside the document, and barely a passing mention of free markets and trade.

26   Just as striking is what the constitution does emphasize. The EU objectives include a clear commitment to "sustainable development . . . based on balanced economic growth," a "social market economy," and "protection and improvement of the quality of the environment." The constitution would also "promote peace, . . . combat social exclusion and discrimination, . . . promote social justice and protection, equality between men and women, solidarity between generations, and protection of children's rights."

27   The constitution's Charter of Fundamental Rights goes far beyond our own Bill of Rights and subsequent constitutional amendments. For example, it promises everyone preventive health care, daily and weekly rest periods, an annual period of paid leave, maternity and parental leave, social and housing assistance, and environmental protection.

28   The EU Constitution is something new in human history. Though it is not as eloquent as the French and U.S. constitutions, it is the first governing document of its kind to expand the human franchise to the level of global consciousness. The language throughout the draft consti-

tution speaks of universalism, making it clear that its focus is not a people, or a territory, or a nation, but rather the human race and the planet we inhabit.

29   By decoupling human rights from territoriality, the European Union has ventured into a new political frontier, with far-reaching consequences for the future of the human race. Citizenship, heretofore, has always been attached exclusively to a nation-state. What happens, then, to the very idea of the state when the political rights of its members are conferred and guaranteed by an extraterritorial body? EU citizens have become the first people in the world whose rights are no longer dependent on the nation-state, but, rather, are universal and enforceable by law.

30   The gist of the new constitution is a commitment to respect human diversity, promote inclusivity, champion human rights and the rights of nature, foster quality of life, pursue sustainable development, free the human spirit for deep play, build a perpetual peace, and nurture a global consciousness. Together, these values and goals represent the woof and warp of a fledgling European Dream.

31   Europe's newly emerging dream is already threatening to create a schism with the United States in a number of areas. For example, the European Union forbids capital punishment. Even a person who commits the most heinous of crimes against fellow human beings, including terrorism or genocide, enjoys, in the official words of the European Union, "an inherent and inalienable dignity." The Europeans see their position on the death penalty as going to the very heart of their new dream, and they hope to convince the world of the righteousness of their cause.

32   The growing divisiveness between the American and European dreams manifests itself in other ways. For instance, the U.S. government gave the green light to genetically modified foods in the mid-1990s, and by the end of the decade over half of America's agricultural land was given over to GM crops. No new laws were enacted to govern the potential harmful effects. With its commitment to the precautionary principle and reining in high-risk scientific enterprise, in the name of sustainable development and environmental protection, Europe responded quite differently. Massive opposition to GM crops led to a de facto moratorium and tough new EU protections covering this technology.

33   Although it's too early to tell exactly how successful the "United States" of Europe will ultimately prove to be, in an era when our identities (and problems) extend beyond borders, no nation will be able to go it alone 25 years from now. The European states are the first to understand and act upon the emerging realities of a globally interdependent world. Others will follow.

The Future of a Dream

34 While I am an enthusiastic supporter of Europe's new experiment, my one real reservations is that I'm not sure how thick the European Dream is. Is Europe's commitment to cultural diversity and peaceful coexistence substantial enough to withstand the kind of terrorist attacks that we experienced on 9/11 or that Spain experienced on 3/11? Would Europeans remain committed to the principles of inclusivity and sustainable development were the world economy to plunge into a deep and prolonged downturn, maybe even a global depression?

35 These are the kinds of challenges that test the mettle of a people and the vitality and viability of their dream. Regardless of what others might think about America, the American Dream has stood the test, in good times and bad. We never lost hope in our dream, until very recently, even in the darkest hours. Will Europeans be able to say the same about their own nascent dream?

36 Having spent nearly 20 years of my life working in both Europe and America, I wonder whether the Europeans' sense of hope is sufficient to the task of sustaining a new vision for the future. Dreams require optimism, a sense that one's hopes can be fulfilled. Americans are flushed with hope and optimism; Europeans, as a people, are less so. Still, they are guardedly hopeful about their new union. And public opinion surveys show that a younger generation is measured in its optimism. Perhaps that's all we can or should expect. The unexamined optimism that has been so characteristic of the American spirit has not always served us well. In a world of increasing global threats, tempered enthusiasm balanced against a realistic assessment of risks might be more appropriate.

37 But there's also a deep pessimistic edge ingrained in the European persona—understandable, perhaps, after so many misbegotten political and social experiments, and so much camage over the centuries. Failures can dash hopes. But they can also make a people stronger, more resilient, and wiser. Overcoming cynicism is going to be as difficult and challenging for Europeans as overcoming naive optimism is for Americans.

38 These are tumultuous times. The European Dream is a beacon of light in a troubled world. It beckons us to a new age of inclusivity, diversity, quality of life, sustainability, universal human rights, the rights of nature, and peace on earth. We Americans used to say that the American Dream is worth dying for. The new European Dream is worth living for. ∎

CHAPTER 21

Science and Ethics

Dolly the sheep

The Ethics of Science and Technology

Item: In November 2004, couples with a family history of cancer were given an unusual permission by the Human Fertilization and Embryology Authority in Great Britain—they were allowed to select for human fertilization embryos free of those defective genes. Critics immediately complained about this effort to create "designer babies," drawing comparisons with Adolph Hitler's interest in creating a "super-race" of genetically enhanced Aryans and raising concerns about the possibility that "better" human beings might be constructed that have one or another advantage over "natural" people.

Item: Early in 2005 in the United States, members of the National Academy of Sciences were finishing a recommendation report on the legal and ethical status of "chimeras"—hybrid creatures created by implanting one animal's stem cells into the fetal matter of a different species. Several living creatures have been "invented" and patented in recent years, raising the question of the possibility of others: mice with human brains? or pigs bioengineered to produce human blood? or even a genetically plausible hybrid between humans and chimpanzees?

Item: On Thanksgiving Day 2001, teenager Shawn Woolley committed suicide after (his mother claims) weeks of twelve-hour stints on the online role-playing game EverQuest addled

> "Twenty-first century technologies—genetics, nanotechnology, and robotics—are so powerful they can spawn whole new classes of accidents and abuses."
>
> —BILL JOY, SUN MICROSYSTEMS

his neurochemical condition. In fact, do electronically mediated experiences like playing EverQuest, not to mention similar experiences that may soon make the transition from science fiction to reality, have mind-and-body effects on the human condition? And what about the widespread use of Prozac and other mind-altering drugs: do they threaten to change our sense of what human nature is at its core? No wonder science fiction movies and narratives are so popular—characters like "The Terminator," hybrids of human and nonhuman, seem possible in the not very distant future.

These three items, brought to our attention by Jeffrey Pruchnic, highlight some of the ethical issues related to science and technology that people are grappling with these days. True, science and technology, central enterprises in our culture, have always raised difficult moral and ethical questions. Whether it is environmental protection (the subject of Chapter 18), or medicine, or genetic engineering, or animal rights, or the teaching of evolution, or computer technologies, or space exploration, or military weapons technology, science and technology command our attention and our committed arguments because they challenge our assumptions about what is possible and push the limits of what we think of as ethical.

Contemporary Arguments

But the items we have cited point to something new: developing technologies are calling into question human nature itself. What are we to make of scientific developments that offer the potential for tremendous human benefits—if they also have the potential to change our very natures? Here we include arguments on three especially important and compelling developments related to science and human nature.

The first is nanotechnology. M.I.T. researcher K. Eric Drexler coined the term because "nano" literally means "one billionth": nanotechnology refers to the science of creating molecule-sized materials and machines. Occupying the space between biology and engineering, nanotechnologists promise to create new things that fundamentally change the ways we work and live. As Spiderman, *Star-Trek: The Next Generation,* and popular magazines such as *Forbes* and *Wired* all indicate, nanotechnology promises to be "the next big thing." Nano skin creams are on the market, nano-enhanced tennis balls are used in the Davis Cup, and microscopic silicon chips run computer games. More importantly, nanotechnologists are developing micro-machines that might radically improve water quality or benefit agriculture or clean up toxic wastes or make obsolete our reliance on oil by improving the efficiency of solar power. Others might enter the human body to repair tissue. Nanomaterials hundreds of times stronger than steel might make possible ten-pound autos or airplanes.

But is nanotechnology safe? Could dangerous nanoparticles escape and cause great damage? And what about its implications for the way human beings think of themselves? Will nanotechnology widen the gap between haves and have-nots around the globe? Those very serious questions are raised here in essays by Bill Joy and Francis Fukuyama. We also include a response to Joy and Fukuyama by Ralph C. Merkle, in the form of an interview.

The second new technology under watch is cloning. When, in February 1997, the English scientist Ian Wilmut announced that he had successfully cloned a ewe named Dolly, people around the world began to debate the wisdom of research that could lead to the cloning of human beings. Would cloning lead to all sorts of frightening mutations? Such fears gained credibility when Dolly died prematurely. Moreover, would cloning change fundamentally our sense of what it means to be human? Would it usurp the prerogative of God in the creation of human life?

On the other hand, cloning might offer a way for infertile couples to have children. Or it might offer the possibility of developing replacement parts for damaged organs, or lead to improvements in the care of certain genetic diseases. Would a ban on cloning be an unfortunate restriction on the human drive to know? In short, do the benefits of cloning counterbalance the risks? Here we offer two informed and informative arguments that attempt to answer such questions.

Finally, to conclude this chapter we offer an Issue in Focus on embryonic stem cell research. No doubt you have read and heard a great deal about stem cell research because of highly publicized appeals on its behalf by Christopher Reeve and Ron Reagan (at the 2004 Democratic National Convention). Here we provide not only Reagan's speech and responses to it, but also background information that you will need to understand the issue—and perhaps to write about it yourself.

BILL JOY

Why the Future Doesn't Need Us

Bill Joy (born 1954) is a cofounder of Sun Microsystems and was the chief scientist there until 2003. He played a major role in developing an early form of UNIX, a computer operating system, as well as other computer technologies, such as the JAVA programming language. "Why the Future Doesn't Need Us" appeared in the April 2000 Wired *magazine, a monthly periodical that covers cultural, political, and economic impacts of technology. The article, which expresses a surprisingly critical position on*

*technology, created a large stir—see the interview with Ralph C. Merkle
that follows this selection.*

I

1   From the moment I became involved in the creation of new technologies, their ethical dimensions have concerned me, but it was only in the autumn of 1998 that I became anxiously aware of how great are the dangers facing us in the 21st century. I can date the onset of my unease to the day I met Ray Kurzweil, the deservedly famous inventor of the first reading machine for the blind and many other amazing things.

2   Ray and I were both speakers at George Gilder's Telecosm conference, and I encountered him by chance in the bar of the hotel after both our sessions were over. I was sitting with John Searle, a Berkeley philosopher who studies consciousness. While we were talking, Ray approached and a conversation began, the subject of which haunts me to this day.

3   I had missed Ray's talk and the subsequent panel that Ray and John had been on, and they now picked right up where they'd left off, with Ray saying that the rate of improvement of technology was going to accelerate and that we were going to become robots or fuse with robots or something like that, and John countering that this couldn't happen, because the robots couldn't be conscious.

4   While I had heard such talk before, I had always felt sentient robots were in the realm of science fiction. But now, from someone I respected, I was hearing a strong argument that they were a near-term possibility. I was taken aback, especially given Ray's proven ability to imagine and create the future. I already knew that new technologies like genetic engineering and nanotechnology were giving us the power to remake the world, but a realistic and imminent scenario for intelligent robots surprised me.

5   It's easy to get jaded about such breakthroughs. We hear in the news almost every day of some kind of technological or scientific advance. Yet this was no ordinary prediction. In the hotel bar, Ray gave me a partial preprint of his then-forthcoming book *The Age of Spiritual Machines,* which outlined a utopia he foresaw—one in which humans gained near immortality by becoming one with robotic technology. On reading it, my sense of unease only intensified; I felt sure he had to be understating the dangers, understating the probability of a bad outcome along this path.

6   I found myself most troubled by a passage detailing a *dys*topian scenario:

7   First let us postulate that the computer scientists succeed in developing intelligent machines that can do all things better than human beings can do them. In that case presumably all work will be done

by vast, highly organized systems of machines and no human effort will be necessary. Either of two cases might occur. The machines might be permitted to make all of their own decisions without human oversight, or else human control over the machines might be retained.

8   If the machines are permitted to make all their own decisions, we can't make any conjectures as to the results, because it is impossible to guess how such machines might behave. We only point out that the fate of the human race would be at the mercy of the machines. It might be argued that the human race would never be foolish enough to hand over all the power to the machines. But we are suggesting neither that the human race would voluntarily turn power over to the machines nor that the machines would willfully seize power. What we do suggest is that the human race might easily permit itself to drift into a position of such dependence on the machines that it would have no practical choice but to accept all of the machines' decisions. As society and the problems that face it become more and more complex and machines become more and more intelligent, people will let machines make more of their decisions for them, simply because machine-made decisions will bring better results than man-made ones. Eventually a stage may be reached at which the decisions necessary to keep the system running will be so complex that human beings will be incapable of making them intelligently. At that stage the machines will be in effective control. People won't be able to just turn the machines off, because they will be so dependent on them that turning them off would amount to suicide.

9   On the other hand it is possible that human control over the machines may be retained. In that case the average man may have control over certain private machines of his own, such as his car or his personal computer, but control over large systems of machines will be in the hands of a tiny elite—just as it is today, but with two differences. Due to improved techniques the elite will have greater control over the masses; and because human work will no longer be necessary the masses will be superfluous, a useless burden on the system. If the elite is ruthless they may simply decide to exterminate the mass of humanity. If they are humane they may use propaganda or other psychological or biological techniques to reduce the birth rate until the mass of humanity becomes extinct, leaving the world to the elite. Or, if the elite consists of soft-hearted liberals, they may decide to play the role of good shepherds to the rest of the human race. They will see to it that everyone's physical needs are satisfied, that all children are raised under psychologically hygienic conditions, that everyone has a wholesome hobby to keep him busy, and that anyone who may become dissatisfied undergoes "treatment" to cure his "problem." Of course, life will be so purposeless that people will have to be biologically or psychologically engineered either to remove their need for the power process or

make them "sublimate" their drive for power into some harmless hobby. These engineered human beings may be happy in such a society, but they will most certainly not be free. They will have been reduced to the status of domestic animals.[1]

10   In the book, you don't discover until you turn the page that the author of this passage is Theodore Kaczynski—the Unabomber. I am no apologist for Kaczynski. His bombs killed three people during a 17-year terror campaign and wounded many others. One of his bombs gravely injured my friend David Gelernter, one of the most brilliant and visionary computer scientists of our time. Like many of my colleagues, I felt that I could easily have been the Unabomber's next target.

11   Kaczynski's actions were murderous and, in my view, criminally insane. He is clearly a Luddite, but simply saying this does not dismiss his argument; as difficult as it is for me to acknowledge, I saw some merit in the reasoning in this single passage. I felt compelled to confront it.

12   Kaczynski's dystopian vision describes unintended consequences, a well-known problem with the design and use of technology, and one that is clearly related to Murphy's law—"Anything that can go wrong, will." (Actually, this is Finagle's law, which in itself shows that Finagle was right.) Our overuse of antibiotics has led to what may be the biggest such problem so far: the emergence of antibiotic-resistant and much more dangerous bacteria. Similar things happened when attempts to eliminate malarial mosquitoes using DDT caused them to acquire DDT resistance; malarial parasites likewise acquired multi-drug-resistant genes.[2]

13   The cause of many such surprises seems clear: The systems involved are complex, involving interaction among and feedback between many parts. Any changes to such a system will cascade in ways that are difficult to predict; this is especially true when human actions are involved.

14   I started showing friends the Kaczynski quote from *The Age of Spiritual Machines;* I would hand them Kurzweil's book, let them read the quote, and then watch their reaction as they discovered who had written it. At around the same time, I found Hans Moravec's book *Robot: Mere Machine to Transcendent Mind.* Moravec is one of the leaders in robotics research, and was a founder of the world's largest robotics research program, at Carnegie Mellon University. *Robot* gave me more material to try out on my friends—material surprisingly supportive of Kaczynski's argument. For example:

15   Biological species almost never survive encounters with superior competitors. Ten million years ago, South and North America were separated by a sunken Panama isthmus. South America, like Australia today, was populated by marsupial mammals, including pouched equivalents of rats, deers, and tigers. When the isthmus connecting North and South America rose, it took only a few thou-

sand years for the northern placental species, with slightly more effective metabolisms and reproductive and nervous systems, to displace and eliminate almost all the southern marsupials.

16   In a completely free marketplace, superior robots would surely affect humans as North American placentals affected South American marsupials (and as humans have affected countless species). Robotic industries would compete vigorously among themselves for matter, energy, and space, incidentally driving their price beyond human reach. Unable to afford the necessities of life, biological humans would be squeezed out of existence.

17   There is probably some breathing room, because we do not live in a completely free marketplace. Government coerces nonmarket behavior, especially by collecting taxes. Judiciously applied, governmental coercion could support human populations in high style on the fruits of robot labor, perhaps for a long while.

18   A textbook dystopia—and Moravec is just getting wound up. He goes on to discuss how our main job in the 21st century will be "ensuring continued cooperation from the robot industries" by passing laws decreeing that they be "nice,"[3] and to describe how seriously dangerous a human can be "once transformed into an unbounded superintelligent robot." Moravec's view is that the robots will eventually succeed us— that humans clearly face extinction.

19   I decided it was time to talk to my friend Danny Hillis. Danny became famous as the cofounder of Thinking Machines Corporation, which built a very powerful parallel supercomputer. Despite my current job title of Chief Scientist at Sun Microsystems, I am more a computer architect than a scientist, and I respect Danny's knowledge of the information and physical sciences more than that of any other single person I know. Danny is also a highly regarded futurist who thinks long-term: four years ago he started the Long Now Foundation, which is building a clock designed to last 10,000 years, in an attempt to draw attention to the pitifully short attention span of our society.

20   So I flew to Los Angeles for the express purpose of having dinner with Danny and his wife, Pati. I went through my now-familiar routine, trotting out the ideas and passages that I found so disturbing. Danny's answer—directed specifically at Kurzweil's scenario of humans merging with robots—came swiftly, and quite surprised me. He said, simply, that the changes would come gradually, and that we would get used to them.

21   But I guess I wasn't totally surprised. I had seen a quote from Danny in Kurzweil's book in which he said, "I'm as fond of my body as anyone, but if I can be 200 with a body of silicon, I'll take it." It seemed that he was at peace with this process and its attendant risks, while I was not.

22   While talking and thinking about Kurzweil, Kaczynski, and Moravec, I suddenly remembered a novel I had read almost 20 years

ago—*The White Plague,* by Frank Herbert—in which a molecular biologist is driven insane by the senseless murder of his family. To seek revenge he constructs and disseminates a new and highly contagious plague that kills widely but selectively. (We're lucky Kaczynski was a mathematician, not a molecular biologist.) I was also reminded of the Borg of *Star Trek,* a hive of partly biological, partly robotic creatures with a strong destructive streak. Borg-like disasters are a staple of science fiction, so why hadn't I been more concerned about such robotic dystopias earlier? Why weren't other people more concerned about these nightmarish scenarios?

23   Part of the answer certainly lies in our attitude toward the new—in our bias toward instant familiarity and unquestioning acceptance. Accustomed to living with almost routine scientific breakthroughs, we have yet to come to terms with the fact that the most compelling 21st-century technologies—robotics, genetic engineering, and nanotechnology—pose a different threat than the technologies that have come before. Specifically, robots, engineered organisms, and nanobots share a dangerous amplifying factor: They can self-replicate. A bomb is blown up only once—but one bot can become many, and quickly get out of control.

24   Much of my work over the past 25 years has been on computer networking, where the sending and receiving of messages creates the opportunity for out-of-control replication. But while replication in a computer or a computer network can be a nuisance, at worst it disables a machine or takes down a network or network service. Uncontrolled self-replication in these newer technologies runs a much greater risk: a risk of substantial damage in the physical world.

25   Each of these technologies also offers untold promise: the vision of near immortality that Kurzweil sees in his robot dreams drives us forward; genetic engineering may soon provide treatments, if not outright cures, for most diseases; and nanotechnology and nanomedicine can address yet more ills. Together they could significantly extend our average life span and improve the quality of our lives. Yet, with each of these technologies, a sequence of small, individually sensible advances leads to an accumulation of great power and, concomitantly, great danger.

26   What was different in the 20th century? Certainly, the technologies underlying the weapons of mass destruction (WMD)—nuclear, biological, and chemical (NBC)—were powerful, and the weapons an enormous threat. But building nuclear weapons required, at least for a time, access to both rare—indeed, effectively unavailable—raw materials and highly protected information; biological and chemical weapons programs also tended to require large-scale activities.

27   The 21st-century technologies—genetics, nanotechnology, and robotics (GNR)—are so powerful that they can spawn whole new classes of accidents and abuses. Most dangerously, for the first time, these acci-

dents and abuses are widely within the reach of individuals or small groups. They will not require large facilities or rare raw materials. Knowledge alone will enable the use of them.

28   Thus we have the possibility not just of weapons of mass destruction but of knowledge-enabled mass destruction (KMD), this destructiveness hugely amplified by the power of self-replication.

29   I think it is no exaggeration to say we are on the cusp of the further perfection of extreme evil, an evil whose possibility spreads well beyond that which weapons of mass destruction bequeathed to the nation-states, on to a surprising and terrible empowerment of extreme individuals.

II

30   Nothing about the way I got involved with computers suggested to me that I was going to be facing these kinds of issues.

31   My life has been driven by a deep need to ask questions and find answers. When I was 3, I was already reading, so my father took me to the elementary school, where I sat on the principal's lap and read him a story. I started school early, later skipped a grade, and escaped into books—I was incredibly motivated to learn. I asked lots of questions, often driving adults to distraction.

32   As a teenager I was very interested in science and technology. I wanted to be a ham radio operator but didn't have the money to buy the equipment. Ham radio was the Internet of its time: very addictive, and quite solitary. Money issues aside, my mother put her foot down—I was not to be a ham; I was antisocial enough already.

33   I may not have had many close friends, but I was awash in ideas. By high school, I had discovered the great science fiction writers. I remember especially Heinlein's *Have Spacesuit Will Travel* and Asimov's *I, Robot,* with its Three Laws of Robotics. I was enchanted by the descriptions of space travel, and wanted to have a telescope to look at the stars; since I had no money to buy or make one, I checked books on telescope-making out of the library and read about making them instead. I soared in my imagination.

34   Thursday nights my parents went bowling, and we kids stayed home alone. It was the night of Gene Roddenberry's original *Star Trek,* and the program made a big impression on me. I came to accept its notion that humans had a future in space, Western-style, with big heroes and adventures. Roddenberry's vision of the centuries to come was one with strong moral values, embodied in codes like the Prime Directive: to not interfere in the development of less technologically advanced civilizations. This had an incredible appeal to me; ethical humans, not robots, dominated this future, and I took Roddenberry's dream as part of my own.

35   I excelled in mathematics in high school, and when I went to the University of Michigan as an undergraduate engineering student I took the advanced curriculum of the mathematics majors. Solving math problems was an exciting challenge, but when I discovered computers I found something much more interesting: a machine into which you could put a program that attempted to solve a problem, after which the machine quickly checked the solution. The computer had a clear notion of correct and incorrect, true and false. Were my ideas correct? The machine could tell me. This was very seductive.

36   I was lucky enough to get a job programming early supercomputers and discovered the amazing power of large machines to numerically simulate advanced designs. When I went to graduate school at UC Berkeley in the mid-1970s, I started staying up late, often all night, inventing new worlds inside the machines. Solving problems. Writing the code that argued so strongly to be written.

37   In *The Agony and the Ecstasy,* Irving Stone's biographical novel of Michelangelo, Stone described vividly how Michelangelo released the statues from the stone, "breaking the marble spell," carving from the images in his mind.[4] In my most ecstatic moments, the software in the computer emerged in the same way. Once I had imagined it in my mind I felt that it was already there in the machine, waiting to be released. Staying up all night seemed a small price to pay to free it—to give the ideas concrete form.

38   After a few years at Berkeley I started to send out some of the software I had written—an instructional Pascal system, Unix utilities, and a text editor called vi (which is still, to my surprise, widely used more than 20 years later)—to others who had similar small PDP-11 and VAX minicomputers. These adventures in software eventually turned into the Berkeley version of the Unix operating system, which became a personal "success disaster"—so many people wanted it that I never finished my PhD. Instead I got a job working for Darpa putting Berkeley Unix on the Internet and fixing it to be reliable and to run large research applications well. This was all great fun and very rewarding. And, frankly, I saw no robots here, or anywhere near.

39   Still, by the early 1980s, I was drowning. The Unix releases were very successful, and my little project of one soon had money and some staff, but the problem at Berkeley was always office space rather than money—there wasn't room for the help the project needed, so when the other founders of Sun Microsystems showed up I jumped at the chance to join them. At Sun, the long hours continued into the early days of workstations and personal computers, and I have enjoyed participating in the creation of advanced microprocessor technologies and Internet technologies such as Java and Jini.

40   From all this, I trust it is clear that I am not a Luddite. I have always, rather, had a strong belief in the value of the scientific search for truth and in the ability of great engineering to bring material progress. The Industrial Revolution has immeasurably improved everyone's life over the last couple hundred years, and I always expected my career to involve the building of worthwhile solutions to real problems, one problem at a time.

41   I have not been disappointed. My work has had more impact than I had ever hoped for and has been more widely used than I could have reasonably expected. I have spent the last 20 years still trying to figure out how to make computers as reliable as I want them to be (they are not nearly there yet) and how to make them simple to use (a goal that has met with even less relative success). Despite some progress, the problems that remain seem even more daunting.

42   But while I was aware of the moral dilemmas surrounding technology's consequences in fields like weapons research, I did not expect that I would confront such issues in my own field, or at least not so soon.

43   Perhaps it is always hard to see the bigger impact while you are in the vortex of a change. Failing to understand the consequences of our inventions while we are in the rapture of discovery and innovation seems to be a common fault of scientists and technologists; we have long been driven by the overarching desire to know that is the nature of science's quest, not stopping to notice that the progress to newer and more powerful technologies can take on a life of its own.

44   I have long realized that the big advances in information technology come not from the work of computer scientists, computer architects, or electrical engineers, but from that of physical scientists. The physicists Stephen Wolfram and Brosl Hasslacher introduced me, in the early 1980s, to chaos theory and nonlinear systems. In the 1990s, I learned about complex systems from conversations with Danny Hillis, the biologist Stuart Kauffman, the Nobel-laureate physicist Murray Gell-Mann, and others. Most recently, Hasslacher and the electrical engineer and device physicist Mark Reed have been giving me insight into the incredible possibilities of molecular electronics.

45   In my own work, as codesigner of three microprocessor architectures—SPARC, picoJava, and MAJC—and as the designer of several implementations thereof, I've been afforded a deep and firsthand acquaintance with Moore's law. For decades, Moore's law has correctly predicted the exponential rate of improvement of semiconductor technology. Until last year I believed that the rate of advances predicted by Moore's law might continue only until roughly 2010, when some physical limits would begin to be reached. It was not obvious to me that a new technology would arrive in time to keep performance advancing smoothly.

46   But because of the recent rapid and radical progress in molecular electronics—where individual atoms and molecules replace lithographically drawn transistors—and related nanoscale technologies, we should be able to meet or exceed the Moore's law rate of progress for another 30 years. By 2030, we are likely to be able to build machines, in quantity, a million times as powerful as the personal computers of today— sufficient to implement the dreams of Kurzwell and Moravec.

47   As this enormous computing power is combined with the manipulative advances of the physical sciences and the new, deep understandings in genetics, enormous transformative power is being unleashed. These combinations open up the opportunity to completely redesign the world, for better or worse: The replicating and evolving processes that have been confined to the natural world are about to become realms of human endeavor.

48   In designing software and microprocessors, I have never had the feeling that I was designing an intelligent machine. The software and hardware is so fragile and the capabilities of the machine to "think" so clearly absent that, even as a possibility, this has always seemed very far in the future.

49   But now, with the prospect of human-level computing power in about 30 years, a new idea suggests itself: that I may be working to create tools which will enable the construction of the technology that may replace our species. How do I feel about this? Very uncomfortable. Having struggled my entire career to build reliable software systems, it seems to me more than likely that this future will not work out as well as some people may imagine. My personal experience suggests we tend to overestimate our design abilities.

50   Given the incredible power of these new technologies, shouldn't we be asking how we can best coexist with them? And if our own extinction is a likely, or even possible, outcome of our technological development, shouldn't we proceed with great caution?

Notes

1. The passage Kurzweil quotes is from Kaczynski's "Unabomber Manifesto," which was published jointly, under duress, by *The New York Times* and *The Washington Post* to attempt to bring his campaign of terror to an end. I agree with David Gelernter, who said about their decision:

   "It was a tough call for the newspapers. To say yes would be giving in to terrorism, and for all they knew he was lying anyway. On the other hand, to say yes might stop the killing. There was also a chance that someone would read the tract and get a hunch about the author; and that is exactly what happened. The suspect's brother read it, and it rang a bell.

   "I would have told them not to publish. I'm glad they didn't ask me. I guess."

   (*Drawing Life: Surviving the Unabomber*. Free Press, 1997: 120.)

2. Garrett, Laurie. *The Coming Plague: Newly Emerging Diseases in a World Out of Balance.* Penguin, 1994: 47–52, 414, 419, 452.

3. Isaac Asimov described what became the most famous view of ethical rules for robot behavior in his book *I, Robot* in 1950, in his Three Laws of Robotics: 1. A robot may not injure a human being, or, through inaction, allow a human being to come to harm. 2. A robot must obey the orders given it by human beings, except where such orders would conflict with the First Law. 3. A robot must protect its own existence, as long as such protection does not conflict with the First or Second Law.

4. Michelangelo wrote a sonnet that begins:

   Non ha l' ottimo artista alcun concetto
   Ch' un marmo solo in sè non circonscriva
   Col suo soverchio; e solo a quello arriva
   La man che ubbidisce all' intelleto.

Stone translates this as:

   The best of artists hath no thought to show
   which the rough stone in its superfluous shell
   doth not include; to break the marble spell
   is all the hand that serves the brain can do.

Stone describes the process: "He was not working from his drawings or clay models; they had all been put away. He was carving from the images in his mind. His eyes and hands knew where every line, curve, mass must emerge, and at what depth in the heart of the stone to create the low relief."

(*The Agony and the Ecstasy.* Doubleday, 1961: 6, 144.) ■

FRANCIS FUKUYAMA

Tale of Two Dystopias

Political economist Francis Fukuyama (born 1952) is the Bernard L. Schwartz Professor at Johns Hopkins University. While he has published numerous academic articles, he is perhaps best known as the author of The End of History and the Last Man *(1992), which argues that after the Cold War the citizens of the world basically agreed that liberal democracy is the ideology by which to live. Fukuyama has also authored* Trust: The Social Virtues and the Creation of Prosperity *(1995) and* Our Posthuman Future: Consequences of the Biotechnology Revolution *(2002), from which the excerpt below comes. Fukuyama is concerned about the dangers and inequalities that can arise from the use of biotechnology to shape human nature. Fukuyama currently also serves on the Bush administration's President's Council on Bioethics.*

The threat to man does not come in the first instance from the
potentially lethal machines and apparatus of technology. The
actual threat has always afflicted man in his essence. The rule of
enframing (*Gestell*) threatens man with the possibility that it
could be denied to him to enter into a more original revealing
and hence to experience the call of a more primal truth.

Martin Heidegger, *The Question Concerning Technology*[1]

1   I was born in 1952, right in the middle of the American baby boom.
For any person growing up as I did in the middle decades of the
twentieth century, the future and its terrifying possibilities were defined
by two books, George Orwell's *1984* (first published in 1949) and Aldous Huxley's *Brave New World* (published in 1932).

2   The two books were far more prescient than anyone realized at the
time, because they were centered on two different technologies that
would in fact emerge and shape the world over the next two generations.
The novel *1984* was about what we now call information technology:
central to the success of the vast, totalitarian empire that had been set up
over Oceania was a device called the telescreen, a wall-sized flat-panel
display that could simultaneously send and receive images from each individual household to a hovering Big Brother. The telescreen was what
permitted the vast centralization of social life under the Ministry of Truth
and the Ministry of Love, for it allowed the government to banish privacy
by monitoring every word and deed over a massive network of wires.

3   *Brave New World,* by contrast, was about the other big technological revolution about to take place, that of biotechnology. Bokanovskifi-
cation, the hatching of people not in wombs but, as we now say, in
vitro; the drug soma, which gave people instant happiness; the Feelies,
in which sensation was simulated by implanted electrodes; and the
modification of behavior through constant subliminal repetition and,
when that didn't work, through the administration of various artificial
hormones were what gave this book its particularly creepy ambiance.

4   With at least a half century separating us from the publication of
these books, we can see that while the technological predictions they
made were startlingly accurate, the political predictions of the first book,
1984, were entirely wrong. The year 1984 came and went, with the
United States still locked in a Cold War struggle with the Soviet Union.
That year saw the introduction of a new model of the IBM personal computer and the beginning of what became the PC revolution. As Peter Huber has argued, the personal computer, linked to the Internet, was in fact
the realization of Orwell's telescreen.[2] But instead of becoming an instrument of centralization and tyranny, it led to just the opposite: the democ-

---

[1]Martin Heidegger, *Basic Writings* (New York: Harper and Row, 1957), p. 308.

ratization of access to information and the decentralization of politics. Instead of Big Brother watching everyone, people could use the PC and Internet to watch Big Brother, as governments everywhere were driven to publish more information on their own activities.

5   Just five years after 1984, in a series of dramatic events that would earlier have seemed like political science fiction, the Soviet Union and its empire collapsed, and the totalitarian threat that Orwell had so vividly evoked vanished. People were again quick to point out that these two events—the collapse of totalitarian empires and the emergence of the personal computer, as well as other forms of inexpensive information technology, from TVs and radios to faxes and e-mail—were not unrelated. Totalitarian rule depended on a regime's ability to maintain a monopoly over information, and once modern information technology made that impossible, the regime's power was undermined.

6   The political prescience of the other great dystopia, *Brave New World,* remains to be seen. Many of the technologies that Huxley envisioned, like in vitro fertilization, surrogate motherhood, psychotropic drugs, and genetic engineering for the manufacture of children, are already here or just over the horizon. But this revolution has only just begun; the daily avalanche of announcements of new breakthroughs in biomedical technology and achievements such as the completion of the Human Genome Project in the year 2000 portend much more serious changes to come.

7   Of the nightmares evoked by these two books, *Brave New World*'s always struck me as more subtle and more challenging. It is easy to see what's wrong with the world of *1984:* the protagonist, Winston Smith, is known to hate rats above all things, so Big Brother devises a cage in which rats can bite at Smith's face in order to get him to betray his lover. This is the world of classical tyranny, technologically empowered but not so different from what we have tragically seen and known in human history.

8   In *Brave New World,* by contrast, the evil is not so obvious because no one is hurt; indeed, this is a world in which everyone gets what they want. As one of the characters notes, "The Controllers realized that force was no good," and that people would have to be seduced rather than compelled to live in an orderly society. In this world, disease and social conflict have been abolished, there is no depression, madness, loneliness, or emotional distress, sex is good and readily available. There is even a government ministry to ensure that the length of time between the appearance of a desire and its satisfaction is kept to a minimum. No one takes religion seriously any longer, no one is introspective or has unrequited longings, the biological family has been abolished, no one reads Shakespeare. But no one (save John the Savage,

²Peter Huber, *Orwell's Revenge The 1984 Palmipsest* (New York: Free Press, 1994), pp. 222–228.

the book's protagonist) misses these things, either, since they are happy and healthy.

9   Since the novel's publication, there have probably been several million high school essays written in answer to the question, "What's wrong with this picture?" The answer given (on papers that get A's, at any rate) usually runs something like this: the people in *Brave New World* may be healthy and happy, but they have ceased to be *human beings.* They no longer struggle, aspire, love, feel pain, make difficult moral choices, have families, or do any of the things that we traditionally associate with being human. They no longer have the characteristics that give us human dignity. Indeed, there is no such thing as the human race any longer, since they have been bred by the Controllers into separate castes of Alphas, Betas, Epsilons, and Gammas who are as distant from each other as humans are from animals. Their world has become unnatural in the most profound sense imaginable, because *human nature* has been altered. In the words of bioethicist Leon Kass, "Unlike the man reduced by disease or slavery, the people dehumanized à la *Brave New World* are not miserable, don't know that they are dehumanized, and, what is worse, would not care if they knew. They are, indeed, happy slaves with a slavish happiness."[3]

10   But while this kind of answer is usually adequate to satisfy the typical high school English teacher, it does not (as Kass goes on to note) probe nearly deeply enough. For one can then ask, What is so important about being a human being in the traditional way that Huxley defines it? After all, what the human race is today is the product of an evolutionary process that has been going on for millions of years, one that with any luck will continue well into the future. There are no fixed human characteristics, except for a general capability to choose what we want to be, to modify ourselves in accordance with our desires. So who is to tell us that being human and having dignity means sticking with a set of emotional responses that are the accidental by-product of our evolutionary history? There is no such thing as a biological family, no such thing as human nature or a "normal" human being, and even if there were, why should that be a guide for what is right and just? Huxley is telling us, in effect, that we should continue to feel pain, be depressed or lonely, or suffer from debilitating disease, all because that is what human beings have done for most of their existence as a species. Certainly, no one ever got elected to Congress on such a platform. Instead of taking these characteristics and saying that they are the basis for "human dignity," why don't we simply accept our destiny as creatures who modify themselves?

[3]Leon Kass, *Toward a More Natural Science: Biology and Human Affairs* (New York: Free Press, 1985), p. 35.

11   Huxley suggests that one source for a definition of what it means to be a human being is religion. In *Brave New World,* religion has been abolished and Christianity is a distant memory. The Christian tradition maintains that man is created in God's image, which is the source of human dignity. To use biotechnology to engage in what another Christian writer, C. S. Lewis, called the "abolition of man" is thus a violation of God's will. But I don't think that a careful reading of Huxley or Lewis leads to the conclusion that either writer believed religion to be the *only* grounds on which one could understand the meaning of being human. Both writers suggest that nature itself, and in particular human nature, has a special role in defining for us what is right and wrong, just and unjust, important and unimportant. So our final judgment on "what's wrong" with Huxley's brave new world stands or falls with our view of how important human nature is as a source of values.

12   The aim of my book is to argue that Huxley was right, that the most significant threat posed by contemporary biotechnology is the possibility that it will alter human nature and thereby move us into a "posthuman" stage of history. This is important, I will argue, because human nature exists, is a meaningful concept, and has provided a stable continuity to our experience as a species. It is, conjointly with religion, what defines our most basic values. Human nature shapes and constrains the possible kinds of political regimes, so a technology powerful enough to reshape what we are will have possibly malign consequences for liberal democracy and the nature of politics itself.

13   It may be that, as in the case of *1984,* we will eventually find biotechnology's consequences are completely and surprisingly benign, and that we were wrong to lose sleep over it. It may be that the technology will in the end prove much less powerful than it seems today, or that people will be moderate and careful in their application of it. But one of the reasons I am not quite so sanguine is that biotechnology, in contrast to many other scientific advances, mixes obvious benefits with subtle harms in one seamless package.

14   Nuclear weapons and nuclear energy were perceived as dangerous from the start, and therefore were subject to strict regulation from the moment the Manhattan Project created the first atomic bomb in 1945. Observers like Bill Joy have worried about nanotechnology—that is, molecular-scale self-replicating machines capable of reproducing out of control and destroying their creators.[4] But such threats are actually the easiest to deal with because they are so obvious. If you are likely to be killed by a machine you've created, you take measures to protect yourself. And so far we've had a reasonable record in keeping our machines under control.

15   There may be products of biotechnology that will be similarly obvious in the dangers they pose to mankind—for example, superbugs,

new viruses, or genetically modified foods that produce toxic reactions. Like nuclear weapons or nanotechnology, these are in a way the easiest to deal with because once we have identified them as dangerous, we can treat them as a straightforward threat. The more typical threats raised by biotechnology, on the other hand, are those captured so well by Huxley, and are summed up in the title of an article by novelist Tom Wolfe, "Sorry, but Your Soul Just Died."[5] Medical technology offers us in many cases a devil's bargain: longer life, but with reduced mental capacity; freedom from depression, together with freedom from creativity or spirit; therapies that blur the line between what we achieve on our own and what we achieve because of the levels of various chemicals in our brains.

16   Consider the following three scenarios, all of which are distinct possibilities that may unfold over the next generation or two.

17   The first has to do with new drugs. As a result of advances in neuropharmacology, psychologists discover that human personality is much more plastic than formerly believed. It is already the case that psychotropic drugs such as Prozac and Ritalin can affect traits like self-esteem and the ability to concentrate, but they tend to produce a host of unwanted side effects and hence are shunned except in cases of clear therapeutic need. But in the future, knowledge of genomics permits pharmaceutical companies to tailor drugs very specifically to the genetic profiles of individual patients and greatly minimize unintended side effects. Stolid people can become vivacious; introspective ones extroverted; you can adopt one personality on Wednesday and another for the weekend. There is no longer any excuse for anyone to be depressed or unhappy; even "normally" happy people can make themselves happier without worries of addiction, hangovers, or long-term brain damage.

18   In the second scenario, advances in stem cell research allow scientists to regenerate virtually any tissue in the body, such that life expectancies are pushed well above 100 years. If you need a new heart or liver, you just grow one inside the chest cavity of a pig or cow; brain damage from Alzheimer's and stroke can be reversed. The only problem is that there are many subtle and some not-so-subtle aspects of human aging that the biotech industry hasn't quite figured out how to fix: people grow mentally rigid and increasingly fixed in their views as they age, and try as they might, they can't make themselves sexually attractive to each other and continue to long for partners of reproductive age. Worst of all, they just refuse to get out of the way, not just of their children, but their grandchildren and great-grandchildren. On the other hand, so few people have children or any connection with traditional reproduction that it scarcely seems to matter.

19   In a third scenario, the wealthy routinely screen embryos before implantation so as to optimize the kind of children they have. You can

[4]Bill Joy, "Why the Future Doesn't Need Us," *Wired* 8 (2000): 238–246.
[5]Tom Wolfe, "Sorry, but Your Soul Just Died," *Forbes ASAP*, December 2, 1996.

increasingly tell the social background of a young person by his or her looks and intelligence; if someone doesn't live up to social expectations, he tends to blame bad genetic choices by his parents rather than himself. Human genes have been transferred to animals and even to plants, for research purposes and to produce new medical products; and animal genes have been added to certain embryos to increase their physical endurance or resistance to disease. Scientists have not dared to produce a full-scale chimera, half human and half ape, though they could; but young people begin to suspect that classmates who do much less well than they do are in fact genetically not fully human. Because, in fact, they aren't.

20   Sorry, but your soul just died . . .

21   Toward the very end of his life, Thomas Jefferson wrote, "The general spread of the light of science has already laid open to every view the palpable truth, that the mass of mankind has not been born with saddles on their backs, nor a favored few booted and spurred, ready to ride them legitimately, by the grace of God."[6] The political equality enshrined in the Declaration of Independence rests on the empirical fact of natural human equality. We vary greatly as individuals and by culture, but we share a common humanity that allows every human being to potentially communicate with and enter into a moral relationship with every other human being on the planet. The ultimate question raised by biotechnology is, What will happen to political rights once we are able to, in effect, breed some people with saddles on their backs, and others with boots and spurs?

A Straightforward Solution

22   What should we do in response to biotechnology that in the future will mix great potential benefits with threats that are either physical and overt or spiritual and subtle? The answer is obvious: *We should use the power of the state to regulate it.* And if this proves to be beyond the power of any individual nation-state to regulate, it needs to be regulated on an international basis. We need to start thinking concretely now about how to build institutions that can discriminate between good and bad uses of biotechnology, and effectively enforce these rules both nationally and internationally.

23   This obvious answer is not obvious to many of the participants in the current biotechnology debate. The discussion remains mired at a relatively abstract level about the ethics of procedures like cloning or stem cell research, and divided into one camp that would like to permit everything and another camp that would like to ban wide areas of research and practice. The broader debate is of course an important one, but events are moving so rapidly that we will soon need more practical guidance on how we can direct future developments so that the technol-

[6]Letter to Roger C. Weightman, June 24, 1926, in *The Life and Selected Writings of Thomas Jefferson*, Thomas Jefferson (New York: Modern Library, 1944), pp. 729–730.

ogy remains man's servant rather than his master. Since it seems very unlikely that we will either permit everything or ban research that is highly promising, we need to find a middle ground.

24   The creation of new regulatory institutions is not something that should be undertaken lightly, given the inefficiencies that surround all efforts at regulation. For the past three decades, there has been a commendable worldwide movement to deregulate large sectors of every nation's economy, from airlines to telecommunications, and more broadly to reduce the size and scope of government. The global economy that has emerged as a result is a far more efficient generator of wealth and technological innovation. Excessive regulation in the past has led many to become instinctively hostile to state intervention in any form, and it is this knee-jerk aversion to regulation that will be one of the chief obstacles to getting human biotechnology under political control.

25   But it is important to discriminate: what works for one sector of the economy will not work for another. Information technology, for example, produces many social benefits and relatively few harms and therefore has appropriately gotten by with a fairly minimal degree of government regulation. Nuclear materials and toxic waste, on the other hand, are subject to strict national and international controls because unregulated trade in them would clearly be dangerous.

26   One of the biggest problems in making the case for regulating human biotechnology is the common view that even if it were desirable to stop technological advance, it is impossible to do so. If the United States or any other single country tries to ban human cloning or germline genetic engineering or any other procedure, people who wanted to do these things would simply move to a more favorable jurisdiction where they were permitted. Globalization and international competition in biomedical research ensure that countries that hobble themselves by putting ethical constraints on their scientific communities or biotechnology industries will be punished.

27   The idea that it is impossible to stop or control the advance of technology is simply wrong. We in fact control all sorts of technologies and many types of scientific research: people are no more free to experiment in the development of new biological warfare agents than they are to experiment on human subjects without the latter's informed consent. The fact that there are some individuals or organizations that violate these rules, or that there are countries where the rules are either nonexistent or poorly enforced, is no excuse for not making the rules in the first place. People get away with robbery and murder, after all, which is not a reason to legalize theft and homicide.

28   We need at all costs to avoid a defeatist attitude with regard to technology that says that since we can't do anything to stop or shape developments we don't like, we shouldn't bother trying in the first

place. Putting in place a regulatory system that would permit societies to control human biotechnology will not be easy: it will require legislators in countries around the world to step up to the plate and make difficult decisions on complex scientific issues. The shape and form of the institutions designed to implement new rules is a wide-open question; designing them to be minimally obstructive of positive developments while giving them effective enforcement capabilities is a significant challenge. Even more challenging will be the creation of common rules at an international level, the forging of a consensus among countries with different cultures and views on the underlying ethical questions. But political tasks of comparable complexity have been successfully undertaken in the past. ■

RALPH C. MERKLE

Nanotechnology: Designs for the Future

Ubiquity *is a Web-based publication of the Association for Computing Machinery focusing on a variety of issues related to the information technology industry. In 2000,* Ubiquity *interviewed Ralph C. Merkle, a former research scientist at Xerox Parc; advisor at the Foresight Institute; and nanotechnology theorist at Zyvex, a nanotechnology research and development company. Merkle now teaches and conducts research as a professor at Georgia Tech. His main research interests are nanotechnology (also called molecular manufacturing), cryptography, and cryonics, and he served as executive editor of the journal* Nanotechnology *for several years. In 1998, Merkle won the Feynman Prize in Nanotechnology for his theoretical work. As you will see, the interview excerpted below is partly in response to Bill Joy's "Why the Future Doesn't Need Us," the first selection in this chapter.*

1   UBIQUITY: Bill Joy's recent *Wired* article on the perils of today's advanced technologies—including nanotechnology—has certainly received a lot of attention, and we did a follow-up interview with him in *Ubiquity*. What are your thoughts on that subject?

2   RALPH C.   Well, certainly the idea that nanotechnology would raise con-
    MERKLE   cerns is something that actually was a major impetus for the founding of the Foresight Institute back in 1986—and by 1989, Foresight had its first technical conference on nanotechnology, and in fact Bill Joy spoke at that meeting. So one of

*Ralph C. Merkle, "Nanotechnology: Designs for the Future," a conversation with *Ubiquity* Magazine, June 27, 2000. http://www.acm.org/ubiquity/interviews/r_merkle-l.html. ©2000 Association for Computing Machinery, Inc. Reprinted by permission.

the things that's a bit surprising is that Bill's concerns about nanotechnology seem to be quite recent—just the last year or two—even though the understanding that this particular technology was going to be very powerful and would raise significant concerns has been around for at least a couple of decades.

3 UBIQUITY: Why don't you take a moment now to tell us about the Foresight Institute?

4 MERKLE: The Foresight Institute (http://www.foresight.org/guidelines/index.html) was created primarily to guide the development of nanotechnology, and it was founded in large part because, when you look at where the technology is going, you reach the conclusion that, though it has great potential for good, there are also some concerns which need to be addressed. We've been having a series of gatherings at Foresight now for some years where Senior Associates (people who have pledged to support the Foresight Institute) can get together informally and off the record and discuss the various issues.

5 UBIQUITY: What are the meetings like?

6 MERKLE: The most recent gathering had over 250 people—including Bill Joy, as a matter of fact—and one of the sessions was a discussion of the Foresight guidelines for safe development of nanotechnology. A year and a half ago we had a workshop where we discussed the guidelines and worked out an initial draft, which was discussed at the 1999 gathering at Foresight, and then further modified and updated and then discussed again at the most recent gathering.

7 UBIQUITY: What do you think would explain the sudden increase of concern about this?

8 MERKLE: Well, I can't really address the specifies of Bill Joy's situation. I do know that nanotechnology is an idea that most people simply didn't believe, even though the roots of it go back to a lecture by Richard Feynman in 1959 (http://www.zyvex.com/nanotech/feynman.html). That was a very famous talk in which he basically said the laws of physics should allow us to arrange things molecule by molecule and even atom by atom, and that at some point it was inevitable that we would develop a technology that would let us do this. I don't think that it was taken very seriously at that time, but as the years progressed it gradually began to be more accepted. If you think the technology is infeasible, you don't worry about what it might do and what its potential is. However, as you begin to internalize the fact that this technology is going to arrive and that we are going to have a very powerful manufacturing technology that

will let us build a wide range of remarkable new products, then one of the things that arises is a concern that this new set of capabilities could create new problems, new concerns, and that these should be addressed.

9   UBIQUITY: But not the way Bill Joy is addressing them?

10   MERKLE: One of the things about Bill Joy's original article that concerned me is that he was calling for a relinquishment, as he put it, of research—and I think that's a *very* foolish strategy. If you look at the various strategies available for dealing with a new technology, sticking your head in the sand is not the most plausible strategy and in fact actually makes the situation more dangerous.

11   UBIQUITY: Why so?

12   MERKLE: For at least three reasons. The first, of course, is that we need to have a collective understanding of the new technology in order to ensure that we develop it appropriately. The second reason is that the new technologies that we see coming will have major benefits, and will greatly alleviate human suffering. The third reason is that, if we attempt to block the development of new technology, if we collectively try and say, "These technologies are technologies that are not meant for humans to understand," and we try to back away from them, what we effectively have done is not to block the technologies, we have simply ensured that the most responsible parties will not develop them.

13   UBIQUITY: So you think "relinquishment" is exactly the wrong strategy.

14   MERKLE: Right. Those people who pay no attention to a call for relinquishment, and in particular those people who are least inclined to be concerned about safe development will, in fact, be the groups that eventually develop the technology. In other words, a relinquishment of the new technology, unless it is absolutely 100 percent effective, is not effective at all. If it's 99.99 percent effective, then you simply ensure that the .01 percent who pays no attention to such calls for relinquishment is the group that will develop it. And that actually creates a worse outcome than if the responsible players move forward and develop the technology with the best understanding that they have and the best efforts to ensure that the technology is developed in a safe and responsible fashion.

15   UBIQUITY: Let's go back to the second reason and expand on that to the extent of enumerating what you consider are the most prominent hopes that it offers.

16   MERKLE: Well, certainly what we see today is an entire planet, which has many limitations. I'm not quite sure how to express it, but

certainly if you look at the human condition today, not everyone is well fed. Not everyone has access to good medical care.
Not everyone has the basics—the physical basics that provide
for a healthy and a happy life. And clearly, if you have a lower
cost manufacturing technology, which can build a wide range
of products less expensively, it can build, among other things,
better medical products. Disease and ill health are caused
largely by damage at the molecular and cellular level, yet today's surgical tools are too large to deal with that kind of problem. A molecular manufacturing technology will let us build
molecular surgical tools, and those tools will, for the first time,
let us directly address the problems at the very root level. So
today we see a human population of over six billion people,
many of whom have serious medical conditions, which either
can't be treated or cannot be treated economically. In other
words, we don't have the resources to effectively treat all the
conditions that we see. If we can reduce the cost and improve
the quality of medical technology through advances in nanotechnology, then we can more widely address the medical
conditions that are prevalent and reduce the level of human
suffering. (See http://www.foresight.org/Nanomedicine for
more information about medical applications.)

17 UBIQUITY: And besides the opportunities in medicine? What else?

18 MERKLE: On another level, food; the simple process of feeding the human population. Today because of technological limits there is
a certain amount of food that we can produce per acre. If we
were to have intensive greenhouse agriculture, which would
be something we could do economically, if we could economically manufacture the appropriate computer controlled enclo-
sures that would provide protection and would provide a very
controlled environment for the growth of food we could have
much higher production. It looks as though yields of over 10
times what we can currently grow per acre are feasible if you
control, for example, the CO^2 concentration, the humidity, the
temperature, all the various factors that plants depend on to
grow rapidly. If we control those, if we make those optimal for
the growth of various crops then we can grow more per acre.
And furthermore, we can grow it less expensively because
molecular manufacturing technology is inherently low cost,
and therefore it will let us grow more food more easily.

19 UBIQUITY: What are the implications?

20 MERKLE: The first is that it makes food less expensive. The second is
that many of the people in the world today who are starving

are not starving because there is an inherent inability to produce food, they are starving because they are caught in the middle of political fights and blockades that have been used as political weapons. As a consequence, food is available but it cannot be shipped into an area and so the people in that area suffer the consequences. However, if you have a distributed manufacturing technology, one of the great advantages is that it should let us have a much lower cost infrastructure. In other words, today manufacturing takes place in very large facilities. If you want to build, for example, a computer chip, you need a giant semiconductor fabrication facility. But if you look at nature, nature can grow complex molecular machines using nothing more than a plant.

21 UBIQUITY: Example?

22 MERKLE: Well, a potato, for example, can grow quite easily on a very small plot of land. With molecular manufacturing, in a similar fashion, we'll be able to have distributed manufacturing, which will permit manufacturing at the site using technologies that are low cost and easily available once the core technology has been developed. And as a consequence, you would have people able to build low-cost greenhouse agriculture tools even if there were a blockade because the manufacturing facilities would be widely distributed, and therefore they could avoid the blockade by simply making what they need inside the blockaded region using cheap raw materials and sunlight.

23 UBIQUITY: And if nanotechnology did so much for people's health and food production, what would it do, do you suppose, for their current economic institution? Would it transition to large-scale nanotechnology? Have unintended consequences in terms of disrupting the economy?

24 MERKLE: I think we would see changes in the economy. Previous technologies have made major changes. Old companies that have had major advantages in the past certainly find those advantages go away. Certainly as manufacturing becomes less expensive, then today's major manufacturing companies would find that they would be at a disadvantage in the future. Other companies that are producing intellectual products, software companies or companies that are not dealing with material objects—banks and financial institutions, for example—fundamentally are dealing with a flow of information so would be relatively less affected. I think you would see some major shifts in the economy in that manufacturing companies would

find that what they were doing was either greatly changed or outright replaced. As in any technological revolution, there will be winners and losers. On balance, everyone will come out ahead, although there will be specific instances where particular companies will have major problems, and in fact, will simply not be able to cope with a new environment and presumably suffer the consequences.

25 UBIQUITY: What about the competition between different countries? Would, for example, the severely underdeveloped countries have an ability to do very rapid catch-up?

26 MERKLE: Yes. I think they would. Also, you have to remember that we are looking at a future where to a first approximation everyone is wealthy. Now, there are certain things that are inherently scarce. For example, there is only a certain amount of beach-front property in California. It is going to be scarce, it is going to be expensive, and only a small percentage of the population will be able to afford it. But if you look at other material possessions—housing or electronics—you find that the only limitation is our ability to manufacture them inexpensively. So the first approximation in this future that we're looking at is that everyone will be physically well off. They will have a great abundance in material goods, and as a consequence, I think that will soften and ease some of the conflicts that we see now. One of the issues facing us today is that there are countries where there is a serious lack of resources, the standards of living are very low, and as a consequence this creates a fundamental unease and discomfort in entire populations. If you have a higher standard of living, at least that source of conflict will be greatly reduced. Now, as we all know, there are many potential sources of conflict in the world, but even easing some of them will be very helpful.

27 UBIQUITY: Give us an example of a product that would be improved using molecular manufacturing?

28 MERKLE: The answer that comes most readily to mind is diamonds. Diamond has a better strength-to-weight ratio than steel or aluminum. Its strength-to-weight ratio is more than 50 times that of steel or aluminum alloy. So, it's much stronger and much lighter. If we had a shatterproof variant of diamond, we would have a remarkably light and strong material from which to make all of the products in the world around us. In particular, aerospace products—airplanes or rockets—would benefit immensely from having lighter, stronger materials. So one of the things that we can say with confidence is that we

will have much lighter, much stronger materials, and this will reduce the cost of air flight, and it will reduce the cost of rockets. It will let us go into space for literally orders of magnitude lower cost.

29 UBIQUITY: Has NASA shown any interest in this?

30 MERKLE: Needless to say, they are pursuing research in nanotechnology with the idea of having lighter, stronger materials as one of the significant objectives. There is a whole range of other capabilities, of course, that would be of interest in NASA. For example, lighter computers and lighter sensors would let you have more function in a given weight, which is very important if you are launching things into space, and you have to pay by the pound to put things there.

31 UBIQUITY: Are there any other areas that would be significantly affected by nanotechnology?

32 MERKLE: The other area is in advanced computer technology. The computer hardware revolution has been continuing with remarkable steadiness over the last few decades. If you extrapolate into the future you find that, in the coming decades, we'll have to build molecular computers to keep the computer hardware revolution on track. Nanotechnology will let us do that, and it will let us build computers that are incredibly powerful. We'll have more power in the volume of a sugar cube than exists in the entire world today.

33 UBIQUITY: Can you put any kind of timeframe on that?

34 MERKLE: We're talking about decades. We're not talking about years; we're not talking about a century. We're talking decades—and probably not many decades. ■

KENAN MALIK

The Moral Clone

In May 2001, Kenan Malik, author of Man, Beast, and Zombie *and* The Meaning of Race: Race, History, and Culture in Western Society, *published the following essay in* Prospect *magazine, a British publication on public issues and contemporary culture.*

1   The Pope condemns their work as "abhorrent." Jeremy Rifkin warns that they are striking a "Faustian bargain" which could pave the way to a "commercial eugenics civilization." The object of this hostility is two doctors, the U.S.-based Panayiotis Zavos and the Italian Severino

Antinori, who, in March, declared their intention of helping infertile couples conceive through the use of cloning techniques.

2   From Aldous Huxley's picture of human production lines in *Brave New World* to Michael Marshall Smith's description in his novel *Spares* of farms where the rich keep clones of themselves so that their organs can be "harvested" for transplants, cloning has been a metaphor for the creation of an immoral, inhuman world. The birth in February 1997 of Dolly the sheep transformed such visions from the realms of science fiction to science fact. It seemed only a matter of time before humans could also be duplicated, a prospect greeted with almost universal condemnation. Even Ian Wilmut, Dolly's creator, believes that we should "reject this proposed use of cloning."

3   I want to argue that the current debate about cloning turns the ethical issues on their head. There are no reasons to regard the cloning of humans as unethical. There is, on the other hand, something deeply immoral about a campaign that seeks to block the advancement, not just of reproductive technology but also of other medical techniques based on cloning methods which could save countless lives.

4   There are three main objections to cloning: that it undermines human dignity and personal identity; that it uses people as objects; and that it is unnatural. Opponents argue that it is immoral to create exact copies of people. According to the bioethicist Leon Kass, "the cloned individual will be saddled with a genotype that has already lived. He will not be fully a surprise to the world." Others worry that unethical governments, or even corporations, may institute a programme to create production line people, perhaps even a race of Adolf Hitlers.

5   Such arguments misunderstand both the character of cloning and the nature of human beings. To clone an organism—whether Dolly or Adolf Hitler—scientists take an egg and remove its nucleus, the pail that includes, among other things, the bulk of the DNA. Next, they remove the nucleus from a cell belonging to the adult that is to be cloned and insert it into the egg. The reconstructed egg is stimulated, either electrically or chemically, to trick it into behaving like a fertilized egg. If this is successful, the egg divides and becomes an embryo, which is then transferred into the uterus of a surrogate mother. Pregnancy then follows its normal course.

6   Any human child conceived in this fashion will be the genetic twin of the person who is the cell donor. But to have the same genome is not to be the same person. Genes play an important part in shaping who we are but they are not the only influence on us.

7   If having the same genome means being the same person, then all naturally-born identical twins would be exact duplicates of each other. This is not the case. Identical twins differ in everything from their fin-

gerprints to their personalities. Children conceived with the aid of cloning technology will be even more different from their genetic parents than are most natural twins from each other. Most naturally conceived identical twins grow up in roughly the same environment. Cloned children, on the other hand, will be born into a different family from their "twin," have different parents and siblings, and have different experiences from the day they are born. In other words they will be nothing like their parent whose genome they inherit.

8   Children conceived through cloning will be indistinguishable from children conceived naturally, whether these happen to be identical twins or not. Each will be a unique human being with a unique identity and an unpredictable future.

9   What of the argument that cloning turns human beings into means, not ends? Cloned children, critics say, will simply be the means for their parents' self-aggrandizement. This may well be true, but it is also true for many children born in conventional ways. Twenty years ago opponents of the then-nascent in vitro fertilization (IVF) technology also argued that "test-tube" babies were being treated as objects. Anyone who has witnessed the emotional and financial commitment that couples have to invest in IVF treatment will recognize, however, that such children are very much wanted and treasured by their parents. The same will be true for any cloned child.

10   Faced with the implausibility of most of their arguments, opponents of cloning generally fall back on the claim that cloning is repugnant because it is unnatural. "From time immemorial," Jeremy Rifkin says, "we have thought of the birth of our progeny as a gift bestowed by God or a beneficent nature." According to Rifkin, "the coming together of sperm and egg represents a moment of surrender to forces outside of our control."

11   Cloning is certainly unnatural. But then so is virtually every human activity. The whole point of any medical intervention from taking an aspirin to heart surgery is to ensure that humans are not at the mercy of "forces outside our control." If we were to look upon human conception as simply a "gift from God," then contraception, abortion and IVF would all have to be ruled immoral. Cloning is no more unnatural than IVF. If we are happy to accept the latter (as most people are), then why should we not accept the former too?

12   There is only one argument against human cloning that has any substance. Many experts believe that it is precipitous to attempt to clone human beings today because the procedure is insufficiently safe. It remains difficult to get reconstructed eggs to develop into embryos and many of these embryos show abnormalities. In the case of Dolly, for instance, Ian Wilmut began with 277 reconstructed eggs, of which 29 devel-

oped into embryos. Of these 29 embryos only one resulted in a pregnancy that went to term. Given such problems, the consensus among most scientists is that Zavos and Antinori are being hasty in their plans to clone humans. Cloning techniques have yet to be fine-tuned and the risk of conceiving deformed children is too great. The question of safety, however, is not an ethical one. Ethical injunctions are absolute: under no circumstances should we attempt to clone a human. Safety considerations are relative: when the technology has become more refined, we can proceed.

13   By preventing cloning research, opponents are preventing the development of new treatments that draw upon cloning techniques, and hence are allowing many people to suffer unnecessarily. A case in point is the controversy over "therapeutic cloning." Therapeutic cloning is a means of growing human tissue that fuses the techniques that helped create Dolly with another new medical technology: the ability to grow embryonic stem (ES) cells.

14   The cells of an adult human are highly specialized; under normal circumstances a liver cell will always stay a liver cell, and a skin cell can never become anything else. Stem cells, however, are cells that can develop into any kind of tissue: liver, skin, nerve, heart. The best source of such stem cells are tiny embryos, a few days old. If we could take the nucleus of, say, a healthy cell from a patient with Parkinson's disease and fuse it with an enucleated stem cell, we could grow brain tissue that could potentially replace the patient's damaged cells. Because such tissue would be genetically identical to that of the patient, there would be no problem of tissue rejection. Such a technique could help patients with problems from Parkinson's and Alzheimer's to diabetes, leukemia and even heart disease.

15   Therapeutic cloning is a way of growing human tissues, it has nothing to do with creating new human beings. The embryo is a pinprick of about two dozen cells; because it could potentially be a human life does not mean that it *is* one. Anyone who objects to therapeutic cloning must logically object not only to all forms of abortion but to IVF too, which produces spare embryos in pursuit of a successful pregnancy.

16   According to the *Telegraph,* "The difference between therapeutic cloning, to create 'spare part' organs, and reproductive cloning, to create babies, is only one of purpose—a secondary distinction." In both cases "the embryo is treated as a disposable object, deprived of any humanity." The same "fundamental moral objections," the *Telegraph* claims, "apply to all human cloning."

17   As a result of such arguments, most European states still ban research into therapeutic cloning. Britain finally licensed certain forms of cloning research last year, but only in very limited cases. In the U.S., the Bush administration is expected to ban federal funding for any form of

ES-cell research. In a special report on therapeutic cloning, the journal *Nature* asked recently why it was that only a dozen or so research teams are pursuing work in such a promising area. A large part of the answer, it concluded, was the degree of political restriction.

18   Opponents of cloning like to present the debate as one between an immoral science, hell-bent on progress at any cost, and those who seek to place scientific advancement within a moral framework. But what is moral about allowing unnecessary suffering? Theologians and Luddites are using norms drawn from dogmatic and reactionary visions of life to prevent the alleviation of human suffering. ∎

Charles Krauthammer

Crossing Lines

Charles Krauthammer (born 1950), a syndicated columnist based at the Washington Post, *won the Pulitzer Prize in 1987. He earned an M.D. from Harvard and worked as a psychiatrist and researcher at Massachusetts General Hospital for several years. Krauthammer later assisted the Carter administration with its planning for psychiatric research and then moved on to writing, even acting as a speechwriter for Walter Mondale's 1980 vice presidential bid. His work on bioethics has led him to a position on the President's Council on Bioethics. Krauthammer has contributed to* The New Republic, Time, *and the* Weekly Standard. *"Crossing Lines," subtitled "A Secular Argument Against Research Cloning," first appeared in the April 29, 2002, issue of* The New Republic.

The Problem

1   You were once a single cell. Every one of the 100 trillion cells in your body today is a direct descendent of that zygote, the primordial cell formed by the union of mother's egg and father's sperm. Each one is genetically identical (allowing for copying errors and environmental damage along the way) to that cell. Therefore, if we scraped a cell from, say, the inner lining of your cheek, its DNA would be the same DNA that, years ago in the original zygote, contained the entire plan for creating you and every part of you.

2   Here is the mystery: Why can the zygote, as it multiplies, produce every different kind of cell in the body—kidney, liver, brain, skin—while the skin cell is destined, however many times it multiplies, to remain skin forever? As the embryo matures, cells become specialized and lose their flexibility and plasticity. Once an adult cell has special-

ized—differentiated, in scientific lingo—it is stuck forever in that specialty. Skin is skin; kidney is kidney.

3   Understanding that mystery holds the keys to the kingdom. The Holy Grail of modern biology is regenerative medicine. If we can figure out how to make a specialized adult cell dedifferentiate—unspecialize, i.e., revert way back to the embryonic stage, perhaps even to the original zygotic stage—and then grow it like an embryo under controlled circumstances, we could reproduce for you every kind of tissue or organ you might need. We could create a storehouse of repair parts for your body. And, if we let that dedifferentiated cell develop completely in a woman's uterus, we will have created a copy of you, your clone.

4   That is the promise and the menace of cloning. It has already been done in sheep, mice, goats, pigs, cows, and now cats and rabbits (though cloning rabbits seems an exercise in biological redundancy). There is no reason in principle why it cannot be done in humans. The question is: Should it be done?

5   Notice that the cloning question is really two questions: (1) May we grow that dedifferentiated cell all the way into a cloned baby, a copy of you? That is called reproductive cloning. And (2) may we grow that dedifferentiated cell just into the embryonic stage and then mine it for parts, such as stem cells? That is called research cloning.

6   Reproductive cloning is universally abhorred. In July 2001 the House of Representatives, a fairly good representative of the American people, took up the issue and not a single member defended reproductive cloning. Research cloning, however, is the hard one. Some members were prepared to permit the cloning of the human embryo in order to study and use its component parts, with the proviso that the embryo be destroyed before it grows into a fetus or child. They were a minority, however. Their amendment banning baby-making but permitting research cloning was defeated by 76 votes. On July 31, 2001, a bill outlawing all cloning passed the House decisively.

7   Within weeks, perhaps days, the Senate will vote on essentially the same alternatives. On this vote will hinge the course of the genetic revolution at whose threshold we now stand.

The Promise

8   This is how research cloning works. You take a donor egg from a woman, remove its nucleus, and inject the nucleus of, say, a skin cell from another person. It has been shown in animals that by the right manipulation you can trick the egg and the injected nucleus into dedifferentiating—that means giving up all the specialization of the skin cell

and returning to its original state as a primordial cell that could become anything in the body.

9   In other words, this cell becomes totipotent. It becomes the equivalent of the fertilized egg in normal procreation, except that instead of having chromosomes from two people, it has chromosomes from one. This cell then behaves precisely like an embryo. It divides. It develops. At four to seven days, it forms a "blastocyst" consisting of about 100 to 200 cells.

10   The main objective of cloning researchers would be to disassemble this blastocyst: pull the stem cells out, grow them in the laboratory, and then try to tease them into becoming specific kinds of cells, say, kidney or heart or brain and so on.

11   There would be two purposes for doing this: study or cure. You could take a cell from a person with a baffling disease, like Lou Gehrig's, clone it into a blastocyst, pull the stem cells out, and then study them in order to try to understand the biology of the illness. Or you could begin with a cell from a person with Parkinson's or a spinal cord injury, clone it, and tease out the stem cells to develop tissue that you would reinject into the original donor to, in theory, cure the Parkinson's or spinal cord injury. The advantage of using a cloned cell rather than an ordinary stem cell is that, presumably, there would be no tissue rejection. It's your own DNA. The body would recognize it. You'd have a perfect match.

12   (Research cloning is sometimes called therapeutic cloning, but that is a misleading term. First, because therapy by reinjection is only one of the many uses to which this cloning can be put. Moreover, it is not therapeutic for the clone—indeed, the clone is invariably destroyed in the process—though it may be therapeutic for others. If you donate a kidney to your brother, it would be odd to call *your* operation a therapeutic nephrectomy. It is not. It's a sacrificial nephrectomy.)

13   The conquest of rejection is one of the principal rationales for research cloning. But there is reason to doubt this claim on scientific grounds. There is some empirical evidence in mice that cloned tissue may be rejected anyway (possibly because a clone contains a small amount of foreign—mitochondrial—DNA derived from the egg into which it was originally injected). Moreover, enormous advances are being made elsewhere in combating tissue rejection. The science of immune rejection is much more mature than the science of cloning. By the time we figure out how to do safe and reliable research cloning, the rejection problem may well be solved. And finally, there are less problematic alternatives—such as adult stem cells—that offer a promising alternative to cloning because they present no problem of tissue rejection and raise none of cloning's moral conundrums.

14   These scientific considerations raise serious questions about the efficacy of, and thus the need for, research cloning. But there is a stronger case to be made. Even if the scientific objections are swept aside, even if research cloning is as doable and promising as its advocates contend, there are other reasons to pause.

15   The most obvious is this: Research cloning is an open door to reproductive cloning. Banning the production of cloned babies while permitting the production of cloned embryos makes no sense. If you have factories all around the country producing embryos for research and commerce, it is inevitable that someone will implant one in a woman (or perhaps in some artificial medium in the farther future) and produce a human clone. What then? A law banning reproductive cloning but permitting research cloning would then make it a crime *not* to destroy that fetus—an obvious moral absurdity.

16   This is an irrefutable point and the reason that many in Congress will vote for the total ban on cloning. Philosophically, however, it is a showstopper. It lets us off too early and too easy. It keeps us from facing the deeper question: Is there anything about research cloning that *in and of itself* makes it morally problematic?

Objection I: Intrinsic Worth

17   For some people, life begins at conception. And not just life—if life is understood to mean a biologically functioning organism, even a single cell is obviously alive—but personhood. If the first zygotic cell is owed all the legal and moral respect due a person, then there is nothing to talk about. Ensoulment starts with Day One and Cell One, and the idea of taking that cell or its successor cells apart to serve someone else's needs is abhorrent.

18   This is an argument of great moral force but little intellectual interest. Not because it may not be right. But because it is unprovable. It rests on metaphysics. Either you believe it or you don't. The discussion ends there.

19   I happen not to share this view. I do not believe personhood begins at conception. I do not believe a single cell has the moral or legal standing of a child. This is not to say that I do not stand in awe of the developing embryo, a creation of majestic beauty and mystery. But I stand in equal awe of the Grand Canyon, the spider's web, and quantum mechanics. Awe commands wonder, humility, appreciation. It does not command inviolability. I am quite prepared to shatter an atom, take down a spider's web, or dam a canyon for electricity. (Though we'd have to be very short on electricity before I'd dam the Grand.)

20   I do not believe the embryo is entitled to inviolability. But is it entitled to nothing? There is a great distance between inviolability, on the one hand, and mere "thingness," on the other. Many advocates of re-

search cloning see nothing but thingness. That view justifies the most ruthless exploitation of the embryo. That view is dangerous.

21   Why? Three possible reasons. First, the Brave New World Factor: Research cloning gives man too much power for evil. Second, the Slippery Slope: The habit of embryonic violation is in and of itself dangerous. Violate the blastocyst today and every day, and the practice will inure you to violating the fetus or even the infant tomorrow. Third, Manufacture: The very act of creating embryos for the sole purpose of exploiting and then destroying them will ultimately predispose us to a ruthless utilitarianism about human life itself.

Objection II: The Brave New World Factor

22   The physicists at Los Alamos did not hesitate to penetrate, manipulate, and split uranium atoms on the grounds that uranium atoms possess intrinsic worth that entitled them to inviolability. Yet after the war, many fought to curtail atomic power. They feared the consequences of delivering such unfathomable power—and potential evil—into the hands of fallible human beings. Analogously, one could believe that the cloned blastocyst has little more intrinsic worth than the uranium atom and still be deeply troubled by the manipulation of the blastocyst because of the fearsome power it confers upon humankind.

23   The issue is leverage. Our knowledge of how to manipulate human genetics (or atomic nuclei) is still primitive. We could never construct ex nihilo a human embryo. It is an unfolding organism of unimaginable complexity that took nature three billion years to produce. It might take us less time to build it from scratch, but not much less. By that time, we as a species might have acquired enough wisdom to use it wisely. Instead, the human race in its infancy has stumbled upon a genie infinitely too complicated to create or even fully understand, but understandable enough to command and perhaps even control. And given our demonstrated unwisdom with our other great discovery—atomic power: As we speak, the very worst of humanity is on the threshold of acquiring the most powerful weapons in history—this is a fear and a consideration to be taken very seriously.

24   For example. Female human eggs seriously limit the mass production of cloned embryos. Extracting eggs from women is difficult, expensive, and potentially dangerous. The search is on, therefore, for a good alternative. Scientists have begun injecting human nuclei into the egg cells of animals. In 1996 Massachusetts scientists injected a human nucleus with a cow egg. Chinese scientists have fused a human fibroblast with a rabbit egg and have grown the resulting embryo to the blastocyst stage. We have no idea what grotesque results might come from such interspecies clonal experiments.

25   In October 2000 the first primate containing genes from another species was born (a monkey with a jellyfish gene). In 1995 researchers in Texas produced headless mice. In 1997 researchers in Britain produced headless tadpoles. In theory, headlessness might be useful for organ transplantation. One can envision, in a world in which embryos are routinely manufactured, the production of headless clones—subhuman creatures with usable human organs but no head, no brain, no consciousness to identify them with the human family.

26   The heart of the problem is this: Nature, through endless evolution, has produced cells with totipotent power. We are about to harness that power for crude human purposes. That should give us pause. Just around the corner lies the logical by-product of such power: human-animal hybrids, partly developed human bodies for use as parts, and other horrors imagined—Huxley's Deltas and Epsilons—and as yet unimagined. This is the Brave New World Factor. Its grounds for objecting to this research are not about the beginnings of life, but about the ends; not the origin of these cells, but their destiny; not where we took these magnificent cells from, but where they are taking us.

Objection III: The Slippery Slope

27   The other prudential argument is that once you start tearing apart blastocysts, you get used to tearing apart blastocysts. And whereas now you'd only be doing that at the seven-day stage, when most people would look at this tiny clump of cells on the head of a pin and say it is not inviolable, it is inevitable that some scientist will soon say: Give me just a few more weeks to work with it and I could do wonders.

28   That will require quite a technological leap because the blastocyst will not develop as a human organism unless implanted in the uterus. That means that to go beyond that seven-day stage you'd have to implant this human embryo either in an animal uterus or in some fully artificial womb.

29   Both possibilities may be remote, but they are real. And then we'll have a scientist saying: Give me just a few more months with this embryo, and I'll have actual kidney cells, brain cells, pancreatic cells that I can transplant back into the donor of the clone and cure him. Scientists at Advanced Cell Technology in Massachusetts have already gone past that stage in animals. They have taken cloned cow embryos past the blastocyst stage, taken tissue from the more developed cow fetus, and reimplanted it back into the donor animal.

30   The scientists' plea to do the same in humans will be hard to ignore. Why grow the clone just to the blastocyst stage, destroy it, pull out the inner cell mass, grow stem cells out of that, propagate them in the

laboratory, and then try chemically or otherwise to tweak them into becoming kidney cells or brain cells or islet cells? This is Rube Goldberg. Why not just allow that beautiful embryonic machine, created by nature and far more sophisticated than our crude techniques, to develop unmolested? Why not let the blastocyst grow into a fetus that possesses the kinds of differentiated tissue that we could then use for curing the donor?

31   Scientifically, this would make sense. Morally, we will have crossed the line between tearing apart a mere clump of cells and tearing apart a recognizable human fetus. And at that point, it would be an even smaller step to begin carving up seven- and eight-month-old fetuses with more perfectly formed organs to alleviate even more pain and suffering among the living. We will, slowly and by increments, have gone from stem cells to embryo farms to factories with fetuses in various stages of development and humanness, hanging (metaphorically) on meat hooks waiting to be cut open to be used by the already born.

32   We would all be revolted if a living infant or developed fetus were carved up for parts. Should we build a fence around that possibility by prohibiting any research on even the very earliest embryonic clump of cells? Is the only way to avoid the slide never to mount the slippery slope at all? On this question, I am personally agnostic. If I were utterly convinced that we would never cross the seven-day line, then I would have no objection on these grounds to such research on the inner cell mass of a blastocyst. The question is: Can we be sure? This is not a question of principle; it is a question of prudence. It is almost a question of psychological probability. No one yet knows the answer.

Objection IV: Manufacture

33 Note that while, up to now, I have been considering arguments against research cloning, they are all equally applicable to embryonic research done on a normal—i.e., noncloned—embryo. If the question is tearing up the blastocyst, there is no intrinsic moral difference between a two-parented embryo derived from a sperm and an egg and a single-parented embryo derived from a cloned cell. Thus the various arguments against this research—the intrinsic worth of the embryo, the prudential consideration that we might create monsters, or the prudential consideration that we might *become* monsters in exploiting post-embryonic forms of human life (fetuses or even children)—are identical to the arguments for and against stem-cell research.

34   These arguments are serious—serious enough to banish the insouciance of the scientists who consider anyone questioning their work to be a Luddite—yet, in my view, insufficient to justify a legal ban on stem-cell research (as with stem cells from discarded embryos in fertil-

ity clinics). I happen not to believe that either personhood or ensoulment occurs at conception. I think we need to be apprehensive about what evil might arise from the power of stem-cell research, but that apprehension alone, while justifying vigilance and regulation, does not justify a ban on the practice. And I believe that given the good that might flow from stem-cell research, we should first test the power of law and custom to enforce the seven-day blastocyst line for embryonic exploitation before assuming that such a line could never hold.

35   This is why I support stem-cell research (using leftover embryos from fertility clinics) and might support research cloning were it not for one other aspect that is unique to it. In research cloning, the embryo is created with the explicit intention of its eventual destruction. That is a given because not to destroy the embryo would be to produce a cloned child. If you are not permitted to grow the embryo into a child, you are obliged at some point to destroy it.

36   Deliberately creating embryos for eventual and certain destruction means the launching of an entire industry of embryo manufacture. It means the routinization, the commercialization, the commodification of the human embryo. The bill that would legalize research cloning essentially sanctions, licenses, and protects the establishment of a most ghoulish enterprise: the creation of nascent human life for the sole purpose of its exploitation and destruction.

37   How is this morally different from simply using discarded embryos from in vitro fertilization (IVF) clinics? Some have suggested that it is not, that to oppose research cloning is to oppose IVF and any stem-cell research that comes out of IVF. The claim is made that because in IVF there is a high probability of destruction of the embryo, it is morally equivalent to research cloning. But this is plainly not so. In research cloning there is not a high probability of destruction; there is 100 percent probability. Because every cloned embryo must be destroyed, it is nothing more than a means to someone else's end.

38   In IVF, the probability of destruction may be high, but it need not necessarily be. You could have a clinic that produces only a small number of embryos, and we know of many cases of multiple births resulting from multiple embryo implantation. In principle, one could have IVF using only a single embryo and thus involving no deliberate embryo destruction at all. In principle, that is impossible in research cloning.

39   Furthermore, a cloned embryo is created to be destroyed and used by others. An IVF embryo is created to develop into a child. One cannot disregard intent in determining morality. Embryos are created in IVF to serve reproduction. Embryos are created in research cloning to serve, well, research. If certain IVF embryos were designated as "helper embryos" that would simply aid an anointed embryo in turning into a child, then we would have an analogy to cloning. But, in fact, we don't

know which embryo is anointed in IVF. They are all created to have a chance of survival. And they are all equally considered an end.

40   Critics counter that this ends-and-means argument is really obfuscation, that both procedures make an instrument of the embryo. In cloning, the creation and destruction of the embryo is a means to understanding or curing disease. In IVF, the creation of the embryo is a means of satisfying a couple's need for a child. They are both just means to ends.

41   But it makes no sense to call an embryo a means to the creation of a child. The creation of a child is the *destiny* of an embryo. To speak of an embryo as a means to creating a child empties the word "means" of content. The embryo in IVF is a stage in the development of a child; it is no more a means than a teenager is a means to the adult he or she later becomes. In contrast, an embryo in research cloning is pure means. Laboratory pure.

42   And that is where we must draw the line. During the great debate on stem-cell research, a rather broad consensus was reached (among those not committed to "intrinsic worth" rendering all embryos inviolable) that stem-cell research could be morally justified because the embryos destroyed for their possibly curative stem cells were derived from fertility clinics and thus were going to be discarded anyway. It was understood that human embryos should not be created solely for the purpose of being dismembered and then destroyed for the benefit of others. Indeed, when Senator Bill Frist made his impassioned presentation on the floor of the Senate supporting stem-cell research, he included among his conditions a total ban on creating human embryos just to be stem-cell farms.

43   Where cloning for research takes us decisively beyond stem-cell research is in sanctioning the manufacture of the human embryo. You can try to regulate embryonic research to prohibit the creation of Brave New World monsters; you can build fences on the slippery slope, regulating how many days you may grow an embryo for research; but once you countenance the very creation of human embryos for no other purpose than for their parts, you have crossed a moral frontier.

44   Research cloning is the ultimate in conferring thingness upon the human embryo. It is the ultimate in desensitization. And as such, it threatens whatever other fences and safeguards we might erect around embryonic research. The problem, one could almost say, is not what cloning does to the embryo, but what it does to us. Except that, once cloning has changed us, it will inevitably enable further assaults on human dignity. Creating a human embryo just so it can be used and then destroyed undermines the very foundation of the moral prudence that informs the entire enterprise of genetic research: the idea that, while a human embryo may not be a person, it is not nothing. Because if it is nothing, then everything is permitted. And if everything is permitted, then there are no fences, no safeguards, no bottom. ∎

ISSUE IN FOCUS

Stem Cell Research

Many current debates surround the study and manipulation of life's basic codes: mapping human genes in the Human Genome Project, developing disease- and insect-resistant crops, altering genes to help grow larger poultry, pursuing ways to clone animals or even human beings. Critics of these technologies, in the tradition of many sci-fi thrillers, worry about unforeseen consequences, and those critics often raise questions as well about the ethical implications of intervening in basic life processes. One area of genetic research that has received a great deal of attention lately is that of embryonic stem cell research. On the one hand, stem cell research seems to offer great potential for the treatment of particularly debilitating diseases like Parkinson's and Alzheimer's; on the other hand, the research troubles others because of its reliance on human embryos.

> "It is surely extremely arrogant to believe that a cluster of pre-embryonic cells is worthy of being endowed with the 'sanctity of life.' Nature is profligate with the creation of life. In nearly every species, a huge quantity of reproductive material, at all stages of development, goes to waste. A few little scraps of such material in the form of blastocysts have as much sanctity as a culture in a Petri dish. . . . We are very prone to overrating our own importance. Even a fully grown individual is no more than a speck of living matter in the vastness of the universe."
>
> —MADELINE MACDONALD, LETTER TO THE EDITOR, *THE TIMES* (LONDON), JUNE 23, 2004

The debate over stem cell research in this decade has taken on a very public face through very public people: Michael J. Fox (who suffers from Parkinson's disease), Christopher Reeve (who suffered paralyzing, ultimately fatal spine damage in a riding accident), Nancy Reagan (who cared for former President Ronald Reagan during his ten-year battle with Alzheimer's), Republican Senators Arlen Specter and William Frist (the former suffering from cancer, the latter a physician who serves as Senate Majority Leader), and, at the Democratic National Convention in 2004, the ex-president's son, Ron Reagan. All these people advocate in favor of stem cell research.

Still, there are many others who find stem cell research to be dangerous and/or unethical, and who find its claims to potential miracle cures to be highly exaggerated (and sometimes moti-vated by the prospect of grant money). Some opponents fear that stem cell research, if ap-proved, would lead to and encourage cloning or the use of aborted fetal tissue—or perhaps even to planned pregnancies and subsequent abortions designed to create the necessary stem cells. If opponents of stem cell research lack high-profile advocates like Fox, Reeve, and the Reagans, they do not lack in fervor and or-ganization.

Christopher Reeve

On both sides the arguments can become complex and emotional because they involve highly charged questions in science, ethics, and religion and because they connect with personal tragedies and human loss. In 2001, when President George W. Bush placed restrictions on funding for stem cell research, emotions were running particularly high. In a nationally televised address, he offered the following argument for this re-striction: "Research on embryonic stem cells raises profound ethical questions because extracting the stem cell destroys the embryo and thus de-stroys its potential for life." His policy of restricting research to already exist-ing cell lines, he suggested, still al-lowed researchers "to explore the promise and potential of stem-cell re-search without crossing a fundamen-tal moral line" (quoted in *The Lancet*, March 13, 2004). Bush's compromise did not hold for long, however. While many people appreciated his holding to that "fundamental moral line," oth-ers scoffed at the assertion that hu-man embryos required for stem cell research hold the potential for human life. And the research community has complained that this restriction has hampered their efforts to cure injury and disease, and put them at a disad-vantage among researchers in other countries.

> "If the [Roman Catholic] Church says it is okay to take organs from a person who is brain dead and give them to someone else so that the person will live, I don't see the difference in using [embryonic] cells that will otherwise be thrown away. . . . My faith is simple. I don't believe miracles happen with thunderclaps and lightning. I believe they happen every day when everyday people do extraordinary things to help each other."
>
> —TOM KARLYA, *NEW YORK NEWSDAY*, MAY 23, 2004

The images and words that follow give you a glimpse of some of the ar-guments, visual and verbal, that recur in the debate over stem cell research.

In addition to photos, cartoons, and excerpts, we include Ron Reagan's highly publicized speech at the 2004 Democratic National Convention and two responses to it—one by Steven Milloy, author of *Junk Science Judo* and employed by the conservative Cato Institute, and one by Richard M. Doerflinger, an advocate for pro-life issues employed by the United States Conference of Catholic Bishops. Perhaps you too have personal, moral, religious, or occupational reasons to be concerned about this debate. If so, the words and images that follow can give you a start in understanding the key points in the argument over stem cell research—and perhaps encourage you to write your own essay on the subject.

RON REAGAN

Ron Reagan's Speech at the Democratic National Convention, July 27, 2004

1 Good evening, ladies and gentlemen.

2   A few of you may be surprised to see someone with my last name showing up to speak at a Democratic Convention. Apparently some of

you are not. Let me assure you, I am not here to make a political speech and the topic at hand should not—must not—have anything to do with partisanship.

3   I am here tonight to talk about the issue of research into what may be the greatest medical breakthrough in our or any lifetime: the use of embryonic stem cells—cells created using the material of our own bodies—to cure a wide range of fatal and debilitating illnesses: Parkinson's disease, multiple sclerosis, diabetes, lymphoma, spinal cord injuries, and much more.

4   Millions are afflicted. And every year, every day, tragedy is visited upon families across the country, around the world. Now, it may be within our power to put an end to this suffering. We only need to try.

5   Some of you already know what I'm talking about when I say embryonic stem cell research. Others of you are probably thinking, that's quite a mouthful. Maybe this is a good time to go for a tall cold one. Well, wait a minute, wait a minute.

6   Let me try and paint as simple a picture as I can while still doing justice to the science, the incredible science involved. Let's say that ten or so years from now you are diagnosed with Parkinson's disease. There is currently no cure, and drug therapy, with its attendant side-effects, can only temporarily relieve the symptoms.

7   Now, imagine going to a doctor who, instead of prescribing drugs, takes a few skin cells from your arm. The nucleus of one of your cells is placed into a donor egg whose own nucleus has been removed. A bit of chemical or electrical stimulation will encourage your cell's nucleus to begin dividing, creating new cells which will then be placed into a tissue culture. Those cells will generate embryonic stem cells containing only your DNA, thereby eliminating the risk of tissue rejection. These stem cells are then driven to become the very neural cells that are defective in Parkinson's patients. And finally, those cells—with your DNA—are injected into your brain where they will replace the faulty cells whose failure to produce adequate dopamine led to the Parkinson's disease in the first place.

8   In other words, you're cured.

9   And another thing, these embryonic stem cells, they could continue to replicate indefinitely and, theoretically, can be induced to recreate virtually any tissue in your body.

10   How'd you like to have your own personal biological repair kit standing by at the hospital? Sound like magic? Welcome to the future of medicine.

11   Now by the way, no fetal tissue is involved in this process. No fetuses are created, none destroyed. This all happens in the laboratory at the cellular level.

12   Now, there are those who would stand in the way of this remarkable future, who would deny the federal funding so crucial to basic

research. They argue that interfering with the development of even the earliest stage embryo, even one that will never be implanted in a womb and will never develop into an actual fetus, is tantamount to murder.

13   A few of these folks, needless to say, are just grinding a political axe and they should be ashamed of themselves. But many are well-meaning and sincere. Their belief is just that, an article of faith, and they are entitled to it. But it does not follow that the theology of a few should be allowed to forestall the health and well-being of the many.

14   And how can we affirm life if we abandon those whose own lives are so desperately at risk? It is a hallmark of human intelligence that we are able to make distinctions.

15   Yes, these cells could theoretically have the potential, under very different circumstances, to develop into human beings—that potential is where their magic lies. But they are not, in and of themselves, human beings. They have no fingers and toes, no brain or spinal cord. They have no thoughts, no fears. They feel no pain.

16   Surely we can distinguish between these undifferentiated cells multiplying in a tissue culture and a living, breathing person—a parent, a spouse, a child.

17   I know a child—well, she must be 13 now so I guess I'd better call her a young woman. She has fingers and toes. She has a mind. She has memories. She has hopes. She has juvenile diabetes. Like so many kids with this disease, she's adjusted amazingly well. The insulin pump she wears—she's decorated hers with rhinestones. She can handle her own catheter needle. She's learned to sleep through the blood drawings in the wee hours of the morning.

18   She's very brave. She is also quite bright and understands full well the progress of her disease and what that might ultimately mean: blindness, amputation, diabetic coma. Every day, she fights to have a future.

19   What excuse will we offer this young woman should we fail her now? What might we tell her children? Or the millions of others who suffer? That when given an opportunity to help, we turned away? That facing political opposition, we lost our nerve? That even though we knew better, we did nothing?

20   And, should we fail, how will we feel if, a few years from now, a more enlightened generation should fulfill the promise of embryonic stem cell therapy? Imagine what they would say of us who lacked the will.

21   No, we owe this young woman and all those who suffer—we owe ourselves—better than that. We are better than that. We are a wiser people, a finer nation.

22   And for all of us in this fight, let me say: we will prevail. The tide of history is with us. Like all generations who have come before ours, we are motivated by a thirst for knowledge and compelled to see others in need as fellow angels on an often difficult path, deserving of our compassion.

23   In a few months, we will face a choice. Yes, between two candidates and two parties, but more than that. We have a chance to take a giant stride forward for the good of all humanity. We can choose between the future and the past, between reason and ignorance, between true compassion and mere ideology.

24   This—this is our moment, and we must not falter.

25   Whatever else you do come November 2, I urge you, please, cast a vote for embryonic stem cell research.

26   Thank you for your time. ■

STEVEN MILLOY

Ron Reagan Wrong on Stem Cells

July 16, 2004

1   Ron Reagan, the younger son of the late Republican president, announced this week that he would give a prime-time address in support of stem cell research at the Democratic National Convention in Boston later this month.

Demonstrators line a sidewalk outside Robert Wood Johnson University Hospital in New Brunswick, N.J., during a forum on the state's stem cell research initiative, Wednesday, May 12, 2003. New Jersey Gov. James E. McGreevey signed an agreement at the forum to create the first state-supported stem-cell research institute, which would be constructed near the hospital. (AP Photo/Daniel Hulshizer)

2   "Ron Reagan's courageous pleas for stem cell research add a powerful voice to the millions of Americans hoping for cures for their children, for their parents and for their grandparents," said a spokesman for John Kerry to the Associated Press.

3   Reagan told the *Philadelphia Inquirer* that the speech was intended "to educate people about stem cell research" rather than be critical of President George Bush. But the Kerry campaign seems to want to scare people by having the son of the revered late President Ronald Reagan decry President Bush and his pro-life supporters as the major roadblocks to a host of supposedly just-around-the-corner miracle cures for cancer, Alzheimer's, diabetes and other dreaded diseases.

4   It will be a junk-science-fueled spectacle.

5   The controversy centers around the use of stem cells derived from destroyed human embryos. So-called "embryonic stem cells" give rise to all other cells and tissues in the human body and have been touted as possibly yielding treatments for a variety of diseases.

6   Moral concerns over the destruction of human embryos caused President Bush to limit taxpayer funding for embryonic stem cell research to stem cell lines already in existence. Researchers who were counting on taxpayer funding to conduct research on embryonic stem

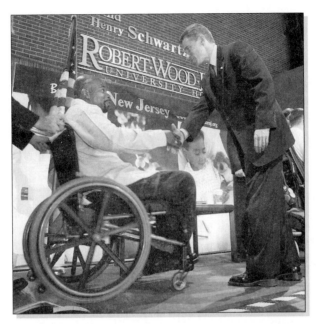

New Jersey Gov. James E. McGreevey, right, greets Wali Mohammed, of Asbury Park, N.J., who suffered a spinal cord injury, as he comes on stage at a forum on the state's stem cell research initiative. McGreevey allocated six and a half million dollars for the project in his proposed budget. (AP Photo/Daniel Hulshizer)

cells—and then rake in millions of dollars from naive investors—were enraged and began a campaign to pressure the President into opening the taxpayer spigots for embryonic stem cell research on the basis of a wide-eyed hope that cures are near at hand.

7   Though embryonic stem cell research advocates euphemistically refer to the current state of research as an "early stage," the unfortunate reality is that the goal of embryonic stem cell therapies is, at this point, more accurately described as a pipe dream. No researcher is anywhere close to significant progress in developing practical embryonic stem cell therapies.

8   Mouse embryonic stem cells were first grown in a laboratory in 1981. It took 20 years to make similar achievements with human embryonic stem cells—and merely growing stem cells is nowhere close to employing those cells in therapies. Embryonic stem cells must be directed to grow into specific cell types and that growth must be controlled—they can proliferate indefinitely in the lab. Uncontrolled stem cell growth may have tumor-forming potential. Because embryonic

stem cells don't come from the patient being treated, there may also be problems associated with immune system rejection following transplantation of foreign stem cells.

9   The difficulty of embryonic stem cell research is underscored by the lack of progress in cancer research. Despite a 30-year, $40-billion "War on Cancer" launched by President Nixon, researchers continue to have great difficulty in controlling, let alone eradicating, the vast majority of cancer cell growth. Conceptually, controlled deployment of "good" stem cells should be vastly more complex than simply destroying "bad" cancer cells.

10   None of this is to say that embryonic stem cell research can't possibly lead to some improvements in biological understanding or future therapeutic treatments, but such speculative progress of who-knows-what value isn't in the foreseeable future. The only thing certain is that the cost of that research will be high. If embryonic stem cell research had real and imminent possibilities, private investors would be pouring capital into research hoping for real and imminent profits. Instead, venture capital firms are contributing to political efforts to get taxpayers to fund research.

11   A proposed ballot initiative in California known as Proposition 71 would provide $3 billion in taxpayer money for stem cell research. Supporters hope to raise $20 million to get the initiative passed. What the venture capitalists seem to be hoping for is that taxpayer funding of stem cell research will increase the value of their stakes in biotech companies. The venture capitalists can then cash out at a hefty profit, leaving taxpayers holding the bag of fruitless research.

12   The spectacle of Ron Reagan at the Democratic Convention will be sad—the disgruntled son of the beloved former president misleading the public with naive hopes while being exploited for political gain by opponents of his father's party. That cynical strategy may get John Kerry a few more votes in November, but it's not going to produce any medical miracles anytime soon, if at all. ■

RICHARD M. DOERFLINGER

Don't Clone Ron Reagan's Agenda

July 28, 2004

1   Ron Reagan's speech at the Democratic convention last night was expected to urge expanded funding for stem cell research using so-called "spare" embryos—and to highlight these cells' potential for treating the Alzheimer's disease that took his father's life.

2   He did neither. He didn't even mention Alzheimer's, perhaps because even strong supporters of embryonic stem cell research say it is unlikely to be of use for that disease. (Reagan himself admitted this on a July 12 segment of MSNBC's *Hardball*.) And he didn't talk about current debates on funding research using existing embryos. Instead he endorsed the more radical agenda of human cloning—mass-producing one's own identical twins in the laboratory so they can be exploited as (in his words) "your own personal biological repair kit" when disease or injury strikes.

3   Politically this was, to say the least, a gamble. Americans may be tempted to make use of embryos left over from fertility clinics, but most polls show them to be against human cloning for any purpose. Other advanced nations—Canada, Australia, France, Germany, Norway—have banned the practice completely, and the United Nations may approve an international covenant against it this fall. Many groups and individuals who are "pro-choice" on abortion oppose research cloning, not least because it would require the mass exploitation of women to provide what Ron Reagan casually calls "donor eggs." And the potential "therapeutic" benefits of cloning are even more speculative than those of embryonic stem cell research—the worldwide effort even to obtain viable stem cells from cloned embryos has already killed hundreds of embryos and produced exactly one stem cell line, in South Korea.

4   But precisely for these reasons, Ron Reagan should be praised for his candor. The scientists and patient groups promoting embryonic stem cell research know that the current debate on funding is a mere transitional step. For years they have supported the mass manufacture of human embryos through cloning, as the logical and necessary goal of their agenda, but lately they have been coy about this as they fight for the more popular slogan of "stem cell research." With his speech Reagan has removed the mask, and allowed us to debate what is really at stake.

5   He claimed in his speech, of course, that what is at stake in this debate is the lives of millions of patients with devastating diseases. But by highlighting Parkinson's disease and juvenile diabetes as two diseases most clearly justifying the move to human cloning, he failed to do his homework. These are two of the diseases that pro-cloning scientists now admit will probably *not* be helped by research cloning.

6   Scottish cloning expert Ian Wilmut, for example, wrote in the *British Medical Journal* in February that producing genetically matched stem cells through cloning is probably quite unnecessary for treating any neurological disease. Recent findings suggest that the nervous system is "immune privileged," and will not generally reject stem cells from a human who is genetically different. He added that cloning is probably useless for auto-immune diseases like juvenile diabetes, where the body mistakenly rejects its own insulin-producing cells as though they were foreign. "In such cases," he wrote, "transfer of

immunologically identical cells to a patient is expected to induce the same rejection."

7   Wilmut's observations cut the ground out from under Ron Reagan's simple-minded claim that cloning is needed to avoid tissue rejection. For some diseases, genetically matched cells are unnecessary; for others, they are useless, because they only replicate the genetic profile that is part of the problem. (Ironically, for Alzheimer's both may be true—cloning may be unnecessary to avoid tissue rejection in the brain, and useless because the cloned cells would have the same genetic defect that may lead to Alzheimer's.) Reagan declared that this debate requires us to "choose between . . . reason and ignorance," but he did not realize which side has the monopoly on ignorance.

8   That ignorance poses an obstacle to real advances that are right before our eyes. Two weeks before Ron Reagan declared that a treatment for Parkinson's may arrive "ten or so years from now," using "the material of our own bodies," a Parkinson's patient and his doctor quietly appeared before Congress to point out that this has already been done. Dennis Turner was treated in 1999 by Dr. Michel Levesque of Cedars-Sinai Medical Center in Los Angeles, using his own adult neural stem cells. Dr. Levesque did not use the Rube Goldberg method of trying to turn those cells into a cloned embryo and then killing the embryo to get stem cells—he just grew Turner's own adult stem cells in the lab, and turned them directly into dopamine-producing cells. And with just one injection, on one side of Turner's brain, he produced an almost complete reversal of Parkinson's symptoms over four years.

9   Turner stopped shaking, could eat without difficulty, could put in his own contact lenses again, and resumed his avocation of big-game photography—on one occasion scrambling up a tree in Africa to escape a charging rhinoceros.

10   Amazingly, while this advance has been presented at national and international scientific conferences and featured on ABC-TV in Chicago, the scientific establishment supporting embryonic stem cell research has almost completely ignored it, and most news media have obediently imposed a virtual news blackout on it. That did not change even after the results were presented to the Senate Commerce Subcommittee on Science, Technology and Space this month. Pro-cloning Senators on the panel actually seemed angry at the witnesses, for trying to distract them from their fixation on destroying embryos.

11   Turner also testified that his symptoms have begun to return, especially arising from the side of his brain that was left untreated, and he would like to get a second treatment. For that he will have to wait Dr. Levesque has received insufficient appreciation and funding for his technique, and is still trying to put together the funds for broader clinical trials—as most Parkinson's foundations and NIH peer reviewers

look into the starry distance of Ron Reagan's dreams about embryonic stem cells.

12   But hey, who cares about real Parkinson's patients when there's a Brave New World to sell? ■

From Reading to Writing

1. In his speech printed here, Ron Reagan made some large claims for embryonic stem cell research; the two respondents to Reagan's speech raised a great many objections to his claims. Do your own research in order to find how much of what Reagan claims is likely to result from stem cell research. Then write a rebuttal to either Reagan's speech or to the responses to it by Milloy and Doerflinger (see Chapter 10 on writing rebuttals).

2. One of the major concerns of those who oppose stem cell research lies in the use of human embryo stem cells—and the source of those stem cells in aborted tissue or in therapeutic cloning. And one of the impediments to public discussion is the fact that highly technical scientific processes and techniques are involved, processes and techniques that lay people imperfectly understand. Do some research to further clarify for yourself and your audience the processes for producing and harvesting stem cells. Then, after looking once again at Chapter 6 on definition arguments, write an essay defining "embryonic stem cells" or "stem cell research" in such a way that you either support or oppose stem cell research.

3. Many people have made arguments against the use of stem cell research by citing religious authorities and traditions. Research the stances of various religions on embryonic stem cell research to see if there is relatively universal concern, or whether there are some religions that support this research. Then write an essay in support or opposition that makes use of the information you turn up.

4. Evaluate President Bush's policy on stem cell research. After summarizing the policy, examine it in the light of aesthetic, practical, and ethical criteria, which are presented on pages 148–50.

5. One of the major methods for convincing people of the necessity of stem cell research is the use of personal examples—narratives—about people who might benefit from this technology. Beginning from your own informed beliefs about the use of embryonic stem cells, write a story that illustrates your position on this topic. If possible, draw

from your personal experience with Parkinson's, childhood diabetes, or some other disease or condition that could be affected by stem cell research. (See Chapter 9 on narrative arguments.)

6. Do a rhetorical analysis of the arguments of Ron Reagan. How is his speech a product of the particular rhetorical situation that he found himself in—before the Democratic National Convention, and before a national television audience? How might have he presented his argument if he had appeared before Republicans? Do you agree with Reagan's assertion that his speech is not political?

7. Based on the guidelines in Chapter 11, write a proposal that defends or undermines the practice of stem cell research.

CHAPTER 22

Privacy

New Challenges to Personal Privacy

The Dog Poop Girl (as she has come to be known) was riding the subway in Seoul, South Korea, one day when her dog decided to "take care of business." According to a *Washington Post* story written by Jonathan Krim on July 7, 2005, the woman (a university student) made no move to clean up the mess, so fellow passengers grew agitated. One of them recorded the scene on a cell phone camera and then posted photos on a Web site. Web surfers came upon the photos and began referring to her as Dog Poop Girl. One thing led to another, and soon her privacy was completely gone: people revealed her true name, began asking for and sharing more information about her, launched blogs commenting about her and her relatives, and generally crackled with gossip about her and her behavior. Ultimately she became the subject of sermons and online discussions, and her story made the national news. In humiliation, Dog Poop Girl withdrew from her university.

A second incident was reported by Felisa Cardona in the *Denver Post* on August 2, 2005. A computer security breach at the University of Colorado left 29,000 students and 7,000 faculty and staff vulnerable to identity theft. It seems that hackers attacked the university computers in order to gain access to the Buff One ID card used by many students and staff. Though no information seems to have ever been used from this attack, 6,000 students had to be issued new cards in order to gain access to their dorms. Moreover, after the incident Colorado officials decided to convert from Social Security number identifications, and many other universities have done the same because they too have been targeted by identity thieves.

> "You have zero privacy now— get over it."
>
> —SCOTT MCNEALY, CEO OF SUN MICROSYSTEMS

These two incidents illustrate some of the new challenges to personal privacy that have been raised by technology developments and by concerns for security in the wake of September 11. There is no doubt that electronic technologies have given people a new degree of personal freedom: cell phones, email, and Web shopping are now routine timesavers. But there is also no doubt that a price has been paid for that freedom: that price is the surveillance side of the Internet and other technologies. In the wake of September 11, other terrorist attacks, and the increased attention to security that has ensued, privacy issues have been an increasing concern in American life as law enforcement officials seek access to information about potential conspiracies and as businesses increasingly gather information about individuals to individualize marketing campaigns, keep an eye out for good (and bad) credit risks, and customize customers.

When is freedom too much freedom? If bloggers act as a posse, tracking down criminals and turning them over to law enforcement, is that appropriate action or vigilante action? What about efforts to replicate what was done to the Dog Poop Girl? Should laws prevent people from publicizing and branding people who seem undesirable? Should people who wish to share secrets—whether the secrets are true or not—have the anonymity and apparent protection afforded by the Internet? Must Internet users simply accept as a fact of life being bombarded by hundreds of unauthorized, unsolicited spam messages? And what are the limits of what government can do to inspect the personal records of citizens? Even in the interests of a good cause, like the prevention of crime and the apprehension of criminals, should government enjoy the rights to snoop that have been granted to it recently by the Patriot Act?

Contemporary Arguments

Is it possible to have both security and freedom in the United States? What is the proper balance between the two? On the one hand, some people support a national ID card (already used, incidentally, in several European nations) or sign up for in-vehicle security systems such as OnStar (always on the watch!) as a safety feature. They root for police to pursue potential terrorists, wink when Internet service providers disclose customer records to government agents if they feel that a crime is being committed, and appreciate being notified that convicted felons have moved into the neighborhood. On the other hand, they also protest when police use wiretaps without explicit legal permission, worry about the ability of global positioning systems to snoop on people from satellites (especially by zeroing in on cell phones or implanted homing devices), and protest when roving surveillance cameras are mounted in stores and at street corners, in public parks and on school playgrounds. Everyone seems to be monitored or monitoring: online data collectors record which Web sites people visit; airlines record data on people's travels; companies routinely perform background checks on potential employees; bus and train companies check passenger lists against records of "suspicious" characters; businesses seek to develop systems that can deliver customized marketing information to particular households and commuters; supermarkets record purchases in order to fine-tune their stocking patterns. In the future, some say, we can look forward to smart cars, smart airports, smart TVs, smart credit cards, and smart homes—all designed to give us certain freedoms, if at the risk of the loss of privacy.

The arguments in this chapter discuss questions related to privacy. Because no case illustrates the tension that exists between freedom and security better than the USA PATRIOT Act of 2001, we look in detail at that Issue in Focus. In addition to cartoons and photographs that dramatize the issue, you will see a short article by former Attorney General John Ashcroft (defending the Patriot Act); a critique of the Patriot Act by David Sarasohn, based on a privacy violation; a blog-based discussion of the case; and additional criticisms of the act from the American Civil Liberties Union and the American Library Association. We also reprint James Bovard's comprehensive warning about the threat to privacy that is being posed by various aspects of the "war on terrorism" as well as something of a counter-argument by David Brin, "Three Cheers for the Surveillance Society!", that overviews the brave new world that is now developing (for better or worse). Paul Saffo explains the not-so-science-fiction possibility of DNA identity theft, Ted Koppel meditates on the "miracles [that] microchip and satellite technology offer"—as well as on the need to oversee how "companies share and exchange their harvest of private data"—and Randall Larsen proposes a national identification card to improve homeland security. Finally, Jeffrey Zaslow offers a warning to students: beware of what you post on blogs, Web sites, and email, because a future employer (or potential spouse!) just may be able one future day to view your every performance!

ISSUE IN FOCUS

Surveillance and Security

Few pieces of legislation in American history have raised passions as much as the USA PATRIOT Act. The name of the bill is both an appeal to the emotions surrounding patriotism in the wake of the September 11 attacks, and an acronym for "Uniting and Strengthening America by Providing

Appropriate Tools Required to Intercept and Obstruct Terrorism." Officially labeled House Resolution 3162, the bill was approved quickly and overwhelmingly by both houses of Congress (98–1 in the Senate, 357–66 in the House) and signed into law by President Bush on October 26, 2001—just six weeks after the terrorist attacks on New York and Washington.

Most provisions of the Patriot Act (the full text of the law runs to over 300 pages) are uncontroversial. They encourage cooperation among law enforcement agencies and speed up a variety of information-gathering processes. But the Patriot Act also attempts to remove hindrances to investigators who were looking for those responsible for the terrorist attacks. Those barriers included limited access to individuals' private email and Internet accounts as well as to bank, credit card, telephone, voice mail, and library records. In addition to compromising some of those barriers, the act requires increased vigilance at entry points to the United States.

> Although liberty and freedom ring out loud and clear throughout the Constitution and democracy, providing amendments and laws, protecting individuals' rights and privacy, they are not absolute. They are tethered to responsibility and must yield when confronted with the safety, security, and survival of the nation and society, even if collateral innocence becomes a victim. Such action, ironically, would be necessary in order to preserve the Constitution and democracy that created them.
>
> —BUCK SMITH, SUN CITY, CALIF., LETTER TO LOS ANGELES TIMES, AUGUST 4, 2004

Because of the speed with which this wide-ranging bill was passed, much of the debate surrounding it has come after it became law—particularly since some of its provisions contained "sunset arrangements" that were set to expire December 31, 2005. (The expiration date was later extended to June 30, 2006.) The possibility of such expirations, the persistence of acts of terrorism worldwide, the war in Iraq, and the worries of civil libertarians have fueled continuing debate on the Patriot Act and on the broader question: What is the proper balance between the security and safety of citizens and the civil liberties guaranteed by the Constitution, including the right to privacy? After all, the fourth amendment in the Bill of Rights guarantees "the right of the people to be secure in their persons, houses, papers, and effects, against unreasonable searches and seizures, . . . and no warrants shall issue, but upon probable cause, supported by oath or affirmation, and particularly describing the place to be searched, and the persons or things to be seized."

In the years after 2001, particularly but not only during the election season of 2004, the Patriot Act has continued to be debated. President Bush, his then-Attorney General John Ashcroft, and others since have contended

Judith Krug, director of intellectual freedom for the American Library Association, wears a button that reads "another 'hysteric' librarian for freedom" as she talks to reporters Thursday, Feb. 26, 2004, at the Public Library Association National Meeting in Seattle. Krug was speaking out against aspects of the Patriot Act that can potentially give the government access to bookstore and library records. The button refers to a speech in September of 2003 where Attorney General John Ashcroft referred to claims by the ACLU and library associations that the Patriot Act allows the FBI to snoop into Americans' reading habits as "baseless hysteria." (AP Photo/Ted S. Warren)

that the Patriot Act should be made permanent and even extended in certain ways. They have asked Congress to consider new clauses that would allow a denial of bail in terrorism cases and easier access to time-sensitive records. But others, including Democratic presidential candidate John Kerry (though he voted in favor of the Patriot Act when it was first passed) have questioned whether certain parts of the act infringe too much on civil liberties, especially by giving police increased access to citizens' private records. Those critics seek safeguards against investigations of computers, medical and financial records, and libraries, and they worry about wiretap surveillance by government investigators without a judge's review. (For a summary of objections to the Patriot Act, see the following Web page on the Electronic Privacy Information Center's Web site: <www.epic.org/privacy/terrorism/usapatriot>.)

Mike Keefe's editorial cartoons regularly appear in the *Denver Post*. This one was published on May 27, 2005.

A Chronology of the Patriot Act

Sept. 13, 2001. Senate debates wiretap and anti-terrorism proposals.

Sept. 19, 2001. Administration presents draft anti-terrorism bill.

Sept. 20, 2001. Public Safety and Cyber Security Act of 2001 is introduced by Rep. Lamar Smith, chairman, House Subcommittee on Crime.

The ACLU, endorsed by other civil liberties groups, releases "In Defense of Freedom at a Time of Crisis" statement.

Sept. 22, 2001. American Library Association reacts to the Sept. 11th attack and issues a statement on the confidentiality and privacy of library records.

Sept. 23, 2001. Senator Graham proposes Anti-Terrorism Bill.

Sept. 24, 2001. Bush Administration submits its own anti-terrorism legislation to Congress.

Oct. 2, 2001. The PATRIOT Act is introduced by Representatives Sensenbrenner and Conyers.

Oct. 5, 2001. Another proposal, the Uniting and Strengthening America (USA) Act, is introduced by Senator Leahy.

Oct. 12, 2001. USA Act is passed by the House.

Oct. 24, 2001. House passes Uniting and Strengthening America by Providing Appropriate Tools Required to Intercept and Obstruct Terrorism (USA PATRIOT) Act of 2001. The new bill, H.R. 3162, is the result of negotiations between the House and Senate anti-terrorism bills (H.R. 2975 and S. 1510). See http://www.cdt.org/security/011023hr3162floordebate.txt for details.

Oct. 25, 2001. Senate passes the USA PATRIOT Act. The vote was 98–1 with only Senator Russ Feingold voting against it. See http://www.cdt.org/security/011025senate.txt for Senate debate, including a detailed statement by Senator Leahy.

Oct. 26, 2001. President Bush signs the USA PATRIOT Act into law in a Rose Garden Ceremony.

Source of Chronology: http://www.unc.edu/courses/2003spring/law/357c/001/projects/hunterb/Patriotact/background.htm.

In this section, you will find a chronology of events in the history of the bill, arguments on either side, and a series of responses—in words and in images—that can help you to recover (and enter) the debate surrounding this momentous legislation. In particular, you might consider the American Library Association resolution that was written in response to this law and which is reprinted here, as well as the American Civil Liberties Union (ACLU) statement "In Defense of Freedom at a Time of Crisis," and two essays on the controversy—one by John Ashcroft and one by David Sarasohn. We also reproduce several entries from a blog discussion of the Patriot Act.

All of this, of course, only scratches the surface of this issue. But it prompt possible areas for further thinking, research, and writing that can help you enter this important argument about security, privacy, and surveillance.

AMERICAN CIVIL LIBERTIES UNION

In Defense of Freedom at a Time of Crisis

1 On September 11, 2001 thousands of people lost their lives in a brutal assault on the American people and the American form of government. We mourn the loss of these innocent lives and insist that those who perpetrated these acts be held accountable.

2 This tragedy requires all Americans to examine carefully the steps our country may now take to reduce the risk of future terrorist attacks.

3 We need to consider proposals calmly and deliberately with a determination not to erode the liberties and freedoms that are at the core of the American way of life.

4 We need to ensure that actions by our government uphold the principles of a democratic society, accountable government and international law, and that all decisions are taken in a manner consistent with the Constitution.

5 We can, as we have in the past, in times of war and of peace, reconcile the requirements of security with the demands of liberty.

6 We should resist the temptation to enact proposals in the mistaken belief that anything that may be called anti-terrorist will necessarily provide greater security.

7 We should resist efforts to target people because of their race, religion, ethnic background or appearance, including immigrants in general, Arab Americans and Muslims.

8 We affirm the right of peaceful dissent, protected by the First Amendment, now, when it is most at risk.

9   We should applaud our political leaders in the days ahead who have the courage to say that our freedoms should not be limited.

10   We must have faith in our democratic system and our Constitution, and in our ability to protect at the same time both the freedom and the security of all Americans. ■

AMERICAN LIBRARY ASSOCIATION COUNCIL

Resolution on the USA Patriot Act and Related Measures That Infringe on the Rights of Library Users

1   WHEREAS, The American Library Association affirms the responsibility of the leaders of the United States to protect and preserve the freedoms that are the foundation of our democracy; and

2   WHEREAS, Libraries are a critical force for promoting the free flow and unimpeded distribution of knowledge and information for individuals, institutions, and communities; and

3   WHEREAS, The American Library Association holds that suppression of ideas undermines a democratic society; and

4   WHEREAS, Privacy is essential to the exercise of free speech, free thought, and free association, and, in a library, the subject of users' interests should not be examined or scrutinized by others; and

5   WHEREAS, Certain provisions of the USA PATRIOT Act, the revised Attorney General Guidelines to the Federal Bureau of Investigation, and other related measures expand the authority of the federal government to investigate citizens and non-citizens, to engage in surveillance, and to threaten civil rights and liberties guaranteed under the United States Constitution and Bill of Rights; and

6   WHEREAS, The USA PATRIOT Act and other recently enacted laws, regulations, and guidelines increase the likelihood that the activities of library users, including their use of computers to browse the Web or access e-mail, may be under government surveillance without their knowledge or consent; now, therefore, be it

7   RESOLVED, That the American Library Association opposes any use of governmental power to suppress the free and open exchange of knowledge and information or to intimidate individuals exercising free inquiry; and, be it further

This cartoon by Tom Toles, a syndicated cartoonist whose work appears in many newspapers and magazines, was published in the *Washington Post* and elsewhere on May 22, 2005.

8 RESOLVED, That the American Library Association encourages all librarians, library administrators, library governing bodies, and library advocates to educate their users, staff, and communities about the process for compliance with the USA PATRIOT Act and other related measures and about the dangers to individual privacy and the confidentiality of library records resulting from those measures; and, be it further

9 RESOLVED, That the American Library Association urges librarians everywhere to defend and support user privacy and free and open access to knowledge and information; and, be it further

10 RESOLVED, That the American Library Association will work with other organizations, as appropriate, to protect the rights of inquiry and free expression; and, be it further

11 RESOLVED, That the American Library Association will take actions as appropriate to obtain and publicize information about the surveillance of libraries and library users by law enforcement agencies and to assess the impact on library users and their communities; and, be it further

12 RESOLVED, That the American Library Association urges all libraries to adopt and implement patron privacy and record retention policies that affirm that "the collection of personally identifiable information should only be a matter of routine or policy when necessary for the fulfillment of the mission of the library" (ALA Privacy: An Interpretation of the Library Bill of Rights); and, be it further

13 RESOLVED, That the American Library Association considers sections of the USA PATRIOT Act are a present danger to the constitutional rights and privacy rights of library users and urges the United States Congress to:

1. provide active oversight of the implementation of the USA PATRIOT Act and other related measures, and the revised Attorney General Guidelines to the Federal Bureau of Investigation;
2. hold hearings to determine the extent of the surveillance on library users and their communities; and
3. amend or change the sections of these laws and the guidelines that threaten or abridge the rights of inquiry and free expression; and, be it further

14 RESOLVED. That this resolution be forwarded to the President of the United States, to the Attorney General of the United States, to Members of both Houses of Congress, to the library community, and to others as appropriate.

Adopted by the ALA Council, January 29, 2003 ∎

JOHN ASHCROFT

The Patriot Act: Wise Beyond its Years

1 The Patriot Act turns three today [October 26, 2004], but its age belies its experience—and its phenomenal success. Over the past 36 months, the Patriot Act has proved itself to be an indispensable tool that the men and women of law enforcement use to combat terrorism and to compile a record of accomplishment that has grown even as their responsibility for the safety of Americans has increased.

2   The Patriot Act enhanced communication on every level of law enforcement to combat terrorist threats, while also giving investigators the same tools to use in terrorism cases that they were using to combat other serious threats.

3   Armed with these tools, U.S. intelligence and law enforcement agents have pursued and captured operatives in the war on terrorism from Florida to New York, from Virginia to Oregon and points in between. Since Sept. 11, 2001, 368 individuals have been charged and 194 have been convicted.

4   Despite the documented successes in keeping Americans safe from terrorism, the Patriot Act rarely receives its due, and indeed is often portrayed in an outright false light.

5   Take the latest example. Just last month, several major news organizations erroneously reported that a federal judge in New York had overturned "an important surveillance provision" of the Patriot Act. In fact, the judge ruled on the Electronic Communications Privacy Act—sponsored by Sen. Patrick Leahy (D., Vt.) and passed in 1986, 15 years before the Patriot Act. Both the *New York Times* and the *Washington Post* were forced to print corrections the next day.

6   Time and again, the image of the Patriot Act is at odds with the facts on the ground. Three years ago today, Congress passed, and President Bush signed, a piece of long-overdue legislation that has been critical to keeping Americans safe and free. The parade of witnesses that appeared before the 9/11 Commission spoke of the importance of the Patriot Act. Former Attorney General Janet Reno and many others credited the Patriot Act with updating the law to deal with terrorists, and, most critically, for tearing down the "wall" in terrorism investigations that restricted the communication and cooperation between law enforcement and intelligence officials.

7   This new ability to share information helped U.S. law enforcement, working with German authorities, to break up an alleged al Qaeda fund-raising plot in Germany. Here in the United States, the Patriot Act helped federal, state and local law enforcement dismantle the "Portland Seven" terrorist cell in Oregon, as well as cells in Seattle and New York, and alleged terrorist financers in Florida and Texas.

8   The Patriot Act has also been successful in updating anti-terrorism and criminal laws to bring law enforcement up to date with technology. Pre-Patriot Act, a new court order was required to continue surveillance of a suspected terrorist whenever he switched phones. The Patriot Act gave anti-terrorism investigators the same authority that investigators in criminal cases had to get a single court order allowing surveillance of every phone a suspect uses. Common sense dictates that tools that help fight the drug lords should be available to protect the American people from terrorist attacks.

9   The Patriot Act also increased penalties for not only these who commit terrorist acts, but for those who provide support to terrorists as well. In particular, the Act enhanced law enforcement's ability to crack down on unlicensed foreign money transmittal businesses, a favored method of financing for terrorists. Prosecutors in New Jersey recently used the Patriot Act to convict Yehuda Abraham, whose services were used in a plot to sell shoulder-fired surface-to-air missiles to terrorists with the understanding that they were going to be used to shoot down U.S. commercial aircraft.

10   The Patriot Act has proved its usefulness beyond the war on terrorism in protecting our most vulnerable citizens from harm. During the course of drafting and debating the Patriot Act in 2001, Congress wisely decided to provide some investigative tools for all criminal investigations, including terrorism investigations.

11   The result? In pedophile and kidnapping investigations, for example, a delay can literally mean the difference between life and death for a child. For years, investigators could subpoena some information from Internet service providers. But filing subpoenas to get information quickly to identify and locate a suspect could cost life-saving time.

12   Section 210 of the Patriot Act changed that. In Operation Hamlet, sexual predators were using the Internet to exchange photos and videotapes of children being sexually abused. Sometimes the abusers molested children while running a live feed via a Web cam; this allowed other child sexual abusers to watch in real-time online. Investigators used the Patriot Act to quickly obtain subpoenas for information from Internet service providers. The sexual predators were identified, and 19 were convicted. More than 100 children were spared further harm.

13   The Patriot Act has helped law enforcement achieve more safety and security for the American people without any abuse of civil liberties. Misleading rhetoric aside, not a single instance of abuse under the Act has been cited by any court, the Congress or the Justice Department's own Inspector General—not one.

14   The public has expressed overwhelming support for the Patriot Act in opinion poll after opinion poll. They know what the 9/11 Commission affirmed: that for the past three years, America's families and communities have been safer, and their freedom is enhanced because of the president's resolve and leadership, the foresight of Congress in enacting these vital tools, and the courageous men and women on the front lines who have used the Patriot Act to protect our lives and liberties. ■

DAVID SARASOHN

The Patriot Act on Trial

1   **B**randon Mayfield is the Justice Department's worst nightmare. Not because he's done anything illegal or dangerous to American security but because he hasn't.

2   That simple reality, now repeatedly admitted and apologized for, is likely to give both the Justice Department and the Patriot Act their most pointed courtroom challenge since the act was passed. This summer in Portland saw the first hearing on three lawsuits—featuring a media superstar lawyer, more government lawyers than could fit at the defense table, the Fourth Amendment, a claim for major damages and repeated concerns expressed by US senators—taking on the post-9/11 operations of the Justice Department.

3   The case began in March 2004 after the terrorist bombings in Madrid, when the Spanish government found a partial fingerprint in a bag containing detonators. Spanish officials sent a digital copy of the partial print to the FBI, which ran it through its 40 million fingerprints and came up with a match for Mayfield, in the system because of a teenage arrest.

4   Checking him out, the FBI found that Mayfield was a Muslim convert who attended the Bilal Mosque, a suburban temple also attended by some members of the Portland 7—convicted for trying to go to Afghanistan to fight with the Taliban against the United States. In fact, Mayfield, an attorney, had represented one of the Portland 7 in a child custody case. The FBI became extremely interested. But by April the Spanish were saying that the Mayfield match was "conclusively negative." The FBI then sent a team to Spain—although reportedly never asking to see the original print—which reportedly returned saying the Spanish were satisfied, although the Spanish kept saying that they weren't.

5   By late April the FBI picked up a rumor that the European media were about to go public with the Mayfield story, and decided to move. Telling Federal Judge Robert Jones that the fingerprint was a "100 percent match," the FBI got a warrant to arrest Mayfield as a "material witness." (This June the ACLU reported that in a sharp increase in the practice, seventy people have been detained as material witnesses since 9/11—all but one of them Muslim.) On May 6, 2004, Mayfield was taken to federal prison, where he spent the first week in lockdown.

6   As an attorney, he knew that the lack of actual charges against him was not reassuring. Mayfield asked his federal public defender three questions—Could he be sent to Spain? Could he be tried for the bombing? Could he be executed if convicted?—and was told that the answer to all three was yes. Except, as he kept telling people, it wasn't his

fingerprint. After he'd spent two weeks in custody, when the Spanish told the FBI they had now matched the fingerprint to an Algerian, the FBI finally agreed, released Mayfield and apologized.

7   A month later Mayfield was telling the Portland City Club, "We need to be safe and secure in our homes, not just from the bad guys but the government as well." And he didn't even know then just how much he needed such protection.

8   The FBI repeatedly insisted that the problem was just a simple, unfortunate law enforcement mistake, and had absolutely nothing to do with the new powers of the Patriot Act. But Mayfield was certain that his home and office had been the object of "sneak and peek" searches. It took until March 2005—almost a full year after the FBI had arrested, released and then apologized to Mayfield—for the Justice Department to admit: "Mr. Mayfield is hereby notified that the following property was seized, altered or reproduced during [Foreign Intelligence Surveillance Act] searches of his residence: three hard drives of three desktop computers and one loose hard drive were copied; several documents in the residence were digitally photographed; ten DNA samples were taken and preserved on cotton swabs and six cigarette butts were seized for DNA analysis; and approximately 335 digital photographs were taken of the residence and the property therein. . . . Mr. Mayfield is also hereby notified that he was the target of electronic surveillance and other physical searches authorized pursuant to FISA."

9   It took another two weeks for the admission—in the course of testimony by Attorney General Alberto Gonzales to the House judiciary committee—that, well, yes, the FBI had used the Patriot Act in the Mayfield case. Gonzales insisted, "I might add that based on what I know today—and I'm limited in what I can say because this matter is in litigation—I don't believe that the Brandon Mayfield case is an example where there was a misuse or abuse of a provision of the Patriot Act."

10   Senators weren't so sure. Later, Senator Russell Feingold noted that the Mayfield case "had a big effect on the whole attitude that anybody who criticized the law really wasn't concerned about terrorism." Senator Patrick Leahy, the ranking Democrat on the Judiciary Committee, argued at another committee hearing on the Patriot Act, "I'm thinking of Brandon Mayfield, the Portland attorney," against whom the FBI had no real evidence except that he "did hang out with Muslims." Conservative Republican Larry Craig seemed to evoke the Mayfield case without mentioning it when he told the committee, "I find it very difficult to believe that the federal government can enter my home, strip my hard drive, go through my records and then exit out the back door without telling me they were there."

11   By then Mayfield was moving on his three lawsuits against the federal government—an effort that gained momentum in June with the court-ordered release of an FBI internal memo, dated before his arrest,

noting that the bureau had insufficient evidence to charge him with anything but should arrest him before the media got the story. First, he wants back everything the FBI seized in searches that the government now admits had no national security justification; the government says it needs the information for its legal defense. Second, he's seeking financial damages. Finally, he's challenging the Patriot Act clause that makes it so much easier for the government to do searches. Previously, under the Foreign Intelligence Surveillance Act, the only justification for a secret search was acquiring information on foreign intelligence. Under the Patriot Act that need only be part of the reason, greatly widening the areas where the Justice Department can seek—and apparently always get—a warrant for such a search.

12   To one of Mayfield's attorneys, Elden Rosenthal of Portland, the sneak-and-peek expansion abandons the Fourth Amendment unnecessarily. "We won World War I, we won World War II, we won the cold war within throwing out the right of Americans to be secure in their homes, without throwing out the Fourth Amendment," Rosenthal says.

13   On July 15 Federal Judge Ann Aiken held a preliminary hearing in Portland on government efforts to dismiss Mayfield's lawsuits. The day featured the first courtroom appearance of Mayfield's other attorney, celebrity lawyer and CNN legal commentator Gerry Spence, who charged that the FBI arrested Mayfield only because of his Muslim identity, even when there was no evidence he'd ever been to Spain or left Portland. "I am sure that had it been Billy Graham, or one of Billy Graham's children, the FBI might have said that we'd better check it out," he mused. "No airline tickets. How did he get over there to Spain? Must have been that magic carpet. The Muslim magic carpet." To Spence—looking, with his swept-back gray pompadour touching his collar, like a retired gunfighter who'd gone into corporate security—the point of the trial was clear: "Although they say, 'We're really sorry,' we haven't had an opportunity to say if sorry is enough."

14   Two weeks later Aiken agreed, rejecting government efforts to dismiss the lawsuits, rejecting motions to remove the FBI fingerprint experts as defendants and ordering the government to release all information about the searches and what it was holding.

15   With more preliminary motions, potential appeals on motions, discovery and a trial ahead, Brandon Mayfield's case against the government has years to go. But in a fairly spectacular development, the Patriot Act itself is at last on trial—although unlike Mayfield, it's not being held in lockdown. ∎

'Sneak and Peek' Blog Entries

Cleared Oregon lawyer Brandon Mayfield's case, described in the previous selection by David Sarasohn, provides an excellent example of the danger of the Patriot's Act's so-called Sneak and Peek provisions—an end run around the Fourth Amendment's requirement that authorities notify the residents of a home when they have been inside to search for evidence.

Mayfield called attention to the fact that someone was repeatedly entering his modest white house when the family was out. The Mayfields would arrive home to find window blinds adjusted much higher than any one could reach. Footprints left in the living room's plush white carpet were larger than any of those belonging to Mayfield, his wife, Mona, and his two sons.

When the Mayfield case began gaining attention, Internet discussion groups began taking up the case in earnest. For example, after Mayfield appeared at a press conference (where he denounced the secret break-ins of his home and stated, "This is the state of affairs we find ourselves in today . . . living in a climate of fear"), discussions of the USA Patriot Act were carried out in a number of blogs. The blog entries which follow are a sample of the ones which appeared on talkleft.com

Comments

Posted by Typical Repug Response at May 27, 2004 12:43 PM

Well, obviously, if he were innocent, he would have nothing to fear from his family's house being broken into on a daily basis. I say they should hang him just to be safe.

Posted by Typical Repug Response at May 27, 2004 12:44 PM

Also, "Mayfield"? Isn't that a French name?

Posted by kdog at May 27, 2004 12:50 PM

To all the posters who rant and rave about the left and Stalin, doesn't the policy of secret sneak and peek searches seem Stalin-esque to you? Or is it that if a Republican does something that Stalin would do, then it's ok?

Posted by Darryl Pearce at May 27, 2004 12:56 PM

Ralphie was right. You're either a bully, a toady, or one of the hapless rabble of victims.
—ventura county, ca

Posted by MS at May 27, 2004 01:11 PM

Scarey when we can all be violated if someone (an angry neighbor?) calls us "possible terrorists."

The Bill of Rights wasn't intended to have exceptions. ("This applies to citizens and people living in this country, except if we suspect you're bad." Hope our Supremes recognize that.

Posted by rvman at May 27, 2004 03:40 PM

What constitutional violation? You might claim these searches were "unreasonable", but would they have been more "reasonable" had they been done when the Mayfields were home? I say no—a search is a search, it is either reasonable or not, and doing it stealthily doesn't make it less reasonable.

Stalinesque would involve Mr. Mayfield being "disappeared". Stalinesque is what happened in the Padilla case—holding folks arrested in the US without trial or charge. This isn't Stalinesque, this is just a little spooky.

Your ordinary search involves the cops essentially tearing the place apart, breaking stuff. Would this have been preferable? I'm not sure I wouldn't rather that all searches be carried out under the premise that, after the cops leave, you shouldn't be able to tell they were there. (Whether the residents knew or not.)

Posted by Darryl Pearce at May 27, 2004 04:17 PM

I propose a law where sneak-and-peak investigators do *at least two chores* while they're in the house—garbage out, dishes done... stuff like that.

Posted by The One True b!X at May 27, 2004 04:23 PM

The problems with the Mayfield case aren't just a matter of false evidence and secret searches. It's also that the original FBI affidavit was a smear against being Muslim.

Posted by Anonymous at May 27, 2004 04:32 PM

Darryl: Tee hee.

Posted by conscious angel at May 27, 2004 05:04 PM

Patriot Act is just the worst act passed since the founding of the republic. What a stupid move and abdication by our senators and representatives. We need to call them on the voting carpet for this one.

Posted by letharjk at May 27, 2004 05:28 PM

Okay, lawyers. If I hook up a guillotine above my window, and an agent just happens to get his little pointy head chopped off sneaking into my house, am I breaking any laws?

Posted by Ray Radlein at May 27, 2004 09:20 PM

Okay, lawyers. If I hook up a guillotine above my window, and an agent just happens to get his little pointy head chopped off sneaking into my house, am I breaking any laws?

Deadfall traps are generally illegal (people have rigged them up to deter burglars, after all, so there is some precedent).

Posted by Sonny Lions at May 28, 2004 02:20 AM

He's just lucky they didn't leave evidence implicating him, just to cover up the fact that they'd blamed the wrong guy all along. Not all people, given that level of power, remain honest.

Posted by HM at June 8, 2004 11:27 AM

to *rvman*:
Once it gets to the point where people are 'disappeared', then it will too late to complain.

That is why we are complaining now.

From Reading to Writing

Because the Patriot Act intersects with so many basic American freedoms and ideals, the possibilities for arguments that pertain to it are equally wide-ranging. Here are some possibilities:

1. Further examine the outcries of those critical of the Patriot Act, and consider writing a rebuttal of those arguments. (Consult Chapter 10 on writing a rebuttal.)

2. In a causal argument (see Chapter 7), consider how the technological age in which we live exacerbates the privacy issue. Since computers can more rapidly assemble information and have a much greater capacity for accessing it, could it be that traditional laws that concern privacy should not be applied to computer technologies?

3. Some have suggested that the Patriot Act violates some basic Constitutional rights of Americans. Evaluate the act according to that criterion (see Chapter 8). Read the Bill of Rights, read specific provisions of the Patriot Act, and argue whether, in your estimation, it does seem to violate the spirit or letter of that part of the Constitution.

4. Or evaluate the act according to its effects: Has the act actually helped in the war on terrorism? Has it actually led to any civil rights violations?

5. Consider the title of this bill, the USA PATRIOT Act, and other recent initiatives such as the "war on terror," "Operation Enduring Freedom," "No Child Left Behind," and "The Defense of Marriage Act." What effect does the name given to particular legislation have? Are the titles useful or misleading?

6. Analyze the visual images associated with this issue that are reproduced here, building on Chapter 5 of this book. What is the nature of the arguments made in those visuals? How do they work to persuade an audience?

7. Offer a narrative argument (such as the ones described in Chapter 9) that contributes to the debate on the Patriot Act. How does a single incident, drawn from the news or from an interview by you or from your own experience, contribute to the debate on the Patriot Act? Or can you write a short story, perhaps with a science-fiction or futuristic slant, that relates to the issue?

JAMES BOVARD

Federal Surveillance: The Threat to Americans' Security

Author of several books, including Lost Rights: The Destruction of American Liberty *(1994),* Terrorism and Tyranny: Trampling Freedom, Justice, and Peace to Rid the World of Evil *(2003), and* The Bush Betrayal *(2004), James Bovard is a contributing editor of* The Freeman: Ideas on Liberty *(where the argument below was published early in 2004), a publication of the Foundation for Economic Education.* The Freeman *takes a libertarian stance, focusing on natural rights, reason, and individual liberties. Bovard has also written articles for* The Wall Street Journal, *the* American Spectator, The New York Times, Reader's Digest, The New Republic, *the* Washington Post, *and* Newsweek.

1   Since the terrorist attacks on 9/11 the Bush administration has launched many new surveillance programs in the name of home-

land security. When critics raised questions about the potential abuses of the new powers, some administration supporters insisted that Bush's new surveillance policies were benign because there was no evidence the programs were being abused.

2   But the key to understanding new government intrusions is that horror stories do not surface in the first 72 hours after a new power is granted. The machinery of government takes time to deploy and expand. It takes time for the impact of precedents to expand, for the agents all along the line to get the message that they are not entitled to go much further than before. We must look to history to see what is likely to happen once the government is unleashed.

3   In May 2002, after revelations that the FBI missed many warning signs before 9/11, Attorney General John Ashcroft announced that he was effectively abolishing restrictions on FBI surveillance of Americans' everyday life. Those restrictions were first imposed in 1976 after pervasive FBI abuses were revealed. At that time, Attorney General Edward Levi announced guidelines to curtail FBI agents' intrusions into the lives of Americans who were not criminal suspects.

4   At his May 30 announcement Ashcroft declared that, after 9/11, "we in the leadership of the FBI and the Department of Justice began a concerted effort to free the field agents—the brave men and women on the front lines—from the bureaucratic, organizational, and operational restrictions and structures that hindered them from doing their jobs effectively."[1] He complained that in the past FBI agents were required "to blind themselves to information that everyone else [was] free to see."

5   However, as the Center for Democracy and Technology, a Washington non-profit organization, noted, "The FBI was never prohibited in the past from going to mosques, political rallies and other public places, to observe and record what was said, but in the past it had to be guided by the criminal nexus—in deciding what mosques to go to and what political meetings to record, it had to have some reason to believe that terrorism might be discussed."[2] A *New York Times* editorial warned that the new guidelines "could mean that F.B.I. agents will show up at the doors of people who order politically unpopular books on Amazon.com or make phone calls to organizations critical of the government."[3]

6   Ashcroft's announcement concluded with the mandatory invocation of freedom consecrating each Bush power grab: "These guidelines will also be a resource to inform the American public and demonstrate that we seek to protect life and liberty from terrorism and other criminal violence with a scrupulous respect for civil rights and personal freedoms. The campaign against terrorism is a campaign to affirm the values of freedom and human dignity. . . . Called to the service of our nation, we are called to the defense of liberty for all men and women." When Bush was asked about the new FBI guidelines at a photo oppor-

tunity that same day, he declared, "the initiative that the attorney general will be outlining today will guarantee our Constitution."[4]

7   Ashcroft talked as if the old guidelines on FBI surveillance were simply the result of a long-ago outbreak of temporary insanity among liberals. Ashcroft declared: "In its 94-year history, the Federal Bureau of Investigation has been . . . the tireless protector of civil rights and civil liberties for all Americans."[5]

8   The 1976 guidelines were put in place in response to a report by the Senate Select Committee to Study Governmental Operations that detailed many FBI abuses over the preceding decades. For 15 years, from 1956 to 1971, the FBI ran COINTELPRO (Counterintelligence Programs) to actively subvert groups and people that the FBI considered threats to national security or to the established political and social order. Over 2,300 separate operations were carried out to incite street warfare between violent groups, to wreck marriages, to get people fired, to smear innocent people by portraying them as government informants, to sic the IRS on people, and to cripple or destroy left-wing, black, communist, or other organizations.[6] The FBI let no corner of American life escape its vigilance; it even worked to expose and discredit "communists who are secretly operating in legitimate organizations and employments, such as the Young Men's Christian Association and Boy Scouts."[7]

Burglary Exposes Scandal

9   Throughout the COINTELPRO period, presidents, congressmen, and other highranking federal officials assured Americans that the federal government was obeying the law and upholding the Constitution. It took a burglary of an FBI office in Media, Pennsylvania, to break the biggest scandal in the history of federal law enforcement. After hundreds of pages of confidential records were commandeered, the "Citizen's Commission to Investigate the FBI" began passing out the incriminating documents to the media.[8] The shocking material sparked congressional and news investigations that eventually (temporarily) shattered the FBI's legendary ability to control its own image.

10   The 1976 Senate report noted that COINTELPRO's origins "are rooted in the Bureau's jurisdiction to investigate hostile foreign intelligence activities on American soil" and that the FBI used the "techniques of wartime." William Sullivan, former assistant to the FBI director, declared, "No holds were barred. . . . We have used [these techniques] against Soviet agents. . . . [The same methods were] brought home against any organization against which we were targeted. We did not differentiate."[9]

11   The FBI sought to subvert many black civil-rights organizations, including the Southern Christian Leadership Conference, Student Nonviolent Coordinating Committee, Deacons for Defense and Justice, and

Congress of Racial Equality. FBI headquarters ordered field offices to, as the Senate report noted, "exploit conflicts within and between groups, to use news media contacts to disrupt, ridicule, or discredit groups; to preclude 'violence-prone' or 'rabble rouser' leaders of these groups from spreading their philosophy publicly; and to gather information on the 'unsavory backgrounds—immorality, subversive activity, and criminal activity—of group members." FBI agents were also ordered to develop specific tactics to "prevent these groups from recruiting young people."[10]

12   Almost any black organization could be targeted for wiretaps. One black leader was monitored largely because he had "recommended the possession of firearms by members for their self-protection."[11] At that time, some southern police departments and sheriffs were notorious for attacking blacks who stood up for their civil rights.[12]

13   The FBI office in San Diego instigated violence between the local Black Panthers and a rival black organization, US (United Slaves Inc.).[13] Agents sent forged letters making accusations and threats to the groups purportedly from their rivals, along with crude cartoons and drawings meant to enrage the recipients. Three Black Panthers and one member of the rival group were killed during the time the FBI was fanning the flames. A few days after shootings in which two Panthers were wounded and one was killed, and in which the US headquarters was bombed, the FBI office reported to headquarters: "Efforts are being made to determine how this situation can be capitalized upon for the benefit of the Counterintelligence Program."

14   The FBI office bragged shortly thereafter: "Shootings, beatings, and a high degree of unrest continues to prevail in the ghetto area of southeast San Diego. Although no specific Counterintelligence action can be credited with contributing to this overall situation, it is felt that a substantial amount of the unrest is directly attributable to this program."[14]

15   The FBI set up a Ghetto Informant Program that continued after COINTELPRO and that had 7,402 informants, including proprietors of candy stores and barbershops, as of September 1972. The informants served as "listening posts" "to identify extremists passing through or locating in the ghetto area, to identify purveyors of extremist literature," and to keep an eye on "AfroAmerican type bookstores" (including obtaining the names of the bookstores' "clientele"). The informants' reports were stockpiled in the FBI's Racial Intelligence Unit.[15]

King Targeted

16   For most of the last five years of his life Martin Luther King was "the target of an intensive campaign by the Federal Bureau of Investigation to 'neutralize' him as an effective civil rights leader," the Senate report

noted. King's "I Have a Dream" speech in Washington in August 1963 was described by the FBI's Domestic Intelligence Division as evidence that King had become "the most dangerous and effective Negro leader in the country." King's home and office were wiretapped and, on 16 occasions, the FBI placed wiretaps in King's motel rooms, seeking information on the "private activities of King and his advisers" to use to "completely discredit" them. The FBI sent a copy of one tape recording directly to King along with a note "which Dr. King and his advisers interpreted as a threat to release the tape recording unless Dr. King committed suicide," the Senate report noted. The FBI offered to play tapes from the hotel rooms for "friendly" reporters. It also sought to block the publication of articles that praised King. An FBI agent intervened with Francis Cardinal Spellman to seek to block a meeting between King and the pope.[16]

17   FBI informants also "set up a Klan organization intended to attract membership away from the United Klans of America. The Bureau paid the informants' personal expenses in setting up the new organization, which had, at its height, 250 members." During the six years Gary Rowe spent as an FBI informant with the Klan, he, along with other Klansmen, had "beaten people severely, had boarded buses and kicked people off; had went [sic] in restaurants and beaten them with blackjacks, chains, pistols." Rowe testified how he and other Klansmen used "baseball bats, clubs, chains, and pistols" to attack Freedom Riders.[17]

18   The FBI continually expanded its racial surveillance investigations, eventually targeting white people who were "known to sponsor demonstrations against integration and against the busing of Negro students to white schools." The FBI also created a national "Rabble Rouser" Index, a "major intelligence program . . . to identify 'demagogues.'"[18]

19   From 1967 to 1972 the FBI paid Howard Berry Godfrey to be an informant with a right-wing paramilitary group in the San Diego area known as the secret Army. The Senate committee discovered that Godfrey or the secret Army was involved in "firebombing, smashing windows . . . propelling lug nuts through windows with sling shots, and breaking and entering." Godfrey took a Secret Army colleague with him to conduct surveillance of the home of a left-wing San Diego State University professor; the colleague fired several shots into the home, badly wounding a woman inside. The Senate report noted "even this shooting incident did not immediately terminate Godfrey as an [FBI] informant." Godfrey subsequently sold explosive material to a subordinate in the Secret Army who bombed the Guild Theater in San Diego in 1972.[19]

20   One FBI informant infiltrated an antiwar group and helped it break into the Camden, New Jersey, Draft Board in 1970. The informant later testified: "Everything they learned about breaking into a building or climbing a wall or cutting glass or destroying lockers, I taught them.

I taught them how to cut the glass, how to drill holes in the glass so you cannot hear it and stuff like that, and the FBI supplied me with the equipment needed. The stuff I did not have, the [FBI] got off their own agents."[20] That sting led to a press conference in which J. Edgar Hoover and Attorney General John Mitchell proudly announced the indictment of 20 people on an array of charges. After learning of the FBI's role in the crime, a jury refused to convict any of the defendants.

21   Some COINTELPRO operations targeted the spouses of political activists, sending them letters asserting that their mates were unfaithful. "Anonymous letters were sent to, among others, a Klansman's wife, informing her that her husband had 'taken the flesh of another unto himself,' the other person being a woman named Ruby, with her 'lust filled eyes and smart aleck figure'; and to a 'Black Nationalist's wife saying that her husband 'been maken it here' with other women in his organization 'and that he gives us this jive bout their better in bed then you.'"[21]

22   One FBI field office bragged that one such letter to a black activist's wife produced the "tangible result" and "certainly contributed very strongly" to the marriage's demise. The FBI targeted the women's liberation movement, resulting in "intensive reporting on the identities and opinions of women who attended" women's lib meetings. One FBI informant reported to headquarters of a meeting in New York: "Each woman at this meeting stated why she had come to the meeting and how she felt oppressed, sexually or otherwise. . . . They are mostly against marriage, children, and other states of oppression caused by men." Women's lib informants were instructed to "go to meetings, write up reports . . . to try to identify the background of every person there . . . [and] who they were sleeping with." The Senate report noted that "the intensive FBI investigation of the Women's Liberation Movement was predicated on the theory that the activities of women in that Movement might lead to demonstrations and violence."[22]

23   The Senate report also described the "snitch jacket" technique— neutralizing a target by labeling him a "snitch" or informant so that he would no longer be trusted—which was used in all COINTELPRO operations. The methods ranged from having an authentic informant start a rumor about the target member, to anonymous letters or phone calls, to faked informants' reports . . . . The "snitch jacket" is a particularly nasty technique even when used in peaceful groups. It gains an added dimension of danger when it is used—as, indeed, it was—in groups known to have murdered informers.[23]

Shotgun Approach

24   The FBI took a shotgun approach toward protesters partly because of its "belief that dissident speech and association should be prevented because they were incipient steps toward the possible ultimate commis-

sion of an act which might be criminal." Some FBI agents may have viewed dissident speech or protests as a "gateway drug" to blowing up the Washington Monument. The Senate report noted:

> The clearest examples of actions directly aimed at the exercise of constitutional rights are those targeting speakers, teachers, writers or publications, and meetings or peaceful demonstrations. Approximately 18 percent of all approved COINTELPRO proposals fell into these categories. The cases include attempts (sometimes successful) to get university and high school teachers fired; to prevent targets from speaking on campus; to stop chapters of target groups from being formed; to prevent the distribution of books, newspapers, or periodicals; to disrupt news conferences; to disrupt peaceful demonstrations, including the SCLC's Washington Spring Project and Poor People's Campaign, and most of the large antiwar marches; and to deny facilities for meetings or conferences.[24]

25   An FBI memo warned that "the anarchist activities of a few can paralyze institutions of learning, [conscription] induction centers, cripple traffic, and tie the arms of law enforcement officials, all to the detriment of our society." The FBI declared: "The New Left has on many occasions viciously and scurrilously attacked the Director [J. Edgar Hoover] and the Bureau in an attempt to hamper our investigation of it and to drive us off the college campuses."

26   The FBI ordered field offices in 1968 to gather information illustrating the "scurrilous and depraved nature of many of the characters, activities, habits, and living conditions representative of New Left adherents."[25] The headquarters directive informed FBI agents across the land: "Every avenue of possible embarrassment must be vigorously and enthusiastically explored. It cannot be expected that information of this type will be easily obtained, and an imaginative approach by your personnel is imperative to its success." One FBI internal newsletter encouraged FBI agents to conduct more interviews with antiwar activists "for plenty of reasons, chief of which are it will enhance the paranoia endemic in these circles and will further serve to get the point across that there is an FBI agent behind every mailbox."[26]

27   A major goal of the COINTELPRO against the New Left operations was to "counter the widespread charges of police brutality that invariably arise following student-police encounters."[27] The FBI was especially incensed at criticisms that Chicago policemen used excessive force when they attacked demonstrators during the 1968 Democratic National Convention. The FBI thus launched an illegal program to smear people the FBI believed had made false assertions of police misconduct.

28   As COINTELPRO continued, the FBI targeted more and more groups and used increasingly vicious tactics. The Senate report noted:

> The White Hate COINTELPRO [that focused primarily on the Klan] used comparatively few techniques which carried a risk of serious physical, emotional, or economic damage to the targets, while the Black Nationalist COINTELPRO used such techniques extensively. The New Left COINTELPRO, on the other hand, had the highest proportion of proposals aimed at preventing the exercise of free speech. Like the progression in targeting, the use of dangerous, degrading, or blatantly unconstitutional techniques also appears to have become less restrained with each subsequent program.

29   The FBI continually discovered new enemies. Nixon aide Tom Charles Huston testified of the program's tendency "to move from the kid with a bomb to the kid with a picket sign, and from the kid with the picket sign to the kid with the bumper sticker of the opposing candidate. And you just keep going down the line."[28]

30   Other federal agencies also trampled citizens' privacy, rights, and lives during the late 1960s and early 1970s. The IRS used COINTELPRO leads to launch audits against thousands of suspected political enemies of the Nixon administration. The U.S. Army set up its own surveillance program, creating files on 100,000 Americans and targeting domestic organizations such as the Young Americans for Freedom, the John Birch Society, and the Anti-Defamation League of B'Nai B'rith.[29]

31   The Senate report on COINTELPRO concluded: "The American people need to be assured that never again will an agency of the government be permitted to conduct a secret war against those citizens it considers threats to the established order. Only a combination of legislative prohibition and Departmental control can guarantee that COINTELPRO will not happen again."[30]

31   The Ford administration derailed legislative reforms in 1976 by promising an administrative fix. Now, 26 years later, Attorney General Ashcroft has thrown the restraints out the window, pretending there was never a valid reason to rein in the FBI.

32   The more information government gathers on people, the more power it will have over them. The more power it has to monitor their peaceful activities, the more intimidated Americans will become. Regardless of the Bush administration's intentions in its war on terrorism, the new federal powers threaten the rights and personal security of American citizens.

Notes

1. "Remarks of Attorney General John Ashcroft," Justice Department Office of Public Affairs, May 30, 2002.

2. Jerry Herman and James X. Dempsey, "CDT's Guide to the FBI Guidelines: Impact on Civil Liberties and Security—The Need for Congressional Oversight," Center for Democracy and Technology, June 26, 2002.

3. Editorial, "An Erosion of Civil Liberties," *New York Times,* May 31, 2002.

4. "Remarks by President George W. Bush during Photo Opportunity at Cabinet Meeting," Federal News Service, May 30, 2002.

5. "Remarks of Attorney General John Ashcroft," Justice Department Office of Public Affairs, May 30, 2002.

6. "Intelligence Activities and the Rights of Americans," Senate Select Committee to Study Governmental Operations with Respect to Intelligence Activities, April 14, 1976.

7. Ibid.

8. Mark Wagenveld, "25 Years Ago, before Watergate, a Burglary Changed History," *Philadelphia Inquirer,* March 10, 1996.

9. "COINTELPRO: The FBI's Covert Action Programs against American Citizens," Final Report of the Senate Committee to Study Governmental Operations with Respect to Intelligence Activities, April 23, 1976.

10. Both quotes taken from ibid.

11. Ibid.

12. Robert J. Cottrol and Raymond T. Diamond, "The Second Amendment: Toward an Afro-Americanist Reconsideration," *Georgetown Law Journal,* December 1991, p. 309.

13. "The FBI's Covert Action Program to Destroy the Black Panther Party," Supplementary Detailed Staff Reports on Intelligence Activities and the Rights of Americans, Final Report of the Select Committee to Study Governmental Operations with Respect to Intelligence Activities United States Senate, Book III, April 23, 1976.

14. Ibid.

15. All quotes taken from "The Use of Informants in FBI Domestic Intelligence Investigations"—Supplementary Detailed Staff Reports on Intelligence Activities and the Rights of Americans—Final Report of the Select Committee to Study Governmental Operations with Respect to Intelligence Activities, United States Senate, April 23, 1976.

16. All quotes from "Intelligence Activities and the Rights of Americans: Dr. Martin Luther King, Jr., Case Study," Book III of the "Final Report of the Select Committee to Study Governmental Operations with Respect to Intelligence Activities, United States Senate," April 23, 1976.

17. All quotes taken from "The Use of Informants."

18. All quotes taken from ibid.

19. Ibid.

20. Ibid.

21. "Intelligence Activities and the Rights of Americans."

22. "COINTELPRO."

23. Ibid.

24. Ibid.

25. Ibid.

26. Wagenveld.

27. "COINTFLPRO."

28. Ibid.

29. "Intelligence Activities and the Rights of Americans."

30. Ibid. ■

DAVID BRIN

Three Cheers for the Surveillance Society!

David Brin (born 1950) provided "Three Cheers," a short version of a longer project he is working on, for the Web publication Salon.com. It appeared on August 3, 2004, on this news and culture Web site founded in 1995. The author of several popular novels, including the Hugo Award-winning science fiction volumes Startide Rising *(1983) and* The Uplift War *(1987), Brin is also a scientist who writes and speaks about contemporary technological advancements. His 1985 novel* The Postman *was made into a popular film in 1997, and his nonfiction work* The Transparent Society *(1998) won the American Library Association's Freedom of Speech award for its examination of privacy and security concerns.*

1   Ten centuries ago, at the previous millennium, a Viking lord commanded the rising tide to retreat. No deluded fool, King Canute aimed in this way to teach flatterers a lesson—that even sovereign rulers cannot halt inexorable change.

2   A thousand years later, we face tides of technology-driven transformation that seem bound only to accelerate. Waves of innovation may liberate human civilization, or disrupt it, more than anything since glass lenses and movable type. Critical decisions during the next few years—about research, investment, law and lifestyle—may determine what kind of civilization our children inherit. Especially problematic are many information-related technologies that loom on the near horizon—technologies that may foster tyranny, or else empower citizenship in a true global village.

3   Typically we are told, often and passionately, that Big Brother may abuse these new powers. Or else our privacy and rights will be violated by some other group. Perhaps a commercial, aristocratic, bureaucratic,

intellectual, foreign, criminal or technological elite. (Pick your favorite bogeyman.)

4   Because one or more of these centers of power might use the new tools to see better, we're told that we should all be very afraid. Indeed, our only hope may be to squelch or fiercely control the onslaught of change. For the sake of safety and liberty, we are offered one prescription: We must limit the power of others to see.

5   Half a century ago, amid an era of despair, George Orwell created one of the most oppressive metaphors in literature with the telescreen system used to surveil and control the people in his novel *1984*. We have been raised to a high degree of sensitivity by Orwell's *self-preventing* prophecy, and others like it. Attuned to wariness, today's activists preach that any growth in the state's ability to see will take us down a path of no return, toward the endless hell of Big Brother.

6   But consider. The worst aspect of Orwell's telescreen—the trait guaranteeing tyranny—was not that agents of the state could use it to see. The one thing that despots truly need is to avoid accountability. In *1984*, this is achieved by keeping the telescreen aimed in just one direction! By preventing the people from looking back.

7   While a flood of new discoveries may seem daunting, they should not undermine the core values of a calm and knowledgeable citizenry. Quite the opposite: While privacy may have to be redefined, the new technologies of surveillance should and will be the primary countervailing force against tyranny.

8   In any event, none of those who denounce the new technologies have shown how it will be possible to stop this rising tide. Consider a few examples:

■ Radio frequency identification (RFID) technology will soon replace the simple, passive bar codes on packaged goods, substituting inexpensive chips that respond to microwave interrogation, making every box of toothpaste or razor blades part of a vast, automatic inventory accounting system. Wal-Mart announced in 2003 that it will require its top 100 suppliers to use RFID on all large cartons, for purposes of warehouse inventory keeping. But that is only the beginning. Inevitably as prices fall, RFID chips will be incorporated into most products and packaging.

■ Supermarket checkout will become a breeze, when you simply push your cart past a scanner and grab a printout receipt, with every purchase automatically debited from your account.

9   Does that sound simultaneously creepy and useful? Well, it goes much further. Under development are smart washers that will read the tags on clothing and adjust their cycles accordingly, and smart medicine cabinets that track tagged prescriptions, in order to warn which ones

have expired or need refilling. Cars and desks and computers will adjust to your preferred settings as you approach. Paramedics may download your health status—including allergies and dangerous drug-conflicts—even if you are unconscious or unable to speak.

10   There's a downside. A wonderful 1960s paranoia satire, *The President's Analyst,* offered prophetic warning against implanted devices, inserted into people, that would allow them to be tracked by big business and government. But who needs implantation when your clothing and innocuous possessions will carry cheap tags of their own that can be associated with their owners? Already some schools—especially in Asia—are experimenting with RFID systems that will locate all students, at all times.

11   Oh, there will be fun to be had, for a while, in fooling these systems with minor acts of irreverent rebellion. Picture kids swapping clothes and possessions, furtively, in order to leave muddled trails. Still, such measures will not accomplish much over extended periods. Tracking on vast scales, national and worldwide, will emerge in rapid order. And if we try to stop it with legislation, the chief effect will only be to drive the surveillance into secret networks that are just as pervasive. Only they will operate at levels we cannot supervise, study, discuss or understand.

12   Wait, there's more. For example, a new Internet protocol (IPv6) will vastly expand available address space in the virtual world.

13   The present IP, offering 32-bit data labels, can now offer every living human a unique online address, limiting direct access to something like 10 billion Web pages or specific computers. In contrast, IPv6 will use 128 bits. This will allow the virtual tagging of every cubic centimeter of the earth's surface, from sea level to mountaintop, spreading a multidimensional data overlay across the planet. Every tagged or manmade object may participate, from your wristwatch to a nearby lamppost, vending machine or trash can—even most of the discarded contents of the trash can.

14   Every interest group will find some kind of opportunity in this new world. Want to protect forests? Each and every tree on earth might have a chip fired into its bark from the air, alerting a network if furtive loggers start transporting stolen hardwoods. Or the same method could track whoever steals your morning paper. Not long after this, teens and children will purchase rolls of ultra-cheap digital eyes and casually stick them onto walls. Millions of those "penny cams" will join in the fun, contributing to the vast IPv6 datasphere.

15   Oh, this new Internet protocol will offer many benefits—for example, embedded systems for data tracking and verification. In the short term, expanded powers of vision *may* embolden tyrants. But over the long run, these systems could help to empower citizens and enhance mutual trust.

16   In the mid-'90s, when I began writing *The Transparent Society,* it seemed dismaying to note that Great Britain had almost 150,000 CCD police cameras scanning public streets. Today, they number in the millions.

17   In the United States, a similar proliferation, though just as rapid, has been somewhat masked by a different national tradition—that of dispersed ownership. As pointed out by UC-San Diego researcher Mohan Trivedi, American constabularies have few cameras of their own. Instead, they rely on vast numbers of security monitors operated by small and large companies, banks, markets and private individuals, who scan ever larger swaths of urban landscape. Nearly all of the footage that helped solve the Oklahoma City bombing and the D.C. sniper episode—as well as documenting the events of 9/11—came from unofficial sources.

18   This unique system can be both effective and inexpensive for state agencies, especially when the public is inclined to cooperate, as in searches for missing children. Still, there are many irksome drawbacks to officials who may want more pervasive and direct surveillance. For one thing, the present method relies upon high levels of mutual trust and goodwill between authorities and the owners of those cameras— whether they be convenience-store corporations or videocam-equipped private citizens. Moreover, while many crimes are solved with help from private cameras, more police are also held accountable for well-documented lapses in professional behavior.

19   This tattletale trend began with the infamous beating of Rodney King, more than a decade ago, and has continued at an accelerating pace. Among recently exposed events were those that aroused disgust (the tormenting of live birds in the Pilgrim's Pride slaughterhouse) and shook America's stature in the world (the prisoner abuse by jailers at Abu Ghraib prison in Iraq). Each time the lesson is the same one: that professionals should attend to their professionalism, or else the citizens and consumers who pay their wages will find out and—eventually— hold them accountable.

20   (Those wishing to promote the trend might look into Project Witness which supplies cameras to underdogs around the world.)

21   Will American authorities decide to abandon this quaint social bargain of shared access to sensors under dispersed ownership? As the price of electronic gear plummets, it will become easy and cheap for our professional protectors to purchase their own dedicated systems of surveillance, like those already operating in Britain, Singapore and elsewhere. Systems that "look down from above" (surveillance) without any irksome public involvement.

22   Or might authorities simply use our networks without asking? A decade ago, the U.S. government fought activist groups such as the Electronic Frontier Foundation, claiming a need to unlock commercial-

level encryption codes at will, for the sake of law enforcement and national defense. Both sides won apparent victories. High-level commercial encryption became widely available. And the government came to realize that it doesn't matter. It never did.

23   Shall I go on?

24   Driven partly by security demands, a multitude of biometric technologies will identify individuals by scanning physical attributes, from fingerprints, iris patterns, faces and voices to brainwaves and possibly unique chemical signatures. Starting with those now entering and leaving the United States, whole classes of people will grow accustomed to routine identification in this way. Indeed, citizens may start to demand more extensive use of biometric identification, as a safety measure against identity theft. When your car recognizes your face, and all the stores can verify your fingerprint, what need will you have for keys or a credit card?

25   Naturally, this is yet another trend that has put privacy activists in a lather. They worry—with some justification—about civil liberties implications when the police or FBI might scan multitudes (say, at a sporting event) in search of fugitives or suspects. Automatic software agents will recognize individuals who pass through one camera view, then perform a smooth handoff to the next camera, and the next, planting a "tail" on dozens, hundreds, or tens of thousands of people at a time.

26   And yes, without a doubt this method could become a potent tool for some future Big Brother. So? Should that legitimate and plausible fear be addressed by reflexively blaming technology and seeking ways to restrict its use? Or by finding ways that technology may work for us, instead of against us?

27   Suppose you could ban or limit a particular identification technique. (Mind you, I've seen no evidence that it can be done.) The sheer number of different, overlapping biometric approaches will make that whole approach fruitless. In fact, human beings fizz and froth with unique traits that can be spotted at a glance, even with our old-fashioned senses. Our ancestors relied on this fact, building and correlating lists of people who merited trust or worry, from among the few thousands that they met in person. In a global village of 10 billion souls, machines will do the same thing for us by prosthetically amplifying vision and augmenting memory.

28   With so many identification methodologies working independently and in parallel, our children may find the word "anonymous" impossibly quaint, perhaps even incomprehensible. But that needn't mean an end to freedom—or even privacy. Although it will undoubtedly mean a redefinition of what we think privacy means.

29   But onward with our scan of panopticonic technologies. Beyond RFID, IPv6 and biometrics there are smart cards, smart highways, smart airports, smart automobiles, smart televisions, smart homes and so on.

30   The shared adjective may be premature. These systems will provide improved service long before anything like actual "artificial intelligence" comes online. Yet machinery needn't be strictly intelligent in order to transform our lives. Moreover, distributed "smart" units will also gather information, joining together in cross-correlating networks that recognize travelers, perform security checks, negotiate microtransactions, detect criminal activity, warn of potential danger and anticipate desires. When these parts fully interlink, the emerging entity may not be self-aware, but it will certainly know the whereabouts of its myriad parts.

31   Location awareness will pervade the electronic world, thanks to ever more sophisticated radio transceivers, GPS chips, and government-backed emergency location initiatives like Enhanced-911 in the United States and Enhanced-112 in Europe. Cellphones, computers and cars will report position and unique identity in real time, with (or possibly without) owner consent. Lives will be saved, property recovered, and missing children found. But these benefits aren't the real reason that location awareness and reporting will spread to nearly every device. As described by science fiction author Vernor Vinge, it is going to happen because the capability will cost next to nothing as an integrated part of wireless technology. In the future, you can assume that almost any electronic device will be trackable, though citizens still have time to debate who may do the tracking.

32   The flood of information has to go someplace. Already databases fill with information about private individuals, from tax and medical records to credit ratings: from travel habits and retail purchases to which movies they recently downloaded on their TiVo personal video recorder. Yahoo's HotJobs recently began selling "self" background checks, offering job seekers a chance to vet their own personal, financial and legal data—the same information that companies might use to judge them. (True, a dating service that already screens for felons, recently expanded its partnership with database provider Rapsheets to review public records and verify a user's single status.) Data aggregators like Acxiom Corp., of Arkansas, or ChoicePoint, of Georgia, go even further, listing your car loans, outstanding liens and judgments, any professional or pilot or gun licenses, credit checks, and real estate you might own—all of it gathered from legal and open sources.

33   On the plus side, you'll be able to find and counter those rumors and slanderous untruths that can slash from the dark. The ability of others to harm you with lies may decline drastically. On the other hand, it will be simple for almost anybody using these methods to appraise the background of anyone else, including all sorts of unpleasant things that are inconveniently true. In other words, the rest of us will be able

to do what elites (define them as you wish, from government to aristo-crats to criminal masterminds) already can.

34   Some perceive this trend as ultimately empowering, while others see it as inherently oppressive. For example, activist groups from the ACLU to the Electronic Privacy Information Center call for European-style legislation aiming to seal the data behind perfect firewalls into separate, isolated clusters that cannot cross-link or overlap. And in the short term, such efforts may prove beneficial. New database filters may help users find information they legitimately need while protecting personal privacy . . . for a while, buying us time to innovate for the long term.

35   But we mustn't fool ourselves. No firewall, program or machine has ever been perfect, or perfectly implemented by fallible human be-ings. Whether the law officially allows it or not, can any effort by mere mortals prevent data from leaking? (And just one brief leak can spill a giant database into public knowledge, forever.) Cross-correlation will swiftly draw conclusions that are far more significant than the mere sum of the parts, adding up to a profoundly detailed picture of every cit-izen, down to details of personal taste.

36   Here's a related tidbit from the *Washington Post:* Minnesota entre-preneur Larry Colson has developed Web Voter, a program that lets Re-publican activists in the state report their neighbors' political views into a central database that the Bush-Cheney campaign can use to send them targeted campaign literature. The Bush campaign has a similar program on its Web site. And here's Colson's response to anyone who feels a pri-vacy qualm or two about this program: "[It's] not as if we're asking for Social Security number and make and model and serial number of car. We're asking for party preference. . . . Party preference is not something that is such a personal piece of data."

37   That statement may be some what true in today's America. We tend to shrug over each other's harmless or opinionated eccentricities. But can that trait last very long when powerful groups scrutinize us, without being scrutinized back? In the long run, tolerance depends on the ability of any tolerated minority to enforce its right to be left alone. This is achieved assertively, not by hiding. And assertiveness is empow-ered by knowledge.

38   The picture so far may seem daunting enough. Only now add a flood of new sensors. We have already seen the swift and inexpensive transformation of mere cellphones into a much more general, portable, electronic tool by adding the capabilities of a digital camera, audio recorder and PDA. But have we fully grasped the implications, when any well-equipped pedestrian might swiftly transform into an ad hoc photo-journalist—or peeping Tom—depending on opportunity or inclination?

39   On the near horizon are wearable multimedia devices, with displays that blend into your sunglasses, along with computational, data-storage and communications capabilities woven into the very clothes you wear. The term "augmented reality" will apply when these tools overlay your subjective view of the world with digitally supplied facts, directions or commentary. You will expect—and rely on—rapid answers to queries about any person or object in sight. In essence, this will be no different than querying your neuron-based memories about people in the village where you grew up. Only we had a million years to get used to tracking reputations that way. The new prosthetics that expand memory will prove awkward at first.

40   Today we worry about drivers who use cellphones at the wheel. Tomorrow will it be distracted pedestrians, muttering to no one as they walk? Will we grunt and babble while strolling along, like village idiots of yore?

41   Maybe not. Having detected nerve signals near the larynx that are preparatory to forming words, scientists at NASA Ames Research Center lately proposed *subvocal speech systems*—like those forecast in my 1989 novel *Earth*—that will accept commands without audible sounds. They would be potentially useful in spacesuits, noisy environments and to reduce the inevitable babble when we are all linked by wireless all the time.

42   Taking this trend in more general terms, *volition sensing* may pick up an even wider variety of cues, empowering you to converse, give commands, or participate in faraway events without speaking aloud or showing superficial signs.

43   Is this the pre-dawn of tech-mediated telepathy? It may be closer than you think. Advertising agencies are already funding research groups that use PET scans and fMRI to study the immediate reactions of test subjects to marketing techniques and images. "We are crossing the chasm," said Adam Koval, chief operating officer of Thought Sciences, a division of Bright House, an Atlanta advertising and consulting firm whose clients include Home Depot, Delta Airlines and Coca-Cola, "and bringing a new paradigm in analytic rigor to the world of marketing and advertising." Those who decry such studies face a tough burden, since all of the test subjects are paid volunteers. But how about when these methods leave the laboratory and hit the street? It is eerie to imagine a future when sensitive devices might scan your very thoughts when you pass by. Clearly there must be limits, only how? Will you be better able to protect yourself if these technologies are banned (and thus driven underground) or *regulated,* with a free market that might offer us all pocket detectors, to catch scanners in the act?

44   Microsoft recently unveiled Sensecam, a camera disguisable as jewelry that automatically records scores of images per hour from the wearer's point of view, digitally documenting an ongoing daily photo-

diary. Such "Boswell machinery" may go far beyond egomania. For example, what good will your wallet do to a mugger when images of the crime are automatically broadcast across the Web? Soon, cyber-witnessing of public events, business deals, crimes and accidents will be routine. In movie parlance, you will have to assume that everybody you meet is carrying a "wire."

45   Meanwhile, you can be sure that military technologies will continue spinning off civilian versions, as happened with infrared night vision. Take "sniffers" designed to warn of environmental or chemical dangers on the battlefield. Soon, cheap and plentiful sensors will find their way into neighborhood storm drains, onto lampposts, or even your home faucet, giving rapid warnings of local pollution. Neighborhood or activist groups that create detector networks will have autonomous access to data rivaling that of local governments. Of course, a better-informed citizenry is sure to be more effective . . .

46   . . . and far more noisy.

47   The same spinoff effect has emerged from military development of inexpensive UAV battlefield reconnaissance drones. Some of the "toys" offered by Draganfly Innovations can cruise independently for more than an hour along a GPS-guided path, transmit 2.4 GHz digital video, then return automatically to the hobbyist owner. In other companies and laboratories, the aim is toward miniaturization, developing micro-flyers that can assist an infantry squad in an urban skirmish or carry eavesdropping equipment into the lair of a suspected terrorist. Again, civilian models are already starting to emerge. There may already be some in your neighborhood.

48   Cheap, innumerable eyes in the sky. One might envision dozens of potentially harmful uses . . . hundreds of beneficial ones . . . and millions of others in between ranging from irksome to innocuous . . . all leading toward a fundamental change in the way each of us relates to the horizon that so cruelly constrained the imagination of our ancestors. Just as baby boomers grew accustomed to viewing faraway places through the magical—though professionally mediated—channel of network television, so the next generation will simply assume that there is always another independent way to glimpse real-time events, either far away or just above the streets where they live.

49   Should we push for yet another unenforceable law to guard our backyards against peeping Toms and their drone planes? Or perhaps we'd be better off simply insisting that the companies that make the little robot spies give us the means to trace them back to their nosy pilots. In other words, looking back may be a more effective way to protect privacy.

50   One might aim for reciprocal transparency using new technology. For example, Swiss researcher Marc Langheinrich's personal digital as-

sistant application detects nearby sensors and then lists what kind of information they're collecting. At a more radical and polemical level, there is the *sousveillance* movement, led by University of Toronto professor Steve Mann. Playing off "surveillance" (overlooking from above). Mann's coined term suggests that we should all get in the habit of looking from below, proving that we are sovereign and alert citizens down here, not helpless sheep. Mann contends that private individuals will be empowered to do this by new senses, dramatically augmented by wearable electronic devices.

51   We have skimmed over a wide range of new technologies, from RFID chips and stick-on penny cameras to new Internet address protocols and numerous means of biometric identification. From database mining and aggregation to sensors that detect chemical pollution or the volition to speak or act before your muscles get a chance to move. From omni-surveillance to universal localization. From eyes in the sky to those that may invade your personal space.

52   Note a common theme. Every device or function that's been described here serves to enhance some human sensory capability, from sight and hearing to memory. And while some may fret and fume, there is no historical precedent for a civilization refusing such prosthetics when they become available.

53   Such trends cannot be boiled down to a simple matter of good news or bad. While technologies of distributed vision may soon empower common folk in dramatic ways, giving a boost to participatory democracy by highly informed citizens, you will not hear that side of the message from most pundits, who habitually portray the very same technologies in a darker light, predicting that machines are about to destroy privacy, undermine values and ultimately enslave us.

54   In fact, the next century will be much too demanding for fixed perspectives. (Or rigid us-vs.-them ideologies.) Agility will be far more useful, plus a little healthy contrariness.

55   When in the company of reflexive pessimists—or knee-jerk optimists—the wise among us will be those saying . . . "Yes, but . . . "

56   Which way will the pendulum of good and bad news finally swing?

57   We are frequently told that there is a fundamental choice to be made in a tragic trade-off between safety and freedom. While agents of the state, like Attorney General John Ashcroft, demand new powers of surveillance—purportedly the better to protect us—champions of civil liberties such as the ACLU warn against surrendering traditional constraints upon what the government is allowed to see. For example, they decry provisions of the PATRIOT Act that open broader channels of inspection, detection, search and data collection, predicting that such steps take us on the road toward Big Brother.

58   While they are right to fear such an outcome, they could not be more wrong about the specifics. As I discuss in greater detail elsewhere, the very idea of a *trade-off* between security and freedom is one of the most insidious and dismal notions I have ever heard—a perfect example of a devil's dichotomy. We modern citizens are living proof that people can and should have both. Freedom and safety, in fact, work together, not in opposition. Furthermore, I refuse to let anybody tell me that I must choose between liberty for my children and their safety! I refuse, and so should you.

59   As we've seen throughout this article, and a myriad other possible examples, there is no way that we will ever succeed in limiting the power of the elites to see and know. If our freedom depends on blinding the mighty, then we haven't a prayer.

60   Fortunately, that isn't what really matters after all. Moreover, John Ashcroft clearly knows it. By far the most worrisome and dangerous parts of the PATRIOT Act are those that remove the tools of supervision, allowing agents of the state to act secretly, without checks or accountability. (Ironically, these are the very portions that the ACLU and other groups have most neglected.)

61   In comparison, a few controversial alterations of procedure for search warrants are pretty minor. After all, appropriate levels of surveillance may shift as society and technology experience changes in a new century. (The Founders never heard of a wiretap, for example.)

62   But our need to watch the watchers will only grow.

63   It is a monopoly of vision that we need to fear above all else. So long as most of the eyes are owned by the citizens themselves, there will remain a chance for us to keep arguing knowledgeably among ourselves, debating and bickering, as sovereign, educated citizens should.

64   It will not be a convenient or anonymous world. Privacy may have to be redefined much closer to home. There will be a lot of noise.

65   But we will not drown under a rising tide of overwhelming technology. Keeping our heads, we will remain free to guide our ships across these rising waters—to choose a destiny of our own. ■

PAUL SAFFO

A Trail of DNA and Data

Paul Saffo is the Roy Amara Fellow at the Institute for the Future, a nonprofit research group located in Silicon Valley that assists organizations with forecasting and future-based planning. A member of the Royal Swedish Academy of Engineering Sciences, Saffo focuses on the long-term impacts of technologies in his numerous essays, some of which have appeared in Fortune, *the* Harvard Business Review, *the* Los Angeles Times, Newsweek, The New York Times, *and* Wired. *The argument reprinted below comes from the April 3, 2005,* Washington Post.

1   If you're worried about privacy and identity theft, imagine this:

2   The scene: Somewhere in Washington. The date: April 3, 2020.

3   You sit steaming while the officer hops off his electric cycle and walks up to the car window. "You realize that you ran that red light again, don't you, Mr. Witherspoon?" It's no surprise that he knows your name; the intersection camera scanned your license plate and your guilty face, and matched both in the DMV database. The cop had the full scoop before you rolled to a stop.

4   "I know, I know, but the sun was in my eyes," you plead as you fumble for your driver's license.

5   "Oh, don't bother with that," the officer replies, waving off the license while squinting at his hand-held scanner. Of course. Even though the old state licensing system had been revamped back in 2014 into a "secure" national program, the new licenses had been so compromised that the street price of a phony card in Tijuana had plummeted to five euros. In frustration, law enforcement was turning to pure biometrics.

6   "Could you lick this please?" the officer asks, passing you a nanofiber blotter. You comply and then slide the blotter into the palm-sized gizmo he is holding, which reads your DNA and runs a match against a national genomic database maintained by a consortium of drug companies and credit agencies. It also checks half a dozen metabolic fractions looking for everything from drugs and alcohol to lack of sleep.

7   The officer looks at the screen, and frowns, "Okay. I'll let you off with a warning, but you really need more sleep. I also see that your retinal implants are past warranty, and your car tells me that you are six months overdue on its navigation firmware upgrade. You really need to take care of both or next time it's a ticket."

8   This creepy scenario is all too plausible. The technologies described are already being developed for industrial and medical applications, and the steadily dropping cost and size of such systems will make them affordable and practical police tools well before 2020. The resulting intrusiveness would make today's system of search warrants and wiretaps quaint anachronisms.

9   Some people find this future alluring and believe that it holds out the promise of using sophisticated ID techniques to catch everyone from careless drivers to bomb-toting terrorists in a biometric dragnet. We have already seen places such as Truro, Mass., Baton Rouge, La. and Miami ask hundreds or thousands of citizens to submit to DNA

mass-testing to catch killers. Biometric devices sensing for SARS symptoms are omnipresent in Asian airports. And the first prototypes of systems that test in real time for SARS, HIV and bird flu have been deployed abroad.

10   The ubiquitous collection and use of biometric information may be inevitable, but the notion that it can deliver reliable, theft-proof evidence of identity is pure science fiction. Consider that oldest of biometric identifiers—fingerprints. Long the exclusive domain of government databases and FBI agents who dust for prints at crime scenes, fingerprints are now being used by electronic print readers on everything from ATMs to laptops. Sticking your finger on a sensor beats having to remember a password or toting an easily lost smart card.

11   But be careful what you touch, because you are leaving your identity behind every time you take a drink. A Japanese cryptographer has demonstrated how, with a bit of gummi bear gelatin, some cyanoacrylic glue, a digital camera and a bit of digital fiddling, he can easily capture a print off a glass and confect an artificial finger that foils fingerprint readers with an 80 percent success rate. Frightening as this is, at least the stunt is far less grisly than the tale, perhaps aprocryphal, of some South African crooks who snipped the finger off an elderly retiree, rushed her still-warm digit down to a government ATM, stuck it on the print reader and collected the victim's pension payment. (Scanners there now gauge a finger's temperature, too.)

12   Today's biometric advances are the stuff of tomorrow's hackers and clever crooks, and anything that can be detected eventually will be counterfeited. Iris scanners are gaining in popularity in the corporate world, exploiting the fact that human iris patterns are apparently as unique as fingerprints. And unlike prints, iris images aren't left behind every time someone gets a latte at Starbucks. But hide something valuable enough behind a door protected by an iris scanner, and I guarantee that someone will figure out how to capture an iris image and transfer it to a contact lens good enough to fool the readers. And capturing your iris may not even require sticking a digital camera in your face—after all, verification requires that the representation of your iris exist as a cloud of binary bits of data somewhere in cyberspace, open to being hacked, copied, stolen and downloaded. The more complex the system, the greater the likelihood that there are flaws that crooks can exploit.

13   DNA is the gold standard of biometrics, but even DNA starts to look like fool's gold under close inspection. With a bit of discipline, one can keep a card sale or a PIN secret, but if your DNA becomes your identity, you are sharing your secret with the world every time you sneeze or touch something. The novelist Scott Turow has already written about a hapless sap framed for a murder by an angry spouse who spreads his DNA at the scene of a killing.

14   The potential for DNA identity theft is enough to make us all wear a gauze mask and keep our hands in our pockets. DNA can of course be easily copied—after all, its architecture is designed for duplication—but that is the least of its problems. Unlike a credit card number, DNA can't be retired and swapped for a new sequence if it falls into the hands of crooks or snoops. Once your DNA identity is stolen, you live with the consequences forever.

15   This hasn't stopped innovators from using DNA as an indicator of authenticity. The artist Thomas Kinkade signs his most valuable paintings with an ink containing a bit of his DNA. (He calls it a "forgery-proof DNA Matrix signature.") We don't know how much of Tom is really in his paintings, but perhaps it's enough for forgers to duplicate the ink, as well as the distinctive brush strokes.

16   The biggest problem with DNA is that it says so much more about us than an arbitrary serial number does. Give up your Social Security number and a stranger can inspect your credit rating. But surrender your DNA and a snoop can discover your innermost genetic secrets— your ancestry, genetic defects and predispositions to certain diseases. Of course we will have strong genetic privacy laws, but those laws will allow consumers to "voluntarily" surrender their information in the course of applying for work or pleading for health care. A genetic marketplace not unlike today's consumer information business will emerge, swarming with health insurers attempting to prune out risky individuals, drug companies seeking customers and employers managing potential worker injury liability.

17   Faced with this prospect, any sensible privacy maven would conclude that DNA is too dangerous to collect, much less use for a task as unimportant as turning on a laptop or working a cash machine. But society will not be able to resist its use. The pharmaceutical industry will need our DNA to concoct customized wonder drugs that will fix everything from high cholesterol to halitosis. And crime fighters will make giving DNA information part of our civic duty and national security. Once they start collecting, the temptation to use it for other purposes will be too great.

18   Moreover, snoops won't even need a bit of actual DNA to invade our privacy because it will be so much easier to access its digital representation on any number of databanks off in cyberspace. Our Mr. Witherspoon will get junk mail about obscure medical conditions that he's never heard of because some direct marketing firm "bot" will inspect his digital DNA and discover that he has a latent disease or condition that his doctor didn't notice at his annual checkup.

19   It is tempting to conclude that Americans will rise up in revolt, but experience suggests otherwise. Americans profess a concern for privacy, but they happily reveal their deepest financial and personal secrets for a

free magazine subscription or cheesy electronic trinket. So they probably will eagerly surrender their biometric identities as well, trading fingerprint IDs for frequent shopper privileges at the local supermarket and genetic data to find out how to have the cholesterol count of a teenager.

20   Biometric identity systems are inevitable, but they are no silver bullet when it comes to identity protection. The solution to identity protection lies in the hard work of implementing system-wide and nationwide technical and policy changes. Without those changes, the deployment of biometric sensors will merely increase the opportunities for snoops and thieves—and escalate the cost to ordinary citizens.

21   It's time to fix the problems in our current systems and try to anticipate the unique challenges that will accompany the expanded use of biometrics. It's the only way to keep tomorrow's crooks from stealing your fingers and face and, with them, your entire identity. ■

Ted Koppel

Take My Privacy, Please!

You know Ted Koppel for his reporting and anchor role on the late-night (and long-running) news show Nightline *(from which he recently retired). However, he has also served ABC News as a diplomatic correspondent, anchor, and bureau chief. As a diplomatic correspondent, he traveled with Henry Kissinger on most of his foreign missions during the Nixon administration. Koppel's awards include 37 Emmys and six Peabody awards, and he is the co-author, with Marvin Kalb, of* In the National Interest *(1977). Koppel's article reprinted here initially appeared on the op/ed page of* The New York Times *on June 13, 2005.*

1   The Patriot Act—brilliant! Its critics would have preferred a less stirring title, perhaps something along the lines of the Enhanced Snooping, Library and Hospital Database Seizure Act. But then who, even right after 9/11, would have voted for that?

2   Precisely. He who names it and frames it, claims it. The Patriot Act, however, may turn out to be among the lesser threats to our individual and collective privacy.

3   There is no end to what we will endure, support, pay for and promote if only it makes our lives easier, promises to save us money, appears to enhance our security and comes to us in a warm, cuddly and altogether nonthreatening package. To wit: OnStar, the subscription vehicle tracking and assistance system. Part of its mission statement, as found on the OnStar Web site, is the creation of "safety, security and peace of mind for drivers and passengers with thoughtful wireless ser-

vices that are always there, always ready." You've surely seen or heard their commercials, one of which goes like this:

4	Announcer:	The following is an OnStar conversation. (Ring)
5	OnStar:	OnStar emergency, this is Dwight.
6	Driver:	(crying) Yes, yes??!
7	OnStar:	Are there any injuries, ma'am?
8	Driver:	My leg hurts, my arm hurts.
9	OnStar:	O.K. I do understand. I will be contacting emergency services.
10	Announcer:	If your airbags deploy, OnStar receives a signal and calls to check on you. (Ring)
11	Emergency services:	Police.
12	OnStar:	This is Dwight with OnStar. I'd like to report a vehicle crash with airbag deployment on West 106th Street.
13	Emergency services:	We'll send police and E.M.S. out there.
14	Driver:	(crying) I'm so scared!
15	OnStar:	O.K., I'm here with you, ma'am; you needn't be scared.

16   Well, maybe just a little scared. Tell us again how Dwight knows just where the accident took place. Oh, right! It's those thoughtful wireless services that are always there. Always, as in any time a driver gets into an OnStar-equipped vehicle. OnStar insists that it would disclose the whereabouts of a subscriber's vehicle only after being presented with a criminal court order or after the vehicle has been reported stolen. That's certainly a relief. I wouldn't want to think that anyone but Dwight knows where I am whenever I'm traveling in my car.

17   Of course, E-ZPass and most other toll-collecting systems already know whenever a customer passes through one of their scanners. That's because of radio frequency identification technology. In return for the convenience of zipping through toll booths, you need to have in your car a wireless device. This tag contains information about your account, permitting E-ZPass to deduct the necessary toll—and to note when your car whisked through that particular toll booth. They wouldn't share that information with anyone, either; that is, unless they had to.

18   The State Department plans to use radio frequency identification technology in all new American passports by the end of 2005. The department wants to be sure that we all move through immigration quickly and efficiently when we return from overseas. Privacy advocates have suggested that hackers could tap into the information stored on these tags, or that terrorists might be able to use them to pinpoint American tourists in a crowd. The State Department assures us that

both concerns are unfounded, and that it will allow privacy advocates to review test results this summer.

19 Radio frequency identification technology has been used for about 15 years now to reunite lost pets with their owners. Applied Digital Solutions, for example, manufactures the VeriChip, a tiny, implantable device that holds a small amount of data. Animal shelters can scan the chip for the name and phone number of the lost pet's owner. The product is now referred to as the HomeAgain Microchip Identification System.

20 Useful? Sure. Indeed, it's not much of a leap to suggest that one day, the VeriChip might be routinely implanted under the skin of, let's say, an Alzheimer's patient. The Food and Drug Administration approved the VeriChip for use in people last October. An Applied Digital Solutions spokesman estimates that about 1,000 people have already had a VeriChip implanted, usually in the right triceps. At the moment, it doesn't carry much information, just an identification number that health care providers can use to tap into a patient's medical history. A Barcelona nightclub also uses it to admit customers with a qualifying code to enter a V.I.P. room where drinks are automatically put on their bill. Possible variations on the theme are staggering.

21 And how about all the information collected by popular devices like TiVo, the digital video recorder that enables you to watch and store an entire season's worth of favorite programs at your own convenience? It also lets you electronically mark the programs you favor, allowing TiVo to suggest similar programs for your viewing pleasure. In February, TiVo announced the most frequently played and replayed commercial moment during the Super Bowl (it involves a wardrobe malfunction, but believe me, you don't want to know), drawing on aggregated data from a sample of 10,000 anonymous TiVo households. No one is suggesting that TiVo tracks what each subscriber records and replays. But could they, if they needed to? That's unclear, although TiVo does have a privacy policy. "Your privacy," it says in part, "is very important to us. Due to factors beyond our control, however, we cannot fully ensure that your user information will not be disclosed to third parties."

22 Unexpected and unfortunate things happen, of course, even to the most reputable and best-run organizations. Only last February, the Bank of America Corporation notified federal investigators that it had lost computer backup tapes containing personal information about 1.2 million federal government employees, including some senators. In April, LexisNexis unintentionally gave outsiders access to the personal files (addresses, Social Security numbers, drivers license information) of as many as 310,000 people. In May, Time Warner revealed that an outside storage company had misplaced data stored on computer backup tapes on 600,000 current and former employees. That same

month, United Parcel Service picked up a box of computer tapes in New Jersey from CitiFinancial, the consumer finance subsidiary of Citigroup, that contained the names, addresses, Social Security numbers, account numbers, payment histories and other details on small personal loans made to an estimated 3.9 million customers. The box is still missing.

23   Whoops!

24   CitiFinancial correctly informed its own customers and, inevitably, the rest of the world about the security breach. Would they have done so entirely on their own? That is less clear. In July 2003, California started requiring companies to inform customers living in the state of any breach in security that compromises personally identifiable information. Six other states have passed similar legislation.

25   No such legislation exists on the federal stage, however—only discretionary guidelines for financial institutions about whether and how they should inform their customers with respect to breaches in the security of their personal information.

26   Both the House and Senate are now considering federal legislation similar to the California law. It's a start but not nearly enough. We need mandatory clarity and transparency, not just with regard to the services that these miracles of microchip and satellite technology offer but also the degree to which companies share and exchange their harvest of private data.

27   We cannot even begin to control the growing army of businesses and industries that monitor what we buy, what we watch on television, where we drive, the debts we pay or fail to pay, our marriages and divorces, our litigations, our health and tax records and all else that may or may not yet exist on some computer tape, if we don't fully understand everything we're signing up for when we avail ourselves of one of these services. ■

RANDALL LARSEN

Traveler's Card Might Just Pave the Way for a National ID Card

1   When my family members fly on an airliner, I would like to think America has a system to ensure that they are not seated next to someone on a terrorist watch list. But this is not the case. The Transportation Security Administration (TSA) does screen passengers against terrorist watch lists, but the system is horribly flawed. It's like putting three dead bolts on the front door and leaving the back door wide open.

2   What ID card do you show at an airport? Most passengers use their driver's licenses. How difficult is it to obtain a counterfeit driver's license? Not very. Seven of the nineteen 9/11 hijackers had Virginia driver's licenses, yet none lived there. America needs a better system for identification.

3   Many Americans worry about creating a national ID card. I have serious concerns, too. But we have reached a point where the lack of an ID card may be a greater threat than the creation of such a system.

4   Sen. Lamar Alexander, R-Tenn., recently changed his mind. Twenty years ago, as governor of Tennessee, he vetoed a bill requiring photos on driver's licenses. He saw it as a breach of privacy. Today, he is calling for national ID cards—with photos and biometrics.

5   Why the change?

6   The reason he and others have changed their minds is that the creation of national ID cards is something akin to medical procedures — they all have risks, but when the risk of inaction becomes greater than the risk of action, action becomes the better choice.

7   Today, 15 European democracies have national ID cards. The United Kingdom debated the issue for several years after 9/11 and has recently decided to move forward with such a system. Our debate should begin now, and it should begin with these four questions:

1. Does an organization and system exist that can ensure ID credentials are properly issued?
2. Does the technology exist to create IDs that cannot be altered or counterfeited?
3. Can we build an affordable system?
4. Does the public feel secure that such a system would protect privacy?

8   Today, the answers are: no, yes, yes, no. It is unlikely that the public will support a national identity system until we can obtain four yeses. Is this possible? Absolutely, but much work is needed.

9   The first question (ensuring credentials are properly issued) will be the most difficult to resolve. It will require that we first answer other questions, many involving immigration and illegal aliens. The last question (privacy) is the one that causes many to object, but technologies exist that can help alleviate those "Big Brother" fears. Even so, a national ID remains, for now, out of reach. But the country is taking incremental steps worth embracing.

10   A month ago, President Bush signed the Real ID Act to establish national standards for state-issued driver's licenses. The good news: It may be a step toward improving identification at airports. The bad news: It won't take effect until 2008, and that may be too late.

Scrutiny by Congress

11   Thursday, the House Committee on Homeland Security will hold a public hearing to examine options for travelers' IDs, including privately issued ones. Frequent travelers could have the option to pay for such a card. They would be fingerprinted, retina-scanned and background-checked so that the TSA could speed them through security.

12   The card, similar to TSA's pilot program "Registered Traveler," would allow TSA to focus on other passengers who might actually have nefarious plans. This is a winning strategy for all homeland security programs—focus resources where the threat is highest.

13   A national identity card is what we ultimately need, but until then, we should consider privately issued travelers cards. They would be voluntary with limited costs to taxpayers and, most important, would assist TSA in ensuring safe travel for my family, and yours. ■

JEFFREY ZASLOW

The End of Youthful Indiscretions: Internet Makes Them Permanent Blots

Jeffrey Zaslow's social commentaries (entitled "Moving On") appeared first on August 12, 2004, in the business-oriented Wall Street Journal, *where he works as a staff writer. Zaslow is the author of* Tell Me All About It: A Personal Look at the Advice Business *(1989) and* Take It from Us: Advice from 262 Celebrities on Everything That Matters—To Them and to You *(1994). Zaslow also has worked as an advice columnist at the* Chicago Sun-Times—*he even replaced Ann Landers for a number of years.*

1   Once upon a time, we all did things in public that quickly became simple private memories.

2   We appeared in grade-school choir concerts, scratching ourselves awkwardly or finding our noses with our fingers. As feisty teens, we wrote angry manifestos for college newspapers. As young adults, we kissed our sweethearts on busy street corners, thrilled by the private publicness of it all.

3   Those public moments were fleeting, and rarely had any bearing on the rest of our lives.

4   But young people today, who live in an age of reality TV and security concerns that led to the Patriot Act, likely won't have that luxury.

While most adults have a Web presence that dates back no further than 1994, today's kids will enter adulthood with far more of their lives in plain view. This could impact their interactions with college-admissions officers, prospective employers, even love interests.

5   Those children's choir concerts that used to be relatively private affairs? They now air repeatedly on school-district cable outlets, allowing any channel surfer to focus on your child's familiarity with his nose.

6   If our teens write political screeds, their words can end up posted forever on Internet Web sites. Every time someone Googles them, their one-time activism will pop up—even it they no longer hold those beliefs.

7   As for stolen kisses: Several million surveillance cameras mounted in public locations now feed footage not just to the police, but also to thousands of community Web sites for all to see.

8   These days, nothing public is private anymore. New parents can now build customized Web sites through OurBabyNews.com, posting photos and details about their baby's young life. The Web sites cost as little as $14.95 a year, and just 10% of customers opt for password protection—the other 90% are open to anybody to peruse.

9   "Camp cams" provide online video and photos of kids' adventures at summer camp for their parents and others to examine. "Hopefully, 30 years from now, you can see images from the summer of 2004," says Ari Ackerman, founder of Bunk1.com, which uploads photos and videos for 2,000 camps. Camp owners decide how secure to make the sites.

10   Meanwhile, teens create confessional Web logs—musings more suited for private diaries—and even after they mature, their adolescent ramblings remain accessible in cyberspace. Job recruiters will increasingly sift through "idiotic blogs" from applicants' teen years, predicts Alan Schlein, a Washington, D.C., consultant who helps businesses find information online. He advises: "Tell your kids to think of the Internet as a public stage that'll still be playing their show 20 years from now."

11   In the cacophony of online revelations, a yearning for privacy can seem quaint. People wonder: Why not expose yourself to the world?

12   I have a colleague who was invited back to his high school this year to receive a distinguished alumni award. If this had happened a decade ago, few people outside his hometown would know about his honor unless he chose to fell them. However, because details of his award appeared online, our company's employee-relations folks found out and posted the news (with his high-school photo) on our in-house Web site for thousands of employees to see. My colleague was embarrassed by the exposure; did people think he had orchestrated the attention?

13   I sympathized with him. In 1991, I wrote a column that happened to include a couple of inane puns. Months later, the International Save the Pun Foundation named me "Punster of the Year" at its annual dinner. I gave an acceptance speech, mustering up a few lame puns. Since

then, when people search for my name online, my punster award pops up, making me seem like a pun fanatic. A public-relations woman recently tried to sweet-talk me into writing about her client; she said she always enjoys my puns. Oh, please!

14   It is true that the face we show the world via the Web often gives others a sense of our accomplishments and interests. But so much of it is out of context and incomplete. Incoming college freshmen today routinely Google their roommates-to-be. That makes it harder for students to reinvent themselves or polish rough edges.

15   Colleges might consider offering required courses on privacy rights and risks. Yes, it is helpful that birth, death, marriage, genealogy and residency records are just a few keystrokes away (anywho.com, anybirthday.com, searchsystems.net). But this ready access also makes it easier for identify thieves, salespeople and stalkers to find us. And it isn't always clear how we should use public records. At NationalAlertRegistry.com, we can learn how many sex offenders are in our neighborhoods, and get maps to their homes. But what do we do with these maps once we download them?

16   As we teach our kids about the decline of privacy, and the moral quandaries of the Internet, we must also be vigilant about protecting ourselves. That means combing the Internet to remove troublesome personal references. It also means being aware that a surveillance or cell-phone camera may capture us in public, or that satellite photos of our homes can be purchased by anyone for $7 at PeopleData.com.

17   In this post-private world, it may be time to redefine ethical behavior. Millions of single people do online searches before dating someone. Deborah Pierce, executive director of Privacy Activism, an advocacy group, argues that it is more polite and ethical to ask for permission first: Do you mind if I Google you?

It is hard to picture people asking each other that question.

18   But talking about the issue might remind our kids they still have a right to privacy, and that they should afford a measure of privacy to others. ◼

CHAPTER 23

Regulating Substances, Regulating Bodies

Drug Use and Public Safety

The U.S. prison population—now at 2.1 million— has more than quadrupled since the early 1980s, which means that our nation now has the highest rate of incarceration in the world (http:// www.ojrusdoj.gov/bjs/prisons.htm). As Jeremy Rifkin indicates in an essay published later in this book, although only 4 percent of the world population is in the United States, the United States "boasts" a quarter of the entire world's prison population. A great many of those in prison are nonviolent drug offenders, usually small-timers who need help with their own addictions. In the late 1980s, in the face of a crack epidemic that was then ravaging the nation's cities and claiming the lives of citizens as prominent as Boston Celtics draftee Len Bias, legislators and law enforcement agents cracked down by instituting mandatory minimum sen-

> An estimated 80–100 million Americans have tried marijuana.

tences. Because those who inform on others can often win reduced sentences, small-time drug violators often get stiffer sentences than major dealers. According to *Newsweek,* 6 percent of those in state prisons in 1980 were there for drug violations; in 1996 the figure was 23 percent. In 1980, 25 percent of those in federal prisons were drug violators, while in 2005 the figure had risen to over 60 percent.

Should we be so hard on drug dealers and abusers? Is the "war on drugs" that has been conducted by the federal government (and by the states) since the 1990s going so poorly that it should be abandoned? Many people think so. Often they call attention not only to the figures on incarceration but also to the other social costs associated with strict drug laws. For example, many addicts resist treatment because they fear punishment; instead, they commit crimes to support their bad habits. Widespread urine testing and seizures of drug-related property have threatened basic civil rights and undermined respect for police. Extensions of the drug war have led to conflicts with other nations where drugs are produced. Moreover, if drugs were considered a medical and social problem rather than a criminal one, citizens could be helped rather than sent to prison. Needle-exchange programs could help check the spread of AIDS by reducing the incidence of shared needles. Recognizing that illegal drugs often are no worse and no better than alcohol (legal since the disastrous 1920s experiment known as Prohibition), Californians voted to legalize marijuana use for cancer and

> Of every one hundred people who have smoked marijuana, only twenty-eight have tried cocaine—and only one uses cocaine weekly.

AIDS patients. Many people, drawing from the experiences of other nations, are now calling for moves to decriminalize some kinds of drug use, or at least to reduce penalties and increase treatment. In other words, the war on drugs might be maintained—but without quite so much prison warehousing.

On the other hand, many people argue for a continuing hard line on drugs because of the damage that illegal drugs do. They point to the health risks and social costs—to early deaths, lost work days, and broken lives attributable to substance abuse. In the tradition of Carry Nation and other temperance warriors who successfully lobbied for prohibition of alcohol in the 1920s, they have evidence that drug use (especially cocaine use) has decreased during the years of the war on drugs, that marijuana may be a "gateway drug" to more dangerous substances (because marijuana smokers are far more likely to try other drugs, such as cocaine), and that the war on drugs is worth waging for all sorts of other reasons.

Advocates of a hard line on drugs sometimes take on not only drug kingpins but also others—alcohol producers, Big Tobacco, performance-enhancing drug users. For example, they promote stiff taxes on cigarettes and alcohol on the grounds that making harmful substances expensive discourages

Reformer Carry Nation holding the weapons of her trade: a hatchet for destroying liquor containers and a copy of the Bible.

Androstenedione (aka "andro") is now being marketed in a chewing gum by a California company. The product is expected to be available on the market soon. Andro supposedly increased the libido in German athletes in the 1980s to levels that "bordered on nymphomania."

—WWW.HEALTHCENTRAL.COM (2003)

use and pays for the social costs involved. And they are often proponents of testing athletes for the use of unfair and dangerous performance-enhancing new substances, such as steroids (which promote muscle growth but have harmful side effects), androstenedione (which baseball slugger Mark McGwire used during his pursuit of home-run records), and creatine (a dietary supplement that many athletes feel helps their training). They point to the popularity of such substances among youngsters. They also work to combat binge drinking on campuses, regarding it as a frightening epidemic that encourages date rape, promotes vandalism, and otherwise ruins or undermines the lives of countless college students.

Contemporary Arguments

Should certain substances be rightly regulated—and which ones? Is substance abuse a victimless crime we have to live with in order to preserve a free society? Is education the only proper approach to the problem? If not, what exactly should be done about various drugs, alcohol, tobacco, and other controversial and harmful practices and substances? Just how should we weigh the risks of drug and alcohol use against the social costs of overzealous law enforcement? We offer here a number of arguments related to these questions. You might begin by looking again at the exchange on pages 177–181 between Milton Friedman and William Bennett on the issue of legalizing drugs—and then consider the similar debate below between Joseph A. Califano, Jr., and Eric Schlosser on marijuana. Then look carefully at the "Issue in Focus" on the regulation of smoking and the arguments after that on steroids. Where exactly should the line be drawn between personal freedom and government intervention on behalf of public safety? With that question in mind, you can then examine the arguments that follow: on alcohol, guns, and SUVs.

Finally, consider how visual images serve to regulate bodies indirectly. Photos and other visuals in this part and other parts of *Good Reasons with Contemporary Arguments* suggest how people's identifications with certain body types can motivate them to behave in certain ways. You can see that in advertisements in most magazines. Other examples are addressed in essays by Terrence Rafferty (on films), Ynestra King (on disability), and Evan Wright (on fraternities and sororities).

JOSEPH A. CALIFANO, JR.

The Right Drug to Target: Cutting Marijuana Use

Joseph A. Califano, Jr., is president of the National Center on Addiction and Substance Abuse at Columbia University, a nonprofit research center dealing with all forms of drug abuse. From 1977 to 1979 he was the U.S. Secretary of Health, Education, and Welfare under President Carter. During his political service he led antismoking campaigns—after having quit smoking four packs a day in 1975. Califano is the author of a recently published personal memoir: Inside: A Public and Private Life *(2004). His argument reprinted here appeared in the* Washington Post *on May 17, 2005.*

1   The increased potency of today's marijuana and the greater knowledge we have of the dangers of using marijuana justify the increased attention that law enforcement is giving to illegal possession of the drug. But the disappointing reality is that a nearly 30 percent increase in marijuana arrests does not translate into a comparable reduction in use of the drug. Something more is needed.

2   Rudolph Giuliani's success in slashing New York City's crime rate by, among other things, going after low-level street crimes such as smoking and selling small amounts of marijuana inspired many other mayors to follow suit. When President Bush announced in 2002 a goal of reducing illegal drug use by 10 percent in two years and 25 percent in five years, he knew he had to focus on cutting marijuana use. Eliminating all other illegal drug use combined would not even get him close to his highly touted objective.

3   From the standpoint of protecting children, teens and the public health, reducing marijuana use makes eminent sense. For even though marijuana use has leveled off or waned slightly over the past several years, the number of children and teenagers in treatment for marijuana dependence and abuse has jumped 142 percent since 1992, and the number of teen emergency room admissions in which marijuana is implicated is up almost 50 percent since 1999. Though alcohol remains by

far the teen substance of choice, teens are three times likelier to be in treatment for marijuana than for alcohol (and six times likelier to be in treatment for marijuana than for all other illegal drugs combined).

4   As has been true of tobacco since the 1960s, we've learned a lot about the dangers of marijuana since the 1970s. The drug adversely affects short-term memory, the ability to concentrate, and motor skills. Recent studies indicate that it increases the likelihood of depression, schizophrenia, and other serious mental health problems. Nora Volkow, director of the National Institute on Drug Abuse, has repeatedly expressed concern about the adverse impact of marijuana on the brain, a matter of particular moment for youngsters whose brains are still in the development stage. Volkow has stated: "There is no question marijuana can be addictive; that argument is over. The most important thing right now is to understand the vulnerability of young, developing brains to these increased concentrations of cannabis."

5   The issue of marijuana use (and most illegal drug use) is all about kids. If we can get kids not to smoke marijuana before they reach age 21, they are virtually certain never to do so. So let's do more than trumpet the arrest rate. Let's focus on discouraging children and teens from getting involved with the drug in the first place.

6   This begins with understanding the importance of preventing kids from becoming cigarette smokers. Most kids who smoke cigarettes will not smoke marijuana, but a 2003 survey of 12- to 17-year-olds, conducted by the National Center on Addiction and Substance Abuse (CASA) at Columbia University, reveals that teens who smoke cigarettes are much likelier than non-smokers to try marijuana; they are also likelier to become regular marijuana users.

7   The next question is how to make public policies, including law enforcement approaches, more effective in discouraging marijuana use. Availability is the mother of use, so doing a far better job of reducing availability is high on the list. Beyond that—and recognizing that reducing demand is key to that goal—we should use the increased arrest rate as an opportunity to discourage use.

8   Years ago, while I was visiting Los Angeles, then-Mayor Dick Riordan told me that in his city kids were arrested an average of nine times for possession of marijuana before anything happened to them. I have since discovered that this situation is common in many American communities. Most kids do not even get a slap on the wrist the first few times they're nabbed for smoking a joint. As a result, we let them sink deeper and deeper into drug use, with its dangers to their physical, mental and emotional development and its risk of addiction.

9   I am not suggesting that we put kids in jail for smoking pot. But why not treat a teen arrested for marijuana use much the same way we treat a teen arrested for drunk driving? Why not require kids arrested

for marijuana possession to attend classes to learn about the dangers of marijuana use and to develop some skills (and the will) to decline the next time they are offered the drug? The incentive to attend such classes would be the threat of the alternative; for the first couple of arrests, loss of a driver's license or a fine stiff enough to hurt; for continued use, a few nights in a local prison. Getting kids to attend sessions designed to discourage their marijuana use would give some practical meaning to increased law enforcement and would bring reductions in drug use more in line with increased arrest rates.

10   These steps will help, but the fact is that we cannot arrest our way out of the teen marijuana problem when (in a recent CASA survey) 40 percent of 12- to 17-year-olds report that they can buy the drug within a day, and 21 percent say they can buy it within an hour.

11   Parents are the first line of defense. Parents must understand that the drug available today is far more potent than what they might have smoked in the 1970s. For their children, smoking marijuana is not a harmless rite of passage but rather a dangerous game of Russian roulette. ■

Eric Schlosser

Make Peace with Pot

Author of the best-selling book Fast Food Nation *(2001), which explains how the fast-food industry dominates everything from cattle farming to teenage jobs to scientific labs, Eric Schlosser contributes frequently to the* Atlantic Monthly *magazine. Having published as well a book—*Reefer Madness *(2003)—about the criminalization of marijuana and the drug's importance to the economy, he continues to work at the juncture of economics, the legal system, and cultural norms. "Make Peace with Pot" appeared in the April 26, 2004, edition of* The New York Times. *Shortly after the essay was published, the United States Supreme Court ruled that the federal government can prosecute citizens who use marijuana for medicinal purposes, even in states where medical marijuana is allowed.*

1   Starting in the fall, pharmacies in British Columbia will sell marijuana for medicinal purposes, without a prescription, under a pilot project devised by Canada's national health service. The plan follows a 2002 report by a Canadian Senate committee that found there were "clear, though not definitive" benefits for using marijuana in the treatment of chronic pain, multiple sclerosis, epilepsy and other ailments. Both Prime Minister Paul Martin and Stephen Harper, leader of the opposition conservatives, support the decriminalization of marijuana.

2   Oddly, the strongest criticism of the Canadian proposal has come from patients already using medical marijuana who think the government, which charges about $110 an ounce, supplies lousy pot. "It is of incredibly poor quality," said one patient. Another said, "It tastes like lumber." A spokesman for Health Canada promised the agency would try to offer a better grade of product.

3   Needless to say, this is a far cry from the situation in the United States, where marijuana remains a Schedule 1 controlled substance, a drug that the government says has a high potential for abuse, no accepted medical uses, and no safe level of use.

4   Under federal law it is illegal to possess any amount of marijuana anywhere in the United States. Penalties for a first marijuana offense range from probation to life without parole. Although 11 states have decriminalized marijuana, most still have tough laws against the drug. In Louisiana, selling one ounce can lead to a 20-year prison sentence. In Washington State, supplying any amount of marijuana brings a recommended prison sentence of five years.

5   About 700,000 people were arrested in the United States for violating marijuana laws in 2002 (the most recent year for which statistics are available)—more than were arrested for heroin or cocaine. Almost 90 percent of these marijuana arrests were for simple possession, a crime that in most cases is a misdemeanor. But even a misdemeanor conviction can easily lead to time in jail, the suspension of a driver's license, the loss of a job. And in many states possession of an ounce is a felony. Those convicted of a marijuana felony, even if they are disabled, can be prohibited from receiving federal welfare payments or food stamps. Convicted murderers and rapists, however, are still eligible for those benefits.

6   The Bush administration has escalated the war on marijuana, raiding clinics that offer medical marijuana and staging a nationwide roundup of manufacturers of drug paraphernalia. In November 2002 the Office of National Drug Control Policy circulated an "open letter to America's prosecutors" spelling out the administration's views. "Marijuana is addictive," the letter asserted. "Marijuana and violence are linked . . . no drug matches the threat posed by marijuana."

7   This tough new stand has generated little protest in Congress. Even though the war on marijuana was begun by President Ronald Reagan in 1982, it has always received strong bipartisan support. Some of the toughest drug war legislation has been backed by liberals, and the number of annual marijuana arrests more than doubled during the Clinton years. In fact, some of the strongest opposition to the arrest and imprisonment of marijuana users has come from conservatives like William F. Buckley, the economist Milton Friedman, and Gary Johnson, the former Republican governor of New Mexico.

8   This year the White House's national antidrug media campaign will spend $170 million, working closely with the nonprofit Partnership for a Drug-Free America. The idea of a "drug-free America" may seem appealing. But it's hard to believe that anyone seriously hopes to achieve that goal in a nation where millions of children are routinely given Ritalin, antidepressants are prescribed to cure shyness, and the pharmaceutical industry aggressively promotes pills to help middle-aged men have sex.

9   Clearly, some recreational drugs are thought to be O.K. Thus it isn't surprising that the Partnership for a Drug-Free America originally received much of its financing from cigarette, alcohol and pharmaceutical companies like Hoffmann-La Roche, Philip Morris, R. J. Reynolds and Anheuser-Busch.

10   More than 16,000 Americans die every year after taking nonsteroidal anti-inflammatory drugs like aspirin and ibuprofen. No one in Congress, however, has called for an all-out war on Advil. Perhaps the most dangerous drug widely consumed in the United States is the one that I use three or four times a week: alcohol. It is literally poisonous; you can die after drinking too much. It is directly linked to about one-quarter of the suicides in the United States, almost half the violent crime and two-thirds of domestic abuse. And the level of alcohol use among the young far exceeds the use of marijuana. According to the Justice Department, American children aged 11 to 13 are four times more likely to drink alcohol than to smoke pot.

11   None of this should play down the seriousness of marijuana use. It is a powerful, mind-altering drug. It should not be smoked by young people, schizophrenics, pregnant women and people with heart conditions. But it is remarkably nontoxic. In more than 5,000 years of recorded use, there is no verified case of anybody dying of an overdose. Indeed, no fatal dose has ever been established.

12   Over the past two decades billions of dollars have been spent fighting the war on marijuana, millions of Americans have been arrested and tens of thousands have been imprisoned. Has it been worth it? According to the government's National Household Survey on Drug Abuse, in 1982 about 54 percent of Americans between the ages of 18 and 25 had smoked marijuana. In 2002 the proportion was . . . about 54 percent.

13   We seem to pay no attention to what other governments are doing. Spain, Italy, Portugal, the Netherlands and Belgium have decriminalized marijuana. This year Britain reduced the penalty for having small amounts. Legislation is pending in Canada to decriminalize possession of about half an ounce (the Bush administration is applying strong pressure on the Canadian government to block that bill). In Ohio, possession of up to three ounces has been decriminalized for years—and yet liberal marijuana laws have not transformed Ohio into a hippy-dippy

paradise; conservative Republican governors have been running the state since 1991.

14   Here's an idea: people who smoke too much marijuana should be treated the same way as people who drink too much alcohol. They need help, not the threat of arrest, imprisonment and unemployment.

15   More important, denying a relatively safe, potentially useful medicine to patients is irrational and cruel. In 1972 a commission appointed by President Richard Nixon concluded that marijuana should be decriminalized in the United States. The commission's aim was not to encourage the use of marijuana, but to "demythologize it." Although Nixon rejected the commission's findings, they remain no less valid today: "For the vast majority of recreational users," the 2002 Canadian Senate committee found, "cannabis use presents no harmful consequences for physical, psychological or social well-being in either the short or long term."

16   The current war on marijuana is a monumental waste of money and a source of pointless misery. America's drug warriors, much like its marijuana smokers, seem under the spell of a powerful intoxicant. They are not thinking clearly. ■

ISSUE IN FOCUS

Regulating Tobacco

In 1998 the attorneys general in 46 states, five U.S. territories, and the District of Columbia reached a landmark agreement with America's most important tobacco companies concerning damages caused by smoking, and the marketing and promotion of tobacco products. According to the settlement, tobacco companies must pay more than $200 billion over 25 years to cover costs associated with smoking-related diseases, restrict their advertising and offer counterads, support smoking-cessation efforts, and especially take steps to discourage children from taking up smoking. Cigarette manufacturers cannot use cartoon characters in ads, cannot advertise in media that are especially accessible to children (e.g.,

According to a March 2004 General Accounting Office report, 54 percent of money from the tobacco lawsuit settlement is spent on budget shortfalls, 17 percent on treating smoking-related illnesses, and just 2 percent on tobacco prevention.

—*WALL STREET JOURNAL* EDITORIAL, JULY 20, 2004

shopping malls, buses, sports arenas, and video game arcades), cannot pay for product placements in movies and television shows, and cannot promote smoking through free merchandise such as caps, shirts, and backpacks.

In addition, as you have no doubt noticed, airlines no longer permit passengers to smoke, smoking is prohibited in many public places such as schools and office buildings, and public accommodations such as restaurants must accommodate nonsmokers. There is nearly universal agreement that cigarette smoking causes lung cancer, heart disease, emphysema, and other diseases, and warnings to that effect have appeared on cigarette packages and ads for decades. In 1964, when 70 million Americans smoked, the first Surgeon General's Report on Smoking and Health launched what became a series of reports on the link between smoking and various diseases. Those reports promoted a new era of industry regulation and consumer lawsuits that have reduced the incidence of smoking in American life.

Since the agreement on the health hazards and since the implementation of warnings and regulations, smoking among teenagers and adults has decreased modestly but perceptibly, and nonsmokers feel more comfortable away from distracting and dangerous secondhand smoke. However, restrictions on smoking remain controversial. On the one hand, risks to public health caused by smoking seem to cry out for intervention. When the government inspects food, insists on safe work

SURGEON GENERAL'S WARNING: Smoking By Pregnant Women May Result in Fetal Injury, Premature Birth, And Low Birth Weight.

For a commentary on Joe Camel, see page 684.

"A free man is at liberty to decide what he will eat, drink, read, watch, and listen to. A free man is at liberty to take risks with his money when he invests, with his career choices when he decides on an occupation, and with his life when he . . . decides what pleasures of the present are worth the possibility of a shorter and less healthy life in the future. And a free man, by logical extension, is at liberty to decide to smoke and in what quantities."

—RICHARD EBELING, WRITING IN
THE FREEMAN, JULY/AUGUST 2004

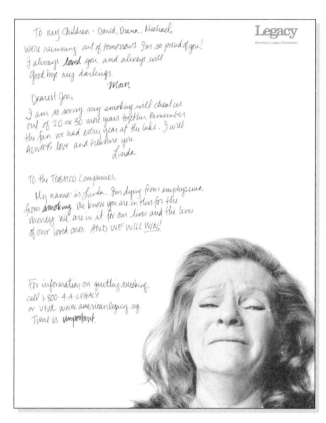

To my Children - David, Diana, Michael,
We're running out of tomorrows. I'm so proud of you!
I always loved you and always will
Good bye my darlings.
                              Mom

Dearest Jon,
I am so sorry my smoking will cheat us
out of 20 or 30 more years together. Remember
the fun we had every year at the lake. I will
Always love and treasure you
                              Linda

To the TOBACCO Companies,
My name is Linda. I'm dying from emphysema
from smoking. We know you are in this for the
money. We are in it for our lives and the lives
of our loved ones. AND WE WILL WIN!

For information on quitting smoking,
call 1-800-4-A-LEGACY
or visit www.americanlegacy.org
Time is important.

Legacy
American Legacy Foundation®

The American Legacy Foundation, based in Washington, D.C., is dedicated to "building a world where young people reject tobacco and where anyone can quit," according to its Web site (<www.americanlegacy.org>). Among other things, the foundation places antismoking ads in the mass media. The one published here appeared in *The New Yorker* in September 2002.

environments, and requires drivers to wear seat belts, should it not regulate smoking as well? On the other hand, some consumer freedom advocates worry that restrictions on smoking (and other habits) violate Americans' right to personal choice. Should the government be interfering with the production, sale, and consumption of consumer products? In a free society, should government be educating citizens to adopt particular lifestyles and avoid certain habits? Is it right for the government to require high taxes on consumer products that it deems dangerous? Where should that power begin and end? If smoking can be restricted, then why not place similar restrictions on beer and other alcoholic beverages, since the social costs associated with alcohol use are similarly high? And what about placing restrictions on certain kinds of foods, such as the burgers and fries sold in fast-food restaurants? Or on products like SUVs, dietary supplements, and firearms?

On these pages are brief arguments that address questions like these, questions that are also addressed by the selections on other topics in this chapter—marijuana, obesity, alcohol, firearms, steroids, and so forth. Tobacco companies continue to advertise their products widely, continue to be sued because of ads they place in magazines popular with young people,

Garry Trudeau (born 1948) won the Pulitzer Prize for his comic strip "Doonesbury" in 1975. A graduate of Yale University, Trudeau began making fun of bigwigs while in college, and his widely syndicated cartoons continue to satirize prominent figures and address current controversies. The strip published here appeared in January 2002.

continue to define their practices—see, for example, the Philip Morris Web site at <www.philipmorrisusa.com>—and continue to generate opposition from organizations like the American Legacy Foundation. Here we reprint an ad from the American Legacy Foundation's "truth" campaign, a cartoon by Garry Trudeau that is critical of Big Tobacco, an argument that restrictions on smoking should be spread worldwide—and a defense of individual freedom to smoke by Walter E. Williams. As you read, decide where you stand on the issue of whether or not to regulate tobacco (and other harmful consumer products). Where should the line be drawn between personal freedom and social responsibility?

DOUGLAS BETTCHER AND CHITRA SUBRAMANIAM

The Necessity of Global Tobacco Regulations

Douglas Bettcher served as the coordinator of the World Health Organization's 2005 Framework Convention on Tobacco Control (FCTC)— a gathering that sought to reduce tobacco use (and its related health problems) worldwide. Chitra Subramaniam is a news correspondent for the Indian Express *who also worked on the WHO's Global Tobacco Control initiative. She studied both at New Delhi and Stanford and has worked for several Indian newspapers. The author of* India Is for Sale *(1997), she earned a reputation by exposing the Bofors arms scandal, an affair in which a Swedish gun manufacturer paid significant kickbacks to Indians in exchange for an arms deal. Both authors endorse the FCTC treaty, which became international law on February 27, 2005, and includes bans on some forms of advertising and the control of tobacco use in public places. "The Necessity of Global Tobacco Regulations" first appeared in the December 5, 2001,* Journal of the American Medical Association.

1   While multinational tobacco companies market high tar and nicotine cigarettes worldwide, in developing countries they advertise these products with techniques that are banned in their home countries.[1] Of the 8.4 million deaths that tobacco is expected to cause by 2020, 70% will occur in transitional countries.[2]

2   Global legislation must hold tobacco companies to the same standards of safety in developing markets that they are held to in their industrialized home markets. To create such global legislation, the World Health Organisation's (WHO's) 191 member states are currently negotiating a legally binding international agreement, the Framework Convention on Tobacco Control (FCTC), which may include legally binding rules on tobacco smuggling, international standardization, disclosure of product contents, and package design and labeling.[3]

3   The ethical basis of the FCTC is the principle that a multinational corporation has a nondelegable duty to protect citizens from harm caused by its products. This includes the duty to ensure that all activities are conducted with the highest standards of safety and to provide all necessary information and warnings regarding the activity involved.[4] In addition, the "negative harm" principle of business ethics requires that, in their operations abroad, corporations have an obligation not to add to the suffering and deprivation of people.

4   Tobacco companies have argued that people should be allowed to consume products of their choice freely.[5] However, a recent World Bank report cites three ways in which the choice to buy tobacco products dif-

fers from the purchase of other consumer goods. First, many smokers are not aware of the high probability of disease and premature death their choice to smoke entails, and thus, their consent to be exposed to harm is uninformed. Children and teenagers in particular may not have the capacity to assess properly information on the health effects of smoking. Second, the highly addictive nature of nicotine, particularly as it is delivered in a manufactured cigarette, limits the tobacco user's freedom to choose not to smoke.[6] Third, smokers impose both direct and indirect costs on other non-consenting individuals. These failures to meet "free" market standards provide a rationale for demand-reduction interventions.[7]

5   Beyond this theoretical justification for action, there is also a practical one. Tobacco companies have shown themselves to be incapable of self-regulation.[8] Despite the fact that cigarette smoke contains some 4000 different constituents, 60 of which are known carcinogens,[9] there is evidence that tobacco companies have failed to perform inhouse smoking and health research, and that this failure was, in part, the result of tobacco company efforts to mislead the public about the health effects of smoking.[10]

6   The tobacco companies have deliberately increased the addictive potential of cigarettes through their well-documented strategy of manipulating nicotine levels. Furthermore, a WHO committee concluded that tobacco companies had conspired to undermine the agency's tobacco control programs around the world. The committee made 58 recommendations to protect against the subterfuge of the tobacco industry.[11]

7   During a global public hearing in October 2000, the WHO supported measures and policies to restrict youth access to tobacco. Recently, three major tobacco companies proposed weak voluntary global marketing standards, but such measures are known to have only limited impact on youth and adult consumption of tobacco.[12] At the same time, tobacco companies opposed comprehensive advertising bans and price increases, interventions that have had a measurable and sustained impact to decrease tobacco use.

8   Tobacco companies have an ethical responsibility to minimize the harm caused by their products in developing countries and to adhere to the same safety standards in developing countries that they use in their home countries.

9   They have proven themselves unwilling or unable to meet this responsibility voluntarily, and the cost of this failure is enormous. The kind of legally binding global regulation of dangerous practices that the FCTC could provide has become necessary.

Notes

1. Giddens, A. Globalization. Available at: news.bbc.co.uk/hi/english/static/ events/reith_99/week1/week1/week1.htm. Accessed November 14, 2001.

2. Murray, C. L., and Lopez, A. D. Alternative projections of mortality and disability by cause 1990–2020: Global Burden of Disease Study. *Lancet,* 1997; 349:1498–1504.

3. Taylor, A. L., and Bettcher, D. W. WHO Framework Convention on Tobacco Control: A global "good" for public health. *Bull World Health Organ.* 2000;78:920–929.

4. Finzen, B. A., and Walburn, R. B. *Union Carbide Corporation's Liability for the Bhopal Disaster. Multinational Enterprise Liability.* Westport, Conn: Quorom Books; 1990:145–150.

5. British American Tobacco. Answer to frequently asked question: "How can you justify being in the business of selling a product that is harmful to people's health?" Available at: http://www.bat.com. Accessed November 14, 2001.

6. Hurt, R. D., and Robertson, C. R. Prying open the tobacco industry's secrets about nicotine. *JAMA.* 1998;280:1173–1181.

7. Jha, P., and Chaloupka, F. J., eds. *Curbing the Epidemic: Governments and the Economics of Tobacco Control.* Washington, DC: World Bank; 1999:3–4.

8. Richards, J. W., Tye, J. B., and Fischer, P. M. The tobacco industry's code of advertising in the United States: Myth and reality. *Tob Control.* 1996; 5:295–311.

9. Shopland, D. Machine Testing for constituent levels in cigarettes. Monograph: *Advancing Knowledge on Regulating Tobacco Products.* Paper presented at International Conference: Advancing Knowledge on Regulating Tobacco Products. Oslo, Norway, 9–11 February 2000.

10. Zeltner, T., Kessler, D., Martiny, A., and Randera, F. *Tobacco Company Strategies to Undermine Tobacco Control Activities at the World Health Organization.* Report of the Committee of Experts on Tobacco Industry Documents, July 2000:229–243.

11. Goldman, L. K., and Glantz, S. A. Evaluation of antismoking advertising campaigns. *JAMA.* 1998;279:772–777.

12. Philip Morris' comments on the Framework Convention for Tobacco Control for the Public Hearings on the FCTC, October 12–13, 2000. Available at: http://www3.who.int/whosis/fctc/fctc.cfm. Accessed November 14, 2001. ∎

WALTER E. WILLIAMS

Nazi Tactics

Walter E. Williams (born 1936) serves as the John M. Olin Distinguished Professor of Economics at George Mason University. While his scholarly work has appeared in American Economic Review, Social Science Quarterly, Economic Inquiry, *and the* Journal of Labor Economics, *he is best known for his conservative commentaries in popular publications such as* Reader's Digest, The Wall Street Journal, *and* Newsweek, *and through his syndicated weekly column entitled "A Minority View." His books include* The State Against Blocks *(1982),* America: A Minority Viewpoint *(1982),* All It Takes Is Guts *(1987),* South Africa's War on Capitalism *(1989), and* More Liberty Means Less Government *(1999). Williams makes numerous television and radio appearances, talking about economic issues and challenges to personal liberty and frequently drawing parallels with Nazi Germany. The article reprinted here was first published in 2003 in* The Freeman: Ideas on Liberty, *which is published by the Foundation for Economic Education and claims to emphasize reason, natural rights, and individual liberties and to attract a readership interested in academic and political issues.*

1 Prior to the 1930s, Germany was Europe's most hospitable country for Jews. While Jews were only 1 percent of the population, they were one-fourth of Germany's law and medical students. In some German cities, Jews were the majority of doctors. While Jews were only 5 percent of the Berlin Population in 1905, they paid 31 percent of all income taxes collected. For Germany as a whole, Jewish income was more than three times the national average. In his book, *Migration and Cultures,* Thomas Sowell adds that Jews were so highly integrated into German economic and social life that in nearly half of all Jewish marriages during the 1920s one of the spouses was gentile. During World War I, Jewish-American publications were investigated and prosecuted by the U.S. government for writing favorably about Germany, a nation at war with the United States.

2 Much of German history has been one of racial toleration. This is partially seen by their anti-slavery positions in Brazil and the United States. In the United States, Germans had a large hand in assisting runaway slaves by way of the "underground railroad." Germans also had an established reputation of getting along well with American Indians.

3 So why the story about pre-Nazi Germany? I think examining it raises an interesting question that few bother to answer; namely, if Germany was so hospitable to Jews, relative to other countries, how in the world did the Holocaust happen? There are several alternative explanations, such as Hitler's massive consolidation of government power. Then there's the fact that German culture places high values on regimentation and obedience to authority. An important part of the answer of how Germans came to accept Jewish persecution was a massive and successful Nazi Jewish-vilification program. Teaching Germans to think of Jews as inferiors and as responsible for the post–World War I economic devastation made it possible for Germans to accept the mistreatment of Jews.

4 You say, "Okay, you're right, but what's the relevance to us?" There are about 40 million Americans who smoke cigarettes. Prior to the 1980s, all efforts to curb tobacco use relied on arguments pertaining

to the health risks borne by smokers. The only way to achieve today's level of sustained attack on smokers and tobacco companies was to create an argument that tobacco smoke harmed not only smokers but others as well. Thanks to a fraudulent Environmental Protection Agency study on secondhand smoke, "Respiratory Health Effects of Passive Smoking," we have today's tobacco regulations. This is despite devastating evidence that EPA's study made subjective judgments, failed to account for important factors that could bias the results, and relaxed a crucial scientific standard to achieve the result the researchers were looking for.

5   The "relaxed" scientific standard was the EPA's lowering of the confidence interval applied to its analysis from the more standard 95 percent to 90 percent—in effect, doubling the chance of error. A federal court in *Flue-Cured Tobacco Cooperative Stabilization Corporation v. EPA* added that the EPA "disregarded information and made findings based on selective information . . . ; deviated from its risk assessment guidelines; failed to disclose important [opposition] findings and reasoning; and left significant questions without answers."

6   As a result of both official and non-official fraudulent claims about the health effects, as well as the health-care costs, of smoking, there has been widely successful vilification of cigarette smokers and tobacco manufacturers. Lawmakers have little hesitance in imposing confiscatory tobacco taxes, in some jurisdictions of one to three dollars per pack. Zealous lawmakers and other public officials have attempted to ban smoking on streets and in parks. In at least a couple of jurisdictions there have been attempts to outlaw smoking in one's own home or apartment under the flimflam reasoning that neighbors are injured by secondhand smoke. Americans don't mind at all seeing their fellow Americans huddled in the winter outside their workplaces in order to have a cigarette. In the state of Washington, a condemned prisoner was denied a last request for a cigarette. Last summer, California banned smoking in some of its prisons.

7   None of this could have happened during a much more civilized era in our country. Nazi-like vilification tactics had to be employed to convince decent Americans that smokers and tobacco companies deserved any harsh treatment.

All Should Be Concerned

8   I'm by no means suggesting that smokers are headed off to concentration camps and gas chambers, although they might have been in Germany because Hitler was a rabid anti-cigarette zealot. Instead, I'm suggesting that the cigarette-smoker vilification campaign is something about which we all should be concerned, whether we smoke cigarettes or not. These people who want to control our lives are almost finished with smokers; but never in history has a tyrant arisen one day and then

decided to tyrannize no more. The nation's tyrants have now turned their attention to the vilification of fast-food chains such as McDonald's, Burger King, Wendy's, and KFC, charging them with having created an addiction to fatty foods. Thus, the tyrants claim, fast-food chains have contributed to obesity-related problems and growing health-care costs. Like the anti-tobacco zealots, they call for regulation, compensation for injury, and taxes on foods they deem to be nonnutritious. In addition to fast-food chains, these tyrants have targeted soft drink and candy manufacturers. Chinese and Mexican restaurants are also in their sights because they have meal servings deemed to be too large.

9   In their campaign against fast-food chains, restaurants, and soda and candy manufacturers, the nation's food Nazis always refer to the anti-tobacco campaign as the model for their agenda. ■

From Reading to Writing

1. Analyze the argument by either Walter E. Williams or Douglas Bettcher and Chitra Subramaniam: How is each argument the product of its audience and purpose? What sources of argument (ethical appeal, emotional appeal, logical appeals, and good reasons) does each author choose and why? (See Chapter 4 for information on rhetorical analysis.)

2. Compare the various photos and ads that appear on the preceding pages. What visual argument does each photo or ad make? How does it support its argument? (See Chapter 5 for information on analyzing visuals.)

3. Write an argument that makes its point by defining a key term related to the regulation of substances like smoking. You might choose to change someone's attitude by redefining "freedom" or "government regulation" or "advertising" in such a way that your definition supports your views on regulating substances like smoking. (See Chapter 6 for more on writing definition arguments.)

4. Propose a certain policy concerning the regulation of smoking or some other substance that is an issue in your community. For instance, should your campus permit beer to be purchased by fans at athletic events? What should be a proper policy on performance-enhancing drugs in college athletics? (See Chapter 11 for advice.)

5. Write a rebuttal of an article related to tobacco, alcohol, steroids, or obesity that you notice in your local newspaper. (See Chapter 10.) Consider whether you wish to show the weakness in the article, whether you wish to counter-argue, or both.

6. Write an essay that recounts a personal experience of yours that makes an argumentative point related to smoking. What exactly does your personal experience with tobacco lead you to believe? See Chapter 9 for advice on narrative arguments.

Drugstore Athlete

Malcolm Gladwell (born 1963) has been writing for some time about fascinating cultural developments of one kind or another—why crime can drop suddenly, how a particular book becomes a best seller, the rise of hair coloring products for women and suicide rates in Micronesio, the fascination for Ritalin, the spread of coffee. In 2000 he published The Tipping Point, *a book that investigates a number of cultural phenomena as if they were "social epidemics" that spread in the same way that infectious diseases do. Gladwell was a reporter, often on science, for the* Washington Post *from 1987 to 1996; since then his work has often appeared in* The New Yorker, *as did the following piece (September 10, 2001).*

1.

1   At the age of twelve, Christiane Knacke-Sommer was plucked from a small town in Saxony to train with the elite SC Dynamo swim club, in East Berlin. After two years of steady progress, she was given regular injections and daily doses of small baby-blue pills, which she was required to take in the presence of a trainer. Within weeks, her arms and shoulders began to thicken. She developed severe acne. Her pubic hair began to spread over her abdomen. Her libido soared out of control. Her voice turned gruff. And her performance in the pool began to improve dramatically, culminating in a bronze medal in the hundred-metre butterfly at the 1980 Moscow Olympics. But then the Wall fell and the truth emerged about those little blue pills. In a new book about the East German sports establishment, *Foust's Gold*, Steven Ungerleider recounts the moment in 1998 when Knacke-Sommer testified in Berlin at the trial of her former coaches and doctors:

2   "Did defendant Gläser or defendant Binus ever tell you that the blue pills were the anabolic steroid known as Oral-Turinabol?" the prosecutor asked. "They told us they were vitamin tablets." Christiane said, "just like they served all the girls with meals." "Did defendant Binus ever tell you the injection he gave was Depot-Turinabol?" "Never," Christiane said, staring at Binus until the slight, middle-aged man

looked away. "He said the shots were another kind of vitamin." "He never said he was injecting you with the male hormone testosterone?" the prosecutor persisted. "Neither he nor Herr Gläser ever mentioned Oral-Turinabol or Depot-Turinabol," Christiane said firmly. "Did you take these drugs voluntarily?" the prosecutor asked in a kindly tone. "I was fifteen years old when the pills started," she replied, beginning to lose her composure. "The training motto at the pool was, "You eat the pills, or you die. It was forbidden to refuse."

3   As her testimony ended, Knacke-Sommer pointed at the two defendants and shouted. "They destroyed my body and my mind!" Then she rose and threw her Olympic medal to the floor.

4   Anabolic steroids have been used to enhance athletic performance since the early sixties, when an American physician gave the drugs to three weight lifters, who promptly jumped from mediocrity to world records. But no one ever took the use of illegal drugs quite so far as the East Germans. In a military hospital outside the former East Berlin, in 1991, investigators discovered a ten-volume archive meticulously detailing every national athletic achievement from the mid-sixties to the fall of the Berlin Wall, each entry annotated with the name of the drug and the dosage given to the athlete. An average teenage girl naturally produces somewhere around half a milligram of testosterone a day. The East German sports authorities routinely prescribed steroids to young adolescent girls in doses of up to thirty-five milligrams a day. As the investigation progressed, former female athletes, who still had masculinized physiques and voices, came forward with tales of deformed babies, inexplicable tumors, liver dysfunction, internal bleeding, and depression. German prosecutors handed down hundreds of indictments of former coaches, doctors, and sports officials, and won numerous convictions. It was the kind of spectacle that one would have thought would shock the sporting world. Yet it didn't. In a measure of how much the use of drugs in competitive sports has changed in the past quarter century, the trials caused barely a ripple.

5   Today, coaches no longer have to coerce athletes into taking drugs. Athletes take them willingly. The drugs themselves are used in smaller doses and in creative combinations, leaving few telltale physical signs, and drug testers concede that it is virtually impossible to catch all the cheaters, or even, at times, to do much more than guess when cheating is taking place. Among the athletes, meanwhile, there is growing uncertainty about what exactly is wrong with doping. When the cyclist Lance Armstrong asserted last year, after his second consecutive Tour de France victory, that he was drug-free, some doubters wondered whether he was lying, and others simply assumed he was, and wondered why he had to. The moral clarity of the East German scandal—with its coercive coaches, damaged athletes, and corrupted competitions—has

given way to shades of gray. In today's climate, the most telling moment of the East German scandal was not Knacke-Sommer's outburst. It was when one of the system's former top officials, at the beginning of his trial, shrugged and quoted Brecht: "Competitive sport begins where healthy sport ends."

2.

6   Perhaps the best example of how murky the drug issue has become is the case of Ben Johnson, the Canadian sprinter who won the one hundred metres at the Seoul Olympics, in 1988. Johnson set a new world record, then failed a post-race drug test and was promptly stripped of his gold medal and suspended from international competition. No athlete of Johnson's calibre has ever been exposed so dramatically, but his disgrace was not quite the victory for clean competition that it appeared to be.

7   Johnson was part of a group of world-class sprinters based in Toronto in the nineteen-seventies and eighties and trained by a brilliant coach named Charlie Francis. Francis was driven and ambitious, eager to give his athletes the same opportunities as their competitors from the United States and Eastern Europe; and in 1979 he began discussing steroids with one of his prize sprinters, Angella Taylor. Francis felt that Taylor had the potential that year to run the two hundred metres in close to 22.90 seconds, a time that would put her within striking distance of the two best sprinters in the world, Evelyn Ashford, of the United States, and Marita Koch, of East Germany. But, seemingly out of nowhere. Ashford suddenly improved her two-hundred-metre time by six-tenths of a second. Then Koch ran what Francis calls, in his autobiography, *Speed Trap,* a "science fictional" 21.71. In the sprints, individual improvements are usually measured in hundredths of a second; athletes, once they have reached their early twenties, typically improve their performance in small, steady increments, as experience and strength increase. But these were quantum leaps, and to Francis the explanation was obvious. "Angella wasn't losing ground because of a talent gap," he writes; "she was losing because of a drug gap, and it was widening by the day." (In the case of Koch, at least, he was right. In the East German archives, investigators found a letter from Koch to the director of research at VEB Jenapharm, an East German pharmaceutical house, in which she complained, "My drugs were not as potent as the ones that were given to my opponent Brbel Eckert, who kept beating me." In East Germany, Ungerleider writes, this particular complaint was known as "dope-envy.") Later, Francis says, he was confronted at a track meet by Brian Oldfield, then one of the world's best shot-putters:

8   "When are you going to start getting serious?" he demanded. "When are you going to tell your guys the facts of life?" I asked him how he could tell they weren't already using steroids. He replied that the muscle density just wasn't there. "Your guys will never be able to compete against the Americans—their careers will be over," he persisted.

9   Among world-class athletes, the lure of steroids is not that they magically transform performance—no drug can do that—but that they make it possible to train harder. An aging baseball star, for instance, may realize that what he needs to hit a lot more home runs is to double the intensity of his weight training. Ordinarily, this might actually hurt his performance. "When you're under that kind of physical stress." Charles Yesalis, an epidemiologist at Pennsylvania State University, says, "your body releases corticosteroids, and when your body starts making those hormones at inappropriate times it blocks testosterone. And instead of being anabolic—instead of building muscle—corticosteroids are catabolic. They break down muscle. That's clearly something an athlete doesn't want." Taking steroids counteracts the impact of corticosteroids and helps the body bounce back faster. If that home-run hitter was taking testosterone or an anabolic steroid, he'd have a better chance of handling the extra weight training.

10   It was this extra training that Francis and his sprinters felt they needed to reach the top. Angella Taylor was the first to start taking steroids. Ben Johnson followed in 1981, when he was twenty years old, beginning with a daily dose of five milligrams of the steroid Dianabol, in three-week on-and-off cycles. Over time, that protocol grew more complex. In 1984, Taylor visited a Los Angeles doctor, Robert Kerr, who was famous for his willingness to provide athletes with pharmacological assistance. He suggested that the Canadians use human growth hormone, the pituitary extract that promotes lean muscle and that had become, in Francis's words, "the rage in elite track circles." Kerr also recommended three additional substances, all of which were believed to promote the body's production of growth hormone: the amino acids arginine and ornithine and the dopamine precursor L-dopa. "I would later learn," Francis writes, "that one group of American women was using three times as much growth hormone as Kerr had suggested, in addition to 15 milligrams per day of Dianabol, another 15 milligrams of Anavar, large amounts of testosterone, and thyroxine, the synthetic thyroid hormone used by athletes to speed the metabolism and keep people lean." But the Canadians stuck to their initial regimen, making only a few changes: Vitamin B_{12}, a non-steroidal muscle builder called inosine, and occasional shots of testosterone were added; Dianabol was dropped in favor of a newer steroid called Furazabol; and L-dopa, which turned out to cause stiffness, was replaced with the blood-pressure drug Dixarit.

11   Going into the Seoul Olympics, then, Johnson was a walking pharmacy. But—and this is the great irony of his case—none of the drugs that were part of his formal pharmaceutical protocol resulted in his failed drug test. He had already reaped the benefit of the steroids in intense workouts leading up to the games, and had stopped Furazabol and testosterone long enough in advance that all traces of both supplements should have disappeared from his system by the time of his race—a process he sped up by taking the diuretic Moduret. Human growth hormone wasn't—and still isn't—detectable by a drug test, and arginine, ornithine, and Dixarit were legal. Johnson should have been clean. The most striking (and unintentionally hilarious) moment in *Speed Trap* comes when Francis describes his bewilderment at being informed that his star runner had failed a drug test—for the anabolic steroid stanozolol. "I was floored," Francis writes:

12   To my knowledge, Ben had never injected stanozolol. He occasionally used Winstrol, an oral version of the drug, but for no more than a few days at a time, since it tended to make him stiff. He'd always discontinued the tablets at least six weeks before a meet, well beyond the accepted "clearance time." . . . After seven years of using steroids, Ben knew what he was doing. It was inconceivable to me that he might take stanozolol on his own and jeopardize the most important race of his life.

13   Francis suggests that Johnson's urine sample might have been deliberately contaminated by a rival, a charge that is less preposterous than it sounds. Documents from the East German archive show, for example, that in international competitions security was so lax that urine samples were sometimes switched, stolen from a "clean" athlete, or simply "borrowed" from a noncompetitor. "The pure urine would either be infused by a catheter into the competitor's bladder (a rather painful procedure) or be held in condoms until it was time to give a specimen to the drug control lab," Ungerleider writes. (The top East German sports official Manfred Höppner was once in charge of urine samples at an international weight-lifting competition. When he realized that several of his weight lifters would not pass the test, he broke open the seal of their specimens, poured out the contents, and, Ungerleider notes, "took a nice long leak of pure urine into them.") It is also possible that Johnson's test was simply botched. Two years later, in 1990, track and field's governing body claimed that Butch Reynolds, the world's four-hundred-metre record holder, had tested positive for the steroid nandrolone, and suspended him for two years. It did so despite the fact that half of his urine-sample data had been misplaced, that the testing equipment had failed during analysis of the other half of his sample, and that the lab technician who did the test identified Sample H6 as positive—and Reynolds's sample was numbered H5. Reynolds lost the prime years of his career.

14   We may never know what really happened with Johnson's assay, and perhaps it doesn't much matter. He was a doper. But clearly this was something less than a victory for drug enforcement. Here was a man using human growth hormone, Dixarit, inosine, testosterone, and Furazabol, and the only substance that the testers could find in him was stanozolol—which may have been the only illegal drug that he hadn't used. Nor is it encouraging that Johnson was the only prominent athlete caught for drug use in Seoul. It is hard to believe, for instance, that the sprinter Florence Griffith Joyner, the star of the Seoul games, was clean. Before 1988, her best times in the hundred metres and the two hundred metres were, respectively, 10.96 and 21.96. In 1988, a suddenly huskier FloJo ran 10.49 and 21.34, times that no runner since has even come close to equalling. In other words, at the age of twenty-eight—when most athletes are beginning their decline—Griffith Joyner transformed herself in one season from a career-long better-than-average sprinter to the fastest female sprinter in history. Of course, FloJo never failed a drug test. But what does that prove? FloJo went on to make a fortune as a corporate spokeswoman. Johnson's suspension cost him an estimated $25 million in lost endorsements. The real lesson of the Seoul Olympics may simply have been that Johnson was a very unlucky man.

3.

15   The basic problem with drug testing is that testers are always one step behind athletes. It can take years for sports authorities to figure out what drugs athletes are using, and even longer to devise effective means of detecting them. Anabolic steroids weren't banned by the international Olympic Committee until 1975, almost a decade after the East Germans started using them. In 1996, at the Atlanta Olympics, five athletes tested positive for what we now know to be the drug Bromantan, but they weren't suspended, because no one knew at the time what Bromantan was. (It turned out to be a Russian-made psycho-stimulant.) Human growth hormone, meanwhile, has been around for twenty years, and testers still haven't figured out how to detect it.

16   Perhaps the best example of the difficulties of drug testing is testosterone. It has been used by athletes to enhance performance since the fifties, and the International Olympic Committee announced that it would crack down on testosterone supplements in the early eighties. This didn't mean that the I.O.C. was going to test for testosterone directly, though, because the testosterone that athletes were getting from a needle or a pill was largely indistinguishable from the testosterone they produce naturally. What was proposed, instead, was to compare the level of testosterone in urine with the level of another hormone, epitestosterone, to determine what's called the T/E ratio. For most people, under normal circumstances, that ratio is 1:1, and so the theory was that if testers found a lot more testosterone than epitestosterone it

would be a sign that the athlete was cheating. Since a small number of people have naturally high levels of testosterone, the I.O.C. avoided the risk of falsely accusing anyone by setting the legal limit at 6:1.

17   Did this stop testosterone use? Not at all. Through much of the eighties and nineties, most sports organizations conducted their drug testing only at major competitions. Athletes taking testosterone would simply do what Johnson did, and taper off their use in the days or weeks prior to those events. So sports authorities began randomly showing up at athletes' houses or training sites and demanding urine samples. To this, dopers responded by taking extra doses of epitestosterone with their testosterone, so their T/E would remain in balance. Testers, in turn, began treating elevated epitestosterone levels as suspicious, too. But that still left athletes with the claim that they were among the few with naturally elevated testosterone. Testers, then, were forced to take multiple urine samples, measuring an athlete's T/E ratio over several weeks. Someone with a naturally elevated T/E ratio will have fairly consistent ratios from week to week. Someone who is doping will have telltale spikes—times immediately after taking shots or pills when the level of the hormone in his blood soars. Did all these precautions mean that cheating stopped? Of course not. Athletes have now switched from injection to transdermal testosterone patches, which administer a continuous low-level dose of the hormone, smoothing over the old, incriminating spikes. The patch has another advantage; once you take it off, your testosterone level will drop rapidly, returning to normal, depending on the dose and the person, in as little as an hour. "It's the peaks that get you caught," says Don Catlin, who runs the U.C.L.A. Olympic Analytical Laboratory. "If you took a pill this morning and an unannounced test comes this afternoon, you'd better have a bottle of epitestosterone handy. But, if you are on the patch and you know your own pharmacokinetics, all you have to do is pull it off." In other words, if you know how long it takes for you to get back under the legal limit and successfully stall the test for that period, you can probably pass the test. And if you don't want to take that chance, you can just keep your testosterone below 6:1, which, by the way, still provides a whopping performance benefit. "The bottom line is that only careless and stupid people ever get caught in drug tests," Charles Yesalis says. "The elite athletes can hire top medical and scientific people to make sure nothing had happens, and you can't catch them."

4.

18   But here is where the doping issue starts to get complicated, for there's a case to be made that what looks like failure really isn't—that regulating aggressive doping, the way the 6:1 standard does, is a better idea

than trying to prohibit drug use. Take the example of erythropoietin, or EPO. EPO is a hormone released by your kidneys that stimulates the production of red blood cells, the body's oxygen carriers. A man-made version of the hormone is given to those with suppressed red-blood-cell counts, like patients undergoing kidney dialysis or chemotherapy. But over the past decade it has also become the drug of choice for endurance athletes, because its ability to increase the amount of oxygen that the blood can carry to the muscles has the effect of postponing fatigue. "The studies that have attempted to estimate EPO's importance say it's worth about a three-, four-, or five-per-cent advantage, which is huge," Catlin says. EPO also has the advantage of being a copy of a naturally occurring substance, so it's very hard to tell if someone has been injecting it. (A cynic would say that this had something to do with the spate of remarkable times in endurance races during that period.)

19   So how should we test for EPO? One approach, which was used in the late nineties by the International Cycling Union, is a test much like the T/E ratio for testosterone. The percentage of your total blood volume which is taken up by red blood cells is known as your hematocrit. The average adult male has a hematocrit of between thirty-eight and forty-four per cent. Since 1995, the cycling authorities have declared that any rider who had a hematocrit above fifty per cent would be suspended—a deliberately generous standard (like the T/E ratio) meant to avoid falsely accusing someone with a naturally high hematocrit. The hematocrit rule also had the benefit of protecting athletes' health. If you take too much EPO, the profusion of red blood cells makes the blood sluggish and heavy, placing enormous stress on the heart. In the late eighties, at least fifteen professional cyclists died from suspected EPO overdoses. A fifty-per-cent hematocrit limit is below the point at which EPO becomes dangerous.

20   But, like the T/E standard, the hematocrit standard had a perverse effect: it set the legal limit so high that it actually encouraged cyclists to titrate their drug use up to the legal limit. After all, if you are riding for three weeks through the mountains of France and Spain, there's a big difference between a hematocrit of forty-four per cent and one of 49.9 per cent. This is why Lance Armstrong faced so many hostile questions about EPO from the European press—and why eyebrows were raised at his five-year relationship with an Italian doctor who was thought to be an expert on performance enhancing drugs. If Armstrong had, say, a hematocrit of forty-four per cent, the thinking went, why wouldn't he have raised it to 49.9, particularly since the rules (at least, in 2000) implicitly allowed him to do so. And, if he didn't, how on earth did he win?

21   The problems with hematocrit testing have inspired a second strategy, which was used on a limited basis at the Sydney Olympics and this summer's World Track and Field Championships. This test measures a

number of physiological markers of EPO use, including the presence of reticulocytes, which are the immature red blood cells produced in large numbers by EPO injections. If you have a lot more reticulocytes than normal, then there's a good chance you've used EPO recently. The blood work is followed by a confirmatory urinalysis. The test has its weaknesses. It's really only useful in picking up EPO used in the previous week or so, whereas the benefits of taking the substance persist for a month. But there's no question that, if random EPO testing were done aggressively in the weeks leading to a major competition, it would substantially reduce cheating.

22   On paper, this second strategy sounds like a better system. But there's a perverse effect here as well. By discouraging EPO use, the test is simply pushing savvy athletes toward synthetic compounds called hemoglobin-based oxygen carriers, which serve much the same purpose as EPO but for which there is no test at the moment. "I recently read off a list of these new blood-oxygen expanders to a group of toxicologists, and none had heard of any of them," Yesalis says. "That's how fast things are moving." The attempt to prevent EPO use actually promotes inequity: it gives an enormous advantage to those athletes with the means to keep up with the next wave of pharmacology. By contrast, the hematocrit limit, though more permissive, creates a kind of pharmaceutical parity. The same is true of the T/E limit. At the 1986 world swimming championships, the East German Kristin Otto set a world record in the hundred-metre freestyle, with an extraordinary display of power in the final leg of the race. According to East German records, on the day of her race Otto had a T/E ratio of 18:1. Testing can prevent that kind of aggressive doping; it can insure no one goes above 6:1. That is a less than perfect outcome, of course, but international sports is not a perfect world. It is a place where Ben Johnson is disgraced and FloJo runs free, where Butch Reynolds is barred for two years and East German coaches pee into cups—and where athletes without access to the cutting edge of medicine are condemned to second place. Since drug testers cannot protect the purity of sport, the very least they can do is to make sure that no athlete can cheat more than any other.

5.

23   The first man to break the four-minute mile was the Englishman Roger Bannister, on a windswept cinder track at Oxford, nearly fifty years ago. Bannister is in his early seventies now, and one day last summer he returned to the site of his historic race along with the current world-record holder in the mile, Morocco's Hicham El Guerrouj. The two men chatted and compared notes and posed for photographs. "I feel as if I am looking at my mirror image," Bannister said, indicating El Guer-

rouj's similarly tall, high-waisted frame. It was a polite gesture, an attempt to suggest that he and El Guerrouj were part of the same athletic lineage. But, as both men surely knew, nothing could be further from the truth.

24   Bannister was a medical student when he broke the four-minute mile in 1954. He did not have time to train every day, and when he did he squeezed in his running on his hour-long midday break at the hospital. He had no coach or trainer or entourage, only a group of running partners who called themselves "the Paddington lunch time club." In a typical workout, they might run ten consecutive quarter miles—ten laps—with perhaps two minutes of recovery between each repetition, then gobble down lunch and hurry back to work. Today, that training session would be considered barely adequate for a high-school miler. A month or so before his historic mile, Bannister took a few days off to go hiking in Scotland. Five days before he broke the four-minute barrier, he stopped running entirely, in order to rest. The day before the race, he slipped and fell on his hip while working in the hospital. Then he ran the most famous race in the history of track and field. Bannister was what runners admiringly call an "animal," a natural.

25   El Guerrouj, by contrast, trains five hours a day, in two two-and-a-half-hour sessions. He probably has a team of half a dozen people working with him; at the very least, a masseur, a doctor, a coach, an agent, and a nutritionist. He is not in medical school. He does not go hiking in rocky terrain before major track meets. When Bannister told him, last summer, how he had prepared for his four-minute mile, El Guerrouj was stunned. "For me, a rest day is perhaps when I train in the morning and spend the afternoon at the cinema," he said. El Guerrouj certainly has more than his share of natural ability, but his achievements are a reflection of much more than that: of the fact that he is better coached and better prepared than his opponents, that he trains harder and more intelligently, that he has found a way to stay injury free, and that he can recover so quickly from one day of five-hour workouts that he can follow it, the next day, with another five-hour workout.

26   Of these two paradigms, we have always been much more comfortable with the first: we want the relation between talent and achievement to be transparent, and we worry about the way ability is now so aggressively managed and augmented. Steroids bother us because they violate the honesty of effort: they permit an athlete to train too hard, beyond what seems reasonable. EPO fails the same test. For years, athletes underwent high-altitude training sessions, which had the same effect as EPO—promoting the manufacture of additional red blood cells. This was considered acceptable, while EPO is not, because we like to distinguish between those advantages which are natural or earned and those which come out of a vial.

27   Even as we assert this distinction on the playing field, though, we defy it in our own lives. We have come to prefer a world where the distractable take Ritalin, the depressed take Prozac, and the unattractive get cosmetic surgery to a world ruled, arbitrarily, by those fortunate few who were born focused, happy, and beautiful. Cosmetic surgery is not "earned" beauty, but then natural beauty isn't earned, either. One of the principal contributions of the late twentieth century was the moral deregulation of social competition—the insistence that advantages derived from artificial and extraordinary intervention are no less legitimate than the advantages of nature. All that athletes want, for better or worse, is the chance to play by those same rules. ■

FRANK SHORTER

Testimony Before the Subcommittee on Commerce, Trade, and Consumer Protection

As he reveals in his testimony here, Frank Shorter (born 1947) ran the marathon in the Olympics twice, becoming the first American in 64 years to win the event when he finished first in Munich in 1972. Shorter earned a law degree in 1974, has worked as a sports commentator, and started his own athletic supply company. He also served for three years as chairperson of the U.S. Anti-Doping Agency, which attempts to deter drug use among American athletes and is responsible for drug testing related to the Olympics and other international competitions. Shorter offered the following words at a hearing before Congress on May 18, 2005, during a session investigating steroid abuse in athletics that also "starred" Sammy Sosa and Mark McGwire.

1   Mr. Chairman, members of the Committee, good morning. My name is Frank Shorter. I want to thank the Committee for its interest in this important subject and for the invitation to testify. Today, I am here as an athlete who competed in international Olympic sport for more than ten years. I am also here as the former Chairman of the United States Anti-Doping Agency (USADA). Accordingly, my comments are from the perspective of an athlete who values an effective anti-doping program and as someone who truly understands the challenges inherent in creating and operating such a program.

2   We value sport in our society because it builds character and promotes teamwork, dedication and commitment. Sport requires honesty

and respect for the rules and fellow competitors. It leaves a legacy of health that can last a lifetime. Sport brings communities together, it creates role models for our kids and it inspires dreams. These are all reasons why sport occupies a special place in our schools and in our society at large. When athletes enhance their performance by doping, it is cheating of the worst kind and it undermines all of these important values of sport. When an athlete is successful through doping it sends a clear message to all athletes: the new price of achieving your dreams is compromising your integrity and risking your health. Athletes who perform outstanding physical feats through doping make sport nothing more than another circus act unworthy of any place in our schools or our social fabric.

3   All sports organizations, amateur or professional, must be truly committed to the same goal: the compete eradication of doping in sports. We owe it to the clean athletes competing today and the young athletes just beginning to chase their dreams to ensure that success in sports does not require the use of drugs.

4   I can tell you what it feels like to have your dream compromised by the drug use of another. In 1972 I won the gold medal for the United States in the marathon at the Olympics in Munich. Four years later, I ran an even better race but finished second at the Olympics in Montreal. I lost that race to an East German. At the time we all expected, and later it was confirmed, that in 1976 the East Germans were benefiting from a state sponsored doping program. I knew I could have improved my chance of winning by taking steroids, but I never even considered it. I chose to compete clean and as a result, I finished second.

5   In discussing anti-doping programs I hear the term "athlete's rights" used frequently. To me the greatest right an athlete has is the right to compete in clean sport on a level playing field. The question we all need to ask is: what is the best way to protect the rights of clean athletes and remove the long shadow that steroids and other drugs have cast over sport in the United States?

6   In the Olympic movement, both throughout the world and in the United States, the quest to eradicate doping has recently led to two significant shifts in the way anti-doping programs are operated. The first shift has been towards harmonization of anti-doping rules, including penalties, across all sports. The second significant change has been the effort to externalize anti-doping programs and shift the responsibility for testing and adjudicating away from the sports and instead place that responsibility with an independent and transparent agency.

7   At the world level, this paradigm shift resulted in the creation of the World Anti-Doping Agency (WADA), as the independent agency charged with the anti-doping responsibilities formally performed by the International Olympic Committee. The effort to harmonize anti-doping

rules across sport led to the creation of a uniform document the World Anti-Doping Code, which was based largely based on the USADA model. While it is not often that most of the world can come together and agree on something that is exactly what this uniform standard represents. All Olympic sports organizations throughout the world and most governments, including the United States government, have agreed to these principles and endorsed this model as the most effective framework for the fight against doping in sports.

8   Formerly, each international federation was responsible for creating its own anti-doping rules. The result was a wide variety of penalty and testing provisions that had little continuity across sports. Now that each sport has adopted the Olympic model, all athletes in the Olympic movement operate under the same rules and face the same consequences if they decide to cheat. Accordingly, all Olympic athletes, from the top track athletes and cyclists, who are full time professionals, to the best curlers, handball players, or sailors in the world, are all subject to the same anti-doping rules, procedures and penalties.

9   The Olympic standards effectively balance athletes' rights to a fair system, with the need for effective penalties designed to hold all athletes accountable for their decisions. First, the Olympic model is fair to athletes. For example, it ensures that athletes, who have a valid medical need for a substance that is otherwise prohibited, can obtain a therapeutic use exemption or "TUE" in advance of a competition. Accordingly, where an athlete can prove that he or she would experience a significant impairment to health if the medication is withheld, that there are no reasonable alternatives and that the medication will not produce an additional enhancement to the athlete's performance, an athlete will receive advance permission to continue taking that medication.

10   While athletes who are taking medication for a legitimate reason are protected, the standards greatly improve the chances of stopping an athlete who considers doping or who is doping and holds that athlete accountable through a fair adjudication system. Importantly, the Olympic model provides for both in-competition testing and out-of-competition, no advance notice testing. Comprehensive out-of-competition testing is fundamental to an effective anti-doping program because steroids are often taken well in advance of competition.

11   The Olympic standards also provide for substantial penalties for those athletes who do cheat. A first offense for taking a steroid results in a two-year suspension. A second violation results in a lifetime ban. Unfortunately, in today's society where the rewards of success in sport are great, the penalty for doping must be strong enough to be an effective deterrent.

12   Another important feature of the Olympic model is a standardized list of prohibited substances. An international committee of experts is

specifically tasked with reviewing and updating the list of prohibited substances. As we have all learned through the on-going BALCO investigation, those who are trying to cheat the system are constantly innovating in their effort to obtain an unfair advantage over their competitors. Accordingly the list of prohibited substances must be both broad in nature and constantly revised in order to be effective.

13   For all of these reasons, if a sports organization is truly committed to fighting doping in sports, I think the first step is to adopt testing and enforcement standards similar to that of the Olympic movement. I believe the second important action should be to place the responsibility for doping in the hands of an independent and transparent agency, as the United States Olympic Committee (USOC) did when it created USADA.

14   In the 1990s, the world did not view the United States as being committed to preventing doping among its Olympic athletes. The system of self-regulation by the various sports led to perceptions of conflict and allegations of attempts to hide doping behavior among United States' athletes. The USOC also recognized that the effectiveness of anti-doping efforts would be improved through centralization of resources and harmonization of regulations and procedures. Accordingly, USADA was formed in 2000. USADA has been recognized by Congress as the independent, national anti-doping agency for Olympic and Paralympic sport in the United States. USADA's mission is to protect and preserve the health of athletes, the integrity of competition and the well-being of sport through the elimination of doping.

15   I served as the Chairman of USADA from 2000 through 2003. During that period I was able to see first hand the benefits of externalizing the responsibility for drug-testing and adjudication. As an independent agency USADA has no conflict of interest. Its function is to protect the rights of clean athletes by conducting its testing and adjudication programs with integrity and transparency to stop those athletes who dope and then hold them accountable for their decision to use drugs for performance enhancement. While no system is perfect, it is clear that the creation of USADA has had a significant impact on the fight against doping among United States Olympic athletes. Now that USADA has been operating for nearly five years as an independent Agency, the United States is considered the world leader in its commitment and in its testing, education, and adjudication systems. There is now simply no doubt that in the Olympic movement the United States is doing everything within its power to eliminate doping by United States athletes.

16   There is still more that can be done in the Olympic movement. For example, USADA needs additional resources for research and testing to combat an ever-increasing sophistication among those committed to cheating. The battle against doping will also never be won without a continual and substantial commitment of resources towards educating

the next generation of athletes of the physical and moral consequences of doping.

17   My hope is that the increasing exposure the problem of doping in sports is receiving through the effort of this Committee and others will result in an increased commitment of resources to the fight against drugs in sport. I also hope that there will soon come a time, where every American sports organization, amateur or professional, will be in a position to say that it is doing everything within its power to eliminate doping in sports. Thank you. ■

DAVID HEMENWAY

Regulation of Firearms

David Hemenway, an economist, is professor of Health Policy at Harvard University. He directs the Harvard Injury Control Research Center and the Harvard Youth Violence Prevention Center—two leading sources of statistical information on violence and injuries in the United States. His books include Monitoring and Compliance: The Political Economy of Inspection *(1985),* Prices and Choices: Microeconomic Vignettes *(third edition, 1993), and* Private Guns, Public Health *(2004). The following argument appeared in the* New England Journal of Medicine, *one of the world's most prestigious medical journals and one that usually publishes experimental and clinical research studies. However, argumentative pieces that are related to public health are also regularly included there.*

1   In the United States, the rates of injury and death due to firearms and the rate of crimes committed with firearms are far higher than those in any other industrialized nation. Every hour, guns are used to kill four people and to commit 120 crimes in our country.

2   Perhaps the most appropriate international comparisons are among the United States and other developed "frontier" countries where English is spoken: Canada, Australia, and New Zealand. These four nations have similar cultures, and all have histories that include the violent displacement of indigenous populations. They also have similar rates of property crime and violence.[1,2] What distinguishes the United States is its high rate of lethal violence, most of which involves guns.

3   Gun-related deaths among children and adolescents are a particular problem in the United States. Among developed nations, three quarters of all murders of children under the age of 14 years occur in this country. More than half of children younger than 14 who commit suicide are Americans, even though the rate of suicide by methods other than firearms among children here is similar to that in other countries.[3]

MADD—Mothers against Drunk Driving—is one of the most respected non-profit organizations in the United States. For the past quarter century MADD has championed the rights of victims of drunk driving and has promoted public awareness of the consequences of drunk driving. The ad on this page was one of many that were displayed on the MADD Web site (www.madd.org) in the summer of 2005.

4   Canada, Australia, and New Zealand all have many guns (though not nearly as many handguns as does the United States). The key difference is that these countries do a much better job than we do of keeping guns out of the wrong hands. Their experience shows that when there are reasonable restrictions, relatively few outlaws can possess or use guns.

5   Success in the United States in reducing motor vehicle injuries—we now have one of the lowest rates of death per vehicle-mile in the world—provides insight into methods that could reduce firearm injuries. In the 1950s, efforts to reduce motor vehicle injuries focused on the driver. Commonly presented statistical data seemed to show that almost all automobile crashes were caused by error on the driver's part. The greatest attention was thus paid to education and enforcement: training motorists to drive better and punishing them for committing safety violations. Despite these well-intentioned efforts, further success in reducing motor vehicle injuries had to await a more comprehensive approach.

6   Eventually, injury-control experts recognized that to increase the safety of driving, it would be more cost effective to try to change the vehicle and the highway environment than to try to change human behavior. People will always make mistakes, and sometimes they will behave recklessly. But when they do, should they die? Should others?

7   Thus, numerous alterations were made both in cars and in roads to make collisions less likely (better brakes, a third brake light, and divided highways, for example) and to make serious injuries more avoidable if there was a collision (collapsible steering columns, nonrupturable gas tanks, breakaway road signs, more advanced emergency medical systems, and so on). No one believes that today's drivers are more careful than those of the 1950s, yet the number of motor vehicle fatalities per mile has been reduced by more than 75 percent.

8   Firearms, like motor vehicles, lawn mowers, and chain saws, are consumer products that cause injury. The safety of virtually every consumer product is regulated by federal or state government. The conspicuous exception is the gun, which, per minute of exposure, is probably the most dangerous of all such products. Unfortunately, because firearms have been deliberately exempted from the oversight of the Consumer Product Safety Commission, we are in the indefensible position of having stronger consumer-protection standards for toy guns—and teddy bears—than for real guns.

9   Stronger safety standards can help make firearms less dangerous. At a restaurant during a recent American Public Health Association convention in Indianapolis, a patron bent over and a derringer fell from his pocket. The gun hit the ground, discharged, and wounded two conven-

tion delegates. This person had a permit to carry the gun, and the firearm met all relevant safety standards—of which there are none.[4] Anecdotes such as this demonstrate why such standards are needed.

10   Survey results reported in this issue of the *Journal* by Teret et al.[5] provide evidence that the majority of Americans want to see guns treated and regulated as consumer products. In nationally representative polls, at least two thirds of all respondents were in favor of six policies that would enhance the safety of new guns. Examples of these policies are childproofing, personalization (which prevents firing by an unauthorized person), and indicators that show whether the gun is loaded. These measures may not substantially reduce gun-related crime, but they are inexpensive and could decrease the number of deaths and injuries that occur each day as a result of unintentional gunshots.

11   In one state, Massachusetts, the attorney general, who is the state officer responsible for protecting consumers' rights, recently issued regulations implementing several of these moderate safety standards for firearms sold in the state. Domestic gun manufacturers and firearm-sports organizations are challenging his authority to ensure, among other things, that firearms are childproof and meet the safety standards required of imported guns.[6] Both these measures are favored by more than 80 percent of gun owners and non-gun owners alike in the national sample polled by Teret et al.[5] We can expect that similar conflicts will develop in other states as new regulatory policies are invoked.

12   These recent polls also show very high public support, among both gun owners and non-gun owners, for innovative policies designed to keep guns out of the wrong hands.[5] One proposed type of law would prohibit the purchase of guns by persons who have been convicted of any one of various felonies, such as assault and battery. Another set of requirements would reduce illegal gun sales by, for example, state adoption of one-gun-per-month laws to decrease gun running across state lines.[7] Such moderate measures would limit the easy access to guns by those most likely to misuse them, while imposing only a slight inconvenience on "decent, law-abiding citizens." Previous surveys have shown that most Americans, most gun owners, and even most selfreported members of the National Rifle Association are in favor of many moderate measures that could reduce gun injuries.[8-10] Unfortunately, most of these measures have not been enacted.

13   The United States has more cars per capita than any other developed nation. Because of reasonable policies to regulate automobiles and roadways, we now have one of the lowest motor vehicle fatality rates. We are also a society with more guns per capita than any other developed nation. We can remain a nation with many guns yet control our gun-injury problem if we take reasonable steps to make firearms safer

and to keep them out of the wrong hands. Few individual gun policies, if enacted alone, would substantially reduce the firearm-injury problem. Similarly, few individual highway-safety initiatives of the past 40 years, by themselves, made a great difference in reducing highway deaths. Together, however, many small policies can have a large effect. It is now quite clear that the implementation of policies focused exclusively on education and enforcement (training in the handling of guns and punishment for criminal violations) is not the most effective way to reduce our firearm-injury problem substantially.

14   Much can be done to decrease the gun problem in the United States without changing the fundamental availability of firearms for most citizens. In the past decade, the public health community has been studying this issue and has suggested many reasonable, feasible policies. Through such policies we can begin to change social norms, as we have with cigarette smoking and motor vehicle injuries. In the case of firearms, the norm to be changed is the one that accepts lethal violence as a part of everyday American life.

References

1. Block R. A cross-national comparison of victims of crime: victim surveys of twelve countries. Int Rev Victimology 1993;2:183–207.

2. Zimring FE, Hawkins G. Crime is not the problem: lethal violence in America. New York: Oxford University Press, 1997.

3. Rates of homicide, suicide, and firearm-related death among children—26 industrialized countries. MMWR Morb Mortal Wkly Rep 1997;46(5):101–5.

4. Bijur P. A funny thing happened on the way to the meeting: on guns and triggers. Inj Prev 1998;4:77.

5. Teret SP, Webster DW, Vernick JS, et al. Support for new policies to regulate firearms—results of two national surveys. N Engl J Med 1998;339:813–8.

6. American Sports Shooting Council v Attorney General. Civil no. 98–0203 in the Suffolk Superior Court, Mass.

7. Weil DS, Knox RC. Effects of limiting handgun purchases on interstate transfer of firearms. JAMA 1996;275:1759–61.

8. Weil DS, Hemenway D. I am the NRA: an analysis of a national random sample of gun owners. Violence Victims 1993;8:377–85.

9. Blendon RJ, Young JT, Hemenway D. The American public and the gun control debate. JAMA 1996;275:1719–22.

10. Young JT, Hemenway D, Blendon RJ, Benson JM. The polls—trends: guns. Public Opin Q 1996;60:634–49. ∎

KEITH BRADSHER

High and Mighty

Keith Bradsher is the former Detroit bureau chief for The New York Times, *so he knows about car culture. In 1997 he won the George Polk Award for his coverage of SUVs and small trucks. The selection below comes from his 2002 book* High and Mighty: SUVs—The World's Most Dangerous Vehicles and How They Got that Way. *His book won the New York Public Library Helen Bernstein Book Award for Excellence in Journalism. Bradsher is now the Hong Kong bureau chief for* The New York Times.

1   Automakers employ thousands of people to figure out which models will be popular next with American buyers, and thousands more to figure out how to promote their latest models. A French medical anthropologist by training, Clotaire Rapaille seems an unlikely person to have reshaped American automotive market research and marketing.

2   Tall and muscular at 60, with sandy blonde hair, Rapaille speaks with a strong French accent, having only moved to the United States at the age of 38. His background makes him an oddity in an industry dominated by the flat Midwestern accents of men (seldom women) who grew up in Midwestern cities like Cleveland, Toledo or Flint. Yet his psychological analysis of how sport utility vehicles appeal to people's most primitive instincts has helped to legitimize the cynical marketing of SUVs.

3   During the 1990s, Rapaille worked on more than 20 projects with David Bostwick, Chrysler's market research director; Francois Castaing, Chrysler's chief of vehicle engineering; and Bob Lutz. Castaing says that he and Lutz believed in gut instinct more than market research in designing new models, and that they showed prototypes to Rapaille only after the initial design work, so as to double-check that their instincts were right. But providing the reality check on possible future models is a considerable responsibility. Because Chrysler was the unquestioned design and marketing leader in Detroit during this period, Rapaille's work also influenced other automakers, with Ford and GM eventually retaining him for projects as well.

4   Clotaire Rapaille was born in Paris on August 10, 1941, less than two months after Hitler's troops occupied the city. His father was an army officer who had just been captured by the Germans and would spend the entire war in a forced labor camp; he would emerge from the camp a broken man. His mother, fearful of the dangers of occupied Paris, sent her baby son out of the city to be raised by his grandmother

in Vallée de Chevreuse, a small town halfway between Paris and the
Normandy coastline.

5   Rapaille's earliest memory is of playing outdoors under his grandmother's watchful eye when he was three, and unexpectedly seeing
some German soldiers running away. "I said, 'How come the Germans
are running away, the Germans never run away,' and then I saw a monster coming out of the forest, an American tank," he recalls. "A big
American with a net on his helmet and flowers took me on the tank and
gave me chocolates and gave me a ride."

6   That experience made an indelible impression. It convinced him
at that early age that he wanted to become an American, because the
French were losers in war while the Germans had been mean to everyone during the occupation.

7   Rapaille's parents and grandparents were nearly wiped out financially by the war. Rapaille put himself through college and graduate
school in Paris by driving a beer delivery truck at night, then began
consulting for Renault and Citroën, two big French automakers, in the
early 1970s.

8   As he studied and then applied principles of psychological research, Rapaille became convinced that a person's first encounter with
an object or idea shaped his or her emotional relationship with it for
life. He would apply that conviction after moving in 1979 to America,
where he became a prominent market researcher who specialized in
psychoanalytic techniques.

9   Relying on the work of Carl Jung, the Swiss psychologist who
founded analytic psychology, Rapaille divides people's reactions to a
commercial product into three levels of brain activity. There is the cor-
tex, for intellectual assessments of a product. There is the limbic, for
emotional responses. And there is the reptilian, which he defines as reactions based on "survival and reproduction."

10   Rapaille focuses his attention on the deepest, most reptilian instincts that people have about consumer products. He seeks to identify
people's archetype of a product, the deepest emotional identity that the
product holds for them based on their earliest encounter with it. His research has led him to some disturbing conclusions about how to sell
sport utility vehicles, which he sees as the most reptilian vehicles of all
because their imposing, even menacing appearance appeals to people's
deep-seated desires for "survival and reproduction."

11   With the detachment of a foreigner, Rapaille sees Americans as increasingly fearful of crime. He acknowledges that this fear is irrational
and completely ignores statistics showing that crime rates have declined
considerably. He attributes the pervasive fear of crime mainly to violent
television shows, violent video games and lurid discussions and images
on the Internet, which make young and middle-aged Americans more

focused on threats to their physical safety than they need to be. At the same time, he argues, the aging of the population means that there are more older Americans, who may pay less attention to violence in the media but are more cautious than young people about personal safety in general.

12   The fear is most intense among today's teenagers, Rapaille has found, attributing the trend to the addition of video games and increasingly menacing toy action figures on top of the steady diet of murders on television that baby boomers had. "There is so much emphasis on violence—the war is every day, everywhere," he said in an interview two weeks before the terrorist attacks of September 11, 2001. The response of teens, he added, is that "They want to give the message, 'I want to be able to destroy, I want to be able to fight back, don't mess with me.'" While teens do not buy many SUVs, youth culture nonetheless tends to shape the attitudes of broad segments of American society.

13   For Rapaille, the archetype of a sport utility vehicle reflects the reptilian desire for survival. People buy SUVs, he tells auto executives, because they are trying to look as menacing as possible to allay their fears of crime and other violence. The Jeep has always had this image around the world because of its heavy use in war movies and frequent appearances in newsreels from the 1940s and 1950s, and newer SUVs share the image. "I usually say, 'If you put a machine gun on the top of them, you will sell them better,'" he said. "Even going to the supermarket, you have to be ready to fight."

14   To reach such conclusions, Rapaille has run dozens of consumer focus groups, or "discoveries," as he prefers to call them. First, he asks a group of 30 people to sit in a windowless room and take turns speaking for an hour about their rational, reasoned responses to a vehicle. "They tell me things I don't really care about, and I don't listen," he said.

15   Then he tells the group to spend another hour pretending to be five-year-old boys from another planet. He asks them to tell him little stories about the vehicle, to get at their emotional responses to the vehicle. But he later discards the notes on these stories as well.

16   What really interests him is the third stage of research. He asks the consumers to lie down on mats and he turns the lights way down in the room. Then he asks each consumer lying in the near darkness to tell him about his or her earliest associations with vehicles, in an attempt to get at their "reptilian" responses to various designs.

17   The answers in these consumer groups have persuaded Rapaille that American culture is becoming frighteningly atavistic and obsessed with crime. He cites as further proof the spread of gated communities and office buildings protected by private security guards, together with the tiny but growing market in the United States for luxury vehicles with bulletproof armor. "I think we're going back to medieval times,

and you can see that in that we live in ghettos with gates and private armies," he said. "SUVs are exactly that, they are armored cars for the battlefield."

18   Even Rapaille says that a few of his ideas are too extreme to be practical. SUV buyers want to be able to take on street gangs with their vehicles and run them down, he said, while hastening that television commercials showing this would be inappropriate. He has unsuccessfully tried to persuade ad agency executives working for Chrysler to buy the television commercial rights to *Mad Max,* the 1979 film that launched Mel Gibson's career. The film shows heavily armed thugs in leather on motorcycles, driving around a post-Apocalyptic Australia and killing people so as to steal their gasoline. Rapaille wanted Chrysler to use computers to insert its SUVs into scenes from the movie, with the vehicle rescuing the hero or heroine from the clutches of one of the movie's nefarious villains in hockey masks. But the idea was dismissed as too controversial. And when I checked with someone in Hollywood, I learned that the rights to *Mad Max* are caught in a legal tangle that would make it nearly impossible to use the film for a commercial.

19   Yet the idea of being civil on the roads has disappeared and SUV design needs to reflect this, Rapaille says. "This is over, people don't care, and for some people, the message is it's *Mad Max* out there, it's a jungle out there and you're not going to kill me, if you attack me I will fight."

20   As a milder alternative, Rapaille admires SUV television ads like the one that showed a Jeep climbing home over a pile of rocks at the bottom of a house's driveway. "Your house has become a castle," he said.

21   When Rapaille came to work for Chrysler, one of his first projects was to define what consumers really saw in the company's Jeeps. His cynical, even brutal view of the world fit perfectly with the "gut" of Bob Lutz, who oversaw Chrysler's light-truck operations in the United States upon his arrival from Ford in 1986. Lutz's corporate empire had grown a lot bigger in 1987, when Chrysler bought American Motors, including its profitable Jeep brand.

22   Lutz insisted on ever more powerful engines mounted in ever taller SUVs and pickup trucks with ever more menacing-looking front ends—an approach enthusiastically recommended by Rapaille. Lutz's instructions were consistent, said David C. McKinnon, Chrysler's director of vehicle exterior design: "Get them up in the air and make them husky." Lutz gave this advice even for two-wheel-drive versions of SUVs that were unlikely ever to go off-road and therefore did not need a lot of height and ground clearance, McKinnon said. Because Chrysler was Detroit's design leader during this period, and Lutz the most influential car

guy in town, Lutz's decisions shaped the way SUVs were designed around the world.

23   The Jeep Grand Cherokee's debut at the Detroit auto show in 1992 was a vintage Lutz moment. With a large crowd of journalists gathered, he drove a Grand Cherokee up the steps of Detroit's convention center and smashed through a plate-glass window to enter the building. A special window had been installed in advance to make this a little less dangerous than it sounds. The television footage was nonetheless great, and established the Grand Cherokee's credentials as a rough-and-tough vehicle.

24   The Dodge Ram full-sized pickup truck came out two years later with a front end that was designed to look as big and menacing as a Mack truck: *USA Today* described it admiringly as the kind of vehicle that would make other motorists want to get out of your way.

25   In his book, *Guts,* Lutz wrote that the Ram's in-your-face styling was carefully chosen even though consumer focus groups showed that most Americans would loathe it. "A whopping 80 percent of the respondents disliked the bold new drop-fendered design. A lot even hated it!" he wrote. However, he explained, "the remaining 20 percent of the clinic participants were saying that they were truly, madly, deeply in love with the design! And since the old Ram had only about 4 percent of the market at the time, we figured, what the hell, even if only half of those positive respondents actually buy, we'll more than double our share! The result? Our share of the pickup market shot up to 20 percent on the radical new design, and Ford and Chevy owners gawked in envy!"

26   Ford and GM did not take the loss of sales lightly. They responded by making the Ford F-series pickups and the Chevrolet Silverado and GMC Sierra pickups more menacing, too. The Ford and GM pickups were then modified to make seven full-sized SUVs: the Ford Excursion, Ford Expedition, Lincoln Navigator, Chevrolet Tahoe, GMC Yukon, Chevrolet Suburban and GMC Yukon XL. Since all of these SUVs shared a lot of the same front-end parts with the pickup trucks on which they were based, the shift led by Dodge Ram toward more menacing front ends caused the entire full-sized SUV market to become more menacing. Close to 90 percent of the parts for a Ford Excursion are the same as for the Ford Super Duty pickup on which it is based, according to Ford. By turning the Ram into a brute, Lutz indirectly fed the highway arms race among SUVs.

27   When it comes to specific vehicles, the Dodge Durango comes closest to fitting Rapaille's Hobbesian view of life as being nasty, brutish and short. The Durango's front end is intended to resemble the face of a savage jungle cat, said Rapaille. The vertical bars across the grille

represent teeth, and the vehicle has bulging fenders over the wheels that look like clenched muscles in a savage jaw.

28   "A strong animal has a big jaw, that's why we put big fenders," Rapaille says.

29   Minivans, by contrast, evoke feelings of being in the womb, and of caring for others, he says. Stand a minivan on its rear bumper and it has the silhouette of a pregnant woman in a floor-length dress. Not surprisingly, minivans are being crowded out of the market by SUVs. Rapaille even dislikes SUVs like the Mercedes M-Class that look a little like minivans.

30   Convertibles are suffering in the marketplace because women worry that they might be assaulted by an intruder who climbs inside, Rapaille contends. "Women were telling me, if you drive a convertible with the top down, the message is 'Rape me.'"

31   The reptilian instinct for survival does not just involve crime fears. Rapaille says. It also shows up in the extent to which people are willing to put other drivers at risk in order to diminish the odds that they will be injured themselves in a crash. In other words, people in touch with their inner reptile are most likely to choose vehicles that look especially likely to demolish other people's cars in collisions.

32   "My theory is the reptilian always wins," he said. "The reptilian says, 'If there's a crash, I want the other guy to die.' Of course, I can't say that aloud."

33   But SUVs cannot just look macho and menacing on the outside, Rapaille believes. Inside, they must be as gentle, feminine and luxurious as possible. Rapaille's argument for this is based on the reptilian instinct for reproduction.

34   "Men are for outside and women are for inside, that's just life; to reproduce men have to take something outside and the women take something inside," Rapaille said. "The inside of an SUV should be the Ritz-Carlton, with a minibar. I'm going to be on the battlefield a long time, so on the outside I want to be menacing but inside I want to be warm, with food and hot coffee and communications."

35   Listen to other auto-market researchers try to define an SUV and you often hear an almost literal echo of Rapaille's advice. "It's aggressive on the outside and it's the Ritz-Carlton on the inside, that's part of the formula," Chrysler's Bostwick said.

36   Rapaille's emphasis on reptilian instincts reflects not only his early encounter with the tank, he says, but also his subsequent, difficult upbringing. Rapaille says that his father never recovered from the psychological damage of his imprisonment, and his parents were divorced after the war. He was then sent off to a Jesuit school in Laval, France, and grew up there. "I had to stay there all year long because no one wanted to take care of me from my family, but I was alive, the reptilian was survival," he says.

37   Rapaille has loved automobiles since boyhood. But while he can now afford to buy an SUV, he doesn't own one. Instead, he owns a Rolls Royce and a Porsche 911. Sport utilities are too tall, he says, and he has a terror of rolling over. He likes the Rolls Royce but loves the Porsche, because it allows him to retain control of his destiny with its nimbleness, excellent brakes and tremendous stability. Compared to an SUV, he says, "A Porsche is safer." He may have emigrated to America, but in this respect he remains a European.

38   Rapaille's work helped automakers begin to understand who buys SUVs and why. But their research has gone far beyond archetypes. Lavishing huge sums, the auto industry has developed year by year an ever more detailed knowledge of what SUV buyers want, and then tapped into these desires with multibillion dollar advertising campaigns that are slick but extremely cynical. ■

TERRENCE RAFFERTY

Kate Winslet, Please Save Us!

Brooklyn native Terrence Rafferty has a special interest in film, and his articles have appeared in The Atlantic, The Village Voice, Film Quarterly, The New York Times, *and many other places. Since 1997 he has been the "critic-at-large" for* GQ *(short for* Gentleman's Quarterly*), a fashion-and-culture magazine geared to young professional men that carried the following argument in May 2001. Do you think the argument would have been constructed differently if it had been published elsewhere?*

1   When I go to the movies these days, I sometimes find myself gripped by a very peculiar sort of nostalgia: I miss flesh. I see skin, I see bones, I see many rocklike outcroppings of muscle, but I rarely see, in the angular bodies up there on the screen—either the hard, sculpted ones or the brittle, anorexic ones—anything *extra,* not even a hint of the soft layer of fatty tissue that was once an essential component of the movies' romantic fantasy, the cushion that made encounters between the sexes seem like pleasant, sensual experiences rather than teeth-rattling head-on collisions. The sleek form-follows-function physiques of today's film stars suggest a world in which power and brutal efficiency are all that matter, in the bedroom no less than in the pitiless, sunseared arena of *Gladiator.* This may well be an accurate reflection of our anxious time, but it's also mighty depressing. When I come out of the multiplex now, I

often feel like the archetypal ninety-eight-pound weakling in the old Charles Atlas ads—like big bullies have been kicking sand in my face for two hours. And that's just the women.

2   This is a touchy area, I realize. Where body type is concerned, an amazingly high percentage of social and cultural commentary is fueled by simple envy, resentment of the young and the buff. A few years ago, when Calvin Klein ads featuring the stunning, waiflike Kate Moss appeared on the sides of New York City buses, they were routinely defaced with bitter-sounding graffiti—FEED ME was the most popular—which was, you had to suspect, largely the product of women who were enraged by her distinctive beauty. (Men, to my knowledge, had few complaints about having to see Moss in her underwear whiz past them on Madison Avenue.) Protesters insisted

Kate Moss, waiflike.

that images such as those in the Klein ads promote eating disorders in impressionable teenage girls. Maybe that's so—I don't have the statistics—but the sheer violence of the attacks on Moss, along with the fact that they seemed to be directed more at the model herself than at the marketing wizards who exploited her, strongly suggested another, less virtuous agenda. The taste of sour grapes was unmistakable.

3   I happened to think Moss looked great—small, but well-proportioned, and mercifully lacking the ropy musculature that had begun to creep into pop-culture images of femininity, in the cunning guise of "empowerment." The Bionic Woman could only dream of the bulging biceps sported by Linda Hamilton in *Terminator 2: Judgment Day* (1991); and Ginger Rogers, even when she was struggling to match steps with Astaire, never had the calf muscles of the mighty Madonna. (Nor would she have wanted them: She was a dancer and not, like Mrs. Ritchie or any of her brood of MTV chicks, a kinky aerobics instructor.) It's understandable, I suppose, that women might have felt the impulse to bulk up during the might-makes-right regimes of Ronald Reagan and George Herbert Walker Bush, when the rippling behemoths of machismo, Arnold and Sly, ruled the screen; in that context, working on one's abs and pecs could be considered a prudent strategy of self-defense. But the arms buildup in the Cold War between the sexes was not a pretty sight. Applied to sex, the doctrine of Mutually Assured Destruction is kind of a bummer. The wages of sinew is the death of romance.

4   At least that's how it looks to people of my generation, whose formative years were the '60s, and to many of Moss's generation (the one commonly designated "X"), who in their youth embraced, for a while, the antipower aesthetic of grunge. What we oversaturated pop-culture consumers consider attractive—i.e., what's sexy in the opposite gender and worth aspiring to in one's own—usually develops in adolescence, as the relevant body parts do, and doesn't change much thereafter. For men older than I am, the perfect woman might have been Sophia Loren or Elizabeth Taylor or Marilyn Monroe or Rita Hayworth or the wartime pinup Betty Grable or (reaching back to the hugely eroticized flapper era) the original It girl, Clara Bow. And for them, the image of the ideal masculine self might have been Cary Grant or Clark Gable or Henry Fonda or Gary Cooper or even, for the less physically prepossessing— OK, shorter—guys, Cagney or Bogart or Tracy. By the time the '60s rocked and rolled into history, some subtle transformations had occurred, primarily in female sexual iconography. While the male stars of that decade remained more or less within the range of body types of their predecessors—Steve McQueen and Sean Connery might have looked a bit more athletic than the old norms demanded, but they wouldn't qualify as hard-bodies by today's standards—the shape of desirability in women distinctly altered, to something less voluptuous and more elongated. The fashions of the era tended to shift the erotic focus southward, from the breasts and the hips down to the legs, which, in a miniskirt, did rather overwhelm all other possible indicators of a woman's sexual allure. Although smaller-chested, leaner-hipped women, such as Julie Christie, stole some thunder from the conspicuously curvaceous, a certain amount of flesh was still required. Minis didn't flatter skinny legs any more than they did chubby ones.

5   So there was, to the avid eyes of teenage boys like me, a fine balance struck in the body aesthetic of the '60s, between, so to speak, length and width, Giacometti and Rubens. And muscles weren't part of the equation. He-men such as Steve Reeves—whose 1959 *Hercules,* a cheap Italian import initiated a spate of "sword and sandal" epics— seemed, to both sexes, ridiculous, vain rather than truly manly. (It's worth noting that in those days it was widely perceived that the primary market for body-building magazines was gay men.) And women? Forget it. The epitome of the muscular gal was the Russian or East German Olympic athlete, an Olga or a Helga, whose gender identity was frequently, and often justly, a matter of some dispute. There's an echo of that attitude in Ridley Scott's 1997 *G.I. Jane,* in which a feminist senator played by Anne Bancroft, trying to select a candidate for the first woman to undergo Navy SEAL training, summarily dismisses several of the beefier applicants on the grounds of ambiguous sexuality. She settles on Demi Moore, who is slender and pretty and, on the evidence of a spectacularly obvious boob job, unquestionably straight.

6   But bodies like Moore's puzzle me. What, exactly, is the empowering element here—the iron she's pumped or the silicone that's been pumped into her chest? My number one teenage crush, Diana Rigg, didn't need either in order to be wholly convincing as kick-ass secret agent Emma Peel in the TV series *The Avengers.* Paired with a dapper male partner, John Steed (played by Patrick Macnee), Mrs. Peel was not only fully empowered but was also by far the more physically active of the two. In her mod pantsuits and go-go boots, she did most of the actual fighting in the kung fu-ish battles that climaxed virtually every episode, while Steed, perhaps mindful of potential damage to his impeccably cut Pierre Cardin suits, generally limited his martial activity to an occasional deft thrust with the umbrella.

7   Maybe if I'd come of age with visions of Madonna dancing in my head, I might find GI Demi devastatingly sexy rather than grotesque, but, objectively, I think the idea that women's power depends on either sculpted muscles or gigantic, orblike breasts (much less both) smacks of desperation. Mrs. Peel wielded her power so coolly, so confidently, and clearly never felt the need to enhance it by strenuous training or expensive medical procedures. Comfort in one's own skin is always appealing, which is probably why, in this sweating, striving, aggressively self-improving era, I find bodies as diverse as Kate Moss's and Kate Winslet's mighty attractive. It's not the body type per se— neither the frail Kate nor the ampler one precisely conforms to my Riggian ideal— but a woman's attitude toward her body that makes her sexy.

8   What's unnerving about today's popculture images of women is how extreme they are—and how much emphasis they place on the *effort* required to correct nature, to retard the aging process, to be all that you can be (and not, God forbid, simply what you are). The ethic of progress through hard work and technology is deeply ingrained in our society, as is the democratic notion that everyone should be whatever he or she wants to be—a noble idea that gets a tad problematic when what everyone wants to be is a star. And every star wants to be a bigger star. As a result, we're seeing, in the movies and on television and in the pages of fashion magazines, increasingly bizarre manifestations of our paradoxical

Kate Winslet from *Titanic* days.

collective need to feel unique and, more, admired. Being really fat, for example, can confer on a person a certain distinction, but not the kind most of us yearn for. (In the old days, for men, a degree of heft often indicated prosperity; the movies embodied their image of financial success in portly figures such as Eugene Pallette and Edward Arnold. No more.) To stand out on the runway these days, a model has to be significantly gaunter—and younger—than even the FEED ME—era Moss. And to make her mark on the screen, an actress has several equally grueling options: starve herself skeletal, go to the gym and get muscular, or—sometimes in perverse combination with one of the previous—have her breasts inflated surgically. In each case, the result is a wild exaggeration of what would be, in moderation, a desirable quality: slimness, fitness or voluptuousness. When I look at women in the movies now, I often feel as if I were gazing not at real people but at cartoon characters—Olive Oyl, Popeye (in drag) and Jessica Rabbit.

9   Of course, there are exceptions: the spectacular Winslet; the cherubic and blissfully unself-conscious Drew Barrymore; the graceful, athletic Asian stars Michelle Yeoh and Maggie Cheung; and (no epithet necessary) Julia Roberts. But too many of the screen's great beauties have been developing a lean and hungry look in recent years. They've felt the burn, and something more than body fat appears to have been eliminated—a certain amount of joy seems to have melted away at the same time. Clearly, we live in extraordinarily ruthless and competitive times; and popular culture is bound to reflect that condition, but I can't think of another age in which the competitive anxieties of the performers themselves were so mercilessly exposed to the public's view. When tough, chunky guys like Cagney squared off against one another in a boxing ring or on the mean streets of New York or Chicago, you sensed that the survival of an entire community of immigrants was at stake; you could see it in every movement of their squat brawler's bodies. And when the Depression was over, those fierce small men just about vanished from the movies, giving way to their larger, better-nourished children, who left the field, in turn, to generations who would be conscious of their bodies without having nearly as much use for them as their ancestors had had. What's at stake for today's action heroes and heroines, all pumped up with no place to go except to the "explosive" climax of a fanciful plot? The steroidal action pictures of the '80s and '90s created a race of pointless Supermen. Everyone in the audience was in on the joke: Bruce Willis and Tom Cruise and Nicolas Cage and Keanu Reeves didn't bulk up to save the world or any recognizable part of it; they did it because starring in an action franchise was, and remains, a surefire means of moving up the Hollywood ladder.

10   As the historian Lynne Luciano points out in her useful new book, *Looking Good: Male Body Image in America,* in a white-collar, service

economy all most of us do with our bodies is compare them with everybody else's. We look, we admire, we envy, we check the mirror, we get dissatisfied, we go back to the old drawing board (the gym, the plastic surgeon, Jenny Craig, whatever). And this strikes many as perfectly reasonable and natural: You have to keep an edge, and you have to *work* on it. Constant vigilance is required for both men and women, and folks are starting to look a little haggard. This applies even to the beautiful people of the silver screen. We can see the strain as they try to hang on to their precarious positions, like Tom Cruise at the beginning of *M.I.2*. And who, aside from the stars themselves, their families and their agents, could possibly care?

11   I haven't used the word *narcissism* yet, and it's long overdue. The unseemly vanity once ascribed to poor Steve Reeves has become the norm in Hollywood, which, kind of hilariously, apparently believes that we're so vain we probably think their movies are about us. I can't come up with another explanation for berserk pictures like David Fincher's *Fight Club* (1999), in which Edward Norton, as a harried white collar Everyman, takes as his guru and alter ego an alarmingly buff *Übermensch* played by Brad Pitt. If the weak box-office returns are any indication, *Fight Club* did not strike the deep chord in the hearts of American men that its makers evidently thought it would, and, to add insult to injury, the picture didn't even provoke the "controversy" that might have validated the artists' sense of their own fearlessness and edginess. The whole spectacle was simply self-important and silly—as silly as *Hercules* and, because no one involved seemed to recognize it, then some.

12   It's time to stop the madness. Sure, we viewers are stressed-out and perhaps slightly self-absorbed, but more of us than Hollywood thinks have some perspective on the absurdities of our lives and the inanities of our culture. Fewer of us than the studios imagine actually believe that a diet or a set of weights or silicone implants will change our lives, even if every movie star worth his or her (pardon the expression) salt apparently does believe it. That's their business, and, as we know—though Hollywood has obviously forgotten—there's *no* business like show business. The feral, predatory creatures prowling across the screen for our amusement are in a world of their own. And although they carry themselves as if they were wolves, magnificent in their power, they're really just coyotes, roaming the hills restlessly for scraps and deluding themselves even more doggedly than Chuck Jones's indefatigable Wile E. At least he knew what he was.

13   In a sense, body image represents the final frontier of postmodernism, the only area as yet untouched by our culture's pervasive irony. It would be useful, I think, for moviemakers to drop the pretense that entertainment is a life-and-death struggle, which only the strong survive. The stars of earlier eras, with their variety of unapologetically eccentric physiques, understood it was all a lovely con, a game played for pleasure:

That's what those discreet little layers of flesh ultimately meant. But what would it take, I wonder, to make today's hardbodies lighten up and laugh at their own desperate exertions or, failing that, merely stop gazing out at us cowed viewers as if they were dying to beat the crap out of us? I don't know, but I suspect that cranky magazine columns won't do the job. A higher power will have to be invoked. Mrs. Peel, you're needed. ■

SUSAN LLEWELYN LEACH

Those Extra Pounds—Are They Government's Business?

Susan Llewelyn Leach often writes about privacy issues and regulation concerns, including articles on identification cards, photograph usage and control, and food regulation. Obesity and food are the concern of her article below, which appeared in the April 28, 2004, edition of the Christian Science Monitor, *which employs Leach as a staff writer. The* Monitor *is a church-founded newspaper, but it has an international scope and readership; for good reason it claims to have maintained a valuable independence since its founding in 1908.*

1 As America's waistline expands and the anti-obesity movement gains momentum, what you eat may soon slip out of the private domain and into the public. Nobody will be regimenting your diet, but the government may start offering more pointed advice and regulating what goes into preprepared foods, among other things. Proposals include a tax on high-fat, low-nutrition food; better school meals; and nutrition labels on restaurant menus.

2 Having the government in your kitchen wouldn't be the first time private habits have come under outside scrutiny. Tobacco, alcohol, and drugs have all gone that route at various points in U.S. history. But where did personal responsibility fall off the bandwagon?

3 The shift of private behavior to public oversight, with new legislation to enforce it, happens in a quantifiable way, says Rogan Kersh, political scientist at Syracuse University's Maxwell School, who is writing a book on the politics of obesity.

4 The first and most significant of several triggers, he explains, is social disapproval. For instance, "it used to be sexy and desirable to smoke. . . . [Now] you're committing some grave moral wrong."

5 As disapproval gains momentum, he says, "public health crusades start to build around these behaviors": Sometimes the science is accurate (the medical establishment is unanimous on the evils of smoking); sometimes the science is a mixed bag (some studies suggest that alcohol

isn't as dangerous as the Prohibitionists claimed); and sometimes the science is completely spurious (Victorian physicians warned that too much sex would maim, blind, or kill).

6   Despite almost two thirds of Americans being overweight, the U.S. is paradoxically one of the most antifat biased countries in the world. And that bias has only intensified in recent decades. Only a couple of brief periods in the 20th century showed a return to the acceptance of corpulence, Professor Kersh says, and both were after the world wars when Americans had undergone deprivation.

7   With social disapproval already widespread, medical science is reinforcing that view. Numerous studies and articles, some more alarmist that others, point to the health consequences of being heavy.

8   The message is no longer that being overweight is not good for you. It's now, "you're killing yourself through your obesity and the government must help you" to change, Kersh says.

9   That sort of shift in reasoning, reframing the problem in terms of a toxic food environment rather than weak will and failing personal responsibility, is key to the government stepping in. The individual is no longer blamed for not pushing back from the table. It's now a social problem.

10   What has helped accelerate that redefinition is the medical bill for dealing with weight-related illnesses, which reached $117 billion last year, according to the U.S. surgeon general, and may soon surpass the toll on healthcare taken by smoking. "When something becomes an economic problem in this country, government tends to act in a more urgent way than if it's a different kind of problem like constitutional rights."

11   "The point is, even though I'm not obese I'm paying for people who are. This really burns Americans and they want their policymakers to act in response," Kersh says. Already, more than 140 anti-obesity laws have been introduced in state legislatures this year.

12   But Sandle Sabo-Russo disputes the health-bill figure. "If a person is large-sized and goes to the doctor for something that has nothing to do with their size, it's often trumped up to be obesity related," says Ms. Sabo-Russo, a member of the board of NAAFA, the National Association to Advance Fat Acceptance and the largest obesity-rights organization in the U.S. "I don't trust what we're getting on that information."

13   She also points out the complexity of the issue. Being obese, or overweight, she says, is not always about food, "There are as many reasons as to how or why people are fat as there are fat people."

14   As for studies on obesity and its consequences, she questions their accuracy because many come from sources with a vested interest. "The first thing we try to look at when a new study comes out is who funded it. If it's funded by Weight Watchers International [for example], I'm not sure I'm going to believe what it says."

15   As societal pressure builds, and government reluctantly eyes new legislation, the courts are already grappling with obesity issues. More and more class-action lawsuits are taking aim at the food industry. And of the 10 major cases filed so far, mostly consumer protection suits, five have had some success. McDonald's, for example, had to fork over $12 million for not disclosing that its fries were cooked in beef fat. Pirates Booty paid $4 million over a cheese snack that misstated the amount of fat it contained.

16   Even though no personal-injury suits have yet won in court, a case brought against McDonald's elicited an unusual response from the judge. A man who sued the fast-food chain when he gained large amounts of weight lost his case twice. But the judge spelled out what the plaintiff could have done to make the case stronger and suggested ways obesity cases could be argued.

17   "With judges doing that, trial lawyers are catching on and it's only a matter of time before they strike," says Kersh. The class-action suit. Kersh adds, has its roots in social movements that once took to the streets to demand change. Now large numbers of people can gather together through the courts.

18   Another historical pattern Kersh has identified in this gradual shift away from personal responsibility is the self-help movement. Twelve-step programs which usually spring up in response to medical warnings—Alcoholics Anonymous, Nicotine Anonymous, Overeaters Anonymous and so on—encourage Americans to live healthier lives. When that encouragement doesn't bear fruit fast enough, the users (in this case, the fat) tend to get "demonized" and so do the producers—the food and restaurant industries, who throw temptation the public's way.

19   The government has responded to public concern by telling people to exercise more and eat less—noncontroversial advice, as critics have noted, which won't rock the boat with the food lobby.

20   With the demonization of big tobacco fresh in memory, however, McDonald's and others are trying to minimize their liability by cutting portion sizes, ending supersizing, eliminating school marketing, and offering more salads. The fast-food industry is still big on individual choice, and even NAAFA's Sabo-Russo doesn't want the government legislating menus.

21   The danger of this growing push to trim the fat, Kersh says, is that it takes such a head of steam to change laws that the momentum often carries action beyond what's necessary. He cites Prohibition's 15-year fiasco and the zero-tolerance drug sentencing of the 1980s that is now being rolled back.

22   "Demonization makes very powerful politics, but it makes miserable public policy. You get these all out prohibitions, zero-tolerance policies which in practice are unrealistic and quite unjust," he says. ■

According to the US government, Arnold Schwarzenegger, Tom Cruise, and Sammy Sosa are all obese! Trial lawyers and activists are using these flawed standards to sue food companies and call for higher food taxes!

See how your weight measures up to these famous figures at

ConsumerFreedom.com

Help the nonprofit Center for Consumer Freedom fight trial lawyers and the food police by donating online.

It's no joke.
He claims the food was too cheap so he ate too much!

Learn more about the erosion of personal responsibility and common sense. Go to:

ConsumerFreedom.com

The two visual arguments on this page, produced by an organization called Consumer Freedom, ridicule the idea that American Corporations might be responsible for obesity. ■

Ynestra King

The Other Body:
Disability and Identity Politics

Ynestra King (born 1957) is a social activist who lives, works, teaches, and writes in New York City. She published the following argument in Ms. *magazine in the spring of 1993.*

1   Disabled people rarely appear in popular culture. When they do, their disability must be a continuous preoccupation overshadowing all other areas of their character. Disabled people are disabled. That is what they "do." That is what they "are."

2   My own experience with a mobility impairment that is only minority disfiguring is that one must either be a creature of the disability, or have transcended it entirely. For me, like most disabled people (and this of course depends on relative severity), neither extreme is true. It is an organic, literally embodied fact that will not change—like being a woman. While it may be possible to "do gender," one does not "do disability." But there is an organic base to both conditions that extends far into culture, and the meaning that "nature" has. Unlike being a woman, being disabled is not a socially constructed condition. It is a tragedy of nature, of a kind that will always exist. The very condition of disability provides a vantage point of a certain lived experience in the body, a lifetime of opportunity for the observation of reaction to bodily deviance, a testing ground for reactions to persons who are readily perceived as having something wrong or being different. It is fascinating, maddening, and disorienting. It defies categories of "sickness" and "health," "broken" and "whole." It is in between.

3   Meeting people has an overlay: I know what they notice first is that I am different. And there is the experience of the difference in another person's reaction who meets me sitting down (when the disability is not apparent), and standing up and walking (when the infirmity is obvious). It is especially noticeable when another individual is flirting and flattering, and has an abrupt change in affect when I stand up. I always make sure that I walk around in front of someone before I accept a date, just to save face for both of us. Once the other person perceives the disability, the switch on the sexual circuit breaker often pops off—the connection is broken. "Chemistry" is over. I have a lifetime of such experiences, and so does every other disabled woman I know.

4   White middle-class people—especially white men—in the so-called First World have the most negative reactions. And I always recognize studied politeness, the attempt to pretend that there's nothing to notice (this is the liberal response—Oh, you're black? I hadn't noticed). Then there's the do-gooder response, where the person falls all over her/himself, insisting on doing everything for you; later they hate you; it's a form of objectification. It conveys to you that that is all they see, rather like a man who can't quit talking with a woman about sex.

5   In the era of identity politics in feminism, disability has not only been an added cross to bear, but an added "identity" to take on—with politically correct positions, presumed instant alliances, caucuses to join, and closets to come out of. For example, I was once dragged across a room to meet someone. My friend, a very politically correct lesbian feminist, said, "She's disabled, too. I thought you'd like to meet her." Rather than argue—what would I say? "I'm not interested in other disabled people," or "This is my night off"? (The truth in that moment was like the truth of this experience in every other moment, complicated and difficult to explain)—I went along to find myself standing before someone strapped in a wheelchair she propels by blowing into a tube with a respirator permanently fastened to the back of the chair. To suggest that our relative experience of disability is something we could casually compare (as other people stand by!) demonstrates the crudity of perception about the complex nature of bodily experience.

6   My infirmity is partial leg paralysis. I can walk anywhere, climb stairs, drive a car, ride a horse, swim, hang-glide, fly a plane, hike in the wilderness, go to jail for my political convictions, travel alone, and operate heavy equipment. I can earn a living, shop, cook, eat as I please, dress myself, wash and iron my own clothes, clean my house. The woman in that wheelchair can do none of these fundamental things, much less the more exotic ones. On a more basic human level I can spontaneously get my clothes off if I decide to make love. Once in bed my lover and I can forget my disability. None of this is true of the woman in the wheelchair. There is no bodily human activity that does not have to be specially negotiated, none in which she is not absolutely "different." It would take a very long time, and a highly nuanced conversation, for us to be able to share experiences as if they were common. The experience of disability for the two of us was more different than my experience is from the daily experience of people who are not considered disabled. So much for disability solidarity.

7   With disability, one is somewhere on a continuum between total bodily dysfunction—or death—and complete physical wholeness. In some way, this probably applies to every living person. So when is it

that we call a person "disabled"? When do they become "other"? There are "minor" disabilities that are nonetheless significant for a person's life. Color blindness is one example. But in our culture, color blindness is considered an inconvenience rather than a disability.

8   The ostracization, marginalization, and distortion response to disability are not simply issues of prejudice and denial of civil rights. They reflect attitudes toward bodily life, an unease in the human skin, and an inability to cope with contingency, ambiguity, flux, finitude, and death.

9   Visibly disabled people (like women) in this culture are the scapegoats for resentments of the limitations of organic life. I had polio when I was seven, finishing second grade. I had excelled in everything, and rarely missed school. I had one bad conduct notation—for stomping on the boys' blocks when they wouldn't let me play with them. Although I had leg braces and crutches when I was ready to start school the next year, I wanted desperately to go back and resume as much of the same life as I could. What I was not prepared for was the response of the school system. They insisted that I was now "handicapped" and should go into what they called "special education." This was a program aimed primarily at multiply disabled children, virtually all of whom were mentally retarded as well as physically disabled. It was in a separate wing of another school, and the children were completely segregated from the "normal" children in every aspect of the school day, including lunch and recreational activities. I was fortunate enough to have educated, articulate parents and an especially aggressive mother; she went to the school board and waged a tireless campaign to allow me to come back to my old school on a trial basis—the understanding being that the school could send me to special education if things "didn't work out" in the regular classroom.

10   And so began my career as an "exceptional" disabled person, not like the *other* "others." And I was glad. I didn't want to be associated with those others either. Apart from the objective limitations caused by the polio, the transformation in identity—the difference in worldly reception—was terrifying and embarrassing, and it went far beyond the necessary considerations my limitations required.

11   My experience as "other" is much greater and more painful as a disabled person than as a woman. Maybe the most telling dimension of this knowledge is my observation of the reactions of others over the years, of how deeply afraid people are of being outside the normative appearance (which is getting narrower as capitalism exaggerates patriarchy). It is no longer enough to be thin; one must have ubiquitous muscle definition, nothing loose, flabby, or ill-defined, no fuzzy boundaries. And of course, there's the importance of control. Control over aging, bodily processes, weight, fertility, muscle tone, skin quality, and

movement. Disabled women, regardless of how thin, are without full bodily control.

12   I see disabled women fight these normative standards in different ways, but never get free of negotiating and renegotiating them. I did it by constructing my life around other values and, to the extent possible, developing erotic attachments to people who had similar values, and for whom my compensations were more than adequate. But at one point, after two disastrous but steamy liaisons with a champion athlete and a dancer (during which my friends pointed out the obvious unkind truth and predicted painful endings), I discovered the worlds I had tried to protect myself from: the disastrous attraction to "others" to complete oneself. I have seen disabled women endure unspeakably horrible relationships because they were so flattered to have such a conventionally attractive individual in tow.

13   And then there's the weight issue. I got fat by refusing to pay attention to my body. Now that I'm slimming down again, my old vanities and insecurities are surfacing. The battle of dieting can be especially fraught for disabled women. It is more difficult because exercising is more difficult, as is traveling around to get the proper foods, and then preparing them. But the underlying rage at the system that makes you feel as if you *are* your body (female, infirm) and that everything else is window dressing—this also undermines the requisite discipline. A tempting response is to resort to an ideal of self as bodiless essence in which the body is completely incidental, and irrelevant.

14   The wish that the body should be irrelevant has been one of my most fervent lifelong wishes. The knowledge that it isn't is my most intense lifelong experience.

15   I have seen other disabled women wear intentionally provocative clothes, like the woman in a wheelchair on my bus route to work. She can barely move. She has a pretty face, and tiny legs she could not possibly walk on. Yet she wears black lace stockings and spike high heels. The other bus occupants smile condescendingly, or pretend not to notice, or whisper in appalled disbelief that this woman could represent herself as having a sexual self. That she could "flaunt" her sexual being violates the code of acceptable appearance for a disabled woman. This woman's apparel is no more far out than that of many other women on our bus—but she refuses to fold up and be a good little asexual handicapped person.

16   The well-intentioned liberal new campaigns around "hire the handicapped" are oppressive in related ways. The Other does not only have to demonstrate her competence on insider terms; she must be better, by way of apologizing for being different and rewarding the insiders for letting her in. And the happy handicapped person, who has had

faith placed in her/him, must vindicate "the race" because the politics of tokenism assumes that there are in fact other qualifications than doing the job.

17   This is especially prejudicial in a recession, where there are few social services, where it is "every man for himself." Disabled people inevitably have greater expenses, since assistance must often be paid for privately. In the U.S., public construction of the disabled body is that one either is fully disabled and dysfunctional/unemployable (and therefore eligible for public welfare) or totally on one's own. There is no in-between—the possibility of a little assistance, or exceptions in certain areas. Disabled people on public assistance cannot work or they will lose their benefits. (In the U.S. ideology that shapes public attitudes and public policy, one is either fully dependent or fully autonomous.) But the reality of human and organic life is that everyone is different in some way; there is no such thing as a totally autonomous individual. Yet the mythology of autonomy perpetuates in terrible ways the oppression of the disabled. It also perpetuates misogyny—and the destruction of the planet.

18   It may be that this clear lack of autonomy—this reminder of mortal finitude and contingency and embeddedness of nature and the body—is at the root of the hatred of the disabled. On the continuum of autonomy and dependence, disabled people need help. To need help is to feel humiliated, to have failed. I think this "help" issue must be even harder for men than women. But any disabled person is always negotiating both the provisionality of autonomy and the rigidity of physical norms.

19   From the vantage point of disability, there are some objective and desirable aspects of autonomy. But they have to do with independence. The preferred protocol is that the attendant or friend perform the task that the disabled person needs done in the way the disabled person *asks it to be done.* Assistance from friends and family is a negotiated process, and often maddening. For that reason most disabled people prefer to live in situations where they can do all the basic functions themselves, with whatever special equipment or built-ins are required.

20   It's a dreadful business, this needing help. And it's more dreadful in the U.S. than in any place in the world, because our heroes are dynamic overcomers of adversity, and there is an inevitable cultural contempt for weakness.

21   Autonomy is on a continuum toward dependency and death. And the idea that dependency could come at any time, that one could die at any time, or be dismembered or disfigured, and still have to live (maybe even *want to live*) is unbearable in a context that understands and values autonomy in the way we moderns do.

22   I don't want to depict this experience of unbearability as strictly cultural. The compromising of the human body before its natural time

is tragic. It forces terrible hardship on the individual to whom it occurs. But the added overlay of oppression on the disabled is intimately related to the fear of death, and the acknowledgement of our embeddedness in organic nature. We are finite, contingent, dependent creatures by our very nature; we will all eventually die. We will all experience compromises to our physical integrity. The aspiration to human wholeness is an oppressive idealism. Socially, it is deeply infantilizing.

23   It promotes a simplistic view of the human person, a static notion of human life that prevents the maturity and social wisdom that might allow human beings to more fully apprehend the human condition. It marginalizes the "different," those perceived as hopelessly wedded to organic existence—women and the disabled. The New Age "human potential movement"—in the name of maximizing human growth—is one of the worst offenders in obscuring the kind of human growth I am suggesting.

24   I too believe that the potential for human growth and creativity is infinite—but it is not groundless. The common ground for the person—the human body—is a place of shifting sand that can fail us at any time. It can change shape and properties without warning; this is an essential truth of embodied existence.

25   Of all the ways of becoming "other" in our society, disability is the only one that can happen to anyone, in an instant, transforming that person's life and identity forever. ∎

Evan Wright

Sister Act

Evan Wright's condemnation of the Greek system—in particular, an exposé of how the sorority system disciplines female bodies in certain ways—appeared in Rolling Stone *in October 1999. You are no doubt aware of* Rolling Stone: *It covers contemporary pop culture, especially music, for a hip audience of under-thirties.*

1   The dogwoods are in bloom here at Ohio State in Columbus, the second-largest university in the United States. Stark residential towers rise to the north and south. A collection of 1950s and 1960s aluminum-

and-glass buildings facing the main thoroughfare have the look of Stalinist architecture. They lend the campus that air of impersonality that many large universities seem to strive for.

2 With more than 35,000 undergrads, including more than 7,000 minority students, OSU can be overwhelming to the sheltered incoming teenager. Still, it is shocking that flocks of OSU's young women are joining sororities, the cornier the better. They are embracing honor badges, sacred oaths and archaic codes of feminine virtue. Seventeen sororities—many housed in expansive mansions along Indianola Avenue and Fifteenth Street—claim a membership of nearly 2,000, and pledge classes have doubled over the past two years.

3 Sorority members say that their organizations make strong female role models and promote ideals of service, sisterhood and leadership. Their success at teaching these values can be judged during OSU's Greek week, the oldest celebration of college fraternal organizations in the land. "Greek week," its organizers say, "is a chance for the Greek community to come together and shine on campus."

4 A solemn event on the Greek-week calendar is Alcohol Awareness Day. For twenty-four hours, all sorority sisters and fraternity brothers pledge to abstain from liquor. To help get them through it, organizers have planned a night of Survival Bingo in Raney Commons, a hall that will seat about 300 ostensibly sober bingo players.

5 Seven sorority presidents gather at a table half an hour prior to the event. Six are blond. All wear beige khaki shorts and white blouses or T-shirts adorned with either Greek letters or Gap and Abercrombie & Fitch logos. Their hair is pulled back straight behind their ears with either hair bands or sunglasses. Each wears silver hoop earrings.

6 Raney Commons fills to capacity with sober, white, clean-cut young people and begins to resemble a fantasy from deep inside the brain of Ronald Reagan, during whose presidency most of these Greeks were born. Black students congregate elsewhere: There are eleven African-American Greek organizations, known as the "black Greeks." The black Greeks evince little interest in joining in with the white Greeks. Leon Coleman, president of all of OSU's black Greeks, says, "In a struggle, sometimes you have to have your own, be around your own."

7 The monotony of the ensuing bingo game is broken only when the number sixty-nine is called. Cheers grow louder when sixty-nine is again called. At last, a hooting fraternity boy is driven over the brink when sixty-nine sounds yet again. He hurls a bingo prize, a bag of Capri-Sun Coolers, at a table packed with sorority sisters. They throw it back, and flocks of the silvery bags arc across the Commons.

8   Preparing to leave, two sorority sisters berate a pledge who has forgotten to carry out their winnings, a case of Sprite.

9   "It's your job to carry it back to the house," one of the elder sisters scolds.

10   "Can't one of you help?" the pledge asks plaintively.

11   "That's your job," explains the other sister. As the pledge trudges back into Raney Commons, the two sisters confer about her performance and leadership potential.

12   "Dude, she is such a whore."

13   "Totally."

14   At 3 A.M., two wobbly-legged sorority girls stand in an alley off Fifteenth Street. A third girl kneels between them on her hands and knees and throws up. Her two friends yank her backward. "Don't get it on you," one of them says. "A sober monitor will smell it."

15   All sororities have a zero tolerance alcohol policy. Many do not even allow a single can of beer in a twenty-one-year-old girl's personal refrigerator.

16   Fraternities, however, are allowed to serve beer in bottles under an elaborate system of ID bracelets, drink cards and monitoring by student sober patrols. They offer the only Greek parties that sorority girls can go to in order to get drunk. Everyone swears that the system works beautifully, and it does, insofar as it allows all Greeks, whatever their ages, to get drunk at pretty much any time of the day or night.

17   Two young women hang out by the main pedestrian crossroads, called the Oval. One has hair dyed lightbulb yellow; the other has dark purple hair braided in strands around alphabet beads. They are both first-year students, and neither would dream of joining a sorority.

18   "Girls in sororities are so conformist," says the yellow-haired one. "They're like Gap clones or something."

19   "I don't know if that's really true or fair," her friend interjects. "Like, I read a survey about sorority girls. It said sorority girls have, like, the highest percentage of pierced clits."

20   She cannot recall in which magazine or scholarly journal she found this fact.

21   The first girl volunteers that her friend from across the hall in her dorm recently pledged with a sorority: "She'll still talk about it now, because she hasn't moved into her house yet. Once they move in, it's kind of like a cult, and they stop speaking to their friends outside the sorority."

22   Yellow hair leads the way to a residential tower on north campus, where her roommate Heather, 18, slouches on a metal cot. Heather is soon to be a resident of Chi Omega's sandstone-and-brick mansion. Her

chestnut hair falls to her jaw line. She smiles frequently and smokes a Marlboro red.

23   Heather says she feels "truly blessed" to have been accepted by her sorority. She was intimidated by the size of OSU, and being a sorority sister makes the university feel like a small college.

24   At the same time, Heather criticizes the cruelty of the rush process, in which some sorority girls rate the appearance of potential pledges down to the straightness of their teeth and the number of zits on their faces. (Other girls have spoken of secret sorority guidebooks that subtract points for frizzy hair and cheese thighs.)

25   Heather alleges that at least one sorority at OSU practices a form of hazing known as the "fat table." She describes it: "You have to strip down to your underwear and bra. You sit on a table, and all your sorority sisters circle the fat and ugly parts of your body with magic markers."

26   Heather says her own sorority is cruelty-free. Even if it weren't, she has little to worry about since her teeth are straight, her body is slim and her skin is as pure as a cold glass of milk.

27   "Some sororities you have to dress definitely a certain way," she elaborates. "You have to have your nails done, your hair perfect. You have to dress up all the time in very nice clothes from Express, the Limited, Gap. Anything with heels for shoes. And for going out, all the girls must have tight, hot-bod sex pants."

28   Heather produces a pair of black Lycra pants and models them, holding them in front of her waist.

29   "My particular brand is called Hot Kiss. Tight, hot sex pants are always black. They flare out at the bottom, and they're tight. They're hip-huggers. You wear these with a tight shirt. Maybe a bare midriff. It depends how much you want to show when you go out at night. Some girls wear these to class. I don't."

30   One of the chief benefits of joining a sorority, she says, is having a brimming social calendar.

31   "We have TGs practically every week. This is just a party at a fraternity house. TGs are a group of fraternity guys and a group of sorority girls getting as drunk as they can and dancing.

32   "A crush party is when you have a crush on someone and you send this little note to them. It says, 'You've been crushed, and if you come to this party, you'll find out who has a crush on you.' Usually, we have this at a bar, so everyone can drink a lot.

33   "The formal is, we have to get all dressed up and go in limos somewhere and dance and drink.

34   "My sorority does a lot of philanthropies. We have parties that raise money for them. We usually go to parks. It has to be somewhere we can drink. Because drinking's a big part of philanthropy.

35   "Sororities are almost like an intense version of Girl Scouts, but with lots of alcohol," she observes.

36   According to Heather, a sorority girl reaches the pinnacle of social achievement when she is lavaliered. "Being lavaliered is when a guy gives you his fraternity pin. It's like a pre-engagement to be engaged.

37   "To wear a guy's fraternity pin is a big thing. And for him to give you his fraternity pin is a big thing, because he'll get the crap beat out of him by his fraternity brothers for doing it. First [the young man and his fraternity brothers] all come to the house and sing a serenade for the girl being lavaliered. Then his brothers have to beat the crap out of him. That way, he only gives his pin to a very special girl."

38   Heather beams; a recent lavaliering party comes to mind.

39   "It goes like this: After a sister is lavaliered, the president calls a meeting. We all get in a big circle and pass a candle around. We sing a song. It's about something in the spring, and in all the seasons, how we'll always be sisters. And whoever has been lavaliered will hold the candle and blow it out.

40   "Sometimes a girl will go up to a boy's bedroom at a TG. The big thing in that type of situation is to get his shirt. She'll come down wearing it, but that's not like being lavaliered at all."

41   Some people say that the Greek system is a sort of apartheid, enabling children from predominately white, upper-middle-class enclaves to safely attend a messily diverse university such as OSU without having to mix with those who are different. Presumably, a sorority is a place where a young white woman can be lavaliered by a fraternity boy, and they can move on to form their own family in a predominately white, upper-middle-class enclave, preferably one that is gated.

42   This theory seems at first to be affirmed when Andrea, a twenty-year-old Alpha Delta Pi, leads the way into her sorority house. She opens the door and enters the all-clear code on the house's burglar alarm. "We have to be safe," she says, pointing south toward a black area of Columbus. "It's total ghetto a few blocks from here. Serious."

43   Andrea is a former cheerleader with scars on her knees from injuries sustained while building a high school homecoming float. As if these credentials weren't enough, she is a straight-A computer-engineering major.

44   She goes into the large, institutional kitchen: "Our cook is a black guy named Bob. He says his wife is a queen in Africa or something." She rolls her eyes with exaggerated disbelief. But later she laughs. "Personally, I'm down with the brown," she says. "Serious. My boyfriend's black."

45   Andrea then describes how, contrary to the apartheid theory, joining a sorority broadened her cultural horizons. She grew up in a rural Ohio town. There were no blacks in her neighborhood, and her high school had a small but active White Knights association, which she describes as a "mini-Ku Klux Klan."

46   "When I got into my sorority," she says, "I found out five of my sisters here were dating black guys. I couldn't believe it. I was like, 'Oh, my God.' I had no idea that went on. And they're, like, marrying these guys, who were really cool.

47   "It was instant attraction when I met my boyfriend. Almost instant. At first, he chased me for a while, because I was, like, scared of the fact that he was black.

48   "I started sleeping with him after we'd been dating not very long. Usually, the rule is I don't sleep with a guy until, like, after two or three months—at least, and a major exchange of gifts at a holiday. Serious. Meet the family, the whole thing. It only took him a month."

49   In the grass outside the student union, a campus lesbian leader and "theoretical feminist" named Mary deconstructs sorority mating rituals. Mary is Hispanic and on full financial aid. She says, "I could never get in. A sorority is a class thing. It's a breeding ground for the next conservative America."

50   Mary lights a cigarette: "I like to look at the power constructs of their rituals, like lavaliering, where the guy gives the girl his pin. Like, he goes to the girl and says, 'I'm going to marry you."

51   "So then his fraternity brothers beat the crap out of him because he's negating his power as a single male by making that commitment with the girl. He's compromised his male power.

52   "Then she gets to blow out the candle, and that's ending her power in the sorority. She's saying, 'I'm leaving my sisters because I'm going to go live with this dude, and I'm going let him govern my life.'"

53   "I look at sororities as whorehouses."

54   Mary tamps out her cigarette and enters the student union. A third-floor meeting room has been reserved for the planners of OSU's fourth annual Take Back the Night Rally, billed as a "march and candlelight vigil to protest rape and other forms of violence against women."

55   The meeting, organized largely by radical feminists, is also being supported by two Delta Phi Epsilons, Rachel Glass and Hallie Fleisch. Hallie and Rachel enter wearing khaki Gap sorority uniforms. Rachel, with her short dark hair in a bob, smiles warmly and sits near Mary. Hallie looks around the room with muted horror, as if she is about to undergo a weird hazing ritual. She peeps a barely audible "hi" and drops into a corner.

56   The other women wear an eclectic mix of combat fatigues, Guatemalan peasant dresses and biker leather gear, such as spiked wrist cuffs and dog collars. As they sprawl out on the floor, vast swaths of armpit and leg hair are exposed.

57   The lesbians are chatting about the Live Homosexual Acts event they are planning to stage on the Oval.

58   "We'll have a lesbian and gay volleyball game."

59   "We should have people bring coat hangers and wire cutters to, like, symbolize putting an end to illegal abortions."

60   Mary brings the meeting to order. A blonde in combat boots suggests that everyone should go around, introduce herself and describe her "first crime." It's intended as a humorous icebreaker.

61   Everyone except Hallie laughs.

62   "My first crime," begins the first person up. When I was little, I used to go under the porch and pee."

63   "I don't know if porn is a crime in Ohio," says a girl in glasses that resemble welding goggles, "but when I was in elementary school, I used to write porno stories for my girlfriends and write dirty things about the guys they had crushes on."

64   Rachel relates a story about getting a speeding ticket when she was seventeen.

65   It is now Hallie's turn. She looks up with a pained expression. She struggles to say something, then blurts out, "I can't think of anything I've done wrong."

66   Sensing Hallie's discomfort, the others rush to put her at ease. There is a murmur of "That's OK, Hallie."

67   The first order of business is raised by a woman who would like to exclude men from marching. She argues that men shouldn't participate because they are the principal perpetrators of violence against women.

68   Across the room, a young woman begins to cry. "You all know how I feel," she says. "There's a lot of pain."

69   Somebody else begins to cry, and soon everyone is either sniffling or rubbing somebody's back in a comforting, supportive way—except for Hallie, who looks up with a somewhat annoyed expression and asks, "Shouldn't we have a vote or something?"

70   Rachel raises her hand. "I have something to say. Didn't we already put out a press release saying men were invited? Wouldn't we look dumb if we changed our minds now?"

71   "I guess we have to let them march," someone says.

72   "How about if we have them march, like, forty feet behind us?" suggests somebody else.

73   "It's OK if they march," says the leader who originally wanted to ban men altogether, "but they have to make the posters."

74   When the meeting ends, Rachel Glass discusses the balance between being a sorority girl and a feminist. "I'm probably one of the only self-defined, outspoken feminists in my sorority," Rachel says. A senior who is graduating at the end of the summer with a degree in women's studies, Rachel describes herself as coming from an affluent background, "a completely shallow, materialistic culture which pushed me into sorority life."

75   She takes issue with fraternity men, whom she feels view sorority sisters merely as "bodies," but cherishes the sorority's sisterhood and opportunities for leadership, which she feels have made her a strong woman. Her sorority experience was complemented by her exposure to feminism. Both influences have made her stronger and more capable of dealing with a sometimes confusing and hostile male-dominated world. Rachel cites an experience in which she drew on her strength as a feminist.

76   "A [sorority] friend and I were walking home from a party junior year and we got sexually assaulted," she says. "We were walking down the street and this guy totally grabbed my friend's ass. She stopped in her tracks, and she was like, 'Oh, my God! That guy just touched me.' We were like, 'Oh, my God; oh, my God.' We started walking away really fast. He just, like, unzipped his pants, whipped it out and started jerking off. We both felt violated.

77   "But I coped with it a lot better than she did, and I think that was due to being a feminist and being a women's-studies major and understanding, like, the system of patriarchy and how women are oppressed. I just got angry.

78   "My friend very much internalized it. She blamed herself and was like, 'I shouldn't have worn these tight black pants tonight.' "

79   Reggaefest falls on the day after Greek week ends, but the Kappa Sigma frat brothers who host the event see it as the last big Greek blowout of the year before exams and the farewell of another graduating class.

80   Reggaefest is open to the public and offers four bands performing on the grassy slope in front of the Kappa Sig house, the former governor's mansion. Up to 8,000 people are expected to show.

81   Orange cyclone fencing cordons off the streets surrounding the Kappa Sig grounds. It is drizzling. Columbus police in white caps and shirts that make them resemble sinister ice-cream men with guns mill around beneath a canopy by the stage.

82   Nearby, a campus administrator is having a heated discussion with Jeff, a Kappa Sig organizer of the event. The administrator has smelled alcohol on the breath of Kappa Sigs and their sorority "goddesses" (sorority sisters invited to the private, VIP Kappa Sig house

party in exchange for selling tickets) manning the front entrances. Reggaefest is a designated alcohol-free event.

83   Jeff is a lanky, twenty-three-year-old senior political-science major. His attempt to mollify the administrator is hampered by the fact that his own breath reeks of beer, and he is slurring.

84   Jeff finally walks away shouting, "Reggaefest has been voted the Number Two party in America! Now the administration won't even let us serve alcohol! The American people need to know what's happening."

85   Jeff enters the Kappa Sig house. A long-neck Bud appears in his hand as he climbs the stairs. The frat house bears all the signs of wear and tear from heavy partying. Carpets are crusty, walls scuffed and punched in. The halls smell like a truck-stop men's room. A sign tacked to the wall from two nights ago says, "Tonight is May Fifth, Cinco de Mayo. Dress Like Mexicans!"

86   The unofficial, private VIP Kappa Sig party is being held on the third floor. Woozy sorority goddesses stumble through the narrow halls.

87   Two of them, Jenn and Tricia, raise beers and drunken grins. "They try to come down on us," says Jenn. "But we still set it off!"

88   Jenn turns to Tricia: "You know what less alcohol means."

89   "More drugs!" they scream in unison, clinking bottles and guzzling.

90   "Do I have beer on my pants?" Jenn pulls up the tail of the men's shirt she's wearing. A dark stain runs down her pants' butt seam and disappears between her legs. Could be beer; could be pee.

91   Another girl comes by and waves a ruby-red drink under Jeff's nose. "This is a Terry Special. Rum, gin and six different kinds of fruit drinks. It's tasty!"

92   Jeff ignores her. He does an about-face. He clambers down four flights of stairs, leading the way into the basement TG (party) room. There is a mirrored disco ball overhead. The tile floor is so sticky with beer, it's like fly paper. Jeff shoves open a steel fire door leading into a dank cement chamber.

93   "You want to know about sorority girls?" asks Jeff. He sits on a loose foundation stone. "This fraternity taught me how to be a gentleman. You know what they call us [the Kappa Sigs]? The Gentlemen on the Hill.

94   "Here's the secret: We learn how to treat girls like ladies."

95   Jeff begins to sing what he calls the "sweetheart song": "You're as pretty as a picture/You're as sweet as you can be/I love you most sincerely/You're all this world to me."

96   He stops. "That's it. When a girl is really special, that's what we do. You serenade her, you pin her, give her a ring, give her a rose."

97   At ten o'clock the Itals are playing, but the lawn in front of the Kappa Sig house is mostly empty. There are just a few hundred dancers, not the expected 8,000.

98   The sorority goddess who had been drinking the Terry Special on the third floor is outside talking excitedly to someone in the darkness. "I want to marry a rich man," she declares. "I want to go to an Ivy League grad school, find a brilliant professor and follow him!"

99   Jeff surveys the dismal turnout. "This party sucks. It's a disgrace. I'm ashamed," he states. "Let's go fuck some sorority girls. It can be arranged. Anyone you want."

100   He stumbles across the lawn. "Fuck a sorority girl," he repeats, apparently forgetting the bull session of twenty minutes ago in which he declared his chivalrous ideals, learned through fraternity life.

101   Jeff climbs under a section of plastic cyclone fence along the driveway. In the darkness there appears to be a row of cinder blocks, perhaps the top of a wall. Jeff steps forward, then disappears. There is a dull thump, like a cantaloupe dropping onto the floor in a super-market.

102   Jeff lies on the asphalt at the bottom of a five foot drop. He springs up, unfazed by his fall. "Anybody see?" he asks.

103   There is an apartment block thirty feet across the yard. Partyers spill out from the yellow light of a sliding porch door.

104   "You want to fuck a sorority girl?" Jeff babbles, leading the way into the apartment. "My Kappa Sig brothers can arrange everything."

105   Inside, girls are piled two and three deep on the couches of a small TV room. They stare ahead, smiling and laughing dully at nothing in particular.

106   There is a large guy in sunglasses. Someone identifies him as a re-cently graduated Kappa Sig. He reaches into his pocket and pulls out a handful of triangle-shaped, blue-green pills. Ecstasy.

107   "Let's double team one of these babes tonight!" he shouts, hand-ing out tabs to all takers.

108   Jeff leans against a sliding door in the entrance. The flesh around his mouth is slack. His forehead looks chalky and damp. His eyes are dull. First-aid manuals commonly describe these symptoms as the ini-tial signs of shock.

109   Jeff's collar is flecked with blood. Partially coagulated blood runs down the back of his neck in the shape of a slug. It is suggested he go back to the Kappa Sig house and seek medical attention, or at least lie down.

110   Jeff weaves back to the Kappa Sig house, cutting a wide swath around the wall that felled him minutes ago. The gentleman on the hill vanishes inside the former governor's mansion.

111   The sorority goddess who had been drinking Terry Specials, then plotting to find a brilliant Ivy League professor, stands on the steps. She is being supported by two fraternity brothers. "I never drink," she babbles. "I'm a good girl. I'm a good girl. I'm really a good girl." ■

CHAPTER 24

Media

Freedom and Restriction of the Media

On October 15, 2004, less than three weeks before the presidential elections, popular Comedy Central comedian Jon Stewart, a guest on CNN's political talk show "Crossfire," got into a celebrated donnybrook with news commentator Tucker Carlson. Stewart, whose hilarious political satire in the form of a mock TV news show sends many Americans to bed with a smile on their faces—he takes particular delight in lampooning the foibles of the Bush administration—took the opportunity of his appearance on "Crossfire" to challenge Carlson about the abysmal level of political commentary in the nation's media. At one point Stewart charged that "Crossfire" and shows like it—he was no doubt thinking of Bill O'Reilly and Rush Limbaugh, "Hardball" and "Hannity and Colmes," "The Capital Gang" and "The Beltway Boys"—are "bad, very bad," for America because they oversimplify discussion and polarize it. "It's hurting America," said Stewart. "Stop, stop, stop, stop, stop hurting America." When Carlson protested that "Crossfire" presents intelligent debate from the political left and right, Stewart was outraged: "[Saying 'Cross-

> The complete transcript of Jon Stewart's appearance on "Crossfire" can be found at <http://politicalhumor.about.com/library/bljonstewartcrossfire.htm>

fire' is a debate show is] like saying pro wrestling is a show about athletic competition. You're doing theater when you should be doing debate. . . . What you do is not honest. What you do is partisan hackery . . . just knee-jerk reactionary talk."

While Stewart was taking his frustrations out on "Crossfire," he was surely also thinking of much more. In the past decade many Americans have been increasingly concerned about certain trends in the popular media: the development of partisan (rather than "fair and balanced") news coverage; the concentration of news outlets and newspapers into the hands of a few powerful corporations; the impact of sensationalistic and one-sided talk radio and talk TV; the effects of the Internet on the political and cultural process; the dubious morality depicted on "reality TV"; the effects of persistent advertising, violence and graphic sexuality, and cultural stereotyping that are associated with films, magazines, and television. Jerry Springer, a former TV news commentator transformed into the host of a trash "reality" show that has concentrated fantastic wealth in his hands, embodies all of the concerns: Is it any wonder, then, that Springer is often mentioned in Ohio as a serious and viable political candidate?

> Congress shall make no law . . . abridging the freedom of speech, or of the press.
>
> —First Amendment to the
> U.S. Constitution

The media is not like other businesses. The nation's founders gave special status to a free and open media by promising that a free press should not be abridged, but since the Constitution was ratified a series of challenges to unfettered freedom of the press has established that the media must operate within the context of other freedoms guaranteed by the Constitution. Just what is the proper balance between freedom and restriction of the media? Here in *Good Reasons with Contemporary Arguments* we present arguments that touch on all of the issues, but three of them in particular.

Contemporary Arguments

The first is the question of whether it is a problem or not that media ownership is becoming increasingly concentrated. In 2003, the Federal Communications Commission seemed to license that concentration when it ruled that companies could own a newspaper and TV station in the same market. The FCC also eased rules in order to permit companies like Clear Channel and Rupert Murdock's News Corporation to own two or even three stations in one area (as long as only one was in the top four in ratings). When the public protested, Congress intervened, but the controversy continues. In a nation that relies on an independent and open media—on a media that is determined to present collectively the full range of voices and perspectives represented in the country—how much concentration is healthy? How much government regulation of nongovernment news sources is appropriate? Here we present a comic strip (by Matt Wuerker) and two essays on media conglomeration: one (by Ben Bagdikian) alerting Americans to potential dangers and the other (by Tom Goldstein) more forgiving of recent developments.

Even as the mass media has been consolidating, a new source of news and information has been developing: the Internet. While most students cannot recall a time when the Internet was not operating, the fact is that only in the past decade or so has the Internet emerged as a significant force in American cultural and political life. Shocked by the prevalence of pornography on the Internet (sometimes including the dissemination of sexually explicit photographs without the permission of the person photographed), by Web sites created by extremist hate groups, or by individuals who offer guns—or advice on bomb construction—on the Internet, many have called for laws regulating the Internet. The 1998 Child Online Protection Act prohibits the publication of materials online that could be harmful to children, and Internet subscription services commonly prohibit users from posting or transmitting messages that are harmful, threatening, defamatory, or obscene. Some universities have disciplined students for posting hate messages on the Internet. Are such policies good or bad? Are restrictions on the Internet violations of the Constitution? How unrestricted should the Internet be? Arguments in this chapter by Cathleen Cleaver and the American Civil Liberties Union articulate the issues, and other, briefer arguments in cartoons and manifestos provide further perspectives. Matt Welch's essay about the new Internet phenomenon—the blog (short for "weblog")—will invite you to ponder how electronic technologies might shape and sharpen political and cultural debates in America in the coming years. Should blogs be regulated as other forms of political advertising are regulated and limited?

> As of July 2005, the blogger audience had grown to 20 percent of newspaper readership and 40 percent of talk radio—and continues to grow rapidly. Over 6 percent of the U.S. population has created a blog.
>
> —Lee Rainie, "The State of Blogging" and "New Data on Blogs and Blogging," <HTTP://WWW.PEWINTERNET.ORG>

The chapter concludes with three arguments that raise questions about some of the subtler effects of the media. Joshua Kurlantzick raises questions about the impact of the Internet on the political process. While some have championed the Internet's capacity to encourage democratic exchange, Kurlantzick worries that it might be having just the opposite effect. Naomi Klein reflects on efforts to curb the pernicious effects of advertising

> If the First Amendment means anything, it means that a state has no business telling a [person], sitting alone in his own house, what . . . he may read or what films he may watch.
>
> —Supreme Court Justice
> Thurgood Marshall, 1969

through "culture jamming." And Michel Marriott explains how videogames, like some films and television shows, by stereotyping African Americans can encourage young people to take destructive actions.

Postscript: In the summer of 2005 CNN cancelled "Crossfire" after 23 years, and it dismissed Tucker Carlson. Jonathan Klein, head of CNN's domestic cable operations, said that he wanted to move away from "head-butting debate shows" like "Crossfire." Is there hope after all? Then again, Carlson simply moved to MSNBC and began a new show. . . .

BEN BAGDIKIAN

Grand Theft: The Conglomeratization of Media and the Degradation of Culture

Author of the 2004 book, The New Media Monopoly *(an update of his earlier* The Media Monopoly, *1983), Ben Bagdikian is dean emeritus of the Graduate School of Journalism at the University of California at Berkeley. He was part of a group that won a Pulitzer Prize for local reporting, and served as assistant managing editor for national news at the* Washington Post. *He has also been honored with a Peabody Award and a Guggenheim Fellowship. Along with his extensive work as a correspondent, Bagdikian served as president of the Lowell Mellett Fund for a Free and Responsible Press. His other books include* In the Midst of Plenty: The Poor in America *(1963) and* The Information Machines: Their Impact on Men and the Media *(1971). "Grand Theft" first appeared in the January/February 2005 issue of* Multinational Monitor, *a journal that focuses on issues related to multinational corporations. The essay that follows it, by Tom Goldstein, is something of an answer to it.*

1 For 25 years, a handful of large corporations that specialize in every mass medium of any consequence has dominated what the majority of people in the United States see about the world beyond their personal experience. These giant media firms, unlike any in the past, thanks to the hands-off attitude of the Federal Communications Commission (FCC) majority, are unhampered by laws and regulation. In the

process, they have been major agents of change in the social values and politics of the United States.

2   They have, in my opinion, damaged our democracy. Given that the majority of Americans say they get their news, commentary and daily entertainment from this handful of conglomerates, the conglomerates fail the needs of democracy every day.

3   Our modern democracy depends not just on laws and the Constitution, but a vision of the real nature of the United States and its people. It is only humane philosophy that holds together the country's extraordinary diversity of ethnicity, race, vastly varied geography and a wide range of cultures. There are imperfections within every individual and community. But underneath it, we expect the generality of our population to retain a basic sense of decency and kindness in real life.

4   We also depend on our voters to approach each election with some knowledge of the variety of ideas and proposals at stake. This variety and richness of issues and ideas were once reflected by competing newspapers whose news and editorial principles covered the entire political spectrum. Every city of any size was exposed to the early Hearst and E. W. Scripps newspapers that were the champions of working people and critics of the rich who exploited workers and used their power to evade taxes. There were middle-of-the-road papers, and a sizeable number of pro-business papers (like the old *New York Sun*). They were, of course, a mixed bag. Not a few tabloids screamed daily headlines of blood and guts.

5   With all of that, the major papers represented the needs and demands of the mass of ordinary people and kept badgering politicians who ignored them.

6   Today, there is no such broad political spectrum and little or no competition among media. There is only a handful of exceptions to the rule of one daily paper per city. On radio and television, Americans see limited ideas and the largest media groups spreading ever-more extreme right-wing politics, and nightly use of violence and sex that tell parents and their children that they live in a cruel country. They have made sex a crude commodity as an inexpensive attention getter. They have made sex, of all things, boring.

7   Instead of newsboys earlier in the nineteenth century hawking a variety of papers to the people leaving their downtown factories and offices for home, we have cars commuting between suburbs with radio turned to news of traffic and crime. At home, TV is the major home appliance. What it displays day and night is controlled by a handful of giant media conglomerates, heavily tilted to the political right. And all of them have substantial control of every medium—newspapers, magazines, books, radio, television and movies.

8   The giant conglomerates with this kind of control are Time Warner, the largest media company in the world; Rupert Murdoch's

News Corporation, which owns the Fox networks, a steady source of conservative commentary; Viacom, the old CBS with similarly heavy holdings in all the other important media; Bertelsmann, the German company with masses of U.S. publications, book houses, and partnerships with the other giant media companies; Disney, which has come a long way from concentrating on Mickey Mouse and now, in the pattern of its fellow giants, owns 164 separate media properties from radio and TV stations to magazines and a multitude of other outlets in print and motion picture companies; and General Electric, owner of NBC and its multiple subsidiaries.

9   One radio firm, ClearChannel, the sponsor of Rush Limbaugh and other exclusively right-wing commentators, owns 2,400 stations, dwarfing all other radio outlets in size and audience.

10   In their control of most of our newspapers, the great majority of our radio and television, of our most widely distributed books, magazines and motion pictures, these conglomerates have cheapened what once was a civilized mix of programming.

11   We have large cadres of talented screen writers who periodically complain that they have exciting and touching material that the networks reject in favor of repetitive junk. These writers do it for the money and could quit, as some of them have. But they once got paid for writing original dramas like those of Paddy Chayevsky and other playwrights whose work was heard in earlier days of television.

12   Programs appealing to the variety of our national tastes and variations in politics are so rare they approach extinction. The choices for the majority of Americans are the prime-time network shows that range from the relatively harmless petty jokes and dating games typified by "Seinfeld" to the unrelieved sex and violence of Murdoch's Fox network and "reality" shows in which "real people"—that is, non-professional amateurs—are willingly subjected to contests in sexual seduction, deceit and violation of friendships. Most TV drama is an avalanche of violence.

13   This is not an appeal for broadcasting devoted solely to the nostalgia of "Andy Hardy" and "Little House on the Prairie." Nor is this an appeal for solely serious classics designed for elite audiences (though surely more of such programs would be good). It is an appeal for a richer variety to meet the range of tastes, regional interests, ethnic documentaries and dramas for the millions of Americans who embrace memories of "the old country," as well as other appeals, like of soap operas, popular music and classical music, lectures.

14   Here and there, at later hours of the evening, there are occasional book-and-author, actors-and-producers interviews, as well as talented performers of the contemporary pop forms. But they are rare gems glimpsed through the masses of stereotyped nightly trash.

15   A basic root of the problem is two-fold. One is the domination of our broadcasting by a handful of giant media conglomerates whose performance is measured not just by Nielsen or Arbitron ratings, but what these create on the stock market, whose major investors' standards are, "I don't care how you do it, but if your program doesn't raise your stock market prices, your president and CEO will be out of their jobs."

16   The other is a Federal Communications Commission which, for the last 30 years, has forgotten its mandated task of making certain that broadcasters serve "the public interest." Instead, the present majority members believe that, contrary to broadcast law, the free market of maximized profits is what constitutes the standard for what is in "the public interest."

17   More than 40 years ago, a Commission member, Newt Minow, electrified the industry and most of the listening and viewing public by describing television programming as a "vast wasteland." It was a measure of the standards of that day. It is a measure of today's standard that this would be ignored as the whining of a crank: and defense of today's far more bleak "wasteland" lets the broadcast industry sneer all the way to the bank.

18   The media giants argue that they are only giving people what they want. But that lost much of its democratic gloss when the two Democratic minority members of the FCC at the start of the decade held hearings in major cities across the country to hear what citizens felt about current broadcasting. The hearings were packed with people who testified with seriously documented complaints that they are not getting what they want, and that more concentration would only make the problem worse.

19   Behind these country-wide complaints is the bitter knowledge that, in effect, "The media giants have stolen our property."

20   It is Grand Theft.

21   "Stolen our property" is not just a figure of speech. Communications law established that the American people are the owners of the radio and television frequencies, not the commercial broadcasters.

22   The theft is not just of the electromagnetic frequencies on which the giants broadcast. The theft is also of the inherent and varied needs and wants of the country's real families and individuals, citizens in the real country.

23   That loss tells us that we are in danger of losing some part of what we call "America." ■

TOM GOLDSTEIN

Does Big Mean Bad?

Former dean of Columbia University's Graduate School of Journalism, Tom Goldstein previously held the same position at the University of California at Berkeley. He has written for The New York Times *and* The Wall Street Journal, *and served as press secretary to former New York mayor Edward Koch. Goldstein's articles have appeared in numerous other places, including* Rolling Stone, The Nation, *and* Columbia Law Review. *His books include* The News at Any Cost: How Journalists Compromise Their Ethics to Shape the News *(1985) and* The Lawyer's Guide to Writing Well *(1989). "Does Big Mean Bad?" is one of Goldstein's many articles in the* Columbia Journalism Review. *It comes from the September/October 1998 issue, and in a sense it is an answer to the previous argument, by Ben Bagdikian, though it was actually written first.*

1   In my last incarnation, as dean of the Graduate School of Journalism at the University of California at Berkeley, I once lobbied a top recruiter for a major newspaper chain to hire students from the school. The recruiter then explained why her company had not interviewed anyone from Berkeley for many years. The reason was simple: "Bagdikian."

2   I protested. Ben Bagdikian, the media critic and my predecessor there as dean, is a self-effacing giant in the field. I was missing the point, the recruiter told me. She was convinced that we drilled our students with Ben's anti-chain views, that like some kind of witch doctor he was initiating students into the dark arts of skepticism toward media power. (In fact, in no course did we assign Ben's influential book, *The Media Monopoly.* Shame on us.) Ultimately, the recruiter shed her remarkably thin skin and began hiring Berkeley students.

3   In the honorable ideological tradition of Will Irwin, Upton Sinclair, George Seldes, and I. E. Stone, Bagdikian contends that no commercial power should dominate the news—just as no state power should. The media giants make up, in the haunting phrase he coined, a "private ministry of information."

4   In the first edition of *Media Monopoly,* in 1984, Bagdikian bemoaned that just fifty corporations controlled more than half of the media outlets in this country. He was writing when CNN was in its infancy, when most journalists still used typewriters, and long before the Internet. By 1997, in the book's fifth edition, Bagdikian pegged the "number of media corporations with dominant power in society" at closer to ten. The "new communications cartel," he wrote, has the power to

"surround almost every man, woman, and child in the country with controlled images and words." With that power comes the "ability to exert influence that in many ways is greater than that of schools, religion, parents and even government itself."

5   Bagdikian's role as a media gadfly is gradually being taken over by a new generation, including Mark Crispin Miller, a forceful and original thinker now teaching at New York University. At a duPont-Columbia University Forum called "Is This News?" earlier this year, Miller pointed to "increasing evidence of direct and conscious manipulation of the news process by higher corporate powers and by advertisers generally." Worse, said Miller, is "a system in which the mere fact of ratings anxiety and declining news budgets and the scramble for promotions, simple careerism inside the news business—all these things combine to help produce a kind of seamless trivial spectacle that really doesn't tell us anything."

6   Miller's words are potent, but they are not the last on the subject of the effects of media concentration. Nor are Bagdikian's.

7   The financial markets have certainly spoken. They have richly rewarded some media-company mergers and made stockholders—including journalists—happy folks. Walk into the lobby of a big newspaper these days and you might be confronted with the latest stock price of the paper's parent company.

8   But while few have written compellingly in favor of media giants gobbling up other media giants, some thoughtful observers have made arguments that question the validity of the traditional way of looking at media concentration. In a recent issue of *Newsweek,* columnist Robert Samuelson mulled a survey by the Pew Research Center for the People & the Press documenting the shrinking audience for the television networks' nightly news programs. That survey, combined with the success that his brother, an innkeeper, reaped from advertising on his own Web site, led Samuelson to rethink some basic assumptions.

9   "The notion of a media elite, if ever valid, requires that people get news and entertainment from a few sources dominated by a handful of executives, editors, anchors, reporters, and columnists," Samuelson wrote. "As media multiply the elite becomes less exclusive. Smaller audiences give them less prominence and market power (i.e. salaries)."

10   Writing two years ago in the extraordinary issue of *The Nation* that contained a spider-like chart illustrating the holdings of the four dominant members of "the national entertainment state," Michael Arlen, an uncommonly astute commentator, argued that the specter of a vast, monolithic, all-pervading media has been wildly overdrawn. George Orwell's vision of Big Brother in 1984 was a resoundingly false prophecy. "How disappointing it would have been to Orwell to observe the actual play-out of this romantic drama," Arlen wrote. As proof, he

pointed to "the emergence over the past several decades of a startling cacophony of market-crazed citizens all over the world, with their insistence on two-way communication and their appetite for fragmentation of broadcast authority." These competing views of media power (and there are many, many more) do not cancel each other out. They just underscore that we have no unitary explanation of the extent and impact of media concentration. If journalism is just another business, then the primary scorecard of success is justifiably the verdict of the financial markets.

11   Because of the First Amendment protection it enjoys, journalism is more than another business. Still, we need to know more about what differentiates media concentration from consolidation in other commercial enterprises. We see consolidation among the airlines, military suppliers, banks, brokerage firms, and telephone companies. Look at accounting firms. For years there was the Big Eight. Then, the Big Six. And now, the Big Four.

12   Why do efficiencies of scale work for some businesses and not, say, for journalistic enterprises? With big media ownership in fewer hands, what barriers to entry actually have been erected? (It has been quite a while since anyone tried to start a major metropolitan newspaper. Many have tried recently to start new television networks, but these latter-day broadcasting pioneers are among the very behemoths that so trouble Bagdikian and Miller.) Why is the much-touted buzzword of the early 1990s—synergy—now viewed with such distrust by journalists? Having moved from an age of media scarcity to one of media babble, what new ways do we need to analyze media concentration?

13   For all the Matt Drudges churning away in small rooms, there are signs that the Internet may come to be dominated by big media. In June, Disney agreed to buy a large portion of the search engine company Infoseek. NBC purchased a share of CNET and its online search engine, Snap! These new investments, wrote Matt Welch in the *Online Journalism Review* (www.ojr.org), "further confused the already byzantine web of ownership, business alliances, and competition among the parent companies of the biz/tech sites."

14   In the Internet Age, media concentration bears even closer watching. Ownership needs to be demystified. Customers are entitled to know what corporate entity is responsible for bringing them their news. And this is now getting harder to know, with the emergence of a crop of big media companies not normally associated with journalism. In the next century, will Softbank dominate? Or Vulcan? Or Zapata? Or Intel?

15   Too often, commentary on media concentration has been fragmentary or anecdotal. We need to recast the debate, which shows signs of stagnating. We need to add new perspectives. That is why we should welcome fresh efforts at understanding media concentration. Two recent

efforts are noteworthy. One is Mark Crispin Miller's Project on Media Ownership, now affiliated with New York University, which will detail interlocking ownership. And "Who Owns What" (described above) will appear on the *CJR* Web site, at www.cjr.org. With hard data and hard analysis will come answers to the vital questions that need to be asked about media concentration. ■

C<small>ATHLEEN</small> C<small>LEAVER</small>

The Internet: A Clear and Present Danger?

Cathleen Cleaver was working in Washington, D.C., at the Family Research Council (a research and advocacy organization) as director of legal education when, in October 1997, she delivered the following speech at Boston University. The argument was later posted on a Web site. Outspoken in support of efforts to regulate the Internet, Cleaver often contributes op-ed articles on subjects related to the protection of children and families. She now works as counsel to the U.S. House of Representatives subcommittee on the Constitution.

1 ■ Someone breaks through your firewall and steals proprietary information from your computer systems. You find out and contact a lawyer who says, "Man, you shouldn't have had your stuff online." The thief becomes a millionaire using your ideas, and you go broke, if laws against copyright violation don't protect material on the Internet.

■ You visit the Antiques Anonymous Web site and decide to pay their hefty subscription fee for a year's worth of exclusive estate sale previews in their private online monthly magazine. They never deliver, and, in fact, never intended to—they don't even have a magazine. You have no recourse, if laws against fraud don't apply to online transactions.

■ Bob Guccione decides to branch out into the lucrative child porn market, and creates a Teen Hustler Web site featuring nude adolescents and preteens. You find out and complain, but nothing can be done, if child pornography distribution laws don't apply to computer transmissions.

■ A major computer software vendor who dominates the market develops his popular office software so that it works only with his browser. You're a small browser manufacturer who is completely squeezed out of the market, but you have to find a new line of work, if antitrust laws don't apply online.

■ Finally, a pedophile e-mails your son, misrepresenting himself as a twelve-year-old named Jenny. They develop an online relationship and one day arrange to meet after school, where he intends to rape your son. Thankfully, you learn in advance about the meeting and go there yourself, where you find a forty-year-old man instead of Jenny. You flee to the police, who'll tell you there's nothing they can do, if child-stalking laws don't apply to the Internet.

The Issue

2   The awesome advances in interactive telecommunication that we've witnessed in just the last few years have changed the way in which many Americans communicate and interact. No one can doubt that the Internet is a technological revolution of enormous proportion, with outstanding possibilities for human advancement.

3   As lead speaker for the affirmative, I'm asked to argue that the Internet poses a "clear and present danger," but the Internet, as a whole, isn't dangerous. In fact, it continues to be a positive and highly beneficial tool, which will undoubtedly improve education, information exchange, and commerce in years to come. In other words, the Internet will enrich many aspects of our daily life. Thus, instead of defending this rather apocalyptic view of the Internet, I'll attempt to explain why some industry and government regulation of certain aspects of the Internet is necessary—or, stated another way, why people who use the Internet should not be exempt from many of the laws and regulations that govern their conduct elsewhere. My opening illustrations were meant to give examples of some illegal conduct which should not become legal simply because someone uses the Internet. In looking at whether Internet regulation is a good idea, I believe we should consider whether regulation is in the public interest. In order to do that, we have to ask the question: Who is the public? More specifically, does the "public" whose interests we care about tonight include children?

Children and the Internet

4   Dave Barry describes the Internet as a "worldwide network of university, government, business, and private computer systems, run by a thirteen-year-old named Jason." This description draws a smile precisely because we acknowledge the highly advanced computer literacy of our children. Most children demonstrate computer proficiency that far surpasses that of their parents, and many parents know only what their children have taught them about the Internet, which gives new relevance to Wordsworth's insight: "The child is father of the man." In fact, one could go so far as to say that the Internet is as accessible to many children as it is inaccessible to many adults. This technological evolution is new in

many ways, not the least of which is its accessibility to children, wholly independent of their parents.

5   When considering what's in the public interest, we must consider the whole public, including children, as individual participants in this new medium.

Pornography and the Internet

6   This new medium is unique in another way. It provides, through a single avenue, the full spectrum of pornographic depictions, from the more familiar convenience store fare to pornography of such violence and depravity that it surpasses the worst excesses of the normal human imagination. Sites displaying this material are easily accessible, making pornography far more freely available via the Internet than from any other communications medium in the United States. Pornography is the third largest sector of sales on the Internet, generating $1 billion annually. There are an estimated seventy-two thousand pornographic sites on the World Wide Web alone, with approximately thirty-nine new ex-

JOHN PERRY BARLOW

A Declaration of the Independence of Cyberspace

John Perry Barlow

After seventeen years as a Wyoming rancher who, on the side, wrote songs for the Grateful Dead, John Perry Barlow (born 1947) in the late 1980s began writing about computer-mediated communications. He served on the board of directors of WELL (the Whole Earth `Lectronic Link), posts regularly on the WELL website, and is a cofounder of the Electronic Frontier Foundation, which advocates keeping government regulations out of the Internet. Since May of 1998, he has been a Fellow at Harvard Law School's Berkman Center for Internet and Society.

1   Governments of the Industrial World, you weary giants of flesh and steel, I come from Cyberspace, the new home of Mind. On behalf of the future, I ask you of the past to leave us alone. You are not welcome among us. You have no sovereignty where we gather.

2   We have no elected government, nor are we likely to have one, so I address you with no greater authority than that with which liberty itself always speaks. I declare the global social space we are building to

plicit sex sites every day. Indeed, the *Washington Post* has called the Internet the largest pornography store in the history of mankind.

7   There is little restriction of pornography-related activity in cyberspace. While there are some porn-related laws, the specter of those laws does not loom large in cyberspace. There's an implicit license there that exists nowhere else with regard to pornography—an environment where people are free to exploit others for profit and be virtually untroubled by legal deterrent. Indeed, if we consider cyberspace to be a little world of its own, it's the type of world for which groups like the ACLU have long fought, but, so far, fought in vain.

8   I believe it will not remain this way, but until it changes, we should take the opportunity to see what this world looks like, if for no other reason than to reassure ourselves that our decades-old decisions to control pornography were good ones.

9   With a few clicks of the mouse, anyone, any child, can get graphic and often violent sexual images—the kind of stuff it used to be difficult to find without exceptional effort and some significant personal risk. Anyone with a computer and a modem can set up public sites featuring

---

be naturally independent of the tyrannies you seek to impose on us. You have no moral right to rule us nor do you possess any methods of enforcement we have true reason to fear.

3   Governments derive their just powers from the consent of the governed. You have neither solicited nor received ours. We did not invite you. You do not know us, nor do you know our world. Cyberspace does not lie within your borders. Do not think that you can build it, as though it were a public construction project. You cannot. It is an act of nature and it grows itself through our collective actions.

4   You have not engaged in our great and gathering conversation, nor did you create the wealth of our marketplaces. You do not know our culture, our ethics, or the unwritten codes that already provide our society more order than could be obtained by any of your impositions.

5   You claim there are problems among us that you need to solve. You use this claim as an excuse to invade our precincts. Many of these problems don't exist. Where there are real conflicts, where there are wrongs, we will identify them and address them by our means. We are forming our own Social Contract. This governance will arise according to the conditions of our world, not yours. Our world is different.

6   Cyberspace consists of transactions, relationships, and thought itself, arrayed like a standing wave in the web of our communications. Ours is a world that is both everywhere and nowhere, but it is not where bodies live.

the perversion of their choice, whether it's mutilation of female genitals, eroticized urination and defecation, bestiality, or sites featuring depictions of incest. These pictures can be sold for profit, they can be sent to harass others, or posted to shock people. Anyone can describe the fantasy rape and murder of a specific person and display it for all to read. Anyone can meet children in chat rooms or via e-mail and send them pornography and find out where they live. An adult who signs onto an AOL chat room as a thirteen-year-old girl is hit on thirty times within the first half hour.

10   All this can be done from the seclusion of the home, with the feeling of near anonymity and with the comfort of knowing that there's little risk of legal sanction.

11   The phenomenon of this kind of pornography finding such a welcome home in this new medium presents abundant opportunities for social commentary. What does Internet pornography tell us about human sexuality? Photographs, videos, and virtual games that depict rape and the dehumanization of women in sexual scenes send powerful messages about human dignity and equality. Much of the pornography

7   We are creating a world that all may enter without privilege or prejudice accorded by race, economic power, military force, or station of birth.

8   We are creating a world where anyone, anywhere may express his or her beliefs, no matter how singular, without fear of being coerced into silence or conformity.

9   Your legal concepts of property, expression, identity, movement, and context do not apply to us. They are based on matter. There is no matter here.

10   Our identities have no bodies, so, unlike you, we cannot obtain order by physical coercion. We believe that, from ethics, enlightened self-interest, and the commonweal, our governance will emerge. Our identities may be distributed across many of your jurisdictions. The only law that all our constituent cultures would generally recognize is the Golden Rule. We hope we will be able to build our particular solutions on that basis. But we cannot accept the solutions you are attempting to impose.

11   In the United States, you have today created a law, the Telecommunications Reform Act, which repudiates your own Constitution and insults the dreams of Jefferson, Washington, Mill, Madison, deToqueville, and Brandeis. These dreams must now be born anew in us.

12   You are terrified of your own children, since they are natives in a world where you will always be immigrants. Because you fear them, you entrust your bureaucracies with the parental responsibilities you are too cowardly to confront yourselves. In our world, all the sentiments

freely available without restriction on the Internet celebrates unhealthy and antisocial kinds of sexual activity, such as sadomasochism, abuse, and degradation. Of course, by its very nature, pornography encourages voyeurism.

12   Beyond the troubling social aspects of unrestricted porn, we face the reality that children are accessing it and that predators are accessing children. We have got to start considering what kind of society we'll have when the next generation learns about human sexuality from what the Internet teaches. What does unrestricted Internet pornography teach children about relationships, about the equality of women? What does it teach little girls about themselves and their worth?

13   Opponents of restrictions are fond of saying that it's up to the parents to deal with the issue of children's exposure. Well, of course it is, but placing the burden solely on parents is illogical and ineffective. It's far easier for a distributor of pornography to control his material than it is for parents, who must, with the help of software, search for and find the pornographic sites, which change daily, and then attempt to block them. Any pornographer who wants to can easily subvert these efforts,

and expressions of humanity, from the debasing to the angelic, are parts of a seamless whole, the global conversation of bits. We cannot separate the air that chokes from the air upon which wings beat.

13   In China, Germany, France, Russia, Singapore, Italy, and the United States, you are trying to ward off the virus of liberty by erecting guard posts at the frontiers of Cyberspace. These may keep out the contagion for a small time, but they will not work in a world that will soon be blanketed in bit-bearing media.

14   Your increasingly obsolete information industries would perpetuate themselves by proposing laws, in America and elsewhere, that claim to own speech itself throughout the world. These laws would declare ideas to be another industrial product, no more noble than pig Iron. In our world, whatever the human mind may create can be reproduced and distributed infinitely at no cost. The global conveyance of thought no longer requires your factories to accomplish.

15   These increasingly hostile and colonial measures place us in the same position as those previous lovers of freedom and self-determination who had to reject the authorities of distant, uninformed powers. We must declare our virtual selves immune to your sovereignty, even as we continue to consent to your rule over our bodies. We will spread ourselves across the Planet so that no one can arrest our thoughts.

16   We will create a civilization of the Mind in Cyberspace. May it be more humane and fair than the world your governments have made before. ■

and a recent Internet posting from a teenager wanting to know how to disable the filtering software on his computer received several effective answers. Moreover, it goes without saying that the most sophisticated software can only be effective where it's installed, and children will have access to many computers that don't have filtering software, such as those in libraries, schools, and at neighbors' houses.

Internet Transactions Should Not Be Exempt

14 Opponents of legal restrictions often argue simply that the laws just cannot apply in this new medium, but the argument that old laws can't apply to changing technology just doesn't hold. We saw this argument last in the early '80s with the advent of the videotape. Then, certain groups tried to argue that, since you can't view videotapes without a VCR, you can't make the sale of child porn videos illegal, because, after all, they're just plastic boxes with magnetic tape inside. Technological change mandates legal change only insofar as it affects the justification for a law. It just doesn't make sense that the government may take steps to restrict illegal material in *every* medium—video, television, radio, the private telephone, *and* print—but that it may do *nothing* where people distribute the material by the Internet. While old laws might need re-definition, the old principles generally stand firm.

15 The question of enforcement usually is raised here, and it often comes in the form of: "How are you going to stop people from doing it?" Well, no law stops people from doing things—a red light at an intersection doesn't force you to stop but tells you that you should stop and that there could be legal consequences if you don't. Not everyone who runs a red light is caught, but that doesn't mean the law is futile. The same concept holds true for Internet laws. Government efforts to temper harmful conduct online will never be perfect, but that doesn't mean they shouldn't undertake the effort at all.

16 There's clearly a role for industry to play here. Search engines don't have to run ads for porn sites or prioritize search results to high-light porn. One new search engine even has sex as the default search term. Internet service providers can do something about unsolicited e-mail with hotlinks to porn, and they can and should carefully monitor any chat rooms designed for kids.

17 Some charge that industry standards or regulations that restrict explicit pornography will hinder the development of Internet technology. But that is to say that its advancement *depends upon* unrestricted exhibition of this material, and this cannot be true. The Internet does not belong to pornographers, and it's clearly in the public interest to see that they don't usurp this great new technology. We don't live in a perfect society, and the Internet is merely a reflection of the larger social community. Without some mitigating influences, the strong will exploit the weak, whether a Bill Gates or a child predator.

Conclusion: Technology Must Serve Man

18 To argue that the strength of the Internet is chaos or that our liberty depends upon chaos is to misunderstand not only the Internet but also the fundamental nature of our liberty. It's an illusion to claim social or moral neutrality in the application of technology, even if its development may be neutral. It can be a valuable resource only when placed at the service of humanity and when it promotes our integral development for the benefit of all.

19 Guiding principles simply cannot be inferred from mere technical efficiency or from the usefulness accruing to some at the expense of others. Technology by its very nature requires unconditional respect for the fundamental interests of society.

20 Internet technology must be at the service of humanity and of our inalienable rights. It must respect the prerogatives of a civil society, among which is the protection of children. ■

Fahrenheit 451.2: Is Cyberspace Burning?

The American Civil Liberties Union is famous for its advocacy on a whole range of civil liberties issues. Among other things, it is resolute in its support of First-Amendment freedoms, particularly the rights of free speech and assembly: see www.aclu.org. The following argument about restrictions on the Internet, written mostly by ACLU staff members Ann Beeson, Chris Hansen, and Barry Steinhardt, appeared on the ACLU Web site on March 17, 2002.

Introduction

1 In his chilling (and prescient) novel about censorship, *Fahrenheit 451,* author Ray Bradbury describes a futuristic society where books are outlawed "Fahrenheit 451" is, of course, the temperature at which books burn.

2 In Bradbury's novel and in the physical world people censor the printed word by burning books. But in the virtual world, one can just as easily censor controversial speech by banishing it to the farthest corners of cyberspace using rating and blocking programs. Today, will Fahrenheit, version 451.2, a new kind of virtual censorship, be the temperature at which cyberspace goes up in smoke?

3 The first flames of Internet censorship appeared two years ago, with the introduction of the Federal Communications Decency Act (CDA), outlawing "indecent" online speech. But in the landmark case *Reno* v. *ACLU,* the Supreme Court overturned the CDA, declaring that

the Internet is entitled to the highest level of free speech protection. In other words, the Court said that online speech deserved the protection afforded to books and other printed matter.

4   Today, all that we have achieved may now be lost, if not in the bright flames of censorship then in the dense smoke of the many ratings and blocking schemes promoted by some of the very people who fought for freedom. And in the end, we may find that the censors have indeed succeeded in "burning down the house to roast the pig."

Is Cyberspace Burning?

5   The ashes of the CDA were barely smoldering when the White House called a summit meeting to encourage Internet users to self-rate their speech and to urge industry leaders to develop and deploy the tools for blocking "inappropriate" speech. The meeting was "voluntary," of course: the White House claimed it wasn't holding anyone's feet to the fire.

6   The ACLU and others in the cyber-liberties community were genuinely alarmed by the tenor of the White House summit and the unabashed enthusiasm for technological fixes that will make it easier to block or render invisible controversial speech.

7   Industry leaders responded to the White House call with a barrage of announcements:

- ■ Netscape announced plans to join Microsoft; together the two giants have 90 percent or more of the Web browser market in adopting PICS (Platform for Internet Content Selection), the rating standard that establishes a consistent way to rate and block online content;

- ■ IBM announced it was making a $100,000 grant to RSAC (Recreational Software Advisory Council) to encourage the use of its RSACi rating system. Microsoft Explorer already employs the RSACi ratings system, Compuserve encourages its use and it is fast becoming the de facto industry standard rating system;

- ■ Four of the major search engines, the services which allow users to conduct searches of the Internet for relevant sites, announced a plan to co-operate in the promotion of "self-regulation" of the Internet. The president of one, Lycos, was quoted in a news account as having "thrown down the gauntlet" to the other three, challenging them to agree to exclude unrated sites from search results;

- ■ Following announcement of proposed legislation by Sen. Patty Murray (D-Wash), which would impose civil and ultimately criminal penalties on those who mis-rate a site, the makers of the blocking program Safe Surf proposed similar legislation, the "Online Cooperative Publishing Act."

8   But it was not any one proposal or announcement that caused our alarm; rather, it was the failure to examine the longer-term implications for the Internet of rating and blocking schemes.

9   What may be the result? The Internet will become bland and homogenized. The major commercial sites will still be readily available, they will have the resources and inclination to self-rate, and third-party rating services will be inclined to give them acceptable ratings. People who disseminate quirky and idiosyncratic speech, create individual home pages, or post to controversial news groups, will be among the first Internet users blocked by filters and made invisible by the search engines. Controversial speech will still exist, but will only be visible to those with the tools and know-how to penetrate the dense smokescreen of industry "self-regulation."

10   As bad as this very real prospect is, it can get worse. Faced with the reality that, although harder to reach, sex, hate speech, and other controversial matter is still available on the Internet, how long will it be before governments begin to make use of an Internet already configured to accommodate massive censorship? If you look at these various proposals in a larger context, a very plausible scenario emerges. It is a scenario which in some respects has already been set in motion:

■ First, the use of PICS becomes universal; providing a uniform method for content rating.

■ Next, one or two rating systems dominate the market and become the de facto standard for the Internet.

■ PICS and the dominant rating(s) system are built into Internet software as an automatic default.

■ Unrated speech on the Internet is effectively blocked by these defaults.

■ Search engines refuse to report on the existence of unrated or "unacceptably" rated sites.

■ Governments frustrated by "indecency" still on the Internet make self-rating mandatory and mis-rating a crime.

11   The scenario is, for now, theoretical but inevitable. It is clear that any scheme that allows access to unrated speech will fall afoul of the government-coerced push for a "family-friendly" Internet. We are moving inexorably toward a system that blocks speech simply because it is unrated and makes criminals of those who mis-rate.

12   The White House meeting was clearly the first step in that direction and away from the principle that protection of the electronic word is analogous to protection of the printed word. Despite the Supreme Court's strong rejection of a broadcast analogy for the Internet, government and industry leaders alike are now inching toward the dangerous

and incorrect position that the Internet is like television, and should be rated and censored accordingly.

13   Is cyberspace burning? Not yet, perhaps. But where there's smoke, there's fire.

Free Speech Online: A Victory Under Siege

14   On June 26, 1997, the Supreme Court held in *Reno* v. *ACLU* that the Communications Decency Act, which would have made it a crime to communicate anything "indecent" on the Internet, violated the First Amendment. It was the nature of the Internet itself, and the quality of speech on the Internet, that led the Court to declare that the Internet is entitled to the same broad free speech protections given to books, magazines, and casual conversation.

15   The ACLU argued, and the Supreme Court agreed, that the CDA was unconstitutional because, although aimed at protecting minors, it effectively banned speech among adults. Similarly, many of the rating and blocking proposals, though designed to limit minors' access, will inevitably restrict the ability of adults to communicate on the Internet. In addition, such proposals will restrict the rights of older minors to gain access to material that clearly has value for them.

Rethinking the Rush to Rate

16 This paper examines the free speech implications of the various proposals for Internet blocking and rating. Individually, each of the proposals poses some threat to open and robust speech on the Internet; some pose a considerably greater threat than others.

17 Even more ominous is the fact that the various schemes for rating and blocking, taken together, could create a black cloud of private "voluntary" censorship that is every bit as threatening as the CDA itself to what the Supreme Court called "the most participatory form of mass speech yet developed."

18 We call on industry leaders, Internet users, policy makers, and parents groups to engage in a genuine debate about the free speech ramifications of the rating and blocking schemes being proposed.

19 To open the door to a meaningful discussion, we offer the following recommendations and principles:

Recommendations and Principles

■ Internet users know best. The primary responsibility for determining what speech to access should remain with the individual Internet user: parents should take primary responsibility for determining what their children should access.

■ Default setting on free speech. Industry should not develop products that require speakers to rate their own speech or be blocked by default.

■ Buyers beware. The producers of user-based software programs should make their lists of blocked speech available to consumers. The industry should develop products that provide maximum user control.

■ No government coercion or censorship. The First Amendment prevents the government from imposing, or from coercing industry into imposing, a mandatory Internet ratings scheme.

■ Libraries are free speech zones. The First Amendment prevents the government, including public libraries, from mandating the use of user-based blocking software.

Six Reasons Why Self-Rating Schemes Are Wrong for the Internet

20 To begin with, the notion that citizens should "self-rate" their speech is contrary to the entire history of free speech in America. A proposal that we rate our online speech is no less offensive to the First Amendment than a proposal that publishers of books and magazines rate each and every article or story, or a proposal that everyone engaged in a street

corner conversation rate his or her comments. But that is exactly what will happen to books, magazines, and any kind of speech that appears online under a self-rating scheme.

21   In order to illustrate the very practical consequences of these schemes, consider the following six reasons, and their accompanying examples, illustrating why the ACLU is against self-rating:

Reason #1: Self-Rating Schemes Will Cause Controversial Speech to Be Censored.

22 Kiyoshi Kuromiya, founder and sole operator of Critical Path Aids Project, has a Web site that includes safer sex information written in street language with explicit diagrams, in order to reach the widest possible audience. Kuromiya doesn't want to apply the rating "crude" or "explicit" to his speech, but if he doesn't, his site will be blocked as an unrated site. If he does rate, his speech will be lumped in with "pornography" and blocked from view. Under either choice, Kuromiya has been effectively blocked from reaching a large portion of his intended audience—teenage Internet users as well as adults.

23   As this example shows, the consequences of rating are far from neutral. The ratings themselves are all pejorative by definition, and they result in certain speech being blocked.

24   The White House has compared Internet ratings to "food labels" but that analogy is simply wrong. Food labels provide objective, scientifically verifiable information to help the consumer make choices about what to buy, e.g., the percentage of fat in a food product like milk. Internet ratings are subjective value judgments that result in certain speech being blocked to many viewers. Further, food labels are placed on products that are readily available to consumers unlike Internet labels, which would place certain kinds of speech out of reach of Internet users.

25   What is most critical to this issue is that speech like Kuromiya's is entitled to the highest degree of constitutional protection. This is why ratings requirements have never been imposed on those who speak via the printed word. Kuromiya could distribute the same material in print form on any street corner or in any bookstore without worrying about having to rate it. In fact, a number of Supreme Court cases have established that the First Amendment does not allow government to compel speakers to say something they don't want to say and that includes pejorative ratings. There is simply no justification for treating the Internet any differently.

Reason #2: Self-Rating Is Burdensome, Unwieldy, and Costly.

26 Art on the Net is a large, nonprofit Web site that hosts online "studios" where hundreds of artists display their work. The vast majority of the art-work has no sexual content, although there's an occasional Rubenesque painting. The ratings systems don't make sense when applied to

art. Yet Art on the Net would still have to review and apply a rating to the more than 26,000 pages on its site, which would require time and staff that they just don't have. Or, they would have to require the artists themselves to self-rate, an option they find objectionable. If they decline to rate, they will be blocked as an unrated site even though most Internet users would hardly object to the art reaching minors, let alone adults.

27   As the Supreme Court noted in *Reno* v. *ACLU,* one of the virtues of the Internet is that it provides "relatively unlimited, low-cost capacity for communication of all kinds." In striking down the CDA, the Court held that imposing age-verification costs on Internet speakers would be "prohibitively expensive for noncommercial as well as some commercial speakers." Similarly, the burdensome requirement of self-rating thousands of pages of information would effectively shut most noncommercial speakers out of the Internet marketplace.

28   The technology of embedding the rating is also far from trivial. In a winning ACLU case that challenged a New York state online censorship statute, *ALA* v. *Pataki,* one long-time Internet expert testified that he tried to embed an RSACi label in his online newsletter site but finally gave up after several hours.

29   In addition, the ratings systems are simply unequipped to deal with the diversity of content now available on the Internet. There is perhaps nothing as subjective as a viewer's reaction to art. As history has shown again and again, one woman's masterpiece is another woman's pornography. How can ratings such as "explicit" or "crude" be used to categorize art? Even ratings systems that try to take artistic value into account will be inherently subjective, especially when applied by artists themselves, who will naturally consider their own work to have merit.

30   The variety of news-related sites on the Web will be equally difficult to rate. Should explicit war footage be labeled "violent" and blocked from view to teenagers? If a long news article has one curse word, is the curse word rated individually, or is the entire story rated and then blocked?

31   Even those who propose that "legitimate" news organizations should not be required to rate their sites stumble over the question of who will decide what is legitimate news.

Reason #3: Conversation Can't Be Rated.

32   You are in a chat room or a discussion group, one of the thousands of conversational areas of the Net. A victim of sexual abuse has posted a plea for help, and you want to respond. You've heard about a variety of ratings systems, but you've never used one. You read the RSACi Web page, but you can't figure out how to rate the discussion of sex and

violence in your response. Aware of the penalties for mislabeling, you decide not to send your message after all.

33   The burdens of self-rating really hit home when applied to the vibrant, conversational areas of the Internet. Most Internet users don't run Web pages, but millions of people around the world send messages, short and long, every day, to chat rooms, news groups and mailing lists. A rating requirement for these areas of the Internet would be analogous to requiring all of us to rate our telephone or street corner or dinner party or water cooler conversations.

34   The only other way to rate these areas of cyberspace would be to rate entire chat rooms or news groups rather than individual messages. But most discussion groups aren't controlled by a specific person, so who would be responsible for rating them? In addition, discussion groups that contain some objectionable material would likely also have a wide variety of speech totally appropriate and valuable for minors; but the entire forum would be blocked from view for everyone.

Reason #4: Self-Rating Will Create "Fortress America" on the Internet.

35   You are a native of Papua, New Guinea, and as an anthropologist you have published several papers about your native culture. You create a Web site and post electronic versions of your papers, in order to share them with colleagues and other interested people around the world. You haven't heard about the move in America to rate Internet content. You don't know it, but since your site is unrated none of your colleagues in America will be able to access it.

36   People from all corners of the globe—people who might otherwise never connect because of their vast geographical differences—can now communicate on the Internet both easily and cheaply. One of the most dangerous aspects of ratings systems is their potential to build borders around American- and foreign-created speech. It is important to remember that today, nearly half of all Internet speech originates from outside the United States.

37   Even if powerful American industry leaders coerced other countries into adopting American ratings systems, how would these ratings make any sense to a New Guinean? Imagine that one of the anthropology papers explicitly describes a ritual in which teenage boys engage in self-mutilation as part of a rite of passage in achieving manhood. Would you look at it through the eyes of an American and rate it "torture," or would you rate it "appropriate for minors" for the New Guinea audience?

Reason #5: Self-Ratings Will Only Encourage, Not Prevent, Government Regulation.

38   The webmaster for Betty's Smut Shack, a Web site that sells sexually explicit photos, learns that many people won't get to his site if he either

rates his site "sexually explicit" or fails to rate it at all. He rates his entire Web site "okay for minors." A powerful congressman from the Midwest learns that the site is now available to minors. He is outraged, and quickly introduces a bill imposing criminal penalties for mis-rated sites.

39   Without a penalty system for mis-rating, the entire concept of a self-ratings system breaks down. The Supreme Court that decided *Reno* v. *ACLU* would probably agree that the statute theorized above would violate the First Amendment, but as we saw with the CDA, that won't necessarily prevent lawmakers from passing it.

40   In fact, as noted earlier, a senator from Washington state—home of Industry giant Microsoft, among others—has already proposed a law that creates criminal penalties for mis-rating. Not to be outdone, the filtering software company Safe Surf has proposed the introduction of a virtually identical federal law, including a provision that allows parents to sue speakers for damages if they "negligently" mis-rate their speech.

41   The example above shows that, despite all good intentions, the application of ratings systems is likely to lead to heavy-handed government censorship. Moreover, the targets of that censorship are likely to be just the sort of relatively powerless and controversial speakers, like the groups Critical Path Aids Project, Stop Prisoner Rape, Planned Parenthood, Human Rights Watch, and the various gay and lesbian organizations we represented in *Reno* v. *ACLU.*

Reason #6: Self-Ratings Schemes Will Turn the Internet into a
Homogenized Medium Dominated by Commercial Speakers.

42   Huge entertainment conglomerates, such as the Disney Corporation or Time Warner, consult their platoons of lawyers who advise that their Web sites must be rated to reach the widest possible audience. They then hire and train staff to rate all of their Web pages. Everybody in the world will have access to their speech.

43   There is no question that there may be some speakers on the internet for whom the ratings systems will impose only minimal burdens: the large, powerful corporate speakers with the money to hire legal counsel and staff to apply the necessary ratings. The commercial side of the Net continues to grow, but so far the democratic nature of the Internet has put commercial speakers on equal footing with all of the other noncommercial and individual speakers.

44   Today, it is just as easy to find the Critical Path AIDS Web site as it is to find the Disney site. Both speakers are able to reach a worldwide audience. But mandatory Internet self-rating could easily turn the most participatory communications medium the world has yet seen into a bland, homogenized, medium dominated by powerful American corporate speakers.

Is Third-Party Rating the Answer?

45 Third-party ratings systems, designed to work in tandem with PICS labeling, have been held out by some as the answer to the free speech problems posed by self-rating schemes. On the plus side, some argue, ratings by an independent third party could minimize the burden of self-rating on speakers and could reduce the inaccuracy and mis-rating problems of self-rating. In fact, one of the touted strengths of the original PICS proposal was that a variety of third-party ratings systems would develop and users could pick and choose from the system that best fit their values. But third-party ratings systems still pose serious free speech concerns.

46 First, a multiplicity of ratings systems has not yet emerged on the market, probably due to the difficulty of any one company or organization trying to rate over a million Web sites, with hundreds of new sites, not to mention discussion groups and chat rooms springing up daily.

47 Second, under third-party rating systems, unrated sites still may be blocked.

48 When choosing which sites to rate first, it is likely that third-party raters will rate the most popular Web sites first, marginalizing individual and noncommercial sites. And like the self-rating systems, third-party ratings will apply subjective and value-laden ratings that could result in valuable material being blocked to adults and older minors. In addition, available third-party rating systems have no notification procedure so speakers have no way of knowing whether their speech has received a negative rating.

49 The fewer the third-party ratings products available, the greater the potential for arbitrary censorship. Powerful industry forces may lead one product to dominate the marketplace. If, for example, virtually all households use Microsoft Internet Explorer and Netscape, and the browsers, in turn, use RSACi as their system, RSACi could become the default censorship system for the Internet. In addition, federal and state governments could pass laws mandating use of a particular ratings system in schools or libraries. Either of these scenarios could devastate the diversity of the Internet marketplace.

50 Pro-censorship groups have argued that a third-party rating system for the Internet is no different from the voluntary Motion Picture Association of America ratings for movies that we've all lived with for years. But there is an important distinction: only a finite number of movies are produced in a given year. In contrast, the amount of content on the Internet is infinite. Movies are a static, definable product created by a small number of producers: speech on the Internet is seamless, interactive, and conversational. MPAA ratings also don't come with automatic blocking mechanisms.

The Problems with User-Based Blocking Software in the Home

51   With the explosive growth of the Internet, and in the wake of the recent censorship battles, the marketplace has responded with a wide variety of user-based blocking programs. Each company touts the speed and efficiency of its staff members in blocking speech that they have determined is inappropriate for minors. The programs also often block speech based on keywords. (This can result in sites such as www.middlesex.gov or www.SuperBowlXXX.com being blocked because they contain the keywords "sex" and "XXX.")

52   In *Reno* v. *ACLU,* the ACLU successfully argued that the CDA violated the First Amendment because it was not the least restrictive means of addressing the government's asserted interest in protecting children from inappropriate material. In supporting this argument, we suggested that a less restrictive alternative was the availability of user-based blocking programs, e.g., Net Nanny, that parents could use in the home if they wished to limit their child's Internet access.

53   While user-based blocking programs present troubling free speech concerns, we still believe today that they are far preferable to any statute that imposes criminal penalties on online speech. In contrast, many of the new ratings schemes pose far greater free speech concerns than do user-based software programs.

54   Each user installs the program on her home computer and turns the blocking mechanism on or off at will. The programs do not generally block sites that they haven't rated, which means that they are not 100 percent effective.

55   Unlike the third-party ratings or self-rating schemes, these products usually do not work in concert with browsers and search engines, so the home user rather than an outside company sets the defaults. (However, it should be noted that this "stand-alone" feature could theoretically work against free speech principles, since here, too, it would be relatively easy to draft a law mandating the use of the products, under threat of criminal penalties.)

56   While the use of these products avoids some of the larger control issues with ratings systems, the blocking programs are far from problem-free. A number of products have been shown to block access to a wide variety of information that many would consider appropriate for minors. For example, some block access to safer sex information, although the Supreme Court has held that teenagers have the right to obtain access to such information even without their parents' consent. Other products block access to information of interest to the gay and lesbian community. Some products even block speech simply because it criticizes their product.

57   Some products allow home users to add or subtract particular sites from a list of blocked sites. For example, a parent can decide to allow

access to "playboy.com" by removing it from the blocked sites list, and can deny access to "powerrangers.com" by adding it to the list. However most products consider their lists of blocked speech to be proprietary information which they will not disclose.

58   Despite these problems, the use of blocking programs has been enthusiastically and uncritically endorsed by government and industry leaders alike. At the recent White House summit, Vice President Gore, along with industry and nonprofit groups, announced the creation of www.netparents.org, a site that provides direct links to a variety of blocking programs.

59   The ACLU urges the producers of all of these products to put real power in users' hands and provide full disclosure of their list of blocked speech and the criteria for blocking.

60   In addition, the ACLU urges the industry to develop products that provide maximum user control. For example, all users should be able to adjust the products to account for the varying maturity level of minors, and to adjust the list of blocked sites to reflect their own values.

61   It should go without saying that under no set of circumstances can governments constitutionally require anyone whether individual users or Internet Service Providers to run user-based blocking programs when accessing or providing access to the Internet.

Why Blocking Software Should Not Be Used by Public Libraries

62   The "never-ending, worldwide conversation" of the Internet, as one lower court judge called it, is a conversation in which all citizens should be entitled to participate whether they access the Internet from the library or from the home. Just as government cannot require home users or Internet Service Providers (ISPs) to use blocking programs or self-rating programs, libraries should not require patrons to use blocking software when accessing the Internet at the library. The ACLU, like the American Library Association (ALA), opposes use of blocking software in public libraries.

63   Libraries have traditionally promoted free speech values by providing free books and information resources to people regardless of their age or income. Today, more than 20 percent of libraries in the United States offer free access to the Internet, and that number is growing daily. Libraries are critical to realizing the dream of universal access to the Internet, a dream that would be drastically altered if they were forced to become Internet censors.

64   In a recent announcement stating its policy, the ALA said:

> Libraries are places of inclusion rather than exclusion. Current blocking/filtering software prevents not only access to what some may consider "objectionable" material, but also blocks information protected by the First Amendment. The result is that legal and useful material will inevitably be blocked.

65   Librarians have never been in the business of determining what their patrons should read or see, and the fact that the material is now found on Internet is no different. By installing inaccurate and unreliable blocking programs on library Internet terminals, public libraries, which are almost always governmental entities, would inevitably censor speech that patrons are constitutionally entitled to access.

66   It has been suggested that a library's decision to install blocking software is like other legitimate selection decisions that libraries routinely make when they add particular books to their collections. But in fact, blocking programs take selection decisions totally out of the hands of the librarian and place them in the hands of a company with no experience in library science. As the ALA noted, "(F)ilters can impose the producer's viewpoint on the community."

67   Because, as noted above, most filtering programs don't provide a list of the sites they block, libraries won't even know what resources are blocked. In addition, Internet speakers won't know which libraries have blocked access to their speech and won't be able to protest.

68   Installing blocking software in libraries to prevent adults as well as minors from accessing legally protected material raises severe First Amendment questions. Indeed, that principle that governments can't block adult access to speech in the name of protecting children was one of the key reasons for the Supreme Court's decision in *Reno* v. *ACLU.*

69   If adults are allowed full access, but minors are forced to use blocking programs, constitutional problems remain. Minors, especially older minors, have a constitutional right to access many of the resources that have been shown to be blocked by user-based blocking programs.

70   One of the virtues of the Internet is that it allows an isolated gay teenager in Des Moines, Iowa, to talk to other teenagers around the globe who are also struggling with issues relating to their sexuality. It allows teens to find out how to avoid AIDS and other sexually transmitted diseases even if they are too embarrassed to ask an adult in person or even too embarrassed to check out a book.

71   When the ACLU made this argument in *Reno* v. *ACLU,* it was considered controversial, even among our allies. But the Supreme Court agreed that minors have rights too. Library blocking proposals that allow minors full access to the Internet only with parental permission are unacceptable.

72   Libraries can and should take other actions that are more protective of online free speech principles. First, libraries can publicize and provide links to particular sites that have been recommended for children. Second, to avoid unwanted viewing by passersby (and to protect the confidentiality of users), libraries can install Internet access terminals in ways that minimize public view. Third, libraries can impose "content-neutral" time limits on Internet use.

Conclusion

73 The ACLU has always favored providing Internet users, especially parents, with more information. We welcomed, for example, the American Library Association's announcement at the White House summit of *The Librarian's Guide to Cyberspace for Parents and Kids,* a "comprehensive brochure and Web site combining Internet terminology, safety tips, site selection advice, and more than fifty of the most educational and entertaining sites available for children on the Internet."

74 In *Reno* v. *ACLU,* we noted that federal and state governments are already vigorously enforcing existing obscenity, child pornography, and child solicitation laws on the Internet. In addition, Internet users must affirmatively seek out speech on the Internet; no one is caught by surprise.

75 In fact, many speakers on the Net provide preliminary information about the nature of their speech. The ACLU's site on America Online, for example, has a message on its home page announcing that the site is a "free speech zone." Many sites offering commercial transactions on the Net contain warnings concerning the security of Net information. Sites containing sexually explicit material often begin with a statement describing the adult nature of the material. Chat rooms and newsgroups have names that describe the subject being discussed. Even individual e-mail messages contain a subject line.

76 The preliminary information available on the Internet has several important components that distinguish it from all the ratings systems discussed above: (1) it is created and provided by the speaker; (2) it helps the user decide whether to read any further; (3) speakers who choose not to provide such information are not penalized; (4) it does not result in the automatic blocking of speech by an entity other than the speaker or reader before the speech has ever been viewed. Thus, the very nature of the Internet reveals why more speech is always a better solution than censorship for dealing with speech that someone may find objectionable.

77 It is not too late for the Internet community to slowly and carefully examine these proposals and to reject those that will transform the Internet from a true marketplace of ideas into just another mainstream, lifeless medium with content no more exciting or diverse than that of television.

78 Civil libertarians, human rights organizations, librarians and Internet users, speakers and providers, all joined together to defeat the CDA. We achieved a stunning victory, establishing a legal framework that affords the Internet the highest constitutional protection. We put a quick end to a fire that was all but visible and threatening. The fire next time may be more difficult to detect and extinguish. ■

RUBEN BOLLING

Tom the Dancing Bug Presents

"Tom the Dancing Bug" cartoons are distributed to many publications by the Universal Press Syndicate. This one was produced in 2000.

MATT WELCH

Blogworld and Its Gravity

Weblogs or "blogs" are now quite popular forms of online journaling, reporting, or discussion. Blogs are easily updated Web pages that many people go back to regularly to see updates by an individual about his or her life, or to see news commentary from a particular political viewpoint. Often a person just reads a blog for some time before ever responding, if any response is given at all. With the case of creating blogs through free Internet sites, their numbers are growing rapidly. The associate editor for the online publication Reason Magazine, *Matt Welch here explores how blogs have altered the movement of information and opinions in a post-9/11 world. "Blogworld and Its Gravity" was first published in the* Columbia Journalism Review, *which seeks to keep the public informed about all aspects of the media. Welch has his own blog, which tends toward personal reflections on political issues.*

1   This February, I attended my first Association of Alternative Newsweeklies conference, in the great media incubator of San Francisco. It's impossible to walk a single block of that storied town without feeling the ghosts of great contrarian media innovators past: Hearst and Twain, Hinckle and Wenner, Rossetto and Talbot. But after twelve hours with the AAN, a much different reality set in: never in my life have I seen a more conformist gathering of journalists.

2   All the newspapers looked the same—same format, same fonts, same columns complaining about the local daily, same sex advice, same five-thousand-word hole for the cover story. The people were largely the same, too: all but maybe 2 percent of the city-slicker journalists in attendance were white; the vast majority were either Boomer hippies or Gen X slackers. Several asked me the exact same question with the same suspicious looks on their faces: "So . . . what's your alternative experience?"

3   At the bar, I started a discussion about what specific attributes qualified these papers, and the forty-seven-year-old publishing genre that spawned them, to continue meriting the adjective "alternative." Alternative to what? To the straight-laced "objectivity" and pyramid-style writing of daily newspapers? New Journalists and other narrative storytellers crashed those gates long ago. Alternative to society's oppressive intolerance toward deviant behavior? Tell it to the Osbournes, as they watch *Queer Eye for the Straight Guy.* Something to do with corporate ownership? Not unless "alternative" no longer applies to *Village Voice Media* (owned in part by *Goldman Sachs*) or the New Times chain

(which has been involved in some brutal acquisition and liquidation deals). Someone at the table lamely offered up "a sense of community," but Fox News could easily clear that particular bar.

4   No, it must have something to do with political slant—or, to be technically accurate, political correctness. Richard Karpel, the AAN executive director, joined the conversation, so I put him on the spot: Of all the weeklies his organization had rejected for membership on political grounds, which one was the best editorially? The *Independent Florida Sun,* he replied. Good-looking paper, some sharp writing but, well, it was just too friendly toward the church. "And if there's anything we all agree on," Karpel said with a smile, "it's that we're antichurch."

5   I assumed he was joking—that couldn't be all we have left from the legacy of Norman Mailer, Art Kunkin, Paul Krassner, and my other childhood heroes, could it? Then later I looked up the AAN's Web site to read the admission committee's rejection notes for the *Florida Sun* (which was excluded by a vote of 9–2). "The right-wing church columnist has no place in AAN," explained one judge. "All the God-and-flag shit disturbs me," wrote another. "Weirdly right-wing," chimed a third.

6   The original alternative papers were not at all this politically monochromatic, despite entering the world at a time when Lenny Bruce was being prosecuted for obscenity, Tom Dooley was proselytizing for American intervention in Vietnam, and Republicans ruled the nation's editorial pages. Dan Wolf, co-founder of the trailblazing *Village Voice,* loved to throw darts at what he called "the dull pieties of official liberalism," and founding editors like Mailer were forever trying to tune their antennae to previously undetected political frequencies.

7   The dull pieties of official progressivism is one of many attributes that show how modern alt weeklies have strayed from what made them alternative in the first place. The papers once embraced amateur writers: now they are firmly established in the journalistic pecking order, with the salaries and professional standards to match. They once championed the slogan "never trust anyone over thirty": now their average reader is over forty and aging fast. They have become so ubiquitous in cities over a certain size, during decades when so many other new media formats have sprung up (cable television, newsletters, talk radio, business journals, Web sites), that the very notion that they represent a crucial "alternative" to a monolithic journalism establishment now strains credulity.

8   But there still exists a publishing format that manages to embody all these lost qualities, and more—the Weblog. The average blog, needless to say, pales in comparison to a 1957 issue of the *Voice,* or a 1964 *Los Angeles Free Press,* or a 2003 Lexington, Kentucky, *ACE Weekly,* for that matter. But that's missing the point. Blogging technology has, for the first time in history, given the average Jane the ability to write, edit,

design, and publish her own editorial product—to be read and responded to by millions of people, potentially—for around $0 to $200 a
year. It has begun to deliver on some of the wild promises about the Internet that were heard in the 1990s. Never before have so many passionate outsiders—hundreds of thousands, at minimum—stormed the ram-
parts of professional journalism.

9   And these amateurs, especially the ones focusing on news and
current events, are doing some fascinating things. Many are connecting
intimately with readers in a way reminiscent of old-style metro columnists or the liveliest of the New Journalists. Others are staking the nar-
rowest of editorial claims as their own—appellate court rulings, new
media proliferation in Tehran, the intersection of hip-hop and libertari-
anism—and covering them like no one else. They are forever fact-
checking the daylights out of truth-fudging ideologues like Ann Coulter
and Michael Moore, and sifting through the biases of the *BBC* and Bill
O'Reilly, often while cheerfully acknowledging and/or demonstrating
their own lopsided political sympathies. At this instant, all over the
world, bloggers are busy popularizing under-appreciated print journalists (like *Chicago Sun-Times* columnist Mark Steyn), pumping up stories that should be getting more attention (like the Trent Lott debacle),
and perhaps most excitingly of all, committing impressive, spontaneous
acts of decentralized journalism.

Blogging's Big Bang

10   Every significant new publishing phenomenon has been mid-wifed by a
great leap forward in printing technology. The movable-type printing
press begat the Gutenberg Bible, which begat the Renaissance. Moving
from rags to pulp paved the way for Hearst and Pulitzer. The birth of alternative newspapers coincided almost perfectly with the development
of the offset press. Laser printers and desktop publishing ushered in the
newsletter and the 'zine, and helped spawn the business journal.

11   When it burst onto the scene just ten years ago, the World Wide
Web promised to be an even cheaper version of desktop publishing.
And for many people it was, but you still had to learn HTML coding,
which was inscrutable enough to make one long for the days of typeset-
ting and paste-up. By the late 1990s, I owned a few Web domains and
made a living writing about online journalism, yet if I really needed to
publish something on my own, I'd print up a Word file and take it down
to the local copy shop. Web publishing was theoretically possible and
cheap (if you used a hosting service like Tripod), but it just wasn't easy
for people as dull-witted as I.

12   In August 1999, Pyra Labs changed all that, with a product called
Blogger (responsible, as much as anything, for that terrible four-letter

word). As much of the world knows by now, "Weblog" is usually de-fined as a Web site where information is updated frequently and pre-sented in reverse chronological order (newest stuff on top). Typically, each post contains one and often several hyperlinks to other Web sites and stories, and usually there is a standing list of links to the author's favorite bookmarks. Pyra labs, since bought out by *Google*, had a revo-lutionary insight that made all this popular: every technological require-ment of Web publishing—graphic design, simple coding for things like links, hosting—is a barrier to entry, keeping non-techies out; why not remove them? Blogger gave users a for-dummies choice of templates, an easy-to-navigate five-minute registration process, and (perhaps best of all) Web hosting. All for free. You didn't even need to buy your own do-main: simply make sure joesixpack.blogspot.com wasn't taken, pick a template, and off you go.

13   The concept took off, and new blogging companies like Livejour-nal, UserLand, and Movable Type scrambled to compete. Blogger co-founders Evan Williams, Paul Bausch, and Meg Hourihan, along with Web designer Jason Kottke, and tech writer Rebecca Blood—these were the stars of the first major mainstream-media feature about blogging, a November 2000 *New Yorker* story by Rebecca Mead, who christened the phenomenon "the CB radio of the Dave Eggers generation."

14   Like just about everything else, blogging changed forever on Sep-tember 11, 2001. The destruction of the World Trade Center and the attack on the Pentagon created a huge appetite on the part of the public to be part of The Conversation, to vent and analyze and publicly ponder or mourn. Many, too, were unsatisfied with what they read and saw in the mainstream media. Glenn Reynolds, proprietor of the wildly popular InstaPundit.com blog, thought the mainstream analysis was terrible. "All the talking heads . . . kept saying that 'we're gonna have to grow up, we're gonna have to give up a lot of our freedoms,' " he says. "Or it was the 'Why do they hate us' sort of teeth-gnashing. And I think there was a deep dissatisfaction with that." The daily op-ed diet of Column left and Column Right often fell way off the mark. "It's time for the United Na-tions to get the hell out of town. And take with it CNN warslut Christiane Amanpour." the *New York Post*'s Andrea Peyser seethed on September 21. "We forgive you; we reject vengeance." Colman McCarthy whimpered to the terrorists in the *Los Angeles Times* September 17. September 11 was the impetus for my own blog (mattwelch.com/warblog.html). Jeff Jarvis, who was trapped in the WTC dust cloud on September 11, started his a few days later. "I had a personal story I needed to tell," said Jarvis, a former *San Francisco Examiner* columnist, founding editor of *Entertainment Weekly,* and current president and creative director of Advance.net, which is the Internet wing of the Conde Nast empire.

"Then lo and behold! I discovered people were linking to me and talking about my story, so I joined this great conversation."

15 He wasn't alone. Reynolds, a hyper-kinetic University of Tennessee law professor and occasional columnist who produces techno records in his spare time, had launched InstaPundit the month before. On September 11, his traffic jumped from 1,600 visitors to almost 4,200; now it averages 100,000 per weekday. With his prolific posting pace—dozens of links a day, each with comments ranging from a word to several paragraphs—and a deliberate ethic of driving traffic to new blogs from all over the political spectrum, Reynolds quickly became the "Blogfather" of a newly coined genre of sites: the warblogs. "I think people were looking for context, they were looking for stuff that wasn't dumb," he said. "They were looking for stuff that seemed to them to be consistent with how Americans ought to respond to something like this."

16 There had been plenty of news-and-opinion Weblogs previously—from political journalists such as Joshua Micah Marshall, Mickey Kaus, Andrew Sullivan, and Virginia Postrel; not to mention "amateurs" like Matt Drudge. But September 11 drew unpaid nonprofessionals into the current-events fray. And like the first alternative publishers, who eagerly sought out and formed a network with like-minded mavericks across the country, the post-September 11 Webloggers spent considerable energy propping up their new comrades and encouraging their readers to join the fun. I'd guess 90 percent of my most vocal early readers have gone on to start sites of their own. In April 2002 Reynolds asked InstaPundit readers to let him know if he had inspired any of them to start their own blogs. Nearly two hundred wrote in. (Imagine two hundred people deciding to become a columnist just because Maureen Dowd was so persuasive.) Meanwhile, Blogger alone has more than 1.5 million registered users, and Livejournal reports 1.2 million. No one knows how many active blogs there are worldwide, but Blogcount (yes, a blog that counts blogs) guesses between 2.4 million and 2.9 million. Freedom of the press belongs to nearly 3 million people.

What's the Point?

17 So what have these people contributed to journalism? Four things: personality, eyewitness testimony, editorial filtering, and uncounted gigabytes of new knowledge.

18 "Why are Weblogs popular?" asks Jarvis, whose company has launched four dozen of them, ranging from beachcams on the Jersey shore to a temporary blog during the latest Iraq war. "I think it's because they have something to say. In a media world that's otherwise leached of opinions and life, there's so much life in them."

19 For all the history made by newspapers between 1960 and 2000, the profession was also busy contracting, standardizing, and homogenizing. Most cities now have their monopolist daily, their alt weekly or two, their business journal. Journalism is done a certain way, by a certain kind of people. Bloggers are basically oblivious to such traditions, so reading the best of them is like receiving a bracing slap in the face. It's a reminder that America is far more diverse and iconoclastic than its newsrooms.

20 After two years of reading Weblogs, my short list of favorite news commentators in the world now includes an Air Force mechanic (Paul Palubicki of *sgtstryker.com*), a punk rock singer-songwriter (Dr. Frank of *doktorfrank.com*), a twenty-four-year-old Norwegian programmer (Bjorn Staerk of *http://bearstrong.net/warblog/index.html*), and a cranky libertarian journalist from Alberta, Canada (Colby Cosh). Outsiders with vivid writing styles and unique viewpoints have risen to the top of the blog heap and begun vaulting into mainstream media. Less than two years ago, Elizabeth Spiers was a tech-stock analyst for a hedge fund who at night wrote sharp-tongued observations about Manhattan life on her personal blog; now she's the It Girl of New York media, lancing her colleagues at *Gawker.com,* while doing free-lance work for the *Times,* the *New York Post, Radar,* and other publications. Salam Pax, a pseudonymous young gay Iraqi architect who made hearts flutter with his idiosyncratic personal descriptions of Baghdad before and after the war, now writes columns for *The Guardian* and in July signed a book deal with Grove/Atlantic. Steven Den Beste, a middle-aged unemployed software engineer in San Diego, has been spinning out thousands of words of international analysis most every day for the last two years; recently he has been seen in the online edition of *The Wall Street Journal.*

21 With personality and an online audience, meanwhile, comes a kind of reader interaction far more intense and personal than anything comparable in print. Once, when I had the poor taste to mention in my blog that I was going through a rough financial period, readers sent me more than $1,000 in two days. Far more important, the intimacy and network effects of the blog-world enable you to meet people beyond your typical circle and political affiliation, sometimes with specialized knowledge of interest to you. "It exposes you to worlds that most people, let alone reporter's, never interact with," says Jarvis, whose personal blog (*buzzmachine.com*) has morphed into a one-stop shop for catching up on Iranian and Iraqi bloggers, some of whom he has now met online or face to face.

22 Such specialization and filtering is one of the form's key functions. Many bloggers, like the estimable Jim Romenesko, with his popular journalism forum on Poynter's site, focus like a laser beam on one

microcategory, and provide simple links to the day's relevant news. There are scores dealing with ever-narrower categories of media alone, from a site that obsesses over the *San Francisco Chronicle* (*ChronWatch.com*), to one that keeps the heat on newspaper ombudsmen (*OmbudsGod.blogspot.com*). Charles Johnson, a Los Angeles Web designer, has built a huge and intensely loyal audience by spotting and vilifying venalities in the Arab press (*littlegreenfootballs.com/weblog*). And individual news events, such as the Iraq war, spark their own temporary group blogs, where five or ten or more people all contribute links to minute-by-minute breaking news. Sometimes the single most mustsee publication on a given topic will have been created the day before.

23   Besides introducing valuable new sources of information to readers, these sites are also forcing their proprietors to act like journalists: choosing stories, judging the credibility of sources, writing headlines, taking pictures, developing prose styles, dealing with readers, building audience, weighing libel considerations, and occasionally conducting informed investigations on their own. Thousands of amateurs are learning how we do our work, becoming in the process more sophisticated readers and sharper critics. For lazy columnists and defensive gatekeepers, it can seem as if the hounds from a mediocre hell have been unleashed. But for curious professionals, it is a marvelous opportunity and entertaining spectacle; they discover what the audience finds important and encounter specialists who can rip apart the work of many a generalist. More than just A. J. Liebling-style press criticism, journalists finally have something approaching real peer review, in all its brutality. If they truly value the scientific method, they should rejoice. Blogs can bring a collective intelligence to bear on a question.

24   And when the decentralized fact-checking army kicks into gear, it can be an impressive thing to behold. On March 30, veteran British war correspondent Robert Fisk, who has been accused so often of anti-American bias and sloppiness by bloggers that his last name has become a verb (meaning, roughly, "to disprove loudly, point by point"), reported that a bomb hitting a crowded Baghdad market and killing dozens must have been fired by U.S. troops because of some Western numerals he found on a piece of twisted metal lying nearby. Australian blogger Tim Blair, a free-lance journalist, reprinted the partial numbers and asked his military-knowledgeable readers for insight. Within twenty-four hours, more than a dozen readers with specialized knowledge (retired Air Force, former Naval Air Systems Command employees, others) had written in describing the weapon (U.S. high-speed antiradiation missile), manufacturer (*Raytheon*), launch point (F-16), and dozens of other minute details not seen in press accounts days and weeks later. Their conclusion, much as it pained them to say so: Fisk was probably right.

25   In December 2001 a University of New Hampshire Economics and Women's Studies professor named Marc Herold published a study, based mostly on press clippings, that estimated 3,767 civilians had died as a result of American military action in Afghanistan. Within a day, blogger Bruce Rolston, a Canadian military reservist, had already shot holes through Herold's methodology, noting that he conflated "casualties" with "fatalities," double-counted single events, and depended heavily on dubious news sources. Over the next two days, several other bloggers cut Herold's work to ribbons. Yet for the next month, Herold's study was presented not just as fact, but as an understatement, by the *Guardian,* as well as the *New Jersey Star-Ledger, The Hartford Courant,* and several other newspapers. When news organizations on the ground later conducted their surveys of Afghan civilian deaths, most set the number at closer to 1,000.

26   But the typical group fact-check is not necessarily a matter of war. Bloggers were out in the lead in exposing the questionable research and behavior of gun-studying academics Michael Bellesiles and John Lott Jr. (the former resigned last year from *Emory University* after a blogger-propelled investigation found that he falsified data in his antigun book, *Arming America;* the latter, author of the pro-gun book, *More Guns, Less Crime,* was forced by bloggers to admit that he had no copies of his own controversial self-defense study he had repeatedly cited as proving his case, and that he had masqueraded in online gun-rights discussions as a vociferous John Lott supporter named "Mary Rosh"). The fact-checking bloggers have uncovered misleading use of quotations by opinion columnists, such as Maureen Dowd, and jumped all over the inaccurate or irresponsible comments of various 2004 presidential candidates. They have become part of the journalism conversation.

Breathing in Blogworld

27   Which is not to say that 90 percent of news-related blogs aren't crap. First of all, 90 percent of any new form of expression tends to be mediocre (think of band demos, or the cringe-inducing underground papers of years gone by), and judging a medium by its worst practitioners is not very sporting. Still, almost every criticism about blogs is valid—they often are filled with cheap shots, bad spelling, the worst kind of confirmation bias, and an extremely off-putting sense of self-worth (one that this article will do nothing to alleviate). But the "blogosphere," as many like to pompously call it, is too large and too varied to be defined as a single thing, and the action at the top 10 percent is among the most exciting new trends the profession has seen in a while. Are bloggers journalists? Will they soon replace newspapers?

28   The best answer to those two questions is: those are two really dumb questions; enough hot air has been expended in their name already.

29   A more productive, tangible line of inquiry is: Is journalism being produced by blogs, is it interesting, and how should journalists react to it? The answers, by my lights, are "yes," "yes," and "in many ways." After a slow start, news organizations are beginning to embrace the form. Tech journalists, such as the *San Jose Mercury New*'s Dan Gillmor, launched Weblogs long before "blogger" was a household word. Beat reporting is a natural fit for a blog—reporters can collect standing links to sites of interest, dribble out stories and anecdotes that don't necessarily belong in the paper, and attract a specific like-minded readership. One of the best such sites going is the recently created California Insider blog by the *Sacramento Bee*'s excellent political columnist. Daniel Weintraub, who has been covering the state's wacky recall news like a blanket. Blogs also make sense for opinion publications, such as the *National Review, The American Prospect,* and my employer, *Reason,* all of which have lively sites.

30   For those with time to notice, blogs are also a great cheap farm system for talent. You've got tens of thousands of potential columnists writing for free, fueled by passion, operating in a free market where the cream rises quickly.

31   Best of all, perhaps, the phenomenon is simply entertaining. When do you last recall reading some writer and thinking "damn, he sure looks like he's having fun"? It's what buttoned-down reporters thought of their long-haired brethren back in the 1960s. The 2003 version may not be so immediately identifiable on sight—and that may be the most promising development of all. ■

JOSHUA KURLANTZICK

Dictatorship.com

As foreign editor of The New Republic, *a well-known middle-of-the-road publication on public affairs and contemporary culture, Joshua Kurlantzick has written about many economics and trade issues. He has also written for* U.S. News and World Report, *and has worked as a correspondent in Southeast Asia for* The Economist. *His articles have appeared frequently in such publications as* Foreign Affairs, The Washington Quarterly, World Policy Journal, Atlantic Monthly, *and* Current History. *In the essay below, which appeared in the April 5, 2004, edition of* The New Republic, *Kurlantzick questions common assumptions about the Internet's potential for opening up political discussion and activism.*

1   Last spring, during a trip to Laos, I visited an Internet café in the capital, Vientiane. Inside, the scene reminded me more of the West Village than the heart of a backward, communist nation. Though Laotians threshed rice by hand just a few miles away, the café itself was thoroughly modern. Tourists and local teenagers surfed the Internet on relatively new PCs. On a large screen on one wall, music videos featured Madonna gyrating half-naked. Below, kids seated at a row of computers logged onto pop-culture sites like MTV.com.

2   Yet, despite its trendiness and high-tech appearance, the Internet joint conspicuously lacked one element usually associated with café life: any discussion of current events. Virtually no one in the café spoke with anyone else. Except for the tourists, no one seemed to venture onto news Web pages—this, despite the fact that many Laotians can read Thai and could have accessed uncensored information on news sites based in neighboring (and democratic) Thailand. When I attempted to access the Web pages of exile groups opposed to the authoritarian Vientiane regime, I received an error message saying the pages were not accessible.

3   My experience in the Vientiane café was a sobering antidote to a pervasive myth: that the Internet is a powerful force for democracy. For years, a significant subset of the democratization industry—that network of political scientists, think tanks, and policymakers—has placed its bets (and, in many cases, its money) on the Web's potential to spread liberal ideas in illiberal parts of the world. Whereas once American politicians and democratization groups focused on older technologies, such as radio, today their plans to spread democracy rest in considerable part on programs for boosting Internet access. In early March, Secretary of State Colin Powell told Congress that a crucial part of the Bush administration's democratization initiative will be establishing "American corners" in libraries overseas, complete with Internet kiosks where locals can surf the Web. In the Middle East, American diplomats have touted their recent online interactions with locals, such as Web dialogue between the American consul in Jeddah and Saudis.

4   But world leaders, journalists, and political scientists who tout the Internet as a powerful force for political change are just as wrong as the dot-com enthusiasts who not so long ago believed the Web would completely transform business. While it's true that the Internet has proved itself able to disseminate pop culture in authoritarian nations—not only Laos, but China, Singapore, Saudi Arabia, and elsewhere—to date, its political impact has been decidedly limited. It has yet to topple—or even seriously undermine—its first tyrannical regime. In fact, in some repressive countries the spread of the Internet actually may be helping dictatorships remain in power.

5   Ever since the Internet became a mass medium in the mid-'90s, its advocates have been touting its political potential. In a 1996 appearance at the World Economic Forum in Davos, John Perry Barlow, co-founder of one of the leading Internet freedom organizations, delivered an address titled "Declaration of the Independence of Cyberspace." In it, he announced, "The global social space we are building" will "be naturally independent of the tyrannies [that governments] impose on us." Other leading political theorists, such as Harvard's Joseph Nye, argued that, by increasing information flows within and between countries and providing a space for political organization, the Internet would threaten dictators.

6   With the gauntlet laid down, the Internet became a new focus of America's foreign policy elite. Political science departments began hiring faculty with backgrounds in both political theory and computer science. The National Democratic Institute and other democratization groups in Washington made seminars on utilizing the Web for political discourse a central part of their agenda. In a 1995 study, the Pentagon predicted the Internet would prove a "strategic threat to authoritarian regimes." In 2000, President Clinton told reporters that, "in the new century, liberty will spread by . . . cable modem" and memorably warned that, if China's leaders attempted to crack down on the Web, they would find it as difficult as "trying to nail Jell-O to the wall." In 1999, then-presidential candidate George W. Bush confidently predicted that, if the Internet were to take hold in China, "freedom's genie will be out of the bottle."

7   Since taking office, the Bush administration has focused on programs to expand Web access in the Middle East, such as funding for Internet connections in Arab schools. Margaret Tutwiler, undersecretary of state for public diplomacy and public affairs, recently told Congress that such efforts would help provide people in the Middle East with "a window on the world. . . . It opens up a whole lot of avenues that I think are in our self-interest." Edward Djerejian, chairman of the White House advisory group on public diplomacy, testified that, "given the strategic importance of information technologies, a greater portion of the budget should be directed to tap the resources of the Internet."

8   Academics and journalists, too, have bought into the idea, frequently pointing to increased Internet usage as de facto evidence of political liberalization. "The Internet and globalization," wrote *The New York Times'* Thomas Friedman in 2000, "are acting like nutcrackers to open societies and empower Arab democrats." A year later, when Bashar Assad became president of Syria, the fact that he had once headed a Syrian computer group was taken as evidence that he might be a liberalizer. Saudi Arabia is the most recent beneficiary of this kind of misunderstanding, with media reports crediting the desert kingdom with liberalization based on its burgeoning Internet culture. This March, *The Economist* enthused, "The Internet, the mobile phone and satellite television are all eroding the [Saudi] authorities' control."

9   But little of this excitement is predicated on empirical research. It's true, of course, that Internet usage has surged in many authoritarian nations. In China, the number of people accessing the Web on a regular basis has risen from fewer than one million in 1997 to almost 70 million in 2003. In the Middle East, Internet penetration has nearly doubled in the past five years. It's also true that this increased access has provided some citizens of dictatorships more access to the outside world and helped loosen restrictive cultural norms. By prompting more open discussion of sexuality, for instance, foreign websites may make it easier for Southeast Asian youngsters to talk frankly about sex—a life-and-death proposition in a region decimated by HIV/AIDS.

10   Yet the growth of the Internet has not substantially altered the political climate in most authoritarian countries. In quasi-authoritarian Singapore, where more than 50 percent of the population has regular Internet access, the ruling People's Action Party actually increased its political stranglehold in the last election, winning more than 95 percent of the seats in the legislature. In Malaysia, another country where Internet access is much higher than in most of the developing world, the ruling United Malays National Organization, which has been in power for over two decades, dominated this week's national elections. The State Department's March report on human rights in Burma says, "The Government's extremely poor human rights record worsened. . . . Citizens still did not have the right to change their government." And its annual report on human rights in China, also released in March, said that last year saw "backsliding on key human rights issues" by Beijing—such significant backsliding that the United States is considering censuring China at the U.N. Human Rights Commission. Indeed, nearly all the Chinese political science professors I have spoken with agree that the mainland Chinese democracy movement is weaker now than it was a decade ago. Nor is this unhappy trend limited to the Far East. Since March 2003, the Cuban government has initiated its biggest crackdown on dissent in years. Neither Cuba nor such Middle Eastern nations as Saudi Arabia, Egypt, and Syria have made any recent progress toward democracy, according to Freedom House's 2004 ranking of countries around the world.

11   Why has the Web failed to transform such regimes? In part because, as a medium, the Web is in many ways ill-suited for expressing and organizing dissent. And, even more significantly, because, as a technology, it has proved surprisingly easy for authoritarian regimes to stifle, control, and co-opt.

12   Many Internet advocates forget that, on the most basic level, the Web is a vehicle merely for disseminating information. Someone, in other words, first needs to have access to the information and a willingness to share it. In practice, this means the impact of the Web depends to a

certain degree on local resources—specifically, the existence of opposition networks able to provide evidence of government wrongdoing. This limitation is evident when one compares Malaysia with Singapore. "The Internet has had more impact on politics in Malaysia than in Singapore," says Cherian George, who is writing a book on Internet usage in Southeast Asia. There are several nongovernmental organizations (NGOs) in Malaysia committed to investigating the government; in Singapore, there are virtually none. As a consequence, when activists in Malaysia want to use the Web to highlight human rights abuses, George says, they can draw upon the information amassed by the NGOs from their networks of sources. Singaporeans, by contrast, have no such resources. This is part of the reason James Gomez, founder of the well-known Singaporean dissident website ThinkCentre.org, admits that his organization has not significantly altered local politics by using the Internet.

13   Another shortcoming of the Internet is that it lends itself to individual rather than communal activities. It "is about people sitting in front of a terminal, barely interacting," says one Laotian researcher. The Web is less well-suited to fostering political discussion and debate because, unlike radio or even television, it does not generally bring people together in one house or one room. In Rangoon, the capital of Burma—one of the most repressive nations on earth—groups of men often crowd around radios in tea shops to clandestinely listen to news from the BBC's Burmese service and then discuss what they've heard. Similarly, in bars and cafés in China, people gather around televisions to watch and discuss the news. But, while restaurateurs in the developing world can afford to use a radio or television to lure customers who might have a snack while listening or watching, owners of Internet cafés have to recoup their much higher capital investments. They do this by dividing their establishments into individual terminals and charging each user separately. In fact, in nearly every Internet café I have visited, in Vientiane last year and in Rangoon this winter (as well as in New York and in London), I have watched the same scenes of people sitting in front of individual computer terminals, barely talking to each other.

14   Add to this a still more simple fact about the Internet—that, unlike television or radio, it generally requires users to be literate—and it's not hard to see why democracy advocates in authoritarian countries (and some authoritarian leaders) consider older, broadcast media to be a more effective means of disseminating information and fostering debate. Wang Dan, a well-known Chinese democracy activist, has argued that television and radio are still the best means for communicating dissident messages within China. Western diplomats in Laos concur, telling me that Thai television, available to many Laotians, has more potential than the Internet to subvert the authoritarian Laotian govern-

ment. Likewise, in the Middle East, Islamist organizations—the only groups that have had much success challenging authoritarian regimes in the region—have largely disdained the Web, relying instead on clandestine videos and audiocassettes, which can be watched communally and then passed along from mosque to mosque.

15   In addition to lending itself primarily to individual use, the Internet also fosters a kind of anarchy inimical to an effective opposition movement. Singaporean dissident Gomez says the Web empowers individual members of a political movement, rather than the movement as a whole. Opposition members can offer dissenting opinions at will, thus undermining the leadership and potentially splintering the organization. In combating an authoritarian regime, in other words, there's such a thing as too much democracy. Two of the most successful opposition movements of the last few decades—the South African opposition led by Nelson Mandela and the Burmese resistance led by Aung San Suu Kyi—relied upon charismatic, almost authoritarian leaders to set a message followed by the rest of the movement. The anti-globalization movement, by contrast, has been a prime example of the anarchy that can develop when groups utilize the Web to organize. Allowing nearly anyone to make a statement or call a meeting via the Web, the anti-globalizers have wound up with large but unorganized rallies in which everyone from serious critics of free trade to advocates of witches and self-anointed saviors of famed death-row convict Mumia Abu Jumal have their say. To take just one example, at the anti-globalization World Social Forum held in Mumbai in January, nuanced critics of globalization like former World Bank chief economist Joseph Stiglitz shared space with, as *The New York Times* reported, "a long list of regional causes," including anti-Microsoft and anti-Coca Cola activists.

16   But the Internet's inherent flaws as a political medium are only part of the reason for its failure to spread liberty. More significant has been the ease with which authoritarian regimes have controlled and, in some cases, subverted it. The most straightforward way governments have responded to opposition websites has been simply to shut them down. In Singapore, for example, an online political forum called Sintercom became popular in the mid-'90s as one of the only places where citizens could express political opinions relatively openly. But, following government pressure, Sintercom was shut down in 2001. Since then, according to Shanthi Kalathil and Taylor C. Boas, authors of the recent comprehensive book *Open Networks, Closed Regimes: The Impact of the Internet on Authoritarian Rule,* the scope of online political discussion in Singapore has shrunk. In Malaysia, too, many of the anti-government websites that formed in the mid-'90s have been shuttered, enabling the regime to beat back a liberal reform movement that sprang up five years ago.

17   But nowhere has a regime's ability to corral the Internet been more apparent than in China, the world's largest authoritarian state. Despite President Clinton's prediction, Beijing has proved that it can, in fact, nail Jell-O to the wall. A 2003 study by Jonathan Zittrain and Benjamin Edelman, two Harvard researchers, found that China has created the most extensive system of Internet censorship in the world and has almost completely controlled the impact of the Web on dissent. It has done this, they note, by mandating that all Web traffic go through government-controlled servers and by constructing an elaborate system of firewalls—which prevent access to certain websites—and online monitoring by state security agents. Censored sites include much of the Western media and sites related to Taiwan, democratization, and other sensitive topics. (*The New York Times* won a reprieve only when its former editor appealed personally to former President Jiang Zemin.) In their book, Kalathil and Boas note that Saudi Arabia has constructed similarly comprehensive systems to limit online dissent, expanding their "censorship mechanism to keep pace with the burgeoning sources of objectionable content." What's more, various authoritarian regimes have collaborated with one another to improve their ability to control the Web. As Kalathil and Boas note, China is formally advising Cuba on its Internet policies, while several Middle Eastern states have looked to Singapore as an example in controlling their citizens' Web usage.

18   In such efforts, authoritarian regimes have also benefited from the willingness of Western companies to sell the latest censorship technology. Cybersecurity companies, such as San Jose–based Secure Computing, have competed intensely to sell Web-filtering and -monitoring technology to Riyadh, Beijing, and other repressive governments. One vice president of Websense, a San Diego company that competed for the Saudi contract, told the *Times* in 2001 that it would "be a terrific deal to win." Unsurprisingly, these companies have not made a similar effort to provide cash-poor dissidents in these nations with technology that could enable them to overcome firewalls or conceal their online identities. In a 2002 study, Michael Chase and James Mulvenon, two RAND researchers, found that the Chinese authorities were able to prevent Internet users from accessing anti-monitoring technology 80 percent of the time.

19   China also has co-opted its own local Internet content providers. In 2002, the country's leading Web entrepreneurs signed a pledge vowing to promote self-discipline in Web usage and encourage "the elimination of deleterious information [on] the Internet." Some of these Internet entrepreneurs are former dissidents who fled China after the 1989 Tiananmen uprising but have since abandoned their political activism, returning to China seeking Web fortune. In fact, as Kalathil and Boas note, "Many of China's up-and-coming Internet entrepreneurs see a sub-

stantial . . . role for the government in the Internet sector. . . . [They] have visions for Chinese Internet development that are inherently pragmatic and complementary to state strategy." So much for Barlow's idea that technology workers will reject the "tyrannies" of government.

20   In the past two years, as authoritarian regimes have become more sophisticated in controlling the Web, many of them have been able to leverage that control to create climates of online self-censorship. According to Nina Hachigian, an expert on China at the Pacific Council on International Policy, the knowledge that the Chinese government monitors online activity, combined with Internet laws so broad they could apply to almost any Web surfer, effectively scare most users into avoiding political sites altogether. As Gary Rodan, a Southeast Asia specialist at Murdoch University in Australia, notes in an essay on Singapore in *Political Science Quarterly,* "When extensive networks of political surveillance are already in place and a culture of fear about such practices exists, the impact of monitoring is likely to be strong."

21   To maintain this fear, Internet cops in China launch periodic crackdowns on the Web, arresting and prosecuting Chinese citizens for posting Web items related to democracy or to helping people evade firewalls. Beijing also has shuttered thousands of Internet cafés over the past four years. On a visit to Shanghai in 1999, I noticed numerous new cafés. By 2003, many had been closed. Other authoritarian regimes have used similar bullying tactics to foster climates of self-censorship online. Singapore also has drafted broad Internet laws that could implicate many Web users and, Kalathil and Boas report, has reinforced citizens' paranoia by occasionally arresting people for posting articles critical of the government and by periodically reminding the public that the country's one Internet service provider, which is connected to the government, snoops through users' Web accounts. The Vietnamese government has made owners of Internet cafés responsible for anything users post online and has made a series of arrests over the past two years of people who posted dissident articles. In January, Hanoi sentenced a man who used the Web to criticize the Vietnamese government to seven years in prison.

22 Even beyond its failure to live up to democratizers' dreams, the Web may actually be helping to keep some dictatorships in power. Asian dissidents have told me that the Web has made it easier for authoritarian regimes to monitor citizens. In Singapore, Gomez says, the government previously had to employ many security agents and spend a lot of time to monitor activists who were meeting with each other in person. But, with the advent of the Web, security agents can easily use government-linked servers to track the activities of activists and dissidents. In fact, Gomez says, in recent years opposition groups in Singapore have moved

away from communicating online and returned to exchanging information face-to-face, in order to avoid surveillance.

23   In China, the Web has similarly empowered the authorities. In the past two decades, Beijing's system of monitoring the population by installing informers into businesses, neighborhoods, and other social institutions has broken down—in part because the Chinese population has become more transient and in part because the regime's embrace of capitalism has meant fewer devoted Communists willing to spy for the government. But Beijing has replaced these legions of informers with a smaller group of dedicated security agents who monitor the Internet traffic of millions of Chinese. "The real problem with groups trying to use the Internet is that you are actually more easily monitored if you use online forms of communication than if you just meet in person in secret," one specialist in Chinese Internet usage told me. Indeed, in May 2003 Beijing's security services imprisoned four people for "inciting the over-throw of the Chinese government"; press reports suggested the authorities learned about the dissidents' movements through reports on pro-democracy websites. Later, in February of this year, Beijing charged Du Daobin, a well-known Internet dissident, with "inciting subversion of state power and the over-throw of China's socialist system."

24   In the Middle East, security services have used the Internet in similar ways. In Egypt, police once had to conduct time-consuming stakeouts of bars and clubs to find gay men breaking the laws against homosexuality. Yet, in 2002, the Associated Press reported that a group of state security agents went "online masquerading as gay men . . . [and] arrested men . . . who responded to the ads." In its most recent annual report on human rights in Egypt, the State Department noted, "Egyptian police have continued to target homosexuals using Internet-based sting operations."

25   What's more, authoritarian regimes have begun flooding the Web with their own content, using high-profile websites to actually increase support for the government. Kalathil and Boas report that e-government services "are likely to boost regime legitimacy, particularly in countries [like Singapore and China] where the state has traditionally offered extensive services [such as social welfare programs] in exchange for political support." Singapore has indeed developed one of the most extensive e-government sites in the world, and Hachigian's research shows that nearly one-tenth of all sites in China are directly related to the Beijing regime. Some of these sites, such as the e-government sites for Beijing municipality, are very sophisticated and include sections in which citizens can e-mail Beijing's mayor with suggestions. (There is little evidence, however, that the mayor feels any need to respond to or even read the submissions.)

26   Dictators also have poured money into the websites of state-linked media outlets, helping to make them more appealing than their inde-

pendent competitors. Gomez says that *The Straits Times,* the government-linked newspaper in Singapore with the most sophisticated and comprehensive website, is where nearly everyone in Singapore goes for news. Similarly, the *People's Daily,* a leading party publication in China, now has a very sophisticated Internet presence and has become a leading source of news for wired Chinese. Its chat rooms have become notorious for their nationalistic sentiment—partly the consequence of security bureau Beijing agents logging into the rooms and posting xenophobic statements. Indeed, during crises like the China-U.S. spy-plane incident in 2001 and the run-up to last week's election in Taiwan, Beijing has utilized these chat rooms to whip up patriotic sentiment.

27   In the long run, the Internet may fulfill some of its hype as an engine of liberalization. Gomez told me that small civil society groups that do not attract as much attention from state security agents—professional organizations, charities, religious groups—are where the Internet's true potential is likely to be. Not, in other words, with groups pushing for regime change. Chinese environmental organizations provide an example of how smaller groups can benefit: These single-issue groups, which normally focus on one environmental problem, have used the Web to coordinate meetings. What's more, by empowering small companies, the Web may decrease state control of the economy. In *New Media, New Politics? From Satellite Television to the Internet in the Arab World,* a recent study of technology in the Middle East, Jon Alterman reports that, in countries like the Persian Gulf states, the spread of the Web may allow small, nimble entrepreneurs to challenge the massive, state-linked companies that have been the foundations of autocratic regimes.

28   While recognizing that the Internet is not developing into the political tool many had predicted, governments and private companies could help promote the Web's gradual emergence as a force for change. In the House of Representatives, Christopher Cox has sponsored legislation to allow U.S. companies to more easily export encryption technology, which lets Internet users send coded messages that cannot be monitored by central governments. Other legislators have proposed a U.S. Office of Global Internet Freedom designed to facilitate the reform of Internet policies around the world. Most important, the private sector could push regimes not to crack down on Internet freedoms. Such an idea is not wishful thinking. China, Malaysia, Singapore, and other authoritarian states desperately want to prove that they are modern, First World nations, and mastering the Internet is essential to this image. Malaysia has built a massive "Multimedia Super Corridor" in an attempt to create a local version of Silicon Valley, while Singapore has promoted itself as an "Intelligent Island" hardwired into the Web. Consequently, foreign companies can have some influence over dictators, since, without their assistance, authoritarian regimes cannot realize their pretensions of

modernity. According to *The New York Times,* John Kamm, the former head of Hong Kong's American Chamber of Commerce, once gave a speech at a banquet for Zhou Nan, Beijing's senior representative in the city, in which he asked Zhou to push for the release of a prominent student detained during the Tiananmen Square protest. Though in public Zhou reacted icily to Kamm's request, a month later the student was released.

29   But neither Western governments nor Western companies seem likely to step up to the plate. Since the war on terrorism began, the Bush administration has been at pains not to ruffle Beijing's feathers. (Indeed, in an ironic twist, the White House is now considering Web-surveillance techniques similar to those utilized by the Chinese government.) Meanwhile, as the information-technology sector continues to struggle, most tech companies are unwilling to risk alienating potential clients, such as the Chinese government. In part, this eagerness to jump into bed with Beijing and Riyadh reflects the economic reality of a sector no longer in a state of permanent expansion. And, in part, it represents the transition of the Web from a technology run by civil-libertarian geeks like Barlow to one dominated by relatively conservative, large corporations. "In the mid-1990s, there was this feeling among the Web's early users that it had to be a medium to promote freedom," says author George. "But companies like AOL, they don't share that commitment—they focus on entertainment." Indeed, Yahoo! and America Online have both willingly censored their news content to please authoritarian regimes like China. "I haven't seen any businesses pushing governments in this way," Gomez told me. "People are giving up on the idea of the Internet as a frontier for freedom." ∎

NAOMI KLEIN

Culture Jamming: Ads Under Attack

Naomi Klein (born 1975 in Montreal) is a columnist for The Guardian, *a major British newspaper, and for Canada's important newspaper* The Globe and Mail. *She is the author of* No Logo: Taking Aim at the Brand Bullies *(2000), which examines major corporations' creation of exploitative brand images, and* Fences and Windows: Dispatches from the Front Lines of the Globalization Debate *(2002), a collection of many of her articles about advertising, corporations, and globalization. The article reprinted below is an excerpt from* No Logo *that also appeared in the July 10, 2000,* Brandweek, *a magazine that focuses on marketing and advertising aspects of the business world.*

1 It's Sunday morning on the edge of New York's Alphabet City and Jorge Rodriguez de Gerada is perched at the top of a high ladder, ripping the paper off a cigarette billboard. Moments before, the billboard at the corner of Houston and Attorney sported a fun-loving Newport couple jostling over a pretzel. Now it showcases the haunting face of a child, which Rodriguez de Gerada has painted in rust. To finish it off, he pastes up a few hand-torn strips of the old Newport ad, which form a fluorescent green frame around the child's face.

2 When it's done, the installation looks as the 31-year-old artist had intended: as if years of cigarette, beer and car ads had been scraped away to reveal the rusted backing of the billboard. Burned into the metal is the real commodity of the advertising transaction. "After the ads are taken down," he says, "what is left is the impact on the children in the area, staring at these images."

3 Unlike some of the growing legion of New York guerrilla artists, Rodriguez de Gerada refuses to slink around at night like a vandal, choosing instead to make his statements in broad daylight. For that matter, he doesn't much like the phrase "guerrilla art," preferring "citizen art" instead. He wants the dialogue he has been having with the city's billboards for more than 10 years to be seen as a normal mode of discourse in a democratic society, not as some edgy vanguard act. While he paints and pastes, he wants kids to stop and watch—as they do on this sunny day just as an old man offers to help support the ladder.

4 Rodriguez de Gerada is widely recognized as one of the most skilled and creative founders of culture jamming, the practice of parodying advertisements and hijacking billboards in order to drastically alter their messages. Streets are public spaces, adbusters argue, and since most residents can't afford to counter corporate messages by purchasing their own ads, they should have the right to talk back to images they never asked to see. In recent years, this argument has been bolstered by advertising's mounting aggressiveness in the public domain— painted and projected onto sidewalks; reaching around entire buildings and buses; into schools; onto basketball courts and on the Internet. At the same time, the proliferation of the quasi-public "town squares" of mails and superstores has created more and more space where commercial messages are the only ones permitted. Adding even greater urgency to their cause is the belief among many jammers that concentration of media ownership has successfully devalued the right to free speech by severing it from the right to be heard.

5 All at once, these forces are coalescing to create a climate of semiotic Robin Hoodism. A growing number of activists believe the time has come for the public to stop asking that some space be left unsponsored, and to begin seizing it back. Culture jamming baldly rejects the idea

that marketing—because it buys its way into our public spaces—must be passively accepted as a one-way information flow.

6   The most sophisticated culture jams are not stand-alone ad parodies but interceptions—counter-messages that hack into a corporation's own method of communication to send a message starkly at odds with the one that was intended. The process forces the company to foot the bill for its own subversion, either literally, because the company is the one that paid for the billboard, or figuratively because anytime people mess with a logo, they are tapping into the vast resources spent to make that logo meaningful. Kalle Lasn, editor of Vancouver-based *Adbusters* magazine, uses the martial art of jujitsu as a precise metaphor to explain the mechanics of the jam. "In one simple deft move you slap the giant on its back. We use the momentum of the enemy." It's an image borrowed from Saul Alinsky who, in his activist bible, *Rules for Radicals,* defines "mass political jujitsu" as "utilizing the power of one part of the power structure against another part. . . . [The] superior strength of the Haves becomes their own undoing." So, by rappelling off the side of a 30-by-90-foot Levi's billboard (the largest in San Francisco) and pasting the face of serial killer Charles Manson over the image, a group of jammers attempts to leave a disruptive message about the labor practices employed to make Levi's jeans. In the statement it left on the scene, the Billboard Liberation Front said they chose Manson's face because the jeans were "assembled by prisoners in China, sold to penal institutions in the Americas."

7   The term "culture jamming" was coined in 1984 by the San Francisco audio-collage band Negativland. "The skillfully reworked billboard . . . directs the public viewer to a consideration of the original corporate strategy," a band member states on the album *Jamcon '84.* The jujitsu metaphor isn't as apt for jammers who insist that they aren't inverting ad messages but are rather improving, editing, augmenting or unmasking them. "This is extreme truth in advertising," one billboard artist tells me. A good jam, in other words, is an X-ray of the subconscious of a campaign, uncovering not an opposite meaning but the deeper truth hiding beneath the layers of advertising euphemisms. So, according to these principles, with a slight turn of the imagery knob, the [now] retired Joe Camel turns into Joe Chemo, hooked up to an IV machine. Or Joe is shown about 15 years younger than his usual swinger self.

8   Like Baby Smurf, the "Cancer Kid" is cute and cuddly and playing with building blocks instead of sports cars and pool cues. And why not? Before R.J. Reynolds reached a $206 billion settlement with 46 states, the American government accused the tobacco company of using the cartoon camel to entice children to start smoking. Why not go further, the culture jammers ask, and reach out to even younger would-be

smokers? Apple computers' "Think Different" campaign of famous figures both living and dead has been the subject of numerous simple hacks: a photograph of Stalin appears with the altered slogan "Think Really Different"; the caption for the ad featuring the Dalai Lama is changed to "Think Disillusioned"; and the rainbow Apple logo is morphed into a skull. My favorite truth-in-advertising campaign is a simple jam on Exxon that appeared just after the 1989 Valdez spill: "Shit Happens. New Exxon," two towering billboards announced to millions of San Francisco commuters.

9   Attempting to pinpoint the roots of culture jamming is next to impossible, largely because the practice is itself a cutting and pasting of graffiti, modern art, do-it-yourself punk philosophy and age-old pranksterism. And using billboards as an activist canvas isn't a new revolutionary tactic either. San Francisco's Billboard Liberation Front (responsible for the Exxon and Levi's jams) has been altering ads for 20 years, while Australia's Billboard Utilizing Graffitists Against Unhealthy Promotions (BUG-UP) reached its peak in 1983, causing an unprecedented $1 million worth of damage to tobacco billboards in and around Sydney.

10   It was Guy Debord and the Situationists, the muses and theorists of the theatrical student uprising of Paris, May 1968, who first articulated the power of a simple *detournement,* defined as an image, message or artifact lifted out of its context to create a new meaning. But though culture jammers borrow liberally from the avant-garde art movements of the past—from Dada and Surrealism to Conceplualism and Situationism— the canvas these art revolutionaries were attacking tended to be the art world and its passive culture of spectatorship, as well as the anti-pleasure ethos of mainstream capitalist society. For many French students in the late '60s, the enemy was the rigidity and conformity of the Company Man; the company itself proved markedly less engaging. So where Situationist Asger Jorn hurled paint at pastoral paintings bought at flea markets, today's culture jammers prefer to hack into corporate advertising and other avenues of corporate speech. And if the culture jammers' messages are more pointedly political than their predecessors', that may be because what were indeed subversive messages in the '60s—"Never Work," "It Is Forbidden to Forbid," "Take Your Desires for Reality"—now sound more like Sprite or Nike slogans: Just Feel it. And the "situations" or "happenings" staged by the political pranksters in 1968, though genuinely shocking and disruptive at the time, are the Absolut Vodka ad of 1998—the one featuring purple-clad art school students storming bars and restaurants banging on bottles.

11   In 1993, Mark Dery wrote "Culture Jamming: Hacking, Slashing and Sniping in the Empire of Signs," a booklet published by the Open Magazine Pamphlet Series. For Dery, jamming incorporates such

eclectic combinations of theater and activism as the Guerrilla Girls, who highlighted the art world's exclusion of female artists by holding demonstrations outside the Whitney Museum in gorilla masks; Joey Skagg, who has pulled off countless successful media hoaxes; and Art-fux's execution-in-effigy of arch-Republican Jesse Helms on Capitol Hill. For Dery, culture jamming is anything, essentially, that mixes art, media, parody and the outsider stance. But within these subcultures, there has always been a tension between the forces of the merry prankster and the hardcore revolutionary. Nagging questions re-emerge: are play and pleasure themselves revolutionary acts as the Situationists might argue? Is screwing up the culture's information flows inherently subversive as Skagg would hold? Or is the mix of art and politics just a matter of making sure, to paraphrase Emma Goldman, that somebody has hooked up a good sound system at the revolution?

12   Though culture jamming is an undercurrent that never dries up entirely there is no doubt that for the last five years it has been in the midst of a revival, and one focused more on politics than on pranksterism. For a growing number of young activists, adbusting has presented itself as the perfect tool with which to register disapproval of the multinational corporations that have so aggressively stalked them as shoppers, and so unceremoniously dumped them as workers. Influenced by media theorists such as Noam Chomsky, Edward Herman, Mark Crispin Miller, Robert McChesney and Ben Bagdikian, all of whom have explored ideas about corporate control over information flows, the adbusters are writing theory on the streets, literally deconstructing corporate culture with a waterproof magic marker and a bucket of wheatpaste.

13   Jammers span a significant range of backgrounds, from purer-than-thou Marxist-anarchists who refuse interviews with "the corporate press" to those like Rodriguez de Gerada who work in the advertising industry by day (his paying job, ironically, is putting up commercial signs and superstore window displays) and long to use their skills to send messages they consider constructive. Besides a fair bit of animosity between these camps, the only ideology bridging the spectrum of culture jamming is the belief that free speech is meaningless if the commercial cacophony has risen to the point that no one can hear you. "I think everyone should have their own billboard, but they don't," says Jack Napier (a pseudonym) of the Billboard Liberation Front.

14   On the more radical end of the spectrum, a network of "media collectives" has emerged, decentralized and anarchic, that combines adbusting with zine publishing, pirate radio, activist video, Internet development and community activism. Chapters of the collective have popped up in Tallahassee, Boston, Seattle, Montreal and Winnipeg—often splintering off into other organizations. In London, where adbusting is

AN ARGUMENT ABOUT ALCOHOL

Ads promoting Absolut vodka are among the most recognizable ones that appear in mass circulation magazines. These ads cleverly show Absolut vodka bottles that mimic the shape of common objects in order to indicate the pervasiveness—and social acceptance—of alcohol consumption in general and the consumption of Absolut vodka in particular. As the essay by Naomi Klein indicates, recently an organization called Adbusters has been trying to make people more critical of the ads they consume each day. The ad reprinted here, parodying Absolut ads, represents one of the ways that Adbusters is attempting to educate the public. ■

called "subvertising," a new group has been formed, called the UK Subs after the '70s punk group of the same name. And in the past two years, the real-world jammers have been joined by a global network of online "hacktivists" who carry out their raids on the Internet, mostly by breaking into corporate Web sites and leaving their own messages behind.

15   More-mainstream groups have also been getting in on the action. The U.S. Teamsters have taken quite a shine to the ad jam, using it to build up support for striking workers in several recent labor disputes. For instance, Miller Brewing found itself on the receiving end of a similar jam when it laid off workers at a St. Louis plant. The Teamsters purchased a billboard that parodied a then-current Miller campaign; as *Business Week* reported, "Instead of two bottles of beer in a snowbank with the tagline 'Two Cold,' the ad showed two frozen workers in a snowbank labeled 'Too Cold: Miller canned 88 St. Louis workers'." As organizer Ron Carver says, "When you're doing this, you're threatening multimillion-dollar ad campaigns." One highprofile culture jam arrived in the fall of 1997 when the New York antitobacco lobby purchased hundreds of rooftop taxi ads to hawk "Virginia Slime" and "Cancer Country" brand cigarettes. All over Manhattan, as yellow cabs got stuck in gridlock, the jammed ads jostled with the real ones.

16   The rebirth of culture jamming has much to do with newly accessible technologies that have made both the creation and the circulation of ad parodies immeasurably easier. The Internet may be bogged down with brave new forms of branding, as we have seen, but it is also crawling with sites that offer links to culture jammers in cities across North America and Europe, ad parodies for instant downloading and digital versions of original ads, which can be imported directly onto personal desktops or jammed on site. For Rodriguez de Gerada, the true revolution has been in the impact desktop publishing has had on the techniques available to ad hackers. Over the course of the last decade, he says, culture jamming has shifted "from low-tech to medium-tech to high-tech," with scanners and software programs like Photoshop now enabling activists to match colors, fonts and materials precisely. "I know so many different techniques that make it look like the whole ad was reprinted with its new message, as opposed to somebody coming at it with a spray paint can."

17   This is a crucial distinction. Where graffiti traditionally seek to leave dissonant tags on the slick face of advertising (or the "pimple on the face of the retouched cover photo of America" to use a Negativland image), Rodriguez de Gerada's messages are designed to mesh with their targets, borrowing visual legitimacy from advertising itself. Many of his "edits" have been so successfully integrated that the altered billboards look like originals, though with a message that takes viewers by surprise. Even the child's face he put up in Alphabet City—not a tradi-

tional parody jam—was digitally output on the same kind of adhesive vinyl that advertisers use to seamlessly cover buses and buildings with corporate logos. "The technology allows us to use Madison Avenue's aesthetics against itself," he says. "That is the most important aspect of this new wave of people using this guerrilla tactic, because that's what the MTV generation has become accustomed to—everything's flashy everything's bright and clean. If you spend time to make it cleaner it will not be dismissed."

18   But others hold that jamming need not be so high tech. The Toronto performance artist Jubal Brown spread the visual virus for Canada's targest billboard-busting blitz with nothing more than a magic marker. He taught his friends how to distort the already hollowed out faces of fashion models by using a marker to black out their eyes and draw a zipper over their mouths—presto! Instant skull. For the women jammers in particular, "skulling" fitted in neatly with the "truth in advertising" theory: if emaciation is the beauty ideal, why not go all the way with zombie chic—give the advertisers a few supermodels from beyond the grave? For Brown, more nihilist than feminist, skulling was simply a detournement to highlight the cultural poverty of the sponsored life. ("Buy Buy Buy! Die Die Die!" reads Brown's statement displayed in a local Toronto art gallery.) On April Fool's Day, 1997, dozens of people went out on skulling missions, hitting hundreds of billboards on busy Toronto streets. Their handiwork was reprinted in Adbusters, helping to spread skulling to cities across North America.

19   And nobody is riding the culture-jamming wave as high as *Adbusters,* the self-described "house organ" of the culture-jamming scene. Editor Kalle Lasn, who speaks exclusively in the magazine's enviro-pop lingo, likes to say that we are a culture "addicted to toxins" that are poisoning our bodies, our "mental environment" and our planet. He believes that adbusting will eventually spark a "paradigm shift" in public consciousness. Published by the Vancouver-based Media Foundation, the magazine started in 1989 with 5,000 copies. It now has a circulation of 35,000—at least 20,000 copies of which go to the United States. The foundation also produces "uncommercials" for television that accuse the beauty industry of causing eating disorders, attack North American overconsumption, and urge everyone to trade their cars in for bikes. Most television stations in Canada and the U.S. have refused to air the spots, which gives the Media Foundation the perfect excuse to take them to court and use the trials to attract press attention to their vision of more democratic, publicly accessible media.

20   Culture jamming is enjoying a resurgence, in part because of technological advancements, but also, more pertinently, because of the good old rules of supply and demand. Something not far from the surface of the public psyche is delighted to see the icons of corporate power

subverted and mocked. There is, in short, a market for it. With commercialism able to overpower the traditional authority of religion, politics and schools, corporations have emerged as the natural targets for all sorts of free-floating rage and rebellion. The new ethos that culture jamming taps into is go-for-the-corporate jugular. "States have fallen back and corporations have become the new institutions," says Jaggi Singh, a Montreal-based anticorporate activist. People are just reacting to the iconography of our time." American labor rights activist Trim Bissell goes further, explaining that the thirsty expansion of chains like Starbucks and the aggressive branding of companies like Nike have created a climate ripe for anticorporate attacks. "There are certain corporations which market themselves so aggressively, which are so intent on stamping their image on everybody and every street, that they build up a reservoir of resentment among thinking people," he says. "People resent the destruction of culture and its replacement with these mass-produced corporate logos and slogans. It represents a kind of cultural fascism."

21   Most of the superbrands are of course well aware that the very imagery that has generated billions for them in sales is likely to create other, unintended, waves within the culture. Well before the anti-Nike campaign began in earnest, CEO Phil Knight presciently observed that "there's a flip side to the emotions we generate and the tremendous well of emotions we live off of. Somehow, emotions imply their opposites and at the level we operate, the reaction is much more than a passing thought." The reaction is also more than the fickle flight of fashion that makes a particular style of hip sneaker suddenly look absurd, or a played-to-death pop song become, overnight, intolerable. At its best, culture jamming homes in on the flip side of those branded emotions, and relocuses them, so that they aren't replaced with a craving for the next fashion or pop sensation but tum, slowly on the process of branding itself.

22   It's hard to say how spooked advertisers are about geting busted. Although the U.S. Association of National Advertisers has no qualms about lobbying police on behalf of its members to crack down on adbusters, they are generally loath to let the charges go to trial. This is probably wise. Even though ad companies try to paint jammers as "vigilante censors" in the media, they know it wouldn't take much for the public to decide that the advertisers are the ones censoring the jammers' creative expressions.

23   So while most big brand names rush to sue for alleged trademark violations and readily take each other to court for parodying slogans or products (as Nike did when Candies shoes adopted the slogan "Just Screw It"), multinationals are proving markedly less eager to enter into legal battles that will clearly be fought less on legal than on political grounds. Furthermore, corporations rightly see jammers as rabid atten-

tion seekers and have learned to avoid anything that could garner media coverage for their stunts. A case in point came in 1992 when Absolut Vodka threatened to sue *Adbusters* over its "Absolut Nonsense" parody. The company immediately backed down when the magazine went to the press and challenged the distiller to a public debate on the harmful effects of alcohol.

24 And much to Negativland's surprise, Pepsi's lawyers even refrained from responding to the band's 1997 release, *Dispepsi*—an antipop album consisting of hacked, jammed, distorted and disfigured Pepsi jingles. One song mimics the ads by juxtaposing the product's name with a laundry list of random unpleasant images: "I got fired by my boss. Pepsi/I nailed Jesus to the cross. Pepsi . . . The ghastly stench of puppy mills. Pepsi" and so on. When asked by *Entertainment Weekly* magazine for its response to the album, the soft-drink giant claimed to think it was "a pretty good listen." ■

MICHEL MARRIOTT

The Color of Mayhem

Michel Marriott writes about technology and media for The New York Times. *His many articles have been published elsewhere as well, often in* Newsweek, *and a series of his features inspired Spike Lee's film* New Jersey Drive. *He has also completed a novel,* Hedz. *The following article appeared in* The New York Times *on August 12, 2004. Do you consider it to be a balanced news article, or an argument?*

1 The screen crackles with criminality as a gang of urban predators itch for a kill. The scene erupts into automatic-weapons fire in a drive-by nightmare of screaming car engines, senseless death and destruction set to a thumping rap soundtrack.

2 The action is not part of a new film, but of a video game in development—the latest permutation of *Grand Theft Auto*, one of the most popular game series ever. Partly set in a city resembling gang-ridden stretches of Los Angeles of the 1990s, it features a digital cast of African-American and Hispanic men, some wearing braided hair and scarves over their faces and aiming Uzis from low-riding cars.

3 The sense of place, peril and pigmentation evident in previews of the game, *Grand Theft Auto: San Andreas,* underscores what some critics consider a disturbing trend: popular video games that play on racial stereotypes, including images of black youths committing and reveling in violent street crime.

4   "They are nothing more than pixilated minstrel shows," said Joe Morgan, a telecommunications executive in Manhattan who is black and is helping rear his girlfriend's 7-year-old son, who plays video games. Mr. Morgan argues that games like the *Grand Theft Auto* sequel, which was described glowingly and at length in a game magazine the boy recently brought home, are dangerously reinforcing stereotypes.

5   "A lot of young people are unable to discern between reality and satirical depictions," he said. "It makes them very vulnerable."

6   His complaint echoes a concern that many civil rights and other groups, including the National Association for the Advancement of Colored People, have long raised about stereotyping in movies, and the detrimental impact it may have on racial understanding and relations.

7   The issue, critics say, is not that the games' representation of racial and ethnic minorities is as blatantly threatening as the sort found at hate sites on the Web, where players are asked to gun down virtual black or Jewish characters. Rather, the racial and ethnic depictions and story lines are more subtle, and therefore, some say, more insidious. "It's not just the kinds of stereotyping people generally think of," said Eileen Espejo, a senior associate at Children Now, an advocacy group in Oakland, Calif., that has studied video games. "It is the kind of limiting what characters of color can do and cannot do in the games that sends a message to kids."

8   Video game developers counter that no offense is intended. They say their games are simply parodies, or a reflection of a sort of "browning" of popular culture that transcends race and sells to all in a marketplace captivated by hip-hop styles, themes and attitude.

9   Several games scheduled for wide release this fall or early next year are notable for their portrayal of urban black culture:

■ *Def Jam Fight for NY*, from Electronic Arts, a sort of "MTV Raps" meets "W.W.E. SmackDown!" in which mostly hip-hop-style characters (one with the voice of the rapper Snoop Dogg) slap, kick and pummel one another in locations like a 125th Street train station in Harlem.

■ *25 to Life*, from Eidos Interactive, an "urban action game" set to a hip-hop soundtrack that allows gamers to play as police officers or criminals, and includes lots of images of young gun-toting black gangsters.

■ *Notorious: Die to Drive*, described by its developer, Ubisoft, as featuring "gangsta-style car combat" with players seeking to "rule the streets of four West Coast neighborhoods." Ubisoft's Web site describes the payoff succinctly: "High-priced honeys, the finest bling, and millionaire cribs are just some of the rewards for the notorious few who can survive this most dangerous game. Once you go Notorious, there's no going back."

10   The prominence of black characters in those story lines is all the more striking because of the narrow range of video games in which blacks have been present, if present at all, over the years. A 2001 study by Children Now, for example, found that of 1,500 video-game characters surveyed, 288 were African-American males—and 83 percent of those were represented as athletes.

11   The portrayal of blacks as athletes has taken on a new wrinkle in *NBA Ballers,* released in April by Midway Games (with an "all ages" rating). It not only pits stars of the National Basketball Association, most of them black, in fierce one-on-one matches, but also encourages players to experience a millionaire lifestyle off the court—accumulating virtual cash that can buy mansions, Cadillac Escalades, yachts and attractive "friends." The style of play emphasizes a street-edged aggression, sizzling with swagger and showboating moves on the court.

12   John Vignocchi, a lead designer with Midway who worked on *NBA Ballers,* contends that the world portrayed in such games is one that gamers take for granted. "Hip-hop culture has kind of crossed over," said Mr. Vignocchi, who is white. "Look at what everyone is wearing, at what everyone is listening to." Racial stereotyping, he insisted, is "not the intention of the game."

13   Leon E. Wynter, a cultural critic and author of *American Skin: Big Business, Pop Culture, and the End of White America* (Crown, 2002), said that the infusion of popular aspects of black youth culture into the mainstream American media was a double-edged sword. On one hand, Mr. Wynter said, the game characters bristle with aspects "solidly associated with nonwhite people." "The bad news is that the larger aspects of the humanity of people who happen to be nonwhite are not always transferred," he noted. "This is an extension and reflection of what we're seeing in other forms of entertainment, especially filmed entertainment aimed particularly at predominantly young male audiences."

14   As video games extend their prominence as a mainstream form of entertainment—the *Grand Theft Auto* series alone has sold more than 30 million games since 1998—their share of consumer dollars rivals Hollywood box-office revenues. Video game sales in the United States reached $7 billion last year, according to the Entertainment Software Association. Game hardware, including consoles, added more than $3 billion to that total, industry analysts estimate. But with Hollywood-scale success have come Hollywood-style pressures, including the need for games to "open big" and achieve enough success to sustain lucrative sequels.

15   "Games are attempting to drive market share beyond the traditional 8- to 14-year-old male player," said Michael Gartenberg, research director for Jupiter Research, an Internet consulting firm. Part of that drive, he suggested, involves having video games reflect what has proved to work in popular films. And as in Hollywood, that may mean

subject matter that drives sales even as it draws criticism for gratuitous violence, sexual exploitation or racial insensitivity.

16   In any case, limiting content to realistic, multidimensional portrayals of racial minorities may be unfair to game developers, Mr. Gartenberg suggested. "Video games are fantasies," he said, "and are not attempting to mirror any reality whatsoever."

17   But Esther Iverem, editor and film critic for www.seeingblack. com, a Washington-based Web site offering black opinion on cultural and political matters, said she worried about the effects of games like earlier versions of *Grand Theft Auto* on black youngsters, including her 11-year-old son. "These games don't teach them anything about respect, tolerance and responsibility," Ms. Iverem said, but are instead "validating a much-too-accepted stereotype, an accepted caricature." Others, like the cultural critic Michael Eric Dyson, point out that racial stereotypes conveyed through video games have an effect not only on the self-image of minority youths but also on perceptions among whites. Dr. Dyson, a professor of religious studies and African studies at the University of Pennsylvania, describes some video games as addictive "video crack." "They are pervasive, and their influence profound," he said.

18   Rockstar Games, the publisher of *Grand Theft Auto: San Andreas* (to be released in October for the Sony PlayStation 2), is known for infusing its games with gritty yet cartoonish violence. Players were famously rewarded in earlier *Grand Theft Auto* games for killing prostitutes and, more recently, brutalizing Haitians.

19   After repeated requests for an interview, Rockstar Games responded with an e-mail statement that read in part, "Rockstar Games is a leading publisher of interactive entertainment geared towards mature audiences and makes every effort to market its games responsibly, targeting advertising and marketing only to adult consumers over the age of 17." (While previous games in the *Grand Theft* series are rated Mature, for ages 17 and over, they have a wide following among younger players.)

20   Those associated with the *Def Jam* games were more forthcoming. Kevin Liles, who recently resigned as president of Island Def Jam, which licensed the games, said they had been good for his company and for hip-hop. "We have a sense of responsibility, but we know that games are games," Mr. Liles said. Def Jam's co-founder, Russell Simmons, said the images of hip-hop culture, even those played out in video games, had been good for the country. "The most important thing for race relations in America in the last I don't know how many years is hip-hop." "Now Eminem and 50 Cent think they are the same people," Mr. Simmons said, comparing a popular white rapper with a popular black rapper. "They're faced with the same struggle, and they recognize their common thread of poverty."

21   Mr. Morgan, the telecommunications executive, rejects that argument. In fact, he limits the 7-year-old gamer in his household, Elijah Wilson, to the cartoonish games for Nintendo Game Boy to avoid exposure to content he finds objectionable. "They ingest these images," Mr. Morgan said of racial stereotypes he had found in games like *NBA Ballers*. "The result is a self-fulfilling prophecy, something straight out of central casting."

22   "It won't," Mr. Morgan added emphatically, "happen in my house." ■

Glossary

A

abstract Summary of an article or book

aesthetic criteria Evaluative criteria based on perceptions of beauty and good taste

AltaVista Internet portal with powerful search engine at http://www.altavista.digital.com

analogy An extended comparison of one situation or item to another

APA American Psychological Association

APA documentation Documentation style commonly used in social science and education disciplines

argument In speech and writing, a claim supported by at least one reason

assumption An unstated belief or knowledge that connects a claim with evidence

audience Real or assumed individuals or groups to whom a verbal or written communication is directed

B

bandwagon appeal A fallacy of argument based on the assumption that something is true or correct because "everyone" believes it to be so

bar chart Visual depiction of data created by the use of horizontal or vertical bars that comparatively represent rates or frequencies

because clause A statement that begins with the word *because* and provides a supporting reason for a claim

begging the question A fallacy of argument that uses the claim as evidence for its own validity

bias Personal beliefs which may skew one's perspective or presentation of information

bibliography List of books and articles on a specific subject

brainstorming A method of finding ideas by writing a list of questions or statements about a subject

C

causal argument An argument that seeks to identify the reasons behind a certain event or phenomenon

claim A declaration or assertion made about any given topic

claim of comparison A claim that argues something is like or not like something else

common factor method A method used by scientists identifying a recurring factor present in a given cause–effect relationship

consequence The cause–effect result of a given action

context Of a text, both the combination of author, subject, and audience and the broader social, cultural, and economic influences

contextual analysis A type of rhetorical analysis that focuses on the author, the audience, the time, and the circumstances of an argument

counterargument An argument offering an opposing point of view with the goal of demonstrating that it is the stronger of the two arguments

criteria Standards used to establish a definition or an evaluation

critical reading A process of reading which surpasses an initial understanding or impression of basic content and proceeds with the goal of answering specific questions or examining particular elements

cropping In photography, the process of deleting unwanted parts of an image

cultural assumptions Widely held beliefs in a particular culture that are considered common sense

D

database Large collection of digital information organized for efficient search and retrieval

debate A contest or game where two or more individuals attempt to use arguments to persuade others to support their opinion

definition, argument by An argument made by specifying that something does or does not possess certain criteria

diction The choice and use of words in writing and speech

E

either–or A fallacy of argument that presents only two choices in a complex situation

emotional appeal An argumentation strategy that attempts to persuade by stirring the emotions of the audience

empirical research Research that collects data from observation or experiment

ethos An appeal to the audience based on the character and trustworthiness of the speaker or writer

evaluation argument An argument that judges something based on ethical, aesthetic, and/or practical criteria

evaluation of sources The assessment of the relevance and reliability of sources used in supporting claims

evidence Data, examples, or statistics used to support a claim

experimental research Research based on obtaining data under controlled conditions, usually by isolating one variable while holding other variables constant

F

fallacy of argument Failure to provide adequate evidence to support a claim. See *bandwagon appeal, begging the question, false analogy, hasty generalization, name calling, non sequitur, oversimplification, polarization, post hoc fallacy, rationalization, slippery slope, straw man*

false analogy A fallacy of argument that compares two unlike things as if they were similar

feasibility The potential that a proposed solution can be implemented

figurative language The symbolic transference of meaning from one word or phrase to another, such as with the use of metaphor, synecdoche, and metonymy

firsthand evidence Evidence such as interviews, observations, and surveys collected by the writer

font The specific size and weight of a typeface

freewriting A method of finding ideas by writing as fast as possible about a subject for a set length of time

G

generalization A conclusion drawn from knowledge based on past occurrences of the phenomenon in question

GIF (Graphic Interchange Format) Preferred Web format for images with sharp lines, text, and small images

good reason A reason that the audience accepts as valid

Google Powerful search engine at www.google.com

H

hasty generalization A fallacy of argument resulting from making broad claims based on a few occurrences

HTML (HyperText Markup Language) Display language used for creating Web pages

hypertext Document that allows you to connect to other pages or documents by clicking on links. The Web can be thought of as one huge hypertext

I

idea map A brainstorming tool which visually depicts connections between different aspects of an issue

image editor Software program that allows you to create and manipulate images

intellectual property Any property produced by the intellect, including copyrights for literary, musical, photographic, and cinematic works, patents for inventions, trademarks, and industrial processes

J

JPEG (acronym for Joint Photographic Experts Group) Preferred Web format for photographs

journal A general category that includes popular, trade, and scholarly periodical publications

K

keyword search A Web-based search that uses a robot and indexer to produce results based on a chosen word or words

L

line graph Visual presentation of data represented by a continuous line or lines plotted on specific intervals

logos An appeal to the audience based on reasoning and evidence

M

metaphor A figure of speech using a word or phrase that commonly designates one thing to represent another, thus making a comparison

metonomy A type of figurative language that uses one object to represent another that embodies its defining quality

MLA Modern Language Association

MLA documentation Documentation style commonly used in humanities and fine arts disciplines

N

name calling A fallacy of argument resulting from the use of undefined and therefore meaningless names

narrative arguments A form of argument based on telling stories that suggest the writer's position rather than explicitly making claims

non sequitur A fallacy of argument resulting from connecting together two or more unrelated ideas

O

oversimplification A fallacy in argument caused by neglect of accounting for the complexity of a subject

P

pathos An appeal based on the audience's emotions or deeply-held values

periodical A journal, magazine, or newspaper published at standard intervals, usually daily, weekly, monthly, or quarterly

periodical index Paper or electronic resource that catalogs the contents of journals, magazines, and newspapers

pie chart A circular chart resembling a pie that illustrates percentages of the whole through the use of delineated wedge shapes

plagiarism The improper use of the unauthorized and unattributed words or ideas of another author

polarization A fallacy of argument based on exaggerating the characteristics of opposing groups to highlight division and extremism

popular journal A magazine aimed at the general public; usually includes illustrations, short articles, and advertisements

position argument A general kind of argument in which a claim is made for an idea or way of thinking about a subject

post hoc fallacy A fallacy of argument based on the assumption that events that follow each other have a causal relationship

practical criteria Evaluative criteria based on usefulness or likely results

primary research Information collected directly by the writer through observations, interviews, surveys, and experiments

process of elimination method A means of finding a cause by systematically ruling out all other possible causes

proposal argument An argument that either advocates or opposes a specific course of action

R

rationalization A fallacy of argument based on using weak explanations to avoid dealing with the actual causes

reason In an argument, the justification for a claim

rebuttal argument An argument that challenges or rejects the claims of another argument

reference librarian Library staff member who is familiar with information resources and who can show you how to use them. You can find a reference librarian at the reference desk in your library.

refutation A rebuttal argument that points out the flaws in an opposing argument

rhetorical analysis Careful study of a written argument or other types of persuasion aimed at understanding how the components work or fail to work

rhetorical situation Factors present at the time of writing or speaking, including the writer or speaker, the audience, the purpose of communicating, and the context

S

sans serif type A style of type recognized by blunt ends and a consistency in thickness

scholarly journals Contain articles written by experts in a particular field; also called "peer-reviewed" or "academic" journals

search engine A program that searches information in electronic formats. Web search engines like Google and AltaVista search the entire Web.

secondary research Information obtained from existing knowledge, such as research in the library

secondhand evidence Evidence from the work of others found in the library, on the Web, and elsewhere

serif type A style of type developed to resemble the strokes of an ink pen and recognized by wedge-shaped ends on letter forms

single difference method Finding a cause for differing phenomena in very similar situations by identifying the one element that varies

slippery slope A fallacy of argument based on the assumption that if a first step is taken, additional steps will inevitably follow

straw man A fallacy of argument based on the use of the diversionary tactic of setting up the opposing position in such a manner that it can be easily rejected

sufficiency Refers to the adequacy of evidence supporting a claim

synecdoche A type of figurative language in which a part is used to represent the whole

T

textual analysis A type of rhetorical analysis that focuses exclusively on the text itself

thesis One or more sentences that state the main idea of an argument

trade journals A magazine in which articles and advertisements target individuals of a specific occupation

typeface Styles of type such as serif, sans serif, and decorative

U

URL (Universal Resource Locator) Addresses on the Web

V

visual argument A type of persuasion with images, graphics, or objects

voice In writing, the distinctive style of a writer that gives a sense of the writer as a person

W

Web directory Subject guide to Web pages grouped by topic and sub-topic

Web editors Programs that allow you to compose Web pages

working thesis A preliminary statement of the main claim of an argument, subject to revision

Y

Yahoo Popular Web directory at http://www.yahoo.com

Credits

Text Credits

Thomas Bailey Aldrich, "The Unguarded Gates," 1895.

American Civil Liberties Union (ACLU), "Fahrenheit 451.2: Is Cyberspace Burning?" March 17, 2002. <www.aclu.org>. Reprinted by permission of the American Civil Liberties Union.

American Civil Liberties Union (ACLU), "In Defense of Freedom at a Time of Crisis," September 20, 2001. <www.aclu.org>. Reprinted with permission.

American Library Association Council, "Resolution on the USA Patriot Act and Related Measures That Infringe on the Right of Library Users," January 29, 2003. <www.ala.org>. Reprinted by permission of the American Library Association.

Hadley Arkes, "The Closet Straight," from *National Review*, July 5, 1993. © 1993 by National Review, Inc. 215 Lexington Avenue, New York, NY 10016. Reprinted by permission.

John Ashcroft, "The Patriot Act: Wise Beyond Its Years." Reprinted with permission from *The Wall Street Journal*, October 26, 2004. © 2004 Dow Jones&Company. All rights reserved.

Ben Bagdikian, "Grand Theft: The Conglomeratization of Media and the Degradation of Culture," *Multinational Monitor*, January/February 2005. By permission of Multinational Monitor.

James Baldwin, from *Notes of a Native Son*. Copyright 1955, renewed © 1983 by James Baldwin. Reprinted by permission of Beacon Press, Boston.

John Perry Barlow, "A Declaration of the Independence of Cyberspace." Reprinted with permission of the author.

William Bennett, from open letter that appeared in the Wall Street Journal September 7, 19 and 29 to Milton Friedman by William Bennett. Used by permission of Dr. William J. Bennett.

Grace A. Bernhardt, from Balcones Canyonlands Preserve website, reprinted with permission of Grace A. Bernhardt.

Wendell Berry, "Manifesto: The Mad Farmer Liberation Front" from *Collected Poems: 1957–1982* by Wendell Berry. Copyright © 1985 by Wendell Berry. Reprinted by permission of North Point Press, a division of Farrar, Straus and Giroux, LLC.

Douglas Bettcher and Chitra Subramaniam, "The Necessity of Global Tobacco Regulation," *JAMA*, December 5, 2001; 286: 2737. Reprinted by permission of the American Medical Association.

James Bovard, "Federal Surveillance: The Threat to Americans' Security," *The Freeman*, Jan/Feb 2004. Reprinted with permission from Foundation for Economic Education. All rights reserved.

Keith Bradsher, from *High and Mighty: SUVs—The World's Most Dangerous Vehicles*. Copyright © 2002 by Keith Bradsher. Reprinted by permission of PublicAffairs, a member of Perseus Books, LLC.

David Brin, "Three Cheers for the Surveillance Society!" This article first appeared in *Salon.com*, August 3, 2004, at http://www.Salon.com. An online version remains in the Salon archives. Reprinted with permission.

Patrick J. Buchanan, "To Reunite a Nation," speech given at the Richard Nixon Library on January 18, 2000. Reprinted by permission of Patrick Buchanan.

Jay Budziszewski, "Homophobia: An Unfinished Story" and "The Seeker" from *Boundless E-zine*. Reprinted by permission of Jay Budziszewski.

Joseph A. Califano, Jr., "The Right Drug to Target: Cutting Marijuana Use," *The Washington Post*, May 17, 2005. Reprinted by permission of the author.

Laura Carlsen, "Wal-Mart vs. the Pyramids," Americas Program (Silver City, NM: Interhemispheric Resource Center, October 12, 2004). Reprinted by permission.

Rachel Carson, "The Obligation to Endure" from *Silent Spring* by Rachel Carson. Copyright © 1962 by Rachel L. Carson, renewed 1990 by Roger Christie. Reprinted by permission of Houghton Mifflin Company. All rights reserved.

Linda Chavez, "'The Separation of Church and State' Myth" as appeared in *Jewish World Review*, July 3, 2002. By permission of Linda Chavez and Creators Syndicate, Inc.

Cathleen Cleaver, "The Internet: A Clear and Present Danger?" Speech given at Boston University, October 29, 1997. Reprinted with permission of the author.

Thomas Derr, "Strange Science" from *First Things*, November 2004. Reprinted by permission of First Things.

Richard Doerflinger, "Don't Clone Ron Reagan's Agenda," *The Weekly Standard*, July 28, 2004. Reprinted by permission of the author.

EPA, pie chart "U.S. Produces Most Greenhouse Gases" from Environmental Protection Agency web site on global warming. <www.epa.gov/global_missions/international/projections.html>

700

Magazine, <www.prospect-magazine.co.uk> Reprinted by permission of Prospect.

Michel Marriott, "The Color of Mayhem," *The New York Times*, August 12, 2004. Copyright © 2004 by The New York Times Co. Reprinted with permission.

Jennifer May, "Why are Teenage Girls Dying to be Thin?" Copyright © 2004. Reprinted by permission of the author.

Scott McCloud, pages 2–9 from *Understanding Comics* by Scott McCloud. Copyright © 1993, 1994 by Scott McCloud. Reprinted by permission of HarperCollins Publishers.

Ralph C. Merkle, "Nanotechnology: Designs for the Future," a conversation with *Ubiquity* Magazine, June 27, 2000. http://www.acm.org/ubiquity/interviews/r_merkle_1.html. © 2000 Association for Computing Machiner, Inc. Reprinted by permission.

Steven Milloy, "Ron Reagan Wrong on Stem Cells," as found at <http://www.foxnews/com>, July 16, 2004. Reprinted by permission of Steven Milloy.

N. Scott Momaday, "The Way to Rainy Mountain" from *The Way to Rainy Mountain*. Copyright © 1969. Reprinted by permission of the University of New Mexico Press.

Dan Neal, "Who's Afraid of the Big Bad Wolf" from *National Geographic Online Forum*, May 1998. Reprinted by permission of the author.

Wilfred Owen, "Dulce et Decorum Est," 1921.

James Poniewozik, "Queer Eye for Straight TV," *Time*, March 14, 2005. © 2005 Time Inc. Reprinted by permission.

Anna Quindlen, from *Thinking Out Loud*. Copyright © 1993 by Anna Quindlen. Used by permission of Random House.

Terrence Rafferty, "Kate Winslet, Please Save Us." Copyright © 2001 Condé Nast Publications. All rights reserved. Originally published in *GQ*, May 2001. Reprinted by permission.

Richard Raynor, "What Immigration Crisis?" as appeared in *The New York Times Magazine*, January 7, 1996. © 1996 by Richard Raynor. Reprinted with the permission of the Wylie Agency Inc.

Ron Reagan, speech on the topic of Stem Cell Research given at the Democratic National Convention, July 27, 2004. Reprinted by permission of Ron Reagan.

Jeremy Rifkin, "The European Dream" as excerpted for and appeared in *Utne* Magazine, September/October 2004 from *The European Dream*. Jeremy Rifkin is the author of *The European Dream: How Europe's Vision of the Future is Quietly Eclipsing the American Dream* (Tarcher/Penguin: August 2004). Reprinted by permission of the author.

Gregory Rodriguez, "Why We're the New Irish." From *Newsweek*, May 30, 2005. © 2005 Newsweek, Inc. All rights reserved. Reprinted by permission.

Paul Saffo, "A Trail of DNA and Data," as appeared in *The Washington Post*, April 3, 2005. Reprinted by permission of the author.

David Sarasohn, "The Patriot Act on Trial." Reprinted with permission from the September 26, 2005 issue of *The Nation*. For subscription information, call 1-800-333-8536. Portions of each week's Nation magazine can be accessed at http://www.thenation.com.

Eric Schlosser, "Make Peace with Pot," *The New York Times* Op Ed, April 26, 2004. Reprinted by permission of The New York Times Syndication Sales Corp.

Frank Shorter, Testimony Before the Subcommittee on Commerce, Trade, and Consumer Protection, May 18, 2005.

Leslie Marmon Silko, "The Border Patrol State." First appeared in *The Nation*, October 17, 1994. © 1994 by Leslie Marmon Silko. Reprinted with the permission of the Wylie Agency.

Douglas W. Smith, graph from "Ten Years of Yellowstone Wolves, 1995–2005" from *Yellowstone Science* 13(1), Winter 2005, a publication of the National Park Service, U.S. Department of the Interior.

Erica M. Strausser, "The NRA Blacklist: A Project Gone Mad?" Copyright © 2004. Reprinted by permission of the author.

Andrew Sullivan, "Here Comes the Groom" from *The New Republic*, August 28, 1989. Reprinted by permission of The New Republic. Copyright © 1989 by The New Republic.

TalkLeft.com, Blog, "'Sneaks and Peeks' Used in Oregon Lawyer Case," from May 27, 2004. http://talkleft.com. Reprinted by permission of TalkLeft.com.

Union of Concerned Scientists. "The Impact of Global Warming in North America" rendering of map and two text boxes "Global Warming Fingerprint" and "Global Warming Harbinger" from <http://www.climatehotmap.org/namerica.html> by Union of Concerned Scientists. Reprinted by permission.

Carmen Vazquez, "Appearances." From *Homophobia* by Warren J. Blumenfeld. Copyright © 1992 by Warren J. Blumenfeld. Reprinted by permission of Beacon Press, Boston.

Alice Walker, "Am I Blue?" from *Living by the Word: Selected Writings 1973–1987*. Copyright © 1986 by Alice Walker. Reprinted by permission of Harcourt, Inc.

Matt Welch, "Blogworld and Its Gravity."
Reprinted from *Columbia Journalism Review*,
September/October 2003. © 2003 by Columbia
Journalism Review. Reprinted by permission of
the publisher and the author.

Walter Williams. "Nazi Tactics," *Ideas on Liberty*,
January 2003. Reprinted with permission from
Foundation for Economic Education. All rights
reserved.

Edward O. Wilson, reprinted by permission of the
publisher from "The Conservation Ethic" in
Biophelia: The Human Bond with Other Species by
Edward O. Wilson, pp. 119–123. Cambridge, Mass:
Harvard University Press. Copyright © 1984 by the
President and Fellows of Harvard College.

Evan Wright, "Sister Act." From *Rolling Stone*, October
14, 1999. © 1999 Rolling Stone LLC. All rights
reserved. Reprinted by permission.

Yahoo! Screen Shot "Issues and Causes" in the Yahoo!
Directory. Reproduced with permission of Yahoo!
Inc. © 2005 by Yahoo! Inc. YAHOO! and the
YAHOO! logo are trademarks of Yahoo! Inc.

Jeffrey Zaslow, "The End of Youthful Indiscretions:
Internet Makes Them Permanent Blots" from
"Moving On" in *The Wall Street Journal*, Eastern
Edition, August 12, 2004. Copyright © 2004 by
Dow Jones&Co. Inc. Reproduced by permission of
Dow Jones&Co. Inc. in the format textbook via
Copyright Clearance Center.

Photo Credits

p. 5 left: Cover from SILENT SPRING by Rachel
Carson (Boston: Houghton Mifflin, 2002);
right: Erich Hartmann/Magnum Photos; p. 87
bottom: Hearts © 1996 Benettton Group SpA
Ph O. Toscani; p. 89: Public Service
Announcement provided courtesy of the
Partnership for a Drug Free America ®; p. 100:
© 2003 America's Dairy Farmers and Milk
Processors; p. 299: Environmental Protection
Agency; p. 300: American Lake Scene, 1844
Thomas Cole Gift of Douglas F. Roby
Photograph © 1986 The Detroit Institute of
Arts; p. 307: © Greenpeace/Filip Verbelen; p.
339: Mark Miller Photography; p. 342: Jim &
Jamie Dutcher/GettyImages; p. 344: Mike Keefe,
http://www.InToon.com; p. 346: Robert
Barber/Painet Inc.; p. 350: Courtesy of
MatthewShepherd.org; p. 351: Photofest NYC;
p. 373: *San Francisco Chronicle*; p. 374: *San
Francisco Chronicle*; p. 375: Matt Davies, ©
Tribune Media Services. Reprinted with
Permission. 2007; p. 380: Photo by Ken Ige,
Honolulu Star Bulletin; p. 397: EPA/Landov; p.
403: Matthias Kulka/CORBIS; p. 404: Henry
Payne: © Detroit News/Dist. By United Features
Syndicate, Inc.; p. 405: National Park Service;
p. 406: AP/Wide World Photos; p. 461: Najlah
Feanny/CORBIS SABA; p. 501: Christy

Bowe/CORBIS; p. 502: © 2005 by Vince
O'Farrell and Cagle Cartoons; p. 505: © 2005 by
Mike Keefe and Cagle Cartoons; p. 506: AP
Worldwide/Daniel Hulshizer; p. 507: AP/Wide
Word Photos; p. 513: CORBIS; p. 515:
Reuters/CORBIS; p. 517: AP/Wide World
Photos; p. 518: © 2005 by Mike Keefe and Cagle
Cartoons; p. 521: TOLES © 2005 *The Washington
Post*. Reprinted with permission of UNIVERSAL
PRESS SYNDICATE. All rights reserved; p. 562:
William Manning/CORBIS; p. 563: Kansas
State Historical Society; p. 570:
Maurice/zefa/CORBIS; p. 571: Image courtesy
of The Advertising Archives; p. 572: Courtesy of
the American Legacy Foundation; p. 573:
TRUDEAU © 2001 Reprinted with permission
of UNIVERSAL PRESS SYNDICATE. All rights
reserved. p. 595: Courtesy of Mothers Against
Drunk Driving (MADD); p. 606: Time Life
Pictures/GettyImages; p. 608: LOS ANGELES
DAILY NEW/CORBIS SYGMA; p. 613 top:
Courtesy of The Center for Consumer Freedom;
p. 613 bottom: Courtesy of The Center for
Consumer Freedom; p. 631: GettyImages; p.
637: M. Wuerker; p. 644: Courtesy of John Perry
Barlow; p. 652: © Tribune Media Services, Inc.
All Rights Reserved. Reprinted with permis-
sion; p. 663: TOM THE DANCING BUG ©
Ruben Bolling. Reprinted with permission of
UNIVERSAL PRESS SYNDICATE. All rights re-
served; p. 687: Courtesy www.adbusters.org. All
other photos supplied by Lester Faigley.

Index